AF767280

AMERICAN INTERNATIONAL LAW CASES

Fourth Series

2006

Volume 7

Oceana®
NEW YORK

OXFORD
UNIVERSITY PRESS

Oxford University Press, Inc., publishes works that further Oxford University's objective of excellence in research, scholarship, and education.

Copyright © 2008 by Oxford University Press, Inc.
Published by Oxford University Press, Inc.
198 Madison Avenue, New York, New York 10016

Oxford is a registered trademark of Oxford University Press
Oceana is a registered trademark of Oxford University Press, Inc.

All rights reserved. No part of this publication may be reproduced, stored in a retrieval system, or transmitted, in any form or by any means, electronic, mechanical, photocopying, recording, or otherwise, without the prior permission of Oxford University Press, Inc.

Cataloging-in-Publication information is available from the Library of Congress.

ISBN 978-0-19-537289-2 (2006, Volume 7)

Note to Readers:

This publication is designed to provide accurate and authoritative information in regard to the subject matter covered. It is based upon sources believed to be accurate and reliable and is intended to be current as of the time it was written. It is sold with the understanding that the publisher is not engaged in rendering legal, accounting, or other professional services. If legal advice or other expert assistance is required, the services of a competent professional person should be sought. Also, to confirm that the information has not been affected or changed by recent developments, traditional legal research techniques should be used, including checking primary sources where appropriate.

(Based on the Declaration of Principles jointly adopted by a Committee of the American Bar Association and a Committee of Publishers and Associations.)

You may order this or any other Oxford University Press publication by visiting the Oxford University Press website at www.oup.com

Table of Contents

INTRODUCTORY NOTE

On the Content:

In last year's Introductory Note (for 2005 cases), we emphasized how quickly the field of international law had expanded in the American court system. That phenomenon only gained momentum in 2006. The topics that appeared for the first time in last year's edition of *AILC*, especially Customary International Law and Terrorism in General, received even more extensive treatment by the federal judiciary in 2006. This year's edition of *AILC* therefore explores these ongoing developments in U.S. treatment of international law.

But the rapid growth of other international law issues in 2006 has justified still more additions to the *AILC* List of Subjects in this new edition. Most of the new topics fall within the areas of environmental law, business law, and the law of war. Specifically, the rise in environmental regulation of industry calls for two new subtopics that clarify the distinction between regulatory violations and criminal ones. Likewise, globalization's increasing prevalence has generated numerous new cases that grapple with questions of contract law and the law of personal property in the international context. Lastly, and most significantly, the U.S. government's global war on terror has given rise to so many new and influential cases regarding the pursuit and detention of alleged terrorists that this year's edition of *AILC* includes a new section called Detention, Investigation, and Prosecution of Suspected Terrorists.

Undoubtedly, the current growth in the number and segmentation of international law issues will continue in future years as well. With each year's new edition of *AILC*, we will continue to keep you updated on those new and expanding trends in U.S. courts.

HOW TO USE

Each volume of *American International Law Cases (AILC)* contains a *List of Subjects*, a *List of Abbreviations*, and a *Table of Cases* (by volume). The collection of cases for each year is organized around the *List of Subjects*. Subjects are assigned the same number each year with new subjects added as necessary (see the discussion of new subjects in the Introductory Note to the 2006 edition). This numeration system unifies the collection so that the user can easily locate the topic in any edition of *AILC*. The *Table of Contents* for each volume lists only those subjects covered in the particular edition.

The cases are arranged alphabetically under each subject. Individual Subject Table of Contents for each covered subject provides a complete list of cases dealing with the subject. The Subject Table of Contents includes the page references for both cases printed in the particular volume or other volumes of the edition. Cases are printed under the lowest assigned subject number but are included in the Subject Table of Contents under every subject to which they are applicable. For example, the 2006 edition of *AILC* includes thirteen cases dealing substantially with the issue of which jurisdiction's law a court should apply. That topic constitutes subcategory "3. Choice of Law" under Section III. PROCEDURE in the volume's *Table of Contents*. The Subject Table of Contents for "Choice of Law" cases starts at page 723 of Volume 2, which alphabetically lists all thirteen cases. The full text of ten of those cases appears in Volume 2. The additional three cases dealing with "Choice of Law" are listed with references to the volume and page where they are reproduced. For example, the case *Sisso v. Islamic Republic of Iran* appears on the Subject Table of Contents page for "Choice of Law" (Section III.3.), but the text of the case actually appears in Section III.1 Jurisdiction, in Volume 1, page 407.

To assist the user in finding particular cases or in researching particular topics, the 2006 edition includes in the last volume of the edition a "Subject Index of Cases" as well as an expanded Consolidated Table of Cases.

– To research cases by topic use the *Subject Index of Cases*. The *Subject Index of Cases* lists the titles of *all* cases in the year's entire collection according to subject with a reference to the volume and page number where each case is reproduced.

– To locate cases by title use the *Consolidated Table of Cases*. Cases listed in the alphabetical *Consolidated Table of Cases* are referenced to both the volume, page and topical section where they are reproduced as well as to all the topical sections to which they pertain.

LIST OF SUBJECTS

TABLE OF CASES

Each volume has a Table of Cases covering the materials included in that volume. A Consolidated Table of Cases appears in the last volume.

LIST OF ABBREVIATIONS

Significant abbreviations appearing in *American International Law Cases, 2006* are listed below.

A., A.2d	Atlantic Reporter [1885-1938], *Id.,* 2d Series [1938-date].
App. Div.	Appellate Division Reports [N.Y. 1896-1955].
Bevans	Treaties and Other International Agreements of the United States of America [1776-1949], compiled under the direction of Charles I. Bevans.
B.R.	Bankruptcy Reporter [1979-date].
Cal., Cal.2d	California Reports [1850-1934], *Id.,* 2d Series [1934-date].
Cal. App.	California Appellate Decisions [1905-1940].
Cal. Rptr.	California Reporter [1959-date].
Cir. (1st, 2d, etc.)	Numbered Circuits of United States Courts of Appeal.
C.M.R.	Court Martial Reports [1951-date].
Ct. Cl.	Court of Claims (U.S.) [1863-1982].
Ct. Int'l Trade	Court of International Trade [1980-date].
Cust. Ct.	Customs Court (U.S.) [1938-1980].
D. (N.D., S.D., etc.)	District Court (N.D. Northern District, S.D. Southern District, etc.).
D.C.	District of Columbia.
E.A.S.	Executive Agreement Series (replaced in 1945 by T.I.A.S.).
F. App'x	Federal Appendix [2001-date].
F., F.2d, F.3d	Federal Reporter [1910-date].
F.P.C.	Federal Power Commission Reports [1931-date].
F.R.D.	Federal Rules Decisions [1938-date].
F. Supp., F. Supp.2d	Federal Supplement [1933-date].
Fed. Cir.	Federal Circuit.
Fed. Cl.	Federal Claims Reporter [1992-date].
I.L.M.	International Legal Materials.
L. Ed., L. Ed. 2d	Lawyers' Edition, United States Supreme Court Reports [1754-1956], *Id.,* 2d Series [1956-date].
Misc., Misc. 2d	New York Miscellaneous [1892-1955], *Id.,* 2d Series [1956-date].
M.J.	Military Justice Reporter [1975-date].

N.E., N.E.2d	North Eastern Reporter [1885-1936], *Id.,* 2d Series [1934-date].
N.J.	New Jersey Reports [1948-date].
N.J. Eq.	New Jersey Equity [1830-1948].
N.W., N.W.2d	North Western Reporter [1879-1941], *Id.,* 2d Series [1941-date].
N.Y., N.Y.2d, N.Y.3d	New York Court of Appeals Reports [1846-1956], *Id.*, 2d Series [1956-2003], *Id.*, 3d Series [2004-date].
N.Y.S., N.Y.S.2d	New York Supplement [1888-1937], *Id.,* 2d Series [1937-date].
P., P.2d	Pacific Reporter [1883-1931], *Id.,* 2d Series [1931-date].
S. Ct.	Supreme Court Reporter [1882-date].
S.E., S.E.2d	South Eastern Reporter [1887-1839], *Id.,* 2d Series, [1939-date].
So., So. 2d	Southern Reporter [1886-1941], *Id.,* 2d Series [1941-date].
Stat.	United States Statutes at Large.
S.W., S.W.2d	South Western Reporter [1886-1928], *Id.,* 2d Series [1928-date].
T.C.	Tax Court (U.S.) [1942-date].
T.I.A.S.	Treaties and Other International Acts Series [1945-date].
T.S.	Treaty Series [1908-1945].
U.N.T.S.	United Nations Treaty Series [1946-date].
U.S.	United States Supreme Court Reports [1774-date] (Official).
U.S.C.M.A.	United States Court of Military Appeals [1951-date].
U.S.T.	United States Treaties and Other International Agreements [1950-date].
W.L.	Westlaw [1986-date].

IX. INTERNATIONAL TRADE

1. Regulations

B. Anti-Dumping & Countervailing Duties*

* Cases are indexed under this subject. The full text of these cases is published in the **volume**-page indicated.

BRATSK ALUMINIUM SMELTER
v.
UNITED STATES OF AMERICA

444 F.3d 1369 (Fed. Cir. 2006)
Decided April 10, 2006

Before GAJARSA, Circuit Judge, ARCHER, Senior Circuit Judge, and DYK, Circuit Judge. Opinion for the court filed by Circuit Judge DYK. Dissenting opinion filed by Senior Circuit Judge ARCHER.

OPINION

DYK, *Circuit Judge*.

SUAL Holding and ZAO Kremny (collectively "appellants") appeal from the judgment of the United States Court of International Trade affirming the International Trade Commission's ("Commission") determination that domestic industry was materially injured by reason of silicon metal imports from Russia that were sold at less than fair market value ("LTFV"). We vacate the Court of International Trade's decision and remand for further proceedings.

BACKGROUND

In antidumping proceedings, the Commission is charged with determining whether an industry in the United States has suffered, or is threatened with, material injury by reason of imports. 19 U.S.C. § 1673d(b) (2000). Material injury determinations are particularly difficult where the imports sold at LTFV compete with identical imports not sold at LTFV.

The product involved here is silicon metal. Silicon metal is a commodity product, meaning that it is generally interchangeable regardless of its source. Therefore, price is the primary consideration for purchasers of silicon metal. The market for silicon metal consists of three segments: chemical, primary aluminum, and secondary aluminum. During the pertinent time period there were ten countries, other than the United States, which supplied silicon metal to the U.S. market: Argentina,

Brazil, Canada, China, Korea, Norway, Russia, Saudi Arabia, South Africa, and Spain.

On March 7, 2002, Globe Metallurgical Inc., SIMCALA Inc., and several union groups filed an antidumping petition with the Commission and with the United States Department of Commerce ("Commerce"), alleging that Russian imports of silicon metal at LTFV had materially injured the domestic industry. On February 11, 2003, Commerce rendered its final determination that the subject imports were, or were likely to be, sold at LTFV. On March 24, 2003, the Commission determined that the domestic industry was materially injured by reason of the subject imports.

The Commission relied on market data over a three-year period, 1999-2001, as well as data for specific periods between January-September 2001 and 2002, and, as required by the statute, considered subject import volume, the effect of subject imports on domestic prices, and the impact of subject imports on domestic producers. 19 U.S.C. § 1677(7)(B)(i), (C) (2000). First, the Commission found that subject import volume was significant and that subject import volume increased from 1999 to 2001, while domestic producers lost market share. The Commission also noted, however, that the domestic industry was able to satisfy only a portion of U.S. silicon metal demand.

The Commission next considered what effect subject imports had on domestic prices. The Commission noted that "price is very important in purchasing decisions, given the commodity-like nature of the subject product." Using purchaser price data, the Commission found that during the period of investigation, subject imports almost always undersold the domestic product in all three market segments. In response to the argument that all imports, not just subject imports, undersold the domestic product, the Commission stated that "price data for nonsubject imports shows that imports from Russia have been priced at lower levels than nonsubject imports," and concluded that "in light of subject imports' increasing volumes and their significant underselling of, and high substitutability with, both domestic and nonsubject silicon metal, we find significant price depression by the subject imports." The Commission further noted:

> We recognize that nonsubject imports may have had an independent price depressive effect on domestic silicon metal prices. However, given the significant underselling by subject imports, subject import volume surges during the POI, and the high degree of substitutability between subject imports and the domestic product, we find that subject imports themselves have significantly depressed domestic silicon metal prices in all three customer segments . . . .

Finally, the Commission turned to the impact of subject imports on domestic producers and concluded that, given the significant volume and price effects of the subject imports, subject imports had a significant adverse effect on the domestic industry. The Commission considered the domestic industry's drop in market share, as well as the fact that certain silicon metal furnaces had been closed or converted for other uses. The Commission "acknowledged that domestic industry lost market share to nonsubject imports as well," but concluded that "regardless of the impact of nonsubject imports on the domestic industry, we find, in this investigation, that the surges in subject import volume at prices that undersold and depressed domestic silicon metal prices to a significant degree during the POI had a material adverse impact on the domestic industry."

Appellants[1] argued that our decision in *Gerald Metals, Inc. v. United States, 132 F.3d 716 (Fed. Cir. 1997)* required a specific determination as to whether the nonsubject imports would simply replace the subject imports, with the same impact on domestic products, if the subject imports were excluded from the market. The Commission made no such determination and dismissed our decision in *Gerald Metals* as being factually distinguishable.

Appellants challenged several aspects of the Commission's determination in the Court of International Trade, including whether the Russian imports actually caused injury to the domestic industry. The court made no ruling with respect to the causation issue but remanded the case to the Commission on an unrelated issue. The court noted that it would "consider the remaining issues raised by Plaintiffs upon review of the remand determination." *Bratsk Aluminum Smelter v. United States, 2004 Ct. Intl. Trade LEXIS 70, No. 03-00200, 2004 WL 1385848, at *11 (Ct. Int'l Trade June 22, 2004)*. On remand, the Commission incorporated its initial decision by reference and then clarified some of its findings. On December 3, 2004, the Court of International Trade affirmed the Commission's remand determination "in its entirety" and dismissed the case, stating that "all other issues have been decided . . . ." SUAL Holding and ZAO Kremny timely appealed. We have jurisdiction under 28 U.S.C. § 1295(a)(5).

DISCUSSION

The sole point of contention in this appeal is whether the Commission established that the injury to the domestic industry was "by reason of" the subject imports.[2]

I

The antidumping statute states that the "Commission shall make a final determination of whether . . . an industry in the United States . . . is materially injured . . . . .

---

1 Plaintiffs below, Bratsk Aluminium Smelter and RUAL Trade Limited, filed a voluntary notice of dismissal on December 6, 2004, and are thus not parties to this appeal. However, the remaining plaintiffs, SUAL Holding and ZAO Kremny, continued in the litigation and are appellants in this case.

2 "We apply anew the standard of review applied by the Court of International Trade in its review of the administrative record. We therefore uphold the Commission's determination unless it was arbitrary and capricious or unsupported by substantial evidence on the record, or otherwise not in accordance with law." *Timken U.S. Corp. v. United States, 421 F.3d 1350, 1354 (Fed. Cir. 2005)* (internal citation and quotation marks omitted); 19 U.S.C. § 1516a(b)(1)(B)(i) (2000).

by reason of imports . . . ." 19 U.S.C. § 1673d(b) (2000). In making this determination, the Commission must consider:

> (I) the volume of imports of the subject merchandise,
>
> (II) the effect of imports of that merchandise on prices in the United States for domestic like products, and
>
> (III) the impact of imports of such merchandise on domestic producers of domestic like products, but only in the context of production operations within the United States . . . .19 U.S.C. § 1677(7)(B)(i) (2000). "An affirmative injury determination requires both (1) present material injury and (2) a finding that the material injury is '*by reason of*' the subject imports." *Gerald Metals, Inc., 132 F.3d at 719* (emphasis added). We have previously explained that the "by reason of" requirement "mandates a showing of causal—not merely temporal—connection between the LTFV goods and the material injury." Id. at 720. We have not required the Commission to employ any particular methodology for determining whether this causation element has been met,[3] and the "Commission need not isolate the injury caused by other factors from injury caused by unfair imports . . . ." *Taiwan Semiconductor Industry v. Int'l Trade Comm'n, 266 F.3d 1339, 1345 (Fed. Cir. 2001)* (quoting legislative history of the Uruguay Round Agreements Act); *see also Nippon Steel Corp. v. Int'l Trade Comm'n, 345 F.3d 1379, 1381 (Fed. Cir. 2003)* ("'Dumping' need not be the sole or principal cause of injury."). However, we have made clear that causation is not shown if the subject imports contributed only "minimally or tangentially to the material harm." *Gerald Metals, 132 F.3d at 722*; *see also Nippon Steel Corp., 345 F.3d at 1381*; *U.S. Steel Group v. United States, 96 F.3d 1352, 1361-62 (Fed. Cir. 1996).*

The Commission, like other federal agencies, "must examine the relevant data and articulate a satisfactory explanation for its action . . . . Normally, an agency rule would be arbitrary and capricious if the agency . . . entirely fails to consider an important aspect of the problem." *Motor Vehicle Mfrs. Ass'n v. State Farm Mut. Auto. Ins. Co., 463 U.S. 29, 43, 103 S. Ct. 2856, 77 L. Ed. 2d 443 (1983)*. Where commodity products are at issue and fairly traded, price competitive, non-subject imports are in the market, the Commission must explain why the elimination of subject imports would benefit the domestic industry instead of resulting in the non-subject imports' replacement of the subject imports' market share without any beneficial impact on domestic producers.

In *Gerald Metals*, the Commission determined that Ukrainian imports of pure magnesium at LTFV injured the domestic industry. The Commission's determina-

---

3 In *United States Steel Group v. United States, 96 F.3d 1352 (Fed. Cir. 1996)*, we noted that the Commission uses different methodologies in determining whether the domestic injury was "by reason of" the LTFV imports. Id. at 1361-62. We then found that the antidumping statute "on its face compels no [] uniform methodology, and we are not persuaded that we should create one, even were we so empowered." *Id. at 1362.*

tion did not discuss whether non-subject imports, namely fairly-traded Russian imports, would have replaced all or a greater part of the subject imports. Three dissenting commissioners found that the presence of the non-subject imports undermined the causation determination. *Magnesium from China, Russia, and Ukraine*, U.S. Int'l Trade Comm'n Pub. 2885, Inv. Nos. 731-TA-696-698 at 29 (Chairman Watson, dissenting), 35-36 (Vice Chairman Nuzum, dissenting), and 48 (Comm'r Crawford, dissenting) (May 1995) (final). The dissenters noted that non-subject imports were perfect substitutes for the Ukrainian subject imports and frequently undersold the domestic product just as the Ukrainian imports had. *Magnesium from China, Russia, and Ukraine* at 35 (Vice Chairman Nuzum, dissenting), 45 (Comm'r Crawford, dissenting); *see also Gerald Metals, 132 F.3d at 718-19.*

The Court of International Trade, while acknowledging that the Commission did not discuss the issue of substitutability, affirmed the Commission's finding of material injury. *Gerald Metals, Inc. v. United States, 20 C.I.T. 1065, 937 F. Supp. 930, 935 n.22, 936 (Ct. Int'l Trade 1996).* On appeal, we vacated the court's decision and explained that the Commission must "'take[] into account contradictory evidence or evidence from which conflicting inferences could be drawn.'" *132 F.3d at 720* (quoting *Universal Camera Corp. v. NLRB, 340 U.S. 474, 487, 71 S. Ct. 456, 95 L. Ed. 456 (1951)).* Given that the fairly-traded non-subject imports were substitutable for the Ukrainian subject imports and undersold the domestic product just as the subject imports had, we held that the Commission must explain, in its analysis of the harm caused by the subject imports, why domestic consumers would not have purchased the fairly traded non-subject imports. *See* id. at 718, 720, 721-23.[4]

This court applied the reasoning of *Gerald Metals* in *Taiwan Semiconductor*. There, the Commission—after two remands from the Court of International Trade on the issue of causation—determined that Taiwanese imports of static random access memory chips ("SRAMs") at LTFV had not injured the domestic industry. *266 F.3d at 1342*. The Commission concluded that "the volume of subject imports, and increase in volume [of subject imports], are not sufficient to demonstrate that the subject imports themselves made a material contribution to any injury experienced by the domestic industry." Id. at 1346 (quoting the Commission's Redetermination). In particular, the Commission found that non-subject Korean imports of SRAMs were, like the subject imports, priced lower than the domestic product, and were at times priced lower than the subject imports as well. Id. at 1347. We affirmed the Commission's determination, noting that "substantial evidence supports the fact that the United States market share was impacted largely by non-subject imports," and that "in *Gerald Metals*, as in this case, the record did not show that

---

4 As we explained in *Taiwan Semiconductor Industry v. International Trade Commission, 266 F.3d 1339 (Fed. Cir. 2001)*, "*Gerald Metals* applied the antidumping law as it existed prior to amendment effective on January 1, 1995, by the Uruguay Round Agreements Act (URAA) . . . . The URAA did not deviate from the pre-existing causation standard enunciated in *Gerald Metals*." Id. at 1345.

the subject imports caused the material injury in light of the dominant presence of non-subject imports in the marketplace." Id. at 1345-46, 1347.

Thus under *Gerald Metals*, the increase in volume of subject imports priced below domestic products and the decline in the domestic market share are not in and of themselves sufficient to establish causation. *Gerald Metals* did not, of course, establish a per se rule barring a finding of causation where the product is a commodity product and there are fairly traded imports priced below the domestic product. However, under Gerald Metals, the Commission is required to make a specific causation determination and in that connection to directly address whether non-subject imports would have replaced the subject imports without any beneficial effect on domestic producers.

II

The antidumping investigation here revealed the same conditions that triggered the additional causation inquiry in *Gerald Metals* and Taiwan Semiconductor, as the Commission found silicon metal generally interchangeable regardless of where it is produced. Non-subject imports were present in the U.S. market during the period of investigation and were a significant factor in the U.S. market. As a percentage of total imports (by quantity), non-subject imports accounted for approximately 79.6% in 1999, 82.6% in 2000, and 73.0% in 2001.

Further, while the subject imports generally undersold the domestic product, there was evidence that non-subject imports from Brazil, Canada, Saudi Arabia, and South Africa generally undersold the domestic product during the period of investigation. These circumstances suggest that the elimination of the subject imports from the domestic market might simply have increased the market share of the non-subject imports. *Gerald Metals* thus requires the Commission to explain why—notwithstanding the presence and significance of the non-subject imports—it concluded that the subject imports caused material injury to the domestic industry. While there may be support for the Commission's ultimate determination of material injury in the record here, we find that the Commission did not sufficiently explain its decision in this regard.

The failure of the agency to explain its causation analysis in accordance with *Gerald Metals* is particularly troubling in this case because of the agency's claim that it is not obligated to follow this court's precedent. The Commission sought to dismiss *Gerald Metals* as having no precedential value in other anti-dumping investigations, stating that "the prior Commission investigations cited by respondents are factually distinguishable from the instant investigation." On appeal, the Commission continues to dismiss our precedent by attempting to limit *Gerald Metals* to its "unique facts" and explaining that "the instant investigation is not factually analogous either to *Gerald Metals* or *Taiwan Semiconductor*." Commission's Br. at 33, 35. In particular, the Commission stated that *Gerald Metals* and *Taiwan Semiconductor* are distinguishable because in both of those cases, non-subject import volume increased while the subject import volume decreased or remained the same. The Commission is obligated to follow the holdings of our cases, not to limit those decisions to their particular facts. The holding of *Gerald Metals* is not limited to situations in which non-subject imports increased during the period of review. The obligation under *Gerald Metals* is triggered whenever the antidumping investigation is centered on a commodity product, and price competitive non-subject imports are a significant factor in the market.

In its decision, the Commission also attempted to support the link between subject imports and the domestic injury by pointing out that after subject imports were withdrawn from the market in 2002 following the Department of Commerce's preliminary determination, silicon spot prices increased and prices for eleven domestic contracts increased during the fourth quarter of 2002. That spot prices may have increased after the Russian imports exited the market may be pertinent to the causation question, but that fact does not excuse the Commission's failure to address directly the causation issue in detail as required by *Gerald Metals*. The Commission did not explain how much the spot prices increased, the significance of that increase, or the significance of the eleven contracts for the domestic market.

Finally on appeal, among other things, the Commission argues that the appellant "has not demonstrated" that "nonsubject imports were well positioned to completely fill any void left by the withdrawal of subject imports from the market." Gov't Br. at 35-36. Presumably, this is an argument that non-subject imports could not replace subject imports because producers of non-subject imports lacked the capacity to supply the necessary volume to the U.S. market. Such a finding would certainly be relevant to the causation analysis under *Gerald Metals*. However, it is the Commission's burden, not the subject importer's, to demonstrate that the subject imports themselves caused the domestic injury. *See Gerald Metals, 132 F.3d at 722*. In any event, the Commission's decision made no finding on the capacity issue.

III

In short, the Commission's summary finding of material injury is insufficiently detailed to comply with the requirements of *Gerald Metals*. We therefore vacate and remand the Court of International Trade's decision so that it may remand the case back to the Commission to specifically address whether the non-subject imports would have replaced subject imports during the period of investigation.

In ordering reconsideration by the Commission, we do not suggest that the mere existence of fairly traded commodity imports at competitive prices precludes the Commission from finding material injury. For example, it may well be that non-subject importers lack capacity to replace the subject imports or that the price of the non-subject imports is sufficiently above the subject imports such that the elimination of the subject imports would have benefited the domestic industry. The point is that the Commission has to explain, in a meaningful way, why the non-subject imports would not replace the subject imports and continue to cause injury to the domestic industry.

CONCLUSION

For the foregoing reasons, the decision below is vacated and remanded for further proceedings.

VACATED and REMANDED

COSTS

No costs

DISSENT BY: ARCHER

ARCHER, *Senior Circuit Judge*, dissenting.

The majority states that *Gerald Metals, 132 F.3d 716 (Fed. Cir. 1997)*, "requires the Commission to explain why—notwithstanding the presence and significance of the non-subject imports—it concluded that the subject imports caused material injury to the domestic industry." Maj. op. at 10. While acknowledging that there may be support for the Commission's ultimate determination of material injury in the record here, the majority "finds that the Commission did not sufficiently explain its decision in this regard." *Id.* I disagree.

In my view, the Commission adequately considered the effect of both the subject imports and the interchangeable nonsubject imports on the domestic industry in its determination and found substantial evidence in the record to support its material injury determination. I would, therefore, affirm the Court of International Trade's judgment sustaining the Commission.

The majority appears to take no issue with the Commission's underlying analysis of whether the domestic industry was in fact harmed. The Commission performed the proper analysis and considered the statutorily enumerated factors. *See* 19 U.S.C. § 1677(7)(B)(i) (2000).[1] It concluded that the volume and increase in volume of subject imports, both in absolute terms and relative to apparent domestic consumption and production in the United States, supported a finding of material injury determination. The Commission found that 1) the quantity of subject imports increased overall by 35.8% from 1999 to 2001 and by 38.6% from 2000-2001 (after showing a slight decrease from 1999 to 2000); 2) "the continued increase in subject import volume by 57.6 percent between the interim periods resulted in Russia being the largest single source of silicon metal imports in interim 2002"; and 3) from 1999 to 2001 and from 2000-2001 subject imports outpaced all other imports in gaining U.S. market share.

Given that "price is a key factor in purchasing decisions [to buy silicon metal]", the Commission also concluded that underselling by subject imports supported a material injury determination, "finding that prices have been depressed to a significant degree by the subject imports." Although nonsubject goods have at times also undersold the domestic product, the Commission found that purchaser price data "shows that imports from Russia have been priced at lower levels than nonsubject

---

1 Section 1677(7)(B)(i) of Title 19 of the United States Code states that in making a material injury determination the Commission must consider the following factors:

(I) the volume of imports of the subject merchandise,

(II) the effect of imports of that merchandise on prices in the United States for domestic and like products, and

(III) the impact of imports of such merchandise on domestic producers of domestic like products, but only in the context of production operations within the United States. . . .19 U.S.C. § 1677(7)(B)(i).

imports." Specifically, the Commission noted that imports from Russia undersold South African chemical grade product in all eleven purchaser price comparisons and undersold Brazilian chemical grade product in ten of eleven purchaser price comparisons. In its price analysis, the Commission "recognized that nonsubject imports may have had an independent price depressive effect on domestic silicon metal prices." Ultimately, however, the Commission concluded that

> given the significant underselling by subject imports, subject import volume surges during the [period of interest], and the high degree of substitutability between subject imports and the domestic product, . . . the subject imports themselves have significantly depressed domestic silicon metal prices in all three customer segments (*i.e.*, chemical, primary and secondary aluminum customers).

As part of its material injury determination, the Commission specifically addressed the respondents' argument "that there was no causal nexus between subject imports and the injury suffered by the domestic industry because of the presence of interchangeable and readily available nonsubject imports." The Commission found that "subject imports registered a 4.8 percentage point market share gain while nonsubject imports lost 2.3 percentage points in market share from 2000 to 2001, the same year that the domestic industry suffered an operating loss for the first time during the [period of interest]and idled, closed, or converted many of its silicon metal production facilities." Specifically, the Commission explained that Russian imports' share of total imports increased from 7.3% in the first quarter of 2001 to 26.2%, 31.4%, and 40.1%, respectively, in the remaining three quarters of 2001. Similarly, Russian imports' share of total imports was 31.5% in first quarter 2002 and 36.9% in second quarter 2002, before declining to 11.6% in third quarter 2002, following the Commission's and the Department of Commerce's preliminary determinations in this investigation. The Commission also observed that by quantity, nonsubject import volume increased only by 25.8% from interim 2001 to interim 2002, whereas subject import volume increased by 57.6% during the same period.

In view of this data, the Commission concluded that "the fact that nonsubject imports may have contributed to the domestic industry's continued deterioration toward the end of the period, along with subject imports, does not negate our finding that subject imports themselves had a material adverse impact on the domestic industry." This is precisely the causation analysis necessary in view of *Gerald Metals*. Neither the statute nor *Gerald Metals* imposes the rigidity in findings or analysis that the majority seems to require. Indeed, the *Gerald Metals* opinion acknowledges the "unique circumstances" in that case. *Gerald Metals, 132 F.3d at 722.*

Contrary to the majority's assertion, the Commission here did not "claim that it is not obligated to follow this court's precedent." *Maj. op.* at 10. Rather, the Commission merely noted that Commission investigations are *sui generis* and, because of this, its prior investigations may not always form the basis for clear precedent that transcends different fact patterns. When explaining the factual differences between *Gerald Metals* (and other similar cases[2]) and the present case, the Commission found significant that in *Gerald Metals* subject import volume had decreased, both in absolute terms and relative to domestic consumption, during the last *full year* of the period of interest. These volume trends, explained the Commission, indicated that the significance of LTFV imports diminished during the period of interest, thus suggesting that in *Gerald Metals* any injury to domestic injury was not by reason of the subject imports. Because of the factual differences between *Gerald Metals* and the present case, the Commission determined that "respondents' arguments that *Gerald Metals* precludes an affirmative determination in this investigation [were] unpersuasive."

As summarized above, the Commission performed a proper material injury analysis, including explaining why the subject imports caused material injury to the domestic industry despite the existence of interchangeable nonsubject imports. In fact, the Commission expressly acknowledged its obligation to consider the effect of nonsubject imports in its investigation, citing *Gerald Metals* and *Taiwan Semiconductor*:

We have considered the evidence on nonsubject imports in this investigation and find, notwithstanding the presence of nonsubject imports, that subject imports themselves caused material injury to the domestic industry and did not simply contribute to the injury in a "tangential or minimal way." *Gerald Metals, 132 F.3d at 722*; *Taiwan Semiconductor Industry Assoc. v. United States, 266 F.3d 1339, 1344 (Fed. Cir. 2001).*

I fail to see what more the Commission should be required to do to explain its decision.

---

2 For example, in discussing *Taiwan Semiconductor Industry Assoc. v. United States, 266 F.3d 1339 (Fed. Cir. 2001)*, the Commission noted that this court had affirmed the Commission's redetermination. There the Commission found that, throughout the period of investigation, Taiwanese Static Random Access Memory Semiconductor ("SRAMS") market share, both by value and by quantity, had remained relatively flat. The domestic industry's market share, by quantity, declined by about 15 while the market share of nonsubject imports increased by almost that amount. During the years in which the domestic industry suffered its greatest injury, imports from Taiwan frequently oversold U.S. product. Thus, the Commission was simply noting the clear difference between the fact pattern present in *Taiwan Semiconductor* and the one before it.

CARIBBEAN ISPAT LIMITED
v.
UNITED STATES

450 F.3d 1336 (D.C. Cir. 2006)
Decided May 4, 2006

Mark A. Moran, Steptoe & Johnson LLP, of Washington, DC, argued for plaintiff-appellant. With him on the brief were Matthew S. Yeo and Evangeline Keenan.

Jonathan J. Engler, Attorney, Office of the General Counsel, United States International Trade Commission, of Washington, DC, argued for defendant-appellee. With him on the brief were James M. Lyons, General Counsel and Andrea C. Casson, Assistant General Counsel For Litigation. Of counsel was Karen Veninga Driscoll.

Kathleen W. Cannon, Collier Shannon Scott PLLC, of Washington, DC, argued for defendants-appellees. With her on the brief were Paul C. Rosenthal and R. Alan Luberda.

Before BRYSON, LINN, and PROST, Circuit Judges.

OPINION

BRYSON, *Circuit Judge*.

In August 2001 several domestic producers of steel wire rod filed petitions with the Department of Commerce and the International Trade Commission alleging that imports of steel wire rod from 12 countries, including Trinidad and Tobago, benefited from countervailing subsidies or were sold at less than fair value ("LTFV"). The petitioners further alleged that the imports from those countries, both collectively and from each country separately, had caused material injury to the domestic wire rod industry. Certain preliminary and final determinations relating to the petition have been challenged in various proceedings in the Court of International Trade and in this court. The present appeal is limited to imports from Trinidad and Tobago. In October 2002, the Commission determined that LTFV imports, collectively and from Trinidad and Tobago alone, had caused material injury to the domestic industry. Caribbean Ispat Limited, a Trinidadian producer of steel wire rod, sought review of that determination in the Court of International Trade, but the court upheld the Commission's determination. *Caribbean Ispat Ltd. v. United States, 366 F. Supp. 2d 1300 (Ct. Int'l Trade 2005)*. Caribbean Ispat appeals from that decision.

I

In an antidumping investigation such as the one in this case, the Commission is required to determine whether an industry in the United States is materially injured or threatened with material injury by reason of the imports that are the subject of the investigation. *19 U.S.C. § 1673d(b)(1)* . Section 1677(7) sets forth the factors and methods the Commission is to use in making a materiality determination. The statute requires the Commission, when making a materiality determination, to consider the volume of imports, the price effects of those imports, and the impact of those imports on the affected domestic industry. *19 U.S.C. § 1677(7)(B)(i)*. In addition to those factors, the Commission may consider "such other economic factors as are relevant to the determination." *Id.* § 1677(7)(B)(ii). The effect of nonsubject imports (i.e., the flow of fairly traded goods into the United States) is often a relevant "other economic factor" that the Commission looks at when considering whether a particular domestic injury was caused by the subject imports (i.e., as opposed to having been caused by the fairly traded goods alone).

Section 1677(7)(G)(i) sets forth the general rule that the Commission must cumulate imports from all countries that are subject to the investigation and that it must determine whether the impact of those cumulated imports is causing a material injury to the domestic industry. However, section 1677(7)(G)(ii) provides several exceptions to that general rule. One of those exceptions, mandated by the Caribbean Basin Economic Recovery Act (CBERA), *19 U.S.C. § 1677(7)(G)(ii)(III)*, exempts Caribbean nations from the cumulation rule and requires the Commission to analyze the volume, price effects, and impact of imports from Caribbean nations separately from those from all other countries. Because Trinidad and Tobago is the only Caribbean nation involved in the present investigation, CBERA required the Commission to assess Trinidad and Tobago's imports individually. Caribbean Ispat's appeal focuses on the application of CBERA to the Commission's investigation of imports of steel wire rod from Trinidad and Tobago.

II

The primary dispute in this case pertains to the causation analysis. The parties disagree as to whether and how LTFV imports from non-CBERA countries are assessed in determining whether the domestic industry was materially injured "by reason of" imports from Trinidad and Tobago. The Commission contends, and the Court of International Trade held, that the relevant statutes prohibit the Commission from considering the effect of LTFV imports from non-CBERA countries when weighing the impact of imports from Trinidad and Tobago.[1] Caribbean Ispat contends that CBERA requires the Commission to weigh the impact of imports from Trinidad and Tobago against the impact of all other imports (both LTFV and fairly traded imports), and to determine whether imports from non-CBERA countries are "so significant" as to render the impact of imports from Trinidad and Tobago immaterial.

A

In support of the argument that the statute prohibits the Commission from considering the effect of LTFV imports from non-CBERA countries, the Commission relies on the following passage from the Uruguay Round Agreements Act Statement of Administrative Action (URAASAA):

> Existing U.S. law and legislative history fully implement the causation standard of the 1979 [Tokyo Round] Codes. Thus, existing U.S. law fully implements [the causation provisions of the Agreement on Implementation of Article VI of the General Agreement on Tariffs and Trade 1994 (Antidumping)]. [Those provisions] do include new language requiring WTO signatories to "examine all relevant evidence" including "any known factors, other than the dumped [or subsidized] imports which at the same time are injuring the domestic industry." The obligations embodied in the new language are reflected in the existing statute and legislative history.

H.R. Doc. No. 103-316, vol. 1, at 851-52 (1994), *reprinted in* 1994 U.S.C.C.A.N. 4040. In the Commission's view, that passage limits the scope of the "other economic factors" the Commission may consider, pursuant to *19 U.S.C. § 1677(7)(B)(ii)*, when making a materiality determination. Because the URAASAA notes that existing law allows consideration of factors "other than the dumped imports," the Commission argues that dumped imports from non-CBERA countries cannot be considered when determining whether a CBERA country caused material injury.

That argument reads too much into the URAASAA's brief discussion of causation. First, the passage does not speak to the unique circumstances of CBERA or other non-cumulation provisions. Second, we do not regard the above-quoted passage as Congress's comprehensive and exclusive interpretation of section 1677(7)(B)(ii). The passage does not specifically reference that statute, and the plain language of section 1677(7)(B)(ii) suggests a broad grant of discretion in materiality determinations that allows the Commission to "consider such other economic factors as are relevant." *See also Angus Chem. Co. v. United States, 140 F.3d 1478, 1484 (Fed. Cir. 1998)* (noting that the statute "permissively allows the Commission to consider other relevant factors as well, as the particulars of the case at hand may warrant"). In the present case, the Commission had authority to treat LTFV imports from non-CBERA countries as an "other economic factor," just as the Com-

---

1 The domestic steel wire rod producers do not advance this argument. Rather, they argue that the Commission properly accounted for non-CBERA imports when it concluded that Trinidad and Tobago's imports caused material injury.

mission ordinarily treats fairly traded imports as an "other economic factor" in dumping investigations that do not involve CBERA countries. *See, e.g., Gerald Metals, Inc. v. United States, 132 F.3d 716, 723 (Fed. Cir. 1997)* (remanding because the "Court of International Trade failed to consider properly the presence of fairly-traded Russian imports in affirming the Commission's determination of material injury by reason of the LTFV goods").

In addition to the argument based on the URAASAA, the Commission contends that permitting consideration of the effect of LTFV imports from non-CBERA countries would render the statute internally inconsistent. That is because CBERA allows the Commission to aggregate dumped imports from CBERA and non-CBERA countries when assessing whether the imports from non-CBERA countries are causing a material injury to a domestic industry. Thus, the Commission argues, it would be illogical to compare the impact of imports from Trinidad and Tobago to the cumulated impact of all subject imports, because the cumulated impact includes the impact of imports from Trinidad and Tobago.

The purported inconsistency is avoided by recognizing that the CBERA exception requires a separate and independent analysis of imports from CBERA countries to determine whether those imports are causing a material injury. That separate analysis is required regardless of whether non-CBERA countries are also analyzed in the same investigation. The fact that CBERA imports are factored into the analysis of cumulated imports has no bearing on the separate analysis the Commission is required to undertake to assess the impact of CBERA imports.

The Commission also argues that, pursuant to *Chevron U.S.A., Inc. v. Natural Resources Defense Council, Inc., 467 U.S. 837, 104 S. Ct. 2778, 81 L. Ed. 2d 694 (1984)*, we must defer to the Commission's reasonable interpretation of the statute. The problem with that argument is that the interpretation advanced in the Commission's brief in this case does not represent the Commission's considered, consistent, or formal interpretation of section 1677(7)(B)(ii). To the contrary, in a similar case the Commission has considered the effect of other LTFV imports when determining whether particular imports from a country subject to a similar non-cumulation provision caused a material injury to a domestic industry. *See Pure Magnesium from China and Israel*, USITC Pub. 3467, Inv. Nos. 701-TA-403, 731-TA-895-896, at 23 (Nov. 2001) (comparing the volume of dumped imports from Israel to the volume of dumped imports from China). Similarly, in this case the Commission did not assert that it was barred from considering the effect of dumped goods from non-CBERA countries. Instead, that view was raised, for the first time, in the Commission's brief to the Court of International Trade.

Although *Chevron* deference is not strictly limited to agency decisions that are the result of formal rulemaking or adjudication, an interpretation that is advanced by counsel in the course of litigation—not accompanied by any indication that it is the considered policy of the agency—is not the sort of interpretation that Congress intended to carry the "force of law." *United States v. Mead Corp., 533 U.S. 218, 226-*

27, 121 S. Ct. 2164, 150 L. Ed. 2d 292 (2001); *see also Bowen v. Georgetown Univ. Hosp., 488 U.S. 204, 212-13, 109 S. Ct. 468, 102 L. Ed. 2d 493 (1988)* ("We have never applied [*Chevron* deference] to agency litigating positions that are wholly unsupported by regulations, rulings, or administrative practice. . . . Congress has delegated to the administrative official and not to appellate counsel . . . ." (internal quotation marks omitted)). Thus, *Chevron* deference has no place in this case.

Nor do we see any reason to accord deference under *Skidmore v. Swift & Co., 323 U.S. 134, 65 S. Ct. 161, 89 L. Ed. 124 (1944)*, to the interpretation advanced in the Commission's brief in this litigation. The degree of deference to an agency's interpretations of a statute in the course of administering its statutory responsibilities "has been understood to vary with circumstances, and courts have looked to the degree of the agency's care, its consistency, formality, and relative expertness, and to the persuasiveness of the agency's position." Mead Corp. 533 U.S. at 228; *see also Cathedral Candle Co. v. Int'l Trade Comm'n, 400 F.3d 1352, 1366 (Fed. Cir. 2005)* ("We believe the Supreme Court intends for us to defer to an agency interpretation of the statute that it administers if the agency has conducted a careful analysis of the statutory issue, if the agency's position has been consistent and reflects agency-wide policy, and if the agency's position constitutes a reasonable conclusion as to the proper construction of the statute, even if we might not have adopted that construction without the benefit of the agency's analysis."). The argument proffered in the brief has none of those characteristics. In fact, the Commission's analysis in *Pure Magnesium from China and Israel* suggests that the Commission has recently endorsed an approach that is at odds with the argument advanced in the brief. Moreover, as discussed above, we believe that the reasoning in support of that argument is unpersuasive. Accordingly, we see no reason to defer to the position taken in the brief under the *Skidmore* doctrine.

Thus, the Court of International Trade erred by concluding that the Commission was prohibited from considering the effects of LTFV imports from non-CBERA countries when it assessed imports from Trinidad and Tobago.

B

Caribbean Ispat contends that "the Commission committed legal error because it did not evaluate whether the effects of [Trinidad and Tobago's] imports were material in light of the vastly larger volumes of other subject imports." Additionally, Caribbean Ispat contends that the Commission's analysis "said literally nothing at all" about the effect of fairly traded imports. Caribbean Ispat asserts that if the Commission had properly considered LTFV and fairly traded imports from non-CBERA countries, the Commission would have had to conclude that the effects of those other imports were "so significant" and their presence so "dominant" as to render Trinidad and Tobago's LTFV imports immaterial. The domestic steel rod producers argue that the Commission considered the effect of LTFV and fairly traded imports when it concluded that Trinidad and Tobago's imports were, themselves, having a significant adverse impact on the domestic industry. In light of this court's recent decision in *Bratsk Aluminum Smelter v. United States, 444 F.3d 1369, 2006 U.S. App. LEXIS 8681, No. 05-1213 (Fed. Cir. Apr. 10, 2006)*, however, we cannot uphold the Commission's decision.

In *Bratsk*, we addressed the "by reason of" standard, and explained that

> where commodity products are at issue and fairly traded, price competitive, non-subject imports are in the market, the Commission must explain why the elimination of subject imports would benefit the domestic industry instead of resulting in the non-subject imports' replacement of the subject imports' market share without any beneficial impact on domestic producers.

Id., 2006 U.S. App. LEXIS 8681.

In the present case, the Commission found a "high level of fungibility between subject imports from Trinidad and Tobago and the domestic product, and between subject imports from Trinidad and Tobago and imports from each of the other subject countries." However, the Commission did not specifically address whether Trinidad and Tobago's imports could or would be replaced by other imports so that the domestic industry would not benefit from the removal of Trinidad and Tobago's imports from the U.S. market. Because CBERA required the Commission to treat Trinidad and Tobago's imports separately from all other imports, our holding in *Bratsk* indicates that, in the present case, the "Commission is required to make a specific causation determination and in that connection to directly address whether [other LTFV imports and/or fairly traded imports] would have replaced [Trinidad and Tobago's] imports without any beneficial effect on domestic producers." Id., 2006 U.S. App. LEXIS 8681. The Commission did not make that specific determination in this case. We therefore remand for further consideration of the causation analysis in light of *Bratsk* and our discussion of CBERA in this opinion.

VACATED AND REMANDED.

INTERNATIONAL IMAGING MATERIALS, INC.
v.
UNITED STATES INTERNATIONAL TRADE COMMISSION

Court No. 04-00215 (Ct. Int'l Trade 2006)
Decided January 23, 2006

Before: Richard K. Eaton, Judge

OPINION AND ORDER

[United States International Trade Commission's final negative determination on wax and wax/resin thermal transfer ribbons remanded]

Steptoe & Johnson, LLP (*Richard O. Cunningham*, *Tina Potuto Kimble*, and *Thomas J. Trendl*), for plaintiff.

James M. Lyons, General Counsel, United States International Trade Commission; *Neal J. Reynolds*, Acting Assistant General Counsel, United States International Trade Commission (*Andrea C. Casson*), for defendant.

Wiley Rein & Fielding LLP (*Alan H. Price* and *Daniel B. Pickard*), for defendant-intervenors Armor U.S.A. and Armor, S.A.

Paul, Hastings, Janofsky & Walker LLP (*Hamilton Loeb* and *Alexander W. Koff*), for defendant-intervenors DNP IMS America Corp. and Dai Nippon Printing Co., Ltd.

Eaton, Judge: This matter is before the court following the motion of plaintiff International Imaging Materials, Inc.

("IIMAK") for judgment upon the agency record pursuant to USCIT Rule 56.2. By its motion, IIMAK contests the final negative determinations of the U.S. International Trade Commission ("ITC" or "Commission") in the antidumping duty investigations concerning certain wax and wax/resin thermal transfer ribbons ("TTR") from France and Japan. *See* Certain Wax and Wax/Resin Thermal Transfer Ribbons From France and Japan Determinations, 69 Fed. Reg. 20,949 (Apr. 19, 2004) ("Final Determination"). In its Final Determination, the ITC found that the domestic industry was not injured or threatened with injury by reason of subject imports.

The court has jurisdiction over this matter pursuant to 28 U.S.C. § 1581(c) (2000) and 19 U.S.C. § 1516a (a) (2) (B) (iii) (2000). For the reasons set forth below, this matter is remanded to the ITC for action in accordance with this opinion.

BACKGROUND

TTRs are ink-covered strips of film used in barcode printers and fax machines. *See* Certain Wax and Wax/Resin Thermal Transfer Ribbons from France and Japan, Inv. Nos. 731-TA-1039-1040 (Final), Confidential Views of the Commission (April 2004), Conf. R. Doc. 314 ("ITC Views"). The first two steps in producing TTR, ink-making and coating, are done exclusively by "coaters" that possess the machinery and equipment necessary to perform that work. *Id.* at 3. These steps yield "jumbo rolls." The jumbo rolls are put through two additional production steps, slitting and packaging, by "slitters" before being sold on the open market. *Id.* The additionally-processed product produced by the slitters is known as finished TTR. *Id.* at 3 n.5. Finished TTR falls into two categories: fax TTR, also known as "finished fax TTR" or "slit-fax TTR" and non-fax TTR, also known as "barcode TTR." There are few U.S. sales of imported jumbo rolls because wholly-owned subsidiaries of foreign-based coaters (i.e., U.S.-based slitters) largely consume the rolls themselves to produce finished fax TTR and barcode TTR. *Id.* at 30.[1]

STANDARD OF REVIEW

The court will hold unlawful "any determination, finding, or conclusion found . . . to be unsupported by substantial evidence on the record, or otherwise not in accordance with law . . . ." 19 U.S.C. § 1516a(b)(1)(B)(I). Substantial evidence is "such relevant evidence as a reasonable mind might accept as adequate to support a conclusion." *Consol. Edison Co. v. NLRB*, 305 U.S. 197, 229 (1938) (citations omitted). It "requires 'more than a mere scintilla,' but is satisfied by 'something less than the weight of the evidence.'" *Altx, Inc. v. United States*, 370 F.3d 1108, 1116 (Fed. Cir. 2004) (quoting *Atl. Sugar, Ltd. v. United States*, 744 F.2d 1556, 1562 (Fed. Cir. 1984); *Matsushita Elec. Indus. Co. v. United States*, 750 F.2d 927, 933 (Fed. Cir. 1984)). The existence of substantial evidence is determined "by considering the record as a whole, including evidence that . . . 'fairly detracts from the substantiality of the evidence.'" *Huaiyin Foreign Trade Corp. (30) v. United States*, 322 F.3d 1369, 1374 (Fed. Cir. 2003) (quoting *Atl. Sugar*, 744 F.2d at 1562). In conducting its review, the court's function is not to reweigh the evidence but rather to ascertain "whether there was evidence which could reasonably lead to the Commission's conclusion . . . ." *Matsushita*, 750 F.2d at 933. The possibility of drawing two inconsistent conclusions from the record evidence does not, in itself,

---

1 The ITC "refer[s] to TTR that is slit and packaged as 'finished TTR' but note[s] that parties often used the terms 'slit' or 'slitted' synonymously with 'finished.'" ITC Views at 3 n.5.

prevent the ITCs determinations from being supported by substantial evidence. *Consolo v. Fed. Mar. Comm'n*, 383 U.S. 607, 620 (1966) (citations omitted); *Altx*, 370 F.3d at 1116.

DISCUSSION

Plaintiff makes two primary arguments as to why the ITC s Final Determination is flawed. First it claims that the Commission erred in its definition of the domestic like product and second, that in its volume and price effects analysis, the ITC should have looked beyond the limited competition for jumbo rolls to downstream competition for finished TTR.

I. Domestic Like Product—The ITCs Use of Its Six-Factor Analysis

In order to determine whether a domestic industry is materially injured or threatened with material injury, the ITC must define the domestic like product. *See* 19 U.S.C. § 1677(10). While Commerce determines the scope of its less than fair value investigation, the ITC is responsible for identifying "the corresponding universe of items produced in the United States that are like[,] or in the absence of like, most similar in characteristics and uses with the items in the scope of the investigation." Def.'s Mem. in Opp'n to Pl.'s Mot. J. Agency R. ("Def.'s Mem.") at 15; *see also* 19 U.S.C. § 1677(10). After the ITC has determined what constitutes the domestic like product, it must next examine "the volume of imports, their effect on prices for the domestic like product, and their impact on domestic producers of the domestic like product . . . ." ITC Views at 27; see *also* 19 U.S.C. § 167 7(7)(B)(i)(I)-(III). All of these factors are considered "within the context of the business cycle and conditions of competition that are distinctive to the affected industry." 19 U.S.C. § 1677(7) (C) (iii).

The ITC defines domestic like product by determining whether there are "clear dividing lines" between any of the domestically-produced items that would warrant finding more than one item to be part of the definition or excluding an item from the definition. *NEC Corp. v. Dep't of Commerce*, 22 CIT 1108, 1110, 36 F. Supp. 2d 380, 383 (1998). That is, if the ITC concludes that there are no clear dividing lines between any of the domestically produced items, it then includes them as part of the domestic like product. "The Commission's decision regarding the appropriate domestic like product is a factual determination, where the Commission applies the statutory standard of 'like' or 'most similar in characteristics and uses' on a case-by-case basis." *Id.* The ITCs findings with respect to domestic like product may, but need not, match the scope of the investigation. *See Hosiden Corp. v. Advanced Display Mfrs.*, 85 F.3d 1561, 1568 (Fed. Cir. 1996) (explaining that the ITC has the discretion to determine to what extent the class or kind of merchandise described by Commerce falls within the scope).

In the Final Determination, the ITC used its previously employed six-factor analysis,[2] which compares (1) physical characteristics and uses; (2) interchangeability; (3) channels of distribution; (4) customer and producer perceptions; (5) manufacturing facilities, production processes, and production employees; and (6) price of the domestic products to the subject imports. *See* ITC Views at 8. Using this analysis, the Commission concluded that finished fax TTR was part of the domestic like product. *See id.* at 8-14.

Plaintiff questions the use of the six-factor test, insisting that the ITC erred in not applying a semifinished product analysis, which seeks to determine "whether articles at different stages of processing should be included in the same like product."[3] Br. of IIMAK in Supp. of R. 56.2 Mot. J. Agency R. ("Pl.'s Br.") at 30. As IIMAK explains in its brief:

> Under this [semifinished product] analysis, the ITC examines (1) whether the upstream article is dedicated to the production of the downstream article or has independent uses; (2) whether there are perceived to be separate markets for the upstream and downstream articles; (3) differences in the physical characteristics and functions of the upstream and downstream articles; (4) differences in the costs or value of the vertically differentiated articles; and (5) the significance and extent of the processes used to transform the upstream into the downstream articles.

Pl.'s Br. at 31 n.32. Thus, using IIMAK's preferred methodology, the upstream product jumbo rolls would be compared to the downstream products barcode TTR and finished fax TTR. IIMAK explains:

> Applying the semifinished product analysis in this case would have [led] to the conclusion that [finished] fax TTR is not part of the same like product as certain TTR.[4] Jumbo rolls are not dedicated to the production of [finished] fax TTR. . . . [T]here are separate markets for jumbo and [finished] fax TTR. There are also differences in physical characteristics and functions of jumbo rolls (which are large rolls designed to be slit) and [finished] fax TTR (which are used as a component part in fax machines and come in more advanced packaging). While jumbo rolls are completely

---

2 *See*, e.g., *Acciai Speciali Terni S.p.A. v. United States*, 24 CIT 1064, 1065 and n.4, 118 F. Supp. 2d 1298, 1300 and n.4 (2000)(upholding the ITCs use of its six-factor test); *NMB Singapore Ltd. v. United States*, 27 CIT __, __, 288 F. Supp. 2d 1306, 1326 (2003)(sustaining the ITCs use of the six-factor analysis) .

3 As with the six-factor analysis, the ITC has used the semifinished product analysis in the past. *See, e.g.*, Stainless Steel Bar from Brazil, India, Japan, and Spain, Inv. No. 731-TA- 678, 679, 681, and 682 (Final), USITC Pub. No. 2856 (1995).

4 IIMAK notes that finished fax TTR was specifically excluded from Commerce's scope determination.

> The scope includes jumbo rolls of wax TTR that are used in facsimile and multifunction thermal transfer printing devices . . . jumbo rolls of wax/resin TTR that are used in bar code printing devices . . . and rolls of bar code TTR that have been slit and finished for use in specific printing devices ("finished TTR"). The scope, however, excludes rolls of fax TTR that have been slit and finished for use in other specific printing devices ("finished fax TTR").

ITC Views at 7 (footnote omitted) (internal citation omitted).

> fungible products with little or no distinguishing features between products of the same type, [finished] fax TTR is a tailor-made product. The functions of TTR in jumbo roll form and [finished] fax TTR are also different. Jumbo TTR rolls have no purpose other than slitting. They are, however, primarily slit into subject barcode TTR. [Finished] fax TTR is inserted into fax machines in which it is used for thermal transfer printing.

Pl.'s Br. at 31-32 (internal citations omitted). IIMAK asserts that it is entitled to the use of the semifinished product analysis based on its utilization in previous cases, in particular Chlorinated Isocyanurates From China and Spain, Inv. Nos. 731-TA-1082-1083 (Prelim.), USITC Pub. No. 3705 (2004).[5] Plaintiff contends that the ITC, having previously used the semifinished product analysis, is bound to continue to use it in this case. "The ITC must pick a methodology to apply to certain factual circumstances and only depart from it when it provides a reasoned justification for doing so." Pl.'s Br. at 31.

The ITC maintains that "IIMAK's discussion of ITC factual determinations as though they were precedential is wrong as a matter of law." Def.'s Mem. at 11. In making this claim, the Commission relies on *Ranchers-Cattlemen Action Legal Found. v. United States*, 23 CIT 861, 74 F. Supp. 2d 1353 (1999), in which the Court explained that "[a]n action by the ITC becomes an 'agency practice' when a uniform and established procedure exists that would lead a party, in the absence of notification of change, reasonably to expect adherence to the established practice or procedure." *Id.* at 884-85, 74 F. Supp. 2d at 1374. According to the Commission, ITC decisions must be "'based upon an independent evaluation of the factors with respect to the unique economic situation of each product and industry under investigation.'" *Id.* at 885, 74 F. Supp. 2d at 1374 (quoting *Citrosuco Paulista, S.A. v. United States*, 12 CIT 1196, 1209, 704 F. Supp. 1075, 1087-88 (1988)); *see also Nucor Corp. v. United States*, 28 CIT __, __, 318 F. Supp. 2d 1207, 1247 (2004) (noting that each investigation involves a "'unique combination and interaction of many economic variables . . . .'") (quoting *Ranchers-Cattlemen*, 23 CIT at 891, 74 F. Supp. 2d at 1379). The Commission further contends that IIMAK has not shown that it deviated from an established practice or procedure, since it applied its six-factor analysis, which it had previously employed on a number of occasions. *See* Def.'s Mem. at 11.

The court agrees that the ITC s prior factual determinations cited by IIMAK do not constitute precedent that the Commission is bound to follow. First, as with all investigations, the present fact pattern is not precisely the same as any with which the ITC has been presented. As such, while some of the facts may have appeared

---

5 In that case, the scope included all chemical and physical forms of chlorinated isocyanurates ("isos"), and the ITC concluded that multiple forms of isos were the same like product. Nonetheless, the ITC used the semifinished product analysis to determine whether two different physical forms of isos, granular and tableted, were also part of the like product. IIMAK argues that this decision "stands in direct contradiction of the ITC s position in the instant case." Pl.'s Br. at 31.

in other investigations, the totality of the facts is unique. See, *e.g., Committee for Fair Beam Imports v. United States*, 27 CIT,, slip op. 03-73 at 25 (June 27, 2003) (not reported in the Federal Supplement), *aff'd*, 95 Fed. Appx. 347 (Fed. Cir. 2004) ("[T]he fact that similar patterns are observed in different investigations with regard to some of the variables does not preclude a different interpretation of the patterns after viewing the entire economic environment as a whole."); *see also Citrosuco*, 12 CIT at 1209, 704 F. Supp. at 1087 ("[E]ach injury investigation is *sui generis*, involving a unique combination and interaction of many economic variables; and consequently, a particular circumstance in a prior investigation cannot be regarded by the Commission as dispositive of the determination in a later investigation.") (internal quotation omitted). Nor does the court find that the ITC had established an "agency practice" from which it deviated in this case. As is noted in *Ranchers-Cattlemen*, an agency practice is established when a uniform procedure exists that would lead a party to reasonably expect that the agency would adhere to the procedure. *Id.* at 884-85, 74 F. Supp. 2d at 1374. Here, an examination of the prior investigations cited by both parties reveals that the ITC has chosen the six-factor test in some instances and the semifinished product analysis in others with not wholly dissimilar fact patterns.[6] Thus, IIMAK cannot claim any reasonable expectation that its preferred methodology would be used.

Nonetheless, the ITCs decision to use the six-factor analysis has not been sufficiently explained to justify its utilization in this case. Here, the ITC does nothing more than state its conclusion that "it found the traditional six-factor test to be the more useful to address the issue of whether to include finished fax TTR in the domestic like product because the scope included products that are at the same level of processing as the finished fax TTR." Def.'s Mem. at 26. The Commission further claims that because "[t]he aim of both the traditional six-factor test and the semifinished product analysis is the same - to ascertain whether there is a clear dividing line between products," *id.* at 25, it has the discretion to determine, based (Final) and Invs. Nos. 731-TA-788-793 (Final), USITC Pub. No. 3188 (1999) and in Certain Bearings From China, France, Germany, Hungary, Italy, Japan, Romania, Singapore, Sweden, and the United Kingdom, Inv. Nos. AA1921-143, 731-TA-341, 731-TA-343-345, 731-TA-391-397, and 731-TA-399 (Rev.), USITC Pub. No. 3309 (2000). However, the ITC used the semifinished product analysis in Stainless Steel Bar From Brazil, India, Japan, and Spain, Inv. No. 731-TA-678, 679, 681, and 682 (Final), USITC Pub. No. 2856 (1995) and in Chlorinated Isocyanurates From China and Spain, Inv. No. 731-TA-1082 and 1083 (Prelim.), USITC Pub. No. 3705 (2004) on the particular facts of the investigation, which test is the appropriate one to apply.

Although the ITC is permitted to make varying determinations based on the facts of each case, it may not act arbitrarily. Rather, the ITC must present a "reviewable,

6 For example, the ITC applied its six-factor test in Certain Stainless Steel Plate From Belgium, Canada, Italy, Korea, South Africa, and Taiwan, Invs. Nos. 701-TA-376, 377, and 379

reasoned basis" for its determinations. *Bando Chem. Indus., Ltd. v. United States*, 17 CIT 798, 799 (1993) (not reported in the Federal Supplement). "[An] agency must explain its rationale . . . such that a court may follow and review its line of analysis, its reasonable assumptions, and other relevant considerations." *Allegheny Ludlum Corp. v. United States*, 29 CIT __, __, 358 F. Supp. 2d 1334, 1344 (2005). "Explanation is necessary . . . for this court to perform its statutory review function." *Dastech Int'l, Inc. v. United States*, 21 CIT 469, 475, 963 F. Supp. 1220, 1226 (1997); *see also Asociacion Colombiana de Exportadores de Flores v. United States*, 12 CIT 1174, 1177, 704 F. Supp. 1068, 1071 (1988) ("[R]easons for the choices made among various potentially acceptable alternatives usually need to be explained."). On remand, therefore, the ITC is directed to explain why it is justified in using its six-factor analysis in defining the domestic like product in this case. In doing so, the ITC shall explicitly address why the semifinished product analysis urged by plaintiff is not appropriate here.

II. Volume and Price Effects of Subject Imports[7]

IIMAK next disputes the methodology the ITC used to measure the volume and price effects of the subject imports.[8] In its volume analysis, the ITC measured only imports of jumbo rolls. IIMAK asserts that the proper analysis would have counted as imports the finished TTR produced in the United States from the imported jumbo rolls. Specifically, plaintiff argues that "there can be no dispute" that the jumbo rolls are used merely for transformation into finished TTR (either finished barcode or finished fax TTR) by a U.S. company related to the importer (and thus excluded from the U.S. industry), so that it can be sold to an unrelated customer in the market for finished TTR. Pl.'s Br. at 9. Thus, "the only meaningful way to measure volume factors and price effects of imports on the U.S. industry is based on the volume and prices of the *finished* TTR into which the imported product is made." *Id.* at 9 (emphasis added).[9] IIMAK states that by only looking at the volume and price effects of imported jumbo rolls, the ITC fails to take into account that "competition for TTR sales almost exclusively occurs at the further processed level . . . . There is simply no way to measure the effects on the U.S. market of

7 While it might be assumed that a discussion of this issue could reasonably await the court's findings concerning domestic like product, since both parties agree that the domestic like product contains both jumbo rolls and at least one downstream product, a discussion of plaintiff's claims relating to volume is proper here.

8 In making its injury determination, the Commission shall consider "(I) the volume of imports of the subject merchandise, (II) the effect of imports of that merchandise on prices in the United States for domestic like product, and (III) the impact of imports of such merchandise on domestic producers of domestic like products . . . ." 19 U.S.C. § 1677(7)(B).

9 IIMAK explains its proposed methodology as "measur[ing] imports' effects based on the first point in the distribution chain at which they entered the U.S. market on an arm's length basis. This includes U.S. merchant market sales of both subject imported jumbo rolls and [finished] TTR made from imported subject jumbo rolls." Pl.'s Br. at 10 n.8.

subject imports dedicated to a downstream product if the ITC does not measure the effects at the downstream level." *Id.*

In its ITC Views, the Commission disputes IIMAK's claim that it should measure shipments and market share of subject imports using the downstream product. The ITC explains, "[O]ur finding that the activities of domestic [slitters] are domestic production means that their shipments are domestic shipments." ITC Views at 32-33. In other words, the ITC relies on its finding that the work performed by the domestic slitters rendered them domestic producers and, thus, necessarily excluded their products from being part of subject imports. This being the case, according to the Commission, the only remaining imported product that could be used to measure volume and price effects was the jumbo rolls.

The ITC used its production-related activities test to reach its conclusion that the slitters produce a domestic product. *Id.* The Commission explains:

> First, testimonial evidence by several [slitters] indicated that the initial capital investment necessary to compete effectively in the U.S. market was significant, and included investment in multiple machines necessary to produce the sizes and quantities required by large purchasers. IIMAK's own witness agreed that slitting machines are costly. . . . As to technical expertise involved in U.S. production activities, the ITC found, based on testimony and other evidence presented by [slitters] ITW and Armor, that the level of expertise required for slitting operations is not insignificant. Based on [slitters'] questionnaire responses, the ITC also found that the percentage of value added by slitting and packaging operations (an average of 30 percent of the total cost of the end product) is significant. With respect to employment levels, the ITC noted that all parties, including IIMAK, agreed that slitting and packaging operations are labor intensive, and require employment of a substantial number of employees.

Def.'s Mem. at 27-28 (internal citations omitted); *see also* ITC Views at 15-19 (analyzing the six factors related to production activities that the ITC considers in deciding whether a firm qualifies as a domestic producer).

IIMAK maintains, however, that "[e]ven assuming the Commission correctly found that the converted products undergo substantial processing in the United States,[10] these products still are created for the sole benefit of the foreign respondents and are still within the scope." Pl.'s Br. at 11-12.

The ITC enjoys broad discretion to choose a methodology for measuring volume. *Ceramica Regiomontana, S.A. v. United States*, 10 CIT 399, 404-05, 636 F. Supp. 961, 966 (1986), *aff'd*, 810 F.2d 1137 (Fed. Cir. 1987) ("As long as the agency's methodology and procedures are a reasonable means of effectuating the statutory purpose . . . the court will not impose its own views as to the sufficiency of the agency' s investigation or question the agency's methodology."). Here, the court agrees with the ITCs finding that the U.S.-based slitters engaged in sufficient production-related activities in transforming the jumbo rolls into finished TTR to con-

---

10 It is worth noting that IIMAK did not appeal this finding.

stitute domestic production. *See USEC Inc. v. United States*, 27 CIT __, __, 259 F. Supp. 2d 1310, 1327 (2003) (noting that the production-related activities test focuses on whether "the overall nature of production-related activities in the United States . . . are sufficient for a company to be considered a member of the domestic industry.") (internal quotation omitted). In its ITC Views, the Commission fully lays out its methodology and the facts it relied on in reaching its conclusions. *See* ITC Views at 16 ("[T]he value added by converting operations to the end-product, the number and technical expertise of workers employed by slitters, and their significant capital expenditures all indicate that these companies do not merely engage in low-level processing as petitioner alleges."). That being the case, the court finds that the ITC was justified in excluding finished TTR from its volume and price analysis. As a result, the sole remaining product that could constitute subject merchandise was the jumbo rolls. Thus, the court affirms the Commission's use of jumbo rolls for the purpose of measuring volume and price effects.

III. Substantial Evidence—Indirect Effects

In arguing that the ITC did not support its conclusions with substantial evidence, IIMAK first claims that it did not consider the indirect effects of the subject imports on the domestic industry. IIMAK insists that "[t]he ITC has [previously] determined that a finding of injurious price effects is not limited to instances where there is head-to-head price competition." Pl.'s Br. at 18. Plaintiff provides several examples in its brief:

> [I]n *Canned Pineapple Fruit from Thailand*, Inv. No. 731-TA-706 (Review), USITC Pub. 3417 at 12 (May 2001), the ITC held that prices in one product segment affected prices in another. Similarly, in *Low Enriched Uranium from France, Germany, the Netherlands, and the United Kingdom*, Inv. Nos. 701-TA-409-412 and 731-TA-909 (Final), USITC Pub. 3486 at 11 (February 2002), the ITC found that a small amount of product sold in a commodity spot market has effects on prices of products sold under contract. This Court likewise has held that "{s}ection 1677(7) (C) (ii) permits a finding of injury where an imported product . . . may not be directly substitutable but nonetheless causes price depression or suppression for the lower cost domestic product." *R-M Indus., Inc. v. United States*, 84 8 F. Supp. 2 04, 211 (CIT 1994).

Id. at 18 n.18(footnote omitted). That is, IIMAK claims that the Commission failed to take into account evidence that slitters using imported jumbo rolls gained an advantage due to the lower cost of these rolls. In response, the ITC states that it "took into account . . . that some U.S. production of finished TTR started with jumbo rolls of imported TTR." Def.'s Mem. at 37. The ITC explains:

> Contrary to IIMAK's assertion, the ITC did not ignore IIMAK's argument that [slitters] were driving prices down because they indirectly benefitted from their importation of subject jumbo rolls. The ITC examined this allegation and found that the evidence suggested otherwise. IIMAK overlooks the ITCs statement that the lack of underselling shown in the limited pricing data was corroborated by the average unit value (AUVs) for jumbo rolls. The AUV data show that, for each year of the [period of investigation], subject import unit values of jumbo rolls imported by the [slitters]

> were higher than the unit values of shipments of domestic jumbo rolls. In addition, the ITC observed that the financial performance of the [slitters] that were most dependent on imported jumbo rolls (i.e., the four related party [slitters]) was no better than that of the integrated producers. In light of these facts, the ITC reasonably found that importation of jumbo rolls did not confer a competitive advantage to [slitters] over the rest of the industry.

Id. at 34-35 (internal citations omitted)(footnote omitted).

Thus, the ITC states that

> With respect to IIMAK's arguments concerning "indirect effects" the ITC took into account . . . that some U.S. production of finished TTR started with jumbo rolls of imported TTR. The ITC did not "ignore" the conditions of competition emphasized by IIMAK. . . . As discussed above, the ITC considered IIMAK's argument that the [slitters] indirectly benefitted from the imports. The ITC found that this premise was not supported by the record evidence concerning [average unit values], comparative financial data, industry capacity data, and questionnaire responses. IIMAK may wish the ITC had weighed the evidence in a different manner, but that concern is not sufficient to sustain its appeal.

Id. at 37 (internal citations omitted). This claim is supported by the ITC Views and the evidence cited therein: "The pricing and average unit value data indicate that subject jumbo rolls were priced higher than domestic jumbo rolls, and as such [slitters] did not have a raw material cost advantage over domestic coaters." ITC Views at 35.

An examination of the data used by the ITC in reaching its conclusion reveals that there were no indirect effects of the sales of jumbo rolls because there was indeed no underselling of imported jumbo rolls, nor was there any evidence that the consumers of these rolls benefitted financially from their use. Thus, despite IIMAK's arguments to the contrary, the ITC did examine the possibility of indirect effects and supported its conclusion that there were none with substantial evidence.

IV. Reliability of Measurement of Price Effects

IIMAK next contends that the ITC erred by not using prices for finished TTR to measure the price effects of the subject merchandise imports. In its analysis, the ITC used prices for imports of jumbo rolls. As has been previously noted, there are few open market sales of jumbo rolls. IIMAK argues:

> Price comparison data for products with low volumes are not reliable for purposes of making price comparisons. To the extent that data for low volume products show overselling, the ITC thus should not rely on this overselling to make a negative determination. This Court has held that the ITC reasonably gives less weight to price comparisons for products where there are only a limited number of comparisons.[11]

---

11 IIMAK cites several cases to support its position. *See, e.g., Taiwan Semiconductor Industry Ass'n v. United States*, 24 CIT 914, 925, 118 F. Supp. 2d 1250, 1260 n.15 (2000) ("The record supports the Commission's conclusion that the quantities of products . . . were relatively small.

Pl.'s Br. at 19-20 (internal citations omitted).

IIMAK's argument, in essence, is but another way of saying that it objects to the Commission's sole use of jumbo rolls when measuring volume. The ITC disputes IIMAK's claim that the data it relied on for price comparisons was unreliable due to low product volume, explaining that it relied on these comparisons

> "because there were only small volumes of sales in this category," Def.'s Mem. at 34, not because the ITC failed to adequately investigate prices. In other words, "[s]ince there are not many sales of domestic jumbo TTR on the open market, the volume of shipments represented by the price data was of course small." *Id.* As this court has determined that the Commission is justified in its finding that slitters produce a domestic product, it will not disturb the ITCs use of jumbo rolls based on scarcity of transactions. Beyond showing that the ITC based its conclusions on a small number of transactions because there were, in fact, few transactions, IIMAK has failed to demonstrate that either the data or the conclusions drawn from the data are unreliable. *See* 19 U.S.C. § 1677(7) (c) (1) (affording the ITC broad discretion to determine the best methodology by which to measure volume). This being the case, the court sustains this portion of the ITCs findings.

V. The ITC's Findings Related to Price Movement[12]

Next, IIMAK contends that the ITC ignored pricing evidence calling into question its negative determination.[13] The Commission found that the movement of prices on the U.S. market was unrelated to the prices of subject imports. ITC Views at 34-35. It reached this finding, at least in part, by examining the prices at which "Product 3," which is the slit form of wax/resin products manufactured by IIMAK and other producers, was sold to original equipment manufacturers ("OEMs"). *See* Conf. Staff Rep., Conf. R. Doc. 292 at Table V-6.[14] IIMAK complains of the ITCs

---

Therefore, the Commission reasonably discounted the data regarding [these] products . . . in its analysis.") (internal citations omitted); *R-M Indus., Inc. v. United States*, 18 CIT 219, 228, 848 F. Supp. 204, 211 (1994) (affirming the ITCs decision to not rely on price comparison data where data was limited); *Trent Tube Div., Crucible Mat'ls Corp. v. United States*, 14 CIT 386, 403, 741 F. Supp. 921, 935 (1990) (giving limited weight to evidence of underselling where only a limited number of price comparisons were available).

12 Again, plaintiff's argument concerning the comparison of the subject imports to the domestic like product does not implicate its arguments concerning the inclusion of fax TTR in the definition of domestic like product.

13 Title 19 U.S.C. § 1677 (7) (C) (ii) provides that in evaluating price effects, the Commission shall consider whether

> (I) there has been significant price underselling by the imported merchandise as compared with the price of domestic like products of the United States, and
>
> (II) the effect of imports of such merchandise otherwise depresses prices to a significant degree or prevents price increases, which otherwise would have occurred, to a significant degree.

Id.

14 Table V-6 shows that U.S. prices do not correlate to the prices for the imported product. For example, U.S. prices increased from January through September of 2002, while import

finding of divergent trends, arguing that although U.S. and import prices for sales of Product 3 to OEMs were divergent over the period of investigation, the prices for sales of the same product to slitters/converters and distributors/resellers were strongly correlated.[15] While the ITC explains that it did not use the other products for which it had questionnaire responses because they included some domestic product, *see* ITC Views at 33, it does not provide an explanation in answer to plaintiff's argument. Because the ITC does not address this argument in its papers, on remand, the Commission shall do so, stating with particularity whether plaintiff is correct with respect to its correlation calculations.

VI. Volume—Market Share

In reaching its volume findings, the Commission concluded: "While the increase in absolute quantity of subject imports could be viewed as significant, subject imports grew only slightly relative to domestic consumption and decreased relative to domestic production. Given that fact . . . we do not find subject import volume overall to be significant." ITC Views at 32.

With respect to market share, plaintiff makes two related claims. First, IIMAK claims that the Commission did not take into account the increases in market share of imports during the period of investigation, stating that "the ITC found an increase in subject imports' market share over the period of investigation. It was inappropriate for the ITC to dismiss this increasing market share of the subject imports without explanation." Pl.'s Br. at 22. Thus, IIMAK maintains that the ITC erred by failing to consider even small increases when, for a fungible product such as TTR, "even small market share increases can be injurious." *Id.* Thus, IIMAK insists that these absolute increases in market share, even though small, must be considered.

Second, IIMAK urges that 19 U.S.C. § 1677(7) (C) (i)[16] requires the ITC to consider whether volume and market shares of the subject imports are significant on an

---

prices decreased. Similarly, U.S. prices fluctuated (i.e., decreased, then increased) from April through December of 2001, while import prices steadily declined for one importer and steadily increased for another. Conf. Staff Rep., Conf. R. Doc. 292 at Table V-6.

15 IIMAK states:

> While it is true that U.S. and import prices for sales of Product 3 to OEMs were divergent over the period of investigation, this product/channel combination is only one of four for which the ITC collected price data for sales of slit TTR, and accounted for only [[ ]] of U.S. coaters' shipment volume these four product/channel combinations and [[ ]] of importers'/converters' shipment volumes. For the other three product/channel combinations, there were very strong correlations between U.S. and importer/converter prices for slit TTR.

Pl.'s Mem. at 21-22 (internal citations omitted).

16 The statute states in relevant part, "In evaluating the volume of imports of merchandise, the Commission shall consider whether the volume of imports of the merchandise, or any increase in that volume, either in absolute terms or relative to production or consumption in the United States, is significant." 19 U.S.C. § 1677 (7) (C) (i) .

absolute basis, and that "the ITC s volume findings are limited only to a determination that the increases in the volume and market share are not significant. . . . As such, the ITCs analysis is incomplete in that it did not analyze whether the subject imports' market shares, standing alone, were significant." *Id.* at 23.

As to the second argument, the ITC defends its method of analyzing volume, explaining that "[u]nder the statute, the ITC considers whether the volume of subject imports *or* any increase in that volume, *either* in absolute terms *or* relative to production *or* consumption in the United States is significant." Def.'s Mem. at 32 (emphasis in original). The ITC cites several cases in which the Court has found that any one of the several methods of analyzing volume is sufficient. *See Copperweld Corp. v. United States*, 12 CIT 148, 167, 682 F. Supp. 552, 570 (1988) (explaining that the statutory language, "when read in conjunction with the legislative history[,][17] indicates that disjunctive language was chosen to signify congressional intent that the agency be given broad discretion to analyze import volume in the context of the industry concerned . . . ."); *see also Am. Bearing Mfrs. Ass'n. v. United States*, 28 CIT __, __,

350 F. Supp. 2d 1100, 1108 (2004) ("Congress recognized that in determining the significance of the volume, price effect, and impact of imports in the U.S. market, the ITC must evaluate the facts of each particular case, and the industry involved, and make its material injury determination accordingly."). Thus, both the statute and the cases indicate that the Commission did not exceed the discretion granted it in choosing to rely most heavily on relative comparisons rather than the absolute size of market share.

With respect to the small increase in subject import volume and market share, the ITC observed:

> Subject import volume increased over the period examined, from 295 million msi in 2001 to 373 million msi in 2003, an increase of 26 percent; shipments of subject imports rose 18 percent over the same period.[18] . . . As a percentage of domestic production, subject imports were [[ ]] percent (by quantity) in 2001, 19.7 percent in 2002, and 13.5 percent in 2003. Thus, subject imports, measured as a share of domestic production, actually declined over the period of investigation.

---

17 The legislative history reads in relevant part: "In determining whether an industry is materially injured, as that phrase is used in the bill, the ITC will consider . . . the factors set forth in [the statute] *together with any other factors it deems relevant. . . .*" *Copperweld*, 12 CIT at 167, 682 F. Supp. at 570 (emphasis added) (quoting S. Rep. No. 249, 96th Cong., 1st Sess. 88, *reprinted in* 1979 U.S.C.C.A.N. 381, 474).

18 Specifically, "[s]ubject imports accounted for [[ ]] percent of apparent U.S. consumption (by quantity) in 2001, [[ ]] percent in 2002, and [[ ]] percent in 2003." ITC Views at 31. Thus, subject imports' share of the U.S. market increased less than [[ ]] over the period of investigation.

In contrast, the domestic industry's market share increased significantly over the period of investigation.[19] . . . Coinciding with this increase in domestic market share, nonsubject imports' market share declined . . . over the same period.[20] Thus the domestic industry gained market share at the expense of nonsubject imports during the period of investigation.

ITC Views at 31—32 (citations omitted) (footnote omitted). Based on the forego- ing, the court finds that the ITC conformed to the statute by examining the sig- nificance of volume relative to both production and consumption. While the Com- mission did not explicitly analyze the small absolute increase in imported product market shares, its discussion demonstrates that it was not unmindful of that fact. Therefore, the ITC has satisfied the statutory demands of 19 U.S.C. § 1677 (7) (C) (i) .

VII. Impact

A. Profitability

IIMAK argues (1) that the ITC failed to address what it calls the "anomaly" of declining operating income and profitability at a time of increasing consumption[21] and (2) that slight declines in operating income cited by the ITC "were skewed by one company with large and increasing profitability over the period of investiga-

---

19 Specifically, "[t]he domestic industry's share of apparent U.S. consumption was [[ ]] percent in 2001, [[ ]] percent in 2002, and [[ ]] percent in 2003, for a period-wide increase of [[ ]] percentage points." ITC Views at 32.

20 The market share for nonsubject imports declined by [[ ]] percentage points over the period of investigation. *See* ITC Views at 32.

21 IIMAK relies on Certain Ceramic Station Post Insulators from Japan, Inv. No. 731-TA-1023 (Prelim.), USITC Pub. No. 3578 (2003), to support its argument. In that case, the ITC stated:

> Based on significant declines or sustained weaknesses in most of the performance indicators of the domestic industry during a period of increasing demand and at the same time that the subject merchandise was being imported in significantly increasing quantities and sold at prices significantly below the weighted average of domestic industry sales, we find that the subject imports had a significant adverse impact on the domestic industry.

Id. at 14.

The ITC disputes plaintiff's characterization of its finding in Ceramic Station Post Insulators, stating that in that investigation, "the ITC found sustained weaknesses in most of the perfor- mance indicators of the domestic industry." Def.'s Mem. at 38 (internal quotation omitted). The ITC notes that this "sharply contrasts with the instant case, in which the ITC found not only that the industry was profitable, but also that the industry experienced significant gains in productivity and declining costs, accompanied by increases in production, shipments, and market share." *Id.*

The court finds IIMAK's reliance on Post Insulators from Japan, Inv. No. 731-TA-1023 (Prelim.), USITC Pub. No. 3578 (2003), to be misplaced. There, the ITC found a significant adverse impact on the domestic industry in part based on "significant declines or sustained weaknesses" in most of the performance indicators of the domestic industry. *Id.* at 14. Here, by contrast, several large U.S. producers operated at a profit during the period of investigation.

tion."[22] Pl.'s Br. at 24. IIMAK claims that this company's increases in operating income over the period of investigation were not in line with the experience of the industry. *See id.* at 25. Thus, IIMAK insists that the ITC ignored a significant condition of competition when it did not account for this one company's data having overshadowed the data for the rest of industry. *See id.*

The ITC maintains that the anomaly to which IIMAK refers, i.e., that the domestic industry experienced declining operating income and profitability at a time of increasing consumption, was not in fact an anomaly, since the decline in operating income was slight and the decline in profitability was "marginal." Def.'s Mem. at 37.[23] The ITC also disputes IIMAK's contention that the data were skewed by one company with large and increasing profits by noting that three other companies[24] also operated at a profit throughout the period of investigation. *See id.*[25]

The court finds that the ITC has sufficiently addressed the "anomaly" cited by IIMAK. First, there is little evidence that the conditions set out by plaintiff are abnormal, since the declines in both operating income and profitability were very slight. *See supra* note 23. Second, it is apparent that the facts do not support plaintiff s contention that only one company was profitable during the period of investigation. Thus, the court finds no merit in IIMAK's contentions.

B. The ITC's finding that "alternative factors," not imports, were the cause of price declines over the period of investigation.

The ITC found that several factors other than imports were responsible for declining prices during the period of investigation. In particular, the Commission noted

---

22 IIMAK states:

> Unlike all other coaters, [[ ]] increased its operating income over the period of investigation; in fact, it increased its operating income by [[ ]] percent. It experienced these increases while [[ ]] experienced declines in operating income. Moreover, by the end of the period of investigation, [[ ]]'s operating income constituted [[ ]] percent of the operating income for the industry as a whole. Notably, [[ ]], a product for which there is not subject import competition.

Pl.'s Br. at 24-25.

23 Operating income declined by [[ ]] percent, while declines in operating income as a percentage of net sales (profit) decreased from [[ ]] percent in 2001 to [[ ]] percent in 2003, for a total decline of [[ ]] percent. ITC Views at 38; *see also* Conf. Staff Rep., Conf. R. Doc. 292 at Table C-3.

24 The other U.S. companies that performed profitably were [[ ]]. Def.'s Mem. at 38; *see also* ITC Views at 38 (citing Conf. Staff Rep., Conf. R. Doc. 292 at Table C-3 for its finding that the domestic industry operated profitably during the period of investigation).

25 As previously noted, IIMAK also asserts that [[ ]] produced only [[ ]] TTR. This assertion is unconvincing. As the ITC notes:

> This assertion ignores that [[ ]] . . . Just as the distinctions between [[ ]] do not create clear dividing lines between slit fax TTR and slit barcode TTR, the fact that [[ ]] does not mean its data should be set aside from the data for the rest of the industry.

Def.'s Mem. at 38, 39.

that intra-industry competition was severe, a finding that IIMAK does not dispute. Nevertheless, IIMAK insists that the Commission erred in finding that factors other than imports were responsible for the price declines.

In particular, IIMAK claims that, in finding that Sony Chemical Corporation of America ("Sony") was the downward price leader, the ITC "has ignored data[26] pertaining to other producers and disregarded the data in support of Sony' s claim that it decreased prices to meet import competition." Pl.'s Br. at 25. In support of its claim, IIMAK cites Sony's Prehearing Submission in Support of the Petition, Conf. R. Doc. 253, in which Sony states that it "is not now, and has not been, the price leader in the industry. Rather, to the extent it has reduced prices at all, Sony has done so in order to meet the downward price competition led by global imports." *Id.*

The ITC insists that its conclusion that Sony was the downward price leader is supported by substantial evidence. It explains that it "relied on public statements . . . corroborating that Sony was at the front of an intra-industry price war, and on price data indicating that Sony . . . lowered its prices below those of [others] to gain larger volume sales." Def.'s Mem. at 37. As evidence for its conclusions, the Commission cites the statement of a Sony consultant who later became an executive, who stated that "through aggressive pricing, we believe we can cut our competition numbers from 19 or 20 down to five," and that "[w]e didn't start these price wars, but we're going to finish them." ITC Views at 30-31, 31 n.145. In addition, a large majority of the responding purchasers identified Sony as the price leader in the industry by 2003. *See* ITC Views at 36 n.176.

It is apparent that the ITC has provided substantial evidence showing that Sony was the downward price leader during the period of investigation.

IIMAK next argues that the ITC relied on erroneous data for its finding that price declines were caused by declines in unit costs and increases in productivity. IIMAK claims that the ITCs data, contained in Table D-1, Conf. Staff Rep., Conf. R. Doc. 292, pertained only to U.S. coaters' operations, even though the ITC included some slitters in the domestic industry. Thus, IIMAK argues, any evaluation of the

26 IIMAK contends that Table E-1, on which the ITC relies for its conclusions, actually shows "(1) pervasive underselling of [[[]] and (2) early [[ ]]." Pl.'s Br. at 26 (citing Conf. Staff Rep., Conf. R. Doc. 292).

A review of Table E-1 confirms that in most quarters from 2001 through 2003, the Japanese producers undersold [[ ]] although not every Japanese producer undersold both [[ ]] in every quarter. Moreover, the Japanese producers undersold [[ ]] in only about [[ ]] of the twelve quarters from 2001 through 2003 for which data was provided. The court finds that by showing that the history of declining prices did not show price reductions contemporaneous with imported merchandise underselling, the ITC has provided sufficient evidence to refute IIMAK's claim that domestic price declines resulted *solely* from competition from foreign imports. Rather, the ITC has provided evidence to show that although domestic producers reduced their prices, they did so in large measure in response to severe intra-industry competition and because of increases in both capacity and productivity.

costs for the domestic producers should include the costs of any slitters that are not excluded from the U.S. industry as related parties. Making the proper comparison reveals that unit prices declined by more than unit sales costs for the U.S. producers. Moreover, the correct data show that both gross and operating margins declined, an unlikely phenomenon when costs decline at the same rate as prices. Consequently, the ITC erroneously concluded that price declines were driven by declines in costs.

Pl.'s Br. at 27-28.

An examination of Table D-1 reveals that IIMAK is correct that it pertains only to U.S. coaters' operations, not to slitters. It would appear that the costs of domestic producers should include both coaters and those slitters unrelated to foreign producers. As this omission is unexplained by the Commission, on remand, the ITC is directed to provide an explanation as to why its analysis did not also account for the costs of U.S. non-related party slitters.

Finally, IIMAK contends that even if the factors cited by the ITC were, in fact, partly responsible for the domestic industry's price declines, the Commission did not address the question of whether the subject imports were *also* a cause of the domestic industry's injury. IIMAK argues that a determination that imports are causing material injury under 19 U.S.C. § 1673d(b)(1) "does not require that the imports be the sole or principal cause of the injury," *Nippon Steel Corp. v. Int'l Trade Comm'n*, 345 F.3d 1379, 1381 (Fed. Cir. 2003); therefore, according to plaintiff, the ITC has failed to show that the subject imports are not at least a significant factor in causing the injury suffered by U.S. industry. *Id.* at 29.

Despite IIMAK's claims, however, it is apparent that the ITC has applied the proper standard. Indeed, the Commission made the very finding that IIMAK claims is absent. "We find that . . . imports . . . have not had a significant negative impact on the condition of the domestic industry during the period examined.

As discussed above, we find both the volume of subject imports and price effects of the subject imports not to be significant." ITC Views at 37. Moreover, the ITC specifically addressed price effects relating to imports, stating:

> The pricing data . . . reflect a downward trend for domestic prices during the period of investigation. This trend was the same at the jumbo roll stage of processing and at the finished [TTR] stage. We find that the movement of domestic prices (upward and downward) was largely unrelated to the price of imported merchandise.

Id. at 34-35.[27] Thus, plaintiff's assertion is not supported by the record.

---

27 The ITC relies on Table V-6 of its Staff Report, which indicates that domestic price movements did not move in tandem with the prices of the imported merchandise. *See* Conf. Staff Rep., Conf. R. Doc. 292 at Table V-6.

VIII. The ITC's Determination That the Industry Is Not Threatened With Material Injury

Finally, IIMAK contends that the problems with the ITC's material injury analysis "also infect the ITC's threat analysis, thereby rendering the finding that the industry is not threatened with injury fundamentally flawed as well." Pl.'s Br. at 37. IIMAK explains:

> The ITC found that "the increase in the volume and market share of the subject imports does not indicate a likelihood of substantially increased imports. Subject imports increased only slightly relative to U.S. consumption and decreased relative to U.S. production." Properly measuring imports relative to consumption and production . . . would demonstrate dramatic increases in those export volumes. . . . [Mo reover], [w]hen the ITC conducts a proper pricing analysis, it should find that subject imports had substantial negative price effects.

Id. at 37-38. In addition, IIMAK disputes the ITCs reliance on the domestic industry's "positive and steady performance" for its finding that the U.S. industry was not threatened with injury. *Id.* at 38. IIMAK claims that the ITC never addressed its claim that the industry was only able to maintain its profits "through cost-cutting measures that could not be sustained in the long-run." *Id.*

For its part, the ITC chooses to rest on its prior arguments regarding domestic like product, stating:

> [P]laintiff's claims concerning the ITCs finding of no threat of material injury stem from IIMAK's dissatisfaction with the ITC s definition of domestic like product and the domestic industry. . . . For the same reasons that the court should reject plaintiff's efforts to reweigh the evidence and impose its own preferred methodology on the ITCs present injury analysis, the court should likewise reject plaintiffs claims regarding threat.

Def.'s Mem. at 39.

Here, a discussion of the questions of material injury and threat must await the Commission's response to the remand instructions. As such, the court will address IIMAK's concerns following the ITCs response to those instructions.

CONCLUSION

Based on the foregoing, this matter is remanded to the ITC for action in accordance with this opinion. Remand results are due on April 24, 2006, comments are due on May 24, 2006, and replies to such comments are due on June 5, 2006.

MITTAL CANADA INC.
v.
UNITED STATES

Court No. 05-00689 (Ct. Int'l Trade 2006)
Decided February 10, 2006

OPINION

[Defendant's motion to dismiss is denied, and plaintiff's motion for preliminary injunction is denied.]

Cameron & Hornbostel, LLP (Dennis James, Jr.) for Plaintiff Mittal Canada, Inc.

Peter D. Keisler, Assistant Attorney General; David D. Cohen, Director, Jeanne E. Davidson, Deputy Director; Commercial Litigation Branch, Civil Division, U.S. Department of Justice, (Michael D. Panzera), for Defendant United States.

Collier, Shannon, Scott, PLLC (Mary T. Staley, Paul C. Rosenthal, and Robin H. Gilbert) for Defendant-Intervenors Gerdau Ameristeel Corp. and Keystone Consolidated Industries, Inc.

GOLDBERG, Senior Judge: Before the Court is the motion of Plaintiff Mittal Canada, Inc. ("Plaintiff") for a preliminary injunction under USCIT R. 65(a) to prevent U.S. Customs and Border Protection ("Customs") from liquidating Plaintiff's entries of steel wire rod entered from October 1, 2004 through September 30, 2005 ("the Entries"). On December 30, 2005, the Court granted a temporary restraining order ("TRO") to enjoin the liquidations pending the disposition of the preliminary injunction motion. Underlying the preliminary injunction request is Plaintiff's claim that the U.S. Department of Commerce ("Commerce") issued liquidation instructions that were at odds with the final results of a changed circumstances review initiated by Plaintiff.

Since entry of the TRO, substantial briefing has occurred. Customs has responded to Plaintiff's motion for a preliminary injunction and filed its own motion to dismiss. Plaintiff has filed a motion in reply to Customs' response, and in response to Customs' motion to dismiss. Customs filed a reply to Plaintiff's response to its motion to dismiss. Lastly, Gerdau Ameristeel Corp. and Keystone Consolidated Industries, Inc. (collectively, "Defendant-Intervenors") filed a joint consent motion to intervene, which the Court granted. Defendant-Intervenors also filed a reply to Plaintiff's response to the motion to dismiss. For the reasons that follow, the Court denies Customs' motion to dismiss, and denies Plaintiff's motion for a preliminary injunction.

I. BACKGROUND

On October 29, 2002, Commerce issued an antidumping duty order that applied to certain Canadian steel imports including the Entries. See Carbon and Certain Alloy Steel Wire Rod from Canada, 67 Fed. Reg. 65944 (Oct. 29, 2002) (amended final determination and antidumping duty order) ("the Order"). The Order contemplated a default weighted-average dumping margin of 8.11 percent that applied to all manufacturers/exporters subject to investigation that were not explicitly assessed a lower rate. Specifically, the Order provided that all unliquidated entries that entered on or after April 10, 2002, and before October 7, 2002, be assessed a duty rate of 8.11 percent. See id. at 65945. For all entries occurring "[o]n or after that date of publication of [the Order] in the Federal Register, the Customs service [was instructed to] require . . . a cash deposit equal to the estimated weighted-average antidumping duty margins as noted [in the Order]."[1] Id. Ispat Sidbec Inc. ("Ispat") was one of the Canadian steel manufacturers/exporters entitled to lower duty assessment and cash deposit rates. See id. Ispat was subject to a 3.86 percent assessment rate, as well as a 3.86 percent cash deposit rate. Id. In late 2004, Ispat changed its name to Mittal Canada Inc. Carbon and Certain Alloy Steel Wire Rod from Canada, 70 Fed. Reg. 22845 (May 3, 2005) (preliminary results of changed circumstances review) ("Preliminary Results"). On January 15, 2005, after noticing that Customs was subjecting its entries to the higher default rate of 8.11 percent, Plaintiff requested a changed circumstances review to take account of the name change.

On May 3, 2005, Commerce issued its preliminary review of Plaintiff's changed circumstance review request. The Preliminary Results stated that "Mittal is the successor-in- interest to Ispat." Id. Commerce also described to Plaintiff what consequences of a final results affirmance would be:

> If the above preliminary results are affirmed in [Commerce's] final results, the cash deposit rate most recently calculated for Ispat will apply to all entries of subject merchandise by Mittal entered, or withdrawn from warehouse, for consumption on or after the date of publication of the final results of this changed circumstances review. Id.

---

1 Entries made between October 7, 2002 and October 29, 2002 (the publication date of the Order) were "not liable for the assessment of antidumping duties due to [Commerce's] termination of . . . the suspension of liquidation." Order, 67 Fed. Reg. at 65945.

Commerce's final determination affirmed the Preliminary Results. See Carbon and Certain Alloy Steel Wire Rod from Canada, 70 Fed. Reg. 39484 (July 8, 2005) (final results of changed circumstances review) ("Final Results"). Specifically, Commerce determined that "Mittal is the successor-in-interest to Ispat for antidumping duty cash deposit purposes." Id. at 39485. The Final Results contained a section entitled "Instructions to the U.S. Customs and Border Protection" that appeared immediately after its finding as to the successor-in- interest issue. In that section, Commerce stated its intention to follow the course indicated by the Preliminary Results: "[Commerce] will instruct [Customs] to suspend liquidation of all shipments of the subject merchandise produced and exported by Mittal entered, or withdrawn from warehouse, for consumption, on or after the publication date of this notice at 3.86 percent (i.e., Ispat's cash deposit rate)." Id.

On July 25, 2005, Customs published Commerce's instructions to notify its directors of field operations and port directors. See Def.'s Corrected Mot. to Dismiss and Resp. in Opp. to Mot. for Prelim. Inj., Attach. A (Message No. 5206202 dated July 25, 2005). Those instructions provided that "as a result of [the changed circumstances] review, [Commerce] find[s] that Mittal Canada Inc. is the successor in interest to Ispat Sidbec Inc." Id. The instructions provided further that "shipments by Mittal Canada Inc. of carbon alloy and certain steel wire rod from Canada shall receive the same cash deposit rate as Ispat Sidbec Inc., for all shipments entered or withdrawn from warehouse, for consumption on or after July 8, 2005." Id. Therefore, these cash deposit instructions did not apply to the Entries, which had already entered and for which cash deposits had already been collected.

On December 15, 2005, Customs issued the instructions to its port directors that constitute the nub of this dispute. The port officials were "to assess antidumping duties on merchandise entered, or withdrawn from warehouse, for consumption at the cash deposit or bonding rate in effect on the date of entry." Mem. in Supp. of Pl.'s Mot. for a TRO and Prelim. Inj. Enjoining Liquidation of Entries, Ex. A (Message No. 5349202 dated Dec. 15, 2005) at 1. For the Entries, "the cash deposit . . . rate in effect on the date of entry," id., was the higher 8.11 percent rate. On December 27, 2005, Plaintiff sent a letter to the Commerce's Assistant Secretary for Import Administration requesting that Commerce instruct Customs to assess antidumping duties at no greater than 3.86 percent, the rate to which Ispat imports were formerly entitled, and, according to Plaintiff, to which Plaintiff's imports were entitled as well. See id., Ex. B (Letter to Ass. Sec. of Imp. Admin. Re: Request for Correction of Instructions to Customs/Mittal Canada, Inc. dated Dec. 27, 2005).

Plaintiff then commenced this case on December 30, 2005, petitioning the Court for a TRO and preliminary injunction to stop Customs from liquidating the Entries. In its accompanying memorandum, Plaintiff cited Mukand Int'l, Ltd. v. United States, 29 CIT ___, ___, Slip Op. 05-164, at 15 (Dec. 22, 2005) to support its position that a TRO was necessary to prevent the imminent liquidations, because liquidation would strip the Court's jurisdiction under 28 U.S.C. § 1581(i) to hear Plaintiff's challenge to the instructions. The Court entered the TRO on the same day as a precaution, and ordered a hearing on the maintenance of the TRO and imposition of the preliminary injunction on January 4, 2006.

Customs filed a motion to dismiss for lack of jurisdiction as well as its response to Plaintiff's motion for preliminary injunction on January 3, 2006. The Court held the hearing as scheduled, after which the parties agreed to an expedited briefing schedule.

II. THE COURT HAS JURISDICTION UNDER 28 U.S.C. § 1581(i)

Absent jurisdiction, a court may not proceed in any cause, and must dismiss the case before it. "The requirement that jurisdiction be established as a threshold matter 'spring[s] from the nature and limits of the judicial power of the United States' and is 'inflexible and without exception.'" Steel Co. v. Citizens for a Better Envm't, 523 U.S. 83, 94-95 (1988) (quoting Mansfield, C. & L. M. R. Co. v. Swan, 111 U.S. 379, 384 (1884)); see also USCIT R. 12(h)(3) ("Whenever it appears . . . that the court lacks jurisdiction of the subject matter, the court shall dismiss the action.").

Moreover, the fact that Plaintiff desires preliminary and equitable relief does not mean a court can sidestep the jurisdictional question. In circumstances when the jurisdictional inquiry is inextricably intertwined with consideration of the merits, it may be appropriate for a court to postpone adjudication of the jurisdictional question pending a thorough examination of the merits. See, e.g., PPG Indus., Inc. v. United States, 84 Cust. Ct. 256, C.R.D. 80-5 (1980) (merger of jurisdictional and merits inquiries is appropriate where "the evidentiary facts necessary to controvert the jurisdiction challenged by the defendant concurrently are necessary in the submission and ultimate determination of the . . . action on the merits"). In this case, however, subject matter jurisdiction is not inextricably tied to a proper test of the strength of Plaintiff's claim, and merger of the jurisdictional and merits questions is inappropriate. Instead, jurisdiction is properly treated as a threshold issue, to be examined separately and antecedently.

Plaintiff invokes the residual jurisdiction of the U.S. Court of International Trade ("CIT") under 28 U.S.C. § 1581(i). By its terms, 28 U.S.C. § 1581(i) is an expansive grant of exclusive jurisdiction over certain causes of action against the government:

> [The CIT] shall have exclusive jurisdiction of any civil action commenced against the United States, its agencies, or its officers, that arises out of any law of the United States providing for—
>
> (1) revenue from imports or tonnage;
>
> (2) tariffs, duties, fees, or other taxes on the importation of merchandise for reasons other than the raising of revenue;

(3) embargoes or other quantitative restrictions on the importation of merchandise for reasons other than the protection of the public health or safety; or

(4) administration and enforcement with respect to the matters referred to in paragraphs (1)-(3) of this subsection and subsections (a)-(h) of this section.

28 U.S.C. § 1581(i) (1999).

A lodestar of the CIT's jurisdictional jurisprudence is that a plaintiff may not pursue an action under 28 U.S.C. § 1581(i) if any other subsection of 28 U.S.C. § 1581 "is or could have been available, unless the remedy provided under that other subsection would be manifestly inadequate." Miller & Co. v. United States, 824 F.2d 961, 963 (Fed. Cir. 1987), cert. denied, 484 U.S. 1041 (1988). Thus, if Plaintiff could have obtained its relief under any other subsection of 28 U.S.C. § 1581, then the Court must immediately dismiss the case for lack of subject matter jurisdiction.

Before the Court may assert jurisdiction over the subject matter, it must identify the claim on which Plaintiff seeks relief. In most cases, this exercise is routine; however, this case requires a more searching examination because the parties disagree as to the characterization of Plaintiff's claim. Plaintiff contends it is challenging Commerce's liquidation instructions as arbitrary and capricious or otherwise not in accordance with law. Customs paints Plaintiff's request in a different light, arguing that Plaintiff is really seeking a substantive review of the changed circumstances review.

Plaintiff believes that Commerce's liquidation instructions, because they instructed Customs to liquidate the Entries at the cash deposit rate, failed to take into account the legal fact that "Mittal is the successor-in-interest to Ispat for antidumping duty cash deposit purposes." Final Results, 70 Fed. Reg. at 39485. Plaintiff insists that, despite the Final Results' expressly limited application to "antidumping duty cash deposit purposes[,]" id., the determination of successor-in-interest status required Commerce to assess the lower 3.86 percent rate to all of Plaintiff's unliquidated entries, including those for which the 8.11 percent duty cash deposit had been required. In Plaintiff's view, then, the Final Results articulated a broad legal principle that has collateral effects beyond the express limitation of its language, and when Commerce does not recognize those effects and instruct Customs accordingly, it acts in contravention of law.

Customs, on the other hand, urges the Court to construe Plaintiff's complaint as a belated attempt to obtain the judicial review of the changed circumstances review that would have been available under 28 U.S.C. § 1581(c). In other words, Customs argues that Plaintiff is attempting to dress up a routine § 1581(c) claim in such a way as to avoid § 1581(i)'s jurisdictional bar in cases where 28 U.S.C. § 1581(c) was available, but not invoked.

The language of 28 U.S.C. § 1581(i) fits Plaintiff's version of the case like a glove. After all, 28 U.S.C. § 1581(i)(4) includes civil actions against the United States relating to the "administration and enforcement" of "duties." 28 U.S.C. § 1581(i)(4) (1999). Moreover, several decisions of the U.S. Court of Appeals for the Federal Circuit ("Federal Circuit") establish that a plaintiff may invoke 28 U.S.C. § 1581(i) to test the legality of instructions that are alleged to contravene determinations made in an administrative review. See, e.g., Shinyei Corp. of Am. v. United States, 355 F.3d 1297, 1305 (Fed. Cir. 2004); Consol. Bearings Co. v. United States, 348 F.3d 997, 1002 (Fed. Cir. 2003); cf. Mitsubishi Elecs. Am. v. United States, 44 F.3d 973, 977 (Fed. Cir. 1994) (suggesting that CIT had jurisdiction to hear plaintiff's claim that liquidation instructions conflicted with final antidumping order). In those cases, the Federal Circuit has affirmed that the CIT possesses residual jurisdiction to hold Commerce accountable for the execution of its determinations arising from administrative reviews.[2] Residual jurisdiction is appropriate in those cases because a challenge to liquidation instructions as not in accordance with an administrative review determination is not enumerated among the "reviewable determinations" of 19 U.S.C. § 1516a that form the basis for the CIT's 28 U.S.C. § 1581(c) jurisdiction. See 19 U.S.C. § 1516a(a)(2)(B) (1999).

On the other hand, it is equally straightforward that should the Court construe Plaintiff's claim as a belated request for judicial review of the Final Results, the case must be dismissed. 28 U.S.C. § 1581(c) grants the CIT "exclusive jurisdiction of any civil action commenced under [19 U.S.C. § 1516a]." 28 U.S.C. § 1581(c) (1999). 19 U.S.C. § 1516a, in turn, permits plaintiffs to seek review of "[a] final determination . . . under [19 U.S.C. § 1675]." 19 U.S.C. § 1516a(a)(2)(B)(iii) (1999). One of the "final determinations" that Commerce makes under 19 U.S.C. § 1675 is a review "based on changed circumstances." Id. § 1675(b). Therefore, because Plaintiff could have brought the matter before the Court under 28 U.S.C. § 1581(c), the Court would have no residual jurisdiction over such a claim.

A thorough examination of Plaintiff's motion for preliminary injunction and accompanying papers reveals that Plaintiff is challenging the liquidation instructions as violative of the legal conclusion, embodied in the Final Results, that Plaintiff is the a successor-in-interest to Ispat. Because the Court has 28 U.S.C. § 1581(i) jurisdiction over civil actions that challenge Commerce's issuance of liquidation instructions at odds with its own determinations, see Consol. Bearings, 348 F.3d at 1002, the Court must deny Customs' motion to dismiss for lack of subject matter

2 The cited cases dealt with non-compliance with administrative reviews, which violated explicit regulatory and statutory provisions requiring the results of administrative reviews to be "the basis for the assessment of . . . antidumping duties on entries of merchandise covered by the determination and for deposits of estimated duties." 19 U.S.C. § 1675(a)(2)(C) (1999); see also 19 C.F.R. § 351.212(b)(1) (2005). Under 19 C.F.R. § 351.221, the general regulation governing review procedures, the same principle applies to changed circumstances reviews. That regulation directs Commerce to "promptly after publication of the notice of final results instruct the Customs Service to assess antidumping duties . . . on the subject merchandise covered by the review . . . ." Id. § 351.221(b)(6). If Commerce fails to instruct Customs accordingly, it withholds or delays the execution of its administrative duty, and the CIT must compel the issuance of correct instructions, see 5 U.S.C. § 706(1) (1999).

jurisdiction. In short, Plaintiff is not challenging the Final Results, so there can not be, nor could there ever have been, jurisdiction under 28 U.S.C. § 1581(c). Instead, this suit is about the "'administration and enforcement' of those final results." Id. (quoting 28 U.S.C. § 1581(i)).

The only puzzling aspect of the jurisdictional question is Plaintiff's prior decision not to contest the Final Results before such an appeal became time-barred.[3] Instead of timely contesting the Final Results in the CIT so as to obtain clear language that would have mandated assessment of the 3.86 percent duty rate, Plaintiffs are now alleging Commerce's liquidation instructions contravene the Final Results determination. That argument in effect maintains that the uncontested and unambiguous Final Results mean something different than what they say. Clearly, the Court possesses residual jurisdiction over such a novel argument, but Plaintiff's victory on the jurisdictional issue is pyrrhic.

Since 28 U.S.C. § 1581(c) relief was time-barred, Plaintiff has chosen to pursue another remedial method designed to obtain the identical substantive result (i.e., assessment of duties at 3.86 percent) by different means. By fashioning its dispute as a challenge to defective liquidation instructions, Plaintiff has defined its claim such that the Court has jurisdiction. In the process, however, it has presented a tenuous argument that, for the following reasons, would make preliminary injunctive relief inappropriate.

III. PLAINTIFF'S MOTION FOR A PRELIMINARY INJUNCTION IS DENIED

A preliminary injunction is "extraordinary relief," FMC Corp. v. United States, 3 F.3d 424, 427 (Fed. Cir. 1993), that should be granted sparingly. However, there are circumstances that can, and often do, justify injunctive relief before trial. A court may enter a preliminary injunction when the movant has established (1) that it will suffer irreparable harm if relief is not granted; (2) that the public interest would be better served by the relief requested; (3) that the balance of the hardships tips in the movant's favor; and (4) that the movant is likely to succeed on the merits at trial. See id. (citing Zenith Radio Corp. v. United States, 710 F.2d 806, 809 (Fed. Cir. 1983)).

In deciding whether to grant a preliminary injunction the CIT has a good deal of discretion. See id. (citing Chrysler Motors Corp. v. Auto Body Panels, Inc., 908 F.2d 951, 953 (Fed. Cir. 1990)); Asociación Colombiana de Exportadores de Flores v. United States, 916 F.2d 1571, 1578 (Fed. Cir. 1990). Courts have

3 A plaintiff has thirty days after the date of publication of a Commerce determination in the Federal Register within which to contest that determination in the CIT. See 19 U.S.C. § 1516a(b) (1999). As such, Plaintiff had until August 8, 2005 to commence a case under 28 U.S.C. § 1581(c). Furthermore, Plaintiff slept on its rights by not filing a case brief, see 19 C.F.R. § 351.309(c)(ii), within thirty days after publication of the Preliminary Results on May 3, 2005. The Preliminary Results were clear: the changed circumstances review looked only to the cash deposit rate, and not the assessment rate. At both those points, Plaintiff could have brought to Commerce's attention that it was seeking a more robust form of retroactive relief.

adopted a flexible approach in dealing with motions for preliminary injunctions. In some instances, the weakness of a showing of one factor may be overborne by the strength of others. See FMC Corp., 3 F.3d at 427. In other circumstances, the weakness of a showing of one factor may justify denial of the preliminary injunction motion. Id.

In particular, the likelihood of success and the irreparable harm prongs "are viewed as a 'continuum in which the required showing of harm varies inversely with the required showing of meritoriousness.'" U.S. Ass'n of Imp.'s of Textiles and Apparel v. U.S. Dep't of Commerce, 413 F.3d 1344, 1347 (Fed. Cir. 2005) (quoting Mikohn Gaming Corp. v. Acres Gaming, Inc., 165 F.3d 891, 895 (Fed. Cir. 1998)). Thus, a convincing demonstration of irreparable harm will diminish the required burden of showing a likelihood of success on the merits. When irreparable harm is shown, a party need not show a likelihood of success; a showing of "a fair chance" of prevailing on the merits may entitle the moving party to preliminary injunctive relief.[4] See Atari Games Corp. v. Nintendo of Am., Inc., 897 F.2d 1572, 1577 (Fed. Cir. 1990).

Diminishing the burden of proof required does not, however, obviate the movant's burden to show some real possibility of success on the merits. See FMC Corp., 3 F.3d at 427. A court may not enter a preliminary injunction, even where the irreparable harm is conspicuous and serious,[5] if the court is convinced that the movant stands no chance of success on its underlying claim. See AM Gen. Corp. v. DaimlerChrysler Corp., 311 F.3d 796, 804 (7th Cir. 2002) ("A party with no chance of

---

4 The U.S. Association of Importers decision adverts the CIT to an ambiguity in the preliminary injunction jurisprudence. See U.S. Ass'n of Imp.'s, 413 F.3d at 1347-48. In particular, it is unclear what precedential weight the Mikohn and Atari Games decisions, which were patent cases applying Ninth Circuit law, have in the context of CIT cases. As a result, it is unclear whether the "fair chance" standard should apply to customs and trade plaintiffs seeking preliminary injunctions against the government. Because the Court concludes that Plaintiff has failed to meet its burden even under the liberal "fair chance" standard, this ambiguity does not affect the disposition of Plaintiff's motion.

5 The Court ultimately denies the motion for preliminary injunction because Plaintiff stands little, if any, chance on the merits of its underlying claim, so its decision would be the same even if irreparable harm were present. However, it bears mention that irreparable harm is not present in this case either. Plaintiff's alleged harm—its losing a statutory right to obtain judicial review of the liquidation instructions upon liquidation—is illusory. The Federal Circuit has held that in cases where a plaintiff brings a suit challenging liquidation instructions' compliance with Commerce determinations, the CIT has 28 U.S.C. § 1581(i) jurisdiction to evaluate such a claim, even where the relevant entries are liquidated during the pendency of the case. See Shinyei, 355 F.3d at 1297-1303. Plaintiff's reliance on Zenith Radio is misplaced because in that case, the denial of preliminary injunctive relief would have foreclosed relief to which the plaintiff was otherwise entitled: namely, its right to have a favorable CIT decision apply to its already-entered merchandise. In this case, as in Shinyei, Plaintiff has already preserved its 28 U.S.C. § 1581(i) challenge to the liquidation instructions. As such, denial of the preliminary injunction should not disturb Plaintiff's ability to challenge the instructions after liquidation, and Plaintiff is not threatened with serious harm.

success on the merits cannot attain a preliminary injunction."); Hoechst Diafoil Co. v. Nan Ya Plastics Corp., 174 F.3d 411, 417 (4th Cir. 1999).

In this case, the Court is unable to grant a preliminary injunction because Plaintiff has failed to meet its burden to show either a "likelihood of success on the merits," U.S. Ass'n of Imp.'s, 413 F.3d at 1346, or even a "fair chance" that its underlying claim will succeed, id. at 1347. Even after extensive briefing, Plaintiff has provided no support for its novel contention that a final changed circumstances determination finding that one producer is the successor-in- interest to another producer "for antidumping duty cash deposit purposes," Final Results, 70 Fed. Reg. at 39485, articulates a broader commitment by Commerce to treat that producer as such for duty assessment purposes as well. "[M]ere novelty is [not] sufficient to demonstrate a fair chance of success" on the merits of a claim. U.S. Ass'n of Imp.'s, 413 F.3d at 1347.

A close look at the U.S. antidumping duty assessment regulations and procedures demonstrates why the Final Results limited the application of the successor-in-interest determination to cash deposits, and why therefore Plaintiff's argument that Commerce was obliged to include assessment instructions is untenable. The United States utilizes a "retrospective" duty assessment system under which importers' final liabilities are determined after the actual importation of the merchandise. See 19 C.F.R. § 351.212 (2005). Importers entering merchandise subject to an antidumping duty order are required to make a cash deposit of estimated antidumping duties at the rates included in the final results determination of an antidumping investigation. See id. § 351.211(b)(2). Unless the importer files a request for an administrative review,[6] those entries will be liquidated (and those duties will be assessed) at the deposit rate that applied at the time the merchandise was entered. See id. § 351.212(a). Commerce processes these entries by issuing "clean-up" instructions, see Shinyei, 355 F.3d at 1303, directing Customs to liquidate all unliquidated entries "as entered." This process is referred to as "automatic liquidation," see Okaya (USA), Inc. v. United States, 27 CIT ___, ___, Slip Op. 03-130 at 3 (Oct. 3, 2003), and ensures the smooth functioning of the "retrospective" system. Notably, there is no analogous exception to automatic liquidation for changed circumstance reviews. See 19 C.F.R. § 351.212(b).

An importer may request an administrative review when it believes the cash deposit rate collected at entry should not be the assessment rate. The administrative review typically looks backward twelve months, see id. § 351.213(e), and permits an importer to recoup the excess duties deposited by halting the automatic liquidation process and allowing Commerce to take account of specific information provided by the importers requesting the review. The duty collection system is imprecise and relies on efficient transfer of information from interested parties to Commerce to achieve an accurate final result; to this end, the administrative re-

6 Two other exceptions exist for new shipper reviews, see 19 C.F.R. § 351.214, and expedited antidumping reviews, see id. § 351.215. Neither procedure is relevant to this case.

view process is "the most frequently used procedure" for apprising Commerce of relevant facts needed to "determin[e] final duty liability[.]" Id. § 351.213(a). The regulations also provide guidance for Commerce in computing new assessment rates and instruct Customs to liquidate at those rates the merchandise subject to administrative review. See id. § 351.212(b).

The changed circumstances review similarly allows interested parties to petition Commerce for review of a final determination. See 19 U.S.C. § 1675(b)(1) (1999). The party seeking a revocation or modification of an antidumping order bears the burden of persuasion with respect to whether changed circumstances warrant such revocation or modification. See id. § 1675(b)(3)(A). Most important for the purposes of this case, however, is the fact that unlike an administrative review, a changed circumstances review does not halt the automatic liquidation process by causing Commerce to recalculate assessment rates in the case of an affirmative determination. In the past, Commerce has modified assessment orders during changed circumstances reviews. See, e.g., Leather from Argentina, Wool from Argentina, Oil Country Tubular Goods from Argentina, and Carbon Steel Cold-Rolled Flat Products from Argentina, 62 Fed. Reg. 41361 (Dep't Commerce Aug. 1, 1997) (final results of changed circumstances reviews) (providing retroactive relief by ordering all unliquidated merchandise entered within six years of publication date to be liquidated without regard to the countervailing duty orders then in place). However, such modification of assessment rates does not arise automatically as a result of a changed circumstances review; an interested party must make a specific demand that Commerce instruct Customs to assess different rates for entries as to which estimated duties have already been deposited.

In this case, Plaintiff made no such demand. Plaintiff "requested that [Commerce] determine that it had become the successor-in-interest of Ispat[.]" Preliminary Results, 70 Fed. Reg. at 22845. Commerce, in its Preliminary Results, unambiguously limited the scope of the changed circumstances review to cash deposit rates, and never addressed the possibility that merchandise entered before the changed circumstances review was entitled to the lower Ispat assessment rate: "If the above preliminary results are affirmed in the Department's final results, the cash deposit rate most recently calculated for Ispat will apply to all entries of subject merchandise by Mittal entered, or withdrawn from warehouse, for consumption on or after the date of publication of the final results of this changed circumstances review." Id. (emphasis added).

The Final Results also focused exclusively on the narrow issue of cash deposit rates: "Based on the information provided by Mittal, and the fact that the Department did not receive any comments during the comment period following the preliminary results of this review, the Department hereby determines Mittal is the successor-in-interest to Ispat for antidumping duty cash deposit purposes." 70 Fed. Reg. at 39485 (emphasis added). Commerce then indicated its intention to

> instruct [Customs] to suspend liquidation of all shipments of the subject merchandise produced and exported by Mittal entered, or withdrawn from warehouse, for consumption, on or after the publication date of this notice at 3.86 percent (i.e., Ispat's cash deposit rate). This deposit rate shall remain in effect until publication of the final results of the ongoing administrative review . . . .

Id. Both the Preliminary Results and Final Results plainly address the treatment of Plaintiff's cash deposit rate, and not its assessment rate.

There are no broader conclusions to be divined out of the pellucid Final Results. The changed circumstances review addressed the cash deposit rate treatment of Plaintiff's merchandise. It seems Plaintiff came to an idiosyncratic interpretation of the Final Results, did nothing to convince Commerce of the correctness of such an interpretation, and assumed that Commerce would do something equally idiosyncratic by adopting Plaintiff's interpretation. Plaintiff could have petitioned Commerce for a more explicit form of retroactive duty assessment for already-entered merchandise; instead, it acquiesced to the Final Results' implicit refusal to grant any such relief. Of course, the automatic liquidation instructions eventually arrived for the Entries, and now Plaintiff is seeking to vindicate its erroneous interpretation before the Court.

Because the changed circumstances review did not address the treatment of the Entries at the time of duty assessment, the automatic liquidation system required that duties be assessed at "the cash deposit rate applicable at the time merchandise was entered[,]" 19 C.F.R. § 351.212(a), which was 8.11 percent. These liquidation instructions were in harmony with the statutory and regulatory requirements regarding the assessment of antidumping duties. Because Plaintiff stands little, if any, chance of prevailing on its underlying claim, the Court must deny Plaintiff's motion for a preliminary injunction.

IV. CONCLUSIONS

In light of the foregoing considerations, Customs' motion to dismiss for lack of subject matter jurisdiction is denied. Plaintiff's motion for a preliminary injunction is also denied. A separate order will issue in accordance with these conclusions.

NATIONAL FISHERIES INSTITUTE, INC.
v.
UNITED STATES BUREAU OF CUSTOMS AND BORDER PROTECTION

Court No. 05-00683 (Ct. Int'l Trade 2006)
Decided November 13, 2006

Before: Timothy C. Stanceu, Judge

OPINION

[Granting in part and denying in part plaintiffs' motion for preliminary injunction relief]

Dated: November 13, 2006 *Steptoe & Johnson LLP* (*Eric C. Emerson*, *Gregory S. McCue* and *Michael A. Pass*) for plaintiffs.

Peter D. Keisler, Assistant Attorney General, *David M. Cohen*, Director, *Patricia M. McCarthy*, Assistant Director, Commercial Litigation Branch, Civil Division, United States Department of Justice (*Stephen C. Tosini*); *Chi S. Choy*, Bureau of Customs and Border Protection, United States Department of Homeland Security, of counsel, for defendant.

Stanceu, Judge: Plaintiffs National Fisheries Institute, Inc. ("NFI"), a non-profit trade association, and 27 of its members move, pursuant to USCIT Rules 7 and 65, for an order entering a preliminary injunction against United States Customs and Border Protection ("Customs" or the "Agency"). *Pls.' Mot. for Prelim. Inj.*, attached *Order* at 1; *First Am. Compl.* Attach. 1. Plaintiffs are commercial importers of seafood products, including shrimp products that are subject to six antidumping duty orders issued by the International Trade Administration, United States Department of Commerce ("Commerce"). *First Am. Compl.* at 1, 19-22. Plaintiffs seek a preliminary injunction essentially to preclude Customs, during the pendency of this case, from applying a particular Customs directive, as amended in 2004 and clarified in 2005, when determining the sufficiency of each plaintiff's basic importation and entry bond. *See Pls.' Mot. for Prelim. Inj.* at 2-3. Plaintiffs, who challenge on the merits the individual bond sufficiency determinations by

Customs, also request in their preliminary injunction motion that the court enjoin Customs from considering potential antidumping and countervailing duty liability in determining bond sufficiency and that Customs be directed by the court to allow replacement of any bond used to enter merchandise on or after the date of filing of *Plaintiffs' Motion for Preliminary Injunction* with a superseding bond calculated without regard to antidumping or countervailing duty liabilities. *Id.* at 1; *Mot. to Amend Injunctive Relief Requested* at 2-3.

As required by the customs laws and regulations, a basic importation and entry bond allows Customs to make a monetary demand on the surety that issued the bond should the importer of record (*i.e.*, the "principal" on the bond) fail to meet its legal obligation to "pay duties, taxes, and charges" or fail to comply with another obligation (*i.e.*, a "bond condition") guaranteed by the bond. *See* 19 C.F.R. § 113.62 (2005). An importer breaching a bond condition typically will incur contractual liability to Customs in the form of liquidated damages that may not exceed the limit of liability of the bond, and also will incur contractual liability to indemnify the surety. *See id.* Commercial importers, such as the plaintiffs in this case, typically obtain "continuous" bonds (also referred to as "term" bonds), which cover liabilities resulting from multiple import transactions over a period of time, such as one year. *See id.* § 113.12(b). For commercial importers who conduct frequent import transactions, continuous bonds typically are more practical and economical than "single entry" bonds, which cover the obligations arising from one entry. *See id.* § 113.12(a).

To date, Customs has applied the amendment and the clarification of its bond directive only to importers of shrimp products covered by the six antidumping duty orders. The amendment and the clarification of the bond directive have had the effect of increasing substantially the limits of liability for the continuous bonds that Customs has demanded of the individual plaintiffs. *See Pls.' Mot. for Prelim. Inj.* at 2-3. The member-importers seeking injunctive relief are Admiralty Island Fisheries, Inc., d.b.a. "Aqua Star" ("Aqua Star"); Berdex Seafood, Inc. ("Berdex Seafood"); Censea Inc.; Crystal Cove Seafood Corp.; Eastern Fish Company, Inc. ("Eastern Fish"); Harbor Seafood, Inc.; Icicle Seafoods, Inc.; International Gourmet Fisheries, Inc., d.b.a. "Mid Pacific Seafoods" ("IGF"); Interocean Inc.; L.N. White & Co., Inc.; Mazzetta Company, LLC; McRoberts Sales Co., Inc.; Mseafood Corporation; Newport International; Ocean Cuisine International; Ocean to Ocean Seafood, LLC; Ore-Cal Corp. ("Ore- Cal"); Oriental Foods, Inc. ("Oriental Foods"); Pacific Seafood Group; Red Chamber Co. ("Red Chamber"); Sea Port Products Corporation; Sea Snack Foods Inc.; Southwind Foods LLC, d.b.a. "Great American Seafood Imports Co."; Tampa Bay Fisheries, Inc. ("Tampa Bay"); Thai Royal Frozen Foods Co., Inc.; The Seafood Exchange of Florida; and The Talon Group LLC. *See First Am. Compl.* Attach. 1.

Plaintiffs claim that the application of the amendment and the clarification of the bond directive are causing and will continue to cause them substantial economic harm because of the obligation to post large amounts of collateral with the surety to satisfy the current and impending bond sufficiency determinations by Customs, which plaintiffs consider to be excessive. *See Pls.' Mot. for Prelim. Inj.* at 2-5; *Mem. of P. & A. in Supp. of Pls.' Mot. for Prelim. Inj.* at 15 ("*Pls.' Mem.*"). Plaintiffs argue that the decision of Customs to require continuous bonds sufficient to cover potential antidumping or countervailing duty liability exceeds the Agency's authority under 19 U.S.C. § 1623(a) (2000). *See Pls.' Mot. for Prelim. Inj.* at 5-6; *Pls.' Mem.* at 40-44. They further claim that the selective application of the amendment and the clarification by Customs to shrimp importers is arbitrary and capricious. *See Pls.' Mot. for Prelim. Inj.* at 6; *Pls.' Mem.* at 39-40, 47-50. Plaintiffs maintain that in weighing whether or not to grant the requested injunctive relief, the balance of the hardships and the public interest favor NFI and its members. *See Pls.' Mem* at 50-52.

Defendant contends that plaintiffs' alleged economic hardships "do not rise to the severe level necessary to establish immediate irreparable harm" sufficient to warrant a preliminary injunction. *Def.'s Opp'n to NFI's Mot. For Prelim. Inj.* at 7 ("*Def.'s Opp'n*"). Defendant argues that a preliminary injunction should not be ordered because, in its view, plaintiffs have not established a likelihood of success on the merits. *See id.* at 7-8, 12-23. Defendant submits that because 19 U.S.C. § 1623 grants the Agency "broad authority to protect the revenue by requiring bonds or other security as Customs 'may deem necessary,'" Customs acted reasonably and within its statutory authority when it increased the continuous bond requirements for importers of shrimp. *Id.* at 15 (quoting 19 U.S.C. § 1623(a)). Defendant further submits that "the specter of harm faced by the Government is very real and acute" if Customs is not allowed to protect the revenue of the United States through increased bonding, and that this potential harm outweighs the hardships alleged by the plaintiffs. *Id.* at 24-25. Defendant also argues that the public interest favors the protection of the revenue through resort to continuous bonds of the size Customs determines to be necessary under the amendment and the clarification of the bond directive. *See id.*

During a hearing held at the United States Court of International Trade on March 30 and March 31, 2006, representatives of eight plaintiffs, specifically, Eastern Fish, Ore-Cal, Red Chamber and affiliates IGF and Tampa Bay, Oriental Foods, Berdex Seafood, and Aqua Star, testified in support of the claim that plaintiffs will suffer immediate, irreparable harm absent injunctive relief. On April 5, 2006, a representative from Customs testified to the hardship that Customs will suffer in protecting the potential revenue and in collecting outstanding antidumping duties from shrimp importers if Customs is prevented from applying the new bond formulas.

The court's decision on plaintiffs' motion for preliminary injunctive relief is based on a review of the evidence introduced at the hearing; the transcripts of the oral argument held on April 7, 2006; plaintiffs' motion to amend its request for preliminary injunction relief filed on April 14, 2006; post-hearing briefs submitted by the parties on May 5, 2006; plaintiffs' unopposed motions to amend the *de novo* hearing record to admit limited additional evidence, filed on May 5, 2006 and July 31, 2006; and other relevant papers and proceedings in this case. The court concludes that plaintiffs have not established their entitlement to the particular injunctive relief sought in their amended motion. The court, however, further concludes that limited injunctive relief is appropriate.

The court held an in-chambers conference on July 19, 2006, during which the court discussed with the parties the reasons that the court would not grant the specific preliminary injunction sought by plaintiffs, the court's conclusion that only the eight plaintiffs that presented evidence at the hearing could satisfy the requirement of showing irreparable harm, and the court's view that plaintiffs' showing of likelihood of success on the merits does not support plaintiffs' request to permit plaintiffs "to replace any bond used to enter merchandise on or after February 23, 2006, with a bond calculated without regard to potential antidumping or countervailing duties." *Mot. to Amend Injunctive Relief Requested*, attached *Order* at 3. As discussed in Section II.A.3 of this opinion, such relief is more akin to the restoration of a form of *status quo ante*, rather than a preliminary injunction to preserve the *status quo*, because it would require the court to order the cancellation of bonds, thereby extinguishing all obligations under such bonds, and would require Customs to approve the replacement of such bonds with superseding bonds with lower limits of liability. During the July 19, 2006 conference, the court attempted to facilitate an amicable resolution of the preliminary injunction issue by informing the parties of the court's preliminary conclusions, by reviewing the language of a limited draft injunction prepared by the court, and by soliciting from the parties suggested modifications to the draft that could achieve an administrable preliminary injunction. At that conference, the parties requested a period of time to consult and to seek agreement on language for a preliminary injunction to which all parties could consent. The court initially granted the parties a period of one week to consult. The plaintiffs subsequently requested, and the court granted, additional time for plaintiffs to continue their consultations with defendant.

In response to a USCIT R. 16 letter from the court dated August 17, 2006, defendant filed status reports on August 17 and September 1, 2006, and plaintiffs filed a status report on August 21, 2006, each advising the court of various matters. Of particular importance was that the communications in the status reports indicated to the court that the parties had reached an impasse in their negotiations concerning the preliminary injunction. Plaintiffs' August 21, 2006 status report conveyed plaintiffs' desire to continue negotiations, but interpreted defendant's August 17, 2006 status report as signaling that negotiations were at an end. Believing that negotiations had concluded, plaintiffs' August 21, 2006 status report requested that the court issue a preliminary injunction. Plaintiffs proposed a substantial change to the draft order prepared by the court, requesting that the injunction require Customs to permit any plaintiff "who obtained a new continuous entry bond on or after

February 23, 2006 . . . to change the limit of liability in the new bond" without applying the amendment or the clarification of the bond directive. *Pls.' Status Report* at 2. Defendant's status reports informed the court that defendant continued to oppose any preliminary injunction but also informed the court that Customs currently did not plan to alter the bond requirements for any of the eight plaintiffs that attempted to demonstrate immediate irreparable harm. *Def.'s Status Report* at 1, Aug. 17, 2006; *Def.'s Status Report* at 1-2, Sept. 1, 2006.

Defendant submitted another status report on October 25, 2006, informing the court that Customs had published the previous day a Federal Register notice concerning bond requirements for importers of certain merchandise subject to antidumping and countervailing duty orders. The notice, described later in this opinion, announced changes to the process used to determine bond amounts for importers of Special Category merchandise. Because the notice addressed matters relevant to the situations of the individual plaintiffs, the court held two status conferences with the parties, on October 26 and November 3, 2006. In the second status conference, counsel for defendant informed the court that Customs did not intend to use the process announced in the notice to replace with superseding bonds any of the bonds already required pursuant to the amendment and the clarification, including those bonds under which plaintiffs currently are importing merchandise. The court held another status conference on November 13, 2006, before issuing this opinion.

Based on all proceedings held to date, the court will enter a limited preliminary injunction that generally will preserve the *status quo* with respect to the bond status of the eight plaintiffs identified above. Each of those eight plaintiffs established that it will suffer immediate, irreparable harm, including a serious impairment of its ability to conduct its shrimp importing business, absent a preservation of the *status quo* during the pendency of this case. Plaintiffs demonstrated that they likely will succeed, partially, on the merits in establishing that the balance of the hardships on all parties in this action tips in favor of plaintiffs and that the public interest would be better served if the court grants injunctive relief. The court concludes that the showing made on behalf of the remaining 19 plaintiffs is insufficient to establish that those plaintiffs will suffer immediate, irreparable harm absent a preliminary injunction.

I. Background

Bond Directive 99-3510-004 (the "Bond Directive"), originally issued by Customs on July 23, 1991, established guidelines under which port directors are to assess the adequacy of an importer's continuous bond. *See Monetary Guidelines for Setting Bond Amounts*, Customs Directive 99-3510-004 (July 23, 1991), *available at* http://cbp.gov/linkhandler/cgov/toolbox/legal/directives/3510-004.ctt/3510-004.txt. Prior to the amendment by Customs in 2004, the Bond Directive set a nondiscretionary, minimum continuous bond amount at $50,000 and established a formula by which "the bond limit of liability amount shall be fixed in multiples of

$10,000 [or $100,000] nearest to 10 percent of duties, taxes and fees paid by the importer or broker acting as importer of record during the calender year preceding the date of the [bond] application." *Id.* (setting forth formulas under "Activity 1—Importer or Broker—Continuous"). Whether the bond limit was fixed in multiples of $10,000 or $100,000 depended upon whether the total duty and tax liability for an importer during the calender year preceding its bond application exceeded $1,000,000. *Id.*

Customs, on July 9, 2004, posted on its website the amendment to the Bond Directive at issue in this case (the "Amendment"), which set forth new formulas for calculating minimum continuous bond amounts for importers of agricultural/aquacultural merchandise that is subject to antidumping or countervailing duty orders. *See Amendment to Bond Directive 99-3510-004 for Certain Merchandise Subject to Antidumping/Countervailing Duty Cases* (July 9, 2004), *available at* http://www.cbp.gov/xp/cgov/import/add_cvd/bonds/07082004.xml ("*Amendment*"). Customs cited an "increasing concern regarding the collection of antidumping and countervailing duties, the impact of these collections on the amount of disbursements pursuant to the Continued Dumping and Subsidy Offset Act [of 2000, Pub. L. 106-387 ("Byrd Amendment")] . . . , and continued vigilance by [Customs] to ensure collection of all appropriate antidumping and countervailing duties." *Id.* Customs listed under-collections of antidumping duty liabilities for imports of fresh garlic and crawfish from China as examples of why it deemed it necessary to change the formula for determining minimum bond requirements. *Id.* The Amendment was neither published in the Federal Register nor subjected to the established notice and comment procedures provided for under the Administrative Procedure Act ("APA"), 5 U.S.C. § 553 (2000). Customs did not publish the Amendment in the Customs Bulletin.

The Amendment requires all Customs port directors "to review continuous bonds for importers who import agriculture/aquaculture merchandise subject to antidumping/ countervailing duty cases and obtain larger bonds where necessary." *Id.* A formula contained in the Amendment directs that "in fixing the limit of liability amount," port directors will calculate the product of an importer's antidumping or countervailing duty rate and the value of merchandise subject to antidumping or countervailing duties imported by that importer during the previous year. *Id.* (setting forth the formula as the "[Commerce] rate at Order [multiplied by the] value of imports of merchandise subject to the case by the importer during the previous year"). The Amendment also applies to provisional measures by providing that "[i]f, at any time after [Commerce] issues a preliminary affirmative determination in an agriculture/aquaculture case, [Customs] detects sudden changes in declared values, claimed country of origin, or declared classification, etc., [Customs] will consider such changes to reflect an increased risk." *Id.* The Amendment, in that event, requires port directors to determine the amount of a continuous bond by calculating the product of the importer's deposit rate in effect on the date of entry and the value of merchandise imported during the previous year. *See Amendment* (setting forth the formula as the "[Commerce] deposit rate in effect on date of entry [multiplied by the] value of imports of merchandise subject to the case by the importer during the previous year"). For importers with no prior history of importing agricultural/aquacultural merchandise, the Amendment directs that a sufficient bond amount will be determined by calculating the product of the importer's cash deposit rate in effect on the date of entry and the "estimated annual import value" of the subject imports. *Id.* (setting forth the formula as the "[Commerce] deposit rate in effect on date of entry [multiplied by the] estimated annual import value of the goods subject to the case").

On January 24, 2005, Customs posted on its website a document entitled "Current Bond Formulas," which contained, *inter alia*, the formulas described in the Amendment. *Current Bond Formulas* (Jan. 24, 2005), *available at* http://www.cbp.gov/xp/cgov/import/communications_to_trade/pilot_program/ ("*Current Bond Formulas*"). The document, which was not published in the Federal Register or Customs Bulletin, also states that a "new comprehensive [Customs] Directive will be issued at a later date." *Id.*

On August 10, 2005, Customs posted on its website a clarification to the Amendment of the Bond Directive (the "Clarification"), which established two classes of merchandise, "Special Categories" and "Covered Cases." *See Clarification to July 9, 2004 Amended Monetary Guidelines for Setting Bond Amounts for Special Categories of Merchandise Subject to Antidumping and/or Countervailing Duty Cases* (Aug. 10, 2005), *available at* http://www.cbp.gov/xp/cgov/import/add_cvd/bonds/07082004.xml ("*Clarification*"). The Clarification was not published in the Federal Register or the Customs Bulletin and was not the subject of a notice and comment proceeding. According to the Clarification, "Special Categories of merchandise can be designated where additional bond requirements in the form of greater continuous entry bonds or other security, may be required." *Id.* The Clarification designates only agricultural/aquacultural merchandise as a Special Category. *Id.* The Clarification explains that "[t]he term Covered Cases refers to merchandise within a previously designated Special Category where different standards or formulas for determining the bond amount will be applied." *Id.* Antidumping and countervailing duty investigations and orders pertaining to shrimp are the only Covered Cases that Customs has designated as falling within the agriculture/aquaculture Special Category. *See id.* The Clarification sets forth criteria that Customs is to consider in determining whether imports designated as Special Categories or Covered Cases should be subject to increased bond requirements. *See id.*[1] The Clarification also establishes the procedure for "notice, timing

---

1 The Clarification lists the following criteria: "1. Previous collection problems concerning a specific case or industry involved; 2. The similarity to previous cases or industries experiencing uncollected revenue problems; 3. Whether the merchandise in question had very low duty rates or was duty-free prior to initiation of an antidumping or countervailing duty case; 4. The projected ability of the industry to pay future duty liabilities; 5. Low capitalization of the industry involved such that new or increased duty liabilities create increased risk; 6. Whether

and appeal" of increased bond demands made by Customs for importers of Special Category and Covered Cases merchandise. *See Clarification*.

Because Customs confined its "Covered Cases" designation to shrimp subject to antidumping or countervailing duty proceedings, only importers of certain frozen warmwater shrimp from Brazil, China, Ecuador, India, Thailand and Vietnam, as specified in the scope of the six antidumping duty orders ("subject shrimp"), are subject to the new bond requirements set forth by Customs in the Amendment and the Clarification. Commerce issued amended antidumping duty orders on certain frozen warmwater shrimp from those six countries on February 1, 2005. *See Pls.' Mem.* Ex. 4. Subsequently, Customs issued to all 27 plaintiffs letters advising, pursuant to 19 C.F.R. Part 113, that their continuous bonds have been deemed "insufficient to protect the revenue and insure compliance with [Customs] laws and regulations." *See Pls.' Mem.* Ex. 5 Attach. B, Ex. 6 Attach. B, Ex. 7 Attach. A, Ex. 8 Attach. B, Ex. 9 Attach. C, Ex. 10 Attach. B. The notices of insufficiency established, for each importer, new continuous bond limits of liability and stated that in determining such limits, Customs applied the formula described as "AD/CVD Order (3)," *i.e.*, the "[Commerce] Order rate [multiplied by the] value of imports of merchandise subject to the case by the importer" during the previous year. *See id.*; *Current Bond Formulas* (setting forth the formula under "AD/CVD Order (3)").

On October 24, 2006, Customs published a Federal Register notice (the "Notice") "to provide additional information on the process used to determine bond amounts for importations involving elevated collection risks and to seek public comment on that process." *Monetary Guidelines for Setting Bond Amounts for Importations Subject to Enhanced Bonding Requirements*, 71 Fed. Reg. 62,276, 62,276 (Oct. 24, 2006) ("*Notice*"). The Notice announces changes to the process discussed in the Amendment and the Clarification and, although inviting public comment, makes the changes in the process effective upon publication. *Id.* (stating that "[t]he process published in this Notice is in effect."). The Notice retains the same basic formulas for calculating limits of liability for the continuous bonds required of importers of merchandise in Special Categories. *Id.* at 62,277. The Notice announces, however, that Customs will provide for public notice and comment on the designation of new Special Categories, which it announces will occur according to specified criteria, and also will provide for public notice of the removal of a designation. *Id.*

The Notice does not announce that Customs is changing the current designation of aquaculture merchandise as a Special Category or the current designation of the shrimp antidumping orders as Covered Cases, but it indicates that Customs no longer will designate Covered Cases. "[Customs] will continue to evaluate on an industry wide basis those types of merchandise where additional bond requirements may be needed." *Id.* "However, because importers are only affected when merchandise is subject to different bond requirements, [Customs] will only desig-

---

the industry involved is highly leveraged such that new or increased duty liabilities create increased risk; [and] 7. Any other factors that are deemed relevant."

nate Special Categories, that is, merchandise for which an enhanced bond amount may be required." *Id.* The Notice states, further, that importers of Special Category merchandise "will be offered the opportunity to submit information on their financial condition related to the risk of non-collection for that importer and [Customs] will determine bond amounts based on that information, the importer's compliance history and other relevant information available to [Customs]." *Id.* The Notice indicates, however, that absent exceptional circumstances, Customs will apply the formulas to determine the bond amounts where a submission has not been made by a principal in response to a notice from Customs of a new bond requirement. *Id.*

The Notice announces a new procedure that will apply when an importer of Special Category merchandise makes a submission in response to a notice from Customs of a new bond requirement. The new procedure provides the principal with 30 days to respond and to provide evidence supporting a lower bond amount, including financial information relevant to the importer's ability to pay, such as financial statements and tax returns. *Id.* at 62,278. The Notice provides that Customs will consider this information along with the factors identified in the applicable Customs regulation, 19 C.F.R. § 113.13(b), in determining a new bond requirement. *Id.* This new bond requirement "will not take effect with respect to a principal until 14 days after the date of [Customs'] reply to the principal's response." *Id.* The Notice indicates that Customs intends to exercise discretion in setting new bond amounts. "If [Customs] determines that the principal has a record of compliance with customs laws and regulations and that the principal has demonstrated an ability to pay, [Customs] may decide not to require an increased bond amount even though the principal imports Special Category merchandise." *Id.* The Notice, however, also states that "[a]t any time after [Customs] determines a bond amount for a principal below that provided by the formula, if the principal fails to remain compliant with customs laws and regulations, [Customs] will recalculate the principal's bond amount in accordance with the formulas outlined in this notice." *Id.*

After the issuance of the six antidumping duty orders on subject shrimp, plaintiffs were required to obtain new continuous bonds that secured the amount of liability demanded by Customs. Some of the 27 plaintiffs were unable to secure continuous bonds in the amounts requested by Customs, and as a result these plaintiffs ceased their importation of some or all types of subject shrimp. *See Pls.' Mem.* at 7. Other plaintiffs were able to secure continuous bonds acceptable to Customs to cover their 2005-2006 imports of subject shrimp. The eight plaintiffs that introduced evidence, in addition to the remaining 19 NFI importers, seek injunctive relief to, *inter alia*, restrict Customs from applying the Amendment or the Clarification, or from considering any potential antidumping duty liability, in determining the sufficiency of future continuous bonds.

II. Discussion

The court exercises subject matter jurisdiction pursuant to 28 U.S.C. § 1581(i). *See First Am. Compl.* ¶¶ 2-4 (asserting jurisdiction under 28 U.S.C. § 1581(i)).

That provision provides the Court of International Trade with exclusive jurisdiction over any civil action commenced against the United States that arises out of any law providing for revenue for imports (subsection (i)(1)), tariffs or duties on the importation of merchandise for reasons other than the raising of revenue (subsection (i)(2)), and administration and enforcement with respect to matters referred to in subsections (i)(1) and (i)(2) (subsection (i)(4)). 28 U.S.C. §§ 1581(i)(1), (2) & (4). "The burden is always on the movant to show entitlement to a preliminary injunction." *Reebok Int'l Ltd. v. J. Baker., Inc.*, 32 F.3d 1552, 1555 (Fed. Cir. 1994). In determining whether the court should employ the extraordinary remedy of a preliminary injunction, a court of equity will consider the following four factors: (1) whether the moving party will suffer immediate and irreparable injury absent relief, (2) whether there exists a likelihood of success on the merits, (3) whether the balance of hardship on all the parties favors the moving party, and (4) whether the public interest would be better served by the requested relief. *Zenith Radio Corp. v. United States*, 710 F.2d 806, 809 (Fed. Cir. 1983). The court, in its analysis of these factors, may "weigh the factors together in a sliding scale manner." *See Chilean Nitrate Corp. v. United States*, 11 CIT 538, 539 (1987). No one factor is dispositive. *FMC Corp. v. United States*, 3 F.3d 424, 427 (Fed. Cir. 1993). "[T]he weakness of the showing regarding one factor may be overborne by the strength of the others." *Id.* Consequently, the court need not assign equal weight to each factor. *See id.*; *see also Corus Group PLC v. Bush*, 26 CIT 937, 942, 217 F. Supp. 2d 1347, 1354 (2002), *aff'd on other grounds*, 352 F.3d 1351 (Fed. Cir. 2003).

The court, having considered the evidence put forth by the parties and the arguments addressing the four factors that the parties made in their briefs and during oral argument, concludes that only eight of the plaintiffs—specifically, Eastern Fish, Ore-Cal, Red Chamber, IGF, Tampa Bay, Oriental Foods, Berdex Seafood, and Aqua Star—have established their entitlement to a preliminary injunction. The showings by these eight plaintiffs as to irreparable harm and the likelihood of success on the merits, however, justifies a more limited preliminary injunction than that sought by plaintiffs. Plaintiffs' motion and draft order for a preliminary injunction, as amended on April 14, 2006, seek to prohibit Customs from "relying upon or otherwise considering" the Amendment, the Clarification, or "any potential antidumping or countervailing duty liability on any imported product, when determining the sufficiency of the continuous entry bond for any entry made on or after February 23, 2006," for the 27 plaintiff- importers. *Mot. to Amend Injunctive Relief Requested*, attached *Order* at 1-2. The motion and draft order also seek an order directing Customs to "permit any of the foregoing named companies to replace any bond used to enter merchandise on or after February 23, 2006, with a bond calculated without regard to potential antidumping or countervailing duties." *Id.* at 3. As discussed in this opinion, the court declines to impose the specific remedy sought by plaintiffs. The court, however, will order a limited preliminary injunction that preserves generally the *status quo* with respect to the bond status of these eight plaintiffs during the pendency of these proceedings.

A. Immediate and Irreparable Harm

To meet their burden of establishing immediate and irreparable harm, "plaintiff[s] must prove that unless the injunction is awarded, some harm will result to [them] that cannot be reasonably redressed in a court of law." *Am. Customs Brokers Co. v. U.S. Customs Service*, 10 CIT 385, 386, 637 F. Supp. 218, 220 (1986). "Only a viable *threat of serious harm which cannot be undone* authorizes exercise of a court's equitable power to enjoin before the merits are fully determined." *Zenith Radio Corp.*, 710 F.2d at 809 (citation and internal quotation marks omitted).

To prevail on a motion for preliminary injunction, plaintiffs have the burden of producing "probative evidence" to demonstrate a threat of immediate, irreparable harm. *See Nat'l Hand Tool Corp. v. United States*, 14 CIT 61, 66 (1990). "Failure of [a plaintiff] to bear its burden of persuasion on irreparable harm is ground to deny a preliminary injunction." *Bomont Indus. v. United States,* 10 CIT 431, 437, 638 F. Supp. 1334, 1340 (1986). However, there is no bright line test for determining whether a plaintiff will suffer irreparable harm. *Corus Group PLC*, 26 CIT at 943, 217 F. Supp. 2d at 1354. A plaintiff can satisfy its burden by showing that it will be forced into bankruptcy absent an injunction. *See Queen's Flowers de Columbia v. United States*, 20 CIT 1122, 1125, 947 F. Supp. 503, 506 (1996). Less drastic harm, however, also can satisfy the burden. *See, e.g., Nat'l Juice Prods. Ass'n v. United States*, 10 CIT 48, 54, 628 F. Supp. 978, 984 (1986) (finding that severe disruption to a company's business operations is sufficient to establish irreparable injury); *718 Fifth Ave. Corp. v. United States*, 7 CIT 195, 198 (1984) (stating that "[b]usiness disruption resulting from administrative delay could be sufficient to demonstrate irreparable harm"); *Lois Jeans & Jackets, U.S.A., Inc. v. United States*, 5 CIT 238, 242, 566 F. Supp. 1523, 1527 (1983) (finding that "the real prospect for lost future orders, the lost benefits from its past advertising, substantial expenditures for marketing and promotional efforts, and the loss of plaintiff's reputation in the trade and with the consuming public are significant actual and potential injuries which warrant the extraordinary relief of a preliminary injunction").

1. Contentions of the Parties on Immediate and Irreparable Harm

Plaintiffs allege that absent the requested preliminary injunctive relief, they will continue to suffer immediate, irreparable harm that includes alteration of their buying activities, damage to their long-standing relationships with their customers and suppliers, and loss of sales and business opportunities. *See Post-Hearing Br. in Supp. of Pls.' Mot. for Prelim. Inj.* at 19-28 ("*Pls.' Post-Hearing Br.*"). According to plaintiffs, such harm results from the need to obtain continuous bonds, pursuant to insufficiency notices issued by Customs to plaintiffs, in the excessive amounts calculated by Customs using the bond formulas indicated by the Amendment and the Clarification. *See id.* at 16-17. The excessive bond amounts, plaintiffs contend, are causing sureties to require, as a condition of issuing a bond, a letter of credit in the amount of the bond. *Id.* at 31-32. Plaintiffs further contend that obtaining these letters of credit hinders plaintiffs' ability to finance their businesses efficiently. In this regard, plaintiffs describe a scenario they refer to as "stacking," arguing that, absent preliminary injunctive relief, their credit will remain encumbered until final liquidation of all entries covered by the new continuous bonds, and that, as time goes on, plaintiffs will remain liable under multiple bonds at the same time. *See id.* at 16-17. Plaintiffs contend that the continuous and increasing burdens on their credit availability will impede severely the operation of their businesses and ultimately will force them out of the business of importing shrimp. *See id.* at 17-18. Although plaintiffs presented testimony from representatives of, and documentary evidence concerning, only eight of the 27 importers who filed jointly the *Complaint* and *Amended Complaint* in this action, plaintiffs argue that the court "should make reasonable inferences as to the irreparable harm that will befall the entire group of NFI [i]mporters" if the requested relief is not granted. *Id.* at 35.

Defendant argues that none of the plaintiffs has met its burden of establishing the level of economic harm necessary to warrant the extraordinary remedy of injunctive relief. *See Def.'s Opp'n* 9-12; *Def.'s Post-Hearing Br. in Opp'n to NFI's Mot. for Prelim. Inj.* 10-15 ("*Def.'s Post Hearing Br.*"). Defendant contends specifically that audited financial records, which were provided by two plaintiffs, fail to establish adequate irreparable harm as to those two plaintiffs, and that any findings of fact drawn from those financial statements for purposes of inferring irreparable harm cannot be extrapolated to the remaining plaintiffs. Tr. 851-868; *see Def.'s Post- Hearing Br.* at 12. Further, defendant claims that plaintiffs' arguments relating to lost business opportunities are speculative and indicate only that "the losing bidder was in a weaker financial position than its competitor." *Def.'s Opp'n* at 12. Defendant also maintains that the administrative record establishes that the overall volume of shrimp imports has declined by only 2.6 percent since importers, including plaintiffs, were required to obtain larger bonds and that, despite the testimony of plaintiffs, the shrimp importing industry as a whole is not suffering extraordinary harm. *See id.* at 10; *Def.'s Post-Hearing Br.* at 5; *Def.'s Opp'n* at *Decl. of Bruce W. Ingalls* Attach. B. According to defendant, "one plaintiff's lost business probably ended up in the hands of a different importer of the same product—like in any low margin, commodity industry with a large number of competitors." *Def.'s Opp'n* at 10. Finally, defendant maintains that plaintiffs' "stacking" argument is also mere speculation because "plaintiffs have provided no evidence that insurers intend to require additional collateral for future years." *Id.* at 5; *see Def.'s Post-Hearing Br.* at 4-5.

2. Findings of Fact on Immediate and Irreparable Harm

To establish that NFI and its members will suffer immediate, irreparable harm absent injunctive relief, eight plaintiffs—Eastern Fish, Ore-Cal, Red Chamber, IGF, Tampa Bay, Oriental Foods, Berdex Seafood, and Aqua Star—submitted testimonial and documentary evidence. Through such evidence, plaintiffs sought to demonstrate that all 27 plaintiffs will incur harm if Customs is not preliminarily enjoined from applying the Amendment in determining the sufficiency of plaintiffs' continuous bonds. Based on a preponderance of the evidence presented at trial, the court finds as facts that each of the above-named eight plaintiffs will incur serious, immediate and irreparable harm absent some form of preliminary injunctive relief. Specifically, this harm is the foreseeable result of the cumulative effects of obtaining the additional collateralized letters of credit necessary to secure future continuous bonds in amounts determined pursuant to the new bond requirements of the Amendment and the Clarification. At this time, the court lacks sufficient evidence to make factual findings that would justify preliminary injunctive relief on the basis of immediate and irreparable harm to the remaining 19 plaintiffs. The evidence supporting the findings of fact relevant to whether the eight plaintiffs will suffer immediate and irreparable harm absent injunctive relief is summarized below.

a. Company-Specific Findings of Fact

i. Eastern Fish

Plaintiffs introduced at trial the testimony of Mr. Eric Howard Bloom, President of Eastern Fish. The court found his testimony credible based on his demeanor, demonstrated knowledge of Eastern Fish's business activities, and general knowledge of the business of importing shrimp. His testimony established, by a preponderance of the evidence, the following facts:

1. Eastern Fish, established in 1972, is engaged in the business of importing seafood products, []

2. [ ]

3. []

4. []

5. []

6. []

7. []

ii. Ore-Cal

Plaintiffs introduced at trial the testimony of Mr. Mark Daniel Shinbane, Vice-President of Ore-Cal. The court found his testimony credible based on his demeanor, demonstrated knowledge of Ore-Cal's business activities, and general knowledge of the business of importing shrimp. His testimony established, by a preponderance of the evidence, the following facts: 8. Ore-Cal, for the last 45 years, has engaged in the business of importing shrimp into the United States. Tr. 193. []

9. [ ]

10. []

11. []

12. [ ]

13. []

iii. Red Chamber, IGF, and Tampa Bay

Plaintiffs introduced at trial the testimony of Mr. Richard V. Martin, General Manager of IGF and Executive Consultant to Red Chamber, a company that is affiliated through common ownership with plaintiffs IGF and Tampa Bay. The court found his testimony credible based on his demeanor, demonstrated knowledge of Red Chamber's, IGF's and Tampa Bay's business activities, and general knowledge of the business of importing shrimp. His testimony established, by a preponderance of the evidence, the following facts:

14. Red Chamber, IGF, and Tampa Bay are affiliated through common ownership. Tr. 267. []

15. []

16. []

17. []

18. []

19. []

20. [ ]

21. []

iv. Berdex Seafood

Plaintiffs introduced at trial the testimony of Mr. Donelson S. Berger, President of Berdex Seafood. The court found his testimony credible based on his demeanor, demonstrated knowledge of Berdex Seafood's business activities, and general knowledge of the business of importing shrimp. His testimony established, by a preponderance of the evidence, the following facts:

22. Berdex Seafood is engaged in the business of importing seafood into the United States [ ]

23. []

24. [ ]

25. []

26. []

v. Oriental Foods

Plaintiffs introduced at trial the testimony of Dr. G.V. Reddy, President of Oriental Foods. The court found his testimony credible based on his demeanor, demonstrated knowledge of Oriental Foods' business activities, and general knowledge of the business of importing shrimp. His testimony established, by a preponderance of the evidence, the following facts:

27. Since 1979, Oriental Foods has engaged in the business of importing seafood products. Tr. 486. [ ]

28. []

29. []

30. []

vi. Aqua Star

Plaintiffs introduced at trial the testimony of Mr. Robert Hooey, Senior Executive Vice President of Aqua Star. The court found his testimony credible based on his demeanor, demonstrated knowledge of Aqua Star's business activities, and general knowledge of the business of importing shrimp. His testimony established, by a preponderance of the evidence, the following facts:

31. Aqua Star is engaged in the business of importing seafood, []

32. []

33. [ ]

34. [ ]

b. Summary of Findings of Fact

Through testimony, Eastern Fish, Ore-Cal, Red Chamber, IGF, Tampa Bay, Oriental Foods, Berdex Seafood, and Aqua Star have established that they encountered difficulties in obtaining new bonds in the increased amounts demanded by Customs. *See Findings of Fact* ¶¶ 3-5, 7, 9-10, 13, 15-18, 23-25, 28-29, 32. The difficulties resulted from the need to provide their financial institutions with collateralized letters of credit in amounts that, in most instances, significantly burden plaintiffs' asset-based credit lines. *See Findings of Fact* ¶¶ 1, 4, 8, 10, 14, 17-18, 22, 24, 29, 32, 34; *see also Pls.' Mem.* at 15; *Pls.' Post-Hearing Br.* at 8-9. Because plaintiffs "rely heavily on their lines of credit to conduct their business[es]," Eastern Fish, Ore- Cal, Red Chamber, IGF, Tampa Bay, Oriental Foods, Berdex Seafood, and Aqua Star all reduced their on-hand inventories and declined to pursue tangible business opportunities. *Pls.' Post- Hearing Br.* at 8. In some instances, plaintiffs dropped product lines or scaled back existing or planned product lines. *See Findings of Fact* ¶¶ 5, 13, 16-17, 20-21, 25-26, 30, 33; *Pls.' Post- Hearing Br.* at 4-5. Effects on cash flow resulting from posting collateral to secure irrevocable letters of credit led some plaintiffs to forgo opportunities to supply, develop, and market new products. *See Findings of Fact* ¶¶ 5, 13, 20-21, 25-26, 30, 33. In several instances, some plaintiffs lost spot sales and declined to bid on major orders from supermarket chains and major retail customers because of the restrictions associated with the new bond requirements. *See Findings of Fact* ¶¶ 5, 25, 30, 34. In other instances, some plaintiffs were forced to import shrimp on a delivered duty-paid basis, which reduces profit margins. *See Findings of Fact* ¶¶ 4, 30, 32-33. For a period spanning 2005 and 2006, one of the plaintiffs was unable to secure a sufficient bond and temporarily was forced out of the importing business. *See Findings of Fact* ¶ 32.

The difficulties associated with obtaining sufficient continuous bonds also affect customer and supplier relationships of the eight plaintiffs. The evidence demonstrates that these plaintiffs declined opportunities to pursue business with existing companies and suppliers. Impediments to the ability to import shrimp on a continuous basis and the transition to importing on a delivered duty-paid basis affect plaintiffs' long-standing relationships with customers, who depend upon plaintiffs for supply, and with suppliers, who dedicate a portion of their production for purchase by plaintiffs. *See Findings of Fact* ¶¶ 6, 13, 20, 24-25, 30, 33-34. Some plaintiffs, in order to fulfill certain contracts with customers, must import shrimp from certain countries that are subject to the antidumping duty orders on shrimp, namely India, Thailand, and Vietnam. *See Findings of Fact* ¶¶ 2, 11-12, 20, 26, 33. These plaintiffs considered shrimp products from certain other countries to be unsuitable substitutes for shrimp from India, Thailand, and Vietnam because suppliers in those other countries, according to these plaintiffs, do not have the infrastructure or sanitary standards necessary to become reliable alternative suppliers. *See Findings of Fact* ¶¶ 2, 11, 20, 33.

The liabilities that are secured by plaintiffs' current bonds will extend until liquidation of all entries is final. The date on which final liquidation of those entries will occur is not known. The letters of credit supporting plaintiffs' current bonds will not be extinguished until after final liquidation. If Customs continues to apply the new bond formulas in calculating future bond demands, plaintiffs likely will suffer an additional reduction to their borrowing capacities as a result of securing new letters of credit. Two of the eight plaintiffs that introduced evidence have already suffered such an additional reduction in their borrowing capacities in order to secure new bonds that were issued in the spring of 2006. Such new letters of credit, the liability of which will not be extinguished until some future date, will further deplete plaintiffs' credit and cause plaintiffs significant economic harm. The court finds as a fact that another round of bond demands likely will cause plaintiffs severe irreparable harm, especially in view of the requirement on an importer, imposed by 19 C.F.R. § 113.12(b)(1), to notify Customs of any material changes in importing activities. The court further observes that bond determinations affecting the eight plaintiffs will occur as bonds expire over the next several months, some as early as December 2006. *See Findings of Fact*. Some plaintiffs have testified that such a burden on available credit may lead to additional drastic changes in business operations, including the importation of shrimp and other products on a delivered duty-paid basis. Such changes will lead to additional inefficiencies and, ultimately, reduced profit margins, lost sales, and severed relationships with customers and suppliers. Others have testified that additional reductions in borrowing capacity may restrict them from operating their businesses altogether. 3. Conclusions of Law on Immediate and Irreparable Harm Applicable to the Eight Plaintiffs Eastern Fish, Ore-Cal, Red Chamber, IGF, Tampa Bay, Oriental Foods, Berdex Seafood, and Aqua Star have established, through probative testimony of their representatives and other probative documentary evidence that, absent a preliminary injunction that preserves generally the *status quo*, they will suffer the type of extraordinary harm that seriously threatens the continued operation of their shrimp importing businesses. Their respective showings satisfy the requirements for preliminary injunctive relief. With respect to all eight of these plaintiffs, the harm that will occur absent a *status quo* preliminary injunction includes severe disruption of the plaintiffs' business activities, damage to the plaintiffs' long-standing relationships with their customers and suppliers, lost sales, diminished profits, and foregoing of business opportunities. *See Am. Customs Brokers Co.*, 10 CIT at 387, 637 F. Supp. 2d at 221 (finding irreparable injury where plaintiff provided "evidence of substantial harm to business good will, business reputation and a significant loss of new business."). The court concludes that some form of a preliminary injunction is the only way to protect the plaintiffs from future irreparable injury during the pendency of this case. *See Weinberger v. Romero-Barcelo*, 456 U.S. 305, 312 (1982).

The situation of three of the eight plaintiff-importers differs from that of the other five plaintiff-importers in a significant respect. These three plaintiffs are constrained, in whole or in part, from importing shrimp subject to the antidumping duty orders pursuant to side agreements that they entered into with Customs in order to obtain affordable continuous bonds. They are, in this respect, suffering a different type of harm than that afflicting the other five plaintiff- importers who introduced evidence of harm. As a direct result of the side agreements, these three importers are experiencing a substantial interference with or preclusion of their ability to conduct their shrimp importing businesses. For these three plaintiffs, a preservation of the *status quo* through a preliminary injunction would allow these conditions to remain in place despite the demonstrated harm that the conditions imposed in the side agreements are causing. Moreover, as discussed later in this opinion with respect to the showing of likelihood of success on the merits, these three importers are likely to be able to show that the imposition of the conditions was contrary to the Customs regulations. For this reason, the preliminary injunctive relief that the court will order prohibits the enforcement of the side agreements and the associated restraints on importation of subject merchandise during the pendency of this proceeding.

The harm being suffered by the other five plaintiff-importers that introduced evidence results from the high limits of liability associated with their basic importer's bonds. The court concludes, based on the evidence these five plaintiffs have introduced, that the impending harm will be a direct result of the cumulative burdens occurring as a result of the application of the bond formulas set forth in the Amendment, the Current Bond Formulas, and the Clarification to the next determinations of bond sufficiency. Each of these five plaintiffs will suffer adverse effects from the encumbering of additional credit when they are required to obtain future continuous bonds in amounts calculated pursuant to the new bond formulas required under the Amendment and the Clarification while they remain under the obligations of the continuous bonds Customs already assessed pursuant to those formulas. Two of these five plaintiff- importers received from Customs a second round of insufficiency notices in the spring of 2006 and have been required to encumber additional credit in order to obtain the new bonds, a development the court has considered in reaching its conclusions concerning irreparable harm.

The court concludes that while a limited preliminary injunction that generally preserves the *status quo* is appropriate at this time, the evidence introduced thus far does not establish that the current level of harm being experienced by these five plaintiffs is so disruptive as to qualify them for a preliminary injunction that restores a form of *status quo ante*, *i.e.*, a preliminary injunction that directs Customs to replace the current bonds with bonds based on the same limits of liability as those in place prior to the application of the Amendment and the Clarification. The court recognizes, additionally, that the situations of one or more of these five plaintiffs, or one or more of the other testifying plaintiffs, may change, and may change rapidly, in a way that could necessitate a modification of the preliminary injunction. The court, therefore, will consider motions to modify the preliminary injunction and may order expedited hearings, if necessary.

The court notes the cumulative effects of two successive rounds of bond determinations based on the rigid application of the formulas, and the upcoming third round of bond determinations that will occur over the next several months. The burden imposed by an importer's outstanding letters of credit, which resulted from the application of the formula with little or no adjustment during the previous rounds of bond determinations, affects negatively the financial condition of that importer. The adverse effects will continue and are all but certain to become exacerbated upon the next round of bond determinations, during which the effect of the letters of credit, by weakening the plaintiff-importer's financial condition, may compromise the ability of that plaintiff-importer to qualify for a lower bond determination. The court, for these reasons, is ordering defendant to begin, immediately, a review of the five continuous bonds that have a limit of liability at or above $1.5 million under which these five plaintiffs currently are importing. The court is ordering Customs to review these five continuous bonds so that Customs determines expeditiously, on its own, whether those bonds should be canceled in favor of superseding bonds with lower limits of liability, and so that Customs reports to the court, within 60 days from the date of the Order imposing the preliminary injunction, its conclusions and explains to the court the reasons for those conclusions.

Defendant argues that plaintiffs have not been able to show sufficient injury to their current respective financial conditions to warrant a preliminary injunction. Although plaintiffs have not shown irreparable harm sufficient to qualify for a preliminary injunction restoring a form of *status quo ante,* they have shown sufficient irreparable harm to justify relief that generally preserves the *status quo*. *See* Tr. 749-751, 896-898 (discussing plaintiffs' request for the *status quo*). Defendant's arguments that relate to whether or not the lost business opportunities, declining profit margins, and decreases in volume of shrimp imports are sufficient to establish irreparable harm that already has occurred, are therefore not on point. To establish irreparable harm, plaintiffs "must show a *presently existing threat* and not just the mere possibility of injury." *NSK Ltd. v. United States*, 28 CIT ___, ___, 350 F. Supp. 2d 1128, 1132 (2004) (emphasis added); *see Zenith Radio Corp.*, 710 F.2d at 809; *Elkem Metals Co. v. United States*, 25 CIT 186, 192, 135 F. Supp. 2d 1324, 1331 (2001). Irreparable harm constitutes *potential harm* that cannot be redressed by a legal or an equitable remedy at the conclusion of the proceedings, so that a preliminary injunction is the only way of protecting the plaintiffs. *See Weinberger*, 456 U.S. at 312-318.

Defendant urges the court to conclude that plaintiffs' argument that the "insurers intend to require additional collateral for future years" is pure speculation. *Def.'s Opp'n* at 5. Based on the facts established by the administrative record, *i.e.*, that each surety required an irrevocable letter of credit from plaintiffs who obtained new continuous bonds in 2005 and 2006, the court infers that there is a strong likelihood that sureties similarly will require additional collateral in the future. The facts established on the *de novo* record also support the inference that sureties will require up to 100 percent security for any new or extended continuous bonds, as they have to date. Specifically, the testimony of witnesses for two plaintiffs relating to the requirements imposed on plaintiffs seeking new term bonds corroborates the finding that sureties typically require 100 percent collateral in the situations occasioned by the new bonding requirements. The record also establishes that lending institutions typically reduce credit limits by amounts equal to, or nearly equal to, the amount of a letter of credit used to secure a bond. *See Findings of Fact* ¶¶ 3, 7, 9-10, 18, 24. Moreover, the requirement that plaintiffs must inform Customs of any material changes in the bond applications, such as whether "the value or nature of the merchandise to be imported will change in any material respect during the next year," further supports the inference that if plaintiffs exceed the import capacities on their existing term bonds, Customs, absent a preliminary injunction, will require additional bonding pursuant to the formulas set forth in the Amendment and the Clarification. 19 C.F.R. § 113.12(b)(1)(ii). Plaintiffs have demonstrated that to secure such additional bonding, plaintiffs' sureties are requiring that the bonds be fully collateralized, which in turn requires plaintiffs to further encumber the credit available from their lending institutions. In view of these demonstrated facts and the strong likelihood of cumulating harm, the court considers the review of current bond limits that it is ordering Customs to conduct to be necessary and appropriate.

In its status reports to the court, filed on August 17 and September 1, 2006, defendant informed the court that "Customs and Border Protection ("CBP") currently does not plan to alter the bond requirements for any of the eight plaintiffs that attempted to demonstrate immediate irreparable harm" and that "CBP does not currently intend to render insufficient the bonds of the three of those eight importers whose current bonds are subject to restrictions upon subject shrimp, should those plaintiffs import subject shrimp." *Def.'s Status Report* at 1-2, Aug. 17, 2006; *Def.'s Status Report* at 1, Sept. 1, 2006. Because of this lack of current intention, among other reasons, defendant submits that a preliminary injunction is not warranted. *Def.'s Status Report* at 1-2, Aug. 17, 2006; *Def.'s Status Report* at 2, Sept. 1, 2006. The court does not agree that this representation by defendant is sufficient to preclude the need for a preliminary injunction at this time. The current intention of Customs, absent a preliminary injunction, can change at any time and, without notice to plaintiffs or the court, result immediately in additional burden and disruption to one or more of the eight plaintiffs who presented evidence of irreparable harm. In addition, the aforementioned expiration of term bonds, some of which bonds will expire as early as December 2006, makes the future serious harm even more imminent. The assurance from defendant that Customs does not intend to render insufficient any current bonds of the eight plaintiffs does not address this imminent harm. The court can prevent that harm during the pendency of this proceeding only by enjoining Customs from applying the Amendment, the Current Bond Formulas, and the Clarification to the next determinations of limits of liability, which will occur upon the expiration of the current term bonds of the eight plaintiffs. 4. The Court Will Not Infer that the Remaining 19 Plaintiffs Have Met Their Burden of Establishing Immediate, Irreparable Harm The court will not infer that the remaining 19 plaintiffs will suffer the same type of harm established by Eastern Fish, Ore-Cal, Red Chamber, IGF, Tampa Bay, Oriental Foods, Berdex Seafood, and Aqua Star. The only facts that the court can infer with respect to the remaining plaintiffs are listed in the *Joint Stipulation of Undisputed Facts* filed on March 30, 2006, which are insufficient to establish that those plaintiffs' current financial conditions, lending relationships, or business operations are threatened with irreparable harm. However, the court will consider another motion by any of these remaining plaintiffs for a preliminary injunction or for a hearing at which evidence of immediate, irreparable harm could be introduced.

B. Likelihood of Success on the Merits

To prevail on a motion for injunctive relief, plaintiffs carry the burden of establishing a likelihood of success on the merits. *FMC Corp.*, 3 F.3d at 427; *Zenith Radio Corp.*, 710 F.2d at 809. Plaintiffs have demonstrated a strong likelihood that they will succeed, in part, on the merits of this action.

Plaintiffs brought this action under 28 U.S.C. § 1581(i) to challenge the application of the Amendment and the Clarification in determinations by Customs of the sufficiency of continuous bonds covering plaintiffs' liabilities for import transactions, particularly those transactions involving subject shrimp. *See First Am. Compl.* ¶ 2. In support of their challenge, plaintiffs make several arguments. Plaintiffs primarily argue that the interplay of 19 U.S.C. § 1623, providing for the setting of bond conditions by Customs, and of 19 U.S.C. §§ 1671, 1673, providing for the assessment of antidumping and countervailing duties by Commerce, precludes Customs from considering potential antidumping and countervailing duty liability in determining the sufficiency of a continuous bond. *See id.* ¶¶ 24-28. Plaintiffs' second general argument is that the application of the Amendment and the Clarification to shrimp importers generally and to plaintiffs was arbitrary, capricious, an abuse of discretion, or otherwise not in accordance with law, and was unsupported by substantial evidence. *See id.* ¶¶ 29-31.

1. Plaintiffs Failed to Show a Likelihood of Success for their Arguments that the Statute Precludes Customs From Considering Potential Antidumping Duty Liability in Determining the Sufficiency of a Continuous Bond

Plaintiffs' primary argument is that Customs is precluded by law from considering potential antidumping and countervailing duty liability in determining the sufficiency of a continuous bond. *See id.* ¶¶ 24-28. Plaintiffs argue, specifically, that 19 U.S.C. § 1623(a) "limits [Customs'] authority to require importers to post a bond to 'case[s] in which bond or other security is not specifically required by law.'" *Pls.' Post-Hearing Br.* at 39 (quoting 19 U.S.C. § 1623(a)). According to plaintiffs, cash deposits collected in antidumping and countervailing cases, which are provided for by statute in 19 U.S.C. §§ 1671e(a)(3), 1673e(a)(3), provide "other security" within the meaning of § 1623(a), thereby precluding Customs from requiring additional security for that purpose. *See Pls.' Mem.* at 41. Plaintiffs cite to the legislative history of § 1623(a) in support of their contention that the plain meaning of § 1623(a) confers on Customs authority to impose a bond or other security only in situations where such measures are not provided for by law. *See id.* at 41-42.

Defendant counters that Customs has full statutory authority to consider antidumping or countervailing duty liability in setting the amount of a continuous bond. *See Def.'s Post-Hearing Br.* at 16-19. Rather than limiting the authority of Customs to establish the amount of a term bond, according to defendant, § 1623(a) confers authority upon Customs to impose bond requirements to protect the revenue, including the authority to set a continuous bond amount in the circumstances at issue in this case. *See id.* Defendant further argues that other subsections of § 1623 "demonstrate that [Customs] possesses discretionary authority to protect the revenue by requiring the posting of a bond." *Id.* at 20. Defendant specifically points to § 1623(b), stating that "'[w]henever a bond is required or authorized by a law, regulation, or instruction which . . . [Customs] is authorized to enforce, the Secretary of the Treasury *may*—(1) Except as otherwise specifically provided by law, *prescribe the conditions* and form of such bond . . . and *fix the amount of penalty* thereof.'" *Id.* (quoting 19 U.S.C. § 1623(b)).

The court concludes that plaintiffs have not met their burden of establishing a likelihood of success on the issue of whether Customs is precluded by law from considering potential antidumping or countervailing duty liability in setting the limit of liability for a continuous bond. Subsection (a) of 19 U.S.C. § 1623 provides that the Secretary of the Treasury may by regulation or specific instruction require, or authorize customs officers to require, such bonds or other security as he, or they, may deem necessary for the protection of the revenue or to assure compliance with any provision of law, regulation, or instruction which the Secretary of the Treasury or the Customs Service may be authorized to enforce. 19 U.S.C. § 1623(a). The subsection conditions the authority accorded to the Secretary or to Customs with the introductory phrase, "[i]n any case in which bond or other security is not specifically required by law." *Id.* Read according to its plain meaning, subsection (a) addresses the matter of *when* a bond or other security may be required. Plaintiffs would have the court construe the introductory phrase as a limitation on the authority of the Secretary and Customs to set the limit of liability of a term bond. The only language in subsection (a) that specifically relates to the limit of liability of a term bond allows for bonds "necessary for the protection of the revenue." Subsection (b) of § 1623 applies to various matters pertaining to bonds, regardless of whether the bond is required by statute, regulation, or instruction. It provides that "[w]henever a bond is required or authorized by a law, regulation, or instruction which the Secretary of the Treasury or the Customs Service is authorized to enforce, the Secretary of the Treasury may—(1) Except as otherwise specifically provided by law . . . fix the amount of penalty thereof, whether for the payment of liquidated damages or of a penal sum." *Id.* § 1623(b)(1). The statute further allows the Secretary to "[a]uthorize the execution of a term bond the conditions of which shall extend to and cover similar cases of importations over such period of time, not to exceed one year, or such longer period as he may fix when in his opinion special circumstances existing in a particular instance require such longer period." *Id.* § 1623(b)(3). When read together, the two subsections appear to provide Customs considerable discretion in setting the requirements for term bonds so as to protect the revenue.

In support of their argument, plaintiffs also refer to the legislative history of Section 623 of the 1930 Tariff Act (19 U.S.C. § 1623). Plaintiffs quote a House Report that explains that

> [i]n order to provide for more uniformity in these matters [*i.e.*, matters in the tariff laws pertaining to bonds] and for more elasticity in the requirement for bonds, there is included in the bill as section 623 a provision authorizing the Secretary of the Treasury by regulations to require or to authorize collectors to require such bonds or other security as he or they [may] deem necessary for the protection of the revenue and to assure compliance with the customs laws and regulations. A number of specific pro-

> visions of Titles III and IV requiring bonds in particular cases have been eliminated to correspond with this amendment. *The new provision will authorize the requirement of a bond wherever not specifically required by the law*, but will not permit of the waiving of a bond where an express requirement occurs.

Pls.' Mem. at 42 (quoting H.R. Rep. No. 71-7, at 186 (1929)) (emphasis added in *Pls.' Mem.*). The legislative history relied upon by plaintiffs does not support an inference that Congress intended to limit the authority of Customs in the way that plaintiffs advocate. To the contrary, in enacting Section 623, Congress appears to have endeavored to expand, not limit, the authority of Customs to provide Customs with sufficient authority to protect the revenue and to ensure compliance with the customs laws and regulations.

Plaintiffs further cite to 19 U.S.C. § 1673d(c)(1)(B)(ii) to support their argument that Congress intended to preclude Customs from considering antidumping duty liability in setting the amount of a continuous bond. *Pls.' Mem.* at 44. That statutory provision directs Commerce to "order the posting of a cash deposit, bond, or other security, as the administering authority deems appropriate, for each entry of the subject merchandise in an amount based on the estimated weighted average dumping margin or the estimated all-others rate, whichever is applicable." 19 U.S.C. § 1673d(c)(1)(B)(ii) (2000). The provision is directed at Commerce. The provision is silent on the question of whether Customs, under other Tariff Act provisions, specifically, under 19 U.S.C. § 1623, may require security in addition to the cash deposit if it deems such security necessary to protect the revenue. Plaintiffs, as of yet, have not pointed to a provision of the antidumping laws indicating congressional intent that cash deposits be the exclusive security available to guarantee antidumping and countervailing duty liabilities. Nor have plaintiffs put forth a convincing argument that 19 U.S.C. § 1673d(c)(1)(B)(ii) and 19 U.S.C. § 1623, when read together, preclude Customs from requiring bonding as security for any potential amount by which liquidated duties may exceed the cash deposit. 2. Plaintiffs Established a Likelihood of Success for their Arguments Alleging That Customs' Actions were Arbitrary, Capricious, or an Abuse of Discretion Although plaintiffs' showing of likelihood of success on the merits falls short in some respects, the court concludes that plaintiffs have shown that they are likely to prevail on their argument that the actions taken by Customs in imposing on plaintiffs increased bond requirements pursuant to the Amendment and the Clarification are arbitrary, capricious, or an abuse of discretion and, therefore, must be set aside pursuant to what they contend is the applicable standard of review, as provided in 5 U.S.C. § 706.[2] Plaintiffs contend, *inter alia*, that the administrative record does not support Customs' application of the new bond requirements to shrimp importers. *See*

2 Claims brought under 28 U.S.C. § 1581(i) are reviewed pursuant to § 706 of the APA, which provides for judicial review of agency action alleged to be, *inter alia*, arbitrary, capricious, an abuse of discretion, or otherwise not in accordance with law. Specifically, 5 U.S.C. § 706 provides that [t]o the extent necessary to decision and when presented, the reviewing court shall decide all relevant questions of law, interpret constitutional and statutory provisions, and

Pls.' Post-Hearing Br. at 47-51. In response to questions of the court during the hearing on the preliminary injunction motion, plaintiffs indicated that the action by Customs constitutes a legislative rule that was adopted without appropriate notice and comment procedures. *See id.* at 45-46. Plaintiffs further argued that application of the new formulas solely to importers of shrimp "is not a reasonable response to the problem identified by [Customs]" in the Amendment or the Clarification. *Id.* at 43. Defendant argues that the actions of Customs in setting the amounts of continuous bonds are committed to agency discretion by law and therefore are not subject to the "arbitrary, capricious, or abuse of discretion" standard of review. *See Def.'s Post-Hearing Br.* at 23-26.

The court is not persuaded by defendant's argument regarding the applicability of the standard of review under the APA. Further, the court finds that plaintiffs have established a likelihood of demonstrating that Customs' selective application of the new bond formulas solely to shrimp importers and the stringent manner in which Customs applied the bond formulas to each of the eight shrimp importers who made an evidentiary showing of irreparable harm are "arbitrary, capricious, an abuse of discretion, or otherwise not in accordance with law."

a. The "Arbitrary, Capricious" Standard of Review Applies in this Case

Defendant argues that the actions of Customs in setting the amounts of continuous bonds are committed to agency discretion by law and therefore are not subject to the "arbitrary, capricious, or abuse of discretion" standard of review. *Def.'s Post-Hearing Br.* at 23-26. Defendant's post-hearing brief posits that 5 U.S.C. § 701(a)(2), the APA provision precluding review of agency action that is committed to agency discretion, applies "'if the statute is drawn so that a court would have no meaningful standard against which to judge the agency's exercise of discre-

---

determine the meaning of applicability of the terms of an agency action. The reviewing court shall—

(1) compel agency action unlawfully withheld or unreasonable delayed; and (2) hold unlawful and set aside agency action, findings, and conclusions found to be—

(A) arbitrary, capricious, an abuse of discretion, or otherwise not in accordance with law;

(B) contrary to constitutional right, power, privilege, or immunity;

(C) in excess of statutory jurisdiction, authority, or limitations, or short of statutory right;

(D) without observance of procedure required by law;

(E) unsupported by substantial evidence in a case subject to [5 U.S.C. §§ 556 and 557] or otherwise reviewed on the record of an agency hearing provided by statute; or

(F) unwarranted by the facts to the extent that the facts are subject to trial de novo by the reviewing court.

In making the foregoing determinations, the court shall review the whole record or those parts of it cited by a party, and due account shall be taken of the rule of prejudicial error.

tion.'" *Id.* at 24 (quoting *Heckler v. Chaney*, 470 U.S. 821, 830 (1985)). Defendant submits that 19 U.S.C. § 1623 provides no such meaningful standard. *See id.* at 23. In further reliance on *Heckler v. Chaney*, defendant maintains that judicial review of the Customs bond decisions "is limited to whether: (1) [Customs] exceeded its statutory authority; (2) there was a constitutional violation; or (3) [Customs] violated its own regulation." *Id.* Defendant asserts that none of these three factors is present here. *Id.*

The court rejects defendant's arguments on the standard of review. Plaintiffs challenge the application of the Amendment and the Clarification to shrimp importers and specifically to the individual bond determinations. As part of their showing of a likelihood of success on the merits, plaintiffs have shown a likelihood of establishing that the bond determinations at issue properly are subjected to judicial review under an "arbitrary, capricious, or abuse of discretion" standard. They assert that the court is granted jurisdiction over this action by 28 U.S.C. § 1581(i). *First Am. Compl.* ¶¶ 2-4. In a challenge to agency action brought under 28 U.S.C. § 1581(i), the court is directed by statute to "review the matter as provided in section 706 of title 5." 28 U.S.C § 2640(e) (2000). In pertinent part, section 706 of title 5 directs a court to "hold unlawful and set aside agency action . . . found to be . . . arbitrary, capricious, an abuse of discretion, or otherwise not in accordance with law." 5 U.S.C. § 706(2)(A) (2000). Defendant would have the court decline to apply this standard of review, despite the statutory directive in 28 U.S.C. § 2640(e), based on what defendant considers to be the holding in *Heckler v. Chaney*.

Defendant's argument fails because the Supreme Court's holding in *Heckler v. Chaney* is inapplicable to the facts of this case. *Heckler v. Chaney* presented the question of whether, under the APA and the Federal Food, Drug, and Cosmetic Act, 21 U.S.C. § 301 *et seq.* ("FDCA"), the Food and Drug Administration's ("FDA") refusal to exercise its enforcement authority—specifically, in that case, the FDA's decision not to exercise authority to prohibit the use by States of drugs to carry out capital sentences by lethal injection—may be judicially reviewed. *See Heckler*, 470 U.S. at 828 (explaining that "th[e] case turns on the important question of the extent to which determinations by the FDA *not to exercise* its enforcement authority over the use of drugs in interstate commerce may be judicially reviewed. That decision in turn involves the construction of two separate but necessarily interrelated statutes, the APA and the FDCA."). The holding, and the reasoning, of *Heckler v. Chaney* stem from the longstanding recognition by the Supreme Court that an agency decision not to exercise enforcement authority is generally unsuitable for judicial review because "an agency decision not to enforce often involves a complicated balancing of a number of factors which are peculiarly within its expertise," including "whether agency resources are best spent on this violation or another, whether the agency is likely to succeed if it acts, whether the particular enforcement action requested best fits the agency's overall policies, and, indeed, whether the agency has enough resources to undertake the action at all." *Id.* at 831. The Supreme Court based its holding in *Heckler v. Chaney* in part on 5 U.S.C.

§ 701(a)(2), which disallows review of agency actions "committed to agency discretion by law." *See id.* at 828-33. But the Supreme Court's analysis, and its holding in the case, is confined to the question of whether and how a court should review an agency's refusal to exercise its enforcement authority. Plaintiffs' claims do not challenge any determination by Customs not to exercise enforcement authority but involve, instead, the manner in which Customs exercised its discretion to set the limits of liability for plaintiffs' continuous bonds under 19 U.S.C. § 1623. Defendant's argument glosses over this critical distinction.

The Supreme Court cautioned in *Heckler v. Chaney*, as it had in its earlier decision in *Citizens to Preserve Overton Park v. Volpe*, that the exception to agency review created by 5 U.S.C. § 701(a)(2) is "'a very narrow exception.'" *Id.* at 830 (quoting *Citizens to Preserve Overton Park v. Volpe*, 401 U.S. 402, 410 (1971)). "The legislative history of the Administrative Procedure Act indicates that [the exception] is applicable in those rare instances where 'statutes are drawn in such broad terms that in a given case there is no law to apply.'" *Id.* (quoting S. Rep. No. 79-752, at 26 (1945)).

The court is unable to agree with defendant that there is no law to apply in this case. Under 19 U.S.C. § 1623(b)(3), Customs may authorize a term bond for a period of one year or longer. Customs has general authority under § 1623(b) to prescribe the conditions and form of a bond, including a term bond, and to "fix the amount of penalty thereof, whether for the payment of liquidated damages or of a penal sum." 19 U.S.C. § 1623(b)(1). Read as a whole, § 1623 clarifies that Customs is to exercise its discretion in setting the amounts and conditions of bonds to further the general purpose of ensuring compliance with law and regulation. That general purpose encompasses the more specific purpose of imposing such bond requirements as are necessary to protect the revenue.

Defendant further asserts that Customs did not violate 19 C.F.R. § 113.13, which regulation, in defendant's view, "does not tie the agency's hands in any way beyond the statute." *Def.'s Post-Hearing Br.* at 29. According to defendant, 19 C.F.R. § 113.13 is a "broadly worded regulation" that "only provides guidelines to use in setting bond amounts," and "in no way constricts [Customs'] authority to identify a risk to the revenue and act accordingly." *Id.* at 29-30. Defendant also argues that the Court of Appeals for the Federal Circuit, in *Carolina Tobacco Co. v. Bureau of Customs and Border Protection*, 402 F.3d 1345, 1349-50 (Fed. Cir. 2005), has rejected the notion that an importer is "entitled to an individualized bond determination based upon each prong of section 113.13(b)." *Id.*

In its regulations, Customs implemented 19 U.S.C. § 1623 to require port directors to make individual determinations on bonds, including continuous bonds, and to do so by applying certain guidelines. *See Carolina Tobacco Co.*, 402 F.3d at 1349 (stating that the guidelines in § 113.13(b) "provide suggested standards for government officials to use in performing their duties."). Under 19 C.F.R. § 113.13(b), the port director should at least consider: (1) The prior record of the principal in timely payment of duties, taxes, and charges with respect to the transaction(s) involving such payments; (2) The prior record of the principal in complying with Customs demands for redelivery, the obligation to hold unexamined merchandise intact, and other requirements relating to enforcement and administration of Customs and other laws and regulations; (3) The value and nature of the merchandise involved in the transaction(s) to be secured; (4) The degree and type of supervision that Customs will exercise over the transaction(s); (5) The prior record of the principal in honoring bond commitments, including the payment of liquidated damages; and (6) Any additional information contained in any application for a bond. 19 C.F.R. § 113.13(b). In *Carolina Tobacco Co.*, the Court of Appeals approved of Customs' "regular practice . . . to set the bond at 10 percent of the importer's prior year's activity, and then use the factors in the regulation to determine whether a higher bond is required for a particular importer in order to protect the revenue." 402 F.3d at 1349. The Court of Appeals stated, in *dicta*, that "[e]ven if the Section 113.13(b) regulation required some individualized consideration by Customs of the six factors before setting the amount of the bond, Carolina has not shown that Customs failed to give such consideration in this case." *Id.* at 1350. The Court of Appeals rejected the notion that a port director must consider each of the six factors in determining the limit of liability for a continuous bond. "In considering the factors, the port director may give [the six factors] whatever weight he deems appropriate; he may conclude that particular factors should be given no weight whatsover." *Id.* (citing *Sec'y of Agric. v. Cent. Roig Ref. Co.*, 338 U.S. 604, 613 (1950)).

The court does not construe 19 C.F.R. § 113.13(b) or the holding in *Carolina Tobacco Co.* to support the proposition that an importer is not entitled to an individualized bond determination by the Customs port director that would be upheld under an "arbitrary, capricious, or an abuse of discretion" standard of review. Under 19 U.S.C. § 1623(b) and Customs' own regulations, the Agency is to employ discretion, but that discretion is to be exercised according to statutory purpose and regulatory criteria. The discretion, therefore, is not unlimited. *See Beardmore v. Dep't of Agric.*, 761 F.2d 677, 679 (Fed. Cir. 1985) (stating that "an agency's discretion is not unlimited, and 'reasonableness' cannot cover for arbitrary or capricious action."). Yet, the implication of defendant's argument is that Customs in its broad discretion may set a bond amount that is unreasonable or that would not be sustained under an "arbitrary, capricious, or an abuse of discretion" standard of review. In view of the congressional directive that the court apply that standard in reviewing the agency actions plaintiffs have challenged, the court cannot accept defendant's constrained conception of the judicial review available to importers in the situation in which plaintiffs have brought this case.

Relying on Article III of the Constitution, defendant also contends that "[b]ecause NFI has not alleged that the bonding policy constitutes a 'legislative rule' subject to APA notice and comment procedures, there is no case or controversy concerning this issue." *Def.'s Post-Hearing Br.* at 30. Finally, defendant maintains that the Amendment and the Clarification are akin to "general statements of policy" and, therefore, exempt from the APA notice and comment procedures pursuant to 5 U.S.C. § 553(b)(A). *See id.* at 32-34.

Because plaintiffs have shown a likelihood of establishing that the individual bond determinations will not survive review under an arbitrary and capricious standard, the court need not reach these issues. The court, however, doubts that the requirements of Article III could preclude plaintiffs from challenging the new bond requirements on the ground that they constitute a "legislative rule" that should have been subjected to notice and comment. Defendant contends that because the issue was not raised by plaintiffs, but rather raised by the court during oral argument, the issue is not properly before the court. *See id.* at 30. The court reads nothing in Article III or in precedent that limits a court's ability to consider arguments pertaining to the legality of agency action, in addition to those raised by the parties in their pleadings and their initial papers, so long as the court exercises proper jurisdiction over the matter challenged.

Plaintiffs challenge the new bond requirements on the basis that they are "arbitrary, capricious, an abuse of discretion, or otherwise not in accordance with law." *First Am. Compl.* ¶ 31. Whether the Amendment or the Clarification constitute a "legislative rule" that should have been subjected to notice and comment procedures is an issue that the court, in later ruling on the merits, could address in deciding whether the Customs action satisfies the "in accordance with law" element of the arbitrary and capricious standard of review. At that time, the court may consider evidence introduced by the testifying plaintiffs demonstrating that only those of the eight importers who promised not to import subject shrimp, or to limit such imports, were able to negotiate a lower minimum bond amount than the bond formulas required. *Findings of Fact* ¶¶ 16-17, 24, 32. Such onerous and rigid application of the new bond formulas indicates that Customs may have applied a quasi-legislative rule, which was not subject to the prescriptions of the APA, 5 U.S.C. § 553, rather than afford the eight plaintiffs a case-by-case administrative determination as contemplated by 19 C.F.R. § 113.13. *See New Jersey v. Dep't of Health & Human Servs.*, 670 F.2d 1262, 1281 (3d Cir. 1981) ("The APA notice and comment procedures exist for good reason: to ensure that unelected administrators, who are not directly accountable to the populace, are forced to justify their quasi-legislative rulemaking before an informed and skeptical public."); *Citizens to Save Spencer County v. U.S. EPA*, 600 F.2d 844, 876 (D.C. Cir. 1979) (noting that quasi-legislative rules are subject to 5 U.S.C. § 553). Because the bond demands appear not to have been based on such individual case-by-case determinations, plaintiffs have established that their exists a strong likelihood that Customs' determinations of continuous bond requirements for Eastern Fish, Ore-Cal, Red Chamber, IGF, Tampa Bay, Oriental Foods, Berdex Seafood, and Aqua Star were arbitrary and capricious.

The court need not decide at this time the merits of defendant's argument characterizing the Amendment and the Clarification as "general statements of policy" exempt from APA notice and comment procedures. The court nonetheless observes that the Amendment and the Clarification possibly can be read to modify the subject matter of 19 C.F.R. § 113.13. The Amendment and the Clarification establish new bonding requirements that affect the substantive rights of an entire group consisting of all or nearly all U.S. importers of shrimp.

b. Plaintiffs Established a Likelihood of Success for their Arguments that in the Clarification, Customs Arbitrarily and Capriciously Designated the Shrimp Antidumping Duty Orders as the Only "Covered Cases"

The administrative record supports a conclusion that plaintiffs are likely to demonstrate that Customs arbitrarily and capriciously selected the antidumping duty orders on shrimp as the only "Covered Cases." The Amendment stated three reasons why Customs must reevaluate the way it determines sufficient bond amounts: a heightened concern regarding the under-collection of antidumping and countervailing duties, the effect of such under-collection on the ability of Customs to disburse duties to the domestic industry pursuant to the Byrd Amendment, and the continued vigilance by Customs to collect all appropriate antidumping and countervailing duties from importers. *See Amendment.* Customs, however, did not articulate in the Amendment or the Clarification a reason why antidumping duties on shrimp imports are especially susceptible to under-collection, as opposed to duties on imports of other agricultural or aquacultural products subject to antidumping duty orders, or as opposed to all products subject to such orders. *See Pls.' Mem.* at 47. Due to the unliquidated status of entries subject to the antidumping duty orders on subject shrimp, no record exists demonstrating that significant numbers of shrimp importers are defaulting or have defaulted on any obligation to pay antidumping duties on their imports of shrimp. *See id.* Even were there a record of under-collection of antidumping duties on shrimp imports, such a record would not serve as an explanation of why Customs has not subjected importers in the industries Customs cited in the Amendment as having established histories of under-collection, *i.e.*, importers of crawfish tail meat and garlic from China, to the bonding formulas in the Amendment and the Clarification.[3] When asked at oral argument to explain this paradox, counsel for defendant responded, even more paradoxically, that the new bond formulas were not applied to importers in other agricultural or aquacultural industries because of "legal challenges." *See* Tr. 1059-61.

Although Customs infers that there exists a risk that the duty liability on certain shrimp imports may be subject to "large fluctuations in the dumping margins, and importers who enter and exit the importing business quickly," the administrative record does not appear to support such a finding. *Admin. R.* Ex. 1 at 2. The record

---

3 According to Customs, the amounts of uncollected duties for crawfish tail meat from China for fiscal years 2003, 2004 and 2005 were $85,397,347.58, $170,053,407.56 and $32,370,446.32, respectively. The amount of uncollected duties for garlic from China for fiscal year 2004 was stated to be $24,581,557.26. *See Pls.' Mem.* at 48 & Ex. 12.

does not identify evidence that the initial cash deposits of plaintiffs will be insufficient to cover the final rates of liquidation. Nor does the record identify evidence that importers of shrimp are particularly susceptible to bankruptcy, likely to go out of business, or operating as "sham" or "alter ego successor companies." *Admin. R.* Ex. 7 & Ex. 8 at 1.[4]

Other documents in the administrative record appear to lend further support to plaintiffs' future endeavor to show that the Amendment and the Clarification were imposed arbitrarily or capriciously on shrimp importers. As one example, the administrative record appears to indicate that political considerations influenced the decision by Customs to apply the new bond formulas only to the shrimp importing industry. The document entitled "Periodic Risk Assessment of Material Risks in the Revenue Process" explains that "the uncollected antidumping duties are under the watchful eye and close scrutiny of the domestic industry. With a large amount of funds unavailable for disbursement [under the Byrd Amendment] because of unpaid duty bills, the issue also garners Congressional and media interest." *Admin. R.* Ex. 1 at 2. All of the "uncollected duties" to which Customs refers in the administrative record, however, pertain to imports of agricultural and aquacultural products other than shrimp.

The record shows that Customs explained why it singled out the entries subject to the antidumping duty order on shrimp during an internal power point presentation on May 27, 2004:

> We are proposing a proactive and prospective approach for the purpose of reducing the potential revenue write-off exposure [(*i.e.*, uncollected duties),] that we have experienced in other cases recently. We have chosen shrimp as a first shot at this because we feel we have built a strong risk based case that provides a strong, defensible position for why we are taking these actions. We can can [sic] be sure that we will hear complaints about these actions from importers but in this case, for once, we can also count on support for our actions from the very parties that have been complaining recently, congress and domestic industry.

Admin. R. Ex. 8 at 8. Customs noted that the Ad Hoc Shrimp Action Committee, which is the petitioner in the shrimp antidumping investigations and represents the interests of the domestic industry, is comprised of shrimp producers located mainly in Alabama, Florida, Louisiana, Mississippi, North Carolina, South Carolina and Texas. *See id.*

---

4 The administrative record establishes that 25 current shrimp importers were participating in the Customs-Trade Partnership Against Terrorism ("C-TPAT"), which evidences a cooperative relationship between those importers and Customs in the war against terror. *Admin. R.* Ex. 6 at 3. Although participation in C-TPAT does not lend support to any finding relating to these importers' financial stability, such participation is relevant to a finding that these importers are not "fly-by-night" operations.

In a memorandum by the Deputy Commissioner of Customs entitled "Proposed Bonding Guidelines for Agriculture/Aquaculture Antidumping and Countervailing Duty Cases," Customs stated that

> [p]olitical and domestic interest and scrutiny of [Customs] actions in [antidumping and countervailing duty] collections is intense as a result of the Byrd Amendment which makes [antidumping and countervailing] duty collections available to domestic petitioners. The domestic petitioners in this case are from south and southeastern states that have congressional representation on committees that include the Subcommittee on Homeland Security, International Trade, House Ways & Means, Appropriations, Small Business Affairs, and the Senate Finance Committee. Concern has been raised about [Customs] efforts in the area of collecting [antidumping and countervailing] dut[ies], particularly from Southeast Asia, and this proposal would provide an example of our proactive efforts to address these concerns.
>
> The impact on importers may also generate inquiries and interest from their congressional representatives. The importers are not as geographically concentrated as the domestic industry but are represented on all of the same committees. In fact, three states that account for over 50 percent of the imports of shrimp are also the home to domestic petitioners for the case.

Admin. R. Ex. 14 at 3-4. These statements appear to be relevant to a finding that Customs, rather than basing its determination to apply the new bond formulas only to importers of shrimp on facts in the administrative record demonstrating risk to the revenue particular to shrimp imports, was motivated, at least in part, by domestic political pressures to take action directed against the shrimp importing industry. Even if such considerations were not dispositive in the decision by Customs to confine the action to shrimp importers, plaintiffs may well be able to establish on the merits that the political considerations help support a conclusion of arbitrariness and capriciousness and that "the appearance and integrity of the [agency] decision-making process would have benefited from a more formal procedure." *Sequoia Orange Co. v. Yeutter*, 973 F.2d 752, 758 (9th Cir. 1992), *reh'g denied and amended by*, 985 F.2d 1419 (9th Cir. 1993) (finding invalid an order of the Secretary of Agriculture for failure to comply with the APA).

c. Plaintiffs Established a Likelihood of Success for their Argument that the Application of the Amendment and the Clarification to Eight Individual Plaintiffs Was Arbitrary and Capricious

Based on a review of the administrative record, the court concludes that plaintiffs are likely to succeed in showing that Customs applied the Amendment and the Clarification to Eastern Fish, Ore-Cal, Red Chamber, IGF, Tampa Bay, Oriental Foods, Berdex Seafood, and Aqua Star in an arbitrary and capricious manner. Despite the flexibility granted to port directors by 19 C.F.R. § 113.13 in determining the minimum amount of a bond, the evidence put forth by these plaintiffs demonstrates that Customs, in applying the new bond requirements, did not allow for any meaningful deviation from the formulas set forth in the Amendment and maintained in the Clarification. Rather, Customs strictly applied the formulas, apparently despite the criteria in 19 C.F.R. § 113.13. The administrative record indicates that plaintiffs are likely to succeed in showing that the bond formulas were applied to these plaintiffs for the sole reason that these plaintiffs were importers of shrimp subject to antidumping duty orders.

The obligation to pay antidumping duties that would be secured by a continuous bond is limited to the amount by which the liquidated antidumping duties may exceed the cash deposits. The formulas, however, do not appear to include a factor to adjust for the required cash deposits unless it is assumed that the cash deposits represent only about half of the eventual antidumping duty liability. In response to plaintiffs' arguments, defendant has not advanced a convincing reason why the formulas do not directly take into consideration the cash deposits, which in the ordinary instance would be made by the importer of record and would reduce the amount of unsecured potential antidumping duty liability.[5] Each notice of bond insufficiency issued to the eight plaintiffs by Customs cites, as authority, Part 113 of the Customs regulations. *See, e.g., Pls.' Mem.* Ex. 5 Attach. B, Ex. 6 Attach. B, Ex. 7 Attach. A, Ex. 8 Attach. B, Ex. 9 Attach. C, Ex. 10 Attach. B; *Joint Stipulation of Undisputed Facts* ¶¶ 8-31. As discussed above, § 113.13(b) of the Customs regulations sets forth guidelines for determining the amount of a bond. "In determining whether the amount of a bond is sufficient, the port director . . . should at least consider" factors including an importer's prior record of paying outstanding duty liabilities, an importer's prior record of complying with Customs' demands for redelivery, the degree of supervision that Customs will exercise over the subject transactions, and an importer's prior record of honoring bond commitments. 19 C.F.R. § 113.13(b). As also discussed above, the Court of Appeals for the Federal Circuit in *Carolina Tobacco Co.* stated that a port director, in reviewing the factors listed in § 113.13(b), may accord those factors "whatever weight he deems appropriate" but did not state that Customs may deny an importer an individualized bond determination or imply that Customs need not act reasonably. 402 F.3d at 1350. In determining the minimum bond amounts for Eastern Fish, Ore-Cal, Red Chamber, IGF, Tampa Bay, Oriental Foods, Berdex Seafood, and Aqua Star, the evidence supports a finding that Customs applied the formula AD/CVD Order (3)—*i.e.*, the Commerce Order rate multiplied by the value of imports of merchandise subject to the case by the importer during the previous year—without regard to each importer's individual compliance record. *See Pls.' Mem.* Ex. 5 Attach. B, Ex. 6 Attach. B, Ex. 7 Attach. A, Ex. 8 Attach. B, Ex. 9 Attach. C, Ex. 10 Attach. B;

---

5 In the closing sentence of the Notice, Customs appears to acknowledge that the continuous bond ordinarily would serve as security only for amounts by which the cash deposit is exceeded. *See Notice*, 71 Fed. Reg. at 62,278 ("Congress has provided CBP authority to require security in order to ensure the payment of all duties determined to be due to the United States, including any revenue collection gaps between estimated duty deposits and final assessed duties that the importer fails to satisfy."). The Notice, nevertheless, maintains the basic formulas announced in the Amendment and the Clarification.

Joint Stipulation of Undisputed Facts ¶¶ 8-31; *Findings of Fact* ¶¶ 1, 4, 9, 15, 19, 23, 28, 31-32. Moreover, it appears that Customs did not consider each individual importer's financial condition or ability to pay prospective antidumping duty liabilities, but rather appeared to base the application of the formulas on one critical factor—that the importer engages in the importation of subject shrimp. *Findings of Fact* ¶¶ 1, 4, 9, 15, 19, 23, 28, 32.

Three plaintiff-importers have established a likelihood of success of prevailing in a challenge to their respective bond determinations in yet another respect. As noted above, each of these importers has been required by Customs to accept a limitation on the importation of subject shrimp, in whole or in part, as a condition of obtaining a bond allowing them to continue to import merchandise. With respect to each of the three importers, the limitation is not set forth as a bond condition but is established only in a series of e-mail communications between the plaintiff-importer and the Customs port director. *See Pls.' Mem.* Ex. 7 Attachs. B, C, & E (e-mails from Customs to each of two plaintiffs, including e-mails from Casey Horn of Customs to these importers stating that bonds will be rendered insufficient "immediately" if the importer attempts to import certain aquacultural products covered by antidumping or countervailing duty orders), Ex. 9 Attach. C (e-mails between an importer and Customs, including an e-mail from Casey Horn of Customs to the importer stating that bonds will be rendered insufficient "immediately" if the importer attempts to import certain aquacultural products covered by antidumping or countervailing duty orders). Those communications reveal a likelihood that each of the three importers were, or are likely to be, denied the benefit of the notice procedure required by 19 C.F.R. § 113.13(c), under which an importer must be provided 30 days to obtain a new continuous bond following notice by the port director that the port director has determined a continuous bond to be inadequate "to protect the revenue and insure compliance with the law and regulations." 19 C.F.R. § 113.13(c). Moreover, the conditions were, according to the record evidence, imposed under a degree of duress and without citation to any statutory or regulatory authority.[6]

---

6 The court raised this issue during the July 19, 2006 conference. In response, Customs represented that "the Government will provide notice to the relevant party pursuant to 19 C.F.R. § 113.13(c), should [Customs] find it necessary to render insufficient any bond issued to any of the eight plaintiffs that attempted to demonstrate immediate irreparable harm." *Def.'s Status Report* at 2, Aug. 17, 2006. While committing Customs to providing notice, defendant simultaneously asserts that "pursuant to 19 C.F.R. § 113.13(d), no notice to the principal is required for additional security if the agency believes there [*sic*] the revenue is in jeopardy." *Id.* at 3. Subsection (d) of § 113.13, however, does not allow Customs to dispense with the 30-day notice when rendering a continuous bond insufficient. The regulations state that "[n]otwithstanding the provisions of this section or any other provision of this chapter, if a port director or drawback office believes that acceptance of *a transaction* secured by a continuous bond would place the revenue in jeopardy or otherwise hamper the enforcement of Customs laws or regulations, he shall require additional security." 19 C.F.R. § 113.13(d) (emphasis added). Section 113.13(d) grants to port directors the discretion to review an individual transaction to determine whether that transaction poses a risk to the revenue, *i.e.*, a port director

C. Balance of the Hardships

In evaluating whether to grant a motion for injunctive relief, the court must "determine which party will suffer the greatest adverse effects as a result of the grant or denial of the preliminary injunction." *Ugine-Savoie Imphy v. United States*, 24 CIT 1246, 1250, 121 F. Supp. 2d 684, 688 (2000). Plaintiffs and defendant each contend that the balance of hardships militates in its respective favor.

Plaintiffs allege that "[i]f no injunctive relief is granted, and if [Customs] continues to require bonds to cover potential antidumping duty liability on frozen shrimp, and if sureties continue their collateral demands to issue these bonds, NFI [i]mporters will suffer grievous irreparable harm. By contrast, if the injunction is granted, [Customs] will suffer none." *Pls.' Mem.* at 50-51. According to plaintiffs, Customs will not suffer harm because plaintiffs are required to post cash deposits when entering subject shrimp into the United States for consumption. *Pls.' Mem.* at 51; *see Pls.' Post-Hearing Br.* at 54-56. These cash deposits provide Customs with the type of security "that Congress intended for imports under antidumping and countervailing duty orders." *Pls.' Mem.* at 51. Plaintiffs argue that they are entitled to preliminary equitable relief to "place NFI [i]mporters in exactly the same position as every other importer of every other product subject to antidumping and countervailing duty orders—no better, no worse." *Pls.' Post-Hearing Br.* at 54.

Defendant argues that the balance of hardship favors the protection of the revenue of the United States. According to Customs, "the cash deposit requirement does not, and was never intended to, provide protection for all antidumping and countervailing duties." *Def.'s Opp'n* at 24.

The balance of hardships favors the grant of a limited preliminary injunction. If the Amendment and the Clarification remain in effect and continue to be applied by Customs during the pendency of this litigation in the manner in which Customs has applied them thus far, the eight plaintiffs are likely again to be confronted with the obligation to obtain term bonds of substantial size while their obligations under past term bonds continue. Two plaintiffs already have secured additional bonds to secure their 2006-2007 importations and, not surprisingly, both of these plaintiff-importers were required by their sureties to obtain letters of credit from financial institutions collateralizing the full amount of the bonds. There is little doubt that sureties will require that the eight plaintiffs obtain additional letters of credit from their lenders to post as security for any future term bonds. Defendant does not assert, and cannot credibly assert, that the obligations under the bonds will not continue until all entries thereunder are liquidated—an event which is not imminent. Defendant raises only the unconvincing argument that plaintiffs' assertion that sureties will continue to require collateralization for new bonds is "speculative." The current level of financial pressures on the eight plaintiffs, as established

---

must make the determination on an entry-by-entry basis. Nothing in 19 C.F.R. § 113.13(d) authorizes Customs to eliminate the 30-day notice requirement of § 113.13(c).

by the evidence submitted and those plaintiffs' testimony before the court, can only increase absent a preliminary injunction directed to preserving generally the *status quo* during the pendency of this litigation.

Defendant raises an additional argument concerning alleged transhipment of shrimp, pointing to a "possibility" that certain entries will be assessed antidumping duties at the countrywide rate for China of 112.8 percent.[7] *See Def.'s Post-Hearing Br.* at 37. As to the alleged transhipment, Bruce W. Ingalls, Chief of the Debt Management Branch in the Revenue Division of the Office of Finance, testified during the hearing on April 5, 2006, declaring that

> [a]fter initiation of the antidumping cases, [Customs] noted substantial shifts in import patterns that suggest transhipment of shrimp to circumvent the high tariffs on shrimp. [Customs] and U.S. Immigration and Customs Enforcement representative [*sic*] (ICE) from the Singapore Attaché office visited shrimp producers in Indonesia (a country not subjected to antidumping) that appeared to be of high-risk for transhipment. [Customs] confirmed that three producers commingled Chinese shrimp and exported the merchandise claimed as Indonesian to circumvent the payment of antidumping duties. Fifty-four importers were sourcing shrimp from the three Indonesian producers during the time when Chinese shrimp was commingled.
>
> NFI importers represent approximately 50% of the imported volume. . . . [Customs] has issued CF 29 (Notice of Action) [to notify each importer that Customs is investigating subject imports pursuant to 19 U.S.C. § 1592 and] to demand that antidumping deposits be made for these imports. . . .

Def.'s Opp'n at *Decl. of Bruce W. Ingalls* ¶¶ 18-20. Defendant maintains that the new bonds "are thus the *only* security that the Government possesses with respect to these entries." *Id.* at 24 (citing *Decl. of Bruce W. Ingalls* ¶ 21). According to defendant, this prospective harm outweighs plaintiffs' "hardship," which defendant characterizes as "bear[ing] the risk of their own nonpayment of duties." *Id.* at 25. Defendant also argues that because plaintiffs failed to inform the court of the proceedings initiated by Customs with respect to such alleged transhipments, plaintiffs' "claims should be barred by the doctrine of unclean hands." *Id.* at 27.

The court finds defendant's arguments concerning the alleged transhipment, including the "unclean hands" argument, unconvincing. The court cannot draw conclusions relevant to a preliminary injunction from the investigation under 19 U.S.C. § 1592 to which defendant alludes. Any such investigation has yet to be completed. The facts that eventually may emerge from such an investigation have not yet been found. In any event, the relevant facts are not before the court. Defendant has not introduced evidence in this proceeding that would enable the court to make findings concerning the alleged transhipment and any eventual antidumping duty liability that could be associated with such findings. Any inference drawn

---

7 The countrywide rate for China is the rate assessed to those Chinese exporters who were unable to establish freedom from government control. It is also, ultimately, the highest rate assessed during the investigation.

with respect to an investigation under 19 U.S.C. § 1592, therefore, would be unsupported by evidence and premature. Defendant's "unclean hands" argument is unavailing for this same reason. Moreover, defendant did not introduce evidence at the court's hearing from which the court could conclude that any of the eight plaintiffs engaged in wrongdoing.

Customs has failed to establish to any degree of certainty that the future entries of Eastern Fish, Ore-Cal, Red Chamber, IGF, Tampa Bay, Oriental Foods, Berdex Seafood, and Aqua Star will be assessed upon liquidation any antidumping duties above the cash deposits, or that these plaintiffs are prone to default on future obligations to pay such duties. The United States, through the testimony of Mr. Ingalls and the submission of attachments A through E regarding the possibility of substantially higher final antidumping duty liability, sought to demonstrate the potential loss of revenue if the injunctive relief is granted. *See Def.'s Opp'n* at *Decl. of Bruce W. Ingalls* ¶¶ 10-15 & Attachs. A-E. Mr. Ingalls, however, conceded that the scenarios presented in attachment A are hypothetical.[8] Tr. 652. Moreover, the court does not view as probative Mr. Ingalls's general assertion that the final antidumping duty rates on shrimp are likely to be higher rather than lower because this conclusory statement was not supported by any record evidence. Tr. 653-655, 678-680. Therefore, the arguments raised by Customs regarding potential antidumping duty liabilities and "possible" transhipments of Indonesian and Chinese shrimp are, necessarily, speculative.

Attachment A indicates that the bonds issued to importers of shrimp prior to the six subject antidumping duty orders would cover the liabilities arising from a 28 percent increase in the final antidumping duty rate over the cash deposit rate. *See Def.'s Opp'n* at *Decl. of Bruce W. Ingalls* ¶ 15 & Attach. A. The bonds required by Customs after the implementation of the new bond formulas ensured that Customs would recover the liabilities arising from an 85 percent increase in the final antidumping duty rate. *See id.* ¶ 14 & Attach. A. During his testimony, Mr. Ingalls was asked to identify a situation where every importer, at the end of an administrative review, defaulted on its obligations to pay antidumping duties. Mr. Ingalls could not identify such a situation and testified that he "would find it hard to believe that there is any industry or any sector where you could say for certain that 100 percent don't pay their bills." Tr. 693.

Attachment C also establishes that only five of the eight plaintiffs were consignees of imports from Indonesian shrimp producers that allegedly engaged in the tran-

---

8 Attachment A presents five scenarios by which defendant quantifies the amount of antidumping duties that Customs would be required to collect if it were instructed to liquidate subject entries at a rate 10, 25, 50, 75, or 100 percent higher than the rate at which the cash deposits were collected. *See Def.'s Opp'n* at *Decl. of Bruce W. Ingalls* Attach. A. For example, if $1 million worth of entries were subject to a 10 percent duty rate, the cash deposits would be $100,000. Assuming that those entries were liquidated at a rate that is 50 percent higher than the 10 percent duty rate, Customs, in this example, would be required to collect an additional $50,000 from subject importers. *See id.*; Tr. 626-627.

shipment of Chinese shrimp. *See Def.'s Opp'n* at *Decl. of Bruce W. Ingalls* Attach. C. Although the possibility of circumvention was a critical factor in defendant's balance of the hardship argument—*i.e.*, "the specter of harm faced by the Government is very real and acute"—defendant did not distinguish between the three plaintiffs that did not purchase shrimp from subject Indonesian producers and the five that did. *Def.'s Opp'n* at 24. A review of Attachment C also reveals that the values of imports for three of the five plaintiffs that purchased shrimp from subject Indonesian producers were grossly disproportionate to the levels of security demanded by Customs in the original notices of insufficiency and in subsequent demands.[9] Even assuming that all subject entries of Indonesian shrimp are assessed the China-wide rate, the bond requirements of Customs far exceed the security necessary to cover a 112.8 percent final liquidation rate. Customs has already collected nearly 100 percent security from Eastern Fish, Ore-Cal, Red Chamber, IGF, Tampa Bay, Oriental Foods, Berdex Seafood, and Aqua Star for subject entries made in 2005 through 2006. An agency's action must be reasonable in light of the harm it seeks to redress. *See* 5 U.S.C. § 706(2)(A) (setting forth the "arbitrary, capricious" standard of review that the court is to apply when reviewing certain agency actions); *cf. Pope v. U.S. Postal Serv.*, 114 F.3d. 1144, 1148 (Fed. Cir. 1997) (stating that an "agency's action should be sustained as long as the penalty imposed is reasonable"). These facts lend strong support to a finding that Customs did not evaluate each importer's risk on a case-by-case basis in assessing the amount of additional security needed to cover the "alleged," yet undetermined, risk posed by the possibility of transhipments or increased final dumping margins. Plaintiffs have shown, therefore, that the bond sufficiency determinations likely were not reasonable in light of the situation Customs sought to redress. When balancing the hardships of the parties, the court finds that plaintiffs will suffer greater adverse effects than defendant during the pendency of this litigation if Customs is not enjoined from making additional bond demands according to the Current Bond Formulas, which will necessitate the further serious depletion of plaintiffs' credit. Moreover, because the court will fashion the injunctive relief in a manner that will allow defendant to move for a modification of the injunction to "establish a change in circumstances that would make the original preliminary injunction inequitable," any prospective harm to defendant that later materializes may be remedied. *Favia v. Ind. Univ. of Pa.*, 7 F.3d 332, 340 (3d Cir. 1993); *see Aimcor, Ala. Silicon, Inc. v. United States*, 23 CIT 932, 938, 83 F. Supp. 2d 1293, 1299 (1999) (stating that "courts have inherent power and the discretion to modify injunctions for changed circumstances" (citing *Sys. Fed'n No. 91 v. Wright*, 364 U.S. 642, 647 (1961))).

D. Public Interest

Even when plaintiffs have "overcome the burden of showing the probability of irreparable harm and the likelihood of success on the merits, or alternatively, that the parties have presented serious questions of law and that the balance of the hard-

9 []

ships tips in favor of the plaintiff[s], the court must still protect the public interest." *Associated Dry Goods Corp. v. United States*, 1 CIT 306, 310-11, 515 F. Supp. 775, 779 (1981). For several reasons, the public interest would be best served by the issuance of a preliminary injunction that preserves generally the *status quo* with respect to the bond status of each of the eight plaintiffs that made adequate factual showings of irreparable harm and precludes enforcement of the "agreements" not to import certain subject shrimp.

The public interest is not served by administration of a bond policy that plaintiffs likely will demonstrate to be arbitrary and capricious and, specifically, to be discriminatory with respect to the shrimp importing industry. Nor is the public interest served by the continued application of a regulatory action that plaintiffs are likely to demonstrate is unreasonable and more onerous than necessary to achieve the statutory purposes of 19 U.S.C. § 1623 and the regulatory objectives of 19 C.F.R. § 113. The court recognizes, however, that the public interest is served by ensuring that any equitable remedy adopted for the pendency of the proceedings allows Customs to protect the revenue. Therefore, any injunctive relief must be fashioned in a manner that would allow for modifications under the appropriate circumstances.

E. Scope and Nature of Preliminary Injunctive Relief

Based on plaintiffs' showings of irreparable harm and likelihood of success on the merits, the court concludes that plaintiffs' amended motion for a preliminary injunction seeks relief that is overly broad. As discussed previously, only eight of the 27 plaintiffs have established that, absent a preliminary injunction, they will suffer irreparable harm. Accordingly, the court is ordering preliminary injunctive relief that, at this time, is confined to the bond status of the eight plaintiffs that made a showing of irreparable harm at the court's hearing.

With respect to the eight plaintiffs, the court's preliminary injunction order is narrower in scope than that sought by plaintiffs. Plaintiffs seek an order requiring Customs to allow any plaintiff to replace any continuous basic importer's bond that was used to enter merchandise on or after February 23, 2006. Under plaintiffs' draft order, Customs would be required to allow a plaintiff to replace such a bond "with a bond calculated without regard to antidumping or countervailing duties." *Mot. to Amend Injunctive Relief Requested*, attached *Order* at 3. Were the court to include such a provision in its preliminary injunction order, that order would restore, for most plaintiffs, the *status quo ante* rather than maintain the *status quo*. Such an order would be broader than the showing of irreparable harm that any plaintiff has made. Although the eight plaintiffs have shown that further application of the formulas in the Amendment, the Current Bond Formulas, and the Clarification will cause them irreparable harm, they have not shown that the demonstrated irreparable harm is preventable *only* through a new bond with a limit of liability that is calculated entirely without regard to antidumping duties. Seeking such broad relief without a demonstrated factual basis presumes that no other limit of liability would suffice to preclude additional irreparable harm during the pendency of this case.

Plaintiffs' proposed order also exceeds plaintiffs' showing of likelihood of success on the merits. As discussed previously in this opinion, plaintiffs have shown a likelihood of success of demonstrating that the individual bond determinations for the eight plaintiffs were made in a way that was arbitrary and capricious. Plaintiffs attempted to, but did not, establish a likelihood of success for their argument that Customs is precluded by 19 U.S.C. § 1623 from any consideration of antidumping duties when setting limits of liability for term bonds. This is not to suggest that the court rejects plaintiffs' argument, only that the showing they have made to date falls short of a showing of likelihood of success on the merits with respect to that particular issue. Moreover, an appropriate preliminary injunction considers the balance of hardships and the public interest. The court considers these two factors to be best satisfied by preliminary injunctive relief that is sufficient to avoid the demonstrated irreparable harm during the pendency of the proceeding but that balances the scope of the relief with the government's interest in setting bond limits of liability that are adequate to protect the revenue.

As noted previously, counsel for plaintiffs, in the status report of August 21, 2006, sought a modification to the draft preliminary injunction that the court discussed with the parties at the conference of July 19, 2006. That modification would direct Customs to permit the parties to obtain a change in the limit of liability in any continuous bond obtained on or after February 23, 2006, to a limit of liability that is not determined according to the Amendment or the Clarification, using the procedures of 19 C.F.R. § 113.23(a)(1) and (d), under which Customs may approve a superseding bond. Counsel for plaintiffs informed the court in the August 21, 2006 status report that this superseding bond procedure would be intended for only two of the eight plaintiffs who introduced evidence. The evidence introduced by those two plaintiffs thus far, however, does not establish that the limits of liability in the current bonds, even when considered with the continuing liability under previous bonds, are causing the extraordinary level of harm that would require the court to order Customs to approve superseding bonds at this time. However, the preliminary injunction that the court is ordering will permit Eastern Fish and Ore- Cal, and any other plaintiff, to seek a modification of the preliminary injunction based on a demonstration of changed circumstances.

The preliminary injunction that the court will order is necessary to prevent the imminent harm that will result when the current one-year term bonds expire and must be replaced with new term bonds. As noted previously, that process will begin in December 2006 and continue over the next several months. Application of the Current Bond Formulas will add to the cumulative burden on the credit availability of the eight testifying plaintiffs. The letters of credit resulting from the first two rounds of bond sufficiency determinations already burden plaintiff-importers' credit availability, adversely affect their ability to pay, and therefore impede their ability to qualify for what otherwise would be lower bond limits. Some of the bonds issued during the second round of bond determinations contained limits of liability of $1.5 million or higher, and certain of those bonds were for amounts substantially higher than $1.5 million.

As discussed previously, counsel for defendant indicated in a status conference that the bond sufficiency reviews contemplated under the Notice are prospective only, and that Customs did not intend to review bonds currently in use by the eight plaintiffs to determine whether it is appropriate to cancel and replace the current bonds with superseding bonds with lower limits of liability. Customs stated in the Notice that "[i]f [Customs] determines that the principal has a record of compliance with customs laws and regulations and that the principal has demonstrated an ability to pay, [Customs] may decide not to require an increased bond amount even though the principal imports Special Category merchandise." *Notice*, 71 Fed. Reg. at 62,278. The court notes that the revised position by Customs as announced in the Notice is likely to prejudice some shrimp importers, including certain of the testifying plaintiffs, relative to other shrimp importers. The high limits of liability on bonds currently in place, which resulted from the application of the Current Bond Formulas with little or no discretionary relief from such application, required plaintiffs to incur substantial liability under letters of credit to secure those bonds and thereby adversely affect the plaintiffs' future ability to pay by burdening plaintiffs' credit lines. Consequently, by refusing to reconsider the damaging effects of its previous bond determinations, Customs is perpetuating the harm caused to the affected importers, which harm is likely to become more acute as a result of the impending next round of bond determinations. The court considers the threat of future harm sufficiently serious as to require the court to address it in the preliminary injunction.

The court will order Customs to begin immediately a review of each of the bonds containing limits of liability of $1.5 million or more that currently are in use by any of the eight plaintiffs that testified before the court. Five current bonds fall into this category. The court directs that the review be focused on the question of whether those bonds should be replaced with superseding bonds with lower limits of liability based on the prior record of the principal and on the other factors identified in 19 C.F.R. § 113.13(b). The review must be completed within 60 days of the date of the Order imposing the preliminary injunction, during which period Customs must report to the court its conclusions and the reasons for its conclusions. Thus, the review must occur concurrently with the earliest of the bond sufficiency determinations that will take place upon the expiration of the term bonds currently in place for the eight testifying plaintiffs. The court requires that Customs allow the affected plaintiffs the opportunity to submit relevant information and to comment during the reviews. The court is limiting the required reviews to the five current bonds with limits of $1.5 million or above because of the exigent circumstances and the need of the court to obtain additional information concerning those five bonds.[10] However, nothing in the preliminary injunction precludes Customs from similarly reviewing other bonds of the testifying plaintiffs or any other plaintiffs, including bonds for which the term has expired or that have been terminated but otherwise remain in effect.

Future bond determinations also have a significant effect on the status of this case. Continuous bonds of two of the eight testifying plaintiffs will expire in December 2006. The court, therefore, is directing counsel for the parties to inform the court of the status of their negotiations on the limits of liability in the two continuous bonds that will be in place following the December 2006 expirations.

Finally, the appropriate preliminary injunctive relief must address the special situation presented by the current bond status of three of the testifying plaintiffs. Each is subject to an agreement not to import shrimp, or certain shrimp, that are subject to antidumping duties. One plaintiff is subject to an agreement not to import any aquaculture product subject to antidumping duties. The record reveals that plaintiffs are likely to be able to show that these conditions, which are not bond conditions but the result of side agreements in e-mail correspondence, violate the Customs regulations, including, in particular, the 30-day notice requirement of 19 C.F.R. § 113.13(c). Because these agreements appear to have been imposed contrary to the regulation and under a degree of duress, and because the conditions are causing irreparable harm to each of these three plaintiff-importers, as discussed previously, the court considers it inappropriate to allow these conditions to be enforced during the pendency of this proceeding. However, the limits of bond liability for each of these three plaintiffs may or may not be sufficient to allow Customs to protect the revenue should imports of the subject merchandise resume. The preliminary injunction order, therefore, allows Customs to seek a modification of the injunction for changed circumstances. Any change in a limit of liability must be reasonable in view of the circumstances and consistent with the purposes of 19 U.S.C. § 1623 and the guidelines of 19 C.F.R. § 113.13.

III. Other Motions

During the cross-examination of Mr. Ingalls, plaintiffs moved to strike two statements. Plaintiffs moved to strike the record of testimony proffered with respect to certain additional Customs notices of action (*i.e.*, "Customs Form 29s" or "CF 29s") that had not been included in the administrative record or submitted to the court by defendant. Plaintiffs argued that any such testimony would be hearsay because Mr. Ingalls testified that he had neither seen nor could confirm the actual

---

10 The statute, under 28 U.S.C. § 2643, provides the court with broad discretion to fashion the appropriate relief. "[T]he court . . . may order such further administrative or adjudicative procedures as the court considers necessary to enable it to reach the correct decision" in cases where "the [court] is unable to determine the correct decision on the basis of the evidence presented." 28 U.S.C. § 2643(b). "[T]he [court] may, in addition to the orders specified in [§§ 2643(a) and (b)], order any other form of relief that is appropriate in a civil action, including, but not limited to, . . . injunctions . . . ." 28 U.S.C. § 2643(c)(1).

existence of additional notices of action. *See* Tr. 638, 697. Plaintiffs further moved to strike, on the basis of hearsay, the portions of testimony proffered by Mr. Ingalls that relate to the three Indonesian shrimp producers who are said to have admitted to commingling Chinese shrimp. *See* Tr. 635, 708. The court reserved decision on both rulings.

The testimony elicited from Mr. Ingalls relating to the notices of action contained in Attachment D indicates that Mr. Ingalls has personal knowledge that additional notices of action had been issued. *See Def.'s Opp'n* at *Decl. of Bruce W. Ingalls* Attach. D. When asked on direct examination whether Attachment D contained "all of the CF29s that were sent to the various NFI importers," Mr. Ingalls testified "[n]o, [it] is not an exhaustive list." Tr. 638. Upon cross- examination, when asked how he knew that other CF 29s exist, Mr. Ingalls responded "[w]hen we contacted the ports to get copies [of the CF 29s], some of the ports produced them immediately and other ports didn't, so that led me to believe that there are other CF29s out there having been issued. We just didn't get copies [of the other CF 29s]." Tr. 697. Based on Mr. Ingalls's testimony, his statement appears to be based on personal knowledge. Despite plaintiffs' assertion that someone at Customs told Mr. Ingalls that other CF 29s existed, plaintiffs never so established upon the cross-examination of Mr. Ingalls. *See* Tr. 696-705. Rather, Mr. Ingalls's testimony indicates that he believes that other CF 29s exist based on the fact that Customs requested copies of the CF 29s, some of the ports immediately produced copies, and some of the ports did not. Mr. Ingalls could reach such a conclusion based on his personal knowledge of the case. Plaintiffs did not elicit testimony to the contrary. Plaintiffs' objection and motion to strike the testimony as hearsay are overruled.

Mr. Ingalls's statement that three Indonesian shrimp producers admitted to commingling shrimp, however, is an out-of-court statement offered for the truth of the matter asserted. *See* Tr. 635, 708. Upon cross-examination, plaintiffs asked Mr. Ingalls whether he was "directly told by the Indonesian shrimp producers" as to the information concerning the admissions of commingling. Mr. Ingalls replied, "[d]irectly from the Indonesian—no." Tr. 708. Plaintiffs then asked "[w]as it something you were told by someone else at Customs," to which Mr. Ingalls replied "[y]es." *Id.* The statement is therefore double hearsay: hearsay as stated by the Customs official to Mr. Ingalls and hearsay as stated by Mr. Ingalls before the court. The court is not aware of, and defendant did not point to, an applicable exception that would allow the admission of this hearsay evidence. Defendant's assertion that the admissions by the Indonesian shrimp producers are statements against interest perhaps accounts for the statement by the Indonesian shrimp producers to the Customs official, but it does not allow for the admission of the statement by the Customs official to Mr. Ingalls, as recalled by Mr. Ingalls before the court. *See* Tr. 709. Plaintiff's objection is sustained, and the statement in question is stricken from the record of the hearing transcript.

Finally, the court grants the four additional unopposed motions that remain outstanding: plaintiffs' *Motion to Amend Injunctive Relief Requested*, filed on April 14, 2006 and consented to on May 3, 2006; plaintiffs' *Motion to Re-Open Record of Plaintiffs' Motion for Preliminary Injunction*, filed on May 5, 2006 and consented to on May 31, 2006; defendant's *Consent Motion for an Extension of Time Out of Time to Respond to Plaintiffs' Motion to Supplement the Factual Record*, filed on May 31, 2006 and unopposed by plaintiff; and plaintiffs' *Motion to Re-Open the Record for Plaintiffs' Motion for Preliminary Injunction*, filed on July 31, 2006 and unopposed by defendant.

IV. Conclusion

Upon application of the four factors that the court must consider when determining whether to order a preliminary injunction, the court concludes that the factual assertions and arguments advanced by plaintiffs establish that Eastern Fish, Ore-Cal, Red Chamber, IGF, Tampa Bay, Oriental Foods, Berdex Seafood, and Aqua Star have shown that they are entitled to preliminary injunctive relief. Plaintiffs merit preliminary injunctive relief that imposes restraints and obligations on Customs, but only to the extent required to prevent irreparable harm during the pendency of this proceeding. These eight plaintiffs have not established their entitlement to a preliminary injunction restoring a form of *status quo ante*, which would require Customs to replace current continuous bonds with new continuous bonds for which liability limits are set without regard to antidumping duty liability. The remaining 19 NFI importers have failed to establish that they will suffer immediate, irreparable harm absent injunctive relief. The court will order preliminary injunctive relief accordingly.

ROYAL THAI GOVERNMENT
v.
UNITED STATES

436 F.3d 1330 (Fed. Cir. 2006)
Decided February 1, 2006

Before CLEVENGER, GAJARSA, and PROST, Circuit Judges.

OPINION

PROST, Circuit Judge.

United States Steel Corporation ("U.S. Steel") and the United States separately challenge different aspects of the United States Court of International Trade's decision in favor of the Royal Thai Government ("RTG") and Sahaviriya Steel Industries Public Company Limited ("SSI") that, on remand to the United States Department of Commerce ("Commerce"), resulted in a determination that no countervailable subsidies were provided to the production or exportation of certain hot-rolled carbon steel flat products from Thailand. *See Royal Thai Gov't v. United States, 341 F. Supp. 2d 1315 (Ct. Int'l Trade 2004)* (*"Decision"*); *Royal Thai Gov't v. United States, 341 F. Supp. 2d 1315 (Ct. Int'l Trade 2004)* (*"Remand Order"*); *Royal Thai Gov't v. United States, 2004 Ct. Intl. Trade LEXIS 122, No. 02-00026 (Ct. Int'l Trade Oct. 1, 2004)* (*"Final Judgment"*). In particular, U.S. Steel challenges the Court of International Trade's holdings (1) affirming Commerce's determination that SSI's debt restructuring was not specific; (2) affirming Commerce's decision not to investigate U.S. Steel's allegation of equity infusions; and (3) reversing Commerce's decision to countervail the entire amount of import duty exemptions, also called drawbacks, provided to SSI. The United States only challenges the third holding of the Court of International Trade. We affirm the Court of International Trade on the first two holdings, but reverse on the third.

BACKGROUND

In 2000, Commerce initiated an investigation to assess whether countervailable subsidies were provided to the Thai steel industry. *See Notice of Initiation of Countervailing Duty Investigations: Certain Hot-Rolled Carbon Steel Flat Prod-*

ucts From Argentina, India, Indonesia, South Africa, and Thailand, 65 Fed. Reg. 77,580 (Dec. 12, 2000). Of the several Thai programs that Commerce investigated, one involved import duty exemptions administered by Thailand's Board of Investment (the "BOI"). Another involved debt restructuring. Commerce ultimately concluded that countervailable subsidies were being conferred on hot-rolled steel from Thailand and assigned a countervailing duty rate on SSI. *See Notice of Preliminary Affirmative Countervailing Duty Determination and Alignment With Final Antidumping Duty Determinations: Certain Hot-Rolled Carbon Steel Flat Products From Thailand, 66 Fed. Reg. 20,251 (Apr. 20, 2001)* ("*Preliminary Determination*"); *Final Affirmative Countervailing Duty Determination: Certain Hot-Rolled Carbon Steel Flat Products from Thailand, 66 Fed. Reg. 50410 (Oct. 3, 2001)* ("*Final Determination*"); Issues and Decision Memorandum in the Final Affirmative Countervailing Duty Determination: Certain Hot-Rolled Carbon Steel Flat Products from Thailand (Sept. 21, 2001) ("*Decision Memorandum*").

Two of Commerce's determinations supporting its conclusion are relevant to this appeal. First, Commerce determined that the entire amount of SSI's import duty exemptions were countervailable export subsidies. This determination was based on its finding that RTG did not have a system or procedure in place that was reasonable and effective for the purpose of confirming which inputs were consumed in the production of exported products and in what amounts those inputs were consumed. In particular, Commerce faulted RTG for not isolating and examining what was consumed in the production of the exported products and for not taking into account that some scrap metal generated in the production of hot-rolled steel is recoverable and saleable. Second, Commerce determined that RTG's debt restructuring program was not countervailable. This determination was based on its finding that the debt restructuring program was not specific to SSI. It cited the fact that numerous and diverse industries were invited to participate in the debt restructuring program, that SSI's debt was less than a number of other invited companies, and that SSI's debt was not significantly greater than many other invited companies. It also stated that the primary metal industry, of which SSI is a part, did not have a disproportionate or overwhelming amount of the overall debt.

Also relevant to this appeal, Commerce declined to investigate an allegation by U.S. Steel that a countervailable subsidy exists because RTG injected equity into SSI when SSI was not equityworthy. *See* Memorandum from the Team to the File Regarding New Subsidy Allegation, (Sept. 21, 2001) ("*New Subsidy Allegation Memo*"). Commerce concluded that there was no basis for investigating the allegation. Commerce reviewed the evidence submitted by U.S. Steel and found that it did not establish a reasonable basis to believe or suspect that the company was not equityworthy at the time of its founding. To the contrary, Commerce found evidence indicating that at the time of SSI's founding economic conditions were right for the development of a Thai hot-rolled steel industry. Commerce also noted that U.S. Steel's allegation was untimely.

In response to Commerce's determinations, both SSI and U.S. Steel filed complaints in the Court of International Trade. U.S. Steel challenged Commerce's determination that the debt restructuring was not specific and therefore not countervailable. U.S. Steel also challenged Commerce's refusal to initiate an investigation into the allegation of countervailable equity infusions. Among other things, SSI challenged Commerce's determination to countervail the entire amount of the import duty exemptions.

The Court of International Trade found for SSI on all three of these disputed issues. First, the court upheld Commerce's determination that the subsidy conferred on SSI was not specific. The court found that the actual recipients of the subsidy were not limited in number, that neither SSI nor the steel industry were predominant users of the subsidy or received a disproportionately large amount of the subsidy, and that the manner in which RTG exercised discretion in granting the subsidy did not indicate that SSI or the steel industry was preferred. Decision, 341 F. Supp. 2d at 1317-20.

Second, the Court of International Trade upheld Commerce's decision not to investigate U.S. Steel's allegation of countervailable equity infusions. The court ruled that the allegation did not reasonably appear to be countervailable because there is substantial evidence in the record indicating that SSI was in fact equityworthy at the time the equity infusions were made. It also ruled that, due to the complex nature of equityworthiness evaluations, the allegation was not discovered by Commerce within a reasonable time prior to the completion of the investigation. In addition, the court found that Commerce did not deny U.S. Steel's basic procedural rights by waiting until issuance of the *Final Determination* to notify U.S. Steel that its allegation was insufficient. Id. at 1320-23.

Third, the Court of International Trade overturned Commerce's decision to countervail the entire amount of the import duty exemptions provided to SSI, concluding that Commerce's decision was neither supported by substantial evidence nor in accordance with law. The court based its conclusion on Commerce's interpretation and application of 19 C.F.R. § 351.519, which governs drawback of import charges upon export. The court characterized Commerce's interpretation as requiring that the entire duty exemption be countervailed whenever the system allows for any excess amount of waste (no matter how small), because any excess waste necessarily makes the system unreasonable. According to the court, this interpretation would render meaningless the separate regulatory subsection allowing only the excess portion of the exemption to be countervailed. Furthermore, the court stated that § 351.519 does not draw a distinction between waste that can be resold as scrap and waste that cannot be resold as scrap, and that under the regulation it does not matter what ultimately happens to the waste, so long as there is a normal allowance for waste. The court then reviewed the evidence and concluded that RTG's system does make a normal allowance for waste because it has specific procedures for determining what constitutes waste. In reviewing the evidence, the court faulted

Commerce for relying on two "extraneous" sources of information to support its finding that RTG's waste rate is excessive. Those two sources of information were a parallel antidumping investigation and a financial audit. According to the court, Commerce should have limited its review to determining whether, based on generally accepted commercial practices in Thailand (as opposed to the United States presumably), RTG's system makes a normal allowance for waste. The court also found Commerce's reliance on the "extraneous" sources of information to be misplaced because Commerce did not assess the reasonableness of the waste rates identified in these sources. Id. at 1323-26.

Because countervailing only the excess, rather than the entire, import duty exemption resulted in a countervailing duty rate of less than two percent, and further because Thailand is considered a developing country for purposes of the United States countervailing duty law and therefore the threshold rate for Thailand is two percent, the Court of International Trade remanded the case to Commerce with instructions to find that the total estimated net countervailing subsidy rate is de minimis. Id. at 1326-27; *Remand Order*. Commerce issued a redetermination decision in accordance with the court's instructions, noting its disagreement and reserving its appeal rights. Final Results of Redetermination on Remand (Sept. 15, 2004). The Court of International Trade affirmed. *Final Judgment.*

We have jurisdiction to review the final judgment of the Court of International Trade pursuant to 28 U.S.C. § 1295(a)(5).

DISCUSSION

I

We exercise de novo review over a decision of the Court of International Trade affirming or reversing the final results of an administrative review. *Torrington Co. v. United States, 82 F.3d 1039, 1044 (Fed. Cir. 1996)*. "That is, we 'apply anew' the court's statutorily-mandated standard of review to the administrative review." *Id.* (quoting *PPG Indus., Inc. v. United States, 978 F.2d 1232, 1236 (Fed. Cir. 1992))*. Thus, in this case we will uphold Commerce's determinations, findings, and conclusions unless they are "unsupported by substantial evidence on the record, or otherwise not in accordance with law." 19 U.S.C. § 1516a(b)(1)(B)(i) (2000). While we essentially step into the shoes of the Court of International Trade and duplicate its review, *Allegheny Ludlum Corp. v. United States, 287 F.3d 1365, 1370 (Fed. Cir. 2002)*, in doing so we do not altogether ignore its informed opinion, *Suramerica de Aleaciones Laminadas, C.A. v. United States, 44 F.3d 978, 983 (Fed. Cir. 1994). See also Altx, Inc. v. United States, 370 F.3d 1108, 1116 (Fed. Cir. 2004).*

II

This case presents three issues for us to resolve. We must decide, in light of the Court of International Trade's decision, whether (1) Commerce's determination that the debt restructuring was not specific is supported by substantial evidence and is otherwise in accordance with law; (2) Commerce's determination not to initiate an investigation in the allegation of equity infusion is supported by substantial evidence and is otherwise in accordance with law; and (3) Commerce's determination to countervail the entire amount of the import duty exemptions is supported by substantial evidence and is otherwise in accordance with law.

A. Commerce's Determination that the Debt Restructuring Was Not Specific

As the Court of International Trade recognized, to determine whether a subsidy is de facto specific, Commerce is required to analyze four factors set forth in *19 U.S.C. § 1677(5A)(D)(iii)*. That statutory provision states that a subsidy is specific if one or more of the following situations exists:

> (I) The actual recipients of the subsidy, whether considered on an enterprise or industry basis, are limited in number.
>
> (II) An enterprise or industry is a predominant user of the subsidy.
>
> (III) An enterprise or industry receives a disproportionately large amount of the subsidy.
>
> (IV) The manner in which the authority providing the subsidy has exercised discretion in the decision to grant the subsidy indicates that an enterprise or industry is favored over others.

19 U.S.C. § 1677(5A)(D)(iii) (2000).

U.S. Steel does not separately take issue with Commerce's analysis of each of the four factors. Rather, U.S. Steel generally argues that Commerce erred by only reviewing the distribution of the magnitude of the loans that were restructured rather than the magnitude of the benefits conferred by the restructuring. U.S. Steel would require an analysis that includes two parts: first, for each company Commerce would compare the interest rate and repayment schedule of the loan before restructuring with the rate and schedule of the loan after restructuring to identify the benefit conferred by the restructuring; second, Commerce would compare the benefits between companies and industries to determine specificity.

RTG and SSI (hereinafter, collectively "RTG") as well as the United States contend that requiring Commerce to determine and compare benefits in this manner would result in unreasonably extensive investigations. They also argue that such a requirement would contradict this court's indication in *AK Steel Corp. v. United States* that Commerce should be given latitude in determining specificity:

> Determinations of disproportionality and dominant use are not subject to rigid rules, but rather must be determined on a case-by-case basis taking into account all the facts and circumstances of a particular case. . . . Because Commerce's methodology in determining disproportionality was reasonable, we will not disturb it on appeal.

192 F.3d 1367, 1385 (Fed. Cir. 1999).

We agree with the Court of International Trade that Commerce's determination that the debt restructuring was not specific is supported by substantial evidence and is otherwise in accordance with law. U.S. Steel's suggestion that Commerce should obtain and analyze the terms of each loan before and after restructuring has some appeal, because a loan that includes vastly more favorable terms after restructuring would confer a greater benefit than a similarly sized loan that includes only slightly more favorable terms after restructuring. As a practical matter, however, it is not unreasonable for Commerce to presume that the amount of benefits conferred by debt restructuring would roughly be proportional to the magnitude of the debts that were restructured, and as a result to compare the magnitudes of the debts that were restructured rather than to engage in the extensive investigations and calculations contemplated by U.S. Steel.

In *AK Steel*, this court recognized that "determinations of disproportionality and dominant use are not subject to rigid rules." *Id.* In particular, this court found that Commerce did not err by comparing relative percentage benefits rather than absolute benefits, as requiring a comparison of absolute benefits "could produce an untenable result, i.e., that a benefit conferred on a large company might be disproportionate merely because of the size of the company." *Id.* Thus, this court determined that Commerce had properly exercised the latitude afforded it in determining the appropriate method by which to determine the specificity of benefits conferred by subsidies. Of course, that latitude does not excuse Commerce from choosing a reasonable method for determining the specificity of benefits. Indeed, Commerce itself has recognized that "the analysis of whether an enterprise or industry or group thereof is a dominant user of, or has received disproportionate benefits under, a subsidy program should normally focus on the level of benefits provided," even if sometimes "it may be impracticable or impossible to determine the relative level of benefits." *Countervailing Duties: Final Rule, 63 Fed. Reg. 65,348, 65,359 (Nov. 25, 1998).*

Here, we understand Commerce to have determined that obtaining the necessary information to engage in the extensive calculations contemplated by U.S. Steel was impracticable. Moreover, we understand Commerce to have determined that the magnitude of debt that is restructured is roughly proportional to the benefit conferred by restructuring. We have no reason to disagree with either determination. As a result, in our view Commerce's decision to compare the magnitude of the loans, a relatively simple endeavor, rather than to engage in exhaustive calculations using unavailable pre- and post-restructuring loan terms, was not unreasonable.

For the foregoing reasons, we conclude that Commerce's determination that the debt restructuring was not specific is supported by substantial evidence and otherwise in accordance with law.

B. Commerce's Determination Not to Investigate U.S. Steel's Allegation of Equity Infusion

Commerce only investigates an equity infusion allegation when the allegation is specific and "supported by information establishing a reasonable basis to believe or suspect that the firm received an equity infusion that provides a countervailable benefit." 19 C.F.R. § 351.507(a)(7) (2004). Furthermore, a countervailable "benefit exists to the extent that the investment decision is inconsistent with the usual investment practice of private investors, including the practice regarding the provision of risk capital, in the country in which the equity infusion is made." *Id.* § 351.507(a)(1).

U.S. Steel argues that its allegation of equity infusion met the standard for initiation and that Commerce erred by not initiating an investigation into that allegation. U.S. Steel maintains that it showed that an initial invitation to bid for a steel mill in Thailand with only a moderate level of subsidies resulted in no bids, while a later invitation accompanied by a substantial level of subsidies resulted in several bids. Thus, U.S. Steel argues that RTG clearly and unequivocally induced bidders to invest in an unequityworthy company using the subsidies. It also contends that the evidence of equityworthiness cited by Commerce consisted wholly of self-serving statements by RTG.

We conclude that there is substantial evidence in the record supporting Commerce's determination that U.S. Steel did not submit information establishing a reasonable basis to believe or suspect that SSI received an equity infusion that provides a countervailable benefit. Commerce rejected U.S. Steel's assumption that no reasonable investor would have invested in SSI without the incentives RTG provided because the information in the record did not support that assumption. *New Subsidy Allegation Memo* at 4. While U.S. Steel is correct that Commerce relied on RTG's testimony regarding the economic conditions in Thailand at the time SSI was formed, U.S. Steel is incorrect to the extent it characterizes Commerce as solely relying on self-serving statements by RTG. To the contrary, Commerce indicated that it relied not only on RTG's testimony, but also on exhibits supplied by RTG:

> Evidence on the record indicates that at the time of SSI's founding, economic conditions were right for the development of a Thai hot-rolled steel industry: the economy was growing rapidly and domestic demand for hot-rolled steel was increasing and was being met exclusively by imports. Indeed, the record shows that the BOI promoted a hot-rolled steel industry to meet this increasing domestic demand for hot-rolled steel products. *See e.g.*, RTG Questionnaire Responses and Exhibits.

Id. at 5. Furthermore, those exhibits do support Commerce's conclusions. One of the exhibits includes a report prepared by the United Nations Industrial Development Organization summarizing various studies regarding iron and steel industry development in Thailand. The report indicates that a 1988 study concluded that if "the private sector was to take on the project" the "return on the whole scheme was 10%." The report also indicates that a 1990 study concluded that the "setup of [a] steelmaking plant" was "viable." The report, therefore, supports Commerce's conclusion that Thailand's economic conditions were right for the development of a Thai hot-rolled steel industry.

For the foregoing reasons, we conclude that Commerce's determination not to initiate an investigation into the allegation of equity infusion is supported by substantial evidence and is otherwise in accordance with law. In light of this conclusion, we need not reach Commerce's alternative finding that U.S. Steel's allegation was untimely.

C. Commerce's Determination to Countervail the Entire Amount of Import Duty Exemptions

Commerce's ability to countervail import duty exemptions is governed by 19 C.F.R. § 351.519. In pertinent part, this regulation states:

> (a) (1) (i) Remission or drawback of import charges. In the case of the remission or drawback of import charges upon export, a benefit exists to the extent that the Secretary determines that the amount of the remission or drawback exceeds the amount of import charges on imported inputs that are consumed in the production of the exported product, making normal allowances for waste.
>
> . . . .
>
> (a) (3) (i) Remission or drawback of import charges. If the Secretary determines that the remission or drawback . . . of import charges confers a benefit under paragraph (a)(1) . . . of this section, the Secretary normally will consider the amount of the benefit to be the difference between the amount of import charges remitted or drawn back and the amount paid on imported inputs consumed in production for which remission or drawback was claimed.
>
> . . . .
>
> (a) (4) Exception. Notwithstanding paragraph (a)(3) of this section, the Secretary will consider the entire amount of an exemption, deferral, remission or drawback to confer a benefit, unless the Secretary determines that:
>
>> (i) The government in question has in place and applies a system or procedure to confirm which inputs are consumed in the production of the exported products and in what amounts, and the system or procedure is reasonable, effective for the purposes intended, and is based on generally accepted commercial practices in the country of export . . . . 19 C.F.R. § 351.519 (2004).

Responding to the arguments the United States and U.S. Steel present on appeal, RTG maintains that the Court of International Trade correctly decided that Commerce's decision to countervail the entire import duty exemption was not supported by substantial evidence or was not in accordance with law. RTG argues that the Court of International Trade properly recognized the circularity of the construction Commerce sought to apply to 19 C.F.R. § 351.519. RTG characterizes Commerce as having "countervailed the entire amount of SSI's import duty exemption for what it deemed to be an excessive amount for waste." (Appellee Br. 17.) According to RTG, by doing so Commerce elevated the exception of § 351.519(a)(4) over the rule of § 351.519(a)(3). RTG points out that "waste" is not mentioned in § 351.519(a)(4), and that the only mention of waste is in subsection § 351.519(a)(1). It argues that reading § 351.519(a)(4) as justification for countervailing an entire drawback program "by simply finding an excessive allowance of any magnitude" renders § 351.519(a)(3) meaningless. (Appellee Br. 20.) RTG contends that Commerce should countervail an entire program only when the program is unreasonable. RTG maintains that its system is reasonable based on the acceptable practices in Thailand, and it also faults Commerce for referencing an accounting book that it alleges says nothing about whether waste includes recoverable or saleable scrap.

Next, RTG, relying on a dictionary definition of "waste," contends that "waste that can be sold is still waste." (Appellee Br. 27.) Furthermore, citing 19 C.F.R. § 191.23(c), RTG points out that the U.S. Customs and Border Protection's own drawback regulations only allow drawback on imported input reduced by recoverable and saleable waste. But RTG maintains that these regulations support rather than defeat its arguments because they recognize that "waste encompasses saleable scrap." (Appellee's Br. 31.)

Finally, RTG argues that the Court of International Trade properly rejected Commerce's reliance on the two "extraneous" sources of yield information, the parallel antidumping investigation and the financial audit. It argues that the rejection of Commerce's reliance on these sources of information does not undercut Commerce's statutory authority, because Commerce could have relied on RTG's system. RTG, recognizing that the dispositive question is whether its system reasonably and effectively confirmed normal allowances for waste, argues that its system is reasonable and effective. RTG contends that the two other sources of information only included slightly lower yield factors, and that Commerce never even assessed the reasonableness of the other sources of information.

We conclude that Commerce's determination to countervail the entire amount of the import duty exemptions is supported by substantial evidence and is otherwise in accordance with law. Subsection 351.519(a)(1)(i) provides that a countervailable benefit exists where a program permits a drawback that "exceeds the amount of import charges on imported inputs that are consumed in the production of the exported product, making normal allowances for waste." Moreover, pursuant to § 351.519(a)(4), the "entire amount" of the drawback is countervailable "unless" Commerce finds that

> the government in question has in place and applies a system or procedure to confirm which inputs are consumed in the production of the exported products and in what amounts, and the system or procedure is reasonable, effective for the purposes intended, and is based on generally accepted commercial practices in the country of export . . . .19 C.F.R. § 351.519(a)(4) (2004). Only when Commerce finds that the

> government in question has the system required by § 351.519(a)(4) does it "normally consider the amount of the benefit to be the difference between the amount of import charges remitted or drawn back and the amount paid on imported inputs consumed in production for which remission or drawback was claimed" pursuant to § 351.519(a)(3)(i). Here, following the requirements of § 351.519(a)(4), Commerce determined that RTG's system for determining which inputs are consumed in the exported product, and in what amounts, is not reasonable because the system did not isolate and examine what was consumed in the production of the exported products and it did not consider in its analysis whether any of the scrap was recoverable and saleable. We see no reason to second guess the determination of Commerce that a system that does not account for recoverable and saleable scrap is not a reasonable system. In short, we defer to the expertise of Commerce in concluding that normal allowances for waste do not include allowing drawback on recoverable and saleable scrap. Unlike RTG, we do not fault Commerce for referencing accounting principles discussed in an accounting book to determine that recoverable and saleable scrap cannot be considered waste because it does have value and can be sold. Furthermore, we reject RTG's reliance on a dictionary definition of the term "waste." We also note that, contrary to RTG's argument, U.S. Customs and Border Protection's regulation on this very same issue, *19 C.F.R. § 191.23(c)*, supports Commerce's finding that reasonable systems do not allow drawback on imported inputs that are recoverable and resold.

The Court of International Trade found Commerce's logic to be circular. It understood Commerce to be countervailing the entire duty exemption because Commerce believes that any excess waste necessarily makes a system unreasonable. The court stated that "the problem with [Commerce's] logic is that it renders § 351.519(a)(3)(i) meaningless, because there could never be a situation where only the excessive portion of the exemption would be countervailed." Decision, 341 F. Supp. 2d at 1324. Contrary to the characterization of Commerce's decision by RTG and the Court of International Trade, however, Commerce did not countervail the entire drawback program simply because the program allowed for some amount of excessive drawback. We understand Commerce to have countervailed the entire drawback program because it found that program to be unreasonable for systematically allowing impermissible drawback of recoverable and resaleable scrap, resulting in unduly large amounts of impermissible drawback. We defer to this interpretation and application of § 351.519, Commerce's own regulation, because it is reasonable. *See Lee v. United States, 329 F.3d 817, 822 (Fed. Cir. 2003)* ("A great amount of deference is owed to an agency's interpretation of its own regulations."); *NSK, Ltd. v. Koyo Seiko Co., 190 F.3d 1321, 1326 (Fed. Cir. 1999)* ("We accord substantial deference to Commerce's interpretations of its own regulations."). Commerce's application of § 351.519(a)(4) here does not mean that there could never be a situation where only the excessive portion of the import duty exemption would be countervailed. For example, Commerce might countervail only excess drawback when the excess drawback is caused by random rather than systematic error. As another example, Commerce might only countervail excess drawback that is relatively very small.

RTG agrees that Commerce should countervail an entire program when the program is unreasonable, but maintains that its system is reasonable based on the generally acceptable practices in Thailand. The Court of International Trade agreed. The requirement of a reasonable and effective system, however, is separate from the requirement that the system reflect local commercial practices. According to the text of 19 C.F.R. § 351.519(a)(4), to have only excess drawback countervailed, a system must be (1) reasonable, (2) effective for the purposes intended, and (3) based on generally accepted commercial practices in the country of export. The language of the regulation does not clearly require that Commerce analyze the reasonableness of a system only from the perspective of the home country. Thus, we defer to Commerce's interpretation of its own regulation as allowing the reasonableness of a system to be evaluated using general accounting principles that might not be prevalent in the country of export, as that interpretation of the regulation is reasonable. *See Lee, 329 F.3d at 822*; *NSK, 190 F.3d at 1326*. Applying that principle here, we conclude that Commerce's reference to general accounting principles used outside Thailand was not reversible error.

Finally, we disagree with RTG's argument that the Court of International Trade was correct to disallow consideration of information generated by the parallel antidumping investigation and the financial audit. Commerce should be allowed to verify the data that foreign systems generate using information generated through independent financial and production audits. Indeed, pursuant to *19 U.S.C. § 1677m(i)* and 19 C.F.R. § 351.307, Commerce is required to verify the factual basis for its determinations. And while the Court of International Trade was concerned that Commerce did not assess the reasonableness of the waste rates identified in these sources, Commerce did assess the reasonableness of the waste rates identified by RTG in light of the significant percent differences between the waste rates identified in those sources and RTG's reported waste rate. Investigating the reasonableness of RTG's system in light of these significant percent differences was not improper.

For the foregoing reasons, we conclude that Commerce's determination to countervail the entire amount of the import duty exemptions is supported by substantial evidence and is otherwise in accordance with law.

CONCLUSION

We affirm the Court of International Trade's findings on issues of the specificity of debt restructuring and the allegations of equity infusion, but we reverse its finding that Commerce erred in countervailing the entire amount of the import duty exemptions. We remand the case to the Court of International Trade for further proceedings consistent with this opinion.

AFFIRMED-IN-PART, REVERSED-IN-PART, and REMANDED

TIMKEN U.S.
v.
UNITED STATES

434 F.3d 1345 (Fed Cir. 2006)
Decided January 10, 2006

Before MICHEL, Chief Judge, CLEVENGER and SCHALL, Circuit Judges.

OPINION

MICHEL, *Chief Judge.*

Timken U.S. Corporation and Timken Nadellager, GmbH (collectively "Timken") appeal the United States Court of International Trade's decision upholding the United States Department of Commerce's antidumping duty determination and Commerce's refusal to correct certain alleged errors associated with Timken's home market sales that were relied upon by Commerce in computing the dumping margin for Timken's cylindrical roller bearings exported from Germany to the United States from May 1, 1998 to April 30, 1999. *Timken U.S. Corp. v. United States, 2004 Ct. Int. Trade LEXIS 135, No. 00-09-00454 (Ct. Int'l Trade Oct. 29, 2004).* Because the Court of International Trade did not err in remanding the case to Commerce for investigation of Timken's evidence supporting correction and because Commerce's antidumping duty determination and its refusal to correct the alleged errors on remand were supported by substantial evidence and were in accordance with law, we affirm.

I. BACKGROUND

Like many appeals from the Court of International Trade, this appeal has a somewhat complex history. In 1999, pursuant to Section 751 of the Tariff Act of 1930, Commerce conducted its tenth administrative review of the Antidumping Duty Orders on cylindrical roller bearings ("bearings") from, *inter alia*, Germany for the period of May 1, 1998 to April 30, 1999. Timken imported bearings made in Germany into the United States during that period of time and thus its importations were subject to Commerce's review.

Commerce provided Timken with a questionnaire and requested Timken to identify the channels of distribution for its home market sales. Timken identified five channels: (1) sales of bearings produced by Timken and sold by Timken from its factory to large original equipment manufacturers ("OEMs"); (2) sales of bearings produced by Timken and sold by Timken from its factory to small OEMs; (3) sales of bearings produced by Timken and sold by Timken from its factory to distributors; (4) resales of bearings made by Timken's affiliated marketing entity to OEMs; and (5) resales of bearings made by Timken's affiliated marketing entity to distributors.[1] Timken also described the selling and marketing processes for each of the five channels of distribution. After receiving Timken's response, Commerce verified Timken's categorization of its sales.

Based upon the verification information, Commerce examined Timken's selling activities, the point in the channel of distribution at which the selling activities occurred, and the types of customers that purchased the subject bearings and eventually determined that three of the channels of distribution identified by Timken were for home market sales by Timken itself and the remaining two were for "resales" by Timken's affiliated marketing entity. As a result, Commerce re-designated channel 1 as home market 1 ("HM1"), grouped channels 4 and 5 together and re-designated them as home market 2 ("HM2"), and grouped channels 2 and 3 and re-designated them as home market 3 ("HM3"). In grouping channel 2 with 3 and channel 4 with 5, Commerce essentially determined that the points in which selling activities occurred in these channels were indistinguishable. Commerce then computed a dumping margin of 61.60 percent and published its preliminary results. *See* Preliminary Results of Administrative Review, Antifriction Bearings (Other than Tapered Roller Bearings) and Parts Thereof from France, Germany, Italy, Japan, Romania, Singapore, Sweden and the United Kingdom, 65 Fed. Reg. 18033 (Apr. 6, 2000).

After reviewing Commerce's results, Timken alleged that it had made certain errors, which it characterized as "clerical," in reporting its sales. Specifically, Timken claimed that it "inadvertently and inaccurately" reported seventeen transactions in channel 1 instead of channel 2 or 3. This mistake, Timken claimed, caused

---

1 Commerce and Timken interpret the definition of "large OEMs" under channel 1 and "small OEMs" under channel 2 differently based upon whether the words "large" and "small" refer to the size of the OEM or the size of the product produced by the OEM. Commerce takes the former position, while Timken takes the latter. Indeed, in Commerce's own words:

> It is important to recognize that the term "large original equipment manufacturer," which connotes the level of trade in which such sales were grouped in the final results of review, does not refer to producers of "large original equipment." Rather it refers to large producers of original equipment. That is, the term "large" modifies the type of manufacturer, not the type of product. Final Results of Redetermination Pursuant to Court Remand, *Timken U.S. Corporation and Timken Nadellager, GmbH v. United States*, No. 00-09-00454, slip op. at 7 (June 7, 2004) ("*Remand Determination").* Timken does not so clearly explain its view. However, we are able to infer its position based upon the arguments it made before Commerce, the Court of International Trade, and this court on appeal.

those transactions to be categorized into HM1 instead of HM3, which in turn resulted in an inaccurate dumping margin. Timken contends that the errors occurred because it relied on the customer's name alone in categorizing the sales, rather than on whether the customer used the bearings in large-sized products or small-sized products. Timken divided these errors into three groups: (1) sales of bearings shipped to several large OEMs for use as replacement parts ("Replacement Parts Sales"); (2) sales of bearings shipped to a division of a large OEM for use in small electric tools ("Small Electric Tools Sales"); and (3) sales of bearings shipped to a prototype center of a large OEM for use in prototypes ("Prototype Sales").

Timken requested Commerce to correct these errors before issuing the final results. In support of its request, Timken submitted a "case brief," which included exhibits consisting of invoices and corresponding purchaser orders for the seventeen allegedly miscategorized sales. Commerce applied the test highlighted in Certain Fresh Cut Flowers from Colombia; Final Results of Antidumping Duty Administrative Review, 61 Fed. Reg. 42833 (Aug. 19, 1996), in deciding whether to substitute Timken's new information and recalculate the applicable dumping margin. The first requirement of the so-called "Colombian Flowers Test" is that the error be of a "clerical" nature, not a "methodological error, a substantive error, or an error in judgment." Commerce found that Timken's errors were not "clerical" but instead were due to "errors in judgment." The second requirement of the "Colombia Flowers Test" is that Commerce must be satisfied that the new evidence provided in support of the "clerical" error is reliable. Commerce found that the new information that Timken submitted in its case brief conflicted with information already of record and that the corrections were not offered at the earliest opportunity, thus allegedly preventing Commerce from ascertaining their reliability through the verification process. For these reasons, Commerce declined to correct the asserted errors and issued its final results without any changes. *See* Final Results of Administrative Review, Antifriction Bearings (Other than Tapered Roller Bearings) and Parts Thereof from France, German, Italy, Japan, Romania, Singapore, Sweden and the United Kingdom, 65 Fed. Reg. 49,219 (Aug. 11, 2000).

Timken appealed to the Court of International Trade. *See Timken U.S. Corp. v. United States, 318 F. Supp. 2d 1271 (Ct. Int'l Trade 2004)* ("*Timken I*"). The Court of International Trade rejected Commerce's rigid application of the "Colombia Flowers Test," even though it agreed with Commerce that Timken's error was not "clerical," because the Court of International Trade was concerned that Commerce's application of the test would render a grossly erroneous dumping margin in this case. Id. at 1277. The Court of International Trade also noted that it was unclear what evidence of record Commerce thought contradicted Timken's new evidence and that any corrective information would necessarily be in conflict with information originally submitted to Commerce. Id. at 1279. Accordingly, the Court of International Trade remanded the case to Commerce for further investigation.

On remand, Commerce noted its disagreement with the Court of International Trade's order at the outset. *Remand Determination*, slip op. at 4. Because Commerce posited that the errors in dispute were not "clerical," as determined by the Court of International Trade, these errors did not require correction and there was no need for any further investigation. Despite this position, Commerce of course followed the Court of International Trade's order and reviewed Timken's new evidence, ultimately determining that corrections were not warranted because "the information [Timken] submitted does not substantiate the existence of the alleged error, and, thus, reclassifying [Timken's] sales in a different level of trade would not result in a more accurate dumping margin." *Id.*, slip op. at 8. In reaching that conclusion, Commerce specifically evaluated the new information that Timken submitted for the three groups of allegedly miscategorized sales.

Starting with the first group, Commerce found that Timken's argument that the Replacement Part Sales should have been categorized under channel 3 conflicted with the information of record. Commerce noted that Timken described the bearings it sold under channel 3 in its verified questionnaire as those listed in its "standard catalog," not replacement parts. *Id.*, slip op. at 16. It consequently found that Timken failed to provide a sufficient explanation of why replacement parts should be classified under channel 3. Commerce also observed that the customers of the Replacement Part Sales were large OEMs, not distributors—the customers Timken originally identified for channel 3 sales. *Id.*, slip op. at 16-17. Lastly, Commerce noted that Timken did not provide evidence showing the bearings were, in fact, used as replacement parts. "The merchandise," Commerce reasoned, "very well may have been used for the normal production activities of the large OEMs." *Id.*, slip op. at 17.

Turning to the second group, Commerce found Timken did not provide factual information to substantiate the claim that the customer of the Small Electric Tools Sales, a division of a large OEM, should independently be considered a small OEM under channel 2 instead of a large OEM under channel 1. *Id.*, slip op. at 14-15.

As to the third group, Commerce found that Timken's argument that the Prototype Sales should have been categorized under either channel 2 or 3 conflicted with the information of record. Significantly, it noted that when Timken described the selling function of channel 1 in its verified questionnaire, it specifically mentioned prototype sales, but did not do so for either channel 2 or 3. *Id.*, slip op. at 12-13. Next, Commerce noted that the customer of the Prototype Sales was a large OEM. "That fact alone," Commerce reasoned, "supports the original channel 1 classification." *Id.*, slip op. at 13. It further noted that only two of the invoices submitted by Timken for the Prototype Sales contained the word "Muster," the German equivalent of "sample," thus suggesting that the remaining Prototype Sales did not actually involve prototypes and were instead regular sales to a large OEM. *Id.* Finally, Commerce noted that Timken did not provide any evidence showing that the alleged prototypes were not used in producing original equipment. *Id.*, slip op. at 14.

Timken again appealed to the Court of International Trade, which upheld Commerce's remand determination not to make the requested corrections on the grounds that Timken's corrective information was not sufficiently supported whereas Commerce had verified Timken's original information. *Timken U.S. Corp. v. United States, 2004 Ct. Intl. Trade LEXIS 135, No. 00-09-00454 (Ct. Int'l Trade Oct. 29, 2004)* ("*Timken II*"). The Court of International Trade observed that Commerce met its burden of reviewing the disputed classifications and the corrective information submitted by Timken. It thus concluded that Commerce provided a reasonable explanation for its determination that the dumping margin applicable to Timken's bearing imports was as accurate as possible and that there was no need to make any corrections. *Id.*, slip op. at 24.

Timken timely appeals the Court of International Trade's decision upholding Commerce's remand determination. We have jurisdiction over this appeal pursuant to *28 U.S.C. § 1295(a)(5)*.

II. DISCUSSION

We review a decision of the Court of International Trade in an antidumping duty case *de novo*, applying the same standard of review to Commerce's determination as the Court of International Trade applies. *See Co-Steel Raritan, Inc. v. ITC, 357 F.3d 1294, 1309 (Fed. Cir. 2004)*. Under that standard, we are obligated to affirm the Court of International Trade's decision unless Commerce's determination is "unsupported by substantial evidence on the record, or otherwise not in accordance with law." *19 U.S.C. § 1516a(b)(1)(B)(i) (2000)*. "Substantial evidence" means "such relevant evidence as a reasonable mind might accept as adequate to support a conclusion." *Consol. Edison v. Nat'l Labor Relations Bd., 305 U.S. 197, 229, 59 S. Ct. 206, 83 L. Ed. 126 (1938)*. Notably, "the possibility of drawing two inconsistent conclusions from the evidence does not prevent an administrative agency's finding from being supported by substantial evidence." *Consolo v. Fed. Mar. Comm'n, 383 U.S. 607, 620, 86 S. Ct. 1018, 16 L. Ed. 2d 131 (Fed. Cir. 2001)*.

Timken argues that Commerce's decision not to reclassify its allegedly miscategorized sales is not supported by substantial evidence. Timken asserts that the new information it submitted in its case brief at the preliminary results stage adequately supports the reclassification of its seventeen allegedly miscategorized sales from channel 1 to either channel 2 or 3. More specifically, for its Replacement Part Sales, that the customer was a large OEM, Timken contends, does not automatically mean that all sales were for bearings that would be incorporated into other goods; a large OEM may also purchase bearings to serve as replacement parts. In such case, Timken points out that the nature of sales and the associated selling activities are by definition different. It thus argues that the market in which its bearings were sold governs the classification, not the identity of the customer, contrary to Commerce's determination.

For its Small Electric Tools Sales, Timken claims that the proper classification is ascertainable by resort to its descriptions of channel 1 and channel 2. Timken points out that it described channel 1 as involving "sales to auto motive and other large OEMs" and channel 2 as involving "sales to smaller OEMs such as machinery and other equipment producers." Based up on these descriptions and the fact that the customer sells small electric tools, Timken asserts that the Small Electric Tools Sales necessarily fall under channel 2; that the customer is a division of a large OEM is irrelevant because the only point of distinction between channel 1 and channel 2 is the size of the goods sold.

For its Prototype Sales, Timken argues as it did for the Replacement Part Sales that customer identity does not control classification; rather, the market in which the product was sold dictates whether a particular sale should be categorized in channel 1, 2, or 3. Hence, that the customer of the Prototype Sales was a large OEM is, Timken claims, of no import in deciding whether the Prototype Sales were erroneously categorized in channel 1. Further, it asserts the fact that some invoices contained the word "Muster," while others did not, is not decisive since all Prototype Sales were shipped to the customer's prototype center, as shown on all the invoices.

Finally, Timken contends that the quantity of bearings involved in the allegedly miscategorized sales confirms that they were erroneously included in channel 1. Timken points out that each sale consisted of several hundreds of bearings; sales placed in channel 1, by contrast, involve several thousands of bearings. As such, Timken claims quantity alone demonstrates that its bearing sales were erroneously categorized in channel 1.

The government responds by arguing that Commerce's decision not to reclassify Timken's allegedly miscategorized sales is supported by substantial evidence. Beginning with the Replacement Parts Sales, the government asserts that Timken neither mentioned replacement parts in its descriptions of its channels of distribution nor offered an explanation for why such sales are correctly classified in channel 3 as opposed to channel 1. Turning to Small Electric Tools Sales, the government points out that Commerce correctly determined that Timken provided no evidence to substantiate its claim that the division of a large OEM, which manufactures small electric tools, should be considered a small OEM. Moreover, the government contends that Commerce correctly noted that while sales to a single customer may be classified in different channels of distribution, Timken failed to demonstrate facts sufficient to show that such bifurcation is necessary for the Small Electric Tools Sales. Finally, the government argues that if Commerce were to reclassify all of the Prototype Sales on the basis of only two invoices, it essentially would place unverified information over conflicting, verified information. Even assuming Timken is correct that the sales were truly for prototypes, the government claims that such sales were properly included in channel 1 because Timken mentioned prototype sales only in its description of channel 1, not in its descriptions of channel 2 and 3.

As an alternative ground of affirmance, the government asserts that the Court of International Trade erred in *Timken I* by remanding the case to Commerce for investigation of Timken's new information. Because the Court of International Trade had agreed with Commerce that Timken's alleged errors were not "clerical," the government contends that the Court of International Trade should have simply affirmed Commerce's original refusal pursuant to the "Colombia Flowers Test." Accordingly, the government argues that Commerce's original antidumping duty determination and first refusal to correct should stand.

Timken replies to the government's alternative argument by disputing both Commerce's and the Court of International Trade's characterization of its errors as "errors in judgment." Timken claims that its errors are "clerical" and thus subject to correction under the "Colombia Flowers Test."

A.

Before addressing Timken's argument concerning its new evidence, we focus on the government's challenge to the Court of International Trade's remand order in *Timken I* since this issue potentially is dispositive of the appeal without requiring minute examination of the old and new information on various sales. On the merits, we disagree with the government. Essentially, it contends that the Court of International Trade erred in remanding the case for further investigation solely because it had concurred with Commerce's determination that Timken's errors were not "clerical" in nature. In making this argument, the government seems to advocate a bright-line rule regarding what kinds of errors may be corrected in the context of antidumping duty determinations. Specifically, it argues that once Commerce calculates a dumping margin, an error in the underlying data supplied by an importer to Commerce may be corrected only where it is "clerical" in nature. Surprisingly, counsel for Timken appeared to agree with the government's contention at oral argument. The government does not, however, identify any statute or regulation on point. Instead, it relies solely on our decision in *Alloy Piping Prods. v. Kanzen Tetsu Sdn. Bhd., 334 F.3d 1284 (Fed. Cir. 2003)*, and its own determination in *Certain Fresh Cut Flowers from Colombia, 61 Fed. Reg. at 42834*. Such reliance is, however, misplaced.

In *Alloy Products*, after receiving the final results of Commerce's antidumping duty determination, the importer sought correction of what it described as a "clerical" error made when it provided its original sales information to Commerce. The importer argued that Commerce was absolutely and expressly required to make the correction pursuant to *19 U.S.C. § 1673d(e)* and 19 C.F.R. § 351.224.[2] Commerce

2 Section 1673d(e) states in pertinent part: "The administering authority shall establish procedures for the correction of ministerial errors in final determinations within a reasonable

declined, and both the Court of International Trade and this court affirmed. We recognized that Commerce was not required to correct the "clerical" errors made by the importer because the statute and regulation cited by the importer apply only to "clerical" errors committed *by Commerce itself. 334 F.3d at 1291*. Contrary to the government's implication, however, we did not broadly bar Commerce from correcting "clerical" errors or, for that matter, methodological errors, errors in judgment, or substantive errors made by an importer. Instead, our decision in *Alloy Products* turned on the fact that the importer sought correction of errors at the final result stage, not at the preliminary result stage as in this case. For this reason, the facts in Alloy Products are readily distinguishable from those implicated here.

Separately, a determination by Commerce, like *Certain Fresh Cut Flowers from Colombia*, is not binding on this court. We also disagree with the restrictiveness of the "Colombia Flowers Test." That test, which Commerce states is based on our decision in *NTN Bearing Corp. v. United States, 74 F.3d 1204 (Fed. Cir. 1995)*, imposes six conditions which must be met before Commerce will correct an error made by an importer. The first condition is that the "error in question must be demonstrated to be a clerical error, not a methodological error, an error in judgment, or a substantive error." *Certain Fresh Cut Flowers from* Colombia, 61 Fed. Reg. at 42834. It is perplexing how Commerce could have derived this first condition from NTN Bearing when our holding in that case, as in *Alloy Products*, was premised exclusively on timeliness. Indeed, upon careful review, we do not even find any dicta suggesting a distinction between "clerical" and other types of errors, and Commerce cited none.

More specifically, after receiving the International Trade Administration's ("ITA") preliminary antidumping duty determination, NTN realized that it made two "clerical" errors caused by typographical mistakes. These clerical errors, NTN asserted, caused a substantial increase in its dumping margins. NTN offered corrective information to the ITA and sought to have corrections made before the ITA issued its final determination. The ITA refused because NTN made its request after the deadline for submitting new information had expired and because its new evidence did not adequately demonstrate that errors had occurred. Notably, the ITA did not challenge NTN's characterization of its errors as "clerical." The Court of International Trade affirmed that refusal. We reversed, holding that the ITA abused its discretion in refusing to consider NTN's corrective information because of untimeliness. *NTN Bearing, 74 F.3d at 1208*. At no point in our analysis did we distin-

---

time after the determinations are issued under this section." Section 351.224(e) provides in relevant part: "The Secretary will analyze any comments received and, if appropriate, correct any significant ministerial error by amending the preliminary determination, or correct any ministerial error by amending the final determination or the final results of review (whichever is applicable)."

guish "clerical" errors from other errors such as methodological errors, substantive errors, or errors in judgment. We simply reasoned:

> NTN responded in a timely manner to the preliminary determination, pointing out ITA's clerical errors, as well as its own. ITA corrected its own but not NTN's errors. Correction of NTN's errors would neither have required beginning anew nor have delayed making the final determination. A straightforward mathematical adjustment was all that was required. Failure to make it resulted in the imposition of many millions of dollars in duties not justified under the statute. *Id.* We also noted that while a tension between finality and correct result may arise in some instances, such was not the case in *NTN Bearing* because NTN requested corrections to be made at the preliminary results stage. *Id.* "Preliminary determinations," we observed, "are 'preliminary' precisely because they are subject to change." *Id.*

To the extent that Commerce cites *NTN Bearing* for the source of its distinction between "clerical" and other errors, we surmise that Commerce erroneously extrapolated one where none was stated or intended. We emphasize that our ruling in *NTN Bearing* was based solely on timeliness, not on the type of error. Additionally, we hold that Commerce is free to correct any type of importer error—clerical, methodology, substantive, or one in judgment—in the context of making an antidumping duty determination, provided that the importer seeks correction before Commerce issues its final results and adequately proves the need for the requested corrections. In light of this holding, we need not address Timken's argument that its errors were "clerical" rather than "errors in judgment" as found by Commerce and affirmed by the Court of International Trade.

Finally, the convenience of the bright-line rule that Commerce advocates is troubling. We suspect that it is not uncommon for an importer to make errors in reporting its sales information to Commerce pursuant to an administrative review. We also suspect that most such errors are methodological, substantive or, as in this case, errors of judgment, rather than "clerical" errors. Oddly, it nevertheless appears that Commerce has not issued any regulation addressing whether an importer can correct errors in the information it has submitted, let alone restricted the types of importer errors that are eligible for such correction. By urging this court to embrace Commerce's determination in *Certain Fresh Cut Flowers from Colombia* limiting correction to just "clerical" errors, the government seemingly aims to save itself from having to evaluate corrective information in most cases, regardless whether correction is sought at the preliminary results stage or the final results stage. This court, however, has never discouraged the correction of errors at the preliminary result stage; we have only balanced the desire for accuracy in antidumping duty determinations with the need for finality at the final results stage. We thus have no choice but to conclude that Commerce's position here amounts to *ipse dixit*, which is a very weak basis for any rule. Accordingly, because Timken sought correction of its errors after Commerce issued the preliminary results, but before it issued the final results, we conclude that the Court of International

Trade in *Timken I* did not err in remanding the case to Commerce for an analysis of Timken's new evidence.

B.

Turning to the heart of Timken's appeal, we disagree with Timken that the new evidence it submitted in its case brief, which consisted of invoices and, in most instances, corresponding purchase orders, is strong enough to require reclassification. At the outset, we note that the government contends in general that Commerce would be forced to prefer unverified information over conflicting, verified information if it were to make Timken's requested corrections. On appeal, the government particularly raises this argument with respect to Timken's Prototype Sales. We are struck by the fallacy of such a position; Commerce declines to verify the new information and then rejects it because it is unverified. If Commerce had reason to doubt Timken's corrective information, then it could have, and perhaps should have, performed a second verification. Indeed, the government, we note, does not cite any statute or regulation barring such a second verification.

We now focus on Timken's allegedly miscategorized sales, beginning with the Replacement Part Sales for which there were eight total sales and three different customers, *i.e.*, three sales to the first customer, one to the second customer, and four to the third customer.[3] For sake of clarity, we consider the Replacement Part Sales for each of the three customers separately. For the first customer, one of the purchase orders contained a handwritten notation in German, which Timken contends translates as: "The parts (from the purchase order) are exclusively destined for repair purposes . . . The total annual demand for this purpose are 26 units." Timken explained that the notation applied to the other two purchase orders as well and was added by Mrs. Kleiner, an employee of Timken. According to Timken, Mrs. Kleiner contacted the customer in preparation for the case brief to confirm that the purchased bearings were not used in producing original equipment. Timken does not, however, present any evidence to substantiate her communication with the customer. Commerce was thus in the position of having to accept her notation, knowing full well that it was produced specifically for the purpose of proving the alleged miscategorization. Viewed in this light, we hesitate to fault Commerce for rejecting this evidence over evidence for these particular sales which it previously verified in conjunction with Timken's original submission.

For the second customer, the invoice contained a handwritten German word, which was not easily readable, followed by an equal sign and the words "Replacement Parts." That invoice, along with the corresponding purchase order, also contained a "649" code followed by the words "shipping point." A code sheet provided with

---

3 We note that the parties agreed to keep the identities of Timken's customers, among other things, confidential under the terms of a protective order. We refer only to the customers generally, because of the protective order and because their identities are not critical to the disposition of this appeal anyway.

the two documents listed "central location for replacement parts" for that code. It is, nevertheless, entirely unclear who supplied the handwritten information or when it was added to the invoice. As with the aforementioned Replacement Part Sales, the notation quite possibly was added after Timken decided to argue that it erred in categorizing the sale. Additionally, Timken did not present any evidence about the sale showing that the bearings were, in fact, used as spare parts and were not incorporated into original equipment produced by the customer. Consequently, we conclude that Commerce reasonably rejected this evidence over previously submitted evidence for this customer.

For the third customer, the purchase orders all contained the typed word "ersatzteile," followed by an equal sign and the handwritten words "spare parts." While we do not doubt that German word "ersatzteile" correctly translates as "spare parts" or the equivalent thereof, Timken again did not provide any evidence to substantiate its claim that the bearings actually were used by the customer as spare parts. Commerce particularly noted the absence of such evidence in its determination: "The merchandise very well may have been used for the normal production activities of the large OEMs." *Remand Determination*, slip op. at 17.

As a final consideration applicable to the eight Replacement Part Sales in general, Timken did not offer a persuasive explanation of why, if the sales were really for spare parts, they should be categorized under channel 3 as opposed to channel 1. Indeed, in defining its channels of distribution in response to Commerce's original questionnaire, Timken did not mention replacement part sales in either channel 1 or channel 3. It consequently has no real basis for reclassifying the Replacement Part Sales in channel 3 as opposed to channel 1 or, for that matter, channel 2. Small OEMs under channel 2 are, after all, just as likely to purchase replacement parts as large OEMs under channel 1 or distributors under channel 3. Therefore, since any customer may require and purchase replacement parts, we conclude that customer identity is not a conclusive way for categorizing Timken's sales, but serves as a sound starting point. Here, the parties do not dispute that the three customers who purchased the Replacement Part Sales were all "large OEMs "classified under channel 1. As a result, we conclude that the evidence supporting Commerce's original determination is substantial and that it was justified in refusing to reclassify the Replacement Part Sales from channel 1 to channel 3.

As to the Small Electric Tools Sales, there were four distinct sales, all to a single customer. One of the four invoices contained a handwritten notation showing an asterisk beside the customer name followed by the comment "product division electric tools." Because Timken's argument as to these sales substantially depends on whether the words "large" and "small" modify the size of the producer or the size of the products sold, we are compelled to reach that distinction in this context. If we agree with Timken that the words "large" and "small" modify the size of the goods produced, then Timken is necessarily correct that its Small Electric Tools Sales were miscategorized under channel 1 when they should have been categorized under channel 2. We do not, however, accept Timken's position. Although Timken is in a better position than Commerce to understand and define its various channels of distribution and customers, we nevertheless observe that Timken's argument is not supported by its own descriptions of its channels of distribution. If anything, Timken's descriptions favor Commerce's position that the words "large" and "small" modify the size of the producers. Throughout its descriptions for channel 1 and channel 2, Timken consistently placed the adjectives "large" and "small," respectively, before the noun "OEMs." Moreover, Timken did not clearly describe the goods produced by the OEMs under channel 1 or 2, let alone define those goods as being "large" or "small." Commerce's analysts, like the average reader, would thus grammatically interpret the adjectives "large" and "small" to modify the noun "OEMs." It is entirely counterintuitive, based solely upon the syntax, to read the adjectives as modifying the products manufactured by the OEMs. We, consequently, must reject Timken's contention that a "large" or "small" OEM means an OEM that produces "large" or "small" products. As such, Timken's argument falls apart. Hence, we conclude that Commerce's refusal to reclassify the Small Electric Tools Sales from channel 1 to channel 2 is supported by substantial evidence.

With regard to the Prototype Sales, Timken made five separate sales to a single customer. Two of the invoices associated with those sales contain the German word "Muster." The other three invoices, although missing the word "Muster," were sent to the same location as the other two sales, presumably the customer's prototype testing facility since the shipping address for each sale contained the word "Prototypen." Timken's argument that these sales should be classified under channel 2 or 3 based upon the "Muster" notation and/or shipping address, however, seems contradicted by Timken's own description of its channels of distribution. As Commerce noted, when discussing sales under channel 1, Timken explained:

> [Timken] will develop and supply prototypes ("Muster") which are specially produced for the customer to test, and if the customer approves these units, the parties estimate the quantities to be bought and negotiate a fixed selling price. Thereafter, [Timken] provides further sample units (designated by the suffix "M41"), which are produced under normal production conditions, and if the customer approves these samples, [Timken] is fully approved to supply.

Timken did not make a similar disclosure for either channel 2 or 3, thereby suggesting that it consciously did not contemplate selling prototypes under channel 2 or 3. What is more, the customer is an "automobile and other large OEMs," the very customer defined for channel 1 sales. Thus, this evidence, especially taken together, demonstrates that Commerce was reasonable to refuse to reclassify the Prototype Sales from channel 1 to channel 2 or 3.

Lastly, Timken's argument that the small quantity of bearings involved in each of the seventeen disputed transactions weighs in favor of reclassifying the sales under either channel 2 or 3 is unavailing. None of the channels of distribution, as defined by Timken, contain any numeric limitations. Despite this, Timken claims that the average quantity for a channel 1 sale exceeds 14,000 units, but fails to substantiate its claim with any evidence. Furthermore, we presume that the sale of prototypes likely would only include a few units. The customer, after all, would want to confirm that the prototypes function for their intended usage before buying commercial quantities. Thus, that the seventeen allegedly miscategorized sales involved a small number of bearings compared to the number typically involved in a commercial sale under channel 1 does not alone require reclassifying the Prototype Sales from channel 1 to channel 2 or 3. Nor does it when taken in view of Timken's other new information.

In sum, we hold that Timken's case before Commerce basically involves a failure of proof; none of the new evidence that Timken submitted adequately supports its position that it initially misclassified seventeen sales. Commerce calculated the dumping margin applicable to the bearings Timken imported in the United States during the review period based upon Timken's original information, which it verified. Although this is a close case, we hold that Commerce's original determination was, on the balance of the old and new evidence, supported by substantial evidence and was not contrary to law. The Court of International Trade, therefore, properly affirmed Commerce's antidumping duty determination based on the original information and its refusal to accept Timken's corrective information.

III. CONCLUSION

We conclude that the Court of International Trade in *Timken I* correctly remanded the case to Commerce for investigation of Timken's new evidence because Timken sought correction after Commerce issued the preliminary results, but before it issued the final results and such corrections are not limited to "clerical" errors only. Because we conclude that Commerce had sufficient factual basis for refusing to make the corrections on remand and because its original duty determination was supported by substantial evidence and in accordance with law, we affirm the Court of International Trade's decision in *Timken II* upholding Commerce's rejection of Timken's corrective information and its antidumping duty determination based on Timken's original evidence.

AFFIRMED

IX. INTERNATIONAL TRADE

1. Regulations

C. Trademarks, Copyrights, Patents*

* Cases are indexed under this subject. The full text of these cases is published in the **volume**-page indicated.

BOURDEAU BROS., INC.
v.
INTERNATIONAL TRADE COMMISSION

444 F.3d 1317 (Fed. Cir. 2006)
Decided March 30, 2006

Before SCHALL, Circuit Judge, CLEVENGER, Senior Circuit Judge, DYK, Circuit Judge.

OPINION

CLEVENGER, *Senior Circuit Judge.*

Appellants Bourdeau Bros., Inc. (Bourdeau), Sunova Implement Co. (Sunova), and OK Enterprises (OK), (collectively, appellants) appeal the decision of the United States International Trade Commission (ITC) affirming the Initial Determination and Recommended Remedy Determination (Initial Determination) of Administrative Law Judge Luckern (ALJ) that the importation of certain Deere European version forage harvesters infringed one or more of Deere's federally registered trademarks, *Certain Agric. Vehicles & Components Thereof*, Inv. No. 337-TA-487 (Jan. 13, 2004) (*Initial Determination*), and granting a general exclusion order covering those forage harvesters as well as cease and desist orders against Bourdeau, OK, and other respondents, *Certain Agric. Vehicles & Components Thereof*, Inv. No. 337-TA-487 (Int'l Trade Comm'n Sept. 24, 2004) (*ITC Remedy Determination*). We vacate and remand.

I

On January 8, 2003, Intervenor Deere & Co. (Deere) filed a complaint with the ITC alleging violations of *19 U.S.C. § 1337* (section 1337) by the importation into the United States, and sale in the United States, of certain used agricultural vehicles that infringed United States Registered Trademark Nos. 1, 503,576, 1,502,103, 1,254,339, and 91,860 (the Deere trademarks). In particular, Deere alleged that Deere forage harvesters that had been manufactured solely for sale in Europe (the European version forage harvesters) were being imported into the United States. Deere argued that the European version forage harvesters were materially different from the forage harvesters manufactured and authorized for sale in the United States (the North American version forage harvesters). Thus, Deere claimed that the European version forage harvesters constituted "gray market goods" such that they infringed Deere's trademarks. The ITC commenced an investigation on February 7, 2003. On January 13, 2004, the ALJ issued his Initial Determination in which he found that appellants' importation of used Deere European version forage harvesters violated section 1337. The ALJ recommended that the ITC issue a general exclusion order covering the infringing Deere forage harvesters and cease and desist orders against Bourdeau, OK, and other non-appellant respondents. Appellants filed a Petition for Review on January 23, 2004, and on March 30, 2004, the ITC issued a notice indicating that it had decided not to review the Initial Determination. On May 14, 2004, after analyzing the proposed remedy and the effect of any remedial orders on the public interest, the ITC followed the ALJ's recommendation and issued both the general exclusion order and the cease and desist orders. Appellants timely filed a notice of appeal. We have jurisdiction pursuant to *28 U.S.C. § 1295(a)(6)*.

II

We review the factual findings of the Commission under the substantial evidence standard. *SKF USA, Inc. v. Int'l Trade Comm'n, 423 F.3d 1307, 1312 (Fed. Cir. 2005)*; *see 19 U.S.C. § 1337(c) (2000)*; *5 U.S.C. § 706(2)(E) (2000)*. Thus, we will not overturn the ITC's factual findings if they are supported by such relevant evidence as a reasonable mind might accept as adequate to support a conclusion. *SKF, 423 F.3d at 1312* (quoting *Finnigan Corp. v. Int'l Trade Comm'n, 180 F.3d 1354, 1362 (Fed. Cir. 1999))*. However, we review legal conclusions of the ITC *de novo*. *Id.* (citing *5 U.S.C. § 706(2)(A) (2000)*; *Checkpoint Sys. v. Int'l Trade Comm'n, 54 F.3d 756, 760 (Fed. Cir. 1995))*.

III

Section 1337(a)(1)(C) forbids "the importation into the United States, the sale for importation, or the sale within the United States after importation by the owner, importer, or consignee, of articles that infringe a valid and enforceable United States trademark registered under the Trademark Act of 1946." Thus, section 1337 grants the ITC the power to prevent the importation of goods that, if sold in the United States, would violate one of the provisions of the federal trademark statute, the Lanham Act.

Many of the goods that are forbidden from importation under section 1337 are what are referred to as "gray market goods": products that were "produced by the owner of the United States trademark or with its consent, but not authorized for sale in the United States." *Gamut Trading Co. v. Int'l Trade Comm'n, 200 F.3d 775, 777 (Fed. Cir. 1999)*. The rationale behind preventing importation of these goods is that the public associates a trademark with goods having certain characteristics. Id. at 778-79. To the extent that foreign goods bearing a trademark have different characteristics than those trademarked goods authorized for sale in the United States, the public is likely to become confused or deceived as to which characteristics are properly associated with the trademark, thereby possibly eroding the goodwill of the trademark holder in the United States. Id. at 779.

Thus, gray market theory recognizes both the territorial boundaries of trademarks and a trademark owner's right to control the qualities or characteristics associated with a trademark in a certain territorial region. As such, the basic question in gray market cases "is not whether the mark was validly affixed" to the goods, "but whether there are differences between the foreign and domestic product and if so whether the differences are material." *Id.* We have applied "a low threshold of materiality, requiring no more than showing that consumers would be likely to consider the differences between the foreign and domestic products to be significant when purchasing the product." *Id.*

However, even though the threshold of materiality is low, "a plaintiff in a gray market trademark infringement case must establish that *all or substantially all* of its sales are accompanied by the asserted material difference in order to show that its goods are materially different." *SKF, 423 F.3d at 1315* (emphasis added). As we noted in *SKF*, the sale by a trademark owner of the very same goods that he claims are gray market goods is inconsistent with a claim that consumers will be confused by those alleged gray market goods. *Id.* "To permit recovery by a trademark owner when less than 'substantially all' of its goods bear the material difference . . . would allow the owner itself to contribute to the confusion by consumers that it accuses gray market importers of creating." *Id.* That is, a trademark owner has the right to determine the set of characteristics that are associated with his trademark in the United States; however, a trademark owner cannot authorize the sale of trademarked goods with a set of characteristics and at the same time claim that the set of characteristics should not be associated with the trademark.

This case involves the importation and sale of used forage harvesters manufactured by Deere. Deere sells 5000 and 6000 series forage harvesters in both the United States and Europe through a network of authorized dealers and distributors. The 5000 series is manufactured exclusively in the United States, regardless of the market for which it is destined, while the 6000 series is manufactured exclusively in Germany. Both the 5000 and 6000 series for age harvesters fit generally into two categories: the North American version forage harvesters, which are manufactured for sale in the United States and North America, and the European version forage harvesters, which are manufactured for sale in Europe. Although the North American and European version forage harvesters are sold under the same series numbers, they have certain differences, including labeling differences and differences in certain safety features, discussed at greater length below.

Appellants are involved in the importation into the United States and the resale of used European version forage harvesters of both the 5000 and 6000 series. The ITC determined that the European versions of these forage harvesters are materially different from their North American counterparts and that the importation and sale of these forage harvesters violates section 1337.

IV

As a threshold matter, appellants argue that, because the 5000 series forage harvesters are manufactured in the United States, they are not "gray market goods" and thus that importation and sale of these forage harvesters cannot violate section 1337. Appellants point to the Supreme Court's decision *K Mart Corp. v. Cartier, Inc., 486 U.S. 281, 108 S. Ct. 1811, 100 L. Ed. 2d 313 (1987),* in which the Court, while addressing whether certain Customs regulations were consistent with *19 U.S.C. § 1526*, discussed the meaning of the term "gray market goods." The Court noted that a gray market good is "a foreign-manufactured good, bearing a valid United States trademark, that is imported without the consent of the United States trademark holder." K Mart, 486 U.S. at 285. Although the Court did not purport to exclusively define the term "gray market goods" in *K Mart*, it articulated three of the scenarios in which a gray market may exist:

> The prototypical gray market victim (case 1) is a domestic firm that purchases from an independent foreign firm the rights to register and use the latter's trademark as a United States trademark and to sell its foreign-manufactured products here . . . . The second context (case 2) is a situation in which a domestic firm registers the United States trademark for goods that are manufactured abroad by an affiliated manufacturer . . . and in the third context (case 3), the domestic holder of a United States trademark *authorizes* an independent foreign manufacturer to use it. Usually the holder sells to the foreign manufacturer an exclusive right to use the trademark in a particular foreign location, but conditions the right on the foreign manufacturer's promise not to import its trademarked goods into the United States.

Id. at 286-87 (emphasis in original). Appellants argue that the Court did not include in these three scenarios a case in which a domestic firm manufactures a product in the United States for sale abroad and that good is re-imported to the United States for later sale without the trademark owner's permission. Thus, appellants argue that a good manufactured domestically for export cannot be a "gray market good" and hence cannot violate section 1337.

However, *K Mart* did not address violations of either section 1337 or of the Lanham Act. Rather, the case discussed gray market theory as the background to an analysis of whether certain Customs regulations were consistent with section 526 of the Tariff Act of 1930, *19 U.S.C. § 1526*, which attempted to regulate, for the first time, the importation of "gray market goods." *See K Mart, 486 U.S. at 285-87.* Both the regulation at issue, *19 C.F.R. § 133.21*, and 19 U.S.C. § 1526 specifically refer to "foreign-made articles" or "merchandise of foreign manufacture." Id. at 287-88 (quoting *19 C.F.R. § 133.21 (1987)* and 19 U.S.C. *§ 1526*). Thus, it is not surprising that the Court's description of gray market theory focused on goods of foreign manufacture. Further, the Court noted that "the regulations implementing § 526 . . . have not applied the prohibition to all gray-market goods." Id. at 288.

Thus, *K Mart* should not be read to limit gray market theory, as it is applied in the context of section 1337, to goods of foreign manufacture.

In addition, the ITC has already determined that trademarked goods manufactured in the United States exclusively for sale in foreign countries may violate section 1337 if they are imported into the United States without the trademark owner's permission and if they are materially different from the trademarked goods authorized for sale in the United States. *See Certain Cigarettes & Packaging, Thereof,* Inv. No. 337-TA-424, USITC Pub. 3366, Commission Opinion at 2, n.2 (Int'l Trade Comm'n, Oct. 16, 2000) (*Cigarettes*) (finding that cigarettes manufactured in the United States but intended for sale exclusively abroad violated section 1337). Although the ITC expressly declined to refer to the goods in Cigarettes as "gray market goods," using instead the terms "for-export" or "re-imported," the ITC analyzed whether the goods violated section 1337 using the "material difference" standard we applied in *Gamut*.[1]

Indeed, section 1337(a)(1)(C) makes no reference to the term "gray market." In addition, unlike the statute at issue in K Mart, it does not distinguish between goods of domestic manufacture and goods of foreign manufacture. Rather, the statute simply declares unlawful "the importation into the United States, the sale for importation, or the sale within the United States after importation by the owner, importer, or consignee, of articles that infringe a valid and enforceable United States trademark registered under the Trademark Act of 1946." *19 U.S.C. § 1337(a)(1)(C).*

Finally, although this court noted in *Gamut* that "the term 'gray market goods' refers to genuine goods that *in this case* are of foreign manufacture," we did not expressly limit the term "gray market goods"—nor yet the reach of section 1337—to foreign-manufactured goods. *200 F.3d at 778* (emphasis added). Rather, we noted that "the principle of gray market law is that the importation of a product that was produced by the owner of the United States trademark or with its consent, but not authorized for sale in the United States, may, in appropriate cases infringe the United States trademark." Id. at 777. Thus, gray market law is not concerned with where the good was manufactured, nor is it concerned with whether the trademark owner controlled the manufacture of the product or authorized the use of the trademark on that product in another country. Instead, gray market law is concerned with whether the trademark owner has authorized use of the trademark on that particular product in the United States and thus whether the trademark owner

---

1 Many district courts have also found that the importation or sale of products manufactured domestically exclusively for export may constitute trademark infringement. *See R.J. Reynolds Tobacco Co. v. Premium Tobacco Stores, Inc., 2004 U.S. Dist. LEXIS 13443, 71 USPQ2d 1670, 1673-74 (N.D. Ill. 2004)*; *Am. Home Prods. v. Reliance Trading Co., 2000 U.S. Dist. LEXIS 16489, 55 USPQ2d 1756 (C.D. Cal. 2000)*; *R.J. Reynolds Tobacco Co. v. Premium Tobacco Stores, Inc., 1999 U.S. Dist. LEXIS 10706, 52 USPQ2d 1052, 1054 (N.D. Ill. 1999)*; *Philip Morris, Inc. v. Allen Distribs., Inc., 48 F. Supp. 2d 844, 852 (S.D. Ind. 1999)*; *Philip Morris Inc. v. Cigarettes for Less, 69 F. Supp. 2d 1181, 1184 n.6 (N.D. Cal. 1999), aff'd, 215 F.3d 1333 (9th Cir. 2000).*

has control over the specific characteristics associated with the trademark in the United States.

As such, we agree with the ITC, and we hold that the importation and sale of a trademarked good of domestic manufacture, produced solely for sale abroad and not authorized by the owner of the trademark for sale in the United States, may violate section 1337 if the imported good is materially different from all or substantially all of those goods bearing the same trademark that are authorized for sale in the United States.

V

In order to find a violation of section 1337, the imported goods must be materially different from all or substantially all of those trademarked goods authorized for sale in the United States. The materiality threshold is low, "requiring no more than showing that consumers would be likely to consider the differences between the foreign and domestic products to be significant when purchasing the product, for such differences would suffice to erode the goodwill of the domestic source." *Gamut, 200 F.3d at 779*. Indeed, there need only be one material difference between a domestic and a foreign product in order to determine that the latter is a gray market good eligible for exclusion. *See, e.g.*, id. at 780-82 (affirming ITC finding of material difference based solely on the absence of English-language warning and instructional labels on foreign goods) . However, the "plaintiff . . . must establish that all or substantially all of its sales are accompanied by the asserted material difference in order to show that its goods are materially different." *SKF, 423 F.3d at 1315*.

In this case, the ALJ found that there were numerous differences between the European and North American versions of both the 5000 and 6000 series forage harvesters that a customer in the United States would be likely to consider significant when purchasing the product. *Initial Determination*, slip op. at 19. While, for the most part, the appellants do not contest the existence of differences between the North American and European version forage harvesters, they argue that substantial evidence does not support the ALJ's findings that these differences are material.[2]

However, substantial evidence supports the ALJ's determination that there are several differences between the North American and European version forage harvesters of both the 5000 and 6000 series that a customer would be likely to consider significant when purchasing the product. Both the 5000 and 6000 series harvesters contain differences in safety features that a customer would be likely to consider significant when purchasing the product. First of all, there are material

2 Appellants contest only whether there are differences in the warranty services supplied to North American and European version forage harvesters. However, as noted below, it is unnecessary to address differences in warranty services, as other differences suffice to render the North American and European version forage harvesters materially different.

differences between the lighting configuration and lighting functions of the North American and European forage harvesters, including the type of lights used during transport, the manner in which hazard lights and turn signals function, and whether safety warning lamps exist. There are also material differences between the warning labels and safety decals on the North American forage harvesters, which carry pictures and English writing, and European forage harvesters, which carry only pictures. *See* In re Certain Agric. Tractors Under 50 Power Takeoff Horsepower, 44 USPQ2d 1385, 1402 (Int'l Trade Comm'n 1997) ("*Tractors*") (finding that the absence of English-language warning and instructional labels on foreign goods constituted a material difference), *aff'd*, *Gamut, 200 F.3d 775*.

There are several other material differences between the North American and European versions of both the 5000 and 6000 series forage harvesters. There is a material difference in the hitch mechanism of the North American and European forage harvesters, as the mechanism in the European forage harvesters is not compatible with wagons used in North America. In addition, the operator's manuals of the European version forage harvesters are in the language of the target country, while the American forage harvesters' manuals are in English. Although appellants claim that North American manuals are often provided to purchasers of European version forage harvesters, this only serves to heighten confusion, as the North American and European manuals contain different information due to other differences in the products.

Finally, there are differences in the services provided along with the machines, including the Deere Product Improvement Programs (PIPs) and Service Information System (SIS). Although all three types of Deere's PIPs—mechanical, fix-it fail, and safety—are free to customers who have purchased American forage harvesters, the owners of European forage harvesters only qualify for safety PIPs. Further, the SIS, which records details about past PIPs, differs depending on the PIPs for which a machine is available, such that more information is available for North American forage harvesters than European forage harvesters.[3]

VI

While the ALJ properly determined that there are material differences between the North American and European forage harvesters, Deere did not establish that all

3 In addition to the material differences between North American and European version forage harvesters that are present in both the 5000 and 6000 series, there are several differences specific to the 6000 series forage harvesters, including differences in seatbelts, seat switches, backup alarms, cutterhead alarms, hydraulic lockout switches, and the maximum ground travel speed of the machine. In addition, the ALJ found that the warranty services provided by Deere differ for the North American and European version foreign harvesters. However, in *Gamut, 200 F.3d at 780-82*, we affirmed a finding of trademark infringement based upon a single material difference in the products. Since we have determined that substantial evidence shows several material differences in both lines of forage harvesters, it is unnecessary to address those differences specific to the 6000 series forage harvesters and any differences in warranty coverage.

or substantially all of its sales were accompanied by these asserted material differences. That is, Deere did not establish that all or substantially all of its sales in the United States were of North American forage harvesters.

In their briefing to the ALJ and to this court, appellants argued that Deere actually sold European forage harvesters in the United States through its network of authorized dealers. In particular, appellants argued that, as early as 1997 and continuing through July of 2003, certain Deere dealers with authority from Deere sold used European forage harvesters in the United States. Appellants asserted that more than fifty used European forage harvesters were sold to them by authorized Deere dealers in the United States and in Europe, and that authorized Deere dealers purchased more than ten European forage harvesters from them. Appellants additionally argued that Deere was aware of the sales of European forage harvesters in the United States as early as 1999, but took no action to stop these sales by authorized Deere dealers until at least 2002. Indeed, appellants argued that Deere permitted its corporate employees to assist authorized dealers in the importation, purchase, and sale of European forage harvesters in the United States, and that "in some instances Deere corporate representatives assisted authorized Deere dealers prior to the sale of European harvesters to U.S. customers." Pet. Br. at 21.

In support of its argument that Deere authorized the sales of European forage harvesters in the United States, appellants also noted that Deere installed cutterhead rotational alarms, a safety device, on certain European forage harvesters located in the United States. Further, appellants argued that Deere promoted the sale of European forage harvesters in the United States through its website www.machinefinder.com. This website, which is owned and operated by Deere, allows consumers to search for forage harvesters through the worldwide network of authorized Deere dealers, providing information about individual machines and contact information for their sellers, such that United States consumers can search for European forage harvesters offered for sale by authorized Deere dealers in Europe. Thus, appellants argue that Deere, through its authorized dealers, imported and sold European forage harvesters in the United States.

If appellants are correct that Deere authorized such United States sales of European forage harvesters, and if such sales were sufficient in number to show that not all or substantially all of Deere's United States sales were not materially different, Deere would not be entitled to section 1337 relief. Indeed, the ALJ recognized this point, stating during the hearing that "if John Deere authorizes the importation of [European forage harvesters], then the Staff agree there are no material differences."[4] Transcript of Hearing at 2365, *Certain Agric. Vehicles & Components Thereof*, Inv. No. 337-TA-487 (Sept. 30, 2003).

---

4 We assume that the ALJ's understanding with regard to this point was premised on the Fifth Circuit's opinion in *Martin's Herend Imports, Inc. v. Diamond & Gem Trading U.S.A. Co., 112 F.3d 1296, 1304 (5th Cir. 1997)*, in which the court held that "the sale of even one authorized porcelain piece would have resulted in the denial of relief with respect to all porcelain

Deere responded by arguing that the sales of European forage harvesters in the United States were by a small number of dealers who did not have authority to engage in such sales. Deere claimed that once it learned that these dealers were engaged in the importation and sale of European forage harvesters, it ordered them to cease doing so and threatened to include these dealers as respondents in the instant case. Further, Deere claimed that it informed its dealers that it would no longer provide warranty services for illegally imported European forage harvesters.

Appellants made their assertions regarding the sale of European forage harvesters by authorized Deere dealers in two different contexts. First, appellants asserted affirmative defenses to Deere's claims. Appellants argued that Deere was estopped from asserting its trademark infringement claims because authorized Deere dealers had apparent authority to sell European forage harvesters, Bourdeau's Post-Hearing Reply Br. at 34, and that Deere's claims were barred by its "unclean hands" as it had permitted its authorized dealers to sell European forage harvesters in the United States, *id.* at 41. However, appellants also argued that Deere had failed to establish its prima facie case, *i.e.*, the existence of a material difference between the accused products and products authorized for sale in the United States, because "Deere, through its authorized distribution network, has imported, exported, purchased and sold the *exact same European harvesters* which form the basis of its claims against [appellants]." Bourdeau's Post-Hearing Br. at 13 (emphasis in original). That is, appellants argued that Deere had not established that "all or substantially all of its sales [we] re accompanied by the asserted material difference." *SKF, 423 F.3d at 1315.*

Although the ALJ did not err in rejecting these particular defenses, he never considered these arguments as part of Deere's prima facie case. Relying primarily on the testimony of Deere's corporate witness, Mr. Meister, the ALJ found that *appellants* had failed to bear their burden of proving the affirmative defenses of estoppel and unclean hands. The ALJ noted in particular that appellants "have not established that Deere somehow fraudulently or deceptively used the marks in issue to facilitate the importation of European version [forage harvesters] into the United States" and that the appellants "did not establish the apparent authority of Deere's dealers to authorize gray market imports." *Initial Determination*, slip op. at 147. The ALJ did not find that *Deere* had established that the sales of European forage harvesters by Deere dealers were not authorized, such that all of Deere's sales were of North American forage harvesters, or that, even if the sales of the European forage harvesters were authorized, the number of European forage

---

pieces of 'the same quality from the same product line.'" *SKF, 423 F.3d at 1316* (quoting *Martin's Herend, 112 F.3d at 1304*). However, at the time of the hearing, we had not yet issued our decision in *SKF*, wherein we refined the rule of *Martin's Herend*, holding that "[a] single sale of a nonconforming item typically should not defeat a trademark owner's protection," but that "a trademark owner must show that all or substantially all of its authorized goods are accompanied by each of the claimed material differences to satisfy that standard." *Id.* Thus, the ALJ did not have the benefit of *SKF* when issuing his Initial Determination.

harvesters sold was so small that substantially all of Deere's sales were of North American forage harvesters. Indeed, Deere, in attempting to distinguish *SKF* from the instant case, argues that "Appellants have failed to quantify Deere's overall sales and the relative ration or alleged non-conforming sales, much less established a ratio of non-conforming sale approaching [that of *SKF*]." Deere's Letter of Nov. 17, 2005 at 2. However, *SKF* clearly places the burden on Deere to establish that all or substantially all of the sales were materially different from the alleged gray market goods. Thus, we must remand this case to the ITC for a determination of whether Deere bore its burden under *SKF*.

Indeed, because *SKF* places the burden on Deere of establishing that all or substantially all of the authorized sales in the United States were of North American forage harvesters, the ITC must presume that sales by authorized dealers were in fact authorized by Deere. To hold otherwise would enable a plaintiff to simply disclaim the sales of any products that do not contain the alleged material differences; Deere could disclaim the sales of any European forage harvesters by simply asserting that such sales were not authorized. On remand, Deere may rebut the presumption that all sales by its authorized dealers were authorized. However, Deere bears the burden of proving that sales of European forage harvesters by its authorized dealers were not authorized sales.

Nonetheless, even if Deere cannot establish on remand that the sales of European forage harvesters by authorized Deere dealers were not authorized, it may still prevail if it can establish that the number of sales of European forage harvesters was so small that substantially all of Deere's sales in the United States were of North American forage harvesters, such that substantially all of the authorized sales were of goods bearing the asserted material differences. As the burden of proof to establish trademark infringement is preponderance of the evidence, *see, e.g., KP Permanent Make-Up, Inc. v. Lasting Impression I, Inc., 543 U.S. 111, 120, 125 S. Ct. 542, 160 L. Ed. 2d 440 (2004)*, we hold that Deere must meet its burdens by a preponderance of the evidence.

VII

Finally, the appellants argue that the ITC erred in granting a general exclusion order that did not contain an exception for goods bearing a permanent nonremovable label indicating their origin. However, because we vacate the ITC decision affirming the ALJ's Initial Determination, we do not reach appellants' challenge to the remedy. For the reasons stated above, we vacate and remand.

COSTS

No costs.

VACATE AND REMAND

DOW JONES & COMPANY, INC.
v.
INTERNATIONAL SECURITIES EXCHANGE, INC.

451 F.3d 295 (2d Cir. 2006)
Decided June 16, 2006

ROBERT P. LOBUE, Patterson Belknap Webb & Tyler LLP (Stuart A. Karle, General Counsel, The Wall Street Journal; Deborah T. Revesz, Assistant General Counsel, Dow Jones & Company, Inc.; Adeel A Mangi, Joanne N. Kwong, Patterson Belknap Webb & Tyler LLP, of counsel), New York, NY, for Plaintiff-Appellant Dow Jones & Company, Inc.

R. BRUCE RICH, Weil, Gotshal & Manges LLP (Irwin H. Warren, Elizabeth S. Weiswasser, Benjamin E. Marks, of counsel), New York, NY, for Plaintiff-Appellant The McGraw-Hill Companies, Inc.

ANDREW L. DEUTSCH, DLA Piper Rudnick Gray Cary US LLP (Michael J. Simon, General Counsel, International Securities Exchange, Inc.; Monica P. McCabe, Christine M. Jaskiewicz, DLA Piper Rudnick Gray Cary US LLP, of counsel), New York, NY, for Defendant-Appellee International Securities Exchange, Inc.

PETER J. TOREN, Sidley Austin Brown & Wood LLP (Tracey Russell Seraydarian, of counsel), New York, NY, for Defendant-Appellee The Options Clearing Corporation.

Douglass B. Maynard, Akin Gump Strauss Hauer & Feld LLP (Karol A. Kepchar, James J. Benjamin, Jr., Rex S. Heinke, Michael D. Lockard, of counsel), New York, NY, for Amici Curiae The Nasdaq Stock Market, Inc., Wilshire Associates Incorporated, The FTSE International Limited and Barclays Global Investors, N.A.

David E. Jacoby, Schiff Hardin LLP (Paul E. Dengel, of counsel), New York, NY; Michele L. Odorizzi, Mayer Brown Rowe & Maw, Chicago, IL; for Amici Curiae Chicago Board Options Exchange, Inc., and Board of Trade of the City of Chicago, Inc.

Edward F. Maluf, Bingham McCutchen (Nia Cross, Susanna Y.Y. Chu, of counsel), New York, NY, for Amici Curiae Archipelago Holdings, Inc., Pacific Exchange, Inc., Boston Stock Exchange, Inc., and Boston Options Exchange Group, LLC.

David M. Battan, General Counsel, Interactive Brokers Group LLC, Washington, D.C., for Amicus Curiae Interactive Brokers Group LLC.

Before: LEVAL, SOTOMAYOR, Circuit Judges, and KRAVITZ, District Judge.[1]

OPINION

Leval, *Circuit Judge*:

This appeal raises a narrow and highly specific question—whether an options exchange, by creating, listing, and facilitating the trading of options on shares in an exchange traded fund ("ETF") designed to track a proprietary market index, misappropriates intellectual-property rights of the creator of the index. The district court found no such infringement, and we agree.

Plaintiffs Dow Jones & Company, Inc. ("Dow Jones") and The McGraw-Hill Companies, Inc. ("McGraw-Hill") appeal from the rulings of the United States District Court for the Southern District of New York (Harold Baer, J.), which dismissed their complaints against defendants International Securities Exchange, Inc. ("ISE"), an options exchange, and Options Clearing Corporation ("OCC"), an options clearing agency. Dow Jones appeals also from the denial of its motion for a preliminary injunction.[2]

Each plaintiff is the originator of a widely known index, which reflects an average of the stock market value of the shares in major United States companies. Dow Jones is the creator of the Dow Jones Industrial Average ("DJIA"), which reflects the averages of the stock market value of the shares of thirty leading United States companies. McGraw-Hill, through its Standard & Poor division ("S&P"), is the creator of the S&P 500 Index ("S&P 500"), which reflects the average of the stock market value of the shares of 500 leading United States companies. Dow Jones and McGraw-Hill have each licensed the creation of an ETF, designed to track the performance of its index, and to provide a vehicle for public investment in a pool of securities which reflects the performance of the index. The ETF in each case consists of a basket of securities, being shares of the companies used to calculate the market average, weighted in the same proportions as in the average. Dow Jones licensed the creation of the DIAMONDS ETF, which tracks the performance of the DJIA, and McGraw-Hill licensed the creation of an ETF under the name Stan-

---

1 The Honorable Mark R. Kravitz, United States District Judge for the District of Connecticut, sitting by designation.

2 These two actions were consolidated in the district court, and the appeals were heard in tandem before this court.

dard & Poor Depositary Receipts, or SPDR (pronounced "spider"), which tracks the performance of the S&P 500. By purchasing shares in the DIAMONDS and SPDR funds, members of the public are able to buy and sell shares that are backed by the securities which make up the DJIA and the S&P 500, and therefore rise and fall with those indexes.[3]

Defendant ISE, an options trading exchange, which creates and markets its own indexes, announced in 2005 its intention to offer options trading on shares of DIAMONDS and SPDRs. Defendant OCC, a clearing organization for options trading, announced that it would clear trades in those options on the ISE. Options are contracts which give the purchaser of the option the right, but not the obligation, to buy or sell a security at a specified price (the "strike price"), on or before a specified date. The buyer of a call option has the right to buy the optioned security at a specified price at or before a specified date. The buyer of a put option has the right to sell the optioned security at a specified price at or before a specified date. Although in theory an option contract is to be settled by the purchase or sale of the optioned security in accordance with the rights created by the option contract, in practice settlement is generally effectuated by a cash payment representing the difference between the market price and the strike price.

Following ISE's announcements of its intention to institute trading in options for DIAMONDS and SPDRs, the plaintiffs brought this suit. The complaints allege that by issuing and trading options on DIAMONDS and SPDRs the defendants will misappropriate plaintiffs' intellectual-property interest in the underlying indexes and engage in unfair competition. They allege as well that through the marketing of these options, the defendants will infringe on, and dilute, plaintiffs' trademarks. We conclude that the defendants' intended actions alleged in the complaints do not infringe on any intellectual-property interest or trademark of the plaintiffs.

BACKGROUND

A. Factual Background

The facts asserted in the complaints, viewed in the light most favorable to plaintiffs, are recited below in greater detail.

---

3 The actions of arbitrageurs, coupled with the ETF issuers' readiness at all times to issue new blocks of ETF shares in exchange for portfolios of the underlying securities comprising the tracked index, and vice versa, ensures that, despite growing or diminishing demand for the shares of the ETF, its market value will not deviate significantly from the market value of the securities constituting the fund. While the parties disagree as to how closely the ETFs track their respective indexes, we believe there is no dispute that the actions of arbitrageurs, seeking to profit from any separation that develops between the prices of the ETF shares and the underlying portfolios, will constantly push the two into virtual parity.

1. McGraw-Hill & SPDRs

McGraw-Hill is a company engaged in educational publishing, financial services, business information, and media services. One of its divisions is S&P, which develops and publishes financial indexes, investment analysis, debt ratings, and other financial services. S&P has been calculating and maintaining the S&P 500 Index since 1957. The S&P 500 Index includes a representative sampling of leading companies in major industries and is regarded as a leading benchmark for measuring the stock performance of large United States companies. The composition of the S&P 500 is regularly reviewed and revised by the S&P 500 Index Committee, which from time to time eliminates the stock of a company from the index, replacing it with another. The committee regularly adjusts its calculation of the S&P 500 to reflect changes affecting the capitalization of the component companies.

S&P licenses the use of the S&P 500 to financial institutions as a benchmark against which to measure the performance of publicly traded stocks. It also licenses the use of the S&P 500 as the basis for financial products that utilize the index. These licenses include grants of the right to use the S&P marks in the names of such products and in connection with a licensee's marketing and promotional efforts.

In 1993, by licensing the American Stock Exchange LLC ("Amex"), S&P authorized the creation of the SPDR fund, an ETF designed to track the performance of the S&P 500. The SPDR fund holds a basket of securities that reflects the components of the S&P 500 and their relative weighting within the index. Shares in the SPDR fund, known as SPDRs, thus constitute ownership interests in a unit investment trust holding a portfolio of securities virtually identical to the makeup of the S&P 500. Shares of the SPDR fund are traded on the Amex, just as if they were shares of common stock in a listed company. "SPDR" is a registered trademark of McGraw-Hill.

In early January 2005, ISE announced its intention to institute trading in options on SPDR shares. OCC, which clears options trades on ISE and other exchanges, announced that it would clear SPDR option trades on ISE.

On January 6, 2005, McGraw-Hill filed its complaint in the Southern District of New York to enjoin the defendants from instituting trading in SPDRs options.[4] Its complaint alleges that by creating, listing, and trading SPDR options, the defendants will misappropriate McGraw-Hill's intellectual property and engage in unfair competition under New York law. The complaint also claims that in marketing and promoting SPDR options, ISE will infringe and dilute McGraw-Hill's trademark rights under federal and state law.[5]

---

4 The initial complaint contained claims against ISE and OCC. On March 7, McGraw-Hill voluntarily dismissed its action against OCC without prejudice.

5 McGraw-Hill alleges trademark violations under § 32 and § 43 of the Lanham Act, as well as under New York common law and New York General Business Law § 360-l. The complaint

McGraw-Hill moved for a preliminary injunction, and the district court granted a Temporary Restraining Order ("TRO") pending a ruling on the motion. Prior to the expiration of the TRO, McGraw-Hill and ISE entered into a temporary license agreement permitting ISE to trade SPDR options during the pendency of the litigation without prejudice to the parties' respective positions. ISE moved to dismiss McGraw-Hill's complaint pursuant to Federal Rule of Civil Procedure 12(b)(6).

2. Dow Jones and DIAMONDS

Dow Jones gathers and publishes business and financial news information. Since 1896, Dow Jones has produced and published the DJIA. Since 1928, the DJIA has been based on the stocks of thirty companies, determined by Dow Jones to be leaders in their respective industries. The DJIA is a leading gauge of United States stock market performance. Dow Jones monitors the components of the DJIA and makes changes in the composition of the index for various reasons, including corporate acquisitions and shifts in a component company's core business, or to enhance the DJIA's reflection of the overall market. Dow Jones regularly adjusts the calculation of the DJIA to reflect changes affecting the capitalization of the component companies.

Dow Jones distributes the DJIA to a variety of real-time and delayed market data vendors pursuant to license agreements. Those vendors then redistribute the DJIA as permitted by those licenses. The standard license agreement used by Dow Jones requires information vendors and their subscribers to agree that they will not "use the Index[] as the basis of financial instruments or investment products (e.g., passively-managed funds) without a separate written agreement with Dow Jones for such purpose." Dow Jones also licenses the use of the DJIA for the creation of investment products that track the DJIA.

In 1997, by exclusive license agreement with the Amex, Dow Jones created the DIAMONDS fund, designed to track the DJIA. Like common stock in corporations, DIAMONDS shares are bought and sold on the Amex. By purchasing DIAMONDS shares, members of the public invest in a security which will move in tandem with the movements in the DJIA without having to purchase shares in the thirty companies that make up the DJIA. "DIAMONDS" is a registered trademark of Dow Jones.

Dow Jones has also exclusively licensed the Chicago Board Options Exchange ("CBOE") to create, issue, trade, market, and promote options on the DJIA, as well as options on DIAMONDS shares.[6] The CBOE engages in advertising to pro-

---

also contains a claim for money had and received. We do not discuss the latter claim and deem it waived, as McGraw-Hill has raised no arguments relating to it on appeal.

6 An option on an index, in terms of the legal rights of the parties, functions differently from an option on the shares of an ETF. An option directly on the index does not contemplate the purchase or sale of an ownership interest in a pool of securities. It is simply a bet on the future value of the index. If at the expiration date the index is above the value stated in the option

mote DIAMONDS options to prospective investors and to develop market depth and liquidity. Under the exclusive license, Dow Jones retains the right to review CBOE's marketing materials relating to DIAMONDS options, and to be indemnified by CBOE for claims arising from CBOE's actions. As with the CBOE market for DIAMONDS options, every investment product available in the United States based on the DJIA has been expressly authorized by a license from Dow Jones.

In May 2005, while McGraw-Hill's motion to dismiss was pending, ISE, which had no license for such activity, announced that it would begin to issue and trade options on DIAMONDS, and OCC announced that it would clear those trades. On May 24, Dow Jones brought suit, seeking to enjoin the defendants from issuing, listing, trading, marketing, promoting, and clearing DIAMONDS options. Dow Jones's complaint is almost identical to that of McGraw-Hill. It claims that defendants' proposed actions constitute unfair competition and misappropriation of Dow Jones's intellectual property in creating, maintaining, and disseminating the DJIA, as well as trademark infringement and dilution under federal and state law.[7] Dow Jones moved for a preliminary injunction; the district court granted a temporary restraining order pending its resolution of the motion.

B. The District Court Opinion

The actions by Dow Jones and McGraw-Hill were consolidated on June 7, 2005 pursuant to Federal Rule of Civil Procedure 42(a), and on June 8 and 13 the district court conducted a preliminary injunction hearing on Dow Jones's motion. On September 1, 2005, the district court issued a single opinion denying Dow Jones's motion for a preliminary injunction and dismissing McGraw-Hill's complaint. *See McGraw-Hill Cos. v. Int'l Sec. Exch., Inc., 2005 U.S. Dist. LEXIS 18674, Nos. 05 Civ. 1129, 05 Civ. 4954, 2005 WL 2100518 (S.D.N.Y. Sept. 1, 2005).* In dismissing McGraw-Hill's complaint, the district court added that "if a similar motion is made with respect to Dow's allegations against ISE and OCC, it will likely come to the same result." Id. at *9. On September 7, 2005, Dow Jones, ISE, and OCC stipulated, and the district court so-ordered, that the September 1 decision be deemed a dismissal of Dow Jones's complaint against ISE and OCC under Rule 12(b)(6) for the reasons stated in the district court opinion.

---

contract, the holder of a call option has the contractual right to receive the difference. If at the expiration date the index is below the value stated in the option contract, the holder of a put option has the contractual right to receive the difference.

7 Dow Jones's complaint also contains claims of tortious interference with contract and unjust enrichment. Dow Jones addresses these claims only in a cursory footnote in its initial appellate brief. We therefore deem them waived. *See Tolbert v. Queens College, 242 F.3d 58, 75 (2d Cir. 2001)* ("A contention is not sufficiently presented for appeal if it is conclusorily asserted only in a footnote."); *United States v. Restrepo, 986 F.2d 1462, 1463 (2d Cir. 1993)* ("We do not consider an argument mentioned only in a footnote to be adequately raised or preserved for appellate review."). Moreover, while Dow Jones points out that the district court failed to address these two claims, it presents no meaningful argument as to why they should not have been dismissed.

McGraw-Hill appeals from the dismissal of its complaint; Dow Jones appeals both from the denial of a preliminary injunction and the dismissal of its complaint.

DISCUSSION

We agree with the district court's conclusion, although not necessarily with every aspect of its reasoning, that the complaints fail to state a claim upon which relief may be granted and were therefore properly dismissed. Each complaint asserts two theories of wrongdoing. The first is that, by creating and maintaining the contemplated options markets, the defendants would misappropriate plaintiffs' intellectual property in their proprietary indexes and the ETFs tracking those indexes, and engage in unfair competition. The second is that defendants will infringe on, and dilute, plaintiffs' trademarks. Both sets of allegations are legally insufficient.

A. Misappropriation of Plaintiffs' Intellectual Property in Their Indexes

Plaintiffs claim that in issuing options contracts and providing a marketplace for trading such contracts, defendants engage in unfair competition and misappropriation of the plaintiffs' intellectual property. Plaintiffs have invested time, money, and intellectual creativity into the creation and maintenance of their indexes. Each argues that this gives it an intellectual-property right in the index itself, as well as in an ETF that tracks the index, and in options on shares of such an ETF. We assume, for purposes of this decision-though we do not reach this issue—that each of the plaintiffs possesses an exclusive intellectual—property right in the index it created and in the ETF which has been structured to duplicate the index.

Plaintiffs argue that because they have an intellectual-property right in the index and the ETF that tracks the index, defendants may not create, list, trade, and clear options on the ETF shares without licenses from plaintiffs. In order to succeed on their misappropriation and unfair competition claims, plaintiffs must establish some wrongful appropriation or use of the plaintiffs' intellectual property. *See Telecom Int'l Am., Ltd. v. AT&T Corp., 280 F.3d 175, 198 (2d Cir. 2001)* (affirming grant of summary judgment to defendant on plaintiff's unfair competition and misappropriation claims where plaintiff failed to show "some appropriation of an idea or knowledge in which [plaintiff] had a property interest or a contractual arrangement creating such an interest"); *Roy Export Co. Establishment v. Columbia Broad. Sys., 672 F.2d 1095, 1105 (2d Cir. 1982)* ("An unfair competition claim involving misappropriation usually concerns the taking and use of the plaintiff's property to compete against the plaintiff's own use of the same property."); *Metropolitan Opera Ass'n v. Wagner-Nichols Recorder Corp., 199 Misc. 786, 101 N.Y.S.2d 483, 493 (N.Y. Sup. Ct. 1950)* ("Clearly, some property rights in the plaintiffs and interference with and misappropriation of them by defendants are necessary to a cause of action."), *aff'd* 279 A.D. 632, 107 N.Y.S.2d 795 (1st Dep't 1951). In our view, the conduct attributed to the defendants in the complaints does not constitute a wrongful use or misappropriation under New York law of an intellectual-property interest of the plaintiffs. As a matter of law, therefore, plaintiffs cannot prevail on these claims.[8]

By authorizing the creation of ETFs using their proprietary formulas, and the sale of the ETF shares to the public, the plaintiffs have relinquished any right to control resale and public trading of those shares, notwithstanding the fact that plaintiffs' intellectual property may be embedded in the shares. Owners and would-be owners of ETF shares are free to negotiate with one another for the purchase and sale of the ETF shares plaintiffs have sold to the public. Because plaintiffs have permitted the buying and selling of the ETF shares, plaintiffs may not prevent exchanges from offering marketplaces for buyers and sellers to come together to effectuate their transactions. *See Nasdaq Stock Market, Inc. v. Archipelago Holdings, LLC, 336 F. Supp. 2d 294, 303-04 (S.D.N.Y. 2004)* ("*Archipelago*").

While an option to purchase or sell ETF shares is undoubtedly a new security, distinct from the ETF share itself, in essence it is nothing more than a means of conditional trading in ETF shares. Instead of directly buying and selling the ETF shares, parties enter into contracts creating a right to buy or sell the ETF shares on a future date. We see no reason why the plaintiffs' authorization of public sale of the ETF shares, which contain their proprietary technology, does not necessarily permit option trading in these shares—including the provision of marketplaces and mechanisms for such trading—just as it authorizes straightforward buying and selling of the shares.

Plaintiffs claim that in creating options on the ETF shares, the defendants will misappropriate their indexes. The possibility that, because of their approximate equivalency, defendants might consult the published index values, as a substitute for consulting ETF values, does not make it an infringement of the plaintiffs' rights in the indexes for the defendants to create and host the trading of such options. Plaintiffs intentionally disseminate their index values to inform the public. They cannot complain when the defendants do nothing more than draw information from that publication of the index values. The complaints do not specify any use of the indexes likely to be made by the defendants that would constitute misappropriation.[9]

---

8 Plaintiffs argue that New York's law of unfair competition is a "'broad and flexible doctrine that depends more upon the facts set forth . . . than in most causes of action.'" *Telecom Int'l, 280 F.3d at 197* (quoting *Roy Export, 672 F.2d at 1105*) (ellipsis in original). Whatever the breadth and flexibility of such a claim, it depends upon the allegation of facts that, if true, would constitute misuse of plaintiffs' property. We find no such allegation. (While defendants argue that *Nat'l Basketball Ass'n v. Motorola, Inc., 105 F.3d 841 (2d Cir. 1997)*, severely limits the scope of a misappropriation claim under New York law, *Motorola* did not purport to address the scope of a misappropriation claim where, as here, the information does not fall within the scope of federal copyright law.)

9 Our holding does not address the situation where a proprietary index is employed in the creation of a financial instrument. *See Standard & Poor's Corp. v. Commodity Exchange, Inc., 538 F. Supp. 1063 (S.D.N.Y. 1982), aff'd, Standard & Poor's Corp. v. Commodity Exchange, Inc., 683 F.2d 704 (2d Cir. 1982); Bd. of Trade v. Dow Jones & Co., Inc., 98 Ill. 2d 109, 456 N.E.2d 84, 74 Ill. Dec. 582 (Ill. 1983).*

Cf. Int'l News Serv. v. Associated Press, 248 U.S. 215, 39 S. Ct. 68, 63 L. Ed. 211 (1918); *Nat'l Basketball Ass'n v. Motorola, Inc., 105 F.3d 841 (2d Cir. 1997).*

Prior judicial rulings on similar questions are infrequent. All are consistent with our ruling on these facts. In *Archipelago*, the plaintiff, Nasdaq, had created the Nasdaq-100 index and an ETF, QQQ, which tracked that index. Defendants hosted and facilitated the trading of QQQ shares on the ArcaEx exchange, without a license from Nasdaq. Nasdaq made claims similar to those now advanced by plaintiffs—that by entertaining a market for the trading of QQQ shares, the defendant exchange was misappropriating Nasdaq's intellectual property in those shares. The district court dismissed the claim. The court ruled that, regardless of any intellectual-property interest Nasdaq held in the QQQ fund, no such interest was infringed when an exchange provided a marketplace for the trading of the shares Nasdaq had sold to the public. *Id.*

The opinion relied in part on a Ninth Circuit decision, *Golden Nugget, Inc. v. American Stock Exchange, Inc., 828 F.2d 586 (9th Cir. 1987).* In that case, the Golden Nugget corporation brought suit against the American Stock Exchange, alleging that by issuing, listing, and trading options on Golden Nugget stock without Golden Nugget's consent, the exchange misappropriated Golden Nugget's property, engaged in unfair competition, and infringed on the Golden Nugget trademark. The court dismissed the complaint, ruling essentially that, having sold its stock to the public, Golden Nugget had relinquished "any propriety rights in the shares . . . that would allow it to control the manner or means of resale." Id. at 590; *see also Champion Parts, Inc. v. Oppenheimer & Co., 878 F.2d 1003, 1008 (7th Cir. 1989)* (agreeing with the *Golden Nugget* analysis). The defendants accordingly were free to create options and facilitate trading in the options without offending any property interest of Golden Nugget.

The district court in *Archipelago* reasoned that, just as in *Golden Nugget* no property interest of the plaintiff in shares of its stock owned by its shareholders would permit it to control resale of those shares, Nasdaq did not possess a property interest in QQQ shares owned by investors that would permit it to control a secondary market. *Archipelago, 336 F. Supp. 2d at 303.* We agree with the Archipelago court that once an index creator (or its licensee) has created a fund of securities tracking the index and has sold shares in the fund to the public, those who engage in secondary trading of the fund's shares, or provide a marketplace for such trading, do not infringe on a property interest of the creator of the index and the fund.[10]

---

10 In one respect, we take issue with various pertinent court opinions. Repeatedly, courts have introduced their discussions with the proposition that the crucial question in such cases is whether the plaintiff retains an intellectual-property interest in securities it has sold to the public. *See, e.g.Golden Nugget, 828 F.2d at 590* ("To succeed on any of its claims, Golden Nugget must persuade us that it has a property or other protectable interest in Golden Nugget common stock owned by its shareholders."); *Archipelago, 336 F. Supp. 2d at 303* ("The question that underlies each of the common law causes of action is whether Nasdaq has the type of interest in the QQQ product that is capable of being protected by a license."); *McGraw-Hill,*

The same reasoning applies to options on shares in the DIAMONDS and SPDR funds. As plaintiffs acknowledge in their complaints, the options in question confer on the holder the right, but not the obligation, to buy or sell shares in the ETFs for a specified price on or before a certain date. When ISE creates, lists, and facilitates the trading of these options, and OCC clears trades in these options, the defendants are simply enabling investors to trade in future rights to buy or sell shares of ETFs. *See also Golden Nugget, 828 F.2d at 591.* Our ruling that such action offends no exclusive intellectual-property right of the creators of the indexes and the ETFs is consistent with the judgments in Archipelago and Golden Nugget.[11]

Plaintiffs argue that *Standard & Poor's Corp. v. Commodity Exchange, Inc., 538 F. Supp. 1063 (S.D.N.Y. 1982)* ("*Comex I*"), *aff'dStandard & Poor's Corp. v. Commodity Exchange, Inc., 683 F.2d 704 (2d Cir. 1982)* ("*Comex II*"), and *Board of Trade v. Dow Jones & Co., Inc., 98 Ill. 2d 109, 456 N.E.2d 84, 74 Ill. Dec. 582 (Ill. 1983)* ("*Board of Trade*"), are to the contrary. We disagree because of substantial differences between the contract rights involved in those cases and options on ETF shares.

In *Comex*, defendant Comex, a commodities exchange, was poised to publish the value of the S&P 500 index, giving it the name "Comex 500 Stock Index," and to create, issue, and trade futures contracts based upon that index. These contracts called for settlement in cash, based on the difference between the contracted value and the closing value of the S&P 500. *See Comex I, 538 F. Supp. at 1065.* S&P

---

*2005 U.S. Dist. LEXIS 18674, 2005 WL 2100518, at *1* ("This action poses the question—can there be a valid property right in trading options on index-tracking stocks without a license from the index providers?"). While it is surely true that a plaintiff cannot succeed on a claim of this nature without showing that it has an intellectual-property interest in the securities, it does not follow that the plaintiff will prevail if it makes that demonstration. Ultimately the question is not whether the plaintiff *has* intellectual-property rights in the securities designed according to the plaintiff's proprietary formulas, but rather whether *the actions* of the defendants relating to the markets for those securities *infringe* any property rights of the plaintiff. To illustrate by analogy to trademark rights, in all probability the plaintiff in *Golden Nugget* retained a trademark in the trade name "Golden Nugget." Nonetheless, so long as the defendant did not create confusion by improper use of the "Golden Nugget" name, the making of an option market for the shares (including describing those options by using the "Golden Nugget" name), did not infringe the plaintiff's rights. In this case we express no view as to what property right, if any, plaintiffs retain in the index values released to the public. *Cf. Int'l News Serv. v. Associated Press, 248 U.S. 215, 39 S. Ct. 68, 63 L. Ed. 211 (1918)* (affirming the grant of a preliminary injunction barring International News Service from copying or paraphrasing articles published by the Associated Press in East Coast newspapers and publishing them in West Coast Newspapers). We hold only that the conduct alleged in the complaints does not constitute an infringement of any such property right.

11 Plaintiffs seek to distinguish this case from *Archipelago* by reference to the *Archipelago* court's emphasis on the fact that the defendant exchange had not created a new security linked to the plaintiff's index, *Archipelago, 336 F. Supp. 2d at 303*, which they argue has been done in this case. However, it is the securities created by plaintiffs (i.e., the ETF shares) that depend on the plaintiffs' indexes. By creating options for trading the securities created by plaintiffs, defendants have merely provided a method for buying and selling those securities.

brought suit to restrain Comex from trading a futures contract based on the use of S&P's name or the S&P 500 index.

The district court found that Comex "intended improperly . . . to misappropriate the property of the plaintiff and to trade directly on . . . the S&P 500 Stock Index," id. at 1065, and that "Comex is misappropriating the S&P 500 Index and the skills, expenditures, labor and reputation of S&P in generating and producing the S&P 500 Index, for Comex's own advantage and profit by creating a futures contract based on the S&P 500 Index," id. at 1071. The district court granted a preliminary injunction restraining Comex from marketing and trading the futures contracts based on the S&P 500. To maintain the status quo until trial, the Court of Appeals affirmed the preliminary injunction, but a majority of the court relied only on the public interest in avoiding harm that might befall investors if trading in the options were instituted and then abruptly cut off. Id. at 711-12. The Court of Appeals expressed no view on the merits of the question of infringement.[12]

The district court's grant of a preliminary injunction in Comex I is not a precedent that substantially favors plaintiffs because the facts of that case are significantly different than those before us. In *Comex*, the futures contracts created by the defendants did not give rights in any basket of securities. Their value depended on a number—the number generated by the plaintiff's formula (and copied by defendants). The purchasers of the defendant's contracts bought the right to receive a payment of a size dependent on the number produced by plaintiff's index as of a future date. The factor that most influenced the decisions in *Archipelago* and *Golden Nugget* (as well as in the district court below), the fact that the plaintiff had sold shares to the public and therefore could not control the secondary market for those shares, was not present in *Comex*.

---

12 Plaintiffs contend that the ruling of the Court of Appeals favors their position. However, the court's ruling, expressed in three separate opinions, reached no conclusion as to the merits. Judge Pierce concluded that "the balance of hardships tips decidedly towards S&P" by reason of a risk of irreparable harm to S&P, and that the preliminary injunction was further justified by consideration of the public interest, by reason of the harm that would likely befall investors if trading in the Comex 500 futures were initiated and then abruptly cut off. *Comex II, 683 F.2d at 711-12*. Judge Knapp, sitting by designation, wrote only that "I concur in the result for the reasons expressed by Judge Newman." Id. at 712. Judge Newman wrote:

> When Standard & Poor's enters the business of publishing an index of selected stock issues, there can be little doubt that another company endeavoring to publish the same index would face liability for misappropriation no matter how it merchandised its product and would face liability for trademark infringement if its merchandising created a risk of confusion between its product and that of Standard & Poor's. However, when Standard & Poor's makes its stock index known to the public, different, novel, and, in my judgment, close questions are presented when another company enters a business other than the publishing of stock indices—here the marketing of futures contracts—and in its business uses the Standard & Poor's index as a reference point—here, the settlement price for the contracts. *Id.* Beyond characterizing it as a "close" question, Judge Newman expressed no further view of the merits but concurred in the affirmance of the preliminary injunction to maintain the status quo pending resolution of the merits, solely by reason of the public interest concern identified by Judge Pierce.

We find the same flaw in plaintiffs' reliance on *Board of Trade*, in which the Supreme Court of Illinois held that the attempt by the Chicago Board of Trade to create a futures contract based on an index identical to the DJIA constituted misappropriation of Dow Jones's investment in its index. Board of Trade, 98 Ill. 2d at 121-22. Like *Comex, Board of Trade* involved a defendant's attempt to create index futures that would allow investors to speculate directly on the value of an index copied from the DJIA. Even if this constitutes misappropriation-and we express no view on this matter-it would not affect the outcome in the case before us, in which plaintiffs have licensed the creation of ETFs and the sale of their shares to the public, and ISE is simply creating a mechanism for trading in those shares.

Plaintiffs argue that the district court erred in concluding that options are not a "new product . . . but merely an opportunity to buy or sell the ETF." We agree with plaintiffs that the options created by ISE are a new product. ETF options are securities distinct from ETFs. *See Fry v. UAL Corp., 84 F.3d 936, 938 (7th Cir. 1996)* ("Puts and other stock options are securities within the meaning of the Securities Exchange Act . . . ."); *15 U.S.C. § 77b(a)(1)* (defining "security," for purposes of the Securities Act of 1933, to include an option); *15 U.S.C. § 78c(a)(10)* (defining "security," for purposes of the Securities Exchange Act of 1934, to include an option); SEC Release No. 34-40157, *63 Fed. Reg. 37428 n.26 (July 10, 1998)* (referring to ETF options as a "new securities product"). But this is irrelevant. It does not change the fact that an option, by its very definition, is the right to buy or sell an underlying security. What is critical is not that the options are new securities, but that they are a means for trading financial products the plaintiffs have licensed for sale to the public. Moreover, while we accept as true plaintiffs' assertion that ETF options are generally settled for cash, without transfer of the ETF shares, this does not change the legal right conveyed by the option contract-to buy or sell ETF shares.[13]

---

13 Plaintiffs also argue that the district court erred when it concluded that ETF shares have value independent of the indexes on which they are based because of the securities held by the ETF. *See* McGraw-Hill, 2005 U.S. Dist. LEXIS 18674, 2005 WL 2100518, at *4 ("ETFs have an additional basis for value in that they are worth the combined price of the stocks that comprise the fund, so, while they are still connected to the indexes they track, they do not rely solely on the index for their existence and value."). They claim that this was based on fact-finding inappropriate on a motion to dismiss and was contrary to the allegation in Dow Jones's complaint that "if Dow Jones stopped producing the DJIA and its related services, trading in both DIAMONDS and DIAMONDS options would cease entirely." There is no inconsistency between the district court's observation that ETFs have value independent of the indexes and Dow Jones's allegation that trading in the ETFs would cease if Dow Jones ceased to publish the DJIA. Neither complaint alleges that the ETF shares would have no further value if the plaintiffs ceased to produce their indexes. The district court's observation that the ETFs would have value notwithstanding the cessation of publication of the indexes flows inevitably from the fact, acknowledged in the complaints, that the ETFs own a portfolio of shares in leading United States companies. Furthermore, neither complaint alleges that upon cessation of the publication of the indexes the trustees of the ETFs would not liquidate the ETFs by distributing their securities to the shareholders or selling the securities and giving the proceeds from

B. Trademark Claims

Dow Jones alleges that "ISE's threatened use of the Dow Jones Marks to market or promote DIAMONDS(R)" constitutes trademark infringement and dilution under federal and state law. It also claims that "[b]y approving and clearing ISE's planned DIAMONDS(R) options, with knowledge that ISE lacked a license from Dow Jones, OCC will have contributed to the infringing use of the Dow Jones Marks." These allegations, without more, are insufficient to survive a motion to dismiss under Federal Rule of Civil Procedure 12(b)(6). While "[a] complaint need only 'give the defendant fair notice of what the plaintiff's claim is and the grounds upon which it rests,'" *Phillip v. Univ. of Rochester, 316 F.3d 291, 293 (2d Cir. 2003)* (quoting *Conley v. Gibson, 355 U.S. 41, 47, 78 S. Ct. 99, 2 L. Ed. 2d 80 (1957))*, "[a] pleading . . . [must] contain . . . a short and plain statement of the claim showing that the pleader is entitled to relief," Fed. R. Civ. P. 8(a). The mere assertion that ISE's intended use of the Dow Jones marks would constitute trademark infringement and dilution, without any factual allegations concerning the nature of the threatened use, does not give the defendants fair notice of the claims against them and does not show, by facts alleged, that Dow Jones is entitled to relief. As to the trademark claims, Dow Jones's complaint, "consists of conclusory allegations unsupported by factual assertions" and therefore it "fails even the liberal standard of Rule 12(b)(6)." *De Jesus v. Sears, Roebuck & Co., Inc., 87 F.3d 65, 70 (2d Cir. 1996)* (quoting *Palda v. Gen. Dynamics Corp., 47 F.3d 872, 875 (7th Cir. 1995)*; *see also Smith v. Local 819 I.B.T. Pension Plan, 291 F.3d 236, 240 (2d Cir. 2002)* ("[C]onclusory allegations or legal conclusions masquerading as factual conclusions will not suffice to prevent a motion to dismiss.") (internal quotation marks omitted).

McGraw-Hill's complaint does not suffer from quite the same deficiency as Dow Jones's complaint. In addition to alleging that "ISE's threatened use of the S&P Marks to market or promote SPDR Options" will constitute trademark infringement and dilution, the McGraw-Hill complaint adds that in a January 5, 2005 press release, ISE used the phrase "options on SPDR(R)." Thus, McGraw-Hill appears to be arguing that ISE's use of the term "SPDR" when describing SPDR options constitutes a trademark violation.

---

the sale to the shareholders. The cessation of trading in ETF shares, for whatever reason, might impair their value but would not nullify it.

While Dow Jones has offered no explanation why the ETF shares, which represent ownership interests in a portfolio of valuable securities, would cease to be traded, we recognize the obligation to accept allegations of a complaint in reviewing a motion to dismiss under Rule 12(b)(6). *See Shah v. Meeker, 435 F.3d 244, 248 (2d Cir. 2006)*. Acceptance of this improbable allegation, however, does not affect our judgment. It remains uncontested that plaintiffs authorized the sale of the ETF shares to the public, and in so doing, authorized a market for secondary trading of those shares, which includes options for the purchase and sale of the shares.

We agree with the district court that such a claim fails as a matter of law. While a trademark conveys an exclusive right to the use of a mark in commerce in the area reserved, that right generally does not prevent one who trades a branded product from accurately describing it by its brand name, so long as the trader does not create confusion by implying an affiliation with the owner of the product. *See Polymer Tech. Corp. v. Mimran, 975 F.2d 58, 61-62 (2d Cir. 1992)* ("As a general rule, trademark law does not reach the sale of genuine goods bearing a true mark even though the sale is not authorized by the mark owner."); *Golden Nugget, 828 F.2d at 591* ("Describing [a] product nondeceptively and by name brand has never been a violation of a manufacturer's trademark."); *Prestonettes, Inc. v. Coty, 264 U.S. 359, 368, 44 S. Ct. 350, 68 L. Ed. 731, 1924 Dec. Comm'r Pat. 508 (1924)* ("When the mark is used in a way that does not deceive the public we see no such sanctity in the word as to prevent its being used to tell the truth. It is not taboo."). Thus, the allegation that ISE will use the word "SPDR" in describing the SPDR shares covered by its options does not save the McGraw-Hill complaint from Rule 12(b)(6) dismissal.[14]

CONCLUSION

For the reasons stated above, we affirm the dismissal of the complaints and, as necessarily follows from the insufficiency of a complaint, the denial of a preliminary injunction.

---

14 It is of course possible that the defendants might market options on DIAMONDS and SPDR shares in a manner that would create confusion as to an affiliation with the plaintiffs and result in trademark infringement or dilution. For example, in *Archipelago* the court denied the motion to dismiss Nasdaq's trademark claims where Nasdaq alleged that the language of three particular advertisements regarding QQQ trading on the ArcaEX exchange would confuse the public into thinking that defendants's actions were sponsored by Nasdaq. *Archipelago, 336 F. Supp. 2d at 299, 305*. But the complaints in this case allege nothing of the kind.

PIAZZA'S SEAFOOD WORLD, LLC
v.
BOB ODOM

448 F.3d 744 (5th Cir. 2006)
Decided May 4, 2006

For PIAZZA'S SEAFOOD WORLD, Plaintiff—Counter Defendant—Appellee: Stephen Davis Marx, Chehardy, Sherman, Ellis, Breslin, Murray, Recile & Griffith, Metairie, LA.

For BOB ODOM, Individually and as Commissioner, Louisiana Department of Agriculture & Forestry, Defendant—Counter Claimant—Appellant: Houston T Penn, Office of the Attorney General for the State of Louisiana, Baton Rouge, LA; Clarence James Gelpi, Clark A Richard, Dan Brian Zimmerman, David Sean McFadden, Gelpi & Associates, New Orleans, LA.

Before HIGGINBOTHAM, DeMOSS, and OWEN, Circuit Judges. HIGGINBOTHAM, Circuit Judge, concurring.

OPINION

DeMOSS, Circuit Judge:

This case requires us to decide the constitutionality of two Louisiana statutes, one that regulates the labeling of catfish, LA REV. STAT. ANN. § 3:4617(C) (the "Catfish Statute"), and another that regulates the use of the word "Cajun" on food products, *id.* at § 3:4617(D), (E) (the "Cajun Statute"). Appellee Piazza's Seafood World, LLC ("Piazza") is a Louisiana company that imports seafood and distributes it under the trade names "Cajun Boy" and "Cajun Delight." It sued the Commissioner of the Louisiana Department of Agriculture and Forestry, Mr. Bob Odom, to enjoin the Commissioner from enforcing the Catfish and Cajun Statutes against the company. The district court granted summary judgment in Piazza's favor with respect to the statutes and enjoined the Commissioner from enforcing either statute against Piazza, concluding (1) that the Catfish Statute was preempted by *21 U.S.C. § 343(t)* and (2) that the Cajun Statute, as applied to Piazza, violated the First Amendment. The district court also denied the Commissioner's motion for new trial regarding the Catfish Statute, which the court treated as a motion to reconsider, reiterating that the Catfish Statute was preempted and finding in the alternative that it violated the dormant Foreign Commerce Clause. For the reasons stated below, we affirm.

I. Background and Procedural History

This case represents the next chapter in an ongoing saga regarding the labeling of catfish. In May 2002, Congress passed legislation limiting the class of fish sold in interstate commerce to which the label "catfish" could be applied. *See* Farm Security and Rural Investment Act of 2002, Pub. L. No. 107-171, § 10806(a), 116 Stat. 134, 526-27 (codified at *21 U.S.C. §§ 321d*, 343(t)). This legislation was prompted by increased sales of Vietnamese *Pangasius bocourti* in the United States as "basa catfish." *See* Kerrilee E. Kobbeman, Legislative Note, *Hook, Line and Sinker: How Congress Swallowed the Domestic Catfish Industry's Narrow Definition of this Ubiquitous Bottomfeeder*, 57 ARK. L. REV. 407, 411-18 (2004); *see also* 148 CONG. REC. S3989 (daily ed. May 8, 2002) (statement of Sen. Hutchinson) ("With this provision, we were trying to end the deceptive and economically destructive practice of mislabeling Vietnamese basa . . . ."); 147 CONG. REC. H6267-68 (daily ed. Oct. 4, 2001) (statements of Reps. Barry, Pickering, and Shows) (describing the purposes behind the legislation). The American catfish industry was heavily impacted by the sale of these fish under the catfish name: sales of domestic catfish dropped significantly and domestic catfish farmers were forced to lower their prices. Kobbeman, *supra*, at 411-12; *see also* 147 CONG. REC. H6267-68 (statements of Reps. Barry, Pickering, and Shows) (detailing the impact of foreign catfish on the American market). The new federal catfish labeling law, codified at *21 U.S.C. §§ 321d* and 343(t), provided that the term "catfish" could only be considered "a common or usual name (or part thereof) for fish classified within the family *Ictaluridae*"; "only labeling or advertising for fish classified within that family" could use the term "catfish"; and a food would be deemed misbranded if it purported to be or was represented as catfish, unless it was fish classified within the family *Ictaluridae. 21 U.S.C. §§ 321d, 343(t)*. After this legislation was passed, Vietnamese *Pangasius bocourti*, members of the family *Pangasiidae*, could no longer be labeled catfish; only fish from the family *Ictaluridae*, native to America, could bear the lucrative catfish label.

Around the same time, Louisiana discovered that American *Ictaluridae* were being farmed in China and sold in the United States as catfish, and it passed legislation limiting further the class of fish to which the catfish label could be applied. 2002 La. Sess. Law Serv. 1st Ex. Sess. Act 125 (West). Specifically, Louisiana stated that only *Ictaluridae* grown in the United States could be labeled "catfish." LA. REV. STAT. ANN. § 3:4617(C) (2003).[1] This lawsuit arose out of application of

1 The legislation also defined fish from the family *Anarhichadidae* grown in the United States as catfish; however, that portion of the statute is not at issue in this case because according to the record, Appellee Piazza only sells *Ictaluridae*.

that law, as well as a Louisiana law limiting the use of the word "Cajun" on food products, to an American importer and distributor of Chinese *Ictaluridae*.

Piazza is a Louisiana Limited Liability Company that has been selling seafood wholesale in Louisiana for more than fifty years; thirty years ago, it began marketing some of its products under the trade names "Cajun Boy" and "Cajun Delight,"[2] and today it sells all of its products under those names. Although Piazza originally sold mostly Louisiana seafood, ninety-nine percent of the food products it sells currently are imported from overseas. Its customers are largely institutional buyers that resell Piazza's products to wholesalers and restaurants, but Piazza sells about one percent of its products to grocery stores that resell its products directly to the public. One of the products Piazza sells is Cajun Boy-brand catfish from the family *Ictaluridae* that is imported from China.[3] The catfish and the "Cajun Boy" and "Cajun Delight" trade names are what is at issue in this case.

In March 2004, Commissioner Odom ordered several of Piazza's customers not to "sell, offer for sale, apply, move or remove" any of Piazza's products because the reference to "catfish" on Piazza's Chinese catfish violated Louisiana's Catfish Statute[4]; as a result of this action, 30,000 cases of Piazza's catfish were seized.[5] Piazza brought suit, seeking an injunction against Commissioner Odom to prevent him from enforcing the Catfish Statute against the company. Piazza argued that the Catfish Statute was preempted by *21 U.S.C. § 343(t)* and unconstitutional under the Commerce and Equal Protection Clauses. The district court eventually granted partial summary judgment in Piazza's favor as to the Catfish Statute, finding that the statute was preempted by *21 U.S.C. § 343(t)* because of an actual conflict between the state and federal laws.[6] The court did not address Piazza's alternative constitutional claims regarding the Catfish Statute at that time, although it did mention that it saw potential Commerce Clause problems with the statute.

---

2 Both trade names are registered with the Louisiana Secretary of State.

3 The Chinese catfish are descendants of American catfish imported to China for farming purposes, and the parties agree that they are biologically identical to American catfish.

4 The Catfish Statute read,

> No one shall misrepresent the name, or type of any fruit, vegetable, grain, meat, or fish, including catfish, sold, or offered or exposed for sale, to any actual or prospective consumer. "Catfish" shall mean only those species within the family *Ictaluridae* . . . and grown in the United States of America.*LA. REV. STAT. ANN. § 3:4617(C)* (2003).

5 These cases were later released for sale after Piazza agreed to stamp the word "Chinese" above the word "catfish" on each case. Each case was already marked "Product of China," and the parties do not dispute that Piazza has always marked its foreign products with their country of origin.

6 Section 343(t) states,

> A food shall be deemed to be misbranded—
>
> > If it purports to be or is represented as catfish, unless it is fish classified within the family *Ictaluridae.21 U.S.C. § 343(t)*.

While the original suit was pending, the Louisiana legislature passed House Bill 891, which repealed the "grandfather clause" in Louisiana's Cajun Statute that had previously protected the use of the word "Cajun" in a product name if that name was a trademark or trade name legally registered with the state of Louisiana as of May 15, 2003.[7] Without the protection of the grandfather clause, all of Piazza's inventory violated the Cajun Statute. Piazza accordingly amended its complaint in the district court, seeking a second injunction against Commissioner Odom, this one to prevent the Commissioner from enforcing the Cajun Statute against Piazza.[8] Piazza argued that the Cajun Statute was unconstitutional under the First Amendment and the Commerce, Equal Protection, Due Process, and Takings Clauses. Around the same time, Commissioner Odom filed a motion for new trial as to the Catfish Statute. The district court again found in Piazza's favor, granting partial summary judgment in Piazza's favor as to the Cajun Statute—finding that the statute, as applied to Piazza, violated the First Amendment—and denying the Commissioner's motion for new trial as to the Catfish Statute—reiterating that the Catfish Statute was preempted and finding in the alternative that it violated the dormant Commerce Clause by discriminating against foreign commerce.[9] The

---

7 The Cajun Statute, prior to amendment, read,

> D. No person shall advertise, sell, offer or expose for sale, or distribute food or food products as "Cajun", "Louisiana Creole", or any derivative thereof unless the food or food product would qualify for the ten percent preference for products produced, processed, or manufactured in Louisiana under R.S. 38:2251 and R.S. 39:1595. Food brought into and processed in Louisiana shall not be considered as food or food products made in Louisiana, for purposes of this Section, unless the food has been substantially transformed by processing in Louisiana.
>
> E. No person shall advertise, sell, offer or expose for sale, or distribute food or food products that do not qualify under this Section for labeling as "Cajun", "Louisiana Creole", or any derivative thereof in any packaging that would lead a reasonable person to believe that the food or food product qualifies as "Cajun" or "Louisiana Creole" food or food products, as defined in this Section.
>
> F. The provisions of Subsections D and E of this Section shall not infringe upon rights acquired pursuant to any trademark or trade name legally registered with the state of Louisiana as of May 15, 2003.*LA. REV. STAT. ANN. § 3:4617(D)-(F) (Supp. 2004)*. House Bill 891 repealed subsection (F).

8 Piazza originally amended its complaint to challenge the constitutionality of the repeal of Louisiana Revised Statutes § 3:4617(F), but later amended its complaint again to add a challenge to the constitutionality of the Cajun Statute itself, Louisiana Revised Statutes § 3:4617(D), (E).

9 The district court correctly characterized and analyzed the Commissioner's Rule 59(a) motion for new trial as a Rule 59(e) motion to reconsider entry of summary judgment. *See Patin v. Allied Signal, Inc., 77 F.3d 782, 785 n.1 (5th Cir. 1996)*; *see also Harcon Barge Co. v. D & G Boat Rentals, Inc., 784 F.2d 665, 669-70 (5th Cir. 1986)* ("'Any motion that draws into question the correctness of a judgment is functionally a motion under Civil Rule 59(e), whatever its label.'" (quoting 9 MOORE'S FEDERAL PRACTICE P204.12[1], at 4-67 (1985))). For simplicity's sake, the Commissioner's motion for new trial is referred to as a motion to reconsider throughout the remainder of this opinion.

court never addressed Piazza's alternative constitutional claims regarding the Cajun Statute.

The Commissioner timely appealed the district court's denial of his motion to reconsider as to the Catfish Statute and its partial summary judgment as to the Cajun Statute.[10] He argues on appeal (1) that the district court erred in holding that the Catfish Statute is preempted by *21 U.S.C. § 343(t)*; (2) that the district court erred in reaching its alternate conclusion that the Catfish Statute violates the dormant Commerce Clause; and (3) that the district court erred in holding that the Cajun Statute, as applied to Piazza, violates the First Amendment.

II. The Catfish Statute

Generally, this Court reviews the denial of a motion to reconsider for abuse of discretion. *Fletcher v. Apfel, 210 F.3d 510, 512 (5th Cir. 2000)*. However, if a party appeals from the denial of a Rule 59(e) motion that is solely a motion to reconsider a judgment on its merits, *de novo* review is appropriate. *Id.* Considering Commissioner Odom's arguments on appeal, it is apparent that he "intended to appeal the merits of the underlying [summary] judgment," *id.*; accordingly, we review his claims regarding the Catfish Statute *de novo*.[11]

The district court held that the Catfish Statute violated the dormant Commerce Clause because it was "a protectionist measure that discriminated against foreign commerce in favor of local interests." We agree.

The Commerce Clause states that "Congress shall have Power . . . To regulate Commerce with foreign Nations, and among the several States, and with the Indian Tribes." *U.S. CONST. art. I, § 8, cl. 3*. Although the Commerce Clause speaks only of Congress's power, it has long been understood that there is a dormant or negative aspect of the Commerce Clause that limits the power of the states to regulate commerce. *See Camps Newfound/Owatonna, Inc. v. Town of Harrison, 520 U.S. 564, 571-72, 117 S. Ct. 1590, 137 L. Ed. 2d 852 (1997)*; *Or. Waste Sys., Inc. v. Dep't of Envtl. Quality, 511 U.S. 93, 98-99, 114 S. Ct. 1345, 128 L. Ed. 2d 13 (1994)*; *Dennis v. Higgins, 498 U.S. 439, 447, 111 S. Ct. 865, 112 L. Ed. 2d 969 (1991)*; *New Energy Co. of Ind. v. Limbach, 486 U.S. 269, 273-74, 108 S. Ct. 1803, 100 L. Ed. 2d 302 (1988)*; *see also Nat'l Solid Waste Mgmt. Ass'n v. Pine Belt Reg'l Solid Waste, 389 F.3d 491, 497 (5th Cir. 2004)* (acknowledging the Supreme Court's dormant Commerce Clause jurisprudence). This negative aspect of the Commerce Clause applies both to the Foreign Commerce Clause ("Commerce

---

10 The notice of appeal effectively stayed the proceedings in the district court, where a cross-claim under the Lanham Act, which is not discussed here, is pending.

11 Neither party properly addresses the standard of review this Court should apply with respect to the motion to reconsider. The Commissioner frames his standard of review discussion as though he were directly appealing the motion for summary judgment, which he is not. And Piazza does not discuss the appropriate standard of review at all. However, we, not the parties, determine the appropriate standard of review.

with foreign Nations"), *see, e.g., Wardair Canada, Inc. v. Fla. Dep't of Revenue, 477 U.S. 1, 7-8, 106 S. Ct. 2369, 91 L. Ed. 2d 1 (1986)*, and to the Interstate Commerce Clause ("Commerce . . . among the several States"), *see, e.g., Camps Newfound/Owatonna, Inc., 520 U.S. at 571-72*, although the scope of Congress's power to regulate foreign commerce, and accordingly the limit on the power of the states in that area, is greater, *see, e.g., Kraft Gen. Foods, Inc. v. Iowa Dep't of Revenue and Fin., 505 U.S. 71, 79, 112 S. Ct. 2365, 120 L. Ed. 2d 59 (1992)* (noting that "the constitutional prohibition against state taxation of foreign commerce is broader than the protection afforded to interstate commerce, in part because matters of concern to the entire Nation are implicated" (citation omitted)); Wardair Canada, Inc., 477 U.S. at 8 ("In the unique context of foreign commerce, we have alluded to the special need for federal uniformity: 'In international relations and with respect to foreign intercourse and trade the people of the United States act through a single government with unified and adequate national power.'" (internal quotation marks and citation omitted)); *Japan Line v. Los Angeles, 441 U.S. 434, 446, 99 S. Ct. 1813, 60 L. Ed. 2d 336 (1979)* (stating that "a more extensive constitutional inquiry is required" in Foreign Commerce Clause cases because a state regulation may "impair federal uniformity in an area where federal uniformity is essential").

State regulations violate the dormant Commerce Clause by discriminating against or unduly burdening foreign or interstate commerce. *See, e.g., Or. Waste Sys., Inc., 511 U.S. at 98* (*Interstate Commerce Clause*); *Kraft Gen. Foods, Inc., 505 U.S. at 81* (Foreign *Commerce Clause*). Regulations that facially discriminate are virtually per se invalid, *Camps Newfound/Owatonna, Inc., 520 U.S. at 575* (explaining that discriminatory regulations are strictly scrutinized); *Nat'l Solid Waste Mgmt. Ass'n, 389 F.3d at 497* (same); *see also Kraft Gen. Foods, Inc., 505 U.S. at 81* ("Absent a compelling justification, . . . a State may not advance its legitimate goals by means that facially discriminate against foreign commerce."), whereas regulations that merely burden commerce are valid "unless 'the burden imposed on such commerce is clearly excessive in relation to the putative local benefits.'" Or. Waste Sys., Inc., 511 U.S. at 99 (quoting *Pike v. Bruce Church, Inc., 397 U.S. 137, 142, 90 S. Ct. 844, 25 L. Ed. 2d 174 (1970)).*

In the context of the Interstate Commerce Clause, if a state regulation is found to be nondiscriminatory, the court examines "the nature of the local interest and whether alternative means could achieve that interest with less impact on interstate commerce." *Nat'l Solid Waste Mgmt. Ass'n, 389 F.3d at 501*. "'If a legitimate local purpose is found, then the question becomes one of degree. And the extent of the burden that will be tolerated will of course depend on the nature of the local interest involved, and on whether it could be promoted as well with a lesser impact on interstate activities.'" *Id.* (quoting Pike, 397 U.S. at 142). However, in the context of the Foreign *Commerce Clause*, other considerations come into play: nondiscriminatory state regulations affecting foreign commerce are invalid "if they (1) create a substantial risk of conflicts with foreign governments; or (2) undermine the ability of the federal government to 'speak with one voice' in regulating commercial affairs with foreign states." *New Orleans S.S. Ass'n v. Plaquemines Port, Harbor & Terminal Dist., 874 F.2d 1018, 1022 (5th Cir. 1989)* (quoting Japan Line, 441 U.S. at 446).

Commissioner Odom focuses his arguments on appeal on the Interstate Commerce Clause. He argues that the Catfish Statute does not discriminate against interstate commerce because it does not meet any of the factors listed in *Exxon Corp. v. Governor of Maryland, 437 U.S. 117, 98 S. Ct. 2207, 57 L. Ed. 2d 91 (1978)*, namely, the Catfish Statute "does not prohibit or limit the flow of goods into the state, creates no barriers whatsoever against the importation of goods, does not place added costs on out-of-state goods, and does not distinguish between in-state and out-of-state companies in the wholesale or retail market." The Commissioner misses the point. The problem with the Catfish Statute is not that it discriminates against interstate commerce, but that it discriminates against foreign commerce. And this discrimination appears on the face of the statute: the Catfish Statute treats domestic catfish differently from foreign catfish to the benefit of the former and the detriment of the latter. *See* Or. Waste Sys., Inc., 511 U.S. at 99 (defining discrimination in the Commerce Clause context). Therefore, the Commissioner's citation to *Exxon Corp.* is inapposite. *Exxon Corp.* involved a statute that did not facially discriminate, *see* Exxon Corp., 437 U.S. at 125 ("Plainly, the Maryland statute does not discriminate against interstate goods, nor does it favor local producers and refiners."); accordingly, the Court was using the factors cited by Commissioner Odom to determine whether the statute in question unduly burdened—or had a discriminatory effect on—commerce, *see id. at 125-26*. Those factors are irrelevant in a case involving facial discrimination.[12]

---

12 The Commissioner cites other cases in his reply brief in support of his argument that the Catfish Statute does not discriminate against commerce. We are not persuaded by any. First, the Commissioner is wrong that the differential treatment of products, rather than entities, cannot qualify as discrimination. *See Bacchus Imps., Ltd. v. Dias, 468 U.S. 263, 269 n.8, 104 S. Ct. 3049, 82 L. Ed. 2d 200 (1984)* ("Discrimination between in-state and out-of-state goods is as offensive to the Commerce Clause as discrimination between in-state and out-of-state taxpayers."). Second, an absolute barrier to commerce is not required for discrimination to exist. *See, e.g.*, Or. Waste Sys., Inc., 511 U.S. at 96-100 & (finding patent discrimination where the statute in question simply applied a differential charge to out-of-state entities, and stating "the degree of a differential burden or charge on interstate commerce 'measures only the extent of the discrimination' and 'is of no relevance to the determination whether a State has discriminated against interstate commerce'" (quoting *Wyoming v. Oklahoma, 502 U.S. 437, 455, 112 S. Ct. 789, 117 L. Ed. 2d 1 (1992))*. Finally, a statute that facially discriminates does not have to otherwise burden commerce in order to be strictly scrutinized—the cases the Commissioner cites requiring a burden in addition to discrimination did not involve facial discrimination. *See id.* The overarching problem with Commissioner Odom's arguments is that he fails to recognize that the Catfish Statute's differential treatment of domestic catfish and foreign catfish to the benefit of the former and the detriment of the latter is, without more, facial discrimination subject to strict scrutiny.

Commissioner Odom also challenges the district court's decision by arguing that Congress somehow condoned Louisiana's legislation. We recognize that Congress may permit a state to enact legislation that would otherwise violate the Commerce Clause, but its intent to do so must be "expressly stated." *New Orleans S.S. Ass'n, 874 F.2d at 1022* (citing *S.-Cent. Timber Dev., Inc. v. Wunnicke, 467 U.S. 82, 91-92, 104 S. Ct. 2237, 81 L. Ed. 2d 71 (1984))*. "The fact that the state policy [involved] appears to be consistent with federal policy—or even that state policy furthers the goals we might believe that Congress had in mind—is an insufficient indicium of congressional intent. S.-Cent. Timber Dev., Inc., 467 U.S. at 92. There is no express statement in either of the statutes cited by the Commissioner, § 343(t) or the Lanham Act, regarding the power of the states to enact catfish labeling legislation that discriminates against foreign commerce. *See 21 U.S.C. § 343(t)*; Lanham Act, *15 U.S.C. § 1051 et seq*. The Commissioner relies on his interpretation of the purposes of § 343(t) and the Lanham Act—to prevent the labeling of foreign fish as catfish and to prevent "initial interest confusion," respectively—to support his position that "federal law allows the actions employed by Louisiana," but even if we agreed with his interpretation of those statutes, his reliance on their purposes, rather than their express language, indicates that Congress has made no express statement regarding state catfish labeling laws that discriminate against commerce. A state statute that violates the Commerce Clause cannot be saved by a showing that it is consistent with the purposes behind federal law. S.-Cent. Timber Dev., Inc., 467 U.S. at 92.

Because we find that the Catfish Statute discriminates on its face against foreign commerce, we presume that it is invalid. *See* Kraft Gen. Foods, Inc., 505 U.S. at 81. To overcome this presumption, the Commissioner must demonstrate that the Catfish Statute serves a legitimate local purpose that cannot be adequately served by reasonable nondiscriminatory alternatives. *New Energy Co. of Ind., 486 U.S. at 278*; *see also* Kraft Gen. Foods, Inc., 505 U.S. at 81. This the Commissioner has not done: Because he thinks the Catfish Statute does not discriminate, he only comes forward with evidence that the statute's burden is minimal in relation to its local benefits. This evidence, even if accepted as true, is not enough to satisfy the Commissioner's heightened burden under strict scrutiny review. *See* Camps Newfound/Owatonna, Inc., 520 U.S. at 582 (stating that because the appellant "made no effort to defend the statute under the *per se* rule," the Court would not address whether strict scrutiny was satisfied). Absent a compelling justification, which the Commissioner has not offered, the Catfish Statute is invalid. Because we find that the Catfish Statute violates the dormant Foreign Commerce Clause, we do not address whether it is preempted.[13]

---

13 We also do not address any of Piazza's alternative constitutional claims regarding the Catfish Statute.

III. The Cajun Statute

This Court reviews grants of summary judgment *de novo*, applying the same standard as the district court. *Wheeler v. BL Dev. Corp., 415 F.3d 399, 401 (5th Cir. 2005).* Summary judgment is appropriate if no genuine issue of material fact exists and the moving party is entitled to judgment as a matter of law. FED. R. CIV. P. 56(c). The Court views the evidence in a light most favorable to the non-movant. *Wheeler, 415 F.3d at 401.* The non-movant must go beyond the pleadings and come forward with specific facts indicating a genuine issue for trial to avoid summary judgment. *Celotex Corp. v. Catrett, 477 U.S. 317, 324, 106 S. Ct. 2548, 91 L. Ed. 2d 265 (1986).* A genuine issue of material fact exists when the evidence is such that a reasonable jury could return a verdict for the non-movant. *Anderson v. Liberty Lobby, Inc., 477 U.S. 242, 248, 106 S. Ct. 2505, 91 L. Ed. 2d 202 (1986).* Summary judgment is appropriate, however, if the non-movant "fails to make a showing sufficient to establish the existence of an element essential to that party's case." Celotex, 477 U.S. at 322-23.

The Commissioner argues on appeal that Piazza's First Amendment rights were not violated by the Cajun Statute because Piazza's use of the word "Cajun" in its trade names is misleading and deceptive. He argues alternatively that even if the use of the word "Cajun" is not misleading or deceptive, Louisiana has substantial governmental interests in regulating use of that word that are directly advanced by the Cajun Statute, and the statute is narrowly tailored to achieve those goals. Piazza counters that the Cajun Statute, as applied to Piazza,[14] violates all four prongs of the relevant *Central Hudson* test and thus constitutes an impermissible restriction on Piazza's First Amendment right to use the "Cajun Boy" and "Cajun Delight" trade names.

Central Hudson Gas v. Public Service Commission, 447 U.S. 557, 100 S. Ct. 2343, 65 L. Ed. 2d 341 (1980), supplies the test for determining whether the government has permissibly regulated commercial speech:

> In commercial speech cases . . . a four-part analysis has developed. At the outset, we must determine whether the expression is protected by the First Amendment. For commercial speech to come within that provision, it at least must concern lawful activity and not be misleading. Next, we ask whether the asserted governmental interest is substantial. If both inquiries yield positive answers, we must determine whether the regulation directly advances the governmental interest asserted, and whether it is not more extensive than is necessary to serve that interest.

Cent. Hudson, 447 U.S. at 566. The district court answered *Central Hudson*'s first two inquiries in the affirmative, finding (1) that Piazza's use of the "Cajun Boy" and "Cajun Delight" trade names was only potentially misleading, not actually or inherently misleading, because Piazza largely sells its products to wholesalers and it labels its products with their country of origin and (2) that Louisiana's interest

14 Piazza clarified at oral argument that on appeal it is only challenging the statute as applied.

in protecting Louisianans from misleading and deceptive uses of trade names was substantial. The district court then turned to whether the Cajun Statute directly advanced Louisiana's asserted interest in protecting Louisianans and whether the statute was more extensive than necessary to serve that interest. It answered this inquiry in the affirmative, finding that the state's interest in protecting Louisianans from deception was not enhanced by application of the state statute to Piazza because there was no deception present to be prevented. The court also found that the state statute was more extensive than necessary when applied to Piazza because it contained no exception for sellers like Piazza who disclose truthful information (country of origin) on their food labels that eliminates the deceptive nature of the labeling. The court emphasized that the Cajun Statute was not facially invalid, only invalid as applied to Piazza.

Having carefully reviewed the record, the briefs, and the oral argument of the parties, we affirm the district court's decision as to the Cajun Statute essentially for the reasons stated by the district court.[15]

IV. Conclusion

Accordingly, we AFFIRM the district court's decision to deny Commissioner Odom's motion for new trial as to the Catfish Statute and its decision to grant Piazza's motion for partial summary judgment as to the Cajun Statute.

---

15 We do not address Piazza's alternative constitutional claims regarding the Cajun Statute.

CONCUR

HIGGINBOTHAM, Circuit Judge, concurring:

I concur for the reasons stated by the panel opinion and the thoughtful opinions of the district court. I agree that the Louisiana Statute discriminates against foreign commerce. As was the district court, however, I am persuaded that the preferable approach is to draw upon preemption doctrine. The commerce power hardly lies dormant here. Congress has set down a detailed regulatory scheme addressing the subject of misleading descriptions of the family relationships of catfish and how this kinship is to be described in their sale. The arguments in this case supporting a finding of discrimination against foreign commerce and the justifications for its heightened review rest upon the dominance of federal power in matters of relations with foreign countries not on maintenance of a national economy by the quelling of sibling efforts to gain commercial advantage over sister states.

IX. INTERNATIONAL TRADE

1. Regulations

D. Procedure*

* Cases are indexed under this subject. The full text of these cases is published in the **volume**-page indicated.

LEATHER FORM S.R.L.
v.
KNOLL, INC.

205 F.App'x. 861(2d Cir. 2006)
Decided November 2, 2006

For Appellants: Nicole M. Meyer, Dickinson Wright PLLC (Samuel D. Littlepage, Dickinson Wright PLLC, Washington, DC, Aidan M. McCormack, Erik W. Drewniak, Nixon Peabody LLP, New York, NY, on the brief).

For Appellees:Thomas C. Morrison, Patterson, Belknap, Webb & Tyler LLP (Evan Mandel, Patterson, Belknap, Webb & Tyler LLP, on the brief), New York, NY.

PRESENT: HON. RALPH K. WINTER, HON. JOSEPH M. McLAUGHLIN, HON. CHESTER J. STRAUB, Circuit Judges.

OPINION

SUMMARY ORDER

AFTER ARGUMENT AND UPON DUE CONSIDERATION, IT IS HEREBY ORDERED, ADJUDGED AND DECREED that the judgment of the District Court is AFFIRMED.

Plaintiffs-Appellants Leather Form S.R.L. and Casprini Gruppo Industriale S.P.A. (collectively, "Casprini") appeal the judgment of the District Court for the Southern District of New York (Jed S. Rakoff, *Judge*), declining to exercise jurisdiction under *28 U.S.C. § 2201(a)* over Casprini's declaratory judgment action, and dismissing Casprini's complaint. We assume the parties' familiarity with the facts and issues on appeal.

Casprini brought this action seeking a declaratory judgment regarding a 1965 Agreement between the designer Mies van der Rohe and Knoll, Inc.'s predecessor Knoll Associates, Inc., in which Mr. van der Rohe agreed to "sell, assign and convey all of [his] right, title and interest in [his] designs and the exclusive use of [his] name in connection with [such] sale in the United States and elsewhere."

The 1965 Agreement is governed by New York law pursuant to a choice-of-law provision. Casprini argued below that this language contains a "latent ambiguity," and claimed that extrinsic evidence would show that the signatories to the 1965 Agreement intended to transfer only domestic rights to the designs.

Casprini is currently engaged in the manufacture and sale of the designs in the United States and Europe. In 2003, Knoll, Inc.'s subsidiary, Knoll International S.P.A., brought suit in Germany against one of Casprini's distributors. Casprini intervened in that action, but was not permitted to introduce evidence in support of its "latent ambiguity" theory. On January 21, 2005, the German court held that the 1965 Agreement conveyed worldwide copyrights to Knoll, and enjoined Casprini's distributor from continuing to sell or advertise the designs. This decision is currently on appeal. On February 3, 2005, Knoll International brought a second suit in Germany, this time against Casprini itself. The latter litigation, brought on February 3, 2005, is ongoing. Casprini brought this action in the Southern District of New York on August 5, 2005, seeking a declaration that its manufacture, distribution, sale, offering for sale and advertising of reproductions of certain items of furniture do not infringe upon or otherwise violate any rights claimed by Knoll under the 1965 Agreement. The District Court declined to exercise jurisdiction over Casprini's action.

The Declaratory Judgment Act vests the district courts with discretion to determine whether they will exert jurisdiction over a proposed declaratory action or not. *28 U.S.C. § 2201(a)* ("In a case of actual controversy within its jurisdiction . . . any court of the United States . . . *may* declare the rights and other legal relations of any interested party seeking such declaration . . . .") (emphasis added). "Courts have consistently interpreted this permissive language as a broad grant of discretion to district courts to refuse to exercise jurisdiction over a declaratory action that they would otherwise be empowered to hear." *Dow Jones & Co. v. Harrods Ltd., 346 F.3d 357, 359 (2d Cir. 2003)* (citing, *inter alia*, *Wilton v. Seven Falls Co., 515 U.S. 277, 282-83, 115 S. Ct. 2137, 132 L. Ed. 2d 214 (1995))*. Moreover, "this broad discretion is reviewed deferentially, for abuse of discretion." *Id.*

In exercising its discretion, the District Court considered five factors, all of which it found weighed against taking jurisdiction of the case. These factors are drawn from our decision in *Dow Jones*, in which we re-articulated the two factors traditionally considered in this Circuit, namely "(1) whether the judgment will serve a useful purpose in clarifying or settling the legal issues involved; and (2) whether a judgment would finalize the controversy and offer relief from uncertainty," and recognized that "[o]ther circuits have built upon this test, to ask also: (1) whether the proposed remedy is being used merely for 'procedural fencing' or a 'race to res judicata'; (2) whether the use of a declaratory judgment would increase friction between sovereign legal systems or improperly encroach on the domain of a state or foreign court; and (3) whether there is a better or more effective remedy." *Id.* Where the district court's exercise of discretion is based on these five factors, we will not entertain "argument[s] that the district court should have balanced the various factors differently," but will affirm unless "we . . . believe that the district court's decision is premised on an erroneous view of the law, [or] a clear error of fact." Id. at 360.

In this case, we do not believe that the District Court abused its discretion. In particular, we do not think that the District Court erred in taking into account the tenuous merits of Casprini's case under New York law when considering whether a declaratory judgment would serve a useful purpose.[1] *See* Wilton, 515 U.S. at 287 (holding that "the propriety of declaratory relief in a particular case will depend upon a circumspect sense of its fitness informed by the teachings and experience concerning the functions and extent of federal judicial power. . . . In the declaratory judgment context, the normal principle that federal courts should adjudicate claims within their jurisdiction yields to considerations of practicality and wise judicial administration.").

Nor do we see any error in the District Court's weighing of the remaining factors. We think that the District Court correctly determined that a ruling by a United States court would not serve to finalize the controversy between the parties, which is in Europe; as Casprini concedes, here and below, the declaration of an American court would merely be "instructive" as to the parties' rights in Germany. We see no reason to disturb the District Court's finding that "the instant action is nothing but an attempt to circumvent the holdings and jurisdictions of the German courts," or that the German legal process offers an adequate remedy and will more effectively address the parties' actual dispute. While we do not believe that the risk of friction between legal systems, under these circumstances, is so great that by itself it would require the District Court to decline jurisdiction, given the strength of the other factors we do not think the District Court's decision was an abuse of discretion.

For the foregoing reasons, the judgment of the District Court is AFFIRMED.

---

1 Under well-established New York law, where a contract is unambiguous on its face, extrinsic evidence is not admissible to challenge its meaning. *Nichols v. Nichols, 306 N.Y. 490, 496, 119 N.E.2d 351 (N.Y. 1954)*. A "latent ambiguity is where you show the words apply equally to two different things or subject-matters, and then evidence is admissible to show which of them was the thing or subject-matter intended." *Petrie v. Trustees of Hamilton College, 158 N.Y. 458, 464, 53 N.E. 216 (N.Y. 1899)*. There is no ambiguity in the 1965 Agreement, latent or otherwise, as to the geographic scope of the transfer of rights. The 1965 Agreement plainly transfers "*all* . . . right, title and interest" in the designs, without geographic limitation; moreover, the 1965 Agreement explicitly states that it "sold, assigned and conveyed . . . exclusive *world wide* rights."

MOTIONS SYSTEMS CORPORATION
v.
GEORGE W. BUSH

437 F.3d 1356 (Fed. Cir. 2006)
Decided February 10, 2006

Before MICHEL, Chief Judge, NEWMAN, MAYER, LOURIE, Circuit Judges, CLEVENGER, Senior Circuit Judge, RADER, SCHALL, BRYSON, GAJARSA, LINN, DYK, and PROST, Circuit Judges. Opinion concurring in part and concurring in the judgment filed by Circuit Judge GAJARSA, in which Circuit Judge NEWMAN joins.

OPINION

Opinion for the court filed PER CURIAM.

Motion Systems Corp. ("Motion Systems") brought suit against George W. Bush, President of the United States, and Robert B. Zoellick, United States Trade Representative ("Trade Representative"), in the United States Court of International Trade, challenging the President's determination not to grant import relief to the domestic pedestal actuator industry under section 421 of the U. S.-China Relations Act of 2000, Pub. L. No. 106-286, 114 Stat. 880 (codified at *19 U.S.C. § 2451*) ("section 421"). The Court of International Trade granted judgment in favor of the defendants. *Motion Systems Corp. v. Bush, 342 F. Supp. 2d 1247 (Ct. Int'l Trade 2004)*. Motion Systems appealed and for the reasons set forth below, we affirm.

I

Section 421, added to the Trade Act of 1974 by the U. S.-China Relations Act of 2000, establishes procedures under which the President may provide import relief in the form of "increased duties or other such import restrictions" for domestic industries threatened by "market disruption" caused by increased importation of products from China. *19 U.S.C. § 2451(a) (2000)*.

In accordance with section 421(b)(1), Motion Systems filed a petition with the United States International Trade Commission ("ITC"), alleging that importation of Chinese pedestal actuators had increased rapidly from 2000-2002, resulting in market disruption within the meaning of section 421. At the time, Motions Systems was one of three domestic producers of pedestal actuators, electromechanical devices used principally to raise and lower the seats of mobility scooters and motorized wheelchairs. See Pedestal Actuators from China: Investigation No. TA-421-1, Pub. 3557 (U. S. Int'l Trade Comm'n, Nov. 2002), at 3, 11-16.

Upon receipt of the petition, the ITC promptly investigated "whether products of the People's Republic of China are being imported into the United States in such increased quantities or under such conditions as to cause or threaten to cause market disruption to the domestic producers of like or directly competitive products." *19 U.S.C. § 2451(b)(1)*. On October 18, 2002, the ITC issued an affirmative finding of market disruption and transmitted its report and remedial recommendations to the President and the Trade Representative. See *19 U.S.C. § 2451(f)-(g)*. The ITC recommended that "the President impose a quantitative restriction for a three-year period on imports of the subject pedestal actuators from China," and suggested specific amounts for each year. In accordance with—section 421(h)(1), a summary of the ITC's determination and an invitation for public comment was published in the Federal Register. See Notice of Proposed Measure and Opportunity for Public Comment Pursuant to Section 421 of the Trade Act of 1974: Pedestal Actuators from the *People's Republic of China, 67 Fed. Reg. 71007*-03 (Nov. 27, 2002).

On January 2, 2003, after attempts to negotiate a remedial agreement with China proved unsuccessful, the Trade Representative submitted to the President his recommendations regarding the ITC's determination. However, the President did not provide the requested import relief. Rather, the President concluded that "providing import relief for the U.S. pedestal actuator industry is not in the national economic interest of the United States" because "the import relief would have an adverse impact on the United States economy clearly greater than the benefits of such action." Presidential Determination on Pedestal Actuator Imports from the *People's Republic of China, 68 Fed. Reg. 3157 (Jan. 17, 2003)*. The President found that the ITC's recommended import quota would not likely benefit the domestic pedestal actuator industry, but instead would cause imports to shift to other offshore sources. Moreover, the President found that even if the import quota would provide some benefit to domestic producers of pedestal actuators, this benefit would be substantially outweighed by the increased cost to the downstream purchasers and the ultimate consumers of pedestal actuators. Motion Systems requested reconsideration of the President's determination, which the President denied.

On April 9, 2003, Motion Systems filed suit against the President and the Trade Representative in the Court of International Trade, challenging the President's denial of import relief and seeking declaratory and injunctive relief. The complaint alleged that the President's denial of relief was beyond his statutory authority under section 421, arguing that the President misconstrued the provisions of section 421 specifying the circumstances in which he may deny import relief and that the relevant facts did not support the conclusion that the import relief would have an adverse impact clearly greater than its benefits. The complaint also alleged that the Trade Representative's actions were in error, arguing that he too misconstrued section 421 and that he did not follow proper procedures in conducting the public hearing on the ITC's findings.

The Court of International Trade granted judgment in favor of the defendants, concluding that the President did not exceed his statutory authority and that the President's action was not invalid because of any defect in the procedures followed by the Trade Representative. *Motion Systems, 342 F. Supp. 2d at 1262, 1265.*

II

Section 421 defines the role of the President and the Trade Representative in determining whether to provide import relief for market disruption due to importation of products from China. An ITC investigation into market disruption may be initiated upon the request of the President or the Trade Representative, upon resolution of the House Committee on Ways and Means or the Senate Finance Committee, upon petition by a private entity "which is representative of an industry" in accordance with *19 U.S.C. § 2252(a)*, or by the ITC's own motion. *19 U.S.C. § 2451(b)(1).* If, after an investigation, the ITC makes an affirmative determination of market disruption, it must propose import relief in the form of an "increase in, or imposition of, any duty or other import restrictions necessary to prevent or remedy the market disruption." *19 U.S.C. § 2451(f)*. The ITC must submit to the President and the Trade Representative a report containing its determination and recommendations, along with an explanation thereof, and must make that report available to the public. *19 U.S.C. § 2451(g).*

After receiving this report, and following a period of public notice and comment, the Trade Representative must make a recommendation to the President concerning what action, if any, to take. *19 U.S.C. § 2451(h)*. However, the President has discretion to determine whether import relief should be awarded. Under section 421(k)(1), the President must, within fifteen days of receiving the Trade Representative's final recommendation, "provide import relief . . . unless the President determines that provision of such relief is not in the national economic interest of the United States . . . ." *19 U.S.C. § 2451(k)(1)*. Further, the statute provides that "the President may determine . . . that providing import relief is not in the national economic interest of the United States only if the President finds that the taking of such action would have an adverse impact on the United States economy clearly greater than the benefits of such action." *19 U.S.C. § 2451(k)(2).*

III

No right of judicial review exists to challenge the acts of either the President or the Trade Representative in this case. There is no explicit statutory cause of action granting a petitioner who is denied import relief under section 421 the right to sue the President and the Trade Representative in the Court of International Trade. Thus, Motion Systems has only two potential sources for relief: (1) the Administrative Procedure Act ("APA"), *5 U.S.C. § 701*; or (2) some form of nonstatutory review. Motion Systems acknowledges that it cannot challenge the President's actions under the APA because the President is not an "agency." See *Franklin v. Massachusetts, 505 U.S. 788, 800-01, 112 S. Ct. 2767, 120 L. Ed. 2d 636 (1992).* Thus, Motion Systems must resort to some form of nonstatutory review as its only potential source for relief.

As regards Motion Systems' challenge to the President's actions, this case reduces down to a rather simple issue: Can Motion Systems challenge the President's discretionary actions under *19 U.S.C. § 2451* as outside the scope of authority delegated to him by Congress? *Dalton v. Specter, 511 U.S. 462, 114 S. Ct. 1719, 128 L. Ed. 2d 497 (1994)*, rejected this alternative and thus leaves Motion Systems with no right to judicial review here. Hence, under Dalton, no complaint can lie against the President on the facts of this case.

In Dalton, the plaintiffs challenged the President's decision to close the Philadelphia Naval Shipyard as a violation of the Defense Base Closure and Realignment Act of 1990. 511 U.S. at 464. In Part I, the Court held that a straightforward application of Franklin removes the APA as a statutory alternative for standing because the President is not an "agency." Id. at 468-70. In Part II, the Court took up the alternative ground relied on by the United States Court of Appeals for the Third Circuit: "That whenever the President acts in excess of his statutory authority, he also violates the constitutional separation-of-powers doctrine." Id. at 471. In other words, the Third Circuit had held that if the President's actions are outside the scope of authority delegated to him by the 1990 Act, they can be challenged under a nonstatutory "constitutional" cause of action analogous to Motion Systems' claim in the present case. In Dalton, however, the Court rejected this theory as inconsistent with its precedents.

The Court commented that its precedents "distinguished between claims of constitutional violations and claims that an official has acted in excess of his statutory authority." Id. at 472. The Court pointed to *Youngstown Sheet & Tube Co. v. Sawyer, 343 U.S. 579, 72 S. Ct. 863, 96 L. Ed. 1153, 62 Ohio Law Abs. 417 (1952)*, as an example of a case properly characterized as involving a "constitutional" challenge. Id. at 473. In that case, the Government disclaimed any statutory authority for the President's seizure of steel mills and invoked the Constitution itself as authority for the Presidential action. Id. ("Because no statutory authority was claimed, the case necessarily turned on whether the Constitution authorized the President's actions."). The Court then explained that, in contrast to Youngstown, Dalton involved a statutory claim: "The President is said to have violated the terms of the 1990 Act by accepting procedurally flawed recommendations." Id. at 474. In other words, the President purportedly acted outside the scope of authority delegated to him by the 1990 Act. The Court did not address the extent of available review of

Presidential action for violation of a "statutory mandate," assuming that some such review was available. Id. However, because the Court concluded that the challenged Presidential action was discretionary under the 1990 Act, see id. at 476, the Court held that review was in any event precluded by the longstanding rule that: "[Judicial] review [of Presidential action] is not available when the statute in question commits the decision to the discretion of the President." Id. at 474.

Here, there is no colorable claim that the President exceeded his statutory authority. Instead, this case presents nearly the same situation as in Dalton: Motion Systems alleges the President violated the terms of section 421 by opting to protect national interests over domestic industry without evidentiary support. Motion Systems thus accuses the President of acting beyond the scope of authority delegated to him under the statute. Motion Systems attempts to distinguish Dalton because, in its view, section 421 gives the President only purely ministerial duties. See *Mississippi v. Johnson, 71 U.S. 475, 498, 18 L. Ed. 437 (1866)* (leaving open the question of whether the President can be sued to perform a purely ministerial act under a positive law). To the contrary, section 421 unquestionably grants the President broad discretion to determine "that provision of [import] relief is not in the national economic interest of the United States or . . . that the taking of action . . . would cause serious harm to the national security of the United States." *19 U.S.C. § 2451(k)(1) (2004)*.

Section 421 thus accords the President the same discretion found to remove Presidential action from judicial review in other Supreme Court cases. In *United States v. George S. Bush & Co., Inc., 310 U.S. 371, 60 S. Ct. 944, 84 L. Ed. 1259 (1940)*, upon which Dalton expressly relies, 511 U.S. at 476, the Court dealt with subject matter quite similar to that of this case. The statute at stake in Bush gave the President discretion to increase tariffs, and he had done so. An importer challenged the President's action. This court's predecessor, the Court of Customs and Patent Appeals, invalidated the increased tariff. Notably, the relevant statute in Bush

> provided . . . that the President "shall by proclamation approve the rates of duty and changes in classification and in basis of value specified in any report of the commission under this section, if in his judgment such rates of duty and changes are shown by such investigation of the commission to be necessary to equalize such differences in costs of production."

Bush, 310 U.S. at 376-77 (emphasis added). Like section 421, the statute in Bush limited to some degree the President's discretion. Specifically, the statute in Bush required the President to find that the rates of duty and changes are "necessary to equalize such differences in costs of production" before taking action. Despite this limit on the President's discretion, the Court held that the Presidential decision was not subject to judicial review:

> The President's method of solving the problem was open to scrutiny neither by the Court of Customs and Patent Appeals nor by us. Whatever may be the scope of appellate jurisdiction conferred by § 501 of the Tariff Act of 1930, it certainly does not

> permit judicial examination of the judgment of the President that the rates of duty recommended by the Commission are necessary to equalize the differences in the domestic and foreign costs of production. Id. at 379 (emphasis added).

In *Dakota Central Telephone Co. v. State of South Dakota, 250 U.S. 163, 181, 39 S. Ct. 507, 63 L. Ed. 910 (1919)*, another case upon which Dalton expressly relies, 511 U.S. at 476, the Court dealt with the President's ability to seize control of various communication systems for national security or defense reasons. Notably, the relevant statute in Dakota provided:

> That the President during the continuance of the present war is authorized and empowered, whenever he shall deem it necessary for the national security or defense, to supervise or to take possession and assume control of any telegraph, telephone, marine cable, or radio system or systems, or any part thereof, and to operate the same in such manner as may be needful or desirable for the duration of the war . . . . Dakota, 250 U.S. at 181 (quoting 40 Stat. 904 (1918)) (emphasis added). As in Bush, the statute in Dakota also limited to some degree the President's discretion. Specifically, the statute required the President to determine that seizure was "necessary for the national security or defense." Despite this restriction, the Court again concluded the Presidential action at issue was "beyond the reach of judicial power." Id. at 184. The Court made this determination despite a challenge to the President's action as being unjustifiable at the time the power was exercised. Id. (commenting that the plaintiffs alleged that "there was nothing in the conditions at the time the power was exercised which justified the calling into play of the authority; indeed, the contention goes further and assails the motives which it is asserted induced the exercise of the power"). Thus both Dakota and Bush involved situations where the Court insulated Presidential action from judicial review for abuse of discretion despite the presence of some statutory restrictions on the President's discretion. Similarly, section 421 places some restriction on the President's discretion to grant or deny import relief. But here, there is no colorable claim that the President has violated an explicit statutory mandate. Rather, the issue is whether the President abused his discretion under section 421(k). The President must determine "that provision of [import] relief is not in the national economic interest of the United States or . . . that the taking of action . . . would cause serious harm to the national security of the United States." *19 U.S.C. § 2451(k)(1)*. However, under Dalton, Bush, and Dakota, the President's actions under section 421 are still sufficiently discretionary to preclude judicial review.

Finally, because the acts of the Trade Representative were not final actions, the Court of International Trade also lacked jurisdiction to review those acts. Instead, the Trade Representative's actions were analogous to those of the Secretary in Franklin, a case in which the Secretary's report was "like a tentative recommendation" or "the ruling of a subordinate official" because it was the President who carried the responsibility of transmitting the final report to Congress. Franklin, 505 U.S. at 798 (internal quotation omitted). A subordinate officer's actions become reviewable as final only when they carry a direct and immediate consequence. See *Japan Whaling Ass'n v. Am. Cetacean Soc., 478 U.S. 221, 106 S. Ct. 2860, 92 L. Ed. 2d 166 (1986)* (concluding that the Secretary's certification to the President automatically triggered sanctions and thus was a final action). In this case, the Trade Representative's actions were not final, but only recommendations for Presidential action, and are thus not reviewable.

IV

On the facts of this case, no complaint can lie against either the President or the Trade Representative. The President's actions cannot be challenged because judicial review is unavailable when a statute allegedly violated itself commits a decision to the discretion of the President. The Trade Representative's actions cannot be challenged because they were not final. We therefore affirm the judgment of the Court of International Trade in favor of both defendants.

AFFIRMED

CONCUR

GAJARSA, Circuit Judge, with whom Circuit Judge NEWMAN joins, concurring in part and concurring in the judgment.

The court concludes that the decision not to assess antidumping duties against CCL Industrial Motor Ltd. will stand. I too would sustain that conclusion, but on its merits, not by default. On its merits, this action by the President is within the statutory authority and discretion that Congress assigned to the President; I conclude, therefore, that the action of the President is in accordance with law.

I write separately to express the view that the court is not barred from review of the range of statutory discretion assigned to the President by Congress. On conducting such review, as fully briefed and argued on this appeal, I conclude that the President's decision is within the parameters of the Act of Congress that assigned to the President the responsibility for the balancing of the economic impact of each instance of dumping.[1] It is not the judiciary's role to grade how the President conducts such an economic study, for the statute established only the broad parameter that the President must balance the economic effect on the aggrieved domestic industry against the economic benefit of the cheaper foreign import. However, it is the judiciary's role, and its duty, to review whether the President acted within the statutory parameters. The court's holding that the President's actions cannot be reviewed on any basis is contrary to the statutory assignment and contrary to the structure of our government.

I.

The majority correctly notes that because no right of judicial review is available under the APA, "Motion Systems must resort to some form of nonstatutory review as its only potential source of relief." It then interprets the Supreme Court's decision in Dalton v. Specter to have "rejected" the notion that a litigant could "challenge the President's actions . . . as outside the scope of authority delegated to him by Congress." But Dalton says no such thing, and the majority's interpretation of it represents an unwarranted expansion of the narrow holding of that case.

The general principle underlying the Supreme Court's opinion in Dalton—that discretionary Presidential actions without constitutional implications are not subject to judicial review—is unexceptionable. No one has argued that the President's discretionary actions under § 2451 raise constitutional questions. The question dividing us is, rather, whether a statute delegating to the President qualified discretion is sufficient to render unreviewable whether the Presidential action is pursuant to the statute, and is within the assigned discretionary authority, such that the President

---

1 In accordance with *19 U.S.C. § 2451(k)(1)*, the President is charged to "provide import relief for such industry pursuant to subsection (a) of this section, unless the President determines that provision of such relief is not in the national economic interest of the United States or, in extraordinary cases, that the taking of action pursuant to subsection (a) of this section would cause serious harm to the national security of the United States."

must be dismissed as a defendant without further inquiry. Dalton does not mandate that result.

I note, first, that the majority opinion in Dalton expressly declined to rule on the very proposition for which the majority relies on it: whether nonstatutory review of allegedly ultra vires Presidential action is ever available. The opinion assumed that "some claims that the President has violated a statutory mandate are judicially reviewable outside the framework of the APA." Dalton, 511 U.S. at 474. Justice Blackmun's concurring opinion states strongly, without contravention, that, under the Court's holding, "neither a challenge to ultra vires exercise of the President's statutory authority nor a timely procedural challenge is precluded" from judicial review. Id. at 478 (Blackmun, J., concurring in part and concurring in the judgment).

Second, both the majority and concurring opinions in Dalton rely heavily upon features peculiar to the statute there at issue—notably, the unfettered discretion granted to the President by the statute, which "[did] not at all limit the President's discretion in approving or disapproving the Commission's recommendations." Id. at 476. Section 2451, by contrast, does not grant the President "unqualified" discretion. As the majority concedes, the limitations on the President's discretion in § 2451 make this case less like Dalton and more like United States v. George S. Bush & Co., in which the Supreme Court stated that the President's actions were subject to review for "conformity with the statute." George S. Bush & Co., 310 U.S. at 380. It is significant that two of the cases on which Dalton relies most heavily—George S. Bush & Co. and Chicago & Southern Air Lines v. Waterman S.S. Corp.—both contemplate the availability of judicial review of Presidential actions for "conformity with the statute" or "regularity." Id.; see also *Chicago & Southern Air Lines v. Waterman S.S. Corp., 333 U.S. 103, 105, 68 S. Ct. 431, 92 L. Ed. 568 (1948).*

The D.C. Circuit has repeatedly confirmed the availability of such review. In *Chamber of Commerce v. Reich, 316 U.S. App. D.C. 61, 74 F.3d 1322, 1331 (D. C. Cir. 1996)*, it explained that "Dalton's holding merely stands for the proposition that when a statute entrusts a discrete specific decision to the President and contains no limitations on the President's exercise of that authority, judicial review of an abuse of discretion claim is not available." It has since reiterated that principle on several occasions in cases involving suits directly against the President acting in his official capacity under a statute granting him discretion. See, e.g., *Mountain States Legal Found. v. Bush, 353 U.S. App. D.C. 306, 306 F.3d 1132, 1136 (D. C. Cir. 2002)* (stating that "Courts remain obligated to determine whether statutory restrictions have been violated. In reviewing challenges under the Antiquities Act, the Supreme Court has indicated generally that review is available to ensure that [the President's actions] are consistent with constitutional principles and that the President has not exceeded his statutory authority."); *Tulare County v. Bush, 353 U.S. App. D.C. 312, 306 F.3d 1138, 1141 (D. C. Cir. 2002)* (reviewing whether

Presidential proclamation made pursuant to his discretion under the Antiquities Act was within the "statutory standard").

In addition, this court's own precedent offers ample authority for the proposition that trade-related actions of the President taken pursuant to authority delegated by Congress are subject to review to determine whether that action "falls within his delegated authority, whether the statutory language has been properly construed, and whether the President's action conforms with the relevant procedural requirements." *Florsheim Shoe Co. v. United States, 744 F.2d 787, 795 (Fed. Cir. 1984)*; see also *Maple Leaf Fish Co. v. United States, 762 F.2d 86, 89 (Fed. Cir. 1985)* (concluding that "for a court to interpose" in Presidential decision making, "there has to be a clear misconstruction of the governing statute, a significant procedural violation, or action outside delegated authority"); *Humane Soc'y v. Clinton, 236 F.3d 1320, 1330 (Fed. Cir. 2001)* (concluding that judicial review of discretionary Presidential decision under *16 U.S.C. § 1826a(b)(3)(A)* was not available, but considering whether the President "acted in other than good faith" or "otherwise was in violation of his duties" under the statute). See also *Sneaker Circus, Inc. v. Carter, 566 F.2d 396, 402 (2d Cir. 1977)* (concluding that although judicial review of Presidential trade negotiations was unavailable, the courts had authority to review "the procedures employed by the Executive in concluding these [trade] agreements, procedures which are mandated by statute"); *No Oilport! v. Carter, 520 F. Supp. 334, 347 (W. D. Wash. 1981)* (stating that "it is clear that this court may review . . . the President's actions to determine whether they complied with the procedural requirements imposed by" the Public Utilities Regulatory Act of 1978).

The majority's assertion that Motion Systems fails to state a colorable claim of ultra vires action is dubious. A "colorable claim" is merely one which is not "frivolous." See, e.g., *S. Illinois Carpenters Welfare Fund v. Carpenters, 326 F.3d 919, 923 (7th Cir. 2003)* (holding that "a colorable claim is merely one that is not frivolous"); *Davis v. Featherstone, 97 F.3d 734, 737-38 (4th Cir. 1996)* (holding that "A claim is colorable if it is arguable and nonfrivolous, whether or not it would succeed on the merits."); *Harline v. Drug Enforcement Agency, 148 F.3d 1199, 1203 (10th Cir. 1998)* (holding that a federal claim is not colorable only "if it is immaterial, and made solely for the purpose of establishing [federal] jurisdiction or . . . is wholly insubstantial or frivolous"); *Boettcher v. Sec'y of Health & Human Servs., 759 F.2d 719, 722 (9th Cir. 1985)* (holding that a federal claim is non-colorable only if it is "wholly insubstantial, immaterial, or frivolous"). Here, Motion Systems' complaint was brought against Presidential action taken pursuant to a statute that dictates the scope of the President's authority and the manner of its exercise. The complaint repeatedly describes the President's actions as "ultra vires." It identifies portions of the statute that Motion Systems believes have been violated. To conclude that Motion Systems' claim is non-colorable simply re-defines the notion of colorability to be synonymous with "meritorious." I disagree with the majority's attempt to dispose of the merits without addressing the more difficult jurisdictional question that is necessarily a predicate to such a disposition.

Where, as here, the plaintiff has alleged that the President's actions are "ultra vires," in the sense that the standards for action "imposed by Congress [have] not been met," I read the applicable authorities to permit and indeed to require judicial review of whether or not he acted within the discretionary range of the statutory mandate. I believe Motion Systems has standing to challenge the President's actions for this purpose.

II.

Having determined that standing exists, it is necessary to assess jurisdiction under § 1581(i), which provides that the Court of International Trade shall have exclusive jurisdiction over "any civil action commenced against the United States, its agencies, or its officers" arising out of certain trade and tariff laws. The question is whether the category of "officer" identified in the statute includes the President, for if it does, review authority is assigned by statute, and is not subject to repulse by the court to which it is assigned.

The phrase "the United States . . . or its officers" naturally calls to mind the constitutional class of "officers of the United States," as that term is used in the Appointments Clause, U.S. Const. art. II, § 2, cl. 2, and the Commission Clause, art. II, § 3. Indeed, in cases involving the applicability of statutory references to "officers" of the United States, the courts have generally held that such references are limited to officials who are subject to the provisions of the Appointments Clause. See, e.g., *Steele v. United States, 267 U.S. 505, 507, 45 S. Ct. 417, 69 L. Ed. 761 (1925)* (stating that "the words 'officer of the United States, 'when employed in the statutes of the United States, [are] to be taken usually to have the limited constitutional meaning' of a person appointed under Appointments-clause procedures."); *United States v. Mouat, 124 U.S. 303, 8 S. Ct. 505, 31 L. Ed. 463, 23 Ct. Cl. 490 (1888).*

The question before us here, however, is very different. This case deals not with a Bureau of Prisons doctor (*United States v. Germaine, 99 U.S. 508, 25 L. Ed. 482 (1878)*), a navy paymaster clerk (Mouat), a customs clerk (*United States v. Smith, 124 U.S. 525, 8 S. Ct. 595, 31 L. Ed. 534 (1888)*), or a Naval Academy cadet (*United States v. Perkins, 116 U.S. 483, 6 S. Ct. 449, 29 L. Ed. 700, 21 Ct. Cl. 499 (1886)*), but with the President of the United States—a constitutional official who is plainly not an "officer of the United States" for Appointments Clause purposes but whose office is created by the Constitution itself. The question before us is whether a person holding a constitutionally recognized position, such as the President or a member of Congress, which is not by its terms subject to the provisions of the Appointments Clause, is nevertheless an officer of the United States for statutory purposes.

The Supreme Court has addressed this question directly, and answered it "yes." In *Lamar v. United States, 241 U.S. 103, 36 S. Ct. 535, 60 L. Ed. 912 (1916)*, the

Court considered whether a man impersonating a member of Congress could be charged under a statute making it a crime to "'falsely assume or pretend to be an officer or employee acting under the authority of the United States, or any Department, or any officer of the government thereof. '" *Lamar v. United States, 241 U.S. at 111* (quoting statute). The defendant argued that the indictment stated no offense against him, "because a member of the House of Representatives . . . is not an officer acting under authority of the United States" within the meaning of the statute and unspecified "provisions of the Constitution." Id. at 112.

The Supreme Court disagreed, concluding that "the issue here is not a constitutional one, but who is an officer acting under the authority of the United States within the provisions" of the statute at issue. Id. That question, the Court ruled, "must be solved by the text of the provision, not shutting out as an instrument of interpretation proper light which may be afforded by the Constitution." Id.

Lamar stands for the proposition that where the alleged officer is a constitutionally recognized person, rather than merely a minor government official, the simple presumption of Germaine and its progeny—that statutory references to "officers of the United States" include only such officials as fall within the terms of the Appointments Clause—does not apply. The President, as holder of the constitutional office of the Presidency,[2] is more closely analogous to a member of Congress than to a minor functionary like the prison doctor in Germaine. The analysis used by the Supreme Court in Lamar is, therefore, the applicable analysis here. That analysis requires simple statutory construction undertaken in light of possible constitutional questions.

The first question before the Court, then, is whether Congress, in enacting *28 U.S.C. § 1581(i)*, intended the words "the United States . . . or its officers" to include the President. In considering that question the court should consider the issues addressed by the Supreme Court in Lamar: the ordinary meaning of the word "officer"; the existence of other statutory provisions that consider the President to be an officer; and the consistency of such officer status with Supreme Court and other analogous precedent. See *Lamar, 241 U.S. at 113*. See also *Operation Rescue Nat'l v. United States, 975 F. Supp. 92, 103-04 (D. Mass. 1997)*, aff'd, *147 F.3d 68 (1st Cir. 1998)* (applying Lamar analysis to determine whether members of Congress are "employees" of the government for purposes of the immunity provisions of the Federal Tort Claims Act and concluding that they are both "employees" and "officers"). Second, the court must consider whether the inclusion of the President within the class of officers in § 1581(i) runs afoul of constitutional principles.

---

2 See, e.g., U.S. Const. art. II, § 1, cl. 1 (vesting the executive power in the President, who "shall hold his Office during the Term of four Years"); art. II, § 1, cl. 5 (referring to the "Office of President").

A. Statutory Construction

In interpreting a statute, "our inquiry begins with the statutory text, and ends there as well if the text is unambiguous." *Bedroc Ltd. v. United States, 541 U.S. 176, 183, 124 S. Ct. 1587, 158 L. Ed. 2d 338 (2004)* (Rehnquist, C. J., plurality opinion). In construing statutory language, we begin with the "assumption that the ordinary meaning of [Congress'] language accurately expresses the legislative purpose." *Engine Mfrs. Ass'n v. S. Coast Air Quality Mgmt. Dist., 541 U.S. 246, 252, 124 S. Ct. 1756, 158 L. Ed. 2d 529 (2004)*. The Supreme Court frequently repairs to dictionary definitions to ascertain the "ordinary meaning" of statutory text that does not arise in a technical context. See id. at 252-53 (using dictionary definition to construe Congress' intent in using the word "standard"); see also Lamar, 241 U.S. at 113 (using dictionary definitions to construe Congress' intent in using the word "officer" and concluding that "officer" included members of Congress). Here, the statute applies to "the United States . . . or its officers." *28 U.S.C. § 1581(i)*.

With regard to the "common understanding" of the word "officer," as "expressed in the ordinary, as well as legal, dictionaries," *Lamar, 241 U.S. at 113*, one finds that, "in public affairs," the term "officer" refers to a person "holding office of trust, command, or authority in corporation, government . . . or other institution." Black's Law Dictionary 977 (5th ed. 1979).[3] The magisterial Oxford English Dictionary defines "officer" as, among other things, "a person authoritatively appointed or elected to exercise some function pertaining to public life, or to take part in . . . the management or direction of a public corporation, institution, etc." and "[a] person holding office and taking part in the management or direction of a society or institution, esp. one holding the office of president, treasurer, or secretary; an office-bearer."[4] 10 Oxford English Dictionary 732 (2d. ed. 1989). Ordinary usage confirms these definitions: the officers of a corporation, for example, typically include its president.

The second factor considered by the Supreme Court in Lamar was the existence of other statutes in which the term "officer" was found to include members of Congress. See Lamar, 241 U.S. at 113. The President of the United States may be an "officer" for some statutory purposes, but not for others. Some statutes by their terms include the President in the class of statutory officers. In the Impoundment

---

3 The same dictionary's definitions of "United States officer" and "officer of the United States," are unhelpful here: they apply to situations as in Germaine, Mouat, and Steele, which, as discussed, are irrelevant to the question of whether a constitutional officer (as opposed to a minor executive branch official) is an "officer of the United States."

4 See also Webster's New International Dictionary 1567 (1961) ("One who holds an office: one who is appointed or elected to serve in a position of trust, authority, or command esp. as specif. provided by law"); American Heritage Dictionary 1220 (2000) ("One who holds an office of authority or trust in an organization, such as a corporation or government"); The New Oxford American Dictionary 1188 (2001) ("a holder of a public, civil, or ecclesiastical office"; "a holder of a post in a society, company, or other organization, esp. one who is involved at a senior level of its management").

Control Act, for example, § 686(a) refers to "the President, the Director of the Office of Management and Budget, the head of any department or agency of the United States, or any other officer or employee of the United States." *2 U.S.C. § 686(a)* (emphasis added). The succeeding section empowers the Comptroller General to bring a civil action in district court to force the government to make available necessary budget authority and empowers the district courts to enter an order against "any department, agency, officer or employee of the United States"—a grouping which, read in conjunction with the "or other officer" language of § 686(a), clearly includes the President. See *2 U.S.C. § 687*; see also *3 U.S.C. § 303* (defining "function" to include "any duty, power, responsibility, authority, or discretion vested in *the President or other officer* concerned") (emphasis added).

Other statutes appear to recognize that the President is included in the class of officers by negative implication: the federal law proscribing bribery, for example, applies to persons who are "officers or employees . . . of the United States," but expressly carves out the President from that classification, suggesting that in the absence of the exception the class would include the President. See *18 U.S.C. § 203(a)(1)(B)*, § 202(c).

In addition, the courts have ruled on several occasions that the federal mandamus law, which by its terms applies to "officers and employees of the United States," applies to the President. See, e.g., *Nat'l Treasury Employees Union v. Nixon, 160 U.S. App. D.C. 321, 492 F.2d 587, 602, 616 (D. C. Cir. 1974)* (concluding that the President is subject to mandamus proceedings under *28 U.S.C. § 1361* but refraining from issuing the writ); *Nat'l Wildlife Fed. v. United States, 200 U.S. App. D.C. 53, 626 F.2d 917, 923 (D. C. Cir. 1980)* (holding that "mandamus is not precluded because the federal official at issue is the President of the United States"); *Swan v. Clinton, 321 U.S. App. D.C. 359, 100 F.3d 973, 976 n. 1 (D. C. Cir. 1996)* (finding that the "prerequisites for stating a cause of action under the mandamus statute are met" in an action against President Clinton).

The executive branch's own lawyers have concluded on many occasions that the President is a statutory officer of the United States. In fact, they have done so in this case: government counsel, in the first oral argument conducted in this matter, stated that "the President is an officer of the United States." Executive branch counsel have also concluded, in a reasoned opinion, that a general statutory reference to "officers" included the President. Section 603 of Title 18 of the United States Code prohibits any "officer or employee of the United States" from making certain political contributions. The Office of Legal Counsel, relying in part on legislative history,[5] concluded in a published opinion that "the better view, in our judgment, is that the President does, indeed, fall within the terms of" the statute's class of "officers. "See 3 U.S. Op. Off. Legal Counsel 31, 39 (1979). The Office of Legal Counsel and other executive branch lawyers have considered the Presi-

5 The legislative history of § 1581(i) is silent on the question of who constitutes an "officer" for statutory purposes.

dent to be an officer for a variety of statutory and other purposes. See 38 U.S. Op. Atty. Gen. 445 (April 9, 1936) (construing statute applying to "the Secretary of the Treasury or any other officer of the Government" to include the President as such an officer); 20 U.S. Op. Off. Legal Counsel No. 124 (May 7, 1976) (referring to "an officer who is subject to control and removal by an officer other than the President"); 19 U.S. Op. Off. Legal Counsel 93 (June 3, 1986) (referring to "executive officers other than the President"); 6 U.S. Op. Off. Legal Counsel 751 (December 14, 1982) (referring to "Executive officers other than the President"); 21 U.S. Op. Atty. Gen. 494 (February 11, 1897) (referring to the Secretary of the Treasury or "any other officers save the President"); 13 U.S. Op. Atty. Gen. 479 (referring to the inability of "any officer but the President" to remit a criminal sentence); 1 U.S. Op. Atty. Gen. 566 (September 27, 1822) (referring to the President as "the executive officer of the laws of the country").

Similarly, the President has, on many occasions, referred to himself as an officer. See, e.g., Executive Order No. 11827 (Jan. 4, 1975) (referring to advisory committees "created by the President or any other officer of the Executive Branch" under the Federal Advisory Commission Act); Executive Order No. 11609 (July 26, 1976) ("Delegating Certain Functions Vested in the President to Other Officers of the Government"); Executive Order No. 11480 (September 9, 1969) (referring to actions taken "by the President or by any other officer of the Executive Branch"); Executive Order No. 11435 (January 21, 1968) (referring to actions "of the President or of any other officer of the United States"); Executive Order No. 10994 (February 14, 1962) (referring to prior orders of "the President or . . . any other officer of the Executive Branch"); Executive Order No. 10640 (October 10, 1955) (same); Executive Order No. 10167 (October 11, 1950) (referring to "the President or such other officer as he may designate").

In addition, the Supreme Court has frequently identified the President as an officer, and specifically as "the chief constitutional officer of the United States." *Nixon v. Fitzgerald, 457 U.S. 731, 750, 102 S. Ct. 2690, 73 L. Ed. 2d 349 (1982)*; see also *Clinton v. Jones, 520 U.S. 681, 699 n. 29, 117 S. Ct. 1636, 137 L. Ed. 2d 945 (1997)* (quoting *Fitzgerald); Franklin v. Massachusetts, 505 U.S. 788, 799, 112 S. Ct. 2767, 120 L. Ed. 2d 636 (1992)* (referring to the President as a "constitutional officer"); *Cheney v. U.S. District Court for the District of Columbia, 541 U.S. 913, 916, 158 L. Ed. 2d 225, 124 S. Ct. 1391 (2004)* (Justice Scalia, writing as a single justice, referring to "the President and other officers of the Executive"); *Menard's Heirs v. Massey, 49 U.S. 293, 309, 12 L. Ed. 1085 (1850)* (referring to "the President or some other officer"); *U.S. Ex. Rel. Goodrich v. Guthrie, 58 U.S. 284, 310, 15 L. Ed. 102 (1854)* (McLean, J., dissenting) (stating that "the President, like all the other officers of the government, is subject to the law"); *Embry v. United States, 100 U.S. 680, 685, 25 L. Ed. 772, 15 Ct. Cl. 632 (1879)* (referring to "no officer except the President"); *United States v. McDonald, 128 U.S. 471, 473, 9 S. Ct. 117, 32 L. Ed. 506, 24 Ct. Cl. 524 (1888)* (quoting *Embry); United States v. Am. Bell Tel., 128 U.S. 315, 363, 9 S. Ct. 90, 32 L. Ed. 450, 1888 Dec. Comm'r Pat. 558*

(1888) (referring to "the president . . . or any other officer of the government"); *In re Sealed Case, 121 F.3d 729, 748, 326 U.S. App. D.C. 276 (D. C. Cir. 1997)* (the President is "the chief constitutional officer" of the United States).

Congress has spoken of the President as an "officer" in other contexts: the Senate report addressing the amendment of the apportionment statute at issue in Franklin v. Massachusetts stated explicitly that the amended statute required participation by the President, rather than by the Secretary of Commerce, "so that this function may be served by a constitutional officer." S. Rep. No. 2, 71st Cong., 1st Sess., at 5 (1929) (quoted in *Franklin v. Massachusetts, 505 U.S. at 800*).

Considered together with the Constitution's express identification of the Presidency as an "office"; the consistency of Supreme Court identification of the President as an officer of the United States; and the plain and commonplace understanding of the term "officer" to include public officials like the President, these examples leave no doubt that the President is an officer of the United States. The next question is whether Congress included the President in the class of "officers" defined by *28 U.S.C. § 1581(i)*. I conclude that it did.

Section 1581(i) creates jurisdiction over civil actions against "the United States, its agencies, or its officers," arising out of "any law of the United States providing for—

(1) revenue from imports or tonnage;

(2) tariffs, duties, fees, or other taxes on the importation of merchandise for reasons other than the raising of revenue;

(3) embargoes or other quantitative restrictions on the importation of merchandise for reasons other than the protection of the public health or safety; or

(4) administration and enforcement with respect to the matters referred to in paragraphs (1)-(3) of this subsection and subsections (a)-(h) of this section. 28 U.S.C. § 1581(i).

Section 1581(i) is a "broad jurisdictional grant," enacted by Congress as a "residual" source of jurisdiction to supplement the more specific provisions of § 1581(a)-(h) and "eliminate the confusion which currently exists between the jurisdiction of the district courts and the Court of International Trade," and clarify that "all of the suits of the type specified [in § 1581(i)] are properly commenced only in the Court of International Trade." H.R. Rep. No. 1235, 96th Cong., 2d. Sess. 47 (1980). The "type specified" in § 1581(i) is lawsuits arising out of a broad array of trade laws in which the President, acting on authority delegated by Congress, plays an unusually significant role.

Section 1581(i)(3), for example, applies to actions arising out of "embargoes or other quantitative restrictions on the importation of merchandise for reasons other than the protection of the public health or safety." *28 U.S.C. § 1581(i)(3)*. Embargoes are an element of international affairs in which the President plays a signature, and even dominant, role. See, e.g., *22 U.S.C. § 6032(c)* (ordering the President to "instruct the Secretary of the Treasury and the Attorney General to enforce fully the Cuban Assets Control Regulations"); *50 U.S.C. § 1707(b)* (requiring the President, within 20 days after the start of hostilities with a foreign nation, to "submit to Congress a report setting forth . . . the specific steps the United States has taken . . . to establish a multinational economic embargo"); *22 U.S.C. § 408* (authorizing the President to "employ such part of the land or naval forces of the United States as he may deem necessary to carry out the purposes of" provisions regulating trade with hostile nations); *22 U.S.C. § 2370* (authorizing the President to "establish and maintain a total embargo upon all trade between the United States and Cuba"). More important, perhaps, is the statute's exclusion from its jurisdictional grant of precisely the kinds of embargoes in which the President plays no role. By excluding from jurisdiction suits arising out of embargoes imposed "for the protection of the public health and safety," the statute excludes most existing embargoes, including, for example, those relating to adulterated foods and unapproved drugs (see *21 U.S.C. § 381*), nonconforming products (see *15 U.S.C. § 1192*), and toxic substances (see *15 U.S.C. § 2612*). The provisions of *§ 1581(i)(3)*, in short, are heavily focused on precisely those areas of trade law in which the President is assigned a role. The same is true for § 1581(i)(2), which applies to actions arising out of "tariffs, duties, fees, or other taxes on the importation of merchandise for reasons other than the raising of revenue." *28 U.S.C. § 1581(i)(2)*. The President plays little, if any, role in the revenue-raising portions of the tariff laws, but is assigned a substantial role in the use of tariffs for other purposes. See, e.g., *19 U.S.C. § 2461* (authorizing the President to provide duty-free treatment from certain developing countries, taking "due regard for" considerations such as "the effect such action will have on furthering the economic development of developing countries").

The legislative history of § 1581(i), although not dispositive of this issue, suggests that Congress did not exclude this aspect of the trade laws from the general compass of the Court of International Trade. In the Senate hearings regarding S. 2857—a predecessor to the bill that became the Customs Courts Act of 1980—Assistant Attorney General Babcock, discussing the jurisdictional confusion that S. 2857, and later § 1581, were designed to remedy, cited *Sneaker Circus, Inc. v. Carter, 566 F.2d 396 (2d Cir. 1977)* as an example of the kind of case that should be heard by the then-named Customs Court. Asked whether the proposed legislation would grant the Customs Court jurisdiction to hear Sneaker Circus' suit against the President, Babcock replied that "that is the object, the real object of the bill. The real object is that that case would very clearly be headed for the Customs Court." Senate Hearings on S. 2857, June 23 and 27, 1978, 95th Cong., 2d. Sess., at 65-66. The House Report on the Customs Courts Act also referred specifically to Sneaker Circus—which was heard by the Second Circuit—as an example of the jurisdictional "confusion" that § 1581(i) was intended to remedy. The legislative history suggests that Congress was aware of, and approved of, the possibility that what is now the Court of International Trade could exercise jurisdiction over suits under the trade laws, not excluding those actions performed by the President and other officers of the United States.

I conclude, therefore, that Congress intended § 1581(i)'s reference to "officers" to include the President of the United States, subject to constitutional implications, to which I now turn. See *Lamar, 241 U.S. at 112* (concluding that although "the issue here is not a constitutional one," it must be considered in the "proper light . . . afforded by the Constitution").

B. Constitutional Considerations

To address the issues presented by this appeal, the court need not reach the overall implications of whether the President is or is not an "officer of the United States" for constitutional purposes.[6] It need only consider whether the designation of the President of the United States as an officer of the United States in administration of the trade statute raises intractable constitutional difficulties. I conclude that it does not.

The Constitution repeatedly designates the Presidency as an "Office, "which surely suggests that its occupant is, by definition, an "officer."[7] See, e.g., U.S. Const. art. I, § 3, cl. 5; art. II, § 1, cl. 1; art. II, § 1, cl. 5; art. II, § 1, cl. 6; art. II, § 1, cl. 8; amend. XXII, § 1; amend. XXV, §§ 1, 3, 4. An interpretation of the Constitution in which the holder of an "office" is not an "officer" seems, at best, strained. It is true, however, that our understanding of the category of "officers of the United States" comes primarily from the Appointments Clause and the jurisprudence associated with it.[8] The Appointments Clause and the Commissions Clause, by their terms,

---

6 There has been lively academic debate on that issue, mostly as an offshoot of discussions of legislative succession. Akhil Amar and Vikram Amar conclude that the President is an "Officer of the United States" for constitutional purposes. See Akhil Reed Amar and Vikram David Amar, Is the Presidential Succession Law Constitutional?, 48 Stan. L. Rev. 113, 136 n. 143 (1995) ("If an acting President, wielding the full and awesome executive power of the United States, is not an 'Officer of the United States, 'what is he?") Steven Calabresi agrees. See Steven G. Calabresi, The Political Question of Presidential Succession, 48 Stan. L. Rev. 155, 158 n. 24 (1995) ("The best reading . . . is that the President and the Vice President are the 'Officers of the United States' contemplated by the language in the Appointments Clause referring to "all other Officers of the United States, whose Appointments are not herein otherwise provided for.") John Manning disagrees. See John F. Manning, Not Proved: Some Lingering Questions About Legislative Succession to the Presidency, 48 Stan. L. Rev. 141, 146 (1995) (questioning whether one who "holds" the office of the Presidency is therefore an "officer of the United States.").d

7 If this is not sufficiently obvious on its face, see, e.g., 10 Oxford English Dictionary 732 (2d. ed. 1989), defining "officer" as "one who holds an office."

8 The full text of the Appointments Clause reads: [The President] shall nominate, and by and with the Advice and Consent of the Senate, shall appoint Ambassadors, other public Ministers and Consuls, Judges of the supreme Court, and all other Officers of the United States, whose Appointments are not herein otherwise provided for, and which shall be established by Law: but the Congress may by Law vest the Appointment of such inferior Officers, as they think

apply to all "officers of the United States" and all "civil officers of the United States," respectively. See id. at art. II, § 2, cl. 2; art. II, § 3; art. II, § 4. Those clauses, and other constitutional provisions,[9] contemplate a class of "officers" inferior in status to the President, who nominates and commissions them. The key features of that class are nomination by the President, appointment with the advice and consent of the Senate, commission by the President, and removal by impeachment. It is plain that the President is not an "officer of the United States" for Appointments Clause, Commission Clause, or Oath of Office Clause purposes.[10]

The question then remains whether the inapplicability of those clauses to the President creates a constitutional barrier to his inclusion as an "officer" for purposes of § 1581(i). I conclude that it does not, for two reasons. First, although the Appointments Clause and its relations do contemplate a class of "Officers of the United States" that is inferior to and does not include the President, there is reason to believe that the inferior class of appointed officials denominated as "Officers of the United States" is nonexclusive. That is, the Constitution suggests that high elected officials—including the President and members of Congress—are officers for constitutional or statutory purposes despite their separate status from persons governed by the Appointments Clause. Second, the constitutional principles and values that underlie the Appointments Clause and the limitations it places upon the officials to whom it applies are not threatened by the identification of the President as an "officer" for purposes of section 1581(i).

---

proper, in the President alone, in the Courts of Law, or in the Heads of Departments. Art. II, § 2, cl. 2.

9 See, e.g., the Oath of Office Clause, art. VI, cl. 3 (requiring an oath of office for, inter alia, "all executive and judicial officers"). The President's oath of office is separately required by Article II, Section 2, clause 8, suggesting that he is not among the "executive officers" governed by Article VI, clause 3.

10 The Impeachment Clause presents a slightly different case. That clause provides for impeachment of "The President, Vice-President and all civil officers of the United States. "U.S. Const. art. II, § 4. This is ambiguous on its face: depending on which canon of construction one prefers, it might mean that impeachment applies to all civil officers of the United States and also to the President and Vice-President, who are not such officers; or it might mean that that the President and Vice-President are examples of the category of civil officers of the United States. It could be read, in other words, to support two contradictory interpretations of the President's status as officer. No less a constitutional authority than Justice Story appears to have held contradictory views about whether the President and Vice-President are "civil officers". In one passage of his Commentaries, for example, he argued that the Impeachment Clause "does not even consider [the President and Vice President] officers of the United States," because "it says, 'the president, vice-president, and all civil officers (not all other civil officers) shall be removed . . . .The language of the clause, therefore, would rather lead to the conclusion that they were enumerated as contradistinguished from, rather than as included in, the description of civil officers of the United States.'" Joseph Story, Commentaries on the Constitution of the United States 2, § 791 (1833). Only a few pages before, however, Story described the remedy of impeachment as being "strictly confined *to civil officers of the United States, including the President and Vice-President.*" Id. at § 787 (emphasis added).

The Incompatibility Clause, Art. I, § 6, cl. 2, for example, makes clear that members of Congress cannot hold appointed office under the United States, but the courts have consistently concluded that members of Congress are "officers of the United States" for purposes of various federal statutes. See, e.g., *Lamar, 241 U.S. 103, 36 S. Ct. 535, 60 L. Ed. 912*; *Operation Rescue Nat'l v. United States, 975 F. Supp. at 103-04* (holding that a member of Congress is an officer of the United States for purposes of *28 U.S.C. § 2671*); *Maddox v. Williams, 855 F. Supp. 406 (D. D.C. 1994)*, aff'd, *314 U.S. App. D.C. 85, 62 F.3d 408 (D. C. Cir. 1995)* (holding that a member of Congress is an officer of the United States for purposes of *28 U.S.C. § 1442(a)*); *Williams v. Brooks, 945 F.2d 1322, 1324 n. 2 (5th Cir. 1991)* (same); *Richards v. Harper, 864 F.2d 85, 86 (9th Cir. 1988)* (same); *Hill Parents Ass'n v. Giaimo, 287 F. Supp. 98, 99 (D. Conn. 1968)* (same); *Preston v. Edmondson, 263 F. Supp. 370, 372 (N. D. Okla. 1967)* (same).

The Senate itself has concluded that Senators are not "officers of the United States"[11] for purposes of the Impeachment Clause,[12] but do hold a "civil office" in the government of the United States for purposes of an oath-of-office statute.[13]

In addition, consideration of the constitutional principles embodied in the Appointments Clause and the limitations it places on "Officers of the United States" leads us to conclude that those principles are unthreatened by the identification of the President as an officer for statutory purposes. The constitutional clauses governing "officers" serve to ensure that the responsible agents of government are subject to defined constitutional controls—primarily nomination, appointment, consent, and impeachment. These requirements exist to effect two core constitutional principles: political accountability and separation of powers. See, e.g., *Edmond v. United States, 520 U.S. 651, 660, 117 S. Ct. 1573, 137 L. Ed. 2d 917 (1997)* (stating that

---

11 Note also that the statute at issue in the oath-of-office debate applied to persons holding "offices" under the United States government, but specifically excepted the President of the United States—suggesting the understanding that without such an exception the President would have been subject to the statute.

12 This principle has been accepted since 1799, when the Senate, presented with articles of impeachment against Senator William Blount, concluded after four days of debate that a Senator was not a "civil officer of the United States" for purposes of the Impeachment Clause. See Senate J., 5th Cong., 3d Sess., 17 December 1798-10 January 1799.

13 See Cong. Globe, 28th Cong., 1st Sess., 26 January 1864 (floor debate regarding whether legislation requiring an oath of office for "every person elected or appointed to any office of honor or profit under the Government of the United States, either in the civil, military, or naval departments of the public service" applied to Senators). Despite bitter opposition, proponents of the view that a Senate seat is a civil office of the United States prevailed by a vote of 28-11. The arguments made by the prevailing Senators anticipated, with remarkable precision, the Supreme Court's analysis in Lamar fifty years later: Senator Sumner of Massachusetts, for example, arguing successfully for the position that Senators did hold "offices" for purposes of the statute, noted that the constitutional definition of "officers of the United States" was not controlling, and pointed to the common understanding of the word "officer, "dictionary definitions of same, and other constitutions and statutes that assumed the officer status of legislators. Cf. Lamar, 241 U.S. at 112-13.

"the Appointments Clause was designed to ensure public accountability"); see also *Weiss v. United States, 510 U.S. 163, 186, 114 S. Ct. 752, 127 L. Ed. 2d 1 (1994)* (Souter, J., concurring in the judgment) (stating that "the Appointments Clause separates the Government's power but also provides for a degree of intermingling, all to ensure accountability"); *Freytag v. Comm'r, 501 U.S. 868, 878-80, 111 S. Ct. 2631, 115 L. Ed. 2d 764 (1991)* (emphasizing the separation-of-powers principles "embedded in the Appointments Clause," which are "structural and political" and articulate "a limiting principle" for both the executive and Congress).

To the extent that the qualifications demanded of "Officers of the United States" are rooted in the need to provide political accountability to officials exercising significant government authority, there is clearly no harm in identifying the President—the most politically accountable of all national figures—as such an officer. To the extent that those qualifications are based upon separation of powers principles, those considerations arise not in the identification of the President as an officer of the United States, but in the substance of what Congress is attempting to achieve by that identification. It is difficult to understand, in the context of section 1581, how the mere exercise of jurisdiction over the President threatens the separation of powers. In this regard it is sufficient to note that the President's duties under the Trade Act were delegated by Congress. There is no doubt that, to the extent Congress chose to grant the President discretion in exercising those duties, the exercise of his discretion within the statutory assignment is not subject to judicial review. Whether the courts may exercise jurisdiction over the President—in order, for example, to review whether the President acted "in full conformity with the statute," as permitted in the trade context by the Supreme Court's decision in George S. Bush & Co.—is a wholly different question, and one that does not significantly implicate the separation of powers.

There remains one issue that merits discussion. The Supreme Court, in Franklin v. Massachusetts, has held that the President is not an "agency" subject to suit under the Administrative Procedure Act. In Franklin, the Court declared, "out of respect for the separation of powers and the unique constitutional status of the President," that it would not subject the President to a statutory provision without an "express statement by Congress" that the provision was meant to include the President. *Franklin v. Massachusetts, 505 U.S. at 800-01.*

Franklin is readily distinguishable from the present case. First, as a matter of plain meaning, the President is an unlikely candidate for "agency" status. The common-sense answer to the question, "Is the President an 'agency'?" seems to be "clearly not." The common-sense answer to the question, "Is the President an 'officer of the United States'?" is clearly "yes." Indeed, the government's own counsel, at oral argument, answered that question affirmatively. Second, by its own terms, Franklin applies only to a statutory provision that would make the President's "performance of his statutory duties" reviewable for "abuse of discretion." Id. at 801. It says nothing about the less troubling circumstance in which the President's actions are reviewed only for conformity with the statutory grant.

In addition, there is no suggestion in Franklin that there is any significant historical support for the notion that the term "agency" includes the President. There is, however, massive historical support—in the Constitution itself, in two centuries of Supreme Court jurisprudence, in significant opinions of the lower courts, in federal statutes, and in myriad other sources—for the proposition that the President is an "officer" of his country. The use of the word "officer" in § 1581(i)—a statute that creates jurisdiction over matters of international trade in which the President exercises significant delegated authority—is an "express statement" that the President is subject to jurisdiction under that statute. In this connection, I note that Franklin itself expressly refers to the President as a "constitutional officer." Id. at 799.

Finally, I note that whereas the identification of the President as an "agency" for APA purposes would potentially expose the President to litigation on innumerable causes of action, the identification of the President as an officer for purposes of § 1581(i) would subject him to jurisdiction only in the limited context of actions arising out of specified areas of trade law—an area in which the President has traditionally been subject to jurisdiction. See, e.g., *George S. Bush & Co.; Florsheim Shoe Co. v. United States, 744 F.2d at 795*; *Maple Leaf Fish Co., 762 F.2d at 89.* In short, the case at bar presents very different issues than those faced by the Supreme Court in Franklin.

I conclude, therefore, that the phrase "the United States . . . or its officers" in the statute encompasses the President of the United States. Motion Systems therefore has a right to judicial review of the President's actions, and the Court of International Trade properly exercised jurisdiction over that action.

III.

Having concluded that this action was properly before the Court of International Trade, it is necessary to consider the merits of that court's decision. The President is charged by statute to balance the economic impact on the American manufacturer who is injured by competition with "dumped" foreign goods, against the benefit to the importer and potentially to the consumer of lower foreign prices. Such an economic analysis involves the responsibilities and interests of government, industry, labor, and the consumer, and the balancing thereof was quite reasonably assigned by Congress to the topmost official of the executive branch. However, this assignment did not remove trade law from its constitutional design: the assignment was made by the legislative arm, which is responsible for trade and customs law; it is administered by the executive arm, as for most laws; and challenge to the law or its administration, when raised by "case or controversy," is the responsibility and authority of the judicial arm. I agree with the conclusion of the Court of International Trade that there is "no basis to conclude that the President's decision is based on a 'clear misunderstanding of the governing statute' or that it constituted 'action outside his delegated authority.'" I would affirm its decision on the merits.

CONCLUSION

We granted this rehearing en banc to consider several significant questions of law. The majority has avoided most of these issues in favor of the dubious proposition, never advanced by any party to this action, that Motion Systems has no right to any judicial review of Presidential action taken pursuant to the statute. In order to avoid the very issues we took this case en banc to resolve, the majority misreads and misapplies applicable Supreme Court authority and, in so doing, adopts an indefensibly cramped view of the judiciary's constitutional role as a check and balance to its coordinate and coequal branches of government.

When Congress has delegated its constitutional authority to the President, and the statute contemplates presidential action within statutory parameters, the courts must determine whether these parameters were respected. The judicial role is to review whether the presidential action is in performance of the statutory assignment, and the extent of executive discretion in that performance. No court, until today, has held that all inquiry is foreclosed as to whether the action complained of is within the statutory assignment and the discretionary authority assigned by Congress. I respectfully object to the majority's unwarranted disruption of the constitutional balance under which we all serve.

IX. INTERNATIONAL TRADE

2. Business & Finance

A. In General*

* Cases are indexed under this subject. The full text of these cases is published in the **volume**-page indicated.

IN RE: CANADIAN IMPORT ANTITRUST LITIGATION
v.
PFIZER, INC.

470 F.3d 785 (8th Cir. 2006)
Decided November 30, 2006

Before LOKEN, Chief Judge, JOHN R. GIBSON, and COLLOTON, Circuit Judges.

OPINION

COLLOTON, Circuit Judge.

Plaintiffs, a group of consumers and organizations from Minnesota who have purchased prescription drugs in the United States from the defendant drug companies in the United States, filed suit pursuant to § 4 of the Clayton Act, *15 U.S.C. § 15*, for damages caused by alleged violations of § 1 of the Sherman Antitrust Act, *15 U.S.C. § 1*, and pursuant to § 16 of the Clayton Act, *15 U.S.C. § 26*, seeking injunctive relief. Plaintiffs also alleged violations of various state statutes concerning restraint of trade. The gravamen of the complaint was that the defendants unlawfully conspired to suppress the importation of Canadian prescription drugs for personal use. The district court[1] dismissed the federal antitrust claim and declined to exercise supplemental jurisdiction over the remaining state law claims. We affirm.

I.

The plaintiffs filed suit on May 19, 2004, alleging that the defendants had "engaged in a concerted course of conduct designed to prevent brand name prescription drugs purchased from Canadian pharmacies from entering the United States." (Complaint, R. Doc. No. 1, at P18). According to the complaint, the conduct eliminated a legal source of prescription drugs and caused American consumers to

1 The Honorable Joan N. Ericksen, United States District Judge for the District of Minnesota, adopting the reports and recommendations of the Honorable Jonathan Lebedoff, Chief United States Magistrate Judge for the District of Minnesota.

pay higher drug prices. The plaintiffs alleged that the defendant drug companies engaged in anti-competitive conduct, including: (1) requiring Canadian pharmacies to certify that they were not selling prescription drugs to persons whom the pharmacies knew or should have known were taking the drugs outside the country, (2) monitoring orders of Canadian pharmacies and limiting their purchases to historical levels, (3) creating "blacklists" of pharmacies that were suspected of selling drugs to American consumers and directing wholesalers not to sell to the blacklisted pharmacies, and (4) cutting off supplies to wholesalers who did not comply with their policies. (*Id.* at P36). The plaintiffs alleged that this conduct violated the Sherman Act, and the antitrust and unfair competition statutes of twenty-three states and the District of Columbia. (*Id.* at PP28, 73, 82).

The district court consolidated several similar cases, and the plaintiffs filed an amended complaint on September 30, 2004. The defendants moved to dismiss the complaint for failure to state a claim. *See Fed. R. Civ. P. 12(b)(6)*. Two defendants, AstraZeneca PLC and Novartis AG, also moved to dismiss for lack of personal jurisdiction and improper venue. A magistrate judge recommended granting the motion to dismiss on the Sherman Act claims. The report concluded that because the importation of Canadian prescription drugs was prohibited by the Federal Food, Drug, and Cosmetic Act ("FFDCA"), the plaintiffs could not demonstrate that they have an injury "of the kind the federal antitrust laws were designed to prevent." The magistrate judge also recommended that the state-law claims against AstraZeneca and Novartis be dismissed for lack of personal jurisdiction and improper venue.

On review of the reports and recommendations, the district court concluded that the plaintiffs lacked standing to pursue their federal antitrust claims because the allegedly anticompetitive behavior discouraged only unlawful importation of drugs and not lawful activity that the Sherman Act was designed to protect. In particular, the court found that drugs imported from Canada, even when imported for personal use, were "misbranded" under the laws of the United States because their labels did not bear the required "Rx only" symbol. After dismissing the federal claims, the court declined to exercise supplemental jurisdiction over the remaining state claims and dismissed them without prejudice. The court also denied the motions to dismiss for lack of personal jurisdiction as moot.

II.

We review the district court's grant of a motion to dismiss *de novo*. *Farm Credit Servs. of Am. v. American State Bank, 339 F.3d 764, 767 (8th Cir. 2003)*. A complaint is properly dismissed for failing to state a claim when the plaintiffs can prove no set of facts that would entitle them to relief. *Conley v. Gibson, 355 U.S. 41, 45-46, 78 S. Ct. 99, 2 L. Ed. 2d 80 (1957)*.

The district court's decision to dismiss the federal claims was premised on its conclusion that federal law prohibits the importation of prescription drugs from

Canada for personal use. Plaintiffs continue to assert that the common assumption that such importation is unlawful is based purely on "myth," and that no federal statute actually precludes a citizen from carrying prescription drugs purchased in Canada into the United States.

The United States Food and Drug Administration ("FDA") repeatedly has expressed the view that virtually all importation of drugs into the United States by individual consumers violates the FFDCA, because the drugs are not approved in accordance with *21 U.S.C. § 355*, are not labeled as required by *21 U.S.C. § 352*, or are dispensed without a valid prescription in contravention of *21 U.S.C. § 353(b)(1)*. The FDA's Office of Compliance has cautioned that "[d]rugs from foreign countries do not have the same assurance of safety as drugs actually regulated by the FDA," due to the risk that counterfeit or unapproved drugs will be sent to consumers, and also because "[w]ithout regulation of repackaging, storage conditions, and many other factors, drugs delivered to the American public from foreign countries may be very different from FDA approved drugs with respect to formulation, potency, quality, and labeling." (Appellees' App. at 8-9). The district court in this case focused on one aspect of the approval process—the labeling requirements—and observed that it is illegal to import drugs whose labels do not comport with the statutory and regulatory requirements.

We agree with the district court's conclusion that the Canadian prescription drugs at issue are not labeled in conformity with federal law, and that importation of the drugs is therefore prohibited. Federal law requires that a drug shall be deemed "misbranded if at any time prior to dispensing the label of the drug fails to bear, at a minimum, the symbol 'Rx only,'" *21 U.S.C. § 353(b)(4)(A)*, and the introduction of misbranded drugs into interstate commerce is prohibited. *Id.* § 331(a). Drugs that are dispensed by Canadian pharmacies are labeled "Pr," as opposed to "Rx only." Plaintiffs argue that the Canadian symbol is the "functional equivalent" of "Rx only," but federal law does not provide for functional equivalence in labeling. The drugs do not "bear, at a minimum, the symbol 'Rx only,'" and they are therefore "misbranded."

The plaintiffs argue that the even if the drugs are misbranded under federal law when they are distributed to Canadian pharmacists, the American labeling requirements do not apply to the drugs after they are dispensed by a pharmacy, because of the so-called "pharmacist's exception" set forth in *21 U.S.C. § 353(b)(2)*. That provision says that "any drug dispensed by filling or refilling a written or oral prescription of a practitioner licensed by law to administer such drug shall be exempt from the requirements of section 352 of this title," with some exceptions. *Id.* The exemption in § 353, however, applies only to the requirements in § 352. The "Rx only" requirement appears in § 353(b)(4), and it is not exempted by § 353(b)(2).

More fundamentally, that the Canadian drugs are mislabeled under federal law illustrates why the Canadian drugs are "unapproved" drugs within the meaning of *21 U.S.C. § 355*, and thus prohibited from importation on that basis as well.

The FFDCA comprehensively regulates the manufacture, importation, and sale of prescription drugs. Before a new drug may be introduced into interstate commerce, the FDA must approve the manufacturing process, labeling, and packaging. *21 U.S.C. § 355(b)(1)*. The approval process addresses the chemical composition of the drug, *id.* § 355(b)(1)(B), (C), the drug's safety and effectiveness, *id.* § 355(b)(1)(A), and elements of the drug's distribution, such as "the methods used in, and the facilities and controls used for, the manufacture, processing, and packing" of the drug, *id.* § 355(b)(1)(D), and the "labeling proposed to be used" for the drug. *Id.* § 355(b)(1)(F). The approval process is specific to each manufacturer and each product. *See* 21 C.F.R. § 314.50.

Drugs that are manufactured and distributed in Canada are not approved pursuant to this statutory framework. The approval process requires, among other things, that a manufacturer provide "the proposed text of the labeling for the drug." 21 C.F.R. § 314.50(c). Because foreign labeling differs from domestic labeling, approval granted to a particular manufacturer for a particular product to be distributed in the United States does not constitute approval of another drug—even one with the same chemical composition—to be distributed in Canada with different labeling, and then imported into the United States.

This is not, as plaintiffs would have it, merely a "hyper-technical" violation of the FFDCA. It is, rather, a manifestation of a congressional plan to create a "closed system" designed to guarantee safe and effective drugs for consumers in the United States. *Vermont v. Leavitt, 405 F. Supp. 2d 466, 472 (D. Vt. 2005)*. Drugs that are not properly labeled for sale under federal law sometimes may be similar in substance to those that are sold legally within the United States. In other cases, however, they may be drugs with chemical compositions that are not yet approved by the FDA, drugs not manufactured in accordance with FDA rules, or drugs not transported or stored in a manner that is deemed safe by the FDA. The plaintiffs have attempted to limit this action to drugs that are "the same" as drugs sold legally in the United States except for the labeling, but the labeling requirements cannot be segregated from other FFDCA requirements in this way. Instead, they work in conjunction with the other statutory standards and FDA regulations to create a system that excludes non-compliant and potentially unsafe pharmaceuticals. This "closed system" ensures that approved prescription drugs are "subject to FDA oversight" and are "continuously under the custody of a U.S. manufacturer or authorized distributor," thus helping to ensure that the quality of drugs used by American consumers is consistent and predictable. *United States v. Rx Depot, Inc., 290 F. Supp. 2d 1238, 1241-42 (N.D. Okla. 2003)*.

Congress recently has legislated against the backdrop of this closed system with respect to the very topic of the importation of prescription drugs from Canada. In 2000 and 2003, Congress enacted amendments to the FFDCA that would permit limited importation of certain prescription drugs from Canada by pharmacists, wholesalers, or individuals, *21 U.S.C. § 384(b), (j)*, but only if the Secretary of

Health and Human Services first certifies that the importation would "pose no additional risk to the public's health and safety" and that it would "result in a significant reduction in the cost of covered products" for American consumers. *21 U.S.C. § 384(l)* ; *see* Medicare Prescription Drug, Improvement, and Modernization Act, Pub. L. No. 108-173, § 1121, 117 Stat. 2066, 2464-69 (2003); *see also* Medicine Equity and Drug Safety Act, Pub. L. No. 106-387, § 745, 114 Stat. 1549A-35 (2000). Three Secretaries of Health and Human Services in the last two presidential administrations have declined to make the requisite certifications. (Appellees' App. at 109, 111-13); *Montgomery County v. Leavitt, 445 F. Supp. 2d 505, 510 (D. Md. 2006)*.

That Congress created a special procedure for authorizing importation of prescription drugs from Canada supports our conclusion that the pre-existing system established by the FFDCA does not permit such importation. While it is true that no federal statute by its express terms bans importation of prescriptions drugs from Canada, such an explicit country-by-country prohibition is unnecessary to accomplish the task. By creating the comprehensive regulatory system described above, Congress has effectively precluded importation of these drugs absent the sort of special authorization contemplated by *21 U.S.C. § 384*.

Plaintiffs argue alternatively that even if personal importation of prescription drugs from Canada is illegal, they nonetheless may pursue an action under the federal antitrust laws based on the defendants' allegedly anti-competitive behavior. Unlike a governmental entity, however, *see, e.g., FTC v. Indiana Fed'n of Dentists, 476 U.S. 447, 106 S. Ct. 2009, 90 L. Ed. 2d 445 (1986)*, a private plaintiff must demonstrate that he has suffered an "antitrust injury" as a result of the alleged conduct of the defendants, and that he has standing to pursue a claim under the federal antitrust laws. Because § 4 of the Clayton Act was designed primarily as a remedial provision, private plaintiffs proceeding thereunder must prove an "injury of the type that the antitrust laws were intended to prevent and that flows from that which makes defendants' acts unlawful." *Brunswick Corp. v. Pueblo Bowl-O-Mat, Inc., 429 U.S. 477, 489, 97 S. Ct. 690, 50 L. Ed. 2d 701 (1977)*. Injunctive relief under § 16 of the Clayton Act is likewise available only to plaintiffs who have suffered an injury cognizable under § 4. *Cargill, Inc. v. Monfort of Colo., Inc., 479 U.S. 104, 111-13, 107 S. Ct. 484, 93 L. Ed. 2d 427 (1986)*.

The requisite antitrust injury must "reflect the anticompetitive effect either of the violation or of the anticompetitive acts made possible by the violation," and represent "the type of loss that the claimed violations . . . would be likely to cause." Brunswick Corp., 429 U.S. at 489. To determine whether the requirements of antitrust standing are satisfied, we also consider the causal connection between the alleged antitrust violation and harm to the plaintiff, the directness or indirectness of the asserted injury, and the degree to which the alleged damages are speculative in a § 4 action. *Associated Gen. Contractors of Cal., Inc. v. Cal. State Council of*

Carpenters, 459 U.S. 519, 537-45, 103 S. Ct. 897, 74 L. Ed. 2d 723 (1983); *see Cargill, 479 U.S. at 110 n.5.*

We agree with the district court that plaintiffs have not established antitrust standing to pursue their federal antitrust claims. Plaintiffs allege that they are injured by increased prices for prescription drugs in the United States, which they say result from their inability to import less expensive drugs distributed by Canadian pharmacies. As we have explained, however, the importation of drugs from Canada is prohibited by federal law. The absence of competition from Canadian sources in the domestic prescription drug market, therefore, is caused by the federal statutory and regulatory scheme adopted by the United States government, not by the conduct of the defendants. Consequently, the alleged conduct of the defendants did not cause an injury of the type that the antitrust laws were designed to remedy. *See RSA Media, Inc. v. AK Media Group., Inc., 260 F.3d 10, 15 (1st Cir. 2001)* (plaintiff lacked antitrust standing where it "was not excluded from the market for outdoor billboards because of [defendant's] threats," but rather "because of the Massachusetts regulatory scheme that prevents new billboards from being built"); *City of Pittsburgh v. West Penn Power Co., 147 F.3d 256, 265 (3d Cir. 1998)* (City suffered no antitrust injury and had no antitrust standing because "any injury suffered by the City did not flow from the defendants' conduct, but, rather, from the realities of the regulated environment in which all three were actors"); 2 P. Areeda & H. Hovenkamp, *Antitrust Law* § 338, at 320 (2d ed. 2000) (explaining that antitrust standing is lacking where "a force other than the antitrust violation fully accounts for the plaintiff's injury").

The plaintiffs do allege that prior to the alleged anti-competitive conduct of the defendants, Americans were able to import prescription drugs from Canada for personal use, because the FDA declined to enforce a legal prohibition on personal importation of Canadian drugs. They do not allege, however, that the government's lack of enforcement resulted in the injury alleged in their complaint—*i.e.*, increased prices for prescription drugs in the United States—presumably because the chain of causation would be too speculative to support such an assertion. To establish antitrust standing based on higher drug prices in the United States, the plaintiffs would have to prove that absent the alleged anti-competitive conduct of the defendants, pharmacists and wholesalers in Canada would sell additional prescription drugs to American consumers, Americans routinely would travel to Canada to fill their prescriptions, those consumers would avoid enforcement when transporting their prescriptions illegally across the border, and the number of consumers engaging in this illegal behavior would be so large as to drive down prices in the United States. These "vaguely defined links" in the chain of causation, even if alleged by the plaintiffs, would be insufficient to establish antitrust standing. *See* Associated Gen. Contractors, 459 U.S. at 540.

Finally, the plaintiffs argue that the district court abused its discretion when it dismissed their state law claims. When a district court dismisses federal claims over which it has original jurisdiction, the balance of interests usually "will point toward declining to exercise jurisdiction over the remaining state law claims." *Carnegie-Mellon Univ. v. Cohill, 484 U.S. 343, 350 n.7, 108 S. Ct. 614, 98 L. Ed. 2d 720 (1988)*; *see also Gibson v. Weber, 433 F.3d 642, 647 (8th Cir. 2006)*; *28 U.S.C. § 1367(c)(3)*. The district court's decision to dismiss the state law claims was in accord with these principles. The advent of the Class Action Fairness Act, Pub. L. No. 109-2, 119 Stat. 4 (2005), and the potential for the future removal of the state claims to federal court, are not sufficient grounds to require the district court to retain federal jurisdiction.

The judgment of the district court is affirmed.

GUAM INDUSTRIAL SERVICES, INC.
v.
DONALD H. RUMSFELD

Civil Action No. 05-1599 (D.D.C. 2006)
Decided July 24, 2006

MEMORANDUM OPINION GRANTING THE DEFENDANTS' MOTION FOR SUMMARY JUDGMENT[1]

I. INTRODUCTION

The plaintiff, Guam Industrial Services ("Guam Shipyard"), is a shipyard in Guam which claims that the United States Navy's bid proposal and contract procurement practices violate the terms of a contract (hereinafter, "the Ship Manager Contract" or "SMC") executed by the Maritime Administration ("MARAD") on behalf of the Department of Transportation ("DOT"). The plaintiff also claims that the Navy's bid proposal and contract procurement practices violate the terms of a memorandum of agreement ("MOA") between MARAD and the Department of Defense ("DoD"). Guam Shipyard seeks to enjoin the defendants[2] from soliciting bid proposals and contracting for repairs of Navy vessels from shipyards not located in either the United States or Guam.

Before the court is the defendants' motion for summary judgment as to the plaintiff's claims under the SMC and the MOA. Because the SMC permits repairs for naval vessels designated as prepositioned ships, it does not prevent the defendants

1 The defendants characterized their motion as a motion to dismiss or for summary judgment. Because the defendants motion relies on extrinsic evidence, the court treats it herein as a motion for summary judgment. *Bastin v. Fed. Nat'l Mortgage Ass'n*, 104 F.3d 1392, 1395 (D.C. Cir. 1997).

2 The defendants are Donald Rumsfeld, Secretary of the U.S. Department of Defense ("DoD"), Norman Mineta, Secretary of the Department of Transportation ("DOT"), John Jamain, Acting Administrator of the Maritime Administration ("MARAD"), and Gordon England, Secretary of the Department of Navy ("Navy"). The court substitutes the current Secretary of the Navy, Donald C. Winter, acting in his official capacity, for his predecessor Gordon R. England. FED. R. CIV. P. 25(d)(1).

from contracting for repairs to the SS Petersburg by foreign ship repair facilities. Furthermore, because 10 U.S.C. § 7310 does not apply to the SS Petersburg, the MOA does not constrain IASC from executing repair contracts with foreign ship repair facilities. For these reasons, the court grants the defendants' motion for summary judgment as to the plaintiff's claims.

II. BACKGROUND

A. Factual Background

The plaintiff is a shipyard located in the U.S. Territory of Guam. Mem. Op. (Aug. 24, 2005) ("Aug. Mem. Op.") at 2. The Guam Shipyard employs approximately two hundred and fifty people—all U.S. citizens—and is "the only United States-citizen owned and controlled shipyard that can service United States Navy, Military Sealift Command ("MSC"), and MARAD ships that are under the jurisdiction of the Secretary of Navy and located in the Pacific and Indian Oceans." *Id.*

A select group of Navy vessels are part of the Navy's Prepositioning Program, a program funded and administered by the Navy and controlled by the Navy's Sealift Command. *Id.* These ships are positioned by the Navy in strategic oceanic locations, "making it possible to deploy equipment, fuel, and supplies to support U.S. military forces on short notice during times of war or as a result of other contingencies." *Id.*

The Navy also maintains a fleet of maritime vessels in the Unites States Ready Reserve Force ("RRF"), which are a select group of ships within the National Defense Reserve Fleet. *Id.* at 3. They are maintained by the DOT's MARAD and are funded from the Navy-controlled National Defense Sealift Fund. *Id.*

The Navy vessel SS Petersburg is designated both within the Navy's Prepositioning Program and MARAD's National Defense Reserve Fleet. *Id.* While on assignment as a vessel in the RRF, the SS Petersburg is maintained and controlled by the DOT's MARAD, but when activated under the Navy's strategic Prepositioning Program, the vessel is maintained and controlled by the Navy and the Navy's Military Sealift Command. *Id.*

The SS Petersburg has been located or "prepositioned" in the U.S. Territory of Guam at the Delta-Echo Pier in Apra Harbor for the past three years. *Id.* Daily control of the SS Petersburg is delegated to one of the three Maritime Prepositioning Ship squadrons ("MSPRONs"). *Id.* The vessel's specific mission while located in Guam is to provide offshore petroleum distribution services to the Defense Logistic Agency. *Id.*

IASC is a corporation that provides ship management services to MARAD for the SS Petersburg. *Id.* Under the terms of the Ship Manager Contract ("SMC") with MARAD, IASC solicited bids for drydock work and repairs of the SS Petersburg on June 21, 2005. *Id.* In response to this solicitation, the plaintiff submitted a bid proposal. *Id.* On August 16, 2005, IASC accepted a bid from the Keppel Shipyard in Singapore for repairs to the SS Petersburg. *Id.*

B. Procedural Background

On August 10, 2005, the plaintiff filed its complaint in this case, and on August 23, 2005, the plaintiff filed a motion for a temporary restraining order ("TRO"). In its motion for a TRO, the plaintiff sought to temporarily enjoin the defendants from servicing the Naval vessel SS Petersburg by the Singaporean Shipyard. Aug. Mem. Op. at 1-2. Because the repair work was set to commence on August 23, 2005, the court ordered extremely expedited briefing on the legal issues presented. The following day, the court issued a memorandum opinion denying the plaintiff's motion for a TRO. Aug. Mem. Op. The court ruled that the plaintiff failed to demonstrate any of the four elements required for a TRO. *See* Mem. Order (Sept. 30, 2005) at 2. Specifically, the court ruled that the Secretary of the Navy's interpretation of 10 U.S.C. § 7310 was entitled to deference under the *Chevron* doctrine[3] and was reasonable, and that the plaintiff failed to support the contention that it had standing to challenge the provisions of the memorandum of agreement between the DoD and MARAD. Mem. Order at 2.

On December 19, 2005, the court issued a memorandum opinion dismissing part of the plaintiff's claims. Mem. Op. (Dec. 19, 2005) ("Dec. Mem. Op."). The court concluded that the Secretary of Navy's interpretation provided a reasonable definition of those vessels falling under the jurisdiction of the Secretary of the Navy. *Id.* at 11. Under this definition, RRF vessels (like the SS Petersburg) are not subject to the "Buy America"[4] requirement in 10 U.S.C. § 7310(a). *Id.* Accordingly, the court dismissed the plaintiff's statutory claims. *Id.*

The court reserved judgment on the plaintiff's claims under the MOA and under the SMC pending further briefing by the parties. *Id.* at 2. The court now turns to these remaining claims.

III. ANALYSIS

A. Legal Standard for a Motion for Summary Judgment

Summary judgment is appropriate when "the pleadings, depositions, answers to interrogatories, and admissions on file, together with the affidavits, if any, show that there is no genuine issue as to any material fact and that the moving party is entitled to a judgment as a matter of law." FED. R. CIV. P. 56(c); *see also Celotex Corp. v. Catrett*, 477 U.S. 317, 322 (1986); *Diamond v. Atwood*, 43 F.3d 1538, 1540 (D.C. Cir. 1995). To determine which facts are "material," a court must look

---

3 Chevron U.S.A., Inc. v. Natural Res. Def. Council, Inc., 467 U.S. 837, 842-43 (1984).

4 Section 7910(a) is a "Buy America" provision which directs the Department of the Navy to contract with United States shipyards in the repair and maintenance of vessels under its jurisdiction. 10 U.S.C. § 7910(a); *Guam Indus. Servs., Inc. v. United States*, No. 03- 706C (Fed. Cl. 2003) at 3.

to the substantive law on which each claim rests. *Anderson v. Liberty Lobby, Inc.*, 477 U.S. 242, 248 (1986). A "genuine issue" is one whose resolution could establish an element of a claim or defense and, therefore, affect the outcome of the action. *Celotex*, 477 U.S. at 322; *Anderson*, 477 U.S. at 248.

In ruling on a motion for summary judgment, the court must draw all justifiable inferences in the nonmoving party's favor and accept the nonmoving party's evidence as true. *Anderson*, 477 U.S. at 255. A nonmoving party, however, must establish more than "the mere existence of a scintilla of evidence" in support of its position. *Id.* at 252. To prevail on a motion for summary judgment, the moving party must show that the nonmoving party "fail[ed] to make a showing sufficient to establish the existence of an element essential to that party's case, and on which that party will bear the burden of proof at trial." *Celotex*, 477 U.S. at 322. By pointing to the absence of evidence proffered by the nonmoving party, a moving party may succeed on summary judgment. *Id.*

In addition, the nonmoving party may not rely solely on allegations or conclusory statements. *Greene v. Dalton*, 164 F.3d 671, 675 (D.C. Cir. 1999); *Harding v. Gray*, 9 F.3d 150, 154 (D.C. Cir. 1993). Rather, the nonmoving party must present specific facts that would enable a reasonable jury to find in its favor. *Greene*, 164 F.3d at 675. If the evidence "is merely colorable, or is not significantly probative, summary judgment may be granted." *Anderson*, 477 U.S. at 249-50 (internal citations omitted).

C. The Court Grants the Defendants' Motion for Summary Judgment as to the Plaintiff's Claims Under the Ship Manager Contract

The plaintiff claims that the SMC executed by MARAD is binding on IASC and prohibits IASC from contracting with foreign ship repair facilities for repairs to the SS Petersburg. Compl., Prayer for Relief ¶¶ 4, 6. The plaintiff bases its claim on a specific provision of a 1996 version of the SMC ("1996 SMC"), which states that "[a]ll repair and or upgrading work required in conjunction with the contract . . . shall be accomplished in a U.S. shipyard or a U.S. ship repair facility, unless the work is an emergency." Compl. ¶ 30 (citing 1996 SMC).[5]

Although both the plaintiff and the defendants agree that this version of the SMC has been superceded, Pl.'s Mot. for Recons. ¶ 2; Defs.' Opp'n to Pl.'s Mot. for TRO at 12, the plaintiff maintains that "all subsequent MARAD ship manager contracts contain[ ] similar requirements [as the 1996 SMC]," Compl. ¶ 31; Pl.'s Mot. for Recons. ¶ 2. The plaintiff is incorrect. Since the year 2000, SMCs have provided that "[a]ll repair and/or upgrading work required in conjunction with the contract . . . shall be accomplished in a U.S. ship repair facility, unless the work is for emergency, or mission essential repairs, *or for pre-positioned ships which*

5 The defendants assert that the plaintiff, in fact, references a 1993 version of the SMC. Defs.' Supp. Mem. at 11 n. 4. Because this discrepancy is not material to the resolution of the plaintiff's claims, the court need not inquire further.

are deployed overseas, or for any vessel forward deployed outside of the United States." Defs.' Mot. ("Defs.' Mot."), Ex. 3 ("Cahill Decl."), Attach. C ("Ship Manager Contract"), Section 2.4.6 (emphasis added).

The plaintiff acknowledges that the SS Petersburg is part of the MSC Prepositioning Program and that it has been prepositioned in Guam. Compl. ¶¶ 13, 18. Moreover, a 2000 version of the SMC includes the SS Petersburg in a list of prepositioned vessels.[6] Defs.' Supp. Mem. at 11 n. 5 (referencing the 2000 Ship Manager Contract, Technical Exhibit 8). Because the SS Petersburg is a prepositioned ship deployed overseas, it is exempt from the SMC clause requiring repair work in a U.S. repair facility. Accordingly, the court grants the defendants' motion for summary judgment as to the plaintiff's claim under the SMC.

D. The Court Grants the Defendants' Motion for Summary Judgment as to the Plaintiff's Claims Under the Memorandum of Agreement

DoD and MARAD, on behalf of the DOT, entered into the MOA on August 26, 1997 for the purpose of identifying "the relationship and responsibilities of the DoD and the DOT in the administration of the [National Defense Reserve Fleet] program, including: the acquisition, lay- up, berthing and maintenance of ships in the RRF[.]" Defs.' Mot., Ex. 7 ("MOA") ¶ 2. Both the plaintiff and the defendants agree that the MOA has not been superceded and remains "an operative government policy statement and interpretation of its own duties." Pl.'s Mot. for Recons. ¶¶ 2-3; Defs.' Opp'n to Pl.'s Mot. for Recons. at 5.

Federal agencies are required to "follow their own rules, even gratuitous procedural rules that limit otherwise discretionary actions." *Steenholdt v. FAA*, 314 F.3d 633, 639 (D.C. Cir. 2003) (citing *United States ex rel. Accardi v. Shaughnessy*, 347 U.S. 260 (1954)). The touchstone of the "*Accardi* doctrine," as it is oft referred, is an agency's demonstrated intent to be bound to its own rules. *Nat'l Latino Media Coal. v. FCC*, 816 F.2d 785, 788 n.2 (D.C. Cir. 1987). "The 'binding' quality of a particular rule or statement will depend on whether the agency intended to establish a 'substantive' rule, one which is not merely interpretive but which creates or modifies rights that can be enforced against the agency." *Id.* Therefore, interpretive rules and policy statements alone will not bind an agency. *See id.*; *see also Vietnam Veterans of Am. v. Sec'y of the Navy*, 843 F.2d 528, 537-38 (D.C. Cir. 1988) (distinguishing between statements which suggest an intent to bind agency discretion and "interpretive rules or policy statements" which are not binding and from which the agency remains free to deviate).

The plaintiff argues that the MOA shows the DoD's and MARAD's clear intents to be bound to "the obligation to repair and maintain RRF ships in domestic ship-

---

6 Because neither the plaintiff nor the defendants have supplied the court with Technical Exhibit 8 (or its equivalent) of the 2005 version, the court has no information as to whether the 2005 SMC designates the SS Petersburg as a prepositioned vessel, though the plaintiff has not argued to the contrary.

yards in accordance with Section 7310(a)[.]" Pl.'s Supp. Mem. at 9. The plaintiff, however, concedes that the MOA is "an operative government policy statement and interpretation of its own duties," Pl.'s Mot. for Recons. ¶¶ 2-3. And because government agencies are not bound by their policy statements and interpretive rules, *Nat'l Latino Media Coalition*, 816 F.2d at 788 n.2, the MOA is not binding on MARAD or the DoD. *Vietnam Veterans*, 843 F.2d at 537-38; *see also Rochon v. Ashcroft*, 319 F. Supp. 2d 23, 29 (D.D.C. 2004), *rev'd on other grounds*, 438 F.3d 1211 (ruling that "litigants may plead themselves out of court by alleging facts that establish defendants' entitlement to prevail").

Nevertheless, the defendants concede that the MOA is binding on DoD and MARAD as parties to the agreement.[7] *See* Defs.' Supp. Mem. at 13 (stating that "parties to an agreement obviously intend to be bound thereby"). But even if the MOA is binding on DoD and MARAD, the court would still grant the defendants' motion for summary judgment. Paragraph 5(b) of the MOA requires that, "[a]ll shipyard and ship repair facility work to RRF ships will be accomplished by MARAD (either directly or through its ship operating companies) and performed in the United States (except for necessary voyage repairs while overseas), in accordance with statute and DOT regulations." MOA ¶ 5(b).

The plaintiff urges the court to read the phrase "in accordance with statute" as "in accordance with 10 U.S.C. § 7310(a)." Pl.'s Supp. Mem. at 9 (stating that "[p]aragraph 5(b) of this binding contract expresses a clear interagency recognition of the obligation to repair and maintain RRF ships in domestic shipyards in accordance with Section 7310(a)"). Surprisingly, the plaintiff's own reading of Paragraph 5(b) undermines its position. Under this reading, the defendants would be bound by 10 U.S.C. § 7310(a). But, as the court has previously noted, "RRF vessels [are excluded] from the 'Buy America' requirement in 10 U.S.C. § 7310(a)."[8] Dec. Mem. Op. at 11.

---

7 The defendants do not, however, accept the plaintiff's underlying assumption that Guam Shipyard is an intended beneficiary of the MOA and that it has standing to enforce the agreement. Defs.' Supp. Mem. at 13. The court previously noted the plaintiff's failure to analyze its standing to enforce the provisions of an agreement to which it is not a party. Aug. Mem. Op. at 12. For a party to avail itself of the "exceptional privilege" of third party beneficiary status, "a party must 'at least show that [the contract] was intended for his *direct* benefit.'" *Glass v. United States*, 258 F.3d 1349, 1354 (Fed. Cir. 2001) (emphasis in original) (citing *German Alliance Ins. Co. v. Home Water Supply Co.*, 226 U.S. 220, 230 (1912)); *see Data Marketing Co. v. United States*, 107 Fed. Appx. 187, 196 (Fed. Cir. July 8, 2004) (ruling that an interagency agreement did not create third party beneficiary status when the appellant was not referenced directly or indirectly in the agreement). The plaintiff has failed to address this issue directly, and, as the defendants correctly point out, the plaintiff's standing as an intended beneficiary of the MOA is highly questionable at best. Defs.' Supp. Mem. at 13; *Data Marketing*, 104 Fed. Appx. at 196.

8 According to the plaintiff, "[COMSCINST 4007.15A], even if valid, cannot negate [the MOA's] broad, formal expression of interagency intent" to be bound to § 7310(a). Pl.'s Supp. Mem. at 11. The court, however, has already construed COMSCINST 4700.15A as a reason-

Because the plaintiff has produced no applicable DOT regulation requiring domestic repair work to the SS Petersburg and because, under the court's previous ruling, 10 U.S.C. § 7310(a) does not apply to the SS Petersburg, the defendants are not violating the MOA's "in accordance with statute and DOT regulations" provision in contracting with a foreign shipyard. Dec. Mem. Op. at 11. Accordingly, the court grants the defendants' motion for summary judgment as to the plaintiff's claim under the MOA.

IV. CONCLUSION

For the foregoing reasons the court, this 24th day of July, 2006, grants the defendants' motion for summary judgment as to the plaintiff's remaining claims. An order instructing the parties in a manner consistent with this Memorandum Opinion is issued contemporaneously herewith.

able interpretation of § 7310(a). Dec. Mem. Op. at 11. Therefore, any inclusion of § 7310(a) in reading the MOA must account for the Navy's reasonable interpretation of this statute.

U.S. ORDNANCE, INC.
v.
U.S. DEPARTMENT OF STATE

Civil Action No. 05-2304 (D.D.C. 2006)
Decided June 5, 2006

MEMORANDUM OPINION AND ORDER

Plaintiff U.S. Ordnance, Inc. ("USO" or "plaintiff") asks the Court to direct the Department of State (the "Department") and its employees to issue plaintiff a license to export M16 machine guns to foreign countries. In response, defendants have filed a motion to dismiss wherein they argue that the Court lacks subject matter jurisdiction to hear plaintiff's claims. The Court agrees and will therefore grant defendants' motion and dismiss plaintiff's complaint.

BACKGROUND

Plaintiff is a manufacturer and exporter of defense articles. Defendants are the Department and John Hillen, Assistant Secretary of State for Political and Military Affairs; Rose M. Likens, Deputy Secretary (formerly Acting Assistant Secretary of State for Political and Military Affairs); and David M. Trimble, Director of the Office of Defense Trade Controls. In February 2000 plaintiff registered with the Department as a manufacturer and exporter of defense articles pursuant to the Arms Export Control Act ("AECA"), 22 U.S.C. § 2751 *et seq.* From that time until May 2004, plaintiff engaged in the business of manufacturing and exporting defense articles to foreign countries. In May 2004, however, the Department learned that plaintiff allegedly was associated with an individual named Curtis Lynn Debord ("Debord Sr."),[1] who had been indicted in 1997 for violations of § 2778 of the AECA, and therefore was considered as being ineligible to engage in the export of arms under the AECA's implementing regulations—International

1 Debord Senior is the father of Curtis Lee Debord, who is the President, Treasurer, Secretary and sole director and owner of USO.

Traffic in Arms Regulations ("ITAR").[2] *See United States v. Debord*, No. 97-CR-239 (N.D. Cal.) (charging Debord Senior with smuggling arms into the United States, dealing in firearms without a license, entry by false statements, conspiracy, making false statements and witness tampering).[3]

The Department immediately initiated an administrative investigation into Debord Senior's association with plaintiff. By letters dated June 2, June 24, and July 9, 2004, the Department requested information regarding Debord Senior's activities and interest in USO. (Defs.' Exs. 1, 4, 5.) On June 2, 2004, the Department also informed plaintiff that pending the conclusion of the Department's investigation, plaintiff's license applications "would be processed only as transaction exemptions that must be supported by a request meeting strict national security, foreign policy and law enforcement criteria." (Defs.' Mem. at 4; *see also* Defs.' Ex. 1.) According to the Department, "[a]pplication of such license review criteria in effect imposed a policy of denial for plaintiff's export license applications under the ITAR." (Defs.' Mem. at 4.) Furthermore, on June 24, 2004, the Department suspended the licenses it previously had issued to plaintiff. (*See* Defs.' Ex. 4.) At the time of the Department's June 2 and June 24 actions, plaintiff had seven pending license applications. Three of those applications were the subject of transaction exemption requests (which were denied in October 2004), and the other four applications were returned without action because no transaction exemption requests had been submitted. In addition, the Department suspended thirty licenses that it previously had issued to plaintiff.

From June 2004 through April 2005, the Department reviewed information submitted by plaintiff in response to its requests.[4] On April 4, 2005, the Department

---

2 The ITAR is found at 22 C.F.R. §§ 120-130. A person indicted for violating the AECA is generally ineligible pursuant to § 120.1(c) of the ITAR. *See* 22 C.F.R. § 120.1(c). As provided by § 127.1(c), an ineligible person may not obtain any benefit or have any direct or indirect interest in the export of defense articles without disclosure to and approval of the Department's Directorate of Defense Trade Controls ("DDTC"). *See id.* § 127.1(c). Also, §§ 122.2(b), 122.4(a) and 126.13(a) require that the ineligible status of a senior official of a manufacturer or exporter of defense articles be disclosed in its registration submission and any application for an export license. *See id.* §§ 122.2(b), 122.4(a) and 126.13(a). Finally, under § 126.7(a), the Department applies a policy of denial with respect to any application in which an ineligible person is involved. *Id.* § 126.7(a); *see also* 22 U.S.C. § 2778(g)(3)(B) (authorizing denial if there is reasonable cause to believe that the applicant for a license has violated the AECA, including its implementing regulations).

3 In June 2005, the United States District Court for the Northern District of California dismissed the indictment, but as argued by defendant, their subsequent dismissal neither changed nor excused plaintiff's reporting obligations. (*See* Defs.' Mem. at 3 n.4.)

4 According to the Department, plaintiff's responses demonstrate, among other things, "that USO had submitted applications for licenses that may have failed to disclose, as required by the ITAR, that an ineligible person, Debord Sr., served as a senior official from July 2000 to June 2004, had a direct or indirect interest in the transactions, and obtained benefits therefrom by earning over $1 million in salary and bonuses that appeared to be attributable in large part to USO's export of defense articles." (Defs.' Mem. at 4; *see also* Defs.' Exs. 2, 3.)

issued plaintiff a draft charging letter pursuant to § 128.11(b) of the ITAR, which permits the settlement of administrative enforcement actions prior to the issuance of a formal charging letter. (*See* Defs.' Ex. 7.) On October 26, 2005, the Department issued plaintiff another proposed charging letter that alleged 35 violations of the AECA. (Defs. Ex. 10.)

Instead of responding to the Department's October 26, 2005 proposed charging letter, plaintiff initiated this lawsuit on November 29, 2005, seeking an order requiring the Department to process all of its pending license applications and declaring that plaintiff is in full compliance with the ITAR. (*See* Compl. ¶¶ 5, 6.) By letter dated February 3, 2006, plaintiff formally responded to the Department's October 26, 2005 proposed charging letter by asserting that the charges set forth therein are without merit. (Defs.' Ex. 13.) After reviewing plaintiff's letter, the Department, through the DDTC, began "preparations for the process to formally charge USO with violations of AECA and ITAR in an administrative proceeding under Part 128 of the ITAR," which provides for debarment as a penalty for violations of the AECA and the ITAR following a formal administrative proceeding. *See* 22 C.F.R. § 128.1. (Defs.' Mem. at 9.) The Department also, on March 10, 2006, formally denied all of plaintiff's pending license applications. (Defs.' Ex. 14.)

ANALYSIS

I. Plaintiff's Request for Injunctive Relief

Because the Department has now formally denied all of plaintiff's pending license applications, plaintiff's request that the Court order the Department to process these applications has been rendered moot. *See Columbian Rope Co. v. West*, 142 F.3d 1313, 1316 (D.C. Cir. 1998) ("[e]ven where litigation poses a live controversy when filed, the [mootness] doctrine requires a federal Court to refrain from deciding it if events have so transpired that the decision will neither presently affect the parties' rights nor have a more-than-speculative chance of affecting them in the future."); *Better Gov't Ass'n v. Dep't of State*, 780 F.2d 86 (D.C. Cir. 1986) (claims challenging the individual denials of fee waiver requests were moot where the agency had ultimately waived the fees in question); *Barabski v. Buckles*, No. 02-0073 (HHK) (D.D.C., Oct. 31, 2002) (dismissing as moot plaintiff's request for an order requiring Treasury Department to process his applications to import firearms once Treasury has denied the applications).

II. Plaintiff's Request for Declaratory Judgment

A. The Department's Denial of Plaintiff's License Applications

To the extent that plaintiff asks this Court to review the Department's denial of plaintiff's license applications under the Administrative Procedure Act ("APA"), 5 U.S.C. § 701 *et seq.*, this Court has no jurisdiction to do so because the Department's actions fall within its discretionary authority.

Plaintiff claims that jurisdiction is proper under 5 U.S.C. § 706(2), which provides that a reviewing court shall "hold unlawful and set aside agency action . . . found to be (A) arbitrary, capricious, and abuse of discretion, or otherwise not in accordance with law (B) contrary to constitutional right . . . (D) without observance of procedure required by law." 5 U.S.C. § 706(2)(A), (B), and (D). Plaintiff argues that because the Department's charges regarding its alleged violations of the ITAR are without merit, the Department has no basis for its denial of plaintiff's license applications. Further, according to plaintiff, the ITAR provide justiciable standards for the Court to conduct its review.

Defendants rely on 5 U.S.C. § 701(a)(2), which provides that an action, deriving from discretionary authority committed to an agency by law, falls outside the court's jurisdiction and is therefore not subject to judicial review under the APA. Defendants argue that the authority to grant or deny a license for export of defense articles has been committed to the Department's discretion, and therefore, the Department's denial of plaintiff's license applications is unreviewable.

Whether an agency action is committed to the discretion of an agency depends on the nature of the delegation of authority and the statutory language. *See Webster v. Doe*, 486 U.S. 592, 599-600 (1988). This narrow exception to judicial reviewability is especially prevalent in cases involving agency decisions relating to foreign affairs and national security, for, as recognized by the D.C. Circuit, these cases involve "judgments on questions of foreign policy and the national interest" that are not "fit for judicial involvement." *See Dist. No. 1, Pac. Coast Dist., Marine Eng'rs' Beneficial Ass'n v. Mar. Admin.,* 215 F.3d 37, 42 (D.C. Cir. 2000); *see also Legal Assistance for Vietnamese Asylum Seekers v. Dep't of State*, 104 F.3d 1349, 1353 (D.C. Cir. 1997) ("By long-standing tradition, courts have been wary of second-guessing executive branch decisions involving complicated foreign policy matters.").

Moreover, where the language of a statute provides no justiciable standard by which a court can review the agency's exercise of its delegated authority, the matter is treated as committed to the agency's discretion. *See Webster*, 486 U.S. at 600 (a statute allowing the Director of the CIA to terminate employment of any employee whenever he found termination "advisable" for the national interest "fairly exude[d] deference" and thereby precluded judicial review under the APA). In particular, if the statute uses language that permits an executive official, such as the President or another agency official, to take action that the official "deems" in the "national interest," these statutes have been consistently interpreted to preclude judicial review under the APA. *See Zhu v. Gonzales,* 411 F.3d 292, 295 (D.C. Cir. 2005) (construing a statute, which allows the Attorney General to waive a requirement if waiver is in the "national interest," as being committed to the discretion of the Attorney General).

In this case, the AECA's delegation of authority to control arms exports is decidedly one involving foreign affairs and national security. As the Court of Appeals for the Federal Circuit has stated, "the broad statutory delegation in the AECA incorporates the 'historical authority of the President in the fields of foreign commerce." *B-West Imports, Inc. v. United States,* 75 F.3d 633, 636 (Fed. Cir. 1996) (addressing authorization to the President to control arms imports under the AECA). Specifically, the AECA provides that the President, or his delegate, may approve the exportation of defense articles when he determines that such action is "consistent with the foreign policy interests of the United States," 22 U.S.C. § 2751, and "in furtherance of world peace and the security and foreign policy of the United States." *Id.* § 2778(a)(1). Congress has also authorized the Secretary of State to "revoke[], suspend[], or amend[]" an export license "without prior notice, whenever the Secretary deems such action to be advisable." *Id.* § 2791(2)(A). Such express statutory language "fairly exudes deference" to the executive branch, and therefore, precludes judicial review under the APA. *Webster*, 486 U.S. at 600.

Accordingly, given the clear statutory language and the absence of judicially manageable standards to guide the Court's review, it must reject plaintiff's invocation of the APA and decline to review the agency's denial of plaintiff's applications for licenses to export M16 machine guns.

In response to this seemingly insurmountable hurdle, plaintiff attempts to raise a series of arguments, none of which has merit. First, plaintiff claims that the Court has jurisdiction because "the core of the complaint is the deprivation of plaintiff's Due Process Rights guaranteed by the Fifth Amendment." (Pl.'s Opp. at 1.) This claim, however, is noticeably absent from plaintiff's complaint and from its motion for preliminary injunction, but more importantly, it is contrary to well established precedent. Courts have consistently held that a party has no property interests in foreign commerce. *See e.g. The Vessel Abby Dodge v. United States*, 223 U.S. 166, 176-77 (1912) ("[N]o one can be said to have a vested right to carry on foreign commerce with the United States."); *B-West Imports*, 75 F.2d at 638 (government may prevent the import of firearms under the AECA without being subject to a Due Process claim); *Continental Seafoods, Inc. v. Schweiker*, 674 F.2d 38, 42 n.11 (D.C. Cir. 1982) ("Courts must defer to the expertise of the agency charged with exercising Congress' broad power to bar articles from import."). In particular, plaintiff's brief completely ignores the case of *B-West Imports*, where the Federal Circuit explicitly held that there is no protected property right in the importation of defense articles. *B-West Imports*, 75 F.3d at 638. Congress has the constitutional authority to restrict sales of arms to foreign nations, and it has exercised this authority through the AECA. *See id.* Since the AECA controls both imports and exports, the *B-West* analysis applies to this case even though the issue here involves exports rather than imports of defense articles.[5]

5 Moreover, plaintiff's reliance on *Kartseva v. Department of State*, 37 F.3d 1524 (D.C. Cir. 1994), is misplaced. (Pl.'s Opp. at 7.) First, *Kartseva* related to employment, rather than to a business's interest in exporting weapons. Second, and more importantly, the posture of *Kartseva* was different than it is here, for the plaintiff in *Kartseva* experienced a change in legal status, but as explained herein, plaintiff's legal status has not yet been determined.

Second, plaintiff attempts to establish jurisdiction by conflating license denial decisions with a debarment determination by characterizing defendants' "policy of denial" as a "*de facto* debarment." (Pl.'s Opp. at 1.) Debarment, which can only be imposed after a formal administrative proceeding, would permanently deprive plaintiff of any chance to obtain a license under the AECA. *See* 22 C.F.R. § 127.7. Whereas, a decision to deny an export license is not an enforcement action, but rather is an exercise of the broad discretionary granted to the Department. *See id.* at § 126.7(a). Thus, a denial of a license is only a preliminary action, and if a subsequent enforcement action is undertaken, only that action is subject to the procedures of Part 128 of the ITAR. *See id.* at §§ 127.7, 128.

Given the fact that the pending enforcement proceeding has not yet been concluded, plaintiff cannot cure the Court's lack of jurisdiction, since any request at this time for review of the Department's actions would be premature. Under the APA, a court may only exercise judicial review over a "final" agency action "for which there is no other adequate remedy in a court," 5 U.S.C. § 704, and an agency action is only final "to the extent that it imposes an obligation, denies a right or fixes some legal relationship." *Reliable Automatic Sprinkler Co. v. Consumer Prod. Safety Com'n*, 324 F.3d. 726, 731 (D.C. Cir. 2003). Since plaintiff's legal status has yet to be determined, the Department's action cannot be reviewed under the APA.

For this reason as well, plaintiff's final argument that it is entitled to declaratory judgment because it has complied with the ITAR must fail. As previously explained, the determination of whether a party is in compliance with the ITAR has been committed to the discretion of the Executive Branch under the AECA, and a court is without authority to thereby trespass into this terrain. *See Peoples v. U.S. Dept. of Agric.*, 427 F.2d 561, 565 n.9 (D.C. Cir. 1970) ("Of course any lawsuit challenging the validity of an administrative or executive action, whether the relief sought is mandamus, injunction, mandatory injunction or declaratory judgment, is limited by the supervening doctrine that a court cannot by its order trespass into the domain of discretion entrusted by the legislature to the official or agency involved."). At this stage, the Court is without jurisdiction to address the merits of the agency's proposed actions, and thus, it has no power to issue a declaratory judgment.

CONCLUSION

For the foregoing reasons, the Court will GRANT defendants' motion to dismiss [#19] and will DISMISS the above-captioned complaint, based on a lack of jurisdiction.

IX. INTERNATIONAL TRADE

2. Business & Finance

B. Banking & Bankruptcy*

* Cases are indexed under this subject. The full text of these cases is published in the **volume**-page indicated.

UNITED STATES OF AMERICA
v.
MILO I. WORTHING

434 F.3d 1046 (8th Cir. 2006)
Decided January 17, 2006

For UNITED STATES OF AMERICA, Plaintiff—Appellee: Linda Parker Marshall, Asst. U.S. Attorney, U.S. ATTORNEY'S OFFICE, Kansas City, MO.

For MILO I. WORTHING, JR., Defendant—Appellant: Bruce W. Simon, SIMON & SIMON, Kansas City, MO.

MILO I. WORTHING, JR., Defendant—Appellant, Pro se, Otisville, NY.

Before MURPHY, McMILLIAN and GRUENDER, Circuit Judges.

OPINION

McMILLIAN, Circuit Judge.

Milo I. Worthing, Jr., appeals from a final judgment entered in the District Court[1] for the Western District of Missouri, upon a jury verdict, finding him guilty of conspiracy (count 1) and multiple counts of interstate transportation of funds obtained by fraud (counts 2-14), wire fraud (counts 15-19), mail fraud (counts 20-21), and money laundering (counts 22-23), and sentencing him to 10 years imprisonment, 3 years supervised release, restitution of more than $ 5 million, and a special assessment of $ 2,300. For reversal, Worthing argues that the evidence was insufficient to support the jury's verdict, the district court erred in denying his request for a cautionary tail instruction, and the sentence violated *United States v. Booker, 543 U.S. 220, 125 S. Ct. 738, 160 L. Ed. 2d 621 (2005)*. For the reasons discussed below, we affirm the judgment of the district court.

1 The Honorable Fernando J. Gaitan, Jr., United States District Judge for the Western District of Missouri.

BACKGROUND

The government charged that Worthing and others conspired to induce individuals to invest in a high-yield investment scheme involving bank debenture and currency trading programs by promising exorbitant returns and making other false and fraudulent material representations. According to the government's theory of the case and the government's evidence, Worthing was the organizer and leader of the scheme, solicited funds and caused investors to send funds through interstate and foreign commerce, using the wires and the mail, laundered the proceeds through many bank accounts, and lulled investors into not demanding return of their funds by making false and fraudulent representations about the status of their accounts. The government charged that Worthing and others created several trading entities which generated promotional materials and other documents, used a portion of the funds to repay other investors, and lulled investors into believing that they were receiving a return on their investments and in forestalling detection by law enforcement authorities.

According to the government, Worthing represented that he used uncut gemstones to obtain a line of credit and then used those funds to trade bank debentures in multi-million dollar transactions, yielding millions on each transaction. According to Worthing, this was a tremendous investment opportunity, the investments could earn 50% in six months or as much as 100% per month in 10 months, the investments were international and were as "safe as certificates of deposit," the investments were guaranteed by the gemstones and securities and "Lloyd's of London," and the trading programs were regulated by the Federal Reserve, the World Bank, and the International Monetary Fund. Government investigators testified that high-yield investment program schemes have been the subject of multiple warnings and that the features of this program are characteristic of this type of fraudulent scheme. The government investigators testified that high-yield investment program schemes are economic "nonsense" and that there are no legitimate bank debenture trading programs. Investors paid funds to sales representatives or promoters, who forwarded the funds to bank accounts, usually by wire, set up by Worthing or others at his direction, in other states and abroad (especially on the Isle of Man). Investors received written agreements in person or through the mail. Worthing contacted investors by telephone and by fax. According to the government, about 140 individuals "invested" $ 5.3 million, which Worthing did not invest in any trading program and instead spent on personal expenses.

In 2002 Worthing, Billie Brandenburg and others were indicted and charged with conspiracy, wire fraud, mail fraud, interstate transportation of funds obtained by fraud, and money laundering. The case was tried in 2004. Motions to dismiss and for judgment of acquittal were denied. Several defendants pleaded guilty before trial and testified pursuant to cooperation agreements. Worthing did not testify. The jury returned a verdict of guilty on all counts. The district court sentenced Worthing to a total of 10 years imprisonment, three years supervised release, a special assessment of $ 2,300, and restitution of more than $ 5 million. This appeal followed.

SUFFICIENCY OF THE EVIDENCE

Worthing first argues that the evidence was insufficient to convict him. He argues that the government charged that there was a single conspiracy and that the evidence showed instead that there were multiple conspiracies. Worthing argues that the evidence failed to show one overall agreement or his role or the roles of the other co-conspirators in the fraudulent scheme. Worthing also argues that the evidence failed to show that he caused funds to move across state lines or international borders (counts 2-14) or that the use of the mail (counts 20-21) or wires (counts 15-19) was in furtherance of the fraudulent scheme. Worthing also argues that the money laundering counts (counts 22-23) must be dismissed because those counts specifically relied on the wire fraud counts as predicate offenses.

In reviewing the sufficiency of the evidence . . ., the evidence is considered in the light most favorable to the government, evidentiary conflicts are resolved in its favor, and all reasonable inferences are drawn from the evidence in support of the jury's verdict. We will reverse only if no reasonable jury could have found the accused guilty beyond a reasonable doubt. *United States v. Mooney, 401 F.3d 940, 944 (8th Cir. 2005)* (citations omitted); *see United States v. Drews, 877 F.2d 10, 13 (8th Cir. 1989).*

We have carefully reviewed the record and conclude that there was sufficient evidence to support the jury verdict finding him guilty. The evidence established the existence of a single conspiracy among Worthing and others to obtain funds from individuals by fraud, that Worthing knew of the fraudulent scheme and knowingly became a part of the fraudulent scheme, and that the other co-conspirators knew of the general nature and scope of the conspiracy and knowingly joined in the overall scheme. The evidence showed that Worthing was the organizer and leader of the fraudulent scheme and that he directed investors and others (including other co-conspirators) where to send or transfer funds from banks in Missouri to banks or accounts in other states in the United States (for example, Atlanta, Georgia) and the United Kingdom (London), and mailed and faxed documents and communications in furtherance of the conspiracy (for example, documenting investment agreements, promising payment, delaying payment, reassuring investors by falsely assuring them of the status of their investments, discouraging investors from complaining to authorities).

CAUTIONARY TAIL INSTRUCTION

Worthing next argues that the district court erred in refusing to instruct the jury that the testimony of an accomplice and testimony given pursuant to a plea agreement should be considered with greater care and caution than the testimony of an ordinary witness. Worthing argues that the government's evidence included the testimony of cooperating witnesses who had entered into plea agreements with the government in exchange for their testimony and who, at the time of trial, had yet to be sentenced. Worthing argues that under these circumstances a cautionary instruction about the credibility of cooperating witnesses was essential. We disagree.

This court has held that "no 'absolute and mandatory duty is imposed upon the court to advise the jury by instruction that they should consider the testimony of an uncorroborated accomplice with caution.'" The district court's instructions drew the jurors' attention to the various factors impinging upon [the co-conspirator's] credibility as a witness, instructed them to give [the co-conspirator's] testimony such weight as they thought it deserved, and advised them that a witness' guilty plea could not be considered by them as evidence of [the defendant's] guilt.

Furthermore, this court has held that a cautionary instruction is not required where additional evidence is presented that corroborates the accomplice's testimony. The corroborating evidence may be circumstantial and "need only tend to link the defendant with the crime and may be of little weight when taken alone." *United States v. Drews, 877 F.2d at 12-13* (citations omitted).

Although Worthing's proposed instruction was a correct statement of the applicable law on the credibility of cooperating witnesses and was based on the Eighth Circuit Model Jury Instructions, the proposed instruction included the following "cautionary tail" which is not part of the relevant Model Instruction (instruction 4.05a): "You should, however, consider the testimony of each with greater caution and care than that of an ordinary witness." The district court did not abuse its discretion in refusing to give the proposed cautionary tail instruction because the testimony of the cooperating witnesses was corroborated by the other cooperating witnesses, by the investors, and by documents. The instructions given adequately informed the jury about the factors to consider in assessing the credibility of witnesses who had entered into plea agreements with the government, including their hope to receive a reduced sentence for cooperation (instruction 14), advised them not to consider a guilty plea as evidence of Worthing's guilt (instruction 13), and instructed them to give the testimony of the cooperating witnesses such weight as they thought it deserved (instruction 12).

SENTENCING

Worthing finally argues that the district court imposed sentence in violation of *United States v. Booker*. Worthing argues that the district court unconstitutionally imposed sentence based on facts not reflected in the jury verdict or admitted by him. Worthing argues that the base offense level for the most serious offense found by the jury was 6, for a guideline sentencing range of 0-6 months, thus making 6 months the statutory maximum sentence. The presentence investigation report (PSR) recommended enhancements of 28 levels (18 levels for the amount of the loss (more than \$ 2.5 million but less than \$ 7 million), 4 levels for the number of victims (more than 50), 2 levels because a substantial part of the fraud was committed from outside the United States and involved sophisticated means, 4 levels for role in the offense (as organizer and leader of conduct that was otherwise extensive and involved five or more participants)), for a total offense level of 34, for a guideline sentencing range of 151-188 months (at criminal history category I). The government sought a sentence at the upper end of the applicable guideline sentencing range. Worthing objected at sentencing, clearly stating the Sixth Amendment basis for his objection and thus preserving the error for appellate review. He did not object to the amount of loss and argued that, without the other enhancements, the appropriate guideline sentencing range would be 48-60 months.

The district court delayed sentencing pending the Supreme Court's decision in *Booker*. The district court sentenced Worthing to a total of ten years imprisonment.

On appeal Worthing argues that the district court improperly increased his sentence (by more than nine years) on the basis of facts not reflected in the jury verdict or admitted by him, such as his role in the offense and the scope of the fraudulent scheme. He particularly argues that the district court—not the jury—found that the offense conduct was outrageous.

We find no *Booker* error. The district court considered the guidelines as set forth in the PSR but expressly regarded the guidelines as advisory and not mandatory, consistent with the Supreme Court's directions in *Booker*. We have reviewed the district court's use of the term "outrageous" and believe that, read in context, the district court used the term to describe the offense conduct in general and did not make any finding of "outrageousness" (and thus did not rely on any such finding to enhance the offense level). The district court stated that it had intended to sentence at the bottom of the applicable guideline sentencing range but decided that 120 months was sufficient, in light of the evidence and the circumstances of the case. We note that the district court imposed a sentence well below the bottom of the applicable guideline sentencing range calculated on the basis of the enhancements recommended by the PSR (151 months). We hold that the sentence was not unreasonable in light of the sentencing factors set forth in *18 U.S.C. § 3553(a)*.

Accordingly, the judgment of the district court is affirmed

IX. INTERNATIONAL TRADE

2. Business & Finance

C. Taxation*

* Cases are indexed under this subject. The full text of these cases is published in the **volume**-page indicated.

DAVE ARNETT
v.
COMMISSIONER OF INTERNAL REVENUE

Docket No. 8866-03 (T.C. 2006)
Decided January 25, 2006

P is a U.S. citizen who earned wage income while working in Antarctica. P excluded this wage income on his 2001 Federal income tax return. R issued a notice of deficiency in which R determined that the excluded wage income earned in Antarctica is taxable.

Held: The wage income P earned in Antarctica is not excludable from income under sec. 911, I.R.C.

Larry D. Harvey, for petitioner. Randall L. Preheim, for respondent.

OPINION

VASQUEZ, Judge: Respondent determined an $8,066 deficiency in petitioner's 2001 Federal income tax and a $1,613.20 section 6662[1] penalty. After a concession,[2] the sole issue for decision is whether section 911 entitles petitioner to exclude from gross income the wage income he earned in Antarctica in 2001.

This case is before the Court on respondent's motion for summary judgment and petitioner's motion for partial summary judgment under Rule 121. This is the lead case in an unconsolidated group of approximately 150 cases of similarly situated taxpayers who earned wage income in Antarctica and who make similar arguments.

Background At the time of the filing of the petition, petitioner resided in Hayward, Wisconsin. During 2001, petitioner was employed by Raytheon Support Services Co. (Raytheon). Raytheon is under contract with the National Science Foundation

---

1 Unless otherwise indicated, all section references are to the Internal Revenue Code in effect for the year in issue, and all Rule references are to the Tax Court Rules of Practice and Procedure.

2 Respondent conceded that no penalty pursuant to sec. 6662 is due from petitioner for 2001.

(NSF), an agency of the United States, for certain research conducted in Antarctica. During 2001, petitioner, a U.S. citizen, resided and performed services at McMurdo Station in Ross Island, Antarctica.

On his 2001 Federal income tax return, petitioner excluded $48,894 of wage income earned and received as an employee of Raytheon for services performed in Antarctica during tax year 2001.

In the notice of deficiency, respondent determined that the income petitioner earned in Antarctica is taxable and is not excludable under section 911.

Discussion I. Summary Judgment Respondent moved for summary judgment on the issue of whether section 911 entitles petitioner to exclude from U.S. taxation $48,894 of wage income earned and received as an employee of Raytheon for services performed in Antarctica during tax year 2001.

Petitioner moved for partial summary judgment on the issue of whether the income he earned in Antarctica is foreign earned income within the meaning of section 911. Petitioner contends that the income he earned in Antarctica "was not earned from sources within the United States" and that he should be entitled to the foreign earned income exclusion under section 911. Petitioner's motion is for partial summary judgment because even if the Court finds for petitioner that the income he earned in Antarctica is foreign earned income, petitioner must still prove that he otherwise meets the requirements of section 911.

Rule 121(a) provides that either party may move for summary judgment upon all or any part of the legal issues in controversy. Full or partial summary judgment may be granted only if it is demonstrated that no genuine issue exists as to any material fact and that the issues presented by the motion may be decided as a matter of law. See Rule 121(b); Sundstrand Corp. v. Commissioner, 98 T.C. 518, 520 (1992), affd. 17 F.3d 965 (7th Cir. 1994).

We conclude that there is no genuine issue as to any material fact and that a decision may be rendered as a matter of law. II. Gross Income in General Section 61(a) provides that gross income means all income from whatever source derived. Thus, citizens of the United States generally are taxed on income earned outside the United States unless the income is specifically excluded. Specking v. Commissioner, 117 T.C. 95, 101-102 (2001), affd. sub nom. Haessly v. Commissioner, 68 Fed. Appx. 44 (9th Cir. 2003), affd. sub nom. Umbach v. Commissioner, 357 F.3d 1108 (10th Cir. 2003). Exclusions from income are construed narrowly, and taxpayers must bring themselves within the clear scope of the exclusion. Id. III. Section 911 Section 911(a) provides in part that a "qualified individual" may elect to exclude from gross income his or her "foreign earned income". Section 911(b)(2) limits the amount of the exclusion for foreign earned income to $78,000 for 2001.

Section 911(b)(1)(A) defines "foreign earned income" to mean, in general, "the amount received by such individual from sources within a foreign country or countries which constitute earned income attributable to services performed by such individual" during the period set forth in section 911(d)(1). Section 911(b)(1)(B) excludes from foreign earned income certain amounts not relevant to this case.

Section 911(d)(1) defines "qualified individual" for purposes of section 911 to mean: an individual whose tax home is in a foreign country and who is–

> (A) a citizen of the United States and establishes to the satisfaction of the Secretary that he has been a bona fide resident of a foreign country or countries for an uninterrupted period which includes an entire taxable year, or
>
> (B) a citizen or resident of the United States and who, during any period of 12 consecutive months, is present in a foreign country or countries during at least 330 full days in such period.

Section 911(d)(9) authorizes the Secretary to prescribe "regulations as may be necessary or appropriate to carry out the purposes of" section 911. Pursuant to that grant of authority, the Secretary promulgated proposed regulations under section 911 in 1983, see 48 Fed. Reg. 33007 (July 20, 1983), and final regulations in 1985, see T.D. 8006, 1985-1 C.B. 224, that apply to the year in issue.

These regulations are legislative; therefore, they are entitled to Chevron deference and are binding on the courts unless procedurally defective, arbitrary or capricious in substance, or manifestly contrary to the statute. United States v. Mead Corp., 533 U.S. 218, 227 (2001); Chevron U.S.A. Inc. v. Natural Res. Def. Council, Inc., 467 U.S. 837 (1984); Specking v. Commissioner, supra at 115.

The Internal Revenue Code (Code) does not define "foreign country" for purposes of section 911. However, section 1.911- 2(h), Income Tax Regs., provides:

> (h) Foreign country. The term "foreign country" when used in a geographical sense includes any territory under the sovereignty of a government other than that of the United States. It includes the territorial waters of the foreign country (determined in accordance with the laws of the United States), the air space over the foreign country, and the seabed and subsoil of those submarine areas which are adjacent to the territorial waters of the foreign country and over which the foreign country has exclusive rights, in accordance with international law, with respect to the exploration and exploitation of natural resources.

The parties disagree regarding whether this definition of "foreign country" includes Antarctica. If Antarctica is a "foreign country" for purposes of section 911, petitioner may be able to exclude from income the wage income he earned in Antarctica. If Antarctica is not a "foreign country" for purposes of section 911, petitioner must include in income the wage income he earned in Antarctica. IV. Caselaw In Martin v. Commissioner, 50 T.C. 59 (1968), we decided a similar issue—whether a U.S. citizen can exclude income earned in Antarctica. We held that Antarctica is not a foreign country within the meaning of section 911(a)(2) and section 1.911-1(b)(7), Income Tax Regs., as in effect in 1962.

In Martin, the taxpayer, as an employee of a private tax- exempt U.S. organization, took part in an Antarctic expedition. The taxpayer claimed, as does petitioner, that his earnings in Antarctica were exempt from tax under section 911, and the only question raised in this respect in Martin was whether Antarctica is a foreign country.

In finding that Antarctica is not a foreign country within the meaning of section 911(a)(2), we relied on a treaty effective June 23, 1961, between the United States and a number of other nations regarding Antarctica. The Antarctic Treaty, Dec. 1, 1959, 12 U.S.T. 794. The treaty provides that Antarctica is to be used for peaceful purposes, that scientific investigation there is to be encouraged, and that all questions of sovereignty over it are to be put in abeyance.

We also relied on the language of section 1.911-1(b)(7), Income Tax Regs., as in effect at the time, which defined "foreign country" as follows: "The term 'foreign country' means territory under the sovereignty of a government other than that of the United States and includes the air space over such territory. It does not include a possession or Territory of the United States."

We noted that in the light of the international treaty concerning Antarctica, the U.S. Department of State did not consider Antarctica to be under the sovereignty of any government. Therefore we held that Antarctica was not a foreign country within the meaning of the regulations or of section 911 as then in effect. Martin v. Commissioner, supra at 62; see also Rev. Rul. 67-52, 1967-1 C.B. 186.

The treaty regarding Antarctica is still in effect, and therefore Antarctica remains a sovereignless region.[3] Petitioner nevertheless contends that Martin has been overruled and superseded by the holding of the Supreme Court of the United States in Smith v. United States, 507 U.S. 197 (1993), and the holding of the U.S. District Court for the District of Massachusetts in Smith v. Raytheon Co., 297 F. Supp. 2d 399 (D. Mass. 2004).

In Smith v. United States, supra at 198, the issue was "whether the Federal Tort Claims Act (FTCA), 28 U.S.C. §§ 1346(b), 1402(b), 2401(b), 2671-2680 (1998 ed. and Supp. II), applies to tortious acts or omissions occurring in Antarctica, a sovereignless region without civil tort law of its own." The plaintiff, Mrs. Smith, brought a wrongful-death action against the United States under the FTCA for the death of her husband, Mr. Smith. At the time of his death, Mr. Smith was employed as a carpenter at McMurdo Station on Ross Island, Antarctica, for a construction company under contract to the NSF, the same agency that had a contract with Raytheon in the instant case. Mr. Smith died after falling into a crevasse in Antarctica.

3 The treaty was in force as of Jan. 1, 2005. Treaties in Force, http://www.state.gov/documents/organization/53776.pdf.

The Supreme Court held that Antarctica is a foreign country for purposes of the FTCA. Id. at 201-202. The Supreme Court reasoned that Mrs. Smith's claim was barred by the foreign- country exception of the FTCA under 28 U.S.C. sec. 2680(k), which precludes the exercise of jurisdiction over "any claim arising in a foreign country." The Court based its conclusion on the particular language of the FTCA. Id. at 201-205.

In Smith v. Raytheon Co., supra, the U.S. District Court for the District of Massachusetts held that Antarctica is a foreign country for purposes of the Fair Labor Standards Act (FLSA). The plaintiffs claimed that the FLSA required their employer, Raytheon, which had entered into a contract with the NSF to perform services in Antarctica, to pay them overtime for work they performed in Antarctica. Id. at 400. The FLSA requires an employer to pay an employee "at a rate not less than one and one- half times the regular rate at which he is employed" for the hours the employee works in excess of 40 hours per week. 29 U.S.C. sec. 207(a). However, there are several exceptions to this rule including geographical limits. Certain provisions of the FLSA, including section 207, do not apply where employee services are performed within a foreign country. 29 U.S.C. sec. 213(f). The court concluded that Antarctica is a foreign country for purposes of the FLSA and based its conclusion on the particular language of the FLSA. Smith v. Raytheon Co., supra at 401-402.

In the instant case, we are revisiting the same issue we discussed in Martin v. Commissioner, supra. Although the statutory and regulatory provisions discussed in Martin have been modified and there have been caselaw developments since Martin, these changes do not affect the conclusion that petitioner's income earned in Antarctica is subject to tax in the United States and petitioner does not qualify for the foreign earned income exclusion under section 911.

Moreover, both Smith v. United States, supra, and Smith v. Raytheon Co., supra, discuss the issue of whether Antarctica is a foreign country within the context of statutes other than the Code. The provisions of the Code and the applicable regulations are controlling herein. Therefore, we do not find Smith and Raytheon Co. to be controlling, and we will not overrule our holding in Martin that Antarctica is not a foreign country for purposes of the Code. V. Conclusion The foreign earned income exclusion of section 911 applies to amounts received "from sources within a foreign country or countries". As Antarctica is not a foreign country for purposes of the Code, we conclude that petitioner is not entitled to exclude the wage income he earned in Antarctica from income for 2001 pursuant to section 911. See also sec. 863(d) (providing that income earned in Antarctica by a U.S. person is sourced in the United States).

In reaching all of our holdings herein, we have considered all arguments made by the parties, and, to the extent not herein discussed, we find them to be irrelevant or without merit.

To reflect the foregoing,

An appropriate order and decision will be entered granting respondent's motion for summary judgment and denying petitioner's motion for partial summary judgment.

SUN LIFE ASSURANCE COMPANY OF CANADA
v.
DEIRDRE K. MANNA

368 Ill. App. 3d 591 (Ct. App. Ill. 2006)
Decided November 1, 2006

For APPELLANTS: R. Lee Christie, Mary Kay M. Martire, Tracy D. Williams, Belinda S. Morgan, Foley & Lardner LLP, of Chicago.

For APPELLEE: Special Assistant Attorney General Iain D. Johnston, Chief Legal Counsel Robert E. Wagner, Assistant Attorney General Nadine J. Wichern, Lisa Madigan, Attorney General of the State of Illinois.

JUSTICE KARNEZIS delivered the opinion of the court. THEIS, P.J., and GREIMAN J., concur.

OPINION

JUSTICE KARNEZIS delivered the opinion of the court:

The appeal concerns the constitutionality of the State of Illinois's "retaliatory tax" on "alien" insurance companies, insurance companies incorporated or organized under the laws of any country other than the United States (215 ILCS 5/2(h) (West 2004)). Plaintiff Sun Life Assurance Company of Canada (Sun Life) is a life insurance corporation organized under the laws of Canada. Sun Life does insurance business in Illinois and is, therefore, considered an "alien" insurance company under the Illinois Insurance Code (215 ILCS 5/1 et seq. (West 2004)) (the Code). Sun Life asserts that imposition of a retaliatory tax on an alien insurance company violates the uniformity clause of the Illinois Constitution (Ill. Const. 1970, art. IX, § 2), the equal protection clauses of the United States Constitution (U.S. Const., amend. XIV) and Illinois Constitution (Ill. Const. 1970, art. I, § 2) (collectively, the equal protection clause) and the foreign commerce clause of the United States Constitution (U.S. Const., art. I, § 8, cl. 3). We affirm.

BACKGROUND

Pursuant to the Code, three types of insurance companies can do business in Illinois: domestic companies, organized and incorporated under the laws of Illinois (215 ILCS 5/2(f) (West 2004)); "foreign" companies, incorporated or organized under the laws of any state of the United States other than Illinois (215 ILCS 5/2(g) (West 2004)); and "alien" companies. Domestic, foreign and alien insurance companies pay the same privilege tax to do business in Illinois. 215 ILCS 5/409, 5/413 (West 2004). However, in addition to the privilege tax, foreign and alien insurance companies may be subject to a retaliatory tax. 215 ILCS 5/444.1 (West 2004).

Section 444(1) of the Code (215 ILCS 5/444(1) (West 2004)) is titled "Retaliation." It provides that, if the laws of any other state or country require that Illinois companies, as a condition of doing business in that state or country, pay a greater amount of penalties, fees, charges or taxes than Illinois requires in the aggregate for similar purposes of foreign or alien companies to do business in Illinois, then Illinois will assess foreign or alien companies incorporated under the laws of that state or country penalties, fees, charges and taxes in amounts equal to those required in the aggregate for like purposes of Illinois companies doing business in such state or country. 215 ILCS 5/444(1) (West 2004). Essentially, if a foreign or alien insurance company would pay less for the privilege of doing business in Illinois than an Illinois insurance company would be required to pay to do business in the foreign or alien company's home state or country, Illinois will retaliate by requiring the foreign or alien company to make up the difference.

Pursuant to the retaliatory tax section of the Illinois Administrative Code (50 Ill. Adm. Code 2515.10 et seq., amended at 24 Ill. Reg. 10228, eff. July 1, 2000), retaliatory tax is due from a foreign or alien insurance company if the sum of its "State of Illinois' Basis" is less than the sum of its "State of Incorporation's Basis." 50 Ill. Adm. Code 2515.50, amended at 24 Ill. Reg. 10228, eff. July 1, 2000. Defendant the Division of Insurance of the Illinois Department of Financial and Professional Regulation (the Department) calculates the state of incorporation's basis as "the sum of the amounts that an Illinois domiciled company would have PAID in the foreign or alien domiciliary state or country if it transacted similar operations there as did the foreign or alien company in Illinois for [subsequently enumerated fees and taxes] in the foreign or alien company's state or country of domicile." 50 Ill. Adm. Code. 2515.50(c), amended at 24 Ill. Reg. 10228, eff. July 1, 2000.

Sun Life consistently paid the privilege tax for the years it operated in Illinois but never paid a retaliatory tax. Canadian law does not impose a premium tax on life insurance companies. Sun Life's Illinois privilege and retaliatory tax statements show that Sun Life would owe no Canadian tax on its life insurance business in Canada. Because Sun Life owed tax and fees under the Illinois tax law but not under the Canadian tax law, it determined that its Canadian tax basis was not higher than its Illinois tax basis and that it owed no retaliatory tax.

However, section 2515.40 of Title 50 of the Administrative Code defines "State of Incorporation's Basis" as:

> "the taxes, fees and charges that would have been assessed against and paid by an Illinois company if it had similar operation in the state of domicile of the foreign or alien company, as the foreign or alien company had in Illinois, as described in subsection 2515.50(c) of this Part. *If applicable, the state of domicile for the alien company may mean its port or state of entry* ***." (Emphasis added.)

50 Ill. Adm. Code 2515.40, amended at 24 Ill. Reg. 10228, eff. July 1, 2000.[1] Sun Life's port of entry into the Unites States was the State of Michigan. Applying section 2515.40, the Department determined that, for retaliatory taxation purposes, Sun Life's state of incorporation basis would be determined by the tax of Michigan, Sun Life's state of entry. In the aggregate, Michigan imposes higher taxes and fees on Illinois companies doing insurance business in Michigan than Illinois charges on Michigan companies doing the same insurance business in Illinois. Accordingly, basing its retaliatory tax audit on Michigan tax, the Department assessed Sun Life $ 4,010,743 in retaliatory tax for 1997 through 2003.

Sun Life disputed that it owed retaliatory tax, arguing that imposition of the tax on alien insurance companies was unconstitutional. Sun Life filed a declaratory judgment action in the circuit court of Cook County, seeking a finding that the State of Illinois is not authorized to impose a discriminatory retaliatory tax on insurance business conducted by alien companies in Illinois. Sun Life argued that imposition of such a tax violates the uniformity clause of the Illinois Constitution, the equal protection clause and the foreign commerce clause.[2] Sun Life filed a motion for summary judgment in the action and the Department filed a cross-motion for summary judgment. On March 23, 2005, the court granted the Department's motion for summary judgment and denied Sun Life's motion. Sun Life timely appeals, seeking reversal of the court's order and a declaration that, as an alien insurance company, Sun Life is not subject to the retaliatory tax.[3]

---

1 Section 2515.40 of Title 50 of the Administrative Code defines "State of Illinois' Basis" as "the taxes, fees and charges in the aggregate assessed against and paid by a company transacting insurance business in the State of Illinois as described in subsection 2515.50(b) of this Part." 50 Ill. Adm. Code. 2515.40, amended at 24 Ill. Reg. 10228, eff. July 1, 2000.

2 Constitutional issues cannot be decided in an administrative hearing before the Department. 50 Ill. Adm. Code 2500.50(b)(4), adopted at 22 Ill. Reg. 290, eff. December 21, 1998. Concerned that a complaint for administrative review from an adverse decision of the Department would not preserve its constitutional claims, Sun Life opted to file a declaratory judgment action in the circuit court seeking resolution of its constitutional challenge. A plaintiff challenging the validity of a statute on its face need not exhaust administrative remedies prior to filing a declaratory judgment action because a facial attack on the constitutionality of a statute is not dependent on the administrative record for its resolution. *Arvia v. Madigan, 209 Ill.2d 520, 532-33, 809 N.E.2d 88, 97, 283 Ill. Dec. 895 (2004).*

3 The issue of whether the Department correctly determined that Michigan law should be used to determine whether Sun Life owes a retaliatory tax is not before us.

Sun Life argues that the court erred in granting summary judgment to the Department and denying Sun Life's motion for summary judgment because the retaliatory tax violates the uniformity clause, the equal protection clause and the foreign commerce clause. The parties agree that there are no genuine issues of material fact. The only issue is a question of law: whether the State of Illinois may constitutionally impose a retaliatory tax on an alien insurance company that it does not impose on a domestic insurer.[4] We review both a trial court's decision on a motion for summary judgment and the constitutionality of a statute *de novo. City of Chicago v. Holland, 206 Ill. 2d 480, 488, 795 N.E.2d 240, 245, 276 Ill. Dec. 887 (2003).*

Uniformity Clause

The uniformity clause provides that, "[i]n any law classifying the subjects or objects of nonproperty taxes or fees, the classes shall be reasonable and the subjects or objects within each class shall be taxed uniformly. Exemptions, deductions, credits, refunds and other allowances shall be reasonable." Ill. Const. 1970, art. IX, § 2.

The tax classification at issue here consists of all insurance companies covered by the Code: domestic, foreign and alien companies doing insurance business in Illinois. The class does not, as the Department occasionally appears to assume, consist solely of all alien insurers doing business in Illinois. There is no discrimination in the retaliatory tax statute's treatment of alien insurers. The statute applies to all alien insurers uniformly. It does not discriminate against one alien company in favor of another or against companies from a particular country. "The retaliatory tax is not imposed on [alien] corporations *qua* [alien] corporations ***; it is imposed only on corporations whose home States impose more onerous burdens on [Illinois] insurers than [Illinois] otherwise would impose on those corporations." *Western & Southern Life Insurance Co. v. State Board of Equalization of California, 451 U.S. 648, 670 n.23, 68 L. Ed. 2d 514, 532 n.23, 101 S. Ct. 2070, 2084 n.23 (1981).* Whether an alien insurer must actually pay a retaliatory tax depends entirely on the tax laws of its own state of incorporation, not on the retaliatory tax statute. In contrast, the statute does not apply uniformly to all members of the class consisting of all insurance companies covered by the Code. Rather, the tax only applies to foreign and alien insurance companies. It does not apply to domestic insurance companies.

As the party attacking the tax classification, Sun Life is not required to negate every conceivable basis which might support it. *Milwaukee Safeguard Insurance Co. v. Selcke, 179 Ill. 2d 94, 98, 688 N.E.2d 68, 70, 227 Ill. Dec. 731 (1997).* Instead, upon a good-faith uniformity challenge by Sun Life, the Department, as the taxing body, bears the initial burden of producing a justification for the classifications. Milwaukee Safeguard Insurance Co., 179 Ill. 2d at 98, 688 N.E.2d at 71. Sun Life

---

4 Sun Life does not dispute Illinois's right to impose the retaliatory tax on foreign insurance companies, only its right to impose the tax on alien insurance companies such as Sun Life.

then has the burden of persuading the court that the justification offered is unsupported by the facts or insufficient as a matter of law. Milwaukee Safeguard Insurance Co., 179 Ill. 2d at 98-99, 688 N.E.2d at 71.

Sun Life challenged the tax as discriminatory and violative of the uniformity clause because it is imposed on some subjects of the class but not on others, arguably favoring domestic insurance companies over alien insurance companies even though there is no real and substantial difference between alien insurance companies and domestic insurance companies. In response to this good faith uniformity challenge, the Department argued the classification was justified because (1) there was a difference between domestic and alien insurers because alien insurers are more difficult to regulate, a distinction found valid in Milwaukee Safeguard Insurance Co., 179 Ill. 2d at 101, 688 N.E.2d at 72; and (2) the purpose of imposing the retaliatory tax is the legitimate state purpose "to promote the interstate business of domestic insurers by deterring other States from enacting discriminatory or excessive taxes," quoting *Western & Southern Life Insurance Co., 451 U.S. at 668, 68 L. Ed. 2d at 531, 101 S. Ct. at 2083.*

In reviewing the constitutionality of a tax classification, the threshold requirement is that the taxation scheme "be motivated by a legitimate, permissible State purpose." *Springfield Rare Coin Galleries, Inc. v. Johnson, 115 Ill. 2d 221, 232, 503 N.E.2d 300, 305, 104 Ill. Dec. 743 (1986)* (uniformity challenge to Illinois's tax statute excluding Republic of South Africa from tax exemption). In *Western & Southern Life Insurance Co.*, the United States Supreme Court noted that a retaliatory tax's "'ultimate object is not to punish foreign corporations doing business in the state, or retort the actions of the foreign state *** but to induce such foreign state to show the same consideration to corporations of the enacting state doing business therein as is shown to corporations of such foreign state doing business in the enacting state.'" *Western & Southern Life Insurance Co., 451 U.S. at 668-69, 68 L. Ed. 2d at 531, 101 S. Ct. at 2083*, quoting Annotation, *Constitutionality, Construction, Operation, and Effect of Retaliatory Statutes Against Foreign Corporations Doing Business Within the State*, 91 A.L.R. 795 (1934). *Western & Southern* concerned the State of California's imposition of a retaliatory tax on an Ohio insurer doing business in California. In conducting an equal protection analysis of the tax, the court found that there was "no doubt that promotion of domestic industry by deterring barriers to interstate business is a legitimate state purpose." *Western & Southern Life Insurance Co., 451 U.S. at 671, 68 L. Ed. 2d at 532, 101 S. Ct. at 2084*. The fact that California sought to promote its insurance industry by influencing the policies of other states did not render this purpose illegitimate. *Western & Southern Life Insurance Co., 451 U.S. at 671, 68 L. Ed. 2d at 532, 101 S. Ct. at 2084*. Because the Court concluded that California's retaliatory tax was rationally related to this purpose, it held that the tax met the requirements of the federal equal protection clause. *Western & Southern Life Insurance Co., 451 U.S. at 672-74, 68 L. Ed. 2d at 532-35, 101 S. Ct. at 2084-86.*

In *Mutual Life Insurance Co. of New York v. Washburn, 137 Ill. 2d 312, 561 N.E.2d 29, 148 Ill. Dec. 723 (1990)*, our supreme court followed *Western & Southern Life Insurance Co.* and determined that the Department's application of the Illinois retaliatory tax statute to a New York life insurance company met the requirements of the equal protection clause. Mutual Life Insurance Co. of New York, 137 Ill. 2d at 330, 561 N.E.2d at 38-39. It also determined that it did not infringe on the dictates of the uniformity clause. Mutual Life Insurance Co. of New York, 137 Ill. 2d at 332, 561 N.E.2d at 38. The plaintiff had argued that the retaliatory tax, as applied by the Department, violated the equal protection and uniformity provisions of the Illinois Constitution because it taxed some New York companies and not others.

Generally, in order to survive scrutiny under the uniformity clause, a nonproperty tax classification such as the one at issue here must (1) be based on a real and substantial difference between the subjects taxed and those not taxed and (2) bear some reasonable relationship to the object of the legislation or to public policy. *Milwaukee Safeguard Insurance Co. v. Selcke, 179 Ill. 2d 94, 98, 179 Ill. 2d 94, 688 N.E.2d 68, 70, 227 Ill. Dec. 731 (1997)*; Mutual Life Insurance Co. of New York, 137 Ill. 2d at 331, 561 N.E.2d at 38. The *Mutual Life Insurance Co. of New York* court determined, however, that it need not engage in this analysis of the retaliatory tax statute because the tax applied uniformly to all New York companies and there was, therefore, not more than one classification at issue. Mutual Life Insurance Co. of New York, 137 Ill. 2d at 331, 561 N.E.2d at 38. It was the New York taxing provisions and not the retaliatory statute which classified New York companies. Whether a particular New York company was subject to the retaliatory tax was dependent on the vagaries of the New York tax laws and the business experiences of the different insurance companies, which resulted in differing tax bases for the companies in New York. Because the plaintiff presented no compelling reason to find otherwise, the Department's application of the retaliatory statute did not infringe on Illinois's uniformity requirement. Mutual Life Insurance Co. of New York, 137 Ill. 2d at 331-32, 561 N.E.2d at 38.

Citing *Western & Southern* and *Mutual Life Insurance Co. of New York*, Sun Life concedes the right of Illinois to impose a retaliatory tax on foreign insurers doing business in Illinois but argues it does not have the same right regarding alien insurers. However, as Sun Life points out, both cases concern interstate commerce and not international commerce. Can the legitimate principal purpose of retaliatory taxes, "to promote the interstate business of domestic insurers by deterring other States from enacting discriminatory or excessive taxes" (*Western & Southern Life Insurance Co., 451 U.S. at 668, 68 L. Ed. 2d at 531, 101 S. Ct. at 2083*), be reframed in an international context without coming into conflict with the plenary and exclusive power of the federal government to establish and carry out foreign policy (Springfield Rare Coin, 115 Ill. 2d at 233, 503 N.E.2d at 305)? Can a state impose a retaliatory tax in order to, paraphrasing *Western & Southern Life Insurance Co.*, promote the international business of domestic insurers by deterring other countries from enacting discriminatory or excessive taxes when "'[p]ower over external affairs is not shared by the States; it is vested in the national government exclusively'" (Springfield Rare Coin, 115 Ill. 2d at 233, 503 N.E.2d at 305, quoting *United States v. Pink, 315 U.S. 203, 233, 86 L. Ed 796, 819, 62 S. Ct. 552, 567 (1942))*

The United States must speak with "one voice" when dealing with foreign nations, otherwise foreign policy initiatives by a single state could embroil the entire nation in serious international disputes. Springfield Rare Coin, 115 Ill. 2d at 233, 503 N.E.2d at 305. Foreign policy actions by individual states "lead to a lack of uniformity" and the power of the federal government must, therefore, "be left free from local interference." Springfield Rare Coin, 115 Ill. 2d at 233, 503 N.E.2d at 306. Illinois's desire to promote its insurance industry by influencing the policies of other countries arguably flies in the face of the federal government's exclusive power over foreign affairs.

Nevertheless,

> "Despite these broad principles, it would be an obvious oversimplification and wrong to assert that no State law which has any impact whatsoever upon foreign relations may ever stand. For example, the fact that Illinois imposes taxes upon imported products generally can be said to have some effect on foreign nations. Clearly, such incidental, evenhanded burdens do not rise to the level of unconstitutionality. [Citation.] Something more than an indirect or incidental effect is necessary." Springfield Rare Coin, 115 Ill. 2d at 233, 503 N.E.2d at 306.

The precise line of demarcation between incidental and unconstitutional intrusions into foreign affairs is difficult to draw, but general principles to consider are whether the challenged classification (1) is motivated by disapproval of a nation's political and social policies, (2) attempts to make a political statement, (3) is targeted at a single foreign nation or (4) is effectively an economic boycott or an embargo. Springfield Rare Coin, 115 Ill. 2d at 236, 503 N.E.2d at 307 (invalidating statutory amendment exempting from retailer's occupancy tax gold and silver coins issued by Illinois, the United States or any other foreign country *except the Republic of South Africa*; court held exclusion was essentially an economic boycott targeted at a single nation, motivated solely by disapproval of South Africa's policies, and created a risk of conflict between nations).

Here, the retaliatory tax appears to be merely a permissible incidental intrusion on foreign affairs. International commerce is, of course, affected when the Department imposes a retaliatory tax on an alien company. Imposition of that tax necessarily involves a monetary impact on the alien insurer and a resultant monetary impact on the insurer's funds in its home country. However, that impact on the foreign country is incidental. The tax is not directed at one particular nation, being applied to all alien insurers equally. It is not a boycott of alien insurers and is not intended to keep them from doing business in Illinois because of their home country's political or social policies. Accordingly, because the impact of the retaliatory tax is incidental, Illinois' imposition of the tax is not an unconstitutional intrusion into foreign affairs.

Equal Protection Clause

The equal protection clause provides that the states may not "'deny to any person within [their] jurisdiction the equal protection of the laws,'" but does allow reasonable classifications among such persons. *Western & Southern Life Insurance Co., 451 U.S. at 656-57, 68 L. Ed. 2d at 523, 101 S. Ct. at 2077*, quoting U.S. Const., amend. XIV. "[T]he uniformity clause was intended to encompass the *equal protection clause* and add to it even more limitations on government." *Geja's Cafe v. Metropolitan Pier & Exposition Authority, 153 Ill. 2d 239, 247, 606 N.E.2d 1212, 1215, 180 Ill. Dec. 135 (1992)*. Because "[t]he uniformity clause imposes more stringent limitations than the equal protection clause on the legislature's authority to classify the subjects and objects of taxation," "'[i]f a tax is constitutional under the uniformity clause, it inherently fulfills the requirements of the equal protection clause.'" *Allegro Services, Ltd. v. Metropolitan Pier & Exposition Authority, 172 Ill. 2d 243, 249-50, 665 N.E.2d 1246, 1251, 216 Ill. Dec. 689 (1996)*, quoting Geja's Cafe, 153 Ill. 2d at 247, 606 N.E.2d at 1215. Accordingly, because the retaliatory tax on alien insurers is valid under the uniformity clause, it is also valid under the equal protection clause. See *Allegro Services, Ltd., 172 Ill. 2d at 250, 665 N.E.2d at 1251.*

Foreign Commerce Clause

The commerce clause of the U.S. Constitution provides that "Congress shall have Power *** To regulate Commerce with foreign Nations, and among the several States, and with the Indian Tribes." U.S. Const., art. I, § 8, cl. 3. The provision providing Congress's power to regulate commerce with foreign nations is referred to as the foreign commerce clause. Generally, in order for a state to tax goods in interstate commerce in compliance with the domestic commerce clause, it must establish that the tax "is applied to an activity with a substantial nexus with the taxing State, is fairly apportioned, does not discriminate against interstate commerce, and is fairly related to the services provided by the State." Complete Auto Transit, Inc. v. Brady, 430 U.S. 274, 279, 51 L. Ed. 2d 326, 331, 97 S. Ct. 1076, 1079 (1977). When a state seeks to tax foreign commerce, it must satisfy the four-part *Complete Auto Transit* test and then relieve two additional concerns: the enhanced risk of multiple taxation and the need for the federal government to "speak with one voice" when regulating commerce with foreign nations. *Japan Line, Ltd. v. County of Los Angeles, 441 U.S. 434, 449 n.14, 60 L. Ed. 2d 336, 348 n.14, 99 S. Ct. 1813, 1822 n.14 (1979)*. Sun Life argues that the retaliatory tax on alien insurers fails to meet the necessary requirements because it (1) discriminates against international commerce by imposing a tax on alien insurers, in violation of the third criterion of the *Complete Auto Transit* test; and (2) prevents the federal government from speaking with one voice when regulating international commerce by attempting to influence the tax policies of other nations, in violation of the second criterion of the *Japan Line* test.

The Department responds that the McCarran-Ferguson Act (15 U.S.C. § 1011 et seq. (2000)) (the Act) operates to exempt a state's taxation of insurance from application of the commerce clause, foreign or otherwise. The Act states: "Congress hereby declares that the continued regulation and taxation by the several States of the business of insurance is in the public interest, and that silence on the part of the Congress shall not be construed to impose any barrier to the regulation or taxation of such business by the several States." 15 U.S.C. § 1011 (2000). To that end, the Act provides:

> "(a) The business of insurance, and every person engaged therein, shall be subject to the laws of the several States which relate to the regulation or taxation of such business.
>
> (b) No Act of Congress shall be construed to invalidate, impair, or supersede any law enacted by any State for the purpose of regulating the business of insurance, or which imposes a fee or tax upon such business, unless such Act specifically relates to the business of insurance: *Provided*, That after June 30, 1948, the Act of July 2, 1890, as amended, known as the Sherman Act, and the Act of October 15, 1914, as amended, known as the Clayton Act, and the Act of September 26, 1914, known as the Federal Trade Commission Act, as amended [*15 U.S.C. 41 et seq. (2000)*], shall be applicable to the business of insurance to the extent that such business is not regulated by State law."

15 U.S.C. § 1012 (2000). In *Western & Southern Life Insurance Co.*, the U.S. Supreme Court held that "Congress removed all Commerce Clause limitations on the authority of the States to regulate and tax the business of insurance when it passed the McCarran-Ferguson Act." *Western & Southern Life Insurance Co., 451 U.S. at 653, 68 L. Ed. 2d at 520, 101 S. Ct. at 2075*. The Court held that California's retaliatory tax on an Ohio insurance company did not violate the commerce clause because "the McCarran-Ferguson Act *removes entirely any Commerce Clause restriction* upon California's power to tax the insurance business." (Emphasis added.) *Western & Southern Life Insurance Co., 451 U.S. at 655, 68 L. Ed. 2d at 522, 101 S. Ct. at 2076*. Sun Life argues, however, that the McCarran-Ferguson Act only operates to remove domestic commerce clause restrictions upon the states' power to tax the insurance business and does not remove foreign commerce clause restrictions. There is no such limitation in the Act. Although Western & Southern Life Insurance Co. is an interstate commerce case, its pronouncement that the McCarran-Ferguson Act "removes entirely any" commerce clause restrictions on a state's taxation of insurance is categorical. *All* such restrictions are eliminated by the Act. If Congress intended that states could only tax interstate commerce, it failed to say so and the United States Supreme Court has yet to interpret the Act in this manner.

Moreover, even if the McCarran-Ferguson Act does not operate to remove foreign commerce clause restrictions from state taxation of alien insurers, the retaliatory tax does meet the criteria enunciated in Complete Auto Transit and Japan Line, notwithstanding Sun Life's assertion to the contrary. As discussed previously, the retaliatory tax is valid under the uniformity and equal protection clauses, its treatment of alien insurers is not discriminatory given its legitimate state purpose and its impact on the federal government's ability to speak with one voice regarding foreign commerce is negligible. Sun Life is correct that the McCarran-Ferguson Act does not preempt the application of the Constitution and other federal laws to state taxation of insurance. *State Board of Insurance v. Todd Shipyards Corp., 370 U.S. 451, 8 L. Ed. 2d 620, 82 S. Ct. 1380 (1962)*. However, the retaliatory tax more than meets constitutional and federal law requirements and, therefore, does not violate the foreign commerce clause.

For the reasons stated above, we affirm the decision of the circuit court.

Affirmed.

IX. INTERNATIONAL TRADE

2. Business & Finance

D. International Securities & Commodities*

* Cases are indexed under this subject. The full text of these cases is published in the **volume**-page indicated.

GREGORY SCHILLER
v.
TOWER SEMICONDUCTOR LTD.

449 F.3d 286 (2d Cir. 2006)
Decided June 1, 2006

JUDGES: Before: MINER, WESLEY, Circuit Judges, and RAKOFF, District Judge.[1]

OPINION

WESLEY, Circuit Judge:

This case pits an old law against a "novel" argument.[2] Gregory Schiller ("Schiller") individually appeals the dismissal of a shareholder class action complaint filed against Tower Semiconductor Ltd. ("Tower"), its directors, and certain Tower investors. The complaint alleges that a Tower proxy statement issued by defendants was materially misleading and therefore violated §§ 14(a) and 20(a) of the Securities Exchange Act of 1934 ("Exchange Act"), 15 U.S.C. §§ 78n(a), 78t, and certain regulations, including Rule 14a-9, 17 C.F.R. § 240.14a-9 (2004) ("Rule 14a-9"). The United States District Court for the Southern District of New York (Wood, J.) dismissed the complaint on the ground that Tower, an Israeli corporation, was a foreign private issuer and therefore exempt from the strictures of § 14(a) by virtue of Exchange Act Rule 3a12-3, 17 C.F.R. § 240.3a12-3 (2004) ("Rule 3a12-3"). In so doing, the district court rejected the plaintiffs' claim that the Securities Exchange Commission ("SEC" or "the Commission") exceeded its authority in promulgating Rule 3a12-3. We affirm.

---

1 The Honorable Jed S. Rakoff, United States District Judge for the Southern District of New York, sitting by designation.

2 "Novel" is the adjective Judge Kimba Wood used to describe the issue that we are presented with here on appeal in her order dismissing the appellant's claims. *Philippe De Vries v. Tower Semiconductor Ltd.*, 2004 U.S. Dist. LEXIS 29921, No. 03-civ-4999 (S.D.N.Y. August 19, 2004).

BACKGROUND

As the facts of this case are not particularly relevant to the disposition of this appeal, we offer only those necessary to provide context to Schiller's claims. In the year 2000, Tower began to secure financing for the construction of a semiconductor fabrication facility ("Fab 2") in Israel. To this end, Tower entered into agreements with two sets of companies (collectively "Fab 2 Investors"), which agreed to provide Tower with approximately $ 305 million in financing in exchange for stock and credits toward the purchase of semiconductors. The agreements divided the total promised financing into installments and conditioned the payment of each installment upon the attainment of a different construction milestone. At the beginning of 2001, Tower further contracted with two Israeli banks to borrow $ 550 million for the construction project. This loan was conditioned on Tower's ability to comply with a timeline for raising $ 103 million in additional financing.

On March 31, 2002, Tower distributed a proxy statement disclosing that it was currently negotiating with the Israeli banks to reschedule the date by which it had to meet its next financing obligation. The proxy statement sought shareholder approval of a plan under which the Fab 2 Investors would accelerate certain installments of their $ 305 million commitment without regard to the attainment of the corresponding construction milestones in return for seven million shares of Tower stock. The proxy statement explained that once the installments were accelerated, the banks would postpone the date by which Tower had to meet its next financing obligation until the end of July 2002. Tower believed that the plan would "permit us to better pursue our efforts to bring strategic investors and to raise other funding."

While the plan received the necessary votes for approval, not all Tower shareholders were content with the arrangement. Schiller and others voiced their objection by filing a class action in the district court. The complaint alleged that Tower's proxy statement was false and misleading in violation of § 14(a) and Rule 14a-9 and that the Fab 2 Investors and certain members of Tower's board of directors, as control persons, were liable under § 20(a) of the Exchange Act, *15 U.S.C. § 78t*. In particular, the complaint alleged that there was no need for the Fab 2 Investors to accelerate the installments of its $ 305 million commitment because the construction of Fab 2 was on schedule, and therefore it was expected that the construction milestones, upon which the installment payments were conditioned, would be attained. Further, Schiller and his fellow plaintiffs contended that "because the Fab 2 project was proceeding on schedule, and because the [construction milestones] were going to be met in a timely manner, the advancement of the payment date had no value and was not a reason for the [b]anks to defer the dates by which additional financing needed to be obtained."

Defendants mounted a straightforward defense. They argued that Tower is a foreign private issuer and therefore that Rule 3a12-3 removes them from the reach of § 14(a). While plaintiffs contested defendants' characterization of Tower as a foreign private issuer, the district court easily dismissed this argument by pointing out that Tower's capital is located in Israel and that Tower's principal lenders are Israeli banks; the district court also relied on the fact that Tower had filed with the Commission annual reports reserved solely for foreign private issuers. As an alternative argument, plaintiffs challenged the validity of Rule 3a12-3, contending, as Schiller does on appeal, that Rule 3a12-3 exceeds the Commission's exemptive authority under the Exchange Act. The district court explained that "Congress has authorized the SEC to create certain exemptions through rules and regulations, so long as those exemptions are in the public interest and protect investors," and that it could not say that *Rule 3a12-3* is "arbitrary, capricious, or manifestly contrary to the statute." We agree.

DISCUSSION

Section 14(a) of the Exchange Act bars the dissemination of proxy statements "in contravention of such rules and regulations as the Commission may prescribe as necessary or appropriate in the public interest or for the protection of investors." *15 U.S.C. § 78n(a)*. Rule 14a-9 provides that proxy statements are not to be "false or misleading with respect to any material fact." *17 C.F.R. § 240.14a-9(a)*. By its own terms, however, § 14(a) does not apply to "exempted securit[ies]." Section 3(a)(12)(A)(vii) of the Exchange Act defines "exempted securit[ies]" as including

> such other securities . . . as the Commission may, by such rules and regulations as it deems consistent with the public interest and the protection of investors, either unconditionally or upon specified terms and conditions or for stated periods, exempt from the operation of any one or more provisions of this chapter which by their terms do not apply to an "exempted security" or to "exempted securities."

The rule exempting foreign private issuers from § 14(a) is nearly as old as § 14(a) itself. The Commission originally promulgated Rule 3a12-3 in 1935, one year after Congress enacted the Exchange Act.[3] At that time, the only source for the SEC's authority to promulgate such a rule was the combined force of § 14(a) and

---

3 The current version of Rule 3a12-3 provides that "[s]ecurities registered by a foreign private issuer, as defined in Rule 3b-4 (§ 240.3b-4 of this chapter), shall be exempt from section[] 14(a) . . . of the [Exchange] Act." 17 C.F.R. § 240.3a12-3(b). The term "foreign private issuer" is defined as any foreign issuer other than a foreign government except an issuer meeting the following conditions:

> (1) More than 50 percent of the issuer's outstanding voting securities are directly or indirectly held of record by residents of the United States; and
>
> (2) Any of the following:
>
> > (i) The majority of the executive officers or directors are United States citizens or residents;
> >
> > (ii) More than 50 percent of the assets of the issuer are located in the United States; or
> >
> > (iii) The business of the issuer is administered principally in the United States.

17 C.F.R. § 240.3b-4(c) (2004).

§ 3(a)(12)(A)(vii). Thus, when the Commission originally adopted Rule 3a12-3 in 1935, pursuant to its statutory mandate, it explicitly stated that it "deem[ed] it necessary and appropriate in the public interest and for the protection of investors" to adopt the exemption for foreign private issuers. SEC Rule AN 18, Exchange Act Release No. 412 (Nov. 6, 1935), 1935 WL 29303, at *1. It explained that at that time "there [were] relatively few stock issues of foreign issuers listed on American exchanges" and that "a realistic approach ha[d] led to the conclusion that the interests of American investors will be best served by the continuance of these exemptions." SEC Rule AN 18, Exchange Act Release No. 412 (Nov. 6, 1935), 1935 WL 29303, at *1.

In 1964, Congress amended the Exchange Act by adding § 12(g), which extended registration requirements to companies not listed on any exchange but whose assets and shareholders exceed in number certain statutory limitations. *See* Securities Acts Amendments of 1964, Pub. L. No. 88-467, § 2, 78 Stat. 565, 566-68 (1964) (codified at *15 U.S.C. § 78l(g)*) ("1964 Amendments"). At the same time, Congress enacted § 12(h), which authorizes the SEC to create exemptions from a number of provisions of the Exchange Act, including § 14, "if the Commission finds, by reason of the number of public investors, amount of trading interest in the securities, the nature and extent of the activities of the issuer, income or assets of the issuer, or otherwise, that such action is not inconsistent with the public interest or the protection of investors." *Id.* at 568 (codified at *15 U.S.C. § 78l(h)*).

In 1966, the SEC amended Rule 3a12-3. Although preserving much of the 1935 version of the rule, the SEC withdrew the exemption from § 14 and § 16 for securities of foreign private issuers with significant ties to the United States.[4] Registration of Foreign Securities, 30 Fed. Reg. 14,737, 14,738-39 (Nov. 27, 1965). The SEC adopted this amended rule after conducting a study in which the Commission [considered] the extent of the trading market for foreign securities in the United States, the disclosure and reporting requirements and practices in many of the countries whose issuers have securities traded in the United States, the requirements of many leading foreign stock exchanges, and the nature of the information presently furnished to the Commission by foreign issuers having securities registered under the Securities Act of 1933, having securities listed on a national securities exchange, and those for whose securities ADR's [American Depository Receipts] have been issued. *Id.* The Commission has amended *Rule 3a12-3* since 1966. *See, e.g.*, Exchange Act Release No. 16,371, 1979 WL 169934, at *10 (Nov.

---

4 In particular, the exemption was made inapplicable "if more than 50 percent of the outstanding voting securities are held by United States residents and the business of the issuer is administered principally in the United States or 50 percent or more of the members of the Board of Directors are residents of the United States." Exemption of Certain Foreign Issuers, 31 Fed. Reg. 6705, 6705 (May 5, 1966).

29, 1979). Nevertheless, Schiller focuses on the 1966 version of the rule, which he characterizes as "the current version of the relevant exemption."[5]

As noted above, Schiller does not appeal the district court's determination that Tower is a foreign private issuer for purposes of Rule 3a12-3 but rather challenges the validity of Rule 3a12-3 itself. In our opinion, this challenge consists of both a substantive and procedural component. Schiller argues that in light of § 12(h), the Commission was unable to justify Rule 3a12-3—what Schiller refers to as a "blanket exemption" from the proxy solicitation rules—because such an exemption exceeds the Commission's authority. Schiller also argues that even if the Commission could have provided an adequate justification for Rule 3a12-3, it did not. Specifically, Schiller contends that the last time the rule was substantively amended, in 1966, the Commission failed to comply with § 12(h)'s requirements, including the requirement that the Commission make a finding that an exemption is not inconsistent with the protection of investors.

I. Two Preliminary Issues

We begin our analysis of Schiller's claims by noting that our authority to review the Commission's adoption of Rule 3a12-3 does not derive from the Securities Exchange Act but rather from the Administrative Procedure Act ("APA"). To be sure, § 25 of the Exchange Act provides for judicial review of rules promulgated pursuant to §§ 78f, 78i(h)(2), 78k, 78k-1, 78o(c)(5) or (6), 78o-3, 78q, 78q-1, or 78s of Title 15. *15 U.S.C. § 78y(b)(1)*. This judicial review provision makes no mention, however, of rules promulgated pursuant to § 3(a)(12)(A)(vii) (codified at *15 U.S.C. § 78c*) or § 12(h) (codified at *15 U.S.C. § 78l*), the two sections of the Exchange Act that authorize the Commission to create exemptions like Rule 3a12-3. Nevertheless, in the absence of authorization of "special statutory review" under the Exchange Act, there is still "general statutory review" under the APA, *see generally* PETER L. STRAUSS, TODD D. RAKOFF & CYNTHIA R. FARINA, ADMINISTRATIVE LAW 1101, 1104-06 (2003), which authorizes us to review "final agency action for which there is no other adequate remedy in a court," *5 U.S.C. § 704*. That our authority to review *Rule 3a12-3* derives from the APA and not the Exchange Act is relevant to our analysis of the Commission's arguments,

---

5 Presumably because Schiller assumes that the rule was last substantively amended in 1966, his brief makes only a passing reference to the "general exemptive authority" provision that was added to the Exchange Act in 1996. National Securities Markets Improvement Act of 1996, Pub. L. No. 104-290, § 105(b), 110 Stat. 3416, 3424 (codified at 15 U.S.C. § 78mm(a)(1)). Using language similar to that of the two other exemptive authority provisions, the general exemptive authority provision authorizes the Commission to exempt by "rule, regulation, or order, any person, security, or transaction, or any class or classes of persons, securities, or transactions, from any provision or provisions of this title or of any rule or regulation thereunder, to the extent that such exemption is necessary or appropriate in the public interest, and is consistent with the protection of investors." *Id.*

advanced in its amicus brief,[6] for why we should avoid reaching the merits of Schiller's claim.

A. Statute of Limitations

The Commission argues that, at its core, Schiller's claim amounts to nothing more than an allegation of a procedural defect in the Commission's adoption of Rule 3a12-3 and that such procedural challenges must be brought within the relevant statutory time period following promulgation of the rule.[7] In support of its argument, the Commission relies upon a line of precedent in the D.C. Circuit making the applicability of statutory limitation periods to claims challenging agency action dependent upon whether the challenge is procedural or substantive in nature. The D.C. Circuit has explained that while substantive challenges to agency action—for example, claims that agency action is unconstitutional, that it exceeds the scope of the agency's substantive authority, or that it is premised on an erroneous interpretation of a statutory term—have no time bars, "challenges to the *procedural lineage of agency regulations*, whether raised by direct appeal, by petition for amendment or rescission of the regulation or as a defense to an agency enforcement proceeding, will not be entertained outside the [time] period provided by statute." *JEM Broad. Co. v. FCC, 306 U.S. App. D.C. 11, 22 F.3d 320, 325 (D.C. Cir. 1994)*. Underlying the statutory limitations period is a concern for the agency's interest in prompt review and the public's settled expectations regarding agency action. *Id.* While an agency's ultra vires or unconstitutional act might outweigh these policy concerns and therefore justify reaching an otherwise time-barred challenge to agency action, a mere procedural defect does not. *Id.* Accordingly, in *JEM Broadcasting*, the D.C. Circuit found that the plaintiff was time-barred from asserting a claim, brought outside of the statutory limitations period, that the FCC's promulgation of certain rules failed to provide for notice and comment rulemaking in violation of the APA.

In the present case, Schiller asserts that his challenge should not be time-barred because it is substantive, not procedural. As noted above, there does indeed seem to be a substantive component to Schiller's claim. Schiller argues that § 12(h) does not authorize Rule 3a12-3, which Schiller refers to as a "blanket exemption" from

---

6 On January 10, 2006, responding to our request, the Commission filed an amicus brief in opposition to Schiller's position. On February 3, 2006, Schiller filed a reply to the Commission's amicus brief.

7 Although the Commission does not specify what statute it thinks might impose a time bar in this case, we assume that it has in mind *28 U.S.C. § 2401(a)*, the six-year "catch-all statute of limitations for federal claims" that we have previously found applicable to procedural challenges to agency action brought under the APA. See *Polanco v. U.S. Drug Enforcement Admin., 158 F.3d 647, 652 (2d Cir. 1998)*. To be sure, § 25 of the Exchange Act also provides that review shall be conducted within "sixty days after the promulgation of the rule," *15 U.S.C. § 78y(b)(1)*; but that statute of limitations provision only applies if review is sought under § 25 itself, and for reasons already articulated, our review of Rule 3a12-3 must derive from the APA, not from § 25 of the Exchange Act.

the proxy rules. However, Schiller's principal argument—that "the SEC failed to comply with the statutory requirement of making a finding"—appears to be inherently procedural. To be sure, Schiller focuses on procedures created by the Exchange Act, not by the APA. But the policy concerns motivating the D.C. Circuit's rule would appear to support barring procedural challenges regardless of what statute creates the allegedly deficient procedure.

Ultimately, however, we are under no obligation to resolve the issue of whether Schiller's claim is time-barred. Because defendants failed to include this statute-of-limitations defense in their answer to the plaintiff's complaint, we at least have the discretion, and might even be required under Federal Rule of Civil Procedure *§§ 8(c)*, *12(b)*, and *15(a)*, to consider the argument forfeited. *Cf.* Day v. McDonough, U.S. , 126 S. Ct. 1675, 1684, 164 L. Ed. 2d 376 (2006) (holding, in the context of a habeas corpus petition, that it is within the discretion of the courts to either raise a statute of limitations defense on their own motion or to declare such a defense forfeited); id. at 1683 (noting that "[u]nder the Civil Procedure Rules, a defendant forfeits a statute of limitations defense, *see* Fed. Rule Civ. Proc. 8(c), not asserted in its answer, *see* Rule 12(b), or an amendment thereto, *see* Rule 15(a)"). Although we requested that the Commission submit an amicus brief concerning the merits of Schiller's challenge to Rule 3a12-3's validity, we did not ask for briefing on the issue of whether Schiller's claim was time-barred, and what briefing the parties did provide of their own accord regarding this issue is scant to say the least. *See Concourse Rehab. & Nursing Ctr., Inc. v. DeBuono, 179 F.3d 38, 47 (2d Cir. 1999)* (declining to address argument raised for the first time in an appellate amicus brief). Accordingly, we decline to address this issue.

B. Primary Jurisdiction

The Commission also argues that the doctrine of primary jurisdiction requires Schiller to have brought his challenge first to the Commission before proceeding to the district court. Even assuming that the issue of primary jurisdiction is one that we can raise on our own motion, *see Pharm. Research and Mfrs. of Am. v. Walsh, 538 U.S. 644, 674, 123 S. Ct. 1855, 155 L. Ed. 2d 889 (2003)* (Breyer, J., concurring), we do not find the doctrine applicable here.

The Exchange Act does not contain a "primary jurisdiction" provision that would control in this case, although it does provide that "[n]o objection to an order or rule of the Commission, *for which review is sought under* [§ 25 *of the Exchange Act]*, may be considered by the court unless it was urged before the Commission or there was reasonable ground for failure to do so." *15 U.S.C. § 78y(c)(1)* (emphasis added). Once again, § 25 does not provide for judicial review of rules promulgated pursuant to any of the Exchange Act sections authorizing the Commission to create exemptions. Thus, cases that involve an organic statute requiring a litigant to bring his claim first to the agency before filing a complaint in court are distinguishable. *See, e.g., City of Peoria v. Gen. Elec. Cablevision Corp., 690 F.2d 116 (7th Cir. 1982).*

Even when primary jurisdiction is not statutorily required, however, courts may still apply the doctrine as a prudential matter. *See S. Utah Wilderness Alliance v. Bureau of Land Mgmt., 425 F.3d 735, 750 (10th Cir. 2005)* ("Primary jurisdiction is a prudential doctrine designed to allocate authority between courts and administrative agencies."). Although "[n]o fixed formula exists for applying the doctrine of primary jurisdiction," *United States v. W. Pac. R.R. Co., 352 U.S. 59, 64, 77 S. Ct. 161, 1 L. Ed. 2d 126, 135 Ct. Cl. 997 (1956)*, we have generally considered four factors:

> (1) whether the question at issue is within the conventional experience of judges or whether it involves technical or policy considerations within the agency's particular field of expertise;
>
> (2) whether the question at issue is particularly within the agency's discretion;
>
> (3) whether there exists a substantial danger of inconsistent rulings; and
>
> (4) whether a prior application to the agency has been made,

Ellis v. Tribune Television Co., 443 F.3d 71, 82-83 (2d Cir. 2006) (citing *Nat'l Commc'ns Ass'n., Inc. v. AT&T Co., 46 F.3d 220, 222 (2d Cir. 1995))*.

The question in the present case—whether the Commission complied with its statutory mandate in promulgating Rule 3a12-3—does not involve technical or policy considerations within the agency's particular field of expertise but instead simply requires us to engage in an activity—statutory interpretation—that is the daily fare of federal judges. *Cf. Baltimore & Ohio Chicago Terminal R.R. Co. v. Wisconsin Cent. Ltd., 154 F.3d 404, 411 (7th Cir. 1998)* (stating that the doctrine of primary jurisdiction does not extend to pure issues of law). Further, the question presented does not fall particularly within the agency's discretion. For obvious reasons, whether an agency has ignored its statutory mandate is a question for the judiciary, not the agency, to address; this remains true even though in answering the question presented, we might defer to an agency's interpretation of the statute it administers. Because the Commission would normally not be expected to rule on whether it had exceeded its own statutory authority, we likewise do not have to worry about inconsistent rulings. Finally, we note that although the party challenging the agency action (in this case, Schiller) made no prior application to the agency, a fact that would normally weigh against primary jurisdiction, in this case such a fact seems simply irrelevant, given that the question presented is not one that the Commission would be expected to decide. Because three of the four factors weigh against primary jurisdiction in this case—and the fourth turns out to be irrelevant—we conclude that this matter should not be referred to the Commission.[8] We therefore turn to the merits and address Schiller's substantive and procedural challenges to *Rule 3a12-3*.

---

8 We recognize that courts have on occasion observed that the agency itself must be joined as a proper party defendant in a judicial proceeding reviewing the validity of an agency rule.

II. The Merits

A. Substantive Challenge

Schiller's substantive challenge focuses on the common language used in the two Exchange Act sections—§ 12(h) and § 3(a)(12)(A)(vii)—granting the Commission authority to create exemptions to § 14(a). Both contain language to the effect that any exemption that the Commission adopts must be consistent with the public interest and the protection of investors. Schiller insists that this language means that the Commission may not sacrifice *any* investor protection, regardless of the public interest an exemption might serve. In essence, Schiller argues that in order to adopt an exemption to the Exchange Act, the Commission must determine that the exemption does not decrease the level of protection afforded investors in the absence of *any* exemptions. Because Rule 3a12-3 decreases investor protection, Schiller argues, it exceeds the Commission's exemptive authority.

Schiller's interpretation finds support in neither the text nor in basic principles of logic. Nowhere does § 12(h) or § 3(a)(12)(A)(iii) purport to establish a minimum acceptable level of investor protection, let alone a level equal to that imaginable in a parallel universe where the securities laws and regulations exist in a form unadulterated by exemptions. Indeed, § 12(h) explicitly provides that in deciding whether an exemption is appropriate, the Commission may consider factors such as "the number of public investors, amount of trading interest in the securities, the nature and extent of the activities of the issuer, [and] income or assets of the issuer." *15 U.S.C. § 78l(h)*. Had Congress intended to restrain the Commission from adopting exemptions that would sacrifice any investor protection for the sake of other public-interest considerations, then these factors, which clearly are proper considerations for the Commission to take into account, would be entirely irrelevant. Moreover, the fact that § 12(h) provides a non-exclusive list of the factors that might enter the Commission's calculus, as evidenced by the phrase "or otherwise," *id.*, strongly suggests that rather than constrain the Commission's exemptive authority, Congress intended to grant the Commission considerable regulatory discretion in this area. Indeed, when it enacted § 12(h), Congress indicated its understanding that the new section provided the Commission with both "flexibility" and "ample

---

See, e.g., City of Peoria, 690 F.2d at 119-21; *GTE South, Inc. v. Morrison, 199 F.3d 733, 743 (4th Cir. 1999)* ("Congress would not give a court the power to determine the validity of an agency's rules when the agency itself is not a party."). Nevertheless, we have in the past chosen to review the validity of agency rules—including Commission rules—without requiring the agency to be a party to the case. *See, e.g., Feder v. Martin Marietta Corp., 406 F.2d 260, 268 (2d Cir. 1969)*; *B.T. Babbitt, Inc. v. Lachner, 332 F.2d 255, 259 (2d Cir. 1964)*; *cf. United States v. Chestman, 947 F.2d 551 (2d Cir. 1991)* (en banc) (addressing whether the SEC exceeded its statutory authority in promulgating Rule 10b-5 even though the agency was not a party in the underlying federal criminal proceeding involving insider trading). We therefore do not think that the fact that the agency is not a party to the litigation prevents our consideration of the validity of Rule 3a12-3, especially where, as here, the Commission has taken the opportunity to submit an amicus brief defending its actions.

authority to modify, and provide exemptions from, the statutory requirements [of the Exchange Act]." Federal Securities Laws: Legislative History 1869 (Fed. Bar Assoc. Sec. Law Comm., 1983); *see also* LOSS & SELIGMAN, SECURITIES REGULATION 1813 (3d ed. 1989) ("Perhaps of greatest significance . . . is the fact that § 12(h), which Congress accepted just as the Commission drafted it, reflects a recognition that it might be necessary to administer the [Exchange] Act with respect to over-the-counter securities more flexibly than had been necessary for listed securities.").

Additionally, Schiller's reading of the two statutory provisions simply belies simple logic. The practical effect of an exemption—which, after all, renders protections that would otherwise be in force inapplicable with respect to a particular class of securities or issuers—is, everything else being equal, a decrease in the net level of investor protection. Therefore, the prohibition of any decrease in the level of investor protection would at the very least substantially curtail, if not completely eviscerate, the Commission's exemptive authority.[9] Such an effect is clearly at odds with the congressional intent to grant the Commission flexibility in adopting exemptions. We therefore conclude that the most plausible reading of § 12(h), *15 U.S.C. § 78l(h)*, and § 3(a)(12)(A)(vii), *15 U.S.C. § 78c(a)(12)(A)(vii)*, is that the Commission can promulgate an exemption once it has determined that the exemption serves the public interest while at the same time leaving in place adequate investor protections.

B. Procedural Challenge

The gist of Schiller's procedural challenge is that in promulgating Rule 3a12-3, the Commission failed to follow certain procedures required by § 12(h). In particular, Schiller contends that the Commission was required to make a formal finding that the exemption was not inconsistent with the public interest or the protection of investors. That an agency must engage in reasoned decisionmaking is not by any means a novel proposition. With respect to informal rulemakings—those, like the one that gave rise to Rule 3a12-3, that are not required by the organic statute to be undertaken "on the record"—the APA requires that the agency "incorporate

---

9 Schiller suggests that his interpretation would only curtail—not eviscerate—the Commission's exemptive authority because "there are some requirements of rules promulgated under [§] 14 from which a foreign private issuer could be exempted without adversely impacting the protections provided investors." As examples, Schiller points to rules regarding the type of information to be furnished to shareholders or the presentation of the information in a proxy statement. In light of the fact that the securities laws seek to protect investors through disclosure of information, we fail to understand how one could limit the application of rules defining the content and form of the information to be disclosed without altering the level of protection afforded investors. But even assuming that one could carry out such an unlikely feat, the fact remains that § 12(h) does not state that the Commission may only create exemptions to certain rules promulgated pursuant to §§ 12(g), 13, 14, 15(d) and 16 but rather states that the Commission may exempt issuers from the provisions of these sections themselves. *See* § 15 U.S.C. 78l(h) (citing 15 U.S.C. §§ 78l(g), 78m, 78n, 78o(d), and 78p).

in the rules adopted a concise general statement of their basis and purpose." *5 U.S.C. § 553(c)*; *see also Indep. U.S. Tanker Owners Comm. v. Dole, 258 U.S. App. D.C. 6, 809 F.2d 847, 852 (D.C. Cir. 1987)* ("Under the Administrative Procedure Act, when an agency initiates a rulemaking that the governing statute does not require to be undertaken 'on the record,' the agency is nonetheless bound to comply with the requirements for 'notice and comment' rulemaking set out in *5 U.S.C. § 553 (1982)*."). The agency must provide such a statement whenever it adopts "'new rules that *work substantive changes*'" or, as the Commission did in the 1966 amendment to Rule 3a12-3, adopt "'*major substantive legal addition[s]*' to prior regulations." *U.S. Telecom Ass'n v. FCC, 365 U.S. App. D.C. 149, 400 F.3d 29, 34 (D.C. Cir. 2005)* (quoting *Sprint Corp. v. FCC, 354 U.S. App. D.C. 288, 315 F.3d 369, 374 (D.C. Cir. 2003)* and *Appalachian Power Co. v. EPA, 341 U.S. App. D.C. 46, 208 F.3d 1015, 1024 (D.C. Cir. 2000))* (brackets and emphasis in *U.S. Telecom Ass'n*).[10] We have explained that the statement of basis and purpose provision "does not require the agency to supply specific and detailed findings and conclusions of the kind customarily associated with formal proceedings," but rather requires the agency to "publish a statement of reasons that will be sufficiently detailed to permit judicial review." *Nat'l Nutritional Foods Ass'n v. Weinberger, 512 F.2d 688, 701 (2d Cir. 1975).*

Nevertheless, Congress may require an even more detailed statement of basis and purpose, and Schiller claims that Congress did precisely that in enacting § 12(h). *Section 12(h)* provides:

> The Commission may by rules and regulations, or upon application of an interested person, by order, after notice and opportunity for hearing, exempt in whole or in part any issuer or class of issuers from the provisions of subsection (g) of this section or from Section 13, 14, or 15(d) of this title or may be exempt from Section 16 of this title any officer, director, or beneficial owner of securities of any issuer, any security of which is required to be registered pursuant to subsection (g) hereof, upon such terms and conditions and for such period as it deems necessary or appropriate, *if the Commission finds, by reason of the number of public investors, amount of trading interest in the securities, the nature and extent of the activities of the issuer, income or assets of the issuer, or otherwise, that such action is not inconsistent with the public interest or the protection of investors*. The Commission may, for the purposes of any

10 It is not clear whether an agency must follow APA procedures with respect to that part of an amended rule that does not undergo any change. *Cf. United States v. Garner, 767 F.2d 104, 119 (5th Cir. 1985)* (assuming for the sake of argument that a regulation merely reaffirming prior policy and practice need not conform strictly to § 553(c)'s requirement of a statement of basis and purpose). Nevertheless, we need not, and do not, address this argument because no party has raised it. We assume that when it adopted the 1966 amendment, the Commission did have to follow all APA procedural requirements—including the requirement that the Commission publish a statement of basis and purpose—even with respect to that portion of the foreign private issuer exemption that did not change from 1935 to 1966. Since the Commission prevails even under this assumption, there is no reason to decide whether an agency must follow APA procedures with respect to the reaffirmation of prior policy.

of the above-mentioned sections or subsections of this chapter, classify issuers and prescribe requirements appropriate for each such class.

Id. 78 Stat. at 568 (codified at *15 U.S.C. § 78l(h)*) (emphasis added). As already noted, prior to Congress's enactment of § 12(h), *15 U.S.C. § 78l(h)*, in 1964, the Commission's authority to create exemptions to § 14(a), *15 U.S.C. § 78n(a)*, derived from the combined effect of § 14(a)—the terms of which do not apply to an "exempted security"—and § 3(a)(12)(A)(vii), *15 U.S.C. § 78c(a)(12)(A)(vii)*, which defines "exempted security" as such other securities . . . as the Commission may, by such rules and regulations as it deems consistent with the public interest and the protection of investors, either unconditionally or upon specified terms and conditions or for stated periods, exempt from the operation of any one or more provisions of this chapter which by their terms do not apply to an "exempted security" or to "exempted securities."

Section 12(h) enlarged upon the Commission's exemptive authority in § 3(a)(12)(A)(vii) in two principal ways.[11] First, § 12(h) permitted the Commission to act by exemptive order on a case-by-case basis rather than solely by rule or regulation.[12] Commentators have suggested that this expansion of the method employed by the Commission to adopt exemptions is § 12(h)'s "primary use." LOSS & SELIGMAN, *supra*, at 1814. Second, § 12(h) provided the Commission with the authority to exempt issuers of listed securities from sections of the Exchange Act with respect to which the Commission previously lacked any exemptive authority, regardless of the method used. Prior to the passage of § 12(h), the sections of the Exchange Act that, by their terms, did not apply to "exempted securities" included §§ 7(a), 7(c)(1), 9, 11(d), 12(a), 12(g), 14(a) and 16. *See* Richard M. Phillips & Morgan Shipman, *An Analysis of the Securities Acts Amendments of 1964*, 1964 DUKE L. J. 706, 746 n.139 (1964). As noted above, § 3(a)(12)(A)(vii) delegated to the Commission the power to determine which securities would be exempt from these provisions. But § 12(h) extended the Commission's exemptive authority with respect to § 13 and the entirety of § 14. In addition, it removed any doubt concerning the Commission's exemptive authority with respect to §§ 15(d) and 16(b).[13]

---

11 A third obvious difference between the two sources of exemptive authority is that the authority in § 12(h) is to exempt *issuers* rather than *securities* as in § 3(a)(12)(A)(vii). However, this "seems of no particular significance" because any exemption with respect to securities can be recast as an exemption with respect to issuers and vice versa. LOSS & SELIGMAN, *supra*, at 1812.

12 Some have argued that the Commission already possessed the authority to issue exemptive orders and that § 12(h) simply clarified this authority. *See, e.g.*, Richard M. Phillips & Morgan Shipman, *An Analysis of the Securities Acts Amendments of 1964*, 1964 DUKE L. J. 706, 746 n.140 (1964).

13 *See* Phillips & Shipman, *supra*, at 747 n.141. Before the 1964 Amendments, § 15(d) by its own terms did not apply to "any other security which the Commission may by rules and regulations exempt as not comprehended within the purposes [of § 15(d)]." Securities Exchange

In drafting § 12(h), however, Congress did not distinguish between the new grant of authority to act by exemptive order and the *expansion* of previously held exemptive authority to act by rule or regulation. Instead, Congress stated that the Commission may act by *either* method to create exemptions from the five listed Exchange Act sections. Because prior to passage of § 12(h) the Commission could already act by rule or regulation to create exemptions from § 14(a), Congress created an overlap between the coverage of § 3(a)(12)(A)(vii) and § 12(h). It is precisely this overlap that Schiller attempts to exploit to his advantage in this case.

Drawing our attention to the differences in language between § 3(a)(12)(A)(vii) and § 12(h), Schiller urges us to find that § 12(h) requires the Commission, when adopting exemptions to § 14(a), to follow certain procedures that are absent from § 3(a)(12)(A)(vii). According to Schiller, when read in conjunction with § 3(a)(12)(A)(vii), § 12(h) introduces three innovations. First, Schiller contends that the omission of the term "unconditionally" in § 12(h) and the retaining of the phrases "upon terms and conditions" and "for such period as the SEC deems necessary or appropriate" authorizes only exemptions that expire after a stated, "reasonable[]" time period. Second, Schiller argues that the added language in § 12(h) requires the SEC to consider three factors: (i) the number of public investors; (ii) the amount of trading interest in the securities; and (iii) the nature and extent of the activities of the issuer, income or assets of the issuer. Finally, Schiller focuses most of his energy on the replacement of the word "deems" in § 3(a)(12)(A)(vii) with the word "finds" in § 12(h), a change that, according to Schiller, requires the Commission to make not simply a mental determination but rather a specific, published finding that an exemption such as Rule 3a12-3 is not inconsistent with the protection of investors.

Even if we were inclined to read § 12(h) in light of § 3(a)(12)(A)(vii), Schiller's reading is not the most compelling interpretation available, let alone the only one. As Schiller himself concedes, the phrase "and for such period that the Commission deems necessary or appropriate" easily incorporates unlimited periods. The all-important phrase "or otherwise" signifies that the three listed reasons for decision are at most merely non-exhaustive illustrations of the types of considerations the Commission might, but is not required to, take into account. Finally, as the Commission points out in its amicus brief, the word "finds" in § 12(h) easily admits of multiple meanings, including not only "to declare" but also "to determine," BLACK'S LAW DICTIONARY 504 (4th ed. rev. 1968), which is one of the well-accepted meanings of the word "deems" employed in § 3(a)(12)(A)(vii), BLACK'S LAW DICTIONARY 538 (3d ed. 1933).[14] Thus, the more plausible interpretation of

---

Act of 1934, §3, Pub. L. No. 74-621, 49 Stat. 1375, 1379 (1936) (current version codified at *15 U.S.C. §78o(d) (2000)*).

14 We also note that, although Congress can certainly require an agency to follow procedures in addition to those mandated by the APA, Congress generally seems to do so with more specific language than that used in § 12(h). One instructive example is the Clean Air Act. "In 1977, Congress—concerned that the Administrative Procedure Act (APA), *5 U.S.C. § 553,*

§ 12(h) is that it means precisely the same thing as § 3(a)(12)(A)(vii): the Commission may create exemptions from § 14(a) unconditionally, provided that it determines that such exemptions are not inconsistent with the public interest and the protection of investors.

More fundamentally, Schiller's reading of the statute reflects a misapplication of basic principles of statutory construction. This is not a case where the more specific statute should govern the more general, *see, e.g., Carr v. Marietta Corp., 211 F.3d 724, 734 (2d Cir. 2000)*, for the simple reason that the differences in statutory language that Schiller highlights do not in any meaningful way render § 12(h) more specific than § 3(a)(12)(A)(vii). Schiller's argument gains relatively more traction in light of the rule "requiring a change in language to be read, if possible, to have some effect," *Am. Nat'l Red Cross v. S.G., 505 U.S. 247, 263, 112 S. Ct. 2465, 120 L. Ed. 2d 201 (1992)*. However, to make the argument that § 12(h) altered the language of *§ 3(a)(12)(A)(vii)*, one must assume that § 12(h) impliedly repealed § 3(a)(12)(A)(vii), and the "'strong judicial policy disfavoring the inference that a statute has been repealed *sub silentio* by subsequent legislation,' *United States v. Shareef, 634 F.2d 679, 680 (2d Cir. 1980)*, applies with equal force to claims of implied amendment, *St. Martin Evangelical Lutheran Church v. South Dakota, 451 U.S. 772, 787-88, 101 S. Ct. 2142, 68 L. Ed. 2d 612 (1981)*. " *Regan v. Ross, 691 F.2d 81, 87 (2d Cir. 1982)*. Indeed, "'[i]n the absence of some affirmative showing of an intention to repeal [or to amend a statute], the only permissible justification for a repeal [or amendment] by implication is when the earlier and later statutes are irreconcilable.'" *St. Martin Evangelical Lutheran Church, 451 U.S. at 788* (quoting *Morton v. Mancari, 417 U.S. 535, 550, 94 S. Ct. 2474, 41 L. Ed. 2d 290 (1974))*. Because there is no evidence in the statute itself or in the legislative

---

did not provide procedures adequate for the complex scientific issues involved in EPA rulemaking—created new procedures for most rulemaking under the Clean Air Act . . . ." *Small Refiner Lead Phase-Down Task Force v. EPA, 227 U.S. App. D.C. 201, 705 F.2d 506, 518 (D.C. Cir. 1983)*. Congress required the EPA to provide in the rules adopted a "statement of basis and purpose," a phrase that mirrors the language of § 553(c) but for the omission of the qualifiers "concise" and "general." Id. at 519. Congress went on to require that this statement of basis and purpose include specific items that also must be disclosed at the proposed rule stage as well as "'an explanation of the reasons for any major changes in the promulgated rule from the proposed rule' and 'a response to each of the significant comments, criticisms, and new data submitted . . . during the comment period.'" *Id.* (quoting Clean Air Act § 307(d)(6) (codified at *42 U.S.C. § 7607(d)(6)*) (alteration in *Small Refiner Lead Phase-Down Task Force*)). Similarly, the Federal Trade Commission Act requires that when the Federal Trade Commission promulgates certain rules, the agency's statement of basis and purpose must include "(A) a statement as to the prevalence of the acts or practices treated by the rule; (B) a statement as to the manner and context in which such acts or practices are unfair or deceptive; and (C) a statement as to the economic effect of the rule, taking into account the effect on small business and consumers." *15 U.S.C. § 57a(d)(1)*; *see also Katharine Gibbs Sch. (Inc.) v. FTC, 612 F.2d 658, 661 (2d Cir. 1979)*. Had Congress wished to require the Commission to follow certain specific procedures unique to informal rulemakings involving proposed exemptions to the Securities Exchange Act, we believe that it would have done so with more clarity and specificity than that exhibited in Schiller's reading of § 12(h).

history indicating Congress's intention to amend § 3(a)(12)(A)(vii), we would find that § 12(h) amended that earlier section by implication only if the two provisions are irreconcilable. They most certainly are not, as evidenced by the interpretation that we have adopted.

Nor do we think that our reading of § 12(h)—that it authorizes the Commission to create exemptions from § 14(a) unconditionally, provided that it determines that such exemptions are not inconsistent with the public interest and the protection of investors—runs afoul of the canon of statutory construction that "legislative enactments should not be construed to render their provisions mere surplusage." *Dunn v. CFTC, 519 U.S. 465, 472, 117 S. Ct. 913, 137 L. Ed. 2d 93 (1997)*. The Supreme Court has recognized that the "preference for avoiding surplusage constructions is not absolute." *Lamie v. United States Tr., 540 U.S. 526, 536, 124 S. Ct. 1023, 157 L. Ed. 2d 1024 (2004)* (citing *Chickasaw Nation v. United States, 534 U.S. 84, 94, 122 S. Ct. 528, 151 L. Ed. 2d 474 (2001))*. In the present case, this canon of statutory construction seems less significant because any surplusage created is not within a single statutory provision but across statutory provisions located in completely different sections of a larger and extraordinarily complex enactment.

In any event, other interpretive rules, where more convincing, can take precedence over general principles of statutory construction. *Cf. Krause v. Titleserv, Inc., 402 F.3d 119, 128 (2d Cir. 2005)* (rejecting argument based on statutory canon of avoiding surplusage because this canon "'should not take precedence over more convincing reasons'" (quoting *Hakala v. Deutsche Bank AG, 343 F.3d 111, 116 (2d Cir. 2003)))*. In the present case, the text of the statute strongly suggests that Congress did not intend to amend § 3(a)(12)(A)(vii). In particular, § 12(g)(1), which was added to the Exchange Act along with § 12(h) as part of the 1964 Amendments, provides that its registration requirements do not apply to an "exempted security," that is to say, a security exempted under § 3(a)(12)(A)(vii). *See* Securities Acts Amendments of 1964, Pub. L. No. 88-467, § 2, 78 Stat. 565, 566-67 (1964) (codified at *15 U.S.C. §78l(g)*). Yet, § 12(h) also grants the Commission exemptive authority with respect to § 12(g). *Id.*, 78 Stat. at 568 (codified at *15 U.S.C. § 78l(h)*). If, as part of the 1964 Amendments, Congress had intended § 12(h) to impliedly amend § 3(a)(12)(A)(vii), it would not have authorized the Commission to rely upon § 3(a)(12)(A)(vii) to create exemptions from one of the newly added provisions. We do not think that the avoidance of surplusage should outweigh this strong textual evidence of Congress's contrary intent. We therefore conclude that § 12(h), *15 U.S.C. § 78l(h)*, does not require the Commission to make a formal finding or follow the other procedures that Schiller advocates.

C. Whether the Commission Provided Adequate Evidence of Reasoned Decisionmaking

Although Schiller's brief is far from clear on the matter, Schiller seems to argue that even if § 12(h) does not require a formal finding, the Commission still must provide reasons for its determination that an exemption is not inconsistent with the public interest or the protection of investors. As explained above, the agency's obligation to engage in reasoned decisionmaking, at least in the context of informal rulemaking, is typically traced to the APA requirement that the agency "incorporate in the rules adopted a concise general statement of their basis and purpose." *5 U.S.C. § 553(c)*. Instead of relying upon *§ 553*, however, Schiller appears to invoke *§ 12(h)* of the Exchange Act as an independent source for the requirement that the agency articulate reasons for its actions.[15] We have already determined that § 12(h) does not mandate a statement of reasons any more detailed or specific than that required by § 553. Accordingly, we have no reason to decide the precise contours of a reasoned decisionmaking requirement derived from § 12(h) if the Commission provided an adequate statement of basis and purpose under § 553. We conclude that it did.

The adequacy of the Commission's statement in connection with its promulgation of Rule 3a12-3 depends in large part upon what we view as the Commission's statement and what level of detail an adequate statement requires. The answer to the first question would seem to be obvious. The plain language of the APA is clear that whatever the statement is, it must at least be incorporated into the adopted rule. *See 5 U.S.C. § 553(c)* (requiring the agency to "incorporate in the rules adopted a concise general statement of their basis and purpose"). Nevertheless, in defining the boundaries of what constitutes the statement, courts have taken a functional approach and expressed a willingness to look beyond the four corners of the agency's adopting release. Although post hoc rationalizations are never permitted, a court reviewing the adequacy of an agency's statement may take into account "materials made public in the course of rulemaking." *Citizens to Save Spencer County v. EPA, 195 U.S. App. D.C. 30, 600 F.2d 844, 884 (D.C. Cir. 1979)* (citing *Automotive Parts & Accessories Ass'n v. Boyd, 132 U.S. App. D.C. 200, 407 F.2d 330, 338 (D.C. Cir. 1968)* (finding that the statement of basis and purpose should be considered "in the light of the reasons stated by the Administrator's denial of rehearing")); *see also Ala. Ass'n of Ins. Agents v. Bd. of Governors of Fed. Reserve, 533 F.2d 224, 236-37 (5th Cir. 1976)* (stating that in considering the adequacy of the statement of basis and purpose, the reviewing court should take into consideration "extraneous material which may be available to explain the basis and purpose of the agency action"), *as amended by Ala. Ass'n of Ins. Agents v. Bd. of Governors, 558 F.2d 729 (5th Cir. 1977)*.

Courts have likewise adopted a functional approach for determining the level of detail required in an adequate statement of basis and purpose. The D.C. Circuit has stated that "[a]t the least, such a statement should indicate the major issues of policy that were raised in the proceedings and explain why the agency decided to

---

15 Presumably Schiller chose not to rely on § 553 of the APA because it is an obviously procedural requirement that would be subject to the six-year statute of limitations. *See* Part I, *supra* (discussing the statute of limitations applicable to challenges to agency rules). Apparently, Schiller determined that his only chance of avoiding the statutory limitations period would be an argument based not on the APA but on the organic statute itself.

respond to these issues as it did, particularly in light of the statutory objectives that the rule must serve." *Indep. U.S. Tanker Owners Comm., 809 F.2d at 852*. At the same time, however, that same court has recognized that it "will 'uphold a decision of less than ideal clarity if the agency's path may reasonably be discerned.'" *Int'l Bhd of Teamsters, 237 U.S. App. D.C. 89, 735 F.2d 1525, 1531 (D.C. Cir. 1984)* (quoting *Bowman Transp., Inc. v. Ark.-Best Freight Sys., Inc., 419 U.S. 281, 286, 95 S. Ct. 438, 42 L. Ed. 2d 447 (1974))*.

Similarly, in the Second Circuit, we have upheld regulations accompanied by statements of less than ideal clarity. *See New York Foreign Freight Forwarders & Brokers Asso. v. Federal Maritime Com., 337 F.2d 289, 296 (2d Cir. 1964)* (upholding a regulation where the statement explained merely that the rules "have for their purpose the establishment of standards and criteria to be observed and maintained by licensed independent ocean freight forwarders, ocean freight brokers and oceangoing common carriers in the conduct of their business affairs"). And on at least one occasion we have even upheld a regulation with no statement at all where the basis and purpose was obvious. *See Hoving Corp. v. FTC, 290 F.2d 803, 807 (2d Cir. 1961)*; *see also Ala. Ass'n of Ins. Agents, 533 F.2d at 236-37* (citing *Hoving* approvingly); *Tabor v. Joint Bd. for Enrollment of Actuaries, 185 U.S. App. D.C. 40, 566 F.2d 705, 710 (D.C. Cir. 1977)* (citing *Alabama Ass'n of Insurance Agents* approvingly for the same proposition); *Citizens to Save Spencer County, 600 F.2d at 884* & n.201 (citing *Tabor* approvingly for the same proposition); *Cal-Almond, Inc. v. U.S. Dep't of Agric., 14 F.3d 429, 443 (9th Cir. 1993)* (citing *Citizens to Save Spencer County* approvingly for the same proposition). Thus, the caselaw is clear that, taking into account the adopting release as well as any materials or statements that the agency has made public in the course of the rulemaking, we can find a statement adequate if the agency's path of reasoning can be reasonably discerned. In the present case, these principles do not mean that the Commission must demonstrate that Rule 3a12-3 would confer additional protections upon investors or even leave investors with the same level of protection in the absence of the exemption. Rather, based on our reading of the statute, *see* Part II, *supra* (discussing Schiller's substantive challenge), these principles mean that at the most the Commission must indicate that the exemption serves some interest and that it leaves in place adequate investor protections.

Although that requirement is not particularly onerous, the Commission does not give us much to go on. The adopting release accompanying the 1966 Rule is, in the Commission's own words, "fairly brief," and even that characterization is charitable. Nowhere in the adopting release does the Commission provide any reason for adopting a foreign private issuer exemption from § 14(a). The adopting release instead describes the rule that was previously in effect, reports on the amendment adopted, and then explains why the Commission decided not to adopt a sub-section of the amendment, as originally proposed. *See Exemption of Certain Foreign Issuers, 31 Fed. Reg. 6705, 6705 (May 5, 1966)*. We reject the Commission's invitation to read the adopting release alongside statements in the legislative history of the 1964 Amendments that purportedly justify the foreign private issuer exemption. As we have already stated, we will not consider anything other than statements made by the Commission in the course of the rulemaking.

But that does not leave us completely in the dark as to Rule 3a12-3's basis and purpose. In 1965, the Commission issued a notice of proposed rulemaking announcing the proposed amendments to Rule 3a12-3 that were adopted later that year. Registration of Foreign Securities, 30 Fed. Reg. 14,737, 14,737 (1965) ("1965 Notice"). The 1965 Notice includes the Commission's underlying rationale for the proposed amendments.

As the 1965 Notice explains, the proposed amendments to Rule 3a12-3 were the culmination of a study, conducted by the Commission, into the state of the foreign securities markets:

> [T]he Commission consulted with representatives of American brokers, dealers, financial analysts, and the principal banks issuing American Depositary Receipts (ADR's) who are interested in foreign securities, and received recommendations from interested domestic and foreign groups. The Commission also studied the extent of the trading market for foreign securities in the United States, the disclosure and reporting requirements and practices in many of the countries whose issuers have securities traded in the United States, the requirements of many leading foreign stock exchanges, and the nature of the information presently furnished to the Commission by foreign issuers listed . . . on a national securities exchange . . . .*Id.* at 14,738. Importantly, the Commission explained in the 1965 Notice that "[t]he study revealed continuing improvement in the reporting of financial and economic information by foreign issuers." *Id.* The Commission also explained that "[t]his improvement has resulted from changes in foreign corporate laws, stock exchange requirements and increasing voluntary disclosure by the companies themselves." *Id.*

Based on the 1965 Notice, we are easily able to discern the Commission's decision path. In determining whether an exemption from § 14(a) was appropriate, the Commission took into account the available protections for investors in foreign securities—the quality of foreign corporate law, the nature of foreign stock exchange rules, and the amount of information voluntarily disclosed by foreign issuers—which are certainly all relevant considerations. Then, the Commission determined that these protections were adequate in light of the important goal of "maintaining [] existing markets in foreign securities," a goal the Commission recognized in the 1965 Notice and that Congress identified in adopting the Securities Acts Amendments of 1964. *Id.* Accordingly, the Commission must have concluded that Rule 3a12-3, 17 C.F.R. § 240.3a12-3, was not inconsistent with the public interest or the protection of investors.[16] *Id.*

---

16 Even if the Commission never made the underlying study public—and there is no indication on appeal that it did—we do not think that § 553(c)'s requirements of a "concise general statement of [] basis and purpose" would require this additional disclosure. Omitting the underlying study would not hamper our ability to engage in judicial review, which is, once again, the principal purpose of the statement requirement, because the study would certainly be included

CONCLUSION

Although perhaps "novel," Schiller's argument is ultimately unpersuasive. Rule 3a12-3 weathers this storm not because of its impressive longevity. Rather, Rule 3a12-3 survives Schiller's challenge because it was promulgated pursuant to the Commission's statutory mandate. Accordingly, we conclude that Rule 3a12-3 is a valid Commission rule and therefore affirm the judgment of the district court.

---

in the record for review. Moreover, this does not appear to be the type of case where the statement of basis and purpose "leave[s] vital questions, raised by comments which are of cogent materiality, completely unanswered." *United States v. Nova Scotia Food Prods. Corp., 568 F.2d 240, 252 (2d Cir. 1977).* And finally, Schiller has never advanced the argument that the Commission's procedure withheld from "interested persons [the] opportunity to participate in the rulemaking." 5 U.S.C. §553(c).

IX. INTERNATIONAL TRADE

2. Business & Finance

E. White Collar Crime

UNITED STATES OF AMERICA
v.
PAUL J. LEAHY

Nos. 03-4490/03 (3rd Cir. 2006)
Decided February 15, 2006

Before: SCIRICA, Chief Judge, SLOVITER, ALITO,* ROTH, MCKEE, RENDELL, BARRY, AMBRO, FUENTES, SMITH, FISHER, VAN ANTWERPEN, ROSENN** and BECKER Circuit Judges.

* Then Judge, now Justice, Alito was on the panel for this case but was elevated to the United States Supreme Court on January 30, 2006. This opinion is filed by quorum of the panel. 28 U.S.C. § 46(d).

** Judge Rosenn heard oral argument on this case, but passed away on February 7, 2006.

IAN M. COMISKY (Argued), JORDANA COOPER, MATTHEW D. LEE, Blank Rome LLP, 130 North 18th Street, One Logan Square, Philadelphia, PA 19103; ROBERT E. WELSH, JR., Welsh & Recker, 2000 Market Street, Suite 2903, Philadelphia, PA 19103; JEFFREY M. MILLER, Nasuti & Miller, 150 South Independence Mall West, Suite 1064, Philadelphia, PA 19106; ATTORNEYS FOR APPELLANTS PAUL J. LEAHY, TIMOTHY SMITH AND DANTONE INC.

ROBERT EPSTEIN (Argued), DAVID MCCOLGIN (Argued), ELAINE DeMASSE, MAUREEN KEARNEY ROWLEY, Defender Association of Philadelphia, Federal Court Division, 601 Walnut Street, Suite 540 West—The Curtis Center, Independence Square West, Philadelphia, PA 19106; ATTORNEYS FOR APPELLANTS JAMES C. FALLON AND KENNARD GREGG

PATRICK L. MEEHAN, LAURIE MAGID, MARY E. CROWLEY, JOSEPH G. POLUKA, ROBERT A. ZAUZMER (Argued), Office of the United States Attorney, 615 Chestnut Street, Suite 1250, Philadelphia, PA 19106; DAVID FARNHAM, United States Department of Justice, P.O. Box 386, Washington DC 20044; JOSHUA L. DRATEL, Law Offices of Joshua L. Dratel, 14 Wall Street, 28th

Floor, New York, NY 10005; ATTORNEY FOR AMICUS CURIAE PARTY NATIONAL ASSOCIATION OF CRIMINAL DEFENSE LAWYERS

OPINION OF THE COURT

FUENTES, Circuit Judge.

We ordered rehearing en banc in three separate appeals to determine whether the District Courts' orders of restitution and forfeiture violated defendants' Sixth Amendment right to trial by jury.

I. Background

In United States v. Paul J. Leahy, No. 03-4490, following trial, a jury found defendant Dantone, Inc. ("Dantone"), and its two senior managers, defendants Paul Leahy and Timothy Smith, guilty of engaging in, and aiding and abetting, bank fraud in violation of 18 U.S.C. § 1344.[1] Defendants' convictions stemmed from their defrauding various banks out of profits derived from Dantone's auctioning of 311 repossessed and after-lease cars on behalf of the banks. At sentencing, the District Court imposed prison sentences upon Leahy and Smith and entered orders of forfeiture in the sum of $418,657 and restitution in the sum of $408,970, jointly and severally, against all three defendants. Dantone, Leahy and Smith appeal both their convictions and the orders of forfeiture and restitution.[2]

In United States v. Kennard Gregg, No. 04-2912, after being arrested and charged for twice attempting to sell counterfeit money to a government informant, defendant Gregg pled guilty to two counts of dealing in counterfeit obligations in violation of 18 U.S.C. § 473. Gregg was sentenced to six months in prison and three years of supervised release, and ordered to pay restitution to the federal government in the amount of $350. He appeals only the restitution order.

In United States v. James C. Fallon, No. 03-4184, a jury convicted defendant Fallon of one count of wire fraud in violation of 18 U.S.C. § 1341, and three counts of mail fraud in violation of 18 U.S.C. § 1343 in connection with marketing his company's Derma Peel skin treatment without FDA approval. Fallon was sentenced to 12 months in prison and ordered to pay restitution in the amount of $55,235. Fallon appeals both his conviction and the District Court's restitution order.

In these appeals, all five of the defendants—Dantone, Leahy, Smith, Gregg and Fallon—challenge their respective restitution orders on Sixth Amendment grounds, arguing that, in accordance with United States v. Booker, 125 S. Ct. 738 (2005), the facts underlying the orders should have been submitted to a jury and established by proof beyond a reasonable doubt. Additionally, on the same grounds, Dantone,

---

1 This case was tried together with United States v. Dantone, Inc., No. 03-4560, and United States v. Timothy Smith, No. 03- 4542.

2 Defendants' appeal of their criminal convictions in this case, as well as in United States v. Fallon, infra, will be addressed in separate opinions.

Leahy and Smith challenge their orders of forfeiture. We called for rehearing en banc to consider three sentencing issues:

1. Whether the decision of the Supreme Court in Booker applies to forefeiture;

2. Whether orders of restitution are a criminal penalty;

3. Whether Booker applies to orders of restitution under the Victim and Witness Protection Act (the "VWPA")[3] and the Mandatory Victims Restitution Act (the "MVRA").[4] Because, in our view, restitution under the VWPA and the MVRA is not the type of criminal punishment that evokes Sixth Amendment protection under Booker, we conclude that the amount a defendant must restore to his or her victim need not be admitted by the defendant or proved to a jury beyond a reasonable doubt. As to forfeiture, based upon the Supreme Court's decision in Libretti v. United States, 516 U.S. 29 (1995), we conclude that the amount a defendant must forfeit also need not be admitted or proved to a jury beyond a reasonable doubt.

II. Forfeiture and Booker

We consider first the constitutionality of the District Court's forfeiture order in Leahy. Following trial, the District Court entered an order of forfeiture in the sum of $418,657, finding that the Government had proven by a preponderance of the

---

3 The VWPA reads in pertinent part:

> (a)(1)(A) The court, when sentencing a defendant convicted of an offense under this title . . . , other than an offense described in section 3363A(c), may order, in addition to or, in the case of a misdemeanor, in lieu of any other penalty authorized by law, that the defendant make restitution to any victim of such offense . . . . (a)(1)(B)(i) The court, in determining whether to order restitution under this section, shall consider–
>
> > (I) the amount of the loss sustained by each victim as a result of the offense; and
> >
> > (II) the financial resources of the defendant, the financial needs and earning ability of the defendant and the defendant's dependents, and such other factors as the court deems appropriate. (a)(1)(B)(ii) To the extent that the court determines that the complication and prolongation of the sentencing process resulting from the fashioning of an order of restitution under this section outweighs the need to provide restitution to any victims, the court may decline to make such an order.

18 U.S.C. § 3663.

4 Passed by Congress in 1996, the MVRA augmented and partially superseded the VWPA by requiring district courts to impose restitution on defendants convicted of certain offenses without regard to their ability to pay. See 18 U.S.C. § 3663A(a)(1) ("[T]he court shall order, in addition to, or in the case of a misdemeanor, in addition to or in lieu of, any other penalty authorized by law, that the defendant make restitution to the victim of the offense . . . .) (emphasis added). Both the VWPA and the MVRA are enforced via 18 U.S.C. § 3664, which states in pertinent part:

> In each order of restitution, the court shall order restitution to each victim in the full amount of each victim's losses as determined by the court and without consideration of the economic circumstances of the defendant.

18 U.S.C. § 3664(f)(1)(A)

evidence that this sum constituted the defendants' "proceeds" from their fraudulent activity within the meaning of 18 U.S.C. § 982(a)(2).[5] The Leahy defendants contend that the imposition of forfeiture by the District Court under a preponderance of the evidence standard violated their Sixth Amendment right in light of the Supreme Court's decisions in Blakely v. Washington, 542 U.S. 296 (2004), and Booker.

The Leahy defendants' Sixth Amendment argument with respect to forfeiture cannot be reconciled with the Supreme Court's decision in Libretti. In that case, the defendant entered a guilty plea in the middle of trial and agreed in his plea agreement to forfeit considerable property. Libretti, 516 U.S. at 33-34. He subsequently argued that his forfeiture plea colloquy was inadequate, in part because the District Court did not explain the right to a jury determination regarding forfeiture and in part because the District Court failed to obtain his express waiver of that right. Id. at 37-38. The Supreme Court acknowledged that, pursuant to what was then Federal Rule of Criminal Procedure 31(e), a special jury verdict was required to permit an order of forfeiture.[6] Id. at 48-49. It nonetheless concluded that there was no Sixth Amendment right to a jury determination, rejecting the defendant's claim that an express description and waiver of the jury right was a necessary component of the plea proceeding:

> Without disparaging the importance of the right provided by Rule 31(e), our analysis of the nature of criminal forfeiture as an aspect of sentencing compels the conclusion that the right to a jury verdict on forfeitability does not fall within the Sixth Amendment's constitutional protection. Our cases have made abundantly clear that a defendant does not enjoy a constitutional right to a jury determination as to the appropriate sentence to be imposed.

Id. at 49. Libretti thus flatly holds that the Sixth Amendment is not implicated in the forfeiture context. See id. at 40-41 (rejecting defendant's argument that forfeiture "is not 'simply' an aspect of sentencing, but is, in essence, a hybrid that shares elements of both a substantive charge and a punishment imposed for criminal activity").

The Leahy defendants contend that Libretti has been undercut by Blakely and Booker to such an extent that its precedential value has been eroded. Even assum-

---

5 U.S.C. § 982(a)(2) states in pertinent part:

> The court, in imposing sentence on a person convicted of a violation of, or a conspiracy to violate—
>
> > (A) section . . . 1344 of this title, affecting a financial institution . . . . shall order that the person forfeit to the United States any property constituting, or derived from, proceeds the person obtained directly or indirectly, as the result of such violation.

6 Former Rule 31(e) stated: "[I]f the indictment or the information alleges that an interest or property is subject to criminal forfeiture, a special verdict shall be returned as to the extent of the interest or property subject to forfeiture, if any." Rule 31(e) and other procedural rules governing the forfeiture of assets in a criminal case were consolidated into a new Rule 32.2 governing "Criminal Forfeiture."

ing that to be true, we nonetheless note that as a Court of Appeals, we are not free to ignore the Supreme Court's holding in Libretti, nor do we possess the authority to declare that the Supreme Court has implicitly overruled one of its own decisions. See United States v. Ordaz, 398 F.3d 236, 241 (3d Cir. 2005) ("[I]f a precedent of [the Supreme Court] has direct application in a case, yet appears to rest on reasons rejected in some other line of decisions, the Court of Appeals should follow the case which directly controls, leaving to [the Supreme] Court the prerogative of overruling its own decisions.") (quoting Rodriguez de Quijas v. Shearson/American Express, Inc., 490 U.S. 477, 484 (1989)).

Defendants argue in the alternative that Libretti should be distinguished on the grounds that it addressed only the question of whether there exists a Sixth Amendment jury right to forfeiture determinations, not the constitutionally-mandated burden of proof, which they contend must be "beyond a reasonable doubt" after Booker. While there may be some tension between Booker and Libretti to the extent that the Libretti Court cites with approval its earlier statement in McMillan v. Pennsylvania that "[t]here is no Sixth Amendment right to jury sentencing, even where the sentence turns on specific findings of fact," we are not dissuaded from our conclusion that Libretti controls the forfeiture issue here. 516 U.S. at 49 (quoting McMillan, 477 U.S. 79, 93 (1986)).

We further observe that the other Courts of Appeals that have considered this issue have reached the same conclusion. See United States v. Fruchter, 411 F.3d 377, 382-83 (2d Cir. 2005) (rejecting arguments that Sixth Amendment applies to forfeiture and that Booker and Blakely require proof beyond reasonable doubt in forfeiture determinations; further holding that "Libretti remains the determinative decision"), cert. denied sub nom. Braun v. United States, 126 S. Ct. 840 (2005); United States v. Hall, 411 F.3d 651, 655 (6th Cir. 2005) (stating that "we fail to see how Booker . . . allows us to turn our back on the Supreme Court's prior ruling in this area (Libretti)"); United States v. Tedder, 403 F.3d 836, 841 (7th Cir. 2005) (holding in pertinent part that Libretti remains binding Supreme Court precedent with respect to forfeiture and Sixth Amendment) cert. denied, 126 S. Ct. 827 (2005).

For the foregoing reasons, we join our sister Courts of Appeals and hold that, even after Booker, the Sixth Amendment's trial by jury protection does not apply to forfeiture, as Libretti remains Supreme Court authority by which we are bound.[7]

---

7 We note that Booker expressly states that 18 U.S.C. § 3544, a provision of the sentencing law that requires a district court to impose forfeiture on a defendant convicted under RICO, is still "perfectly valid." Booker, 125 S. Ct. at 764 (Breyer, J., remedial majority opinion). Although the forfeiture provision identified in Booker is not the same provision at issue in this case, "Booker itself suggests that a district court's forfeiture determination under [the RICO forfeiture statute] does not offend the Sixth Amendment." Fruchter, 411 F.3d at 382.

III. The Nature of Restitution

Before turning to Booker's applicability to restitution under the MVRA and the VWPA, we consider whether restitution under these statutes is criminal or civil in nature. If we deem restitution to be civil, there is no Sixth Amendment concern because that Amendment's protections apply only to criminal trials. We note first that restitution combines features of both criminal and civil penalties, as it is, on the one hand, a restoration to the victim by defendant of ill-gotten gains, while it is, at the same time, an aspect of a criminal sentence.

This is not the first time we have addressed this issue. In United States v. Syme , after reviewing several of our earlier cases, we stated that "[w]e consider restitution orders made pursuant to criminal convictions to be criminal penalties." 276 F.3d 131, 159 (3d Cir. 2002). Syme accordingly held that "restitution ordered under 18 U.S.C. § 3663 [the VWPA] constitutes 'the penalty for a crime' within the meaning of Apprendi." Id.; see also United States v. Edwards, 162 F.3d 87, 91 (3d Cir. 1998) (holding that restitution ordered under MVRA constitutes punishment for purpose of Ex Post Facto Clause analysis); United States v. Sleight, 808 F.2d 1012, 1020 (3d Cir. 1987) (finding that under Federal Probation Act, restitution "remains inherently a criminal penalty"); United States v. Palma, 760 F.2d 475, 479 (3d Cir. 1985) (holding that restitution ordered under VWPA is criminal penalty).

The Supreme Court has touched on this issue as well. In Pasquantino v. United States, a wire fraud case in which the MVRA applied, the Court noted:

> Petitioners answer that the recovery of taxes is indeed the object of this suit, because restitution of the lost tax revenue to Canada is required under the [MVRA]. We do not think it matters whether the provision of restitution is mandatory in this prosecution. Regardless, the wire fraud statute advances the Federal Government's independent interest in punishing fraudulent domestic criminal conduct, a significant feature absent from all of petitioners' revenue rule cases. The purpose of awarding restitution in this action is not to collect a foreign tax, but to mete out appropriate criminal punishment for that conduct.

125 S. Ct. 1766, 1777 (2005) (footnote omitted and emphasis added). Pasquantino suggests that whether the restitution order being reviewed is mandatory or discretionary does not change the analysis. Moreover, and more importantly, Pasquantino clearly states that an award of restitution under the MVRA or the VWPA is a "criminal punishment."

This latter stance is consistent with earlier Supreme Court precedent. In Kelly v. Robinson, 479 U.S. 36 (1986), the Court reviewed a Connecticut restitution statute in order to determine whether a restitution order was dischargeable in bankruptcy. The Court initially observed that "[t]he criminal justice system is not operated primarily for the benefit of victims." Id. at 52. The Court went on to state that "[a]lthough restitution does resemble a judgment 'for the benefit of' the victim," it is imposed in the context of a criminal sentence and "[t]he victim has no control over the amount . . . or the decision to award" restitution. Id. Additionally, the Court noted that "the decision to impose restitution generally does not turn on the victim's injury, but on the penal goals of the state and the situation of the defendant." Id. Quoting the Bankruptcy Judge who decided the underlying issue, the Court finally observed that [u]nlike an obligation which arises out of a contractual, statutory or common law duty, here the obligation is rooted in the traditional responsibility of a state to protect its citizens by enforcing its criminal statutes and to rehabilitate an offender by imposing a criminal sanction intended for that purpose.

Id. (citation omitted and emphasis added). In sum, the Kelly Court held that restitution granted in a state proceeding as a condition of probation could not be discharged because it constituted a criminal penalty enforced "for the benefit of" the government and did not serve primarily as "compensation for actual pecuniary loss" under § 523(a)(7) of the bankruptcy code.[8] See id. at 51-52.

Of the other Courts of Appeals that have addressed this issue, only the Seventh and Tenth Circuits have held that restitution is a civil rather than a criminal penalty. See United States v. Newman, 144 F.3d 531, 542 (7th Cir. 1998) (holding "restitution authorized by the VWPA (and mandatorily imposed under the MVRA) is not a criminal punishment for purposes of the Ex Post Facto Clause"); United States v. Nichols, 169 F.3d 1255, 1279-80 (10th Cir. 1999) (adopting Seventh Circuit's Newman holding that Ex Post Facto Clause does not bar application of restitution under MVRA). In contrast, the Fifth, Eighth, Ninth, Eleventh and D.C. Circuits recognize that restitution, when ordered in connection with a criminal conviction, is a criminal penalty.[9]

---

8 Section 523(a)(7) reads:

> (a) A discharge under section 727, 1141, 1228(a), 1228(b), or 1328(b) of this title does not discharge an individual debtor from any debt—
>
> . . .
>
> (7) to the extent such debt is for a fine, penalty, or forfeiture payable to and for the benefit of a governmental unit, and is not compensation for actual pecuniary loss, other than a tax penalty—
>
> (A) relating to a tax of a kind not specified in paragraph (1) of this subsection; or
>
> (B) imposed with respect to a transaction or event that occurred before three years before the date of the filing of the petition . . . .

11 U.S.C. § 523(a)(7).

9 See United States v. Rico Indus., Inc., 854 F.2d 710, 714 (5th Cir. 1988) ("Restitution is a criminal penalty."); United States v. Williams, 128 F.3d 1239, 1241 (8th Cir. 1997) ("We conclude an order of restitution under the MVRA is punishment for Ex Post Facto Clause purposes."); United States v. Miguel, 49 F.3d 505, 509 (9th Cir. 1995) ("The [VWPA] also clearly indicates that restitution is a penalty available to sentencing courts regardless of other criminal penalties that may be imposed."); Creel v. Comm'r of Internal Revenue, 419 F.3d 1135, 1140 (11th Cir. 2005) ("[A]n order to pay restitution under 18 U.S.C. § 3663 [the VWPA] is a criminal penalty rather than a civil penalty."); United States v. Bapack, 129 F.3d 1320, 1327 n.13 (D.C. Cir. 1997) (endorsing the Second Circuit's approach in Thompson).

Based upon our reading of Supreme Court precedent, we decline to overturn our precedent in Syme and instead reaffirm our view, consistent with the view of the majority of the Circuits to have addressed this issue, that restitution ordered as part of a criminal sentence is criminal rather than civil in nature.

IV. Restitution and Booker

We next turn to whether Booker applies to orders of restitution. The Leahy defendants were ordered to pay restitution under the VWPA, and the defendants in both Gregg and Fallon were ordered to do so under the MVRA. For purposes of determining whether Booker applies to orders of restitution under these two Acts, we believe the distinction between the permissive language of the VWPA and the mandatory language of the MVRA, see supra notes 3 and 4, is immaterial. See Pasquantino, 125 S. Ct. at 1777 (noting that whether restitution is mandatory or discretionary does not change government's interest in enforcing orders of restitution). The primary issue we must therefore address is whether a defendant's constitutional right to have certain facts found exclusively by a jury beyond a reasonable doubt, or admitted by the defendant, bars a judge from determining the sum of restitution he or she must pay. We hold that Booker extends no such protection to criminals under the Sixth Amendment.

A. Fact-Finding Under the Sixth Amendment

The Sixth Amendment provides that all criminal defendants "shall enjoy the right to a speedy and public trial, by an impartial jury." In the series of recent decisions culminating in Booker, the Supreme Court considered in depth the respective roles of judge and jury in the context of fact-finding and criminal sentencing. The central theme of the Booker line of cases has been that facts increasing the maximum penalty for a crime must be either admitted or proven to a jury beyond a reasonable doubt. The reasoning of these cases also led to a corresponding de-emphasis in the Court's Sixth Amendment jurisprudence on the rigid classification of facts increasing penalties as either elements of a crime or sentencing factors. After Booker, the inquiry governing what facts may be found by judges now turns on the effect of the fact-finding on the defendant's punishment, rather than the fact's legislative classification.

The Court first articulated this principle in Jones v. United States, where it stated in a footnote that "any fact (other than prior conviction) that increases the maximum penalty for a crime must be charged in an indictment, submitted to a jury, and proven beyond a reasonable doubt." 526 U.S. 227, 243 n.6 (1999). The Court affirmed this principle in Apprendi v. New Jersey, where it held that "[o]ther than the fact of a prior conviction, any fact that increases the penalty for a crime beyond the prescribed statutory maximum must be submitted to a jury, and proved beyond a reasonable doubt." 530 U.S. 466, 490 (2000). Four years later, the Court clarified in Blakely that the relevant "statutory maximum" for Apprendi purposes is the maximum sentence a judge may impose based solely on facts reflected in the jury verdict or admitted by the defendant. Blakely, 542 U.S. at 303-04.

In addition to refining its Apprendi holding, the Blakely Court rejected the presumption that "the jury need only find whatever facts the legislature chooses to label elements of the crime, and . . . those it labels sentencing factors—no matter how much they may increase the punishment—may be found by the judge." 542 U.S. at 306. The constitutional problem with such a presumption is that it allows legislatures to subvert the Sixth Amendment jury right by terming practically any fact a "sentencing fact," thereby reducing the number of facts that need to be proven to a jury for conviction. See id. at 306-07 ("The jury could not function as circuitbreaker in the State's machinery of justice if it were relegated to making a determination that the defendant at some point did something wrong, a mere preliminary to a judicial inquisition into the facts of the crime the State actually seeks to punish.") (emphasis in original). This concern, foreshadowed in Apprendi,[10] dovetailed with the Court's greater concern that "[w]hen a judge inflicts punishment that the jury's verdict alone does not allow, the jury has not found all the facts which the law makes essential to the punishment, and the judge exceeds his proper authority." Id. at 304 (internal citation and quotation marks omitted). Thus, the legislative labeling of a fact as an element or sentencing factor is no longer significant in determining whether it may or may not be constitutionally found by a judge. Rather, under Blakely, the central consideration is the effect a given fact may have on a defendant's maximum punishment. In short, for purposes of sentencing under Apprendi and Blakely, whether a fact is labeled a sentencing fact or an element of the offense is of no consequence.

The Booker Court confirmed the insignificance of legislative labeling in this context by asserting that "the characterization of a fact or circumstance as an 'element' or 'sentencing factor' is not determinative of the question 'who decides,' judge or jury." 125 S. Ct. at 749 (citation omitted). More important for our purposes, the Booker Court reaffirmed the reasoning of Apprendi and Blakely and applied it to invalidate the Federal Sentencing Guidelines, holding that "[a]ny fact (other than a prior conviction) which is necessary to support a sentence exceeding the maximum authorized by the facts established by a plea of guilty or a jury verdict must be admitted by the defendant or proved to a jury beyond a reasonable doubt." Id. at 756. Thus, the key inquiry in determining the applicability of Booker to an order of restitution under the VWPA or the MVRA is whether a judge's calculation of the sum a defendant must restore to his or her victim constitutes an increase in punishment exceeding that authorized by plea or jury verdict, in violation of the Sixth Amendment.

---

10 In a footnote, the Apprendi Court commented that "when the term 'sentence enhancement' is used to describe an increase beyond the maximum authorized statutory sentence, it is the functional equivalent of an element of a greater offense than the one covered by the jury's guilty verdict. Indeed, it fits squarely within the usual definition of an 'element' of the offense." 530 U.S. at 494 n.19.

B. Restitution Does Not Exceed the Statutory Maximum

Under both the VWPA and the MVRA, when a defendant is convicted of certain specified offenses, restitution is authorized as a matter of course "in the full amount of each victim's losses." 18 U.S.C. § 3664(f)(1)(A). Hence, under a plain reading of the governing statutory framework, the restitution amount authorized by a guilty plea or jury verdict—the full amount of loss—may not be exceeded by a district court's restitution order; that is, a district court is not permitted to order restitution in excess of that amount. In imposing restitution, a district court is thus by no means imposing a punishment beyond that authorized by jury-found or admitted facts. Though post-conviction judicial fact-finding determines the amount of restitution a defendant must pay, a restitution order does not punish a defendant beyond the "statutory maximum" as that term has evolved in the Supreme Court's Sixth Amendment jurisprudence. See Booker, 125 S. Ct. at 749 (defining "statutory maximum" as "the maximum sentence a judge may impose solely on the basis of the facts reflected in the jury verdict or admitted by the defendant") (citing Blakely, 542 U.S. at 303) (emphasis in original); see also United States v. Sosebee, 419 F.3d 451, 462 (6th Cir. 2005) ("Nor does [] Booker's analysis of the Sixth Amendment affect restitution, because a restitution order for the amount of loss cannot be said to 'exceed the statutory maximum' provided under the penalty statutes."). There can therefore be no Booker violation in the imposition of restitution under the VWPA or the MVRA.

Defendants argue that until a district court makes a factual finding as to the amount of loss, restitution is not authorized in any amount. As we read the statute, once a defendant is convicted of an offense covered by the VWPA or the MVRA, a district court must (or in the case of the VWPA, unquestionably may) order restitution, and in order to fulfill this mandate, the court must determine the amount of loss pursuant to 18 U.S.C. § 3664(f)(1)(A). Under the defendants' view, the conviction itself yields a restitution amount of zero dollars, and the factual finding of the amount of loss therefore increases the sentence beyond the maximum sum authorized by the facts, in violation of Booker. On the contrary, we see the conviction as authorizing restitution of a specific sum, namely the "full amount of each victim's loss"; when the court determines the amount of loss, it is merely giving definite shape to the restitution penalty born out of the conviction.[11] Thus, there is no restitution range under 18 U.S.C. § 3664(f)(1)(A) that starts at zero and ends

---

11 We agree with our dissenting colleagues that "the relevant inquiry is not of form, but of effect–does the required finding [of the amount of loss] expose the defendant to a greater punishment than that authorized by the jury's verdict?" McKee Dis. Op. at 12 (quoting Apprendi, 530 U.S. at 494). As we note throughout this Subsection, however, we do not believe that determining the "full amount of each victim's losses" in any way "exposes" a defendant to a greater punishment than that "authorized by the jury's verdict." Indeed, the jury's verdict automatically triggers restitution in the "full amount of each victim's losses," and under the MVRA restitution is not only "authorized" (as it undoubtedly also is under the VWPA), it is required. We therefore cannot accept our dissenting colleagues assertion that uncovering the specific sum lost by a defendant's victims amounts to exposure to a punishment greater than

at "the full amount of each victim's losses"; rather, the single restitution amount triggered by the conviction under the MVRA, or permitted under the VWPA, is the full amount of loss. For these reasons, we join the Fifth, Sixth, Seventh, Eighth, Ninth and Tenth Circuits and hold that Booker does not apply to orders of restitution under the MVRA and VWPA.[12] This conclusion is consistent with our view that orders of restitution have little in common with the prison sentences challenged by the defendants in Jones, Apprendi, Blakely and Booker. In those cases, the Supreme Court was faced with "exceptional" and "enhanced" sentences that added anywhere from two to ten years to the prison terms authorized by the facts found by the jury or pled to by the defendants. See Blakely, 542 U.S. at 299; see also Booker, 125 S. Ct. at 747 n.1. In contrast, the restitution ordered in Leahy, Gregg and Fallon was explicitly authorized by the defendants' pleas and convictions, and merely required the defendants to return property and proceeds obtained as a result of the offense of conviction.

Restitution is, at its essence, a restorative remedy that compensates victims for economic losses suffered as a result of a defendant's criminal conduct. In this sense, even though restitution is a criminal punishment, it does not transform a defendant's punishment into something more severe than that authorized by pleading to, or being convicted of, the crime charged. Rather, restitution constitutes a return to the status quo, a fiscal realignment whereby a criminal's ill-gotten gains are returned to their rightful owner. In these circumstances, we do not believe that ordering a convicted defendant to return ill-gotten gains should be construed as increasing the sentence authorized by a conviction pursuant to Booker.[13]

---

that authorized by a jury's verdict, as full restitution is explicitly authorized under the two Acts at issue here. This logic of course extends to defendants who plead guilty as well.

12 See United States v. Garza, 429 F.3d 165, 170 (5th Cir. 2005) (per curiam) ("We agree with our sister Circuits, who have uniformly held that judicial fact-finding supporting restitution orders does not violate the Sixth Amendment."); Sosebee, 419 F.3d at 461 (6th Cir. 2005) ("Given existing Sixth Circuit precedent and recent decisions of the other circuits on this issue, we now conclude that Booker does not apply to restitution and, thus, that Sosebee's Sixth Amendment challenge has no merit."); United States v. George, 403 F.3d 470, 473 (7th Cir. 2005) ("We have accordingly held that Apprendi v. New Jersey . . . does not affect restitution . . . and that conclusion is equally true for Booker."); United States v. May, 413 F.3d 841, 849 (8th Cir. 2005) ("[S]everal circuits have affirmatively rejected the notion that Apprendi, Blakely, or Booker affect the manner in which findings of restitution can be made . . . . These cases are persuasive."); United States v. Bussell, 414 F.3d 1048, 1060 (9th Cir. 2005) ("In contrast to its application of the Sentencing Guidelines, the district court's orders of restitution and costs are unaffected by the changes worked by Booker."); United States v. Visinaiz, 428 F.3d 1300, 1316 (10th Cir. 2005) (noting that "Blakely and Booker do not apply to restitution" because "[i]n the Tenth Circuit, restitution is not a criminal punishment") (citations omitted).

13 We recognize, of course, that the key question under the Booker analysis is whether the judicial fact-finding required by the VWPA and the MVRA exposes a defendant to greater punishment than that authorized by a jury verdict or guilty plea. As discussed above, we hold that an order of restitution based on such fact- finding does not violate a defendant's Sixth Amendment rights.

V. Conclusion

For the foregoing reasons, we conclude that restitution under the VWPA and the MVRA is a criminal penalty and that the Sixth Amendment right to jury determinations of certain facts as articulated in Booker does not apply to forfeiture or to orders of restitution imposed as part of a criminal sentence under those two statutes.

SLOVITER, Circuit Judge, concurring.

I approve and join Parts I. and II. of the majority opinion. I join in the judgment of Parts III. and IV. While I believe that Judge McKee's dissent has much to commend it, in the last analysis, I join the majority because the majority opinion persuades me that restitution is not a punishment governed by the Sixth Amendment.

FISHER, Circuit Judge, with whom Judge BARRY joins, concurring in part in the judgment.

I approve and join in Parts I, II, and III of the majority opinion. I concur only in the judgment as to Part IV. I would base our holding that the imposition of restitution did not violate the Sixth Amendment right to a jury trial solely on the conclusion that restitution is not the type of criminal penalty to which the right to a jury trial attaches. As the majority opinion correctly notes, "orders of restitution have little in common with the prison sentences challenged by the defendants in Jones, Apprendi, Blakely and Booker." Maj. Op. at 19. The issue of restitution was not before the United States Supreme Court in any of those decisions, and the Supreme Court gave no indication in those decisions that the right to a jury trial applies to any form of criminal penalty other than imprisonment. Accordingly, I would not reach—and do not join—the majority's conclusion that restitution orders do not constitute an increase in punishment beyond the "statutory maximum" for the offense.

McKEE, Circuit Judge. Concurring in part and dissenting in part with Judges RENDELL, AMBRO, SMITH, and BECKER joining.

Given the Supreme Court's holding in *Libretti v. United States*, 516 U.S. 29 (1995), I agree that a judicial determination of the amount of forfeiture when imposing a criminal sentence does not violate the Sixth Amendment right to a jury trial. Although I find it difficult to reconcile *Libretti* with the Court's subsequent decisions in *Blakely v. Washington*, 542 U.S. 296 (2004), and *United States v. Booker*, 125 S. Ct. 738 (2005), any tension between *Libretti* and those cases must be resolved by the Supreme Court, as the majority explains. *See* Maj. Op. at 9 (citing *United States v. Ordaz*, 398 F.3d 236, 241 (3d Cir. 2005)). I therefore join Section II of the majority opinion. However, for the reasons set forth below, I do not agree that a judge can determine the amount of restitution under either the Mandatory Victims Restitution Act ("MVRA"), 18 U.S.C. § 3663A, or the Victim Witness Protection Act ("VWPA"), 18 U.S.C. § 3663, without violating the Sixth Amendment. Accordingly, I respectfully dissent from Section IV of the majority opinion (captioned, "Restitution and *Booker*").

I.

In *Apprendi v. New Jersey*, 530 U.S. 466 (2000), the Supreme Court stated, "any fact (other than a prior conviction) that increases the maximum penalty for a crime must be charged in an indictment, submitted to a jury, and proven beyond a reasonable doubt." 530 U.S. at 476 (citation omitted). The Court later characterized this as a "bright-line rule." *See Blakely* 542 U.S. at 303.

In *United States v. Syme*, 276 F.3d 131, 159 (3d Cir. 2002), we held that "restitution ordered under 18 U.S.C. § 3663 [the VWPA] constitutes 'the penalty for a crime' within the meaning of *Apprendi*." We therefore had to determine "whether the . . . restitution order increased beyond the statutory maximum the penalties that Syme faced." *Id.* "If so, the [restitution] order violated *Apprendi*." *Id.* We held that *Apprendi* did not apply because the VWPA authorizes restitution as part of the criminal sentence that is imposed upon conviction, and because the statute "does not specify a maximum amount of restitution that a court may order." *Id.* We reasoned that the VWPA "provides guidelines that a sentencing judge may use to determine the amount of restitution, but does not prescribe a maximum amount." *Id.* We concluded that "[t]he *Apprendi* rule does not apply to restitution orders . . . because *Apprendi* applies only to criminal penalties that increase a defendant's sentence 'beyond the prescribed statutory maximum.'" *Id.* (quoting *Apprendi,* 530 U.S. at 490).

However, the Court decided *Blakely* after we decided *Syme*. *Blakely* clarified that "statutory maximum" for Sixth Amendment purposes is not the maximum sentence prescribed for a given offense. Rather, "the 'statutory maximum' for *Apprendi* purposes is the maximum sentence a judge may impose *solely on the basis of the facts reflected in the jury verdict or admitted by the defendant*." *Blakely*, 542

U.S. at 303 (emphasis in original). The Court clarified further by explaining: "In other words, the relevant 'statutory maximum' [for Sixth Amendment purposes] is not the maximum sentence a judge may impose after finding additional facts, but the maximum he may impose *without* any additional findings." *Id.* (emphasis in original). That definition of "statutory maximum" fatally undermines our analysis in *Syme*, and it is why I cannot agree with the majority's conclusion that the Sixth Amendment does not apply to orders of restitution.

A.

In *Blakely*, the Court reasoned that the right to a jury trial "is meant to ensure [the people's] control in the judiciary." *Id.* at 306. The Court explained that requiring any fact (other than a prior conviction) that increases the sentence beyond that authorized by the jury's verdict alone to be proven to the jury "reflects not just respect for longstanding precedent, but the need to give intelligible content to the right of a jury trial." *Id.* at 305. "*Apprendi* carries out this design by ensuring that the judge's authority to sentence derives *wholly* from the jury's verdict." *Id.* (emphasis added). The Court explained that those who "would reject *Apprendi* are resigned to one of two alternatives." *Id.* The first is that the jury need only find facts the legislature labels as "elements of the crime." This alternative would allow the judge to find facts which are tantamount to sentencing factors, whether or not they result in an increase in punishment. *Id.* However, this reduces the jury's findings to "a mere preliminary to a judicial inquisition into the facts of the crime the State *actually* seeks to punish." *Id.* at 307. The second alternative is that "legislatures may establish legally essential sentencing factors *within limits*—limits crossed when, perhaps, the sentencing factor is a 'tail which wags the dog of the substantive offense.'" *Id.* (emphasis in original). This means that "the law must not go *too far*—it must not exceed the judicial estimation of the proper role of the judge." *Id.* (emphasis in original). However, "[w]ith *too far* as the yardstick, it is always possible to disagree with such judgments and never refute them." *Id.* at 308 (emphasis in original). "[T]he very reason the Framers put a jury-trial guarantee in the Constitution is that they were unwilling to trust the government to mark out the role of the jury." *Id.*

The bright-line rule of *Apprendi* ensures that punishment will only be imposed in a manner that is consistent with the Sixth Amendment. It ensures that "the judge's authority to sentence derives wholly from the jury's verdict." *Id.* at 306. Thus, "every defendant has a *right* to insist that the prosecutor prove to a jury all facts legally essential to the punishment." *Id.* at 313 (emphasis in original). In *Booker*, the Court reaffirmed that the Sixth Amendment right "is implicated whenever a judge seeks to impose a sentence that is not solely based on 'facts reflected in the jury verdict or admitted by the defendant.'" *Booker*, 125 S. Ct. at 749.

The *Booker* Court explained that the sentencing scheme at issue in *Blakely* ran afoul of the Sixth Amendment precisely because it "violated the defendant's right to have the jury find the existence of any particular fact that the law makes essential to . . . punishment." *Id.* (internal quotation marks omitted). The judge was able to impose a sentence greater than that authorized by the jury's verdict *alone* merely by finding additional facts. *Id.* As a result, "the judge, not the jury . . . determined the upper limits of sentencing, and the facts determined were not required to be raised before trial or proved by more than a preponderance." *Id.* at 751.

Here, the majority pirouettes around *Apprendi*'s bright-line concept of "statutory maximum" by ignoring the Court's definition of that term while putting a favorable "spin" on restitution. Restitution, we are told, is "not the type of criminal punishment that evokes Sixth Amendment protection under *Booker*." Maj. Op. at 7. While conceding that restitution is a criminal sanction, the majority emphasizes that "orders of restitution have little in common with . . . prison sentences." Maj. Op. at 19. We are reminded that "[r]estitution combines features of both criminal and civil penalties." Maj. Op. at 10-11. However, that focus obfuscates the inquiry and sidesteps the analysis required by *Blakely.*

B.

In *Pasquantino v. United States*, 125 S. Ct. 1766 (2005), the Court discussed the nature of an order of restitution. There, the defendants were charged with wire fraud arising from a scheme to smuggle liquor into Canada to avoid that country's alcohol import taxes. They challenged the prosecution, arguing that the government "lacked a sufficient interest in enforcing the revenue laws of Canada." *Id.* at 1770. The argument arose from the fact that restitution of Canada's lost tax revenue was required by the MVRA. The Court rejected the defendants' argument, stating: "The purpose of awarding restitution in this action [was] not to collect a foreign tax, but to mete out appropriate criminal punishment for that conduct." *Id.* at 1777. Foreign tax collection was only incidental to the criminal prosecution. The primary objective of the prosecution was "deterrence and punishment of fraudulent conduct." *Id.* Restitution furthered that objective even though it also made the victim whole. Thus, in *Syme*, we correctly concluded: "restitution ordered under [the VWPA] constitutes the penalty for a crime within the meaning of *Apprendi*." Maj. Op. at 11 (quoting *Syme*, 276 F.3d at 159).

Here, no less than in *Pasquantino,* whatever compensation results from the defendants' prosecution is merely incidental to their criminal prosecution and sentence. The primary objective of these criminal prosecutions is clearly "deterrence and punishment" of criminal conduct, not ensuring compensation for the victims.

As the majority recognizes, this view of restitution is also required by the Supreme Court's earlier decision in Kelly v. Robinson, 479 U.S. 36 (1986). See Maj. Op. at 12. In Kelly, the Court had to decide if restitution imposed as part of a state criminal sentence was dischargeable in bankruptcy.[14] In resolving that inquiry, the Court noted that restitution, "[u]nlike traditional fines, . . . is forwarded to the victim, and

---

14 11 U.S.C. § 523(a)(7) exempts from discharge any condition a state criminal court imposes as part of a criminal sentence.

may be calculated by reference to the amount of harm the offender has caused." Kelly, 479 U.S. at 52. However, in rejecting the defendant's contention that restitution was subject to discharge under Chapter 7, the Court explained:

> The criminal justice system is not operated primarily for the benefit of victims but for the benefit of society as a whole. . . . Although restitution does resemble a judgment "for the benefit of" the victim, the context in which it is imposed undermines that conclusion. The victim has no control over the amount of restitution awarded or over the decision to award restitution. Moreover, the decision to impose restitution generally does not turn on the victim's injury, but on the penal goals of the State and the situation of the defendant.

Id.

Ignoring their own references to Pasquantino and Kelly, Maj. Op. at 11-12, the majority declares that "restitution is, at its essence, a restorative remedy that compensates victims for economic losses suffered as a result of a defendant's criminal conduct." Maj. Op. at 19 (emphasis added). That view of restitution ignores the Supreme Court's pronouncement that "[t]he purpose of awarding restitution . . . is not [to compensate the victim], but to mete out appropriate criminal punishment for that conduct." Pasquantino, 125 S. Ct. at 1777. That view of restitution is also inconsistent with the bright-line rule of Apprendi.

By ignoring that bright-line rule and redefining restitution's "essence," the majority is able to proclaim that "even though restitution is a criminal punishment, it does not transform a defendant's punishment into something more severe than that authorized by pleading to, or being convicted of, the crime charged." Maj. Op. at 19. My colleagues state "restitution constitutes a return to the status quo, a fiscal realignment whereby a criminal's ill-gotten gains are returned to their rightful owner." Maj. Op. at 19. The pirouette comes full circle once my colleagues conclude: "[i]n these circumstances, we do not believe that ordering a convicted defendant to return ill-gotten gains should be construed as increasing the sentence authorized by a conviction pursuant to *Booker*." Maj. Op. at 19.

However, that is not the question. The issue is not whether returning "ill-gotten gains should be construed as increasing the sentence authorized by a conviction." Maj. Op. at 19. Rather, the question is whether the verdict "*alone*" allows the judge to impose restitution with no additional finding of fact. Obviously, it doesn't. Notwithstanding the jury's verdict, no restitution can be imposed absent a judicial determination of the amount of loss. The fact that the statute "*require[s]*" the judge to find the amount of restitution, *see* Maj. Op. at 17 n.11, does not free the restitution order from the inescapable Sixth Amendment pitfall created when the judge, and not the jury, makes the finding. "The dispositive question . . . 'is one not of form, but of effect.' If a State makes an increase in a defendant's punishment contingent on the finding of a fact, that fact—no matter how the State labels it—must be found by a jury beyond a reasonable doubt." *Ring v. Arizona*, 536 U.S. 2428, 2439 (2002) (quoting *Apprendi*, 530 U.S. at 494; internal citations omitted).

II.

The majority believes that a defendant's conviction for specified offenses authorizes restitution "as a matter of course 'in the full amount of each victim's losses.'" Maj. Op. at 16 (quoting 18 U.S.C. § 3664(f)(1)(A)). Thus, according to my colleagues, the subsequent sentence of restitution "by no means impose[s] punishment beyond that authorized by the jury-found facts. Though the post-conviction judicial fact-finding determines the amount of restitution a defendant must pay, a restitution order does not punish a defendant beyond the 'statutory maximum' as that term has evolved in the Supreme Court's Sixth Amendment jurisprudence." Maj. Op. at 17. However, that analysis ignores the very meaning of "statutory maximum" and the bright-line rule of *Apprendi* that the Court erected to ensure the proper role of judge and jury.

To reiterate, "'statutory maximum' for *Apprendi* purposes is the maximum sentence a judge may impose *solely on the basis of the facts reflected in the jury verdict or admitted by the defendant.*" *Blakely*, 542 U.S. at 303 (emphasis in original). "In other words, the relevant 'statutory maximum' is not the maximum sentence a judge may impose after finding additional facts, but the maximum he may impose *without* any additional findings." *Id.* at 303-04 (emphasis in original). The fact that the jury's verdict authorizes restitution "in the full amount of the victim's loss" by no means allows any restitution to be imposed at all "*without* any additional findings." The jury's verdict allows the judge to make the additional finding, but restitution cannot be ordered on the basis of the jury's verdict *alone*.

A.

The majority's analysis requires that we accept the proposition that an order of restitution rests upon the jury's verdict *alone*, even though no restitution can be imposed until the judge determines the amount of loss. We must also accept that adding a set dollar amount of restitution to a sentence does not "enhance" the sentence beyond that authorized by the jury's verdict alone. I suspect that a defendant who is sentenced to a period of imprisonment and ordered to pay restitution in the amount of $1,000,000 would be surprised to learn that his/her sentence has not been enhanced by the additional penalty of $1,000,000 in restitution. "*Apprendi* held[] [that] every defendant has the *right* to insist that the prosecutor prove to a jury all facts legally essential to the punishment." *Blakely*, 542 U.S. at 313 (emphasis in original). Determining the amount of loss is "legally essential" to an order of restitution.

Yet, my colleagues agree, as they must, that, for Sixth Amendment purposes, "the 'statutory maximum' . . . is the maximum sentence a judge may impose *solely on the basis of the facts reflected in the jury verdict or admitted by the defendant.*" *Id.* at 303 (emphasis in original). They seek to avoid the logical consequence of that rule by suggesting that additional facts required to impose the penalty of restitution are not really "additional facts" at all. However, the Supreme Court has rejected the distinction required by the majority's analysis.

> Whether the judge's authority to impose an enhanced sentence depends on finding a specified fact [i.e. the amount of loss] . . . one of several specified facts . . . or any aggravating fact . . . , it remains the case that the jury's verdict alone does not authorize the sentence.

Id. at 305. I therefore cannot accept the majority's attempt to suggest that restitution is "not really" additional punishment. See Maj. Op. at 19 ("Restitution is, at its essence, a restorative remedy . . . .").

In Blakely, "[t]he application of Washington's sentencing scheme violated the defendant's right to have the jury find the existence of any particular fact that the law makes essential to his punishment." Booker, 125 S. Ct. at 749 (discussing Blakely) (internal quotation marks omitted). The judge there "was required to find additional facts in order to impose the greater . . . sentence." Id. (emphasis in original). Similarly, the sentencing judges in the cases consolidated here were required to find the additional fact of the amount of loss. Thus, as in Booker, the effect of these restitution orders is to impermissibly "increase the judge's power and diminish that of the jury." Id. at 751.

My colleagues claim that the conviction alone authorizes restitution in an undetermined amount, and that the judicial determination of loss "merely [gives] shape to the restitution penalty born out of the conviction." Maj. Op. at 17 (emphasis added). That hairsplitting is analogous to the "constitutionally novel and elusive distinction between 'elements' and 'sentencing factors.'" Apprendi, 530 U.S. at 494. "[T]he relevant inquiry is one not of form, but of effect—does the required finding [of the amount of loss] expose the defendant to a greater punishment than that authorized by the jury's verdict?" Id. Requiring facts that increase the sentence to be proven to a jury is "not motivated by Sixth Amendment formalism, but by the need to preserve Sixth Amendment substance." Booker, 125 S. Ct. at 752. Restitution in any amount greater than zero clearly increases the punishment that could otherwise be imposed.[15]

---

15 The majority's view that "[i]n imposing restitution, a district court is . . . by no means imposing a punishment beyond that authorized by jury-found or admitted facts" is fallacious. To demonstrate that the maximum amount of restitution authorized by the conviction is $0, and any increase beyond that figure requires the District Court to make additional findings of fact, we offer the following.

What, exactly, is the amount of loss? When the judge says to the defendant, "I order you to pay restitution in the amount of ____," what does the judge use to fill in the blank? Certainly it is not enough to say "I order you to pay restitution in the full amount of the victim's loss"; we suspect that the victim might be disappointed with the size of the check he ultimately receives under such a scenario. For this reason, the judge must order restitution *in a specific amount*, and in order to do so, he or she must make *a factual determination* of the size of the victim's loss. It is this factual determination, and not the simple act of conviction, that determines the maximum award that may be imposed. That is why, in this case, the District Court did not

B.

The majority finds some comfort in being able to "join[] the Fifth, Sixth, Seventh, Eighth, Ninth, and Tenth Circuits" in holding "that Booker does not apply to orders of restitution under the MVRA and VWPA." Maj. Op. at 18. However, before Booker was decided, one could have developed an even more impressive list of the courts that had incorrectly concluded that Apprendi does not apply to the federal

---

order restitution "in the full amount of the victim's loss"; instead, it ordered restitution in the amount of $408,970 for Leahy, $55,235 for Fallon, and $350 for Gregg.

Of course, the determination of "the full amount of the victim's loss" plainly is an "additional finding." So, the majority's argument requires us to accept that district courts can somehow impose restitution "in the full amount of the victim's loss" without making a factual determination as to what that amount is. We have many fine district judges in this Circuit, but we know of none capable of this feat.

The majority fails to realize that without additional findings, the maximum sentence that may be imposed in the form of restitution is $0. To see why this is true, consider a typical first-time defendant convicted of possession with intent to distribute in violation of 18 U.S.C. § 841(a)(1). For simplicity's sake, we will focus solely on the issue of drug quantity, and assume that the jury has found that the substance at issue is cocaine and that no other sentencing elements (such as criminal history) are relevant. Under the Guidelines, the District Court could impose a sentence of 10-16 months based solely on the fact of conviction, without making any more factual findings. If the District Court later determines that the defendant possessed more than 25 grams of cocaine, then it may, in accordance with the Guidelines, impose a higher sentence.

In truth, the determination of drug quantity in this scenario is precisely equivalent to the determination of the victim's loss in the restitution example. In the same way that conviction authorizes a judge to impose restitution "in the full amount of the victim's loss," so too does conviction for possession with intent to distribute under 18 U.S.C. § 841(a)(1) authorize the judge to impose "the appropriate Guidelines sentence of incarceration, based on the quantity of the drugs possessed by the defendant."

The only real difference between the two situations is that a judge imposing restitution starts from a baseline of $0 and then makes a determination of fact regarding the actual amount of the victim's loss, while a judge imposing incarceration for violating § 841(a)(1) starts from a baseline of 10-16 months and then makes a determination of fact regarding the actual quantity of drugs sold. Just as the maximum sentence under § 841(a)(1) without additional findings is 10-16 months, the maximum amount of restitution without additional findings is $0.

Of course, the restitution statutes actually authorize or require restitution in the full amount of the victim's loss—just like the Sentencing Guidelines require incarceration in accordance with the quantity of drugs the defendant actually sold. The only relevance of the 10-16 month range is that it is the penalty that may be imposed *without* any additional findings—just like the maximum award of restitution that may be imposed *without* any additional findings is $0. In both cases, however, the judge is required to make additional findings which will increase the sentence beyond the maximum authorized solely by conviction. The distinction that the majority draws between the pre-*Booker* Sentencing Guidelines and restitution under the VWPA or MVRA simply is not a meaningful one. In both cases, the judge makes factual determinations that increase the maximum penalty that may be imposed. For this reason, both schemes run afoul of the Sixth Amendment.

sentencing guidelines.[16] Moreover, the cases the majority cites from other circuit courts are not very helpful.

In United States v. Sosebee, 419 F.3d 451 (6th Cir. 2005), the court rejected a claim that orders of restitution are subject to the Sixth Amendment by concluding that "restitution statutes do not specify a statutory maximum," id. at 461, without ever considering Blakely's definition of that term or even discussing Blakely as part of its Sixth Amendment analysis. In addition, Sosebee attempts to distinguish Booker by referring to the fact that "restitution orders are authorized by statute." Id. at 462. However, the fact that restitution arises from statute rather than a guideline is obviously irrelevant to a Sixth Amendment analysis. Constitutional rights are not subject to legislative repeal. See Ring, 536 U.S. 584. As noted at the outset, "the very reason the Framers put a jury-trial guarantee in the Constitution is that they were unwilling to trust the government to mark out the role of the jury." Blakely, 542 U.S. at 308.[17]

The analysis in *United States v. George*, 403 F.3d 470 (7th Cir. 2005), is driven by the fact that the court considers restitution a civil penalty. The court states: "There is no 'statutory maximum' for restitution; indeed, it is not a criminal punishment but . . . a civil remedy administered for convenience by courts that have entered criminal convictions . . . ." *Id.* at 473.

In *United States v. Garza,* 429 F.3d 165, 169-70 (5th Cir. 2005), the Court of Appeals for the Fifth Circuit also concluded *Booker* does not directly affect the MVRA because it is a statute (as opposed to a guideline), without attempting to explain why that "distinction" is relevant to a Sixth Amendment analysis. With no analysis, the court proclaims that judicial fact-finding for restitution does not violate the Sixth Amendment. The court then states that "even if there were *Booker* error in the restitution order, any error would certainly not be plain under current law." *Id.* at 170. The court used the plain error standard because the defendant had not objected to the order of restitution. The court does not cite *Blakely* in that part of its analysis, nor does it explain why a violation of a Sixth Amendment right to a jury finding would not affect substantial rights as required for plain error under *United States v. Olano*, 507 U.S. 725 (1993).

---

16 United States v. Goodine, 326 F.3d 26, 27 (1st Cir. 2003); *United States v. Luciano*, 311 F.3d 146, 153 (2d Cir. 2002); *United States v. Cepero*, 224 F.3d 256, 268 n.5 (3d Cir. 2000); *United States v. Cannady*, 283 F.3d 641, 649 n.7 (4th Cir. 2002); *United States v. Randle*, 304 F.3d 373, 378 (5th Cir. 2002); *United States v. Harper*, 246 F.3d 520, 530 (6th Cir. 2001); *United States v. Cole*, 298 F.3d 659, 663 (7th Cir. 2002); *United States v. Mora-Higuera*, 269 F.3d 905, 911 (8th Cir. 2001); *United States v. Ochoa*, 311 F.3d 1133, 1135 (9th Cir. 2002); *United States v. Wilson*, 244 F.3d 1208 (10th Cir. 2001); *United States v. Sanchez*, 269 F.3d 1250, 1262 (11th Cir. 2001); *United States v. Fields*, 251 F.3d 1041, 1043 (D.C. Cir. 2001).

17 Sosebee also relies in part upon our holding in *Syme*. *See* 419 F.3d at 461. As I have already explained, our decision there cannot survive *Blakely*.

In *United States v. May*, 413 F.3d 841, 849 (8th Cir. 2005), the Court of Appeals for the Eighth Circuit concluded "that restitution does not have a 'statutory maximum.'" The court also concluded that, even if there had been a *Booker* error, it could not be plain because neither the Supreme Court nor the Eighth Circuit has held that *Booker* applies to restitution. *Id.* However, here again, there is no discussion of what is meant by "statutory maximum" for purposes of the Sixth Amendment.

In *United States v. Bussell*, 414 F.3d 1048, 1060 (9th Cir. 2005), the defendant challenged imposition of costs and restitution, but the challenge to restitution rested on her claim that the court erred in relying upon the *intended* loss rather than the actual loss. With no discussion of *Blakely*, the court decreed: "[i]n contrast to its application of the Sentencing Guidelines, the district court's orders of restitution and costs are unaffected by the changes worked by *Booker*." The court relied upon *United States v. DeGeorge*, 380 F.3d 1203, 1221 (9th Cir. 2004), and *United States v. Chavez*, 627 F.2d 953, 957 (9th Cir. 1980), in reaching this conclusion. However, *Chavez*, was decided in 1980, long before *Apprendi* and *Blakely*. *DeGeorge*, like *Bussell*, states only that restitution orders pursuant to the VWPA are "unaffected by *Blakely*." The court in *DeGeorge* simply cited a 1994 Ninth Circuit case which stated that "restitution determinations under the VWPA are quite different from sentencing determinations under the Sentencing Guidelines." *DeGeorge*, 380 F.3d at 1221 (internal citation omitted). Moreover, the court in *DeGeorge* specifically stated that, because it was reversing on other grounds, "we will not address the *Blakely* issues here; instead, DeGeorge is free to raise them on remand." *Id.* at 1220. Thus, *DeGeorge* does not advance the Sixth Amendment inquiry in *Bussell,* even though the latter court relies upon it.

The final case cited by the majority in support of its restitution determination is *United States v. Visinaiz*, 428 F.3d 1300 (10th Cir. 2005). There, in its brief discussion of restitution under *Blakely* and *Booker*, the court stated: "[i]n the Tenth Circuit, restitution is not criminal punishment." *Visinaiz*, 428 F.3d at 1316. Accordingly, *Visinaiz* does not further the majority's inquiry because the majority properly views restitution as a *criminal* punishment as required by *Pasquantino* and *Kelly*.

III.

In attempting to distinguish restitution from imprisonment, the majority notes that *Apprendi* and its progeny all involved rather substantial increases in terms of incarceration based upon judicial fact-finding. The majority notes that, "[i]n those cases, the Supreme Court was faced with 'exceptional' and 'enhanced' sentences that added anywhere from two to ten years to the prison terms authorized by the facts found by the jury or pled to by the defendants." Maj. Op. at 19.

I agree that this distinction has some merit. For example, the defendant in *Blakely* "was sentenced to prison for more than three years beyond what the law allowed for the crime to which he confessed." *Blakely*, 542 U.S. at 313. However, nothing in the Supreme Court's analysis in *Apprendi* or its progeny (including *Blakely*) suggests that the Supreme Court would tolerate this distinction or that the Sixth Amendment allows it. In fact, the Court says quite the opposite in holding that the Sixth Amendment applies to *any* fact-finding that increases the sentence beyond that which could be imposed based upon the jury's verdict alone. As I have already explained, *Apprendi* requires that "[o]ther than the fact of a prior conviction, any fact that increases the penalty for a crime beyond the prescribed statutory maximum must be submitted to a jury, and proved beyond a reasonable doubt." 530 U.S. at 490. The majority limits that rule to increases in terms of imprisonment. However, that limitation requires us to turn a blind eye to the meaning of "statutory maximum." It merits repeating yet again that "'statutory maximum' for *Apprendi* purposes is the maximum sentence a judge may impose *solely on the basis of the facts reflected in the jury verdict or admitted by the defendant.*" *Blakely*, 542 U.S. at 303 (emphasis in original).[18]

The Court could easily have limited its Sixth Amendment analysis by defining "statutory maximum" as the maximum sentence of incarceration or confinement (rather than punishment) that a judge may impose on the basis of the verdict alone. Given the backdrop of *Pasquantino* and *Kelly*, the Court would almost certainly have used language that would have limited the reach of its analysis to enhancements that result in a deprivation of liberty if the Court intended to restrict the Sixth Amendment as the majority does. The Court could also have limited the reach of *Apprendi* to any fact that "substantially" increases the sentence. The Court did neither.

I submit that it is difficult to read the majority's attempt to rationalize the limits it places on the Court's Sixth Amendment jurisprudence without concluding that, in essence, the majority essentially believes that applying *Apprendi* to orders of restitution simply stretches the Sixth Amendment too far. However, *Blakely* specifically rejects that limitation by noting that the Framers would not have left the "definition of the scope of jury power up to judges' intuitive sense of how far is *too far*." *Blakely*, 542 U.S. at 308. Rather, the Court created a bright-line rule. *Id.* Pursuant to that rule, *any* factual finding (other than a prior conviction) that increases the defendant's punishment beyond that authorized by the jury's verdict

---

18 The Court emphasized this language for a reason, and I cannot deemphasize it as readily as the majority's analysis requires. Even if we could somehow assume that determining the amount of loss did not expose a defendant to greater punishment, determining the amount of loss would still be essential to the restitution order. Therefore, restitution does not rest "*solely on the basis of the facts reflected in the jury verdict or admitted by the defendant.*" Rather, it rests substantially on the judicial determination of the amount of loss. It is therefore somewhat misleading to suggest that the "key question under the *Booker* analysis is whether the judicial fact- finding required by the VWPA and the MVRA exposes a defendant to greater punishment than that authorized by a jury verdict or guilty plea." Maj. Op. at 19, n. 13. Even assuming *arguendo* that a defendant is not exposed to a greater punishment, his/her sentence is still based on facts not found by a jury or admitted in a plea.

alone must be proven beyond a reasonable doubt to a jury or admitted by the defendant. Our decision today cannot be reconciled with that rule.

I do, of course, realize that the precise issue of the application of the Sixth Amendment to restitution orders was not before the Court in *Apprendi* or its progeny. It is therefore quite possible that the Court never considered the precise issue that we are deciding when it crafted those landmark opinions. Nevertheless, given the Court's recent jurisprudence, we are not at liberty to rationalize a distinction between punishment in the form of incarceration on the one hand, and punishment in the form of restitution on the other. Given the clear pronouncements in *Apprendi* and *Blakely*, any such distinction must be drawn by the Court in the first instance, and not by us. *See Ordaz*, 398 F.3d at 241.

A sentencing court may impose restitution under the VWRA, and it *must* do so under the MVRA. I agree with the majority's conclusion that "the distinction between the permissive language of VWPA and the mandatory language of the MVRA is immaterial." Maj. Op. at 14. Under neither statute does the restitution order rest "*solely*" upon the jury's verdict. A finding of loss necessarily is a condition precedent to an order of restitution, and under both statutes, it is the judge who makes the finding. As I have explained, the imposition of this additional criminal penalty based on a fact not found by a jury violates the Sixth Amendment. Therefore, I respectfully dissent from the majority's conclusion that the Sixth Amendment does not apply to orders of restitution.

AMBRO, Circuit Judge, concurring and dissenting in part

I write separately to note my view that both the majority and dissenting opinions are grounded in reasonable interpretations of Booker's effect on restitution. On the one hand, Judge Fuentes' opinion pragmatically avoids an outcome whose consequences—mandating the Government to prove loss amount to a jury beyond a reasonable doubt whenever it seeks restitution for victims—may prove cumbersome to implement. On the other hand, the broad language of Blakely and Booker appears to dictate that any fact controlling the maximum sentence that can be imposed must be admitted or proven to the jury. Thus, as articulated in Judge McKee's dissent, under the federal restitution statutes the amount of loss—because it controls the maximum restitution that can be imposed—must be subject to the Sixth Amendment's jury requirement. Indeed, the difficulty of resolving the question before us, and the fact that Booker nowhere mentions restitution (though, to be fair, restitution was not an issue in Booker), suggest that the Supreme Court did not take restitution penalties into consideration in crafting the Booker remedy. Until the Supreme Court directs us otherwise, however, I believe that the broad language of Booker obligates us to hold that the Sixth Amendment applies to orders of restitution under the MVRA and VWPA. Therefore, I join in its entirety Judge McKee's opinion concurring in part and dissenting in part.

SMITH, Circuit Judge, concurring in part and dissenting in part.

I join in its entirety Judge McKee's opinion concurring in part and dissenting in part. I write separately to note a particular concern arising out of Part IV of the majority opinion.

The majority rests its opinion upon a distinction between the facts "authorizing restitution of a specific sum, namely 'the full amount of each victim's loss'" and the facts "merely giving definite shape to the restitution penalty born out of the conviction." Maj. Op. at 17. The majority implicitly holds that under the Supreme Court's decisions in *Apprendi v. New Jersey*, 530 U.S. 466 (2000), *Blakely v. Washington*, 542 U.S. 296 (2004), and *United States v. Booker*, 125 S.Ct. 738 (2005), only the facts which *authorize a "specific" punishment*, and not the facts which *give "definite shape" to that punishment*, must be charged in an indictment, submitted to a jury, and proven beyond a reasonable doubt I suggest that this is a distinction that district courts will find difficult to understand and apply in other circumstances. Consequently, the majority opinion does not satisfy "the need to give intelligible content to the right of jury trial." *See Blakely*, 542 U.S. at 305. As the Supreme Court explained in *Blakely*, defining a right to a jury trial with intelligible content is a necessary step in protecting the people's ultimate control over the judiciary, as the Framers of the Sixth Amendment intended. *See id.* at 305-06.

Indeed, the Court in *Blakely* explicitly rejected a similar two-step approach to setting criminal punishments–first allowing the jury to determine that the defendant's actions warranted criminal punishment, and then allowing the court to determine the actual details of the crime–for precisely this reason. *See id.* at 306- 07 ("The jury could not function as circuitbreaker in the State's machinery of justice if it were relegated to making a determination that the defendant at some point did something wrong, a mere preliminary to a judicial inquisition into the facts of the crime the State *actually* seeks to punish.") (emphasis in original). Accordingly, because our decision today renders the right to a jury trial considerably less intelligible, and consequently undermines the people's constitutionally-protected right to ultimate control over the judicial branch, I join Judge McKee and respectfully dissent from Part IV of the majority opinion.

UNITED STATES OF AMERICA v. VALENTINE ONWUBIKO OBASI

435 F.3d 847 (8th Cir. 2006)
Decided January 19, 2006

For UNITED STATES OF AMERICA, Plaintiff-Appellee: Joseph Thomas Dixon, III, John Richard Marti, U.S. ATTORNEY'S OFFICE, Minneapolis, MN.

For VALENTINE ONWIBIKO OBASI, Defendant-Appellant: Daniel L. Gerdts, Minneapolis, MN.

Valentine Onwibiko Obasi, Defendant-Appellant, Pro se, Lemon Grove, CA.

Before MURPHY, BRIGHT, and GRUENDER, Circuit Judges. BRIGHT, Circuit Judge, concurring.

OPINION

MURPHY, Circuit Judge.

Valentine Onwubiko Obasi[1] was indicted for mail fraud, wire fraud, and money laundering and was convicted on thirty seven counts by a jury. The district court[2] sentenced him to 33 months and ordered restitution in the amount of $ 368,578.80. Obasi appeals, claiming that the denial of a portion of his request for investigative funds under the Criminal Justice Act (CJA) violated his constitutional rights, that the district court improperly admitted evidence of foreign bank records, and that the prosecutor committed misconduct in eliciting testimony about an absent investor. We affirm.

Obasi placed an advertisement in an insurance industry trade magazine to recruit agents to sell international mutual funds for Oval Financial and Investment Group, Ltd. (Oval). Oval claimed to be a worldwide fund management company that man-

1 Appellant's name appears in this form in the case caption and the district court record, but counsel indicated in briefing and at oral argument that his name is actually Obasi Valentine.

2 The Honorable Michael J. Davis, United States District Judge for the District of Minnesota.

aged over $ 1 billion in funds and offered international mutual funds with guaranteed principal and minimum interest of ten percent. Insurance salesman Jeffrey Rodd responded to the advertisement and signed an agency agreement with Obasi. Rodd recruited a number of Minnesota investors to deposit money in Oval, telling them that the money would be invested in certificates of deposit or mutual funds.

Obasi deceived investors in numerous ways through direct conversations, promotional materials, and presentations made by Rodd. Obasi claimed for example that the investments were insured and guaranteed through the Securities and Investor Protection Corporation and the Federal Deposit Insurance Corporation (FDIC), and he told Rodd that the money was deposited in United States banks. The Minnesota investors received payments from Obasi which he described as interest on their investments but which were frequently late, and he also furnished them false account statements which claimed that their investments were guaranteed. One of these statements claimed an investment in a certificate of deposit insured by the FDIC. When the investors inquired about their funds, Obasi either failed to respond or claimed that he had invested them. He eventually told investors that Oval was bankrupt.

There was evidence at trial that none of the money was ever deposited in certificates of deposit or mutual funds as the investors had been promised. Rather, Obasi used the funds for making payments to previous investors, for stock and options trading, for commission payments to Rodd, and for personal transactions. Some of the funds were sent to Excelsior Bank & Trust in Barbados, despite Obasi's promise to some investors that their funds would be deposited solely in United States banks.

Obasi was indicted on eight counts of mail fraud pursuant to *18 U.S.C. § 1341*, eighteen counts of wire fraud pursuant to *18 U.S.C. §§ 1343* and 2, and four counts of laundering of monetary instruments pursuant to *18 U.S.C. § 1956(a)(1)*. Obasi pled not guilty, and his attorney submitted a request to the district court under the CJA, *18 U.S.C. § 3006A(e)*, for $ 7,500 in funds for an investigator to gather information for his defense. He hoped to collect evidence about Jeffrey Rodd, the Minnesota investors, the Barbados bank in which Obasi had deposited some of the investment funds, witnesses from other alleged fraudulent schemes whom the government might present at trial, and Oval which was based in California. After a magistrate judge[3] certified the request, it was forwarded to the chief judge of the circuit[4] who approved funds in the amount of $ 2,500.

Later at a pretrial conference, Obasi's counsel complained that he had not received the full funding he had requested and needed more funds to investigate the case

---

3 The Honorable James B. Loken, Chief Judge, United States Court of Appeals for the Eighth Circuit.

4 The Honorable James B. Loken, Chief Judge, United States Court of Appeals for the Eighth Circuit.

and to hire an investigator to go to California to examine what he characterized as significant exculpatory evidence. The trial judge responded by explaining that,

> a more detailed explanation has to be given to the court other than saying there's some boxes out in California that if I was free to go get they would show that I was somehow innocent of this case. Something more than that has to be put on the record for the court to make any comments on that or to make any orders dealing with those documents being brought to court.

Obasi's counsel stated that he could not "provide a more detailed explanation at this point" but perhaps he could before trial. Obasi raised the funding issue again within several days, and the court instructed him to submit a written request. Although he agreed to do so, no written request was submitted.

The government notified Obasi six months before trial that it planned to introduce records from Excelsior Bank in Barbados where he had deposited some of the investment funds. The government also turned over copies of the records and a certification from their custodian in compliance with *18 U.S.C. § 3505(a)*, which permits the introduction of records of regularly conducted foreign activity. Obasi's counsel objected to the introduction of any Excelsior Bank records on the grounds that they were hearsay, that the certification was inadequate, and that the records were incomplete and possibly forged. He also mentioned an FBI report which he said had expressed concerns about the completeness and authenticity of the records. The government told the court that the only records it planned to introduce were Obasi's own requests for wire transfers from Excelsior Bank, but it made the complete set of records available to the defense. The district court found that the record certification was adequate, that the documents identified by the government were neither hearsay nor untrustworthy, and that the allegation of incompleteness did not make the records inadmissible.

The government gave notice one month before trial that it intended to present evidence about Hazel Clark, whom it identified as a "prior victim of Obasi's fraud". Clark was an elderly woman who had invested approximately $ 455,000 with Obasi through an intermediary. After her nephew Gary Seawright demanded return of her money, Obasi forwarded payments to him. The government's evidence showed that these payments were made from funds deposited by the Minnesota investors. Obasi filed a motion in limine to exclude the evidence under Fed. R. Evid. 404(b); the motion was denied before trial.

At trial the government introduced evidence that Obasi had fraudulently misrepresented his own background, the status of his company, and the services he was providing. It elicited testimony concerning the dates the Minnesota investors turned over funds to Rodd, the amounts of money invested, and the varied uses Obasi made of the funds received from the investors. Obasi's failure to invest money as promised and his attempts to lull his victims into a false sense of security were evidenced by testimony from Jeffrey Rodd and the investors, as well as by introduction of records showing wire transfer requests made by Obasi to Excelsior Bank, including the dates and the amounts involved.

Gary Seawright testified about Hazel Clark's investment. He told the jury that Clark had invested approximately $ 455,000 with Obasi, that she was a frail woman in her eighties who had moved from a mobile home into assisted living, and that she was no longer able to manage her business affairs. When Seawright began discussing his review of Clark's records, Obasi objected on the grounds of relevance; the objection was overruled. When the prosecutor asked Seawright whether a check sent by Obasi to Clark reflected proceeds from a certificate of deposit or any type of mutual fund, Obasi objected that the question implied that it was he who had defrauded Clark. Obasi moved for a mistrial, but he did not request that the testimony be stricken. The district court overruled his objection and denied the motion for mistrial, and the parties agreed on a stipulation to be read to the jury. Pursuant to that agreement, the court informed the jury that the parties agreed that Obasi had not solicited "the referenced investment from Ms. Hazel Clark and that Ms. Clark received a complete settlement of her investment after a civil suit was brought on her behalf against a third party, Mr. [Renald] Leduc."

The jury returned guilty verdicts on eight counts of mail fraud, twenty five counts of wire fraud[5], and four counts of money laundering. It found that Obasi had caused a loss of $ 378,373.60 through his mail and wire fraud and that the value of funds involved in the money laundering charges was $ 26,150.00. Obasi moved for a new trial based on 1) prosecutorial misconduct by introduction of evidence suggesting that he had perpetrated fraud on an elderly unsophisticated victim and 2) the denial of full funding for his requested investigative services. The district court denied the motion, stating that "any mistaken impression that Seawright's testimony initially left on the jury was corrected by the stipulation that Obasi, himself, agreed upon" and that Obasi had never made a specific showing that he needed more funding. The court also commented that Obasi could have had his own records shipped from California, subpoenaed third party records, or made another ex parte request under the CJA.

Obasi appeals. He contends that the decision of the chief circuit judge to grant only $ 2,500 in funding for an investigator denied him the ability to mount an adequate defense, in violation of his due process, equal protection, and jury trial rights. He also claims that the district court improperly admitted evidence of foreign bank records and that the prosecutor committed misconduct while eliciting testimony about Hazel Clark's investment.

A defendant can submit an ex parte request for investigative services under § 3006A(e) of the CJA if he is unable to afford them. If the court finds that the

---

5 One count of wire fraud had been dismissed before trial on the government's motion because the amount and date of the particular wire transfer had been incorrectly identified in the indictment.

services are "necessary and that the person is financially unable to obtain them," the court shall authorize the services. *Id.* Under the statute any request for over $ 1,600 must be certified by the district court or magistrate judge and approved by the chief judge of the circuit. District court action on the request is committed to its discretion, and "denial or limitation of funds is not grounds for reversal absent a showing of prejudice." *United States v. Bledsoe, 674 F.2d 647, 668 (8th Cir. 1982), cert. denied, 459 U.S. 1040, 103 S. Ct. 456, 74 L. Ed. 2d 608 (1982).* The defendant bears the burden of demonstrating that expert services are necessary. *United States v. Valverde, 846 F.2d 513, 517 (8th Cir. 1988).*

Although Obasi has the right to appeal an individual judge's ruling on his request for funds under the CJA, the situation is different in respect to the decision of the chief judge of the circuit because that judge is acting in an administrative capacity when reviewing the request rather than performing a judicial function. *See United States v. Johnson, 391 F.3d 946, 948-49 (8th Cir. 2004), judgment vacated and remanded* (2005); *United States v. D'Andrea, 612 F.2d 1386, 1387-88 (7th Cir. 1980).* Although a petition for rehearing is available to challenge a determination by an individual circuit judge and the district court decision is subject to appeal, a determination by the chief circuit judge can only be challenged by seeking reconsideration or mandamus in the Supreme Court. *See D'Andrea, 612 F.2d at 1387-88.* In our unvacated opinion in *Johnson*, we agreed with the reasoning in *D'Andrea* and held that:

> The chief judge's decision is neither "a final decision of the district court" under *28 U.S.C. § 1291*, nor an appealable interlocutory order under *28 U.S.C. § 1292*. It is instead an administrative decision that is beyond our jurisdiction.

Johnson, 391 F.3d at 949. We agree with the jurisdictional analysis in these cases.

Although jurisdiction is lacking over Obasi's attempted appeal of the CJA decision by the chief circuit judge, we do have jurisdiction over district court decisions on funding requests under *18 U.S.C. § 3006A(e)* and we review them for abuse of discretion. *See Johnson, 391 F.3d at 949 n. 4.* In order to prevail on his challenge, Obasi must show that the action of the district court prejudiced him. Id. (citing *United States v. Bledsoe, 674 F.2d 647, 668 (8th Cir. 1982)*; *United States v. Bertling, 370 F.3d 818, 820-21 (8th Cir. 2004)).*

Obasi's written funding request only named individuals and institutions from which evidence might be obtained. It did not specify what evidence was needed or justify the amount of funds requested. Counsel said only that he needed travel funds for "additional investigation [in California] concerning Mr. Obasi's investment business, his contacts there, and [to] obtain witnesses located in California." Despite further opportunities before the district court during pretrial and posttrial proceedings, he failed to detail the materials he sought and presented only minimal declarations about their relevance although his offer of proof in his motion for a new trial was somewhat more specific than his earlier descriptions.

Obasi has similarly failed to present on appeal a specific account of his investigative needs or any prejudice suffered. Instead he has simply repeated the general subjects mentioned in his ex parte request and a need for "communications about and advertising from Excelsior Bank and its officers tending to demonstrate that the bank did indeed advertise and represent to Defendant and others that it was a legitimate, approved banking institution and that its deposits were insured and guaranteed." Obasi did not request subpoenas for California witnesses, issue discovery requests, or seek to depose bank officers or employees. The failure to renew the funding request, to clarify the importance of the records, or to seek the records by other means, *see United States v. Kasto, 584 F.2d 268, 273-74 (8th Cir. 1978), cert. denied, 440 U.S. 930, 99 S. Ct. 1267, 59 L. Ed. 2d 486 (1979)*, undercuts Obasi's claim that more funds were necessary or that he was prejudiced by the district court's failure to approve further funding. Obasi has not shown any violation of his constitutional rights.

On appeal Obasi continues his challenge to the Excelsior Bank records as incomplete, as well as his attack on their authenticity and accuracy. He claims that some of the documents appear to have been altered by expunging deposit and credit information and that the summaries were not prepared near the time of the recorded transactions as required under *18 U.S.C. § 3505*. The government offered portions of the records into evidence to show the source of the funds which had been used to pay some investors and which had been represented as interest payments. The government responds that it made a sufficient showing that the wire transfer records were trustworthy and reliable. The records had been validly certified and had been prepared by Obasi himself, and they had been corroborated by Obasi's statements to Minnesota investors about interest payments and by witness testimony about these transfers. They were further supported by evidence showing receipt of the funds by banks in the United States. The government also points out that Obasi is arguing about the trustworthiness of business records which he himself introduced.

Under § 3505 foreign business records may be received unless they reflect untrustworthiness, and the wire transfer requests from Excelsior Bank were properly certified and were corroborated by domestic records and witness testimony. We conclude that these records were shown to be trustworthy and reliable and that the district court did not abuse its discretion in allowing their admission. To the extent that Obasi is challenging summaries of various Excelsior Bank transactions, rather than the wire transfer requests, we note that it was he who introduced them. He claims he introduced the summaries only to demonstrate that the government's exhibits were suspect, but he has not shown that the government exhibits were improper or that he was prejudiced by them.

Obasi alleges that the prosecutor engaged in misconduct depriving him of his constitutional right to a fair trial through a "blatant appeal to the passions and prejudice of the jury in its questioning of Government witness Gary Seawright." Prior to trial the government stated that its purpose in eliciting testimony from Seawright about Hazel Clark was to demonstrate that funds from the Minnesota investors had been used to repay other defrauded investors, rather than having been deposited in certificates of deposit and mutual funds as promised. The court limited the scope of Seawright's testimony to exclude details relating to Clark's lawsuit against Obasi and others. The government contends that Seawright's testimony complied with the district court's order limiting its scope and that any possible prejudice was cured by the stipulation of both sides which was read to the jury. The government argues further that if there were any error in allowing the testimony and denying the motion for a new trial, then it was harmless given the amount of evidence against Obasi.

To show reversible misconduct by a prosecutor, a proponent must show that counsel engaged in improper conduct which "prejudicially affected the defendant's substantial rights so as to deprive the defendant of a fair trial." *United States v. Johnson, 968 F.2d 768, 770 (8th Cir. 1992)*. Obasi asserts that the prosecutor elicited precisely the evidence which was to have been excluded that was "at the heart of the California litigation" brought on behalf of Hazel Clark. He claims that the prosecutor's question to Seawright about the origin of the proceeds returned to Clark suggested that it had been Obasi who fraudulently solicited her money. To avoid any confusion, however, the parties agreed to a stipulation which was read to the jury and which made it clear that the individual who had solicited Clark's investment had been Renald LeDuc.

We conclude that not only did Seawright's testimony not breach the court's limitations on his testimony, but that Obasi was not unduly prejudiced by his testimony. The prejudicial impact of alleged prosecutorial misconduct must be assessed by looking at the "cumulative effect of the misconduct, determining if the court took any curative actions, and gauging the strength of the evidence against the defendant in the context of the entire trial." *United States v. French, 88 F.3d 686, 689 (8th Cir. 1996)*. The focus of the trial was on the fraud perpetrated on the Minnesota investors. Seawright's testimony focused only on the amounts and timing of payments made to Clark. Any prejudice to Obasi by the prosecutor's question, about whether a particular check represented a return from a certificate of deposit or mutual fund, was cured by the fact that Seawright never answered the question and by the joint stipulation read to the jury clarifying that another individual had fraudulently solicited Clark to invest with Obasi. We conclude that any prejudice would have had minimal impact at most on the questions at issue in the trial and that it would consequently be harmless. We conclude Obasi has not shown prosecutorial misconduct.

Because Obasi has not shown that his constitutional rights were violated by the denial of CJA funding for investigation, that the district court improperly admitted evidence, or that the prosecutor committed misconduct, we affirm the judgment of the district court.

CONCUR

BRIGHT, Circuit Judge, concurring.

The *D'Andrea* and *Johnson* cases stand for the proposition that the Chief Judge's decision on funding under Section 3006A of the Criminal Justice Act may not be attacked directly as an interlocutory order. However, that issue may be subject to review in an appeal from a judgment of conviction where the appellant contends the conviction was imposed in violation of his due process right to present an adequate defense. *See Ake v. Oklahoma, 470 U.S. 68, 76-77, 105 S. Ct. 1087, 84 L. Ed. 2d 53 (1985)* ("[A] criminal trial is fundamentally unfair if the State proceeds against an indigent defendant without making certain that he has access to the raw materials integral to the building of an effective defense."); *United States v. Abreu, 202 F.3d 386, 388 (1st Cir. 2000)* ("This court has appellate jurisdiction over § 3006A determinations that impact a defendant's trial or sentence."); *United States v. Bloomer, 150 F.3d 146, 149 (2d Cir. 1998)* (same).

Here, however, Obasi has not shown with the required specificity his need for the full amount of funds that he requested, nor that his defense was prejudiced by lack of funds, nor that he was deprived of due process in the presentation of his defense.

Thus, I concur separately.

UNITED STATES OF AMERICA
v.
FEI YE

436 F.3d 1117 (9th Cir. 2006)
Decided February 2, 2006

Kyle Waldinger, Assistant United States Attorney, San Francisco, California, for the plaintiff-appellant.

Paul B. Meltzer, Santa Cruz, California, for defendant-appellee Fei Ye.

Before: John T. Noonan, A. Wallace Tashima, and William A. Fletcher, Circuit Judges. Opinion by Judge Tashima.

OPINION

TASHIMA, Circuit Judge:

Defendants are charged with possessing stolen trade secrets in violation of the Economic Espionage Act of 1996 ("EEA"), *18 U.S.C. § 1831 et seq.* The district court granted defendants' motion for pre-trial depositions of several expert witnesses whom the government intends to call at trial. The government brings this interlocutory appeal under *18 U.S.C. § 1835*, arguing that the district court erred in granting the motion because the order authorizes and directs the disclosure of trade secrets, and because it is inconsistent with the Federal Rules of Criminal Procedure and the Jencks Act. In the alternative, the government maintains that the district court's order is clearly erroneous and warrants mandamus relief. While we conclude that we do not have appellate jurisdiction under § 1835, we find this case appropriate for mandamus relief.

JURISDICTION

We have jurisdiction over an interlocutory appeal under the EEA when the district court issues "a decision or order . . . authorizing or directing the disclosure of any trade secret." *18 U.S.C. § 1835*. As discussed below, § 1835 does not provide us with jurisdiction over this appeal because the government had already disclosed all of the relevant trade secret materials prior to the making of the order at issue.

We do, however, have jurisdiction over the government's petition for a writ of mandamus under the All Writs Act, *28 U.S.C. § 1651*.

BACKGROUND

Defendants Fei Ye and Ming Zhong were arrested by federal law enforcement agents while attempting to board a flight to China at the San Francisco International Airport. Federal agents simultaneously seized various materials from defendants' personal luggage, homes, and offices, alleged to be trade secrets stolen from four American technology companies. Defendants were subsequently charged with possessing stolen trade secrets with the intent to benefit the People's Republic of China.[1]

Prior to trial, defendants filed a motion for a bill of particulars, for discovery, and to dismiss the indictment. At the hearing on this motion, the prosecutor explained that "all the trade secret materials" in the case had already been provided to defendants pursuant to a protective order months before the indictment was filed. The prosecutor further noted that these materials "discuss and explain what the trade secrets are" and "why they are trade secrets," and that the materials estimated "the values of many of these trade secrets." The district court denied the motion, reasoning that "the indictment explicitly identifies the trade secrets involved" for each count, and that the government had already disclosed more than 8,800 pages of materials, which "describe the substance of each alleged trade secret."

Defendants then filed a motion to depose government witnesses prior to trial. During the hearing on this motion, counsel for Zhong admitted that he was seeking to use the Federal Rules of Criminal Procedure for discovery purposes:

> And [the prosecutor] accuses us of using Rules 15 and 16 to seek discovery.
>
> I don't know whether [co-defendant's counsel] agrees with this, but I do. That's exactly what we're trying to do. We're trying to find a rule that guarantees us notice in this case and whether it be Rule 15, Rule 16, or the Court's inherent power to make this workable, I think the Court clearly has the ability to fashion a remedy.

Defense counsel also acknowledged that he wanted the depositions so that defendants could obtain information on "what exactly is being alleged to be the trade secret and why it is a trade secret in advance of trial." The government opposed the motion, arguing that the prospective deponents "will be available at trial," and that the Federal Rules of Criminal Procedure do not permit pre-trial depositions for discovery purposes.

---

1 The ten-count indictment included conspiracy to commit economic espionage, possession of stolen trade secrets, and foreign transportation of stolen property, in violation of 18 U.S.C. §§ 371, 1831(a)(5), and 1832(a)(5); economic espionage, in violation of 18 U.S.C. § 1831(a)(3); possession of stolen trade secrets, in violation of 18 U.S.C. § 1832(a)(3); and foreign transportation of stolen property, in violation of 18 U.S.C. § 2314.

The district court granted defendants' motion, reasoning that "the fairness and efficiency of the trial process" amounted to "exceptional circumstances" under Rule 15.[2] The government's motion for reconsideration was denied, and the government now brings this interlocutory appeal/petition for mandamus.

DISCUSSION

I. Jurisdiction under 18 U.S.C. § 1835

As a threshold matter, defendants contend that we lack jurisdiction to hear the government's interlocutory appeal under § 1835 because the district court's order does not mandate the disclosure of any trade secret materials that have not already been previously disclosed by the government. We agree.

Section 1835 provides:

> In any prosecution or other proceeding under this chapter, the court shall enter such orders and take such other action as may be necessary and appropriate to preserve the confidentiality of trade secrets, consistent with the requirements of the Federal Rules of Criminal and Civil Procedure, the Federal Rules of Evidence, and all other applicable laws. An interlocutory appeal by the United States shall lie from a decision or order of a district court authorizing or directing the disclosure of any trade secret.*18 U.S.C. § 1835*. The precise scope of our jurisdiction under § 1835 is an issue of first impression.[3]

"The starting point for our interpretation of a statute is always its language." *Cmty. for Creative Non-Violence v. Reid, 490 U.S. 730, 739, 109 S. Ct. 2166, 104 L. Ed. 2d 811 (1989)*. "If the plain language of a statute renders its meaning reasonably clear, [we] will not investigate further unless its application leads to unreasonable or impracticable results." *United States v. Stephens, 424 F.3d 876, 882 (9th Cir. 2005)* (internal quotation marks and citation omitted).

The plain language of the EEA indicates that the government can file an interlocutory appeal pursuant to § 1835 only where a district court's order actually directs or authorizes the disclosure of a trade secret. *See 18 U.S.C. § 1835*. Black's Law Dictionary defines "disclosure" as "the act or process of making known something that was previously unknown." BLACK'S LAW DICTIONARY 477 (7th ed. 1999); *see also* AMERICAN HERITAGE DICTIONARY OF THE ENGLISH LANGUAGE (4th ed. 2000) (defining disclosure as, "to make known (something

---

2 Rule 15(a)(1) provides in relevant part:

> A party may move that a prospective witness be deposed in order to preserve testimony for trial. The court may grant the motion because of exceptional circumstances and in the interest of justice.

Fed. R. Crim. P. 15(a)(1).

3 The Third Circuit is the only court to have exercised jurisdiction over an interlocutory appeal under 18 U.S.C. § 1835. *See United States v. Hsu, 155 F.3d 189 (3d Cir. 1998)*. In *Hsu*, however, the parties agreed that the court had jurisdiction because the district court's order authorized the disclosure of trade secrets that had not been previously released. *See* id. at 193-94.

heretofore kept secret)"). Here, the district court's order did not provide for the disclosure of any trade secret materials. In its opening brief in this court, the government acknowledges that it had already turned over all relevant trade secret materials and documents:

> At the hearing on this motion on October 20, 2003, the prosecutor noted that "all the trade secret materials" in the case had been provided to the defendants pursuant to a protective order months before the indictment was filed, that these materials "discuss and explain what the trade secrets are" and "why they are trade secrets," and that the materials even estimated "the values of many of these trade secrets."

Because the purpose of the district court's order was only to clarify exactly which materials the government contends constitute the protected trade secrets, and all relevant materials had already been turned over, the district court's order does not direct or authorize the "disclosure" of trade secrets as required by the plain language of § 1835. *Cf. Hsu, 155 F.3d at 193-94* (asserting jurisdiction over interlocutory appeal under § 1835 where district court ordered government to turn over trade secret materials that had not been previously "disclosed" to defendants).

Although we need not go beyond the plain language of § 1835, the legislative history of the EEA supports this interpretation. *See* H.R. REP. NO. 104-788, at 13 (1996), *reprinted in* 1996 U.S.C.C.A.N. 4021, 4032. The section-by-section analysis explains that "the intent of [§ 1835] is to preserve the confidential nature of the information and, hence, its value. Without such a provision, owners may be reluctant to cooperate in prosecutions for fear of further exposing their trade secrets to public view, thus further devaluing or even destroying their worth." *Id.* Where the government concedes that it has previously disclosed all of the trade secret materials pursuant to a protective order, and the ordered depositions are subject to the same protective order, the underlying rationale for granting immediate appellate review is absent because there is no risk of "further exposing trade secrets to public view." *Id.*

The government also argues that this Court has jurisdiction over the interlocutory appeal because the district court's order violates § 1835's requirement that such orders be consistent with the Federal Rules of Criminal Procedure and other applicable laws. By its plain language, however, § 1835 grants interlocutory appellate jurisdiction *only* when a district court's order authorizes or directs the disclosure of a trade secret. *See 18 U.S.C. § 1835*. As discussed *supra*, the district court's order does not direct the disclosure of a trade secret. We conclude therefore that we lack jurisdiction over the government's interlocutory appeal under § 1835. Accordingly, the government's appeal must be dismissed.

II. Mandamus relief under 28 U.S.C. § 1651

The government alternatively petitions for a writ of mandamus pursuant to the All Writs Act, *28 U.S.C. § 1651*. *See Miller v. Gammie, 335 F.3d 889, 895 (9th Cir. 2003)* (en banc) (treating notice of appeal as a petition for a writ of mandamus).

The Supreme Court has explained that only "exceptional circumstances amounting to a judicial usurpation of power will justify the invocation of this extraordinary remedy." *Will v. United States, 389 U.S. 90, 95, 88 S. Ct. 269, 19 L. Ed. 2d 305 (1967)* (internal quotation marks and citation omitted). "Nevertheless, review of a discovery order through the exceptional remedy of mandamus may be appropriate in the proper circumstances." *Admiral Ins. Co. v. U.S. Dist. Court, 881 F.2d 1486, 1490 (9th Cir. 1989)*; *see, e.g., United States v. U.S. Dist. Court (DeLorean), 717 F.2d 478, 481 (9th Cir. 1983)* (issuing writ where district court ordered pretrial discovery in violation of Federal Rules of Criminal Procedure). The petitioner must show that its right to issuance of the writ is clear and indisputable. *Bauman v. U.S. Dist. Court, 557 F.2d 650, 656 (9th Cir. 1977) (citing Kerr v. United States Dist. Court for Northern Dist., 426 U.S. 394, 403, 96 S. Ct. 2119, 48 L. Ed. 2d 725 (1976)).*

We apply a five-factor test to determine whether mandamus relief is warranted: (1) whether the petitioner has no other adequate means to attain the relief he or she desires; (2) whether the petitioner will be damaged or prejudiced in a way that is not correctable on appeal; (3) whether the district court's order is clearly erroneous as a matter of law; (4) whether the district court's order is an oft-repeated error, or manifests a persistent disregard of the federal rules; and (5) whether the district court's order raises new and important problems, or issues of law of first impression. *United States v. Amlani, 169 F.3d 1189, 1193-94 (9th Cir. 1999)* (citing *Bauman, 557 F.2d at 654-55*). A petitioner need not establish all five factors, *see Admiral Ins. Co., 881 F.2d at 1491*, and we will weigh the factors together based on the facts of the individual case. *SG Cowen Sec. Corp. v. U.S. Dist. Court, 189 F.3d 909, 913 (9th Cir. 1999)* (citation omitted).

1. Does the government have other adequate means to attain relief?

Discovery orders are generally interlocutory and non-appealable under *28 U.S.C. § 1291*. *Admiral Ins. Co., 881 F.2d at 1490*. Appellate review under *28 U.S.C. § 1292(b)* is also unavailable because the district court did not certify the issue for appellate review.

Defendants maintain, however, that mandamus relief is inappropriate because the government could refuse to comply with the district court's discovery order and appeal the resulting sanction. This argument finds support in the basic principle that "while discovery orders themselves are not generally final for purposes of *section 1291*, parties who face such an order have the option of making the decision final simply by refusing to comply, and appealing the resulting sanction." *United States v. Fernandez, 231 F.3d 1240, 1245 (9th Cir. 2000)* (internal quotation marks and citations omitted); *United States v. Ryan, 402 U.S. 530, 533, 91 S. Ct. 1580, 29 L. Ed. 2d 85 (1971)* ("One who seeks to resist the production of desired information [must choose] between compliance with a trial court's order to produce prior to any review of that order, and resistance to that order with the concomitant possibility of an adjudication of contempt if his claims are rejected on appeal." (citation omitted)).

We have explicitly rejected this argument, however, where "discovery is directed at third-parties who could not be expected" to incur a contempt citation. *SG Cowen, 189 F.3d at 913-14* (*citing In re Grand Jury Subpoena 92-1(SJ), 31 F.3d 826, 829 (9th Cir. 1994)*). While we recognized that a petitioner "could refuse to comply with the discovery orders *directed at it*[,] and then appeal from the contempt order," we reasoned that third-party witnesses were unlikely to do so. *Id.* (emphasis added). Because most of the district court's discovery orders in *SG Cowen* were directed at third-parties, we concluded that the defendant had no alternative remedy for purposes of the first *Bauman* factor. *Id.*; *DeLorean, 717 F.2d at 481* (granting mandamus relief from a district court's discovery order *without* requiring the government to first violate the order and pursue a direct appeal under § 1291).

While defendants cite to *Fernandez* for support, *Fernandez* only provides an example of a situation where the district court sanctioned the government for failing to comply with a discovery order, thereby producing an appealable final order. *Fernandez, 231 F.3d at 1245*. It does not, however, hold that a party must incur a sanction, such as contempt, before it may seek mandamus relief. *See id.* Moreover, *Fernandez* can also be distinguished from the case at bar on the grounds that the government itself was the subject of the discovery order, and therefore, could have refused to comply and thus incurred sanctions. By contrast, the discovery order in this case is directed at third-party witnesses who may choose to comply with the district court's discovery order rather than risk a contempt citation, thereby leaving the government with no alternative grounds for relief. *See SG Cowen, 189 F.3d at 913-14*. Accordingly, the first factor weighs in favor of granting the government's petition.

2. Will the government be damaged in a way not correctable on appeal?

Defendants argue that the discovery order will not result in damage to the government because it will not cause any trade secrets to be disclosed. The potential disclosure of trade secrets, however, is not the only damage resulting from the district court's order. We have previously held that "a petitioner is damaged or prejudiced if his claim will be moot on appeal." *SG Cowen, 189 F.3d at 914*. Because "compliance with a discovery order moots an appeal of that order," the government would therefore suffer damage. *Id.* (*citing Medhekar v. U.S. Dist. Court, 99 F.3d 325, 326-27 (9th Cir. 1996)*).

Moreover, any error would also not be correctable on appeal because, "if defendants are acquitted, the government will be barred by the double jeopardy clause from raising the issue by way of appeal." *United States v. U.S. Dist. Court (Kantor), 858 F.2d 534, 537 (9th Cir. 1988)* (citation omitted). The issue would "be equally unreviewable in case of conviction because the government would not have been prejudiced by the claimed error." *Id.* (citation omitted). Therefore, the second factor also weighs in favor of granting the government's petition.

3. Was the district court's order clearly erroneous?

An order is clearly erroneous for purposes of a mandamus petition if "we are left with the definite and firm conviction that a mistake has been committed." *Wash. Pub. Utils. Group v. U.S. Dist. Court, 843 F.2d 319, 325 (9th Cir. 1987)* (internal quotation marks and citation omitted); *In re Cement Antitrust Litig., 688 F.2d 1297, 1305-07 (9th Cir. 1982)*. Rule 15, which governs the taking of depositions in criminal cases, provides in pertinent part that "[a] party may move that a prospective witness be deposed in order to preserve testimony for trial," and that "the court may grant the motion because of exceptional circumstances and in the interests of justice." *Fed. R. Crim. P. 15(a)(1)*. Unlike in civil cases, however, Rule 15 depositions are not allowed merely for discovery purposes. *United States v. Rich, 580 F.2d 929, 933-34 (9th Cir. 1978)*.

We have previously clarified that Rule 15 "contemplates a party taking the deposition of only his own witness," and "only if the witness may be unable to attend trial." Id. at 934; *United States v. Cutler, 806 F.2d 933, 936 (9th Cir. 1986)*. Here, the district court's order violates the well-established principles governing Rule 15 depositions because the prospective deponents are adverse witnesses; they are available to testify at trial; and the defendants seek discovery, not preservation of testimony. Although the district court's order acknowledges that Rule 15 does not permit depositions for discovery purposes, the court inexplicably proceeded to authorize pre-trial depositions for that very purpose.

The only justification that can be gleaned from the discovery order is that "the witnesses would be less inconvenienced if allowed to state [their] opinions orally as opposed to being required to write them out," and that it would be more efficient "to extract the details of any expert opinion[,] or lack thereof," before trial. The district court also justified its order as ensuring "fairness and efficiency of the trial process." While the district court's belief that it would be more convenient and efficient to allow pretrial depositions may be well-founded, Rule 15 makes no exception for convenience and efficiency. *See Rich, 580 F.2d at 933-34*; *Culter, 806 F.2d at 935-36*.[4] Moreover, the district court cites no case law to support its interpretation of Rule 15, and ignores the extensive body of law that directly contradicts its reasoning. Accordingly, the district court's order was clearly erroneous.

---

4 Although the district court's order does not purport to rely upon Fed. R. Crim. P. 16 to justify its pre-trial deposition order, defendants have referred to Rule 16 as justifying the deposition. It is clear, however, that Rule 16 also does not authorize such an order. *See, e.g.*, *In re United States, 878 F.2d 153, 156 (5th Cir. 1989)* ("Nor can the deposition be authorized under Rule 16, Fed.R.Crim.P. That rule does not mention depositions, which are plainly to be governed by Rule 15.").

4. Is the error an oft-repeated error, or does it manifest a persistent disregard of the federal rules?

Because the district court's discovery order is a clear violation of the well-established legal principles underlying Federal Rules of Criminal Procedure, it is likely not an "oft-repeated" error. Moreover, the government has not argued or presented any evidence to the contrary. Therefore, this factor weighs against the government's petition.

5. Does the district court's order raise a new and important problem, or an issue of first impression?

The district court reasoned that its order was necessary to ensure the "fairness and efficiency of the trial process," and to "establish pretrial procedures for effectively controlling the dissemination of the trade secrets before they are presented in the context of a public jury trial." However, no circuit has recognized any such exception to the Federal Rules of Criminal Procedure. Therefore, the district court's order raises the new and important question of whether the EEA empowers a district court to order depositions for discovery purposes under Rule 15's "exceptional circumstances and in the interest of justice" provision in order to ensure "fairness and efficiency" and "effectively control[] the dissemination" of important trade secrets. Accordingly, this factor weighs in favor of granting the government's petition.

In sum, four of the five *Bauman* factors weigh in favor of granting the government's petition.

CONCLUSION

After weighing all five factors, we conclude that they lean strongly in favor of granting mandamus relief. The district court's order was "wholly unauthorized" and "constitutes a clear and very substantial departure from the fundamental principles governing criminal pretrial and trial procedures in federal court." *In re United States, 878 F.2d at 159*. The government has demonstrated that it has no alternative means of relief and will suffer harm that is not correctable on appeal. *See SG Cowen, 189 F.3d at 913-14*. Finally, the district court's order raises the new and important question of whether the EEA empowers a court to authorize discovery depositions under Rule 15 in order to ensure fairness and efficiency and effectively control the dissemination of important trade secrets.

Accordingly, the government's petition for a writ of mandamus is granted and the district court is directed to rescind its order of November 4, 2004, granting defendant Fei Ye's motion to depose the government's expert witnesses prior to trial.

Appeal DISMISSED; petition for a writ of mandamus GRANTED.

IX. INTERNATIONAL TRADE

2. Business & Finance

F. Agency, Employment, & Labor*

* Cases are indexed under this subject. The full text of these cases is published in the **volume**-page indicated.

FORMER EMPLOYEES OF QUALITY FABRICATING, INC.
v.
UNITED STATES SECRETARY OF LABOR

448 F.3d 1351 (Fed. Cir. 2006)
Decided May 24, 2006

Adam H. Gordon, Collier Shannon Scott, PLLC, of Washington, DC, argued for plaintiff-appellee. With him on the brief was John B. Brew.

Stephen C. Tosini, Attorney, Commercial Litigation Branch, Civil Division, United States Department of Justice, of Washington, DC, argued for defendant-appellant. With him on the brief were Peter D. Keisler, Assistant Attorney General, David M. Cohen, Director, and Patricia M. McCarthy, Assistant Director. Of counsel on the brief was Gary E. Bernstecker, Attorney, Office of the Solicitor, United States Department of Labor, of Washington, DC.

Before NEWMAN, RADER, and PROST, Circuit Judges.

OPINION

RADER, *Circuit Judge*.

The United States Court of International Trade ordered the Department of Labor (Labor) to notify former employees of Quality Fabricating, Inc. (Quality) that they qualify for secondarily-affected worker benefits, to explain these benefits to the former Quality employees, and to provide the court with status updates demonstrating Labor's compliance with the court's order. *Former Employees of Quality Fabricating, Inc. v. U.S. Dep't of Labor*, No. 02-00522 (Ct. Int'l Trade 2005) (Order). Because the Court of International Trade lacks jurisdiction to review Labor's determinations with respect to secondarily-affected worker benefits, this court vacates the Order and remands with instructions to dismiss.

I.

On June 28, 2001, several former Quality employees filed a petition with Labor seeking unemployment benefits stemming from Quality's loss of business with firms that either shifted production to Mexico or Canada, or lost sales because of increased imports from Mexico or Canada. The former Quality employees sought unemployment benefits under one of two programs: (1) benefits as "primarily-affected workers" under the North American Free Trade Agreement-Transitional Adjustment Assistance program (NAFTA-TAA); or (2) benefits as "secondarily-affected workers" under the Job Training Partnership Act (JTPA) or its successor, the Workforce Investment Act (WIA). From a former employee's perspective, these programs provide substantially identical benefits. Nonetheless, these programs apply to different categories of workers.

Before losing employment, primarily-affected workers had employers that were "directly affected" by increased imports from or shifts of production to other countries. The federal government provides benefits targeting primarily-affected workers under various Transitional Adjustment Assistance programs dating back to at least the Trade Act of 1974, codified at *19 U.S.C. § 2291-98*. See *Hampe v. Butler, 364 F.3d 90, 91 (3d Cir. 2004)* (describing the unemployment benefits provided under the Trade Act of 1974).

NAFTA provides a specific program, the NAFTA-TAA program, for those primarily-affected workers affected by shifts in production to or increased imports from Canada and Mexico. *See 19 U.S.C. § 2331 (1993)*. The Trade Act of 2002 combined the benefits programs under NAFTA-TAA and the Trade Act of 1974 and expanded those programs to expressly provide for benefits to "adversely affected secondary workers." *See* Pub. L. No. 107-210, Div .A, Title I, § 123(a), 116 Stat. 944 (2002); *19 U.S.C. § 2272(b) (2002)*. In this case, the primarily-affected worker benefits under the NAFTA-TAA program fall within that Trade Act program.

In contrast to primarily-affected workers, before losing employment, secondarily-affected workers had employers that were "indirectly-affected" by increased imports from or shifts of production to other countries. These secondarily-affected workers had worked for employers that supplied materials and/or components to a primary firm. Unlike primarily-affected workers, secondarily-affected workers did not receive unemployment benefits under the Trade Act of 1974. Instead, the Statement of Administrative Action (SAA) gave Labor the authority to provide secondarily-affected worker benefits under the JTPA. *See* H.R. Doc. No. 103-159, at 672 (1993) ("[T]hrough administrative action, the Secretary of Labor will use existing authority under . . . the Job Training Partnership Act . . . to provide assistance to workers in secondary firms that supply or assemble products produced by firms that are directly affected.") *(SAA); H.R. Rep. 103-361, at 92-93 (1993) reprinted in* 1993 U.S.C.C.A.N. 2552, 2642-43 ("The Secretary of Labor will use existing authority under the [JTPA] program to provide similar assistance to workers in secondary firms that supply or assembly products directly affected by the NAFTA."). At the heart of the present appeal, the parties dispute whether the SAA and the NAFTA Implementation Act, codified at *19 U.S.C. § 3311*, created a secondarily-affected worker benefits program that was incorporated into the Trade Act of 2002 along with the NAFTA-TAA program.

In June, 2001, several former Quality employees filed a petition seeking benefits either as primarily-affected workers or as secondarily-affected workers. After investigation, Labor certified the employees as a secondarily-affected worker group that qualified for benefits under the JTPA/WIA. However, upon publication of findings in the Federal Register, Labor denied the petition as a whole, meaning that the group did not qualify either as primarily-affected or secondarily-affected. *See Notice of Determinations Regarding Eligibility To Apply for Worker Adjustment Assistance and NAFTA Transitional Adjustment Assistance, 67 Fed. Reg. 35,142* (Dep't of Labor May 17, 2002). Thereafter, one of the former Quality employees sent a letter of complaint to the Court of International Trade requesting an appeal of Labor's negative determination.

While the case was pending before the Court of International Trade, Labor discovered that it had not published notice in the Federal Register of the secondarily-affected worker benefits certification. Accordingly, Labor published that notice for the first time. *See Quality Fabricating, Inc., North Huntington, PA; Affirmative Finding Regarding Qualification as a Secondarily-Affected Worker Group Pursuant to the Statement of Administrative Action Accompanying the North American Free Trade Agreement (NAFTA) Implementation Act, 68 Fed. Reg. 53,397* (Dep't of Labor, Sept. 10, 2003). Labor claims to have also provided other forms of notice both before and after discovering the error in the Federal Register. For instance, Labor claims to have faxed a copy of its determination to the state coordinator in Pennsylvania. At trial, however, Labor could not lay a proper foundation for this evidence. Believing proper notice had, at that point, been given for the secondarily-affected worker certification and noting that benefits as secondarily-affected workers were substantially identical to benefits as primarily-affected worker benefits, Labor moved to dismiss the case as moot. Alternatively, Labor moved to dismiss the case for lack of jurisdiction because the Court of International Trade's jurisdiction under *28 U.S.C. §§ 1581(d)(1), (i)(4)* encompasses only disputes under the Trade Act. Labor asserts that the Trade Act did not incorporate the SAA program for secondarily-affected workers.

The trial court disagreed with Labor on both grounds. The Court of International Trade instead asserted jurisdiction to review the secondarily-affected worker benefits issue because the SAA and NAFTA-TAA programs are part of a unified program that falls within the court's particular expertise in trade matters. *Former Employees of Quality Fabricating, Inc. v. U.S. Dep't of Labor, 343 F. Supp. 2d 1272, 1279 (Ct. Int'l Trade 2004)* (Trial Court Decision). The trial court also found that the notice issue was not moot because, even with republication in the Federal Register, Labor had not provided proper notice under its own internal procedures. Id. at 1287. Thus, the trial court ruled for the former Quality employees on the merits and ordered Labor to "exercise all reasonable efforts" to identify the eligible employees, to explain these benefits to the former employees, and to provide the court with status updates demonstrating its compliance with the *Order*. *Order*, slip op. at 1-2. The present appeal followed.

II.

This court reviews decisions of the Court of International Trade about jurisdiction without deference. *Xerox v. United States, 423 F.3d 1356, 1359 (Fed. Cir. 2005)* (citations omitted). In general, "[t]he United States, as sovereign, is immune from suit save as it consents to be sued." *Awad v. United States, 301 F.3d 1367, 1372 (Fed. Cir. 2002)* (quoting *United States v. Sherwood, 312 U.S. 584, 586, 61 S. Ct. 767, 85 L. Ed. 1058 (1941))*. Only an express statute suffices to waive the sovereign immunity of the United States. *West v. Gibson, 527 U.S. 212, 217, 119 S. Ct. 1906, 144 L. Ed. 2d 196 (1999)*; *Yancheng Baolong Biochem. Corp. v. United States, 406 F.3d 1377, 1382 (Fed. Cir. 2005)* (explaining that waivers of sovereign immunity must be "unequivocally expressed" in statutory language) (quoting *Lane v. Pena, 518 U.S. 187, 192, 116 S. Ct. 2092, 135 L. Ed. 2d 486 (1996))*. A waiver statute may assign specific causes of action to specific courts as a condition of consent. *See Humane Soc'y. of United States v. Clinton, 236 F.3d 1320, 1328 (Fed. Cir. 2001)*; *Quality Tooling, Inc. v. United States, 47 F.3d 1569, 1576-77 (Fed. Cir. 1995)*; *NEC Corp. v. United States, 806 F.2d 247, 249 (Fed. Cir. 1986)*. Thus, this court must determine whether a statute unequivocally granted a waiver for adjudication of Labor's eligibility determinations with respect to secondarily-affected worker groups in the Court of International Trade.

In 1980, Congress sought to improve upon the judiciary's ability to handle increasingly complex international trade litigations by replacing the outdated United States Customs Court with a full Article III trial court, the Court of International Trade. *See Customs Courts Act of 1980, Pub. L. No. 96-417, 94 Stat. 1727* (codified primarily at scattered sections of 19 and 28 U.S. C.). Congress intended for this newly formed court to reflect:

> The re-emphasis and clarification of Congress' intent that the expertise and national jurisdiction of the Court of International Trade . . . be exclusively utilized in the resolution of conflicts and disputes arising out of the tariff and international trade laws, thereby eliminating the present jurisdictional conflict between [the Court of International Trade] and the federal district . . . courts. Gregory C. Sisk, *The Trial Courts Of The Federal Circuit: Diversity By Design, 13 Fed. Cir. B.J. 241, 254 (2003)* (quoting H.R. Rep. No. 96-1235, at 28 (1980), reprinted in 1980 U.S.C.C.A.N. 3729, 3739). Because NAFTA is, in effect, a body of trade law (specifically regulating trade between the United States, Canada and Mexico), the statutes implementing NAFTA vested the Court of International Trade with considerable jurisdiction over litigations arising under NAFTA, including Labor's trade adjustment assistance certifications for primarily-affected workers. *See* 28 U.S.C. § 1581(d) (vesting the Court of International Trade with exclusive jurisdiction over Labor's adjustment assistance determinations under the Trade Act); 19 U.S.C. § 2331(c)(2) (1993) (stating that persons petitioning for NAFTA-TAA benefits who are denied affected worker status under the subsection should be automatically evaluated for benefits under the Trade Act of 1974); see *also Former Employees of Sonoco Prods. Co. v. Chao, 372 F.3d 1291 (Fed. Cir. 2004)* (reviewing denied petitions for benefits under *NAFTA-TAA); Former Employees of Barry Callebaut v. Chao, 357 F.3d 1377 (Fed. Cir. 2004)*

(same). The relevant jurisdictional provisions for the Court of International Trade do not, however, waive sovereign immunity nor grant that court jurisdiction to review the determination, administration, and enforcement of *all* trade adjustment assistance certifications by Labor.

Section 1581(d) authorizes the Court of International Trade to review "any final determination of the Secretary of Labor under section 223 of the Trade Act of 1974 with respect to the eligibility of workers for adjustment assistance under such Act." Similarly, section 1581(i)(4) limits the court's review to Labor's administration and enforcement of Trade Act determinations under § 1581(d). Thus, 28 U.S.C. §§ 1581(d), (i)(4) only authorize the trial court to review Labor's actions here if secondarily-affected worker benefits under the SAA fall within the scope of the Trade Act as amended by the NAFTA Implementation Act.

In this regard, nothing in the NAFTA Implementation Act provides secondarily-affected worker benefits under the Trade Act. Rather, 19 U.S.C. § 3311 simply approves the NAFTA with Canada and Mexico, and the SAA proposed to implement the agreement.[1] There is no mention of secondarily-affected worker benefits in § 3311 at all. Thus, some other statute must provide the necessary waiver for adjudication of the secondarily-affected worker benefits issue in the Court of International Trade to be proper.

Turning to the SAA, the SAA explicitly distinguishes between primarily-affected worker benefits under the NAFTA-TAA program and secondarily-affected worker benefits under the JTPA. The SAA explains that only the NAFTA-TAA program was incorporated into the Trade Act. Specifically, the SAA states:

First, sections 501 through 506 of the NAFTA implementing bill amend . . . the Trade Act of 1974 . . . to provide assistance for workers in firms that are directly affected by imports form or shifts in production to Mexico or Canada. Second, through administrative action, the Secretary of Labor will use *existing authority under . . . the Job Training Partnership Act ("JTPA") . . . to provide assistance to workers in secondary firms* that supply or assemble products produced by firms

---

1 The Omnibus Trade and Competitiveness Act of 1988, codified at *19 U.S.C. § 2903*, and section 151 of the Trade Act of 1974, codified at *19 U.S.C. § 2191*, required the President to submit a statement of administrative action to Congress because the North American Free Trade Agreement was negotiated using fast track provisions under these acts. *See* Cindy G. Buys, *An "Authoritative" Statement of Administrative Action: A Useful Political invention Or A Violation Of The Separation Of Powers Doctrine*?, 7 N.Y.U.J. Legis. & Pub. Pol'y 73, 80 (2003) (describing the relationship between SAAs and trade agreements, including NAFTA, that are established under the fast track provisions of U.S. trade law). Specifically, section 2903 required the President:

> (B) after entering into the agreement [to submit] a document to the House of Representatives and to the Senate containing a copy of the final legal text of the agreement, together with—
>
> (i) a draft of an implementing bill, [and]
>
> (ii) a statement of any administrative action proposed to implement the trade agreement . . . .

that are directly affected. H.R. Doc. No. 103-15 9 at 672 (emphasis added). Thus, the SAA explicitly states that secondarily-affected worker benefits fall under the JTPA (succeeded by the WIA). *Id.* Primarily-affected worker benefits, on the other hand, fall under the Trade Act. *See 19 U.S.C. § 2331(c)(2) (1993)*; *Former Employees of Chevron Prods. Co. v. U.S. Sec'y of Labor, 279 F. Supp. 2d 1342, 1345 n.2 (Ct. Int'l Trade 2003)* ("[T]he NAFTA-TAA statute requires that—where petitioning workers are found to be ineligible for NAFTA-TAA benefits—the Labor Department is to automatically evaluate their eligibility for benefits under the TAA statute.") Thus, the SAA does not place secondarily-affected worker benefits within the Trade Act along with the primarily-affected worker benefit program.

Because the SAA separates the secondarily-affected worker and primarily-affected worker programs and the NAFTA Implementation Act does not incorporate the secondarily-affected worker program into the Trade Act, no statute waives immunity nor authorizes suit in the Court of International Trade with respect to Labor's determinations on secondarily-affected worker benefits. Indeed, the trial court concedes that neither the SAA nor the NAFTA Implementation Act, on their faces, grant jurisdiction over the secondarily-affected worker benefits claim. *Trial Court Decision, 343 F. Supp. 2d at 1278*. Without an express waiver of immunity and consent to suit in the Court of International Trade, the trial court lacks authority to proceed further.

This court recognizes that the NAFTA Implementation Act provides judicial review of NAFTA-TAA claims under the Trade Act in the Court of International Trade. This court also recognizes that Labor administers and enforces both primary and secondary claims, often in one combined petition. These aspects of trade law and policy, however, do not constitute an express statutory waiver of sovereign immunity and grant of jurisdiction to the Court of International Trade. Neither this court nor the trial court has authority to create a single coherent trade related program for both primarily- and secondarily-affected workers. Moreover, neither this court nor the trial court may create a unitary plan for judicial review of both programs in a single forum absent express statutory authorization. 28 U.S.C. §§ 1581(d), (i)(4) do not provide that authority.

As previously discussed, the SAA separated the primarily-affected worker benefit program under the Trade Act from the secondarily-affected worker benefit program under the JTPA, and the NAFTA Implementation Act did not incorporate the secondarily-affected worker benefit program into the Trade Act. Thus, no statute requires Labor to administer a single all inclusive benefits program subject to the trial court's jurisdiction. Even if Labor finds administrative efficiency in handling claims for both forms of benefits in one unified petition with one unified investigation, administrative convenience does not create an express statutory waiver for jurisdiction.

For the aforementioned reasons, the Court of International Trade did not possess jurisdiction to consider Labor's determination on secondarily-affected worker benefit eligibility. As for primarily-affected worker benefits, the trial court specifically confirmed that the employees disclaimed any intent to seek primary certification. Because the primarily-affected worker benefit claim was no longer a part of the case when the trial court issued its *Order*, the trial court did not have any jurisdiction over any part of the case.

IV.

In a final note, the Court of International Trade, under *28 U.S.C. § 2643(c)(2)*, has no authority to "grant an injunction or issue a writ of mandamus in any civil action commenced to review a final determination of the Secretary of Labor." Here, the trial court's *Order* directed Labor to take specific steps to notify the employees, explain the benefits to the employees, and report back with status updates. Further, the trial court apparently extended its *Order* to reach federal government agencies and resources beyond Labor by directing utilization of all available "government resources" to locate and provide notice to affected employees. *See Order*, slip op. at 2. However, given the lack of jurisdiction in the Court of International Trade over this case, this court need not reach the question of whether there is any basis upon which the *Order* of the Court directed to the Secretary could possibly be sustained.

V.

For the reasons stated, this court concludes that the Court of International Trade lacks jurisdiction to review Labor's determinations with respect to secondarily-affected worker benefit eligibility. The *Order* of the trial court is hereby vacated, and the case is remanded with instructions to dismiss for lack of jurisdiction.

COSTS

Each party shall bear its own costs.

VACATED and REMANDED

IX. INTERNATIONAL TRADE

2. Business & Finance

G. Sanctions, Attachment, & Seizure of Gov't and Private Assets*

* Cases are indexed under this subject. The full text of these cases is published in the **volume**-page indicated.

ALA KIAIE
v.
ISLAMIC REPUBLIC OF IRAN

Civil Action No. 01-1501 (D.D.C. 2006)
Decided December 29, 2006

MEMORANDUM OPINION

Plaintiffs have filed an Objection to the Report & Recommendation issued by Magistrate Judge Deborah Robinson in this case. Pursuant to 28 U.S.C. § 636(b)(3) and LCvR 72.3(c), the Court reviews the Report & Recommendation *de novo*. Upon consideration of the Objection, the Report & Recommendation, the applicable case law, and the entire record herein, the Court concludes that the Objection will be overruled, and the Report & Recommendation will be adopted. Since Magistrate Judge Robinson concluded that no liability had been established and that, therefore, no damages should be awarded, this case will be dismissed.

Plaintiffs are members of the Kiaie family and the Tavakoli family, who were shareholders in two Iranian corporations: the West Industrial Group ("WIG") and the Western Publishing and Printing Company ("WPPC"). The Defendant, the Islamic Republic of Iran, was properly served and never made any appearance in the case. Default was entered against the Defendant on August 22, 2002. On February 13, 2004, the case was referred to Magistrate Judge Robinson for issuance of a Report & Recommendation as to Defendant's liability and damages. On March 25, 2004, Magistrate Judge Robinson bifurcated liability and damages, and on February 11, 2005, issued her Report & Recommendation. On February 23, 2005, Plaintiffs filed a timely Objection.

The two companies, WIG and WPPC, in which the various Plaintiffs owned various amounts of stock, were seized by the Islamic Republic of Iran during Iran's 1979 Islamic Revolution. Plaintiffs sought compensation for the seizure of their property and the losses they suffered. In the early 1980s, Plaintiffs filed two claims with the Iranian-United States Claims Tribunal ("Tribunal"). Those claims were brought on behalf of members of the two different families and sought compensation for the confiscation of WIG and its subsidiaries. In 1996, the Tribunal issued a ruling concluding that none of the Kiaie Plaintiffs were entitled to relief. In 1997, the Tribunal issued a ruling concluding that one member of the Tavakoli family was entitled to compensation, and awarded her approximately $375,952, plus interest and costs. That award has been paid in full.

Plaintiff Ala Kiaie, who is representing all the Plaintiffs, makes two requests in this litigation: first, that the Court "accept" the award of compensation made by the Tribunal as accurate and, second, that the Court assist Plaintiffs in their efforts to collect their award. Magistrate Judge Robinson concluded that there was no legal authority to grant either of these two requests.

The lead Plaintiff, Mr. Kiaie, is proceeding *pro se*, and the Court gives full consideration to that fact. Mr. Kiaie has submitted a number of different statements of position in this case, all of which the Court has carefully read. Although he is not a lawyer, he is clearly a highly intelligent person, who is very well educated, and has a good command of the English language. Moreover, he has been persistent in his efforts to seek compensation for members of his family and of the Tavakoli family. In light of his demonstrated ability to express himself in the English language and his familiarity with the legal and factual issues in this case, the Court must accept his submissions and arguments as he has presented and phrased them.

There is no dispute that in 1981, the United States entered into the Algiers Accords, in order to resolve a diplomatic crisis which had arisen because Iran seized the American embassy in Tehran and held a number of Americans as hostages. As part of the resolution of that crisis, the United States and Iran entered into the Algiers Accords which provided for an international arbitral tribunal known as the Iranian-United States Claims Tribunal. The Tribunal was located in The Hague and was designated to hear claims brought by Americans against the Government of Iran and vice versa. In exchange, the United States undertook to terminate legal proceedings in American courts brought by Americans against Iran and, most significantly, to unblock more than $1 billion of Iranian assets in the United States. United States v. Sperry Corp., 493 U.S. 52, 55-56 (1999). The Algiers Accords specify that the decisions of the Tribunal shall "operate as a final resolution and discharge of the claims for all purposes." Exec. Order #12294, 46 Fed. Reg. 14111 (1981), Sec. 4.

In this case, the Tribunal issued two decisions, as noted above and as described in some detail in Magistrate Judge Robinson's Report & Recommendation at p. 3, that disposed of all claims presented by the Plaintiffs. Moreover, as the Plaintiffs concede, the one Plaintiff who was awarded compensation by the Tribunal has been paid in full.

In the Objection to the Report & Recommendation, Plaintiffs argue, at p. 1, that the Magistrate Judge has "misapprehended" their arguments. They claim that they are not seeking to review, overturn, or overrule any decision of the Tribunal, but merely request that this Court "acknowledge, adopt, and enforce the Tribunal determinations." Id. at 2. Plaintiffs also claim that they "are not requesting that the Court assist in collection of the money award[ed] by the Tribunal," because it has been collected in full.

However, their earlier submissions are very much to the contrary. Consequently, it is very difficult to understand what Plaintiffs are really claiming. They have stated repeatedly, in their Memorandum of June 28, 2004, in their Supplemental Memorandum of June 30, 2004, and at the status conference before Magistrate Judge Robinson on March 25, 2004, that in addition to seeking "acceptance" of the Tribunal's rulings, they also seek "adjudication" of issues on which they did not prevail before the Tribunal. Finally, they have clearly requested in prior representations, that they seek help in enforcing the Tribunal's awards, even though they deny this in their Objection at p.2 to the Report & Recommendation.

The Magistrate Judge is correct, as a matter of law, that "no statute, treaty, or law gives this Court power to review a decision of the Iranian-United States Claims Tribunal, or to aid in the collection of an award made by the Tribunal." Report & Recommendation, at 6. See also Iran Aircraft Industry v. Avco Corp., 98 F.2d 141, 144-45 (2d Cir. 1992) ("Avco"). Indeed, Plaintiffs concede that "this Court has no authority to overturn or overrule" the Tribunal. Objection at p. 2. Moreover, Avco squarely rejected the argument that the Accords create any mechanism for direct enforcement of Tribunal awards.

Given that this Court has no authority to review decisions of the Tribunal denying relief to the Kiaie family Plaintiffs, and that there is nothing left to enforce in the Tribunal's two decisions relating to this case because the Tavakoli family Plaintiff has received the compensation she was awarded, it is clear that no liability can be established against the Defendant.[1] For these reasons, the Court concludes that the Objection to the Report & Recommendation of Magistrate Judge Robinson must be overruled, and the Report & Recommendation will be adopted.

---

1 To the extent that Plaintiffs are asking this Court to rule on the merits as to the claims of Ala Kiaie, Jacqueline Kiaie, Jubin Kiaie, Anthony Tavakoli and David Tavakoli, their position must be rejected because "the Tribunal was vested with exclusive jurisdiction over claims by nationals of the United States against Iran, claims by nationals of Iran against the United States, and counterclaims arising from the same transactions." Avco, 980 F.2d at 143.

IX. INTERNATIONAL TRADE

2. Business & Finance

H. Travel Bans*

* Cases are indexed under this subject. The full text of these cases is published in the **volume**-page indicated.

IX. INTERNATIONAL TRADE

2. Business & Finance

I. IEEPA

UNITED STATES OF AMERICA
v.
RAFIL DHAFIR

461 F.3d 211 (2d Cir. 2006)
Decided August 24, 2006

STEVEN WARD WILLIAMS, Smith, Sovik, Kendrick & Sugnet, P.C., Syracuse, New York, for Defendant-Appellant.

MICHAEL C. OLMSTED, Assistant United States Attorney (Glenn T. Suddaby, United States Attorney for the Northern District of New York; Brenda K. Sannes, Stephen C. Green, Assistant United States Attorneys, on the brief), Syracuse, New York, for Appellee.

Before: JACOBS, LEVAL, Circuit Judges, RAKOFF, District Judge.*

* The Honorable Jed S. Rakoff, District Judge, United States District Court for the Southern District of New York, sitting by designation.

OPINION

DENNIS JACOBS, *Circuit Judge*:

The sole issue on this appeal is whether the International Emergency Economic Powers Act ("IEEPA") constitutes an appropriate delegation of congressional authority to the executive. The IEEPA authorizes the President to regulate financial transactions with foreign countries or nationals in a time of security crisis, and prescribes criminal penalties for violations of the president's regulations. Defendant-Appellant Osameh Al Wahaidy pled guilty to transferring money into Iraq on three specific occasions in 1999 and 2000, in violation of Executive Orders and regulations issued pursuant to the IEEPA, but preserved his right to bring a constitutional challenge to the statute. Al Wahaidy now appeals from the July 3, 2003 Memorandum Decision and Order of the United States District Court for the Northern District of New York (Mordue, J.) denying his motion to dismiss the indictment on the ground that the IEEPA improperly delegates Congress' authority to define criminal offenses. We affirm.

BACKGROUND

A. The IEEPA

The IEEPA, enacted in 1977 and codified at 50 U.S.C. § 1701 et seq., confers on the President certain powers to respond to any threat to the national security, foreign policy or economy of the United States that is "unusual and extraordinary" and that "has its source in whole or substantial part outside the United States." 50 U.S.C. § 1701(a). The President is granted the power to "investigate, regulate, or prohibit" various commercial activities, including: [i] "any transactions in foreign exchange," [ii] "transfers of credit or payments between, by, through, or to any banking institution, to the extent that such transfers or payments involve any interest of any foreign country or a national thereof," and [iii] "the importing or exporting of currency or securities, by any person, or with respect to any property, subject to the jurisdiction of the United States . . . ." 50 U.S.C. § 1702(a)(1)(A). The President is also authorized to block transactions involving property "in which any foreign country or a national thereof has any interest by any person, or with respect to any property, subject to the jurisdiction of the United States . . . ." 50 U.S.C. § 1702(a)(1)(B). These powers may be exercised only if and when the President declares a national emergency with respect to the threat, 50 U.S.C. § 1701(a), in which event "[t]he President may issue such regulations, including regulations prescribing definitions, as may be necessary for the exercise of the authorities granted by this title." 50 U.S.C. § 1704. The violation of an Executive Order or regulation promulgated pursuant to the IEEPA is punishable by a fine of not more than $ 50,000 and imprisonment for not more than twenty years. *See* 50 U.S.C. § 1705(b).[1] The IEEPA provides, however, that no person shall be held liable for acts or omissions conducted "in good faith." 50 U.S.C. § 1702(a)(3).

The IEEPA reserves a continuing role for Congress. Thus, the IEEPA provides that "[t]he President, in every possible instance, shall consult with the Congress before exercising any of the authorities granted," that he "shall consult regularly with the Congress so long as such authorities are exercised," and that he shall report periodically concerning any actions taken in the exercise of the delegated authority. 50 U.S.C. § 1703. Congress can terminate the President's declaration of emergency "by concurrent resolution pursuant to section 202 of the National Emergencies Act [50 USCS § 1622]." 50 U.S.C. § 1706(b) (emendation in original).

B. The Iraqi Sanctions Executive Orders & Regulations

Following the Iraqi invasion of Kuwait in August, 1990, President George H.W. Bush issued four emergency Executive Orders declaring a national emergency, and prohibiting trade, transportation and financial transactions with Iraq and Kuwait. *See* Exec. Order No. 12722, 55 Fed. Reg. 31803 (August 2, 1990); Exec.

---

1 Section 1706 was amended in 2006 to provide for a maximum sentence of 20 years. At the time Al Wahaidy was sentenced the maximum sentence was 10 years.

Order No. 12723, 55 Fed. Reg. 31805 (August 2, 1990); Exec. Order No. 12724, 55 Fed. Reg. 33089 (August 9, 1990); and Exec. Order No. 12725, 55 Fed. Reg. 33091 (August 9, 1990). Executive Orders 12722 and 12724 blocked the Iraqi government's property and interests in property in the United States and prohibited transactions with entities in Iraq or controlled by the Iraq government. Executive Orders 12723 and 12725 correspondingly blocked the property of the Kuwaiti government and prohibited various transactions with entities in Kuwait or controlled by the Kuwaiti government.

To implement the Executive Orders, the Office of Foreign Assets Control ("OFAC") promulgated regulations providing (in relevant part) that "no U.S. person may commit or transfer, directly or indirectly, funds or other financial or economic resources to the Government of Iraq or any person in Iraq." 31 C.F.R. § 575.210; *see also* 31 C.F.R. § 575.211 (prohibiting the evasion or avoidance of the regulations and any attempt to violate the prohibitions).

The day the President signed Executive Order 12722 declaring a national emergency, the Senate passed a resolution commending the measures taken and urging the President to act immediately to enforce the IEEPA and to impose sanctions against Iraq. *See* S. Res. 318, 101st Cong. (1990). Several days later, the House passed its version of the Sanctions Against Iraq Act of 1990, authorizing economic sanctions under the authority of the IEEPA. H.R. 5431, 101st Cong. (2d Sess. 1990). In November 1990, Congress passed "The Iraqi Sanctions Act", declaring that Congress "supports the actions that have been taken by the President . . . [and] supports the imposition and enforcement of multilateral sanctions against Iraq," and requiring that the President "continue to impose the trade embargo and other economic sanctions with respect to Iraq and Kuwait . . ., pursuant to Executive Orders Numbered 12724 and 12725 (August 9, 1990) and, to the extent they are still in effect, Executive Orders Numbered 12722 and 12723 (August 2, 1990)." Iraqi Sanctions Act, Pub. L. 101-513 § 586, 104 Stat. 1979, 2047-48 (1990).

C. Al Wahaidy's Plea and Conviction

On February 19, 2003, Al Wahaidy was charged in an Indictment, which was superseded on April 23, 2003, by an Information charging three specific instances of "willfully attempt[ing] to violate and evade Executive Order Numbers 12722 and 12724 and the regulations issued under those Executive Orders and under the [IEEPA]" by transferring "funds and other economic resources to one or more persons" in Iraq. The Information alleged that the violations occurred on October 25, 1999, November 9, 1999, and February 23, 2000, and that they involved a total amount of $ 100,000.[2] On April 4, 2003, Al Wahaidy moved to dismiss the charges

2 Al Wahaidy admitted that he and others attempted to transfer funds through Jordan to persons in Iraq, in violation of 31 C.F.R., Subpart B, § 575.210, which is punishable as a violation of IEEPA pursuant to 50 U.S.C. § 1705. Al Wahaidy said he believed the funds were being used to help needy people in Iraq; but the funds were actually used by Iraqi "agents" for a series of undisclosed projects.

on the ground that the IEEPA unconstitutionally delegated legislative authority to the executive branch. On April 23, 2003, Al Wahaidy pled guilty to the charges in the Information, but he preserved his right to challenge the statute's constitutionality. On July 3, 2003, the district court denied Al Wahaidy's motion to dismiss the indictment and upheld the constitutionality of the IEEPA. On August 12, 2005, Al Wahaidy was sentenced to two years probation, 100 hours of community service, and a $ 5000 fine. This appeal ensued.

DISCUSSION

Al Wahaidy argues [i] that the *IEEPA* is an improper delegation to the President of the Congressional authority to create criminal offenses, and [ii] that, in any event, the delegation fails on its own terms because the government has not shown that the executive has complied with the statutory reporting requirements.

A. Constitutionality of the IEEPA

We review the constitutionality of a federal statute *de novo*. *United States v. Awadallah, 349 F.3d 42, 51 (2d Cir. 2003)*.

The Constitution vests in Congress the legislative power to define criminal conduct; but "our jurisprudence" has reached a "practical understanding that . . . Congress simply cannot do its job absent an ability to delegate power under broad general directives." *Mistretta v. United States, 488 U.S. 361, 372, 109 S. Ct. 647, 102 L. Ed. 2d 714 (1989)*. Delegations of congressional authority are upheld "[s]o long as Congress 'shall lay down by legislative act an intelligible principle to which the person or body authorized to [exercise the delegated authority] is directed to conform.'" *Id.* (emendation in original) (quoting *J.W. Hampton, Jr., & Co. v. United States, 276 U.S. 394, 406, 48 S. Ct. 348, 72 L. Ed. 624, Treas. Dec. 42706 (1928)*). Under that standard, impermissible delegation has been rarely found. Since the articulation of the "intelligible principle" test in *J.W. Hampton, Jr.*, the Supreme Court has struck down only two statutes as impermissible delegations. *See A.L.A. Schechter Poultry Corp. v. United States, 295 U.S. 495, 55 S. Ct. 837, 79 L. Ed. 1570 (1935)* (striking down delegation to industry associations comprised of private individuals to create legally binding codes of "fair competition"); *Panama Refining Co. v. Ryan, 293 U.S. 388, 55 S. Ct. 241, 79 L. Ed. 446 (1935)* (striking down blanket delegation to President to criminalize the interstate transport of petroleum). Neither instance involved foreign affairs, a sphere in which delegation is afforded even broader deference. *See Zemel v. Rusk, 381 U.S. 1, 17, 85 S. Ct. 1271, 14 L. Ed. 2d 179 (1965)* ("Congress—in giving the Executive authority over matters of foreign affairs—must of necessity paint with a brush broader than that it customarily wields in domestic areas."); *United States v. Curtiss-Wright Export Corp., 299 U.S. 304, 315-22, 57 S. Ct. 216, 81 L. Ed. 255 (1936)* (explaining why delegations in the foreign affairs context differ from those in the domestic context). Thus a delegation to the executive that may be improper if confined to internal affairs might "nevertheless be sustained on the ground that its exclusive aim is to afford a remedy for a hurtful condition within foreign territory." Curtiss-Wright, 299 U.S. at 315. This indulgence stems from the Constitution: "In this vast external realm, with its important, complicated, delicate and manifold problems, the President alone has the power to speak or listen as a representative of the nation." *Id. at 319*; *see also* Zemel, 381 U.S. at 17.

The Supreme Court has upheld Congressional delegation to the executive—under the IEEPA—to nullify certain attachments and transfers of assets. *See Dames & Moore v. Regan, 453 U.S. 654, 675, 101 S. Ct. 2972, 69 L. Ed. 2d 918 (1981)*; *Regan v. Wald, 468 U.S. 222, 232-33, 104 S. Ct. 3026, 82 L. Ed. 2d 171 (1984)* (holding that regulations promulgated pursuant to the IEEPA and the Trading with the Enemy Act were constitutional); *see also Zemel, 381 U.S. 1, 85 S. Ct. 1271, 14 L. Ed. 2d 179* (upholding the Passport Act of 1926, which gave the Secretary of State the power to grant and issue passports without setting forth standards to guide the use of his discretion). Likewise, this court and our sister circuit courts have upheld such delegations. *See Sardino v. Federal Reserve Bank, 361 F.2d 106, 110 (2d Cir. 1966)* (upholding constitutionality of the Trading with the Enemy Act); *Freedom to Travel Campaign v. Newcomb, 82 F.3d 1431, 1437-38 (9th Cir. 1996)* (upholding constitutionality of Congress' delegation of authority to renew the Cuban embargo solely upon a determination that it is "in the national interest"); *see also United States v. Esfahani, 2006 U.S. Dist. LEXIS 1839, No. 05 Cr. 0255, 2006 WL 163025, at *11 (N.D. Ill. Jan. 17, 2006)* (upholding constitutionality of the IEEPA); *United States v. Anvari-Hamedani, 378 F. Supp. 2d 821 (N.D. Ohio 2005)* (upholding constitutionality of the IEEPA).

The Supreme Court has also upheld particular delegations of authority to define criminal offenses, although not yet in the context of the IEEPA. In *Curtiss-Wright Export Corp., 299 U.S. 304, 57 S. Ct. 216, 81 L. Ed. 255*, the Court upheld a Congressional resolution empowering the President to declare illegal the sale of arms to certain countries (specified by the President), without discussing any special considerations that may be implicated when the President is granted the power to define crimes. *See also United States v. Grimaud, 220 U.S. 506, 517, 31 S. Ct. 480, 55 L. Ed. 563 (1911)* ("[W]hen Congress had legislated and indicated its will, it could give to those who were to act under such general provisions 'power to fill up the details' by the establishment of administrative rules and regulations, the violation of which could be punished by fine or imprisonment fixed by Congress, or by penalties fixed by Congress, or measured by the injury done."). In *Touby v. United States, 500 U.S. 160, 111 S. Ct. 1752, 114 L. Ed. 2d 219 (1991)*, the Supreme Court upheld a delegation of power to the Attorney General to expedite the designation of a substance as "controlled" by bypassing (for a limited time) several of the requirements for permanent scheduling. The *Touby* Court weighed the petitioner's argument that "something more than an 'intelligible principle' is required when Congress authorizes another Branch to promulgate regulations that contemplate criminal sanctions," but declined to decide whether more specific guidance was required, because the statute passed muster even under a heightened standard:

> Our cases are not entirely clear as to whether more specific guidance is in fact required. We need not resolve the issue today. We conclude that § 201(h) passes muster even if greater congressional specificity is required in the criminal context.

Id. at 165-66 (internal citations omitted). The Court concluded the statute "meaningfully constrain[ed] the Attorney General's discretion to define criminal conduct," by requiring that the powers only be exercised when "necessary to avoid an imminent hazard to the public safety," by specifying what constitutes "an imminent hazard," and by requiring notice to and consideration of comments from the Secretary of Health and Human Services. Id. at 166-67 (quoting the statute at issue).

Even if a heightened standard should apply to delegations concerning criminal offenses, the IEEPA's delegation is subject to constraints similar to those found sufficient in *Tou.by*. *See United States v. Arch Trading Co., 987 F.2d 1087, 1093 (4th Cir. 1993)* (comparing IEEPA's provisions with the statute upheld in *Touby*). The IEEPA "meaningfully constrains the [President's] discretion," Touby, 500 U.S. at 166, by requiring that "[t]he authorities granted to the President . . . may only be exercised to deal with an unusual and extraordinary threat with respect to which a national emergency has been declared." 50 U.S.C. § 1701(b). And the authorities delegated are defined and limited. *See* 50 U.S.C. § 1702.

Al Wahaidy argues that *Touby* upheld a temporary power (to define what constitutes a controlled substance under criminal law), whereas the IEEPA gives the President the power "to define conduct as criminal for an unlimited time once a national emergency is declared." The IEEPA delegation is, however, subject to the President's periodic re-affirmation of necessity and is conditioned on reporting to Congress. *50 U.S.C. § 1703*. Moreover, Congress can terminate the President's declaration of emergency. *50 U.S.C. § 1706*.

Certain additional factors not present in *Touby* further weigh in favor of upholding the IEEPA's criminal provisions. Significantly, the IEEPA relates to foreign affairs—an area in which the President has greater discretion. *See Dames & Moore, 453 U.S. at 675*. Additionally, Congress endorsed the President's actions and enacted legislation codifying the sanctions. There is thus no question that "'the will of Congress has been obeyed.'" *Touby, 500 U.S. at 168* (quoting *Skinner v. Mid-America Pipeline Co., 490 U.S. 212, 218, 109 S. Ct. 1726, 104 L. Ed. 2d 250 (1989)*).

B. The President's Compliance with the IEEPA[3]

Al Wahaidy argues in any event that the constitutionality of the delegation depends upon a showing by the government that the President has complied with the statu-

---

3 At oral argument and in subsequent briefing, we learned that *Congress* may have failed to comply with its oversight responsibilities. Specifically, the House of Representatives may not have satisfied its obligation under the National Emergencies Act to meet "each six-month period []after [the declaration of a national emergency] . . . to consider a vote on a joint resolu-

tory reporting requirements imposed upon his exercise of power under the IEEPA.[4] According to Al Wahaidy, only one of the statutorily-required six-month periodic reports was proffered to the district court, and the government thereby failed to sustain its burden of proof. This argument rests on two defective premises.

First, case law does not support the idea that the government bears the burden of proving its compliance with a statute in order to establish the statute's constitutionality. Al Wahaidy cites *dicta* in *Panama Refining Co. v. Ryan, 293 U.S. 388, 55 S. Ct. 241, 79 L. Ed. 446 (1935)*, an opinion that invalidated Congress' delegation to the President to pass a law prohibiting the interstate transport of petroleum products produced in excess of state quotas. 293 U.S. at 414-15. The Supreme Court explained that Congress' delegation failed to "declare[] a policy with respect to that subject[,] . . . [to] set-up a standard for the President's action[,] . . . [or to require] any finding by the President in the exercise of the authority to enact the prohibition." Id. at 415. The Supreme Court further added in *dicta*, "if . . . it were possible to derive a statement of prerequisites to the President's action . . ., it would still be necessary for the President to comply with those conditions and to show that compliance as the ground of his prohibition." Id. at 431. That *dicta* notwithstanding, we are aware of no court that has placed on the government the burden to prove compliance with a statute's requirements in order to defeat a claim that the statute is unconstitutional. *See Heller v. Doe, 509 U.S. 312, 320, 113 S. Ct. 2637, 125 L.*

---

tion to determine whether that emergency shall be terminated." 50 U.S.C. § 1622(b). Whether the House of Representatives' possible inaction affects the validity of the Iraqi sanctions regulations raises complicated and sensitive issues concerning separation of powers. We decline to consider this issue because it was not raised by the defendant or considered by the district court, and the record before us is incomplete.

4 50 U.S.C. § 1703 provides, in part:

> (b) Report to Congress upon exercise of Presidential authorities. Whenever the President exercises any of the authorities granted by this chapter [50 USCS §§ 1701 et seq.], he shall immediately transmit to the Congress a report specifying—
>
> (1) the circumstances which necessitate such exercise of authority;
>
> (2) why the President believes those circumstances constitute an unusual and extraordinary threat, which has its source in whole or substantial part outside the United States, to the national security, foreign policy, or economy of the United States;
>
> (3) the authorities to be exercised and the actions to be taken in the exercise of those authorities to deal with those circumstances;
>
> (4) why the President believes such actions are necessary to deal with those circumstances; and
>
> (5) any foreign countries with respect to which such actions are to be taken and why such actions are to be taken with respect to those countries.
>
> (c) Periodic follow-up reports. At least once during each succeeding six-month period after transmitting a report pursuant to subsection (b) of this section with respect to an exercise of authorities under this chapter [50 USCS §§ 1701 et seq.], the President shall report to the Congress with respect to the actions taken, since the last such report, in the exercise of such authorities, and with respect to any changes which have occurred concerning any information previously furnished pursuant to paragraphs (1) through (5) of subsection (b) . . . .

Ed. 2d 257 (1993) ("'[T]he burden is on the one attacking the legislative arrangement to negative every conceivable basis which might support it . . . .'") (quoting *Lehnhausen v. Lake Shore Auto Parts Co., 410 U.S. 356, 364, 93 S. Ct. 1001, 35 L. Ed. 2d 351 (1973)*); *Usery v. Turner Elkhorn Mining Co., 428 U.S. 1, 15, 96 S. Ct. 2882, 49 L. Ed. 2d 752 (1976)* ("It is by now well established that legislative Acts adjusting the burdens and benefits of economic life come to the Court with a presumption of constitutionality, and that the burden is on one complaining of a due process violation to establish that the legislature has acted in an arbitrary and irrational way."). Second, regardless of who bears the burden of proving compliance with the IEEPA, the present record is not limited to a single report. The government's memorandum in opposition to Al Wahaidy's motion stated that the President had complied with the IEEPA's reporting requirements, drew the court's attention to its website where each of the reports may be found, and included an example of the report. This showing was sufficient; the district court was satisfied, and it does not appear that Al Wahaidy contested the point in the district court. *Cf. Pani v. Empire Blue Cross Blue Shield, 152 F.3d 67, 75 (2d Cir. 1998)* ("It is well established that a district court may rely on matters of public record in deciding a motion to dismiss under Rule 12(b)(6), including case law and statutes.").

Public records reflect that each President has fulfilled his obligations under the IEEPA for the period (1990-2003) in which the relevant Executive Orders and regulations were in place. With respect to the Iraqi sanctions at issue here, President George H.W. Bush coordinated with Congress before and when he invoked his authority under IEEPA, and sent a "Message to Congress" on August 3, 1990 reporting his Executive Order (issued the day before) declaring a national emergency; and each President from 1990 until 2003 sent a report to Congress every six months detailing the sanctions actions. Finally, pursuant to the National Emergencies Act, 50 U.S.C. § 1622, each President has annually reported to Congress in order to continue the national emergency with respect to Iraq.

CONCLUSION

For the foregoing reasons, we affirm the judgment.

IX. INTERNATIONAL TRADE

2. Business & Finance

J. Property Disputes*

* Cases are indexed under this subject. The full text of these cases is published in the **volume**-page indicated.

IX. INTERNATIONAL TRADE

2. Business & Finance

K. Contracts*

* Cases are indexed under this subject. The full text of these cases is published in the **volume**-page indicated.

MICHEL ACEVEDO-REINOSO
v.
IBERIA LINEAS AEREAS DE ESPANA S.A.

449 F.3d 7 (1st Cir. 2006)
Decided May 23, 2006

Before Torruella, Lipez, and Howard, Circuit Judges.

OPINION

LIPEZ, *Circuit Judge*. This case requires us to decide whether a passenger's state tort claim against an international air carrier was preempted by the Warsaw Convention[1] and therefore properly dismissed by the district court. For the reasons set forth below, we vacate the district court's judgment granting the motion to dismiss and remand for further proceedings consistent with this opinion.

I.

The following facts are drawn from the complaint. Michel Acevedo-Reinoso is a citizen of Cuba with legal residence in the United States. At the time of this action, Acevedo-Reinoso resided in Puerto Rico. In October 2002, Acevedo-Reinoso, a banking executive, was invited to participate in an annual convention hosted by the Mortgage Loan Officers Association ("Association") in Madrid, Spain. The Association contracted with a travel agency, The Travel Place, to coordinate all travel arrangements for attendees to the convention. The Travel Place assured Acevedo-Reinoso that he would not require a visa, and instead need only show his Cuban passport and U.S. resident alien card upon entry to Spain. On November 13, 2002, Acevedo-Reinoso and his partner, Maria Pacheco-Gonzalez, a U.S. citizen (collectively, "Plaintiffs"), arrived at the Iberia Lineas Aereas Espanolas, S.A. ("Iberia") airline counter in Puerto Rico to check in. The Iberia agent informed Acevedo-Reinoso and Pacheco-Gonzalez that all immigration documents were in place and gave them their tickets and boarding passes.

---

1 The Convention for the Unification of Certain Rules Relating to International Transportation by Air, Oct. 12, 1929, 49 Stat. 3000, 3014, T.S. 876 (1934), note following *49 U.S.C. § 40105* [hereinafter "Warsaw Convention" or "Convention"].

Upon arriving in Spain on November 14, 2002, a Spanish immigration officer requested passports from all passengers. When Acevedo-Reinoso showed his Cuban passport, the Spanish government ordered his immediate detention. Acevedo-Reinoso was questioned, represented by counsel appointed by the Spanish government, and detained with other allegedly illegal immigrants in a closed room in the airport. Meanwhile, Pacheco-Gonzalez suffered great anguish at seeing her partner detained in front of his peers in the banking industry, mocked by Spanish immigration officers, and humiliated. Acevedo-Reinoso's appointed counsel provided him with several documents for his review. At the behest of a Spanish officer who told him the documents were for his own benefit, Acevedo-Reinoso signed the documents without reading them, and was subsequently told that he would be deported to his country of origin—Cuba. Acevedo-Reinoso suffered great anguish thinking about the punishment he would face at the hands of Cuban authorities upon returning to a country he was forced to leave many years ago, and the suffering—financial and otherwise—of his partner and two children who would be forced to live without him in Puerto Rico.

Later that evening, Acevedo-Reinoso was taken to another room where he was strip-searched and humiliated by a female Spanish officer. He was then taken to a detention room with hundreds of allegedly illegal immigrants, where he was served his first meal of the day and was ordered to pass the night in a cold room that included a row of bunk beds without sheets or blankets. During this time, Acevedo-Reinoso observed Spanish officers beating a young adolescent from Ecuador who stood up to visit the restroom. The following morning, after speaking with Pacheco-Gonzalez about a letter she had obtained from the General Manager of the hotel in Spain assuming responsibility for him during his stay, Acevedo-Reinoso inquired whether he could be sent back to Puerto Rico. Spanish officers declined to accept this proposition. Pacheco-Gonzalez was extremely nervous about her partner's future and the well-being of herself and her children. The following day, Acevedo-Reinoso was escorted by several Spanish guards to an Iberia airplane bound for San Juan, Puerto Rico, detained until airline crew boarded the airplane, and thereafter released.

As a result of the humiliation, emotional distress, and mental anguish they experienced, Plaintiffs sued Iberia, a foreign entity, in federal court, alleging negligence under Puerto Rico law.[2] On February 25, 2003, Iberia brought a motion to dismiss for failure to join as indispensable parties The Travel Company and its owner. That motion was denied. Iberia then filed its answer to Plaintiffs' complaint. After discovery and the entry of a pretrial order, Iberia filed a second motion to dismiss, based on Plaintiffs' failure to state a claim under the Convention, and, in the alternative, under Puerto Rico law. The district court dismissed Plaintiffs' action for failure to state a claim under the Convention. Acevedo-Reinoso appealed.[3]

---

2 Plaintiffs also sued The Travel Place and its owner in the Superior Court of Puerto Rico.

3 Pacheco-Gonzalez did not join this appeal.

II.

We review the district court's grant of Iberia's motion to dismiss de novo. *See SFW Arecibo, Ltd. v. Rodriguez, 415 F.3d 135, 138 (1st Cir. 2005)*. To that end, we accept as true the well-pleaded factual allegations of the complaint, drawing all reasonable inferences in favor of the non-movant, Acevedo-Reinoso. *See* id. at 138-39. "Our goal is to determine whether the complaint, so read, alleges facts sufficient to make out a cognizable claim. In so doing, we are free to affirm on any basis supported by the record." *Carroll v. Xerox Corp., 294 F.3d 231, 241 (1st Cir. 2002)* (internal citations and quotation marks omitted).

A. Applicability of the Warsaw Convention

1. The Warsaw Convention

The Convention, as amended by the Montreal Agreement,[4] governs the liability of international air carriers for "passenger injuries occurring 'on board the aircraft or in the course of any of the operations of embarking or disembarking.'"[5] El Al Israel Airlines, 525 U.S. at 172 (quoting Convention art. 17); *see Langadinos v. American Airlines, Inc., 199 F.3d 68, 70 (1st Cir. 2000)*. The Convention is preemptive: a carrier is not subject to liability under local law for passenger injuries "covered by" the Convention, that is, "all personal injury cases stemming from occurrences on board an aircraft or in embarking or disembarking." El Al Israel Airlines, 525 U.S. at 168 (adopting Government's construction of Convention); *see also* Convention art. 24 (stating that in personal injury cases "covered by" the Convention, "any action for damages, however founded, can only be brought subject to the conditions and limits set out in this convention"[6]). The corollary is also true:

---

4 While "[t]he United States initially adhered to the Warsaw Convention on October 29, 1934," *McCarthy v. Northwest Airlines, Inc., 56 F.3d 313, 316 n.2 (1st Cir. 1995)*, all references to the Convention herein are to that document as modified by Montreal Protocol No. 4. Montreal Protocol No. 4 to Amend the Convention for the Unification of Certain Rules Relating to International Carriage by Air, Signed at Warsaw on Oct. 12, 1929, as amended by the Protocol Done at the Hague on Sept. 8, 1955 [hereinafter Protocol No. 4] reprinted in S. Exec. Rep. No. 105-20, pp. 21-32 (1998). This protocol, "ratified by the Senate on September 28, 1998, amends Article 24 [of the Convention] to read, in relevant part: 'In the carriage of passengers and baggage, any action for damages, however founded, can only be brought subject to the conditions and limits set out in this Convention . . . .'" *El Al Israel Airlines, Ltd. v. Tsui Yuan Tseng, 525 U.S. 155, 174, 119 S. Ct. 662, 142 L. Ed. 2d 576 (1999)* (quoting Convention art. 24, as amended by Montreal Protocol No. 4).

5 Article 17 of the Convention states, in relevant part, that [t]he carrier shall be liable for damage sustained in the event of the death or wounding of a passenger or any other bodily injury suffered by a passenger, if the accident which caused the damage so sustained took place on board the aircraft or in the course of any of the operations of embarking or disembarking.

6 Article 24 of the Convention states that "[i]n the cases covered by article 17 [i.e., personal injury cases]," Convention art. 24(2), "any action for damages, however founded, can only be brought subject to the conditions and limits set out in this convention," Convention art. 24(1).

> the Convention's preemptive effect on local law extends no further than the Convention's own substantive scope. A carrier, therefore, is indisputably subject to liability under local law for injuries arising outside of that scope: *e.g.*, for passenger injuries occurring before any of the operations of embarking or disembarking.

El Al Israel Airlines, 525 U.S. at 172 (internal citations and quotation marks omitted); *see also Commercial Union Ins. Co. v. Alitalia Airlines, S.p.A., 347 F.3d 448, 456 (2d Cir. 2003)* ("As a treaty adhered to by the United States, it is the supreme law of the land and trumps local law *when it applies*.") (emphasis added).

"Treaty interpretation," we have noted, "is a purely legal exercise." *McCarthy, 56 F.3d at 317* (interpreting meaning of "embarking" and "disembarking" under Convention). Therefore, the question [of] whether a passenger's injury was sustained "on board the aircraft or in the course of any of the operations of embarking or disembarking," Convention art. 17, "is a question of law to be decided by the court" based on the facts of each case, *Marotte v. American Airlines, Inc., 296 F.3d 1255, 1259 (11th Cir. 2002). See also Schmidkunz v. Scandinavian Airlines Sys., 628 F.2d 1205, 1207 (9th Cir. 1980)* (same). Since "[t]he terms 'embarking' and 'disembarking' are not specifically defined in the Convention," *Marotte, 296 F.3d at 1259*, and absent some direction from the Supreme Court, which has not yet had occasion to define them, we have found "(1) the passenger's activity at the time of injury, (2) his or her whereabouts when injured, and (3) the extent to which the carrier was exercising control . . . highly relevant in determining the applicability of [the Convention]." *McCarthy, 56 F.3d at 317.*

If the Convention applies (and local law is thereby preempted), the next question is whether the carrier is liable under the Convention. This inquiry involves a determination of whether there was an "accident," i.e., "an unexpected or unusual event or happening that is external to the passenger," *Air France v. Saks, 470 U.S. 392, 405, 105 S. Ct. 1338, 84 L. Ed. 2d 289 (1985)*; whether the passenger suffered a compensable injury, i.e., "death, physical injury, or physical manifestation of injury," *Eastern Airlines, Inc. v. Floyd, 499 U.S. 530, 552, 111 S. Ct. 1489, 113 L. Ed. 2d 569 (1991)*; and whether the accident was a proximate cause of the passenger's injury, *see Langadinos, 199 F.3d at 71.*

2. The District Court Proceeding

The district court held that Plaintiffs' Puerto Rico tort claim was preempted by the Convention because Plaintiffs failed to state a claim for liability under the Convention. According to the district court, "plaintiffs may not sue a carrier pursuant to state law if they are barred from recovering under the convention." The district court noted that Plaintiffs did not allege that "they suffered death, physical injury or physical manifestation of an injury"—one of the requirements for proving liability under the Convention.[7] Rather, Plaintiffs alleged only "humiliation, embar-

7 The district court noted that since Plaintiffs' claim failed to satisfy the injury requirement for liability under the Convention, the court did not need to decide whether Plaintiffs' claim satis-

rassment, and great anguish"—none of which is compensable under the Convention. Since Plaintiffs were barred from recovering under the Convention, the court held that their claim under Puerto Rico law was likewise barred.

3. Application of the Warsaw Convention

Echoing the district court, Iberia notes that since "[t]he Warsaw Convention's dispositions provide the exclusive source of an airline's liability in international flights claims," Acevedo-Reinoso's claim falls short because he does not allege any physical injury or an "accident." Acevedo-Reinoso, on the other hand, argues that the court erroneously assumed the Convention's applicability without resolving the threshold issue of whether his injuries were "sustained . . . on board the aircraft or in the course of any of the operations of embarking or disembarking."[8] Convention art. 17. According to Acevedo-Reinoso, the Convention does not apply—and his Puerto Rico tort claim is therefore not preempted—because he was not embarking or disembarking when he sustained his injuries. Rather, Acevedo-Reinoso argues, his injuries were sustained "in Spain in a detention jail and [in] . . . being deported back to Puerto Rico in front of all the members of the Association."

We agree with Acevedo-Reinoso that the district court erroneously conflated the applicability of the Convention with liability under the Convention. The Convention's applicability rests on a determination of whether the passenger's injury occurred "on board the aircraft or in the course of any of the operations of embarking or disembarking." Convention art. 17. If the Convention applies in a particular case, it is preemptive, and the trier of fact must then determine whether the carrier is liable under the Convention. *See* El Al Israel, 525 U.S. at 161 ("[R]ecovery for a personal injury on board [an] aircraft or in the course of any of the operations of embarking or disembarking, if not allowed under the Convention, is not available at all.") (internal citation and quotation marks omitted); *see* id. at 174 ("[I]n all questions relating to the carrier's liability, it is the provisions of the [C]onvention which apply and [] the passenger does not have access to any other remedies, whether under the common law or otherwise, which may be available within the particular country where he chooses to raise his action." (quoting *Sidhu* v. *British Airways plc*, [1997] 1 All E. R., 193 at 201, 207)). If the Convention is not applicable, it is not preemptive, and the passenger is free to pursue his or her claim under local law. Id. at 171-72 ("[T]he Convention addresses and concerns, only and exclusively, the airline's liability for passenger injuries occurring 'on board

---

fied the "accident" requirement for liability—i.e., whether Plaintiffs alleged that their injury resulted from an unexpected or unusual event or happening external to the passenger.

8 Acevedo-Reinoso also argues that the district court should never have reached the merits of Iberia's second motion to dismiss invoking the applicability of the Convention. According to Acevedo-Reinoso, Iberia waived the arguments raised in the second motion to dismiss by not asserting them earlier in the proceedings. We are unpersuaded by this argument but see no need to discuss it in any detail since we decide this appeal in Acevedo-Reinoso's favor on the merits.

the aircraft or in the course of any of the operations of embarking or disembarking.'" (quoting Convention art. 17)).

Here, the district court assumed the applicability of the Convention, stating that "pursuant to *El Al Israel*, plaintiffs' only basis of redress is the Convention's passenger liability provision." But *El Al Israel* does not support such an assumption. In that case, applicability of the Convention was not at issue because the parties explicitly agreed that "the episode-in-suit occurred in international transportation in the course of embarking." El Al Israel, 525 U.S. at 167. In this case, by contrast, the parties dispute whether Acevedo-Reinoso's damages were sustained "in the course of any of the operations of embarking or disembarking," and, thus, whether the Convention is applicable.

Acevedo-Reinoso argues that Iberia's failure to advise him at the ticket counter of the need for a visa to enter Spain preceded his boarding the plane, and that his subsequent arrest upon arrival in Spain came well after he disembarked from the plane. Iberia, on the other hand, contends that its alleged failure to warn Acevedo-Reinoso at the airport in Puerto Rico and his ensuing arrest in Spain took place during the process of embarking and disembarking, respectively. Because the district court did not address this dispute, there was never any determination that the Convention was applicable and therefore preemptive of Acevedo-Reinoso's claim. *See Marotte, 296 F.3d at 1260-61* (holding that the Convention preempted plaintiffs' state law claims where plaintiffs' injuries "occurred in the process of embarking, as contemplated by the Warsaw Convention"); *see also McCarthy, 56 F.3d at 317* (holding that plaintiff was not engaged in the course of "embarking" under the Convention, based on "(1) the passenger's activity at the time of injury, (2) his or her whereabouts when injured, and (3) the extent to which the carrier was exercising control at the moment of injury"). The district court therefore erred in dismissing Acevedo-Reinoso's claim under the Convention without first determining whether Acevedo-Reinoso's injury occurred on board the airplane or in the process of embarking or disembarking.

B. Liability Under Puerto Rico Law

Even if the Convention is not applicable and therefore not preemptive, Iberia asks us to affirm on a different basis, arguing that the motion to dismiss was properly granted because Acevedo-Reinoso does not state a claim under Puerto Rico law.

1. Contract Claim

Iberia contends that while Acevedo-Reinoso characterizes his claim as sounding only in tort, his claim also sounds in contract, based on the allegation in the complaint that Iberia "breached its contract to travel with Acevedo."[9] Iberia further

9 According to Iberia, "[t]he well-pleaded allegations []form a basic contract: Acevedo would pay a specific monetary amount to Iberia, in exchange for safe transportation to Madrid, Spain."

argues that, as between these two sources of law, "in Puerto Rico contractual law [] control[s] the scenario depicted in the complaint. As a result, Acevedo cannot resort to general principles of tort law but must submit [himself] to the provisions applicable to contracts." Furthermore, because "the parties did not contract for Iberia to assume the duty of verifying that Acevedo's papers were in order for entering Spain, a task that was Acevedo's personal obligation to comply with," Iberia argues that Acevedo-Reinoso's claim fails to state a claim for breach of contract under Article 1054 of the Civil Code of Puerto Rico, P.R. Laws Ann., Tit. 31, § 3018.[10]

Aside from language in the complaint briefly alluding to a contractual claim, Acevedo-Reinoso nowhere argues that Iberia breached a contract. On the contrary, Acevedo-Reinoso asserts that his claim "is without a doubt one in tort," and states in the complaint that his state law claims are "based on Article 1802 of the Civil Code of Puerto Rico"—the Puerto Rico statute governing tort claims, P.R. Laws Ann., Tit. 31, § 5141.[11] Nevertheless, even if we assume that Acevedo-Reinoso's claim sounds in both tort and contract, it does not follow that Puerto Rico contract law provides the remedy. In fact, the opposite is true: where the event that caused the damage results from the breach of both a contractual obligation as well as a noncontractual duty not to cause harm to another, Puerto Rico law holds that an action for damages for breach of contract does not lie. According to the Puerto Rico Supreme Court:

> an action for damages for breach of contract [Article 1054] only lies when the damage suffered *exclusively* arises as a consequence of the breach of an obligation specifically agreed upon, which damage would not occur without the existence of a contract. However . . . a claim for noncontractual damages resulting from the breach of a contract lies if the act that caused the damage constitutes a breach of the general duty not to injure anyone and, at the same time, a breach of contract.*Ramos Lozada v. Orientalist Rattan Furniture Inc., 130 P.R. Dec. 712, 727*, 1992 P.R.-Eng. 755597 (P.R. 1992) (emphasis added). Iberia's argument regarding the application of Puerto Rico contract law is therefore unavailing.

2. Tort Claim

Iberia argues that even if Puerto Rico tort law applies to Acevedo-Reinoso's claim, his claim should still be dismissed. By contrast, Acevedo-Reinoso argues that the complaint adequately states a claim for negligence. We agree with Acevedo-Reinoso. Puerto Rico tort law "imposes responsibility for damages caused by neg-

10 Article 1054 states, in relevant part, that those who in any manner whatsoever act in contravention of the stipulations of [their contractual obligations], shall be subject to indemnify for the losses and damages caused thereby.P.R. Laws Ann., Tit. 31, § 3018; *see also* P.R. Laws Ann., Tit. 31, § 2994 ("Obligations arising from contracts have legal force between the contracting parties, and must be fulfilled in accordance with their stipulations.").

11 Article 1802 states in relevant part that [a] person who by an act or omission causes damage to another through fault or negligence shall be obliged to repair the damage so done.P.R. Laws Ann., Tit. 31, § 5141.

ligence or fault. The necessary elements to prevail in [such a] tort action are: (1) a negligent act or omission, (2) damages, and (3) a causal relationship between them." *Irvine v. Murad Skin Research Lab., 194 F.3d 313, 321-22 (1st Cir. 1999).* The complaint alleges facts addressing each of these elements, stating that Iberia's negligent acts or omissions—i.e., its "fail[ure] to advise [Acevedo-Reinoso] that he needed a visa in order to enter Spain"—caused Acevedo-Reinoso to be "detained by Spanish authorities in Spain, humiliated in front of his peers from the banking industry, and subjected to extensive mental anguish and sufferings."

Iberia's argument that an air carrier has no duty to advise passengers under Puerto Rico law is foreclosed by our decision in *Compagnie Nationale Air France v. Castano, 358 F.2d 203 (1st Cir. 1966).* In that case, three passengers and a relative sued an air carrier under Puerto Rico tort law for failing to advise them that they needed visas to enter Spain. We opined that the Puerto Rico court would . . . hold [that] where there was evidence that the defendant, as an inducement to plaintiffs to purchase passage, had held itself out as a tourist or travel agency, and had negligently failed to provide the information that plaintiffs had reasonably been led to expect, [] damages for negligence would include . . . proximate, though unforeseeable, injury of any sort.Id. at 209. Applying this reasoning to the facts of that case, we held that "the unforeseen suffering occasioned by defendant's failure to perform of the type here claimed can be compensated." *Id.* We noted, however, that "there was a substantial factual issue whether this damage was proximate, and whether the plaintiff or plaintiffs reasonably attempted to mitigate the damages." *Id.*

Here, Acevedo-Reinoso claims that he was injured by the failure of an air carrier to advise him that he needed a visa to enter Spain. The facts alleged by Acevedo-Reinoso in this case are nearly identical to those alleged by the passengers in Castano, and thus are sufficient to state a claim for the negligent failure to advise under Puerto Rico tort law.[12]

---

12 Iberia's attempts to distinguish this case from *Castano* are unavailing. While Castano did not discuss the applicability of the Convention, our determination that Acevedo-Reinoso states a claim under Puerto Rico tort law does not depend on the applicability of the Convention. In fact, Acevedo-Reinoso's tort claim has effect only to the extent that the Convention does *not* apply (and does not preempt the tort claim). In addition, while we vacated three of the verdicts in *Castano* (and dismissed the fourth) and remanded for a new trial, the lack of a final disposition in that case does not render our holding under Puerto Rico law any less binding. *See Room v. Caribe Hilton Hotel, 659 F.2d 5, 8 n.3 (1st Cir. 1981)* (relying on *Castano* for proposition that "[u]nder Puerto Rico law a plaintiff may recover damages for mental suffering"). Finally, while it may be that "Iberia was in no position to induce Acevedo to purchase passage" and did not hold itself out "as a tourist or travel agency," these issues await further factual development at summary judgment or trial. At this stage in the proceedings, for the reasons discussed above, Acevedo-Reinoso has alleged sufficient facts to overcome Iberia's motion to dismiss.

III.

In summary, we hold that the district court erred in granting Iberia's motion to dismiss based on the preemptive effect of the Convention, without first determining whether the Convention in fact applied to this case. On remand, the district court must determine whether Acevedo-Reinoso's injury occurred "in the course of any of the operations of embarking or disembarking." If the district court answers this question in the affirmative, the Convention will apply and will preempt Acevedo-Reinoso's Puerto Rico tort claim, thus limiting his claim to one that meets the requirements of the Convention. If, on the other hand, the district court answers this question in the negative, the Convention will have no application and this case will go forward on the elements of the tort claim set forth under Puerto Rico tort law. We ***vacate*** the district court's judgment granting Iberia's motion to dismiss and ***remand*** for further proceedings consistent with this opinion. Costs of appeal are awarded to appellant.

So ordered.

BERG CHILLING SYSTEMS, INC.
v.
HULL CORPORATION

435 F.3d 455 (3rd Cir. 2006)
Decided January 31, 2006

JOHN J. SOROKO (Argued), PATRICK J. LOFTUS, JAMES H. STEIGERWALD, Duane Morris LLP, Philadelphia, PA, Counsel for Appellant.

MICHAEL O. ADELMAN (Argued), MICHAEL P. DALY, KATHRYN E. BISORDI, Drinker Biddle & Reath LLP, Philadelphia, PA, Counsel for Appellees SP Industries, Inc.

Before: ALITO, AMBRO, and LOURIE,* Circuit Judges. AMBRO, Circuit Judge, Dissenting.

* Honorable Alan D. Lourie, Judge of the United States Court of Appeals for the Federal Circuit, sitting by designation.

OPINION

ALITO, Circuit Judge:

Berg Chilling Systems ("Berg") appeals a judgment entered by the United States District Court for the Eastern District of Pennsylvania. In the earlier proceedings, Berg sought a judgment rendering SP Industries ("SPI") liable for breach of contract, most recently based on the theory that SPI assumed liability when it purchased the assets of an entire division of the Hull Corporation ("Hull"), the original party to the contract. Because we find that SPI did not assume Hull's contractual liability to Berg under any of the exceptions to the traditional corporate rule of successor non-liability, we affirm.

I.

The tangled history of this case began in 1995, when Berg, a Canadian corporation, contracted with a Chinese company, Hua Du Meat Products Company ("Huadu"), to provide an industrial food freeze-drying system (the "Huadu Contract").

The system included several components that Berg planned to acquire from subcontractors and suppliers. One of these subcontractors was Hull, a Pennsylvania entity, with whom Berg eventually contracted to design, engineer, manufacture, test, and modify two freeze dryers. The purchase agreement between Berg and Hull (the "Purchase Agreement") stipulated that the two freeze dryers conform to particular "through-put" specifications, an industry term referring to the dryers' ability to process a certain volume of food at a high quality level within a 24-hour period.

All did not go according to plan. Initially, various logistical and timing issues plagued the manufacture and delivery of the freeze dryers before they were eventually installed at Huadu's facility in China in April 1997, and prepared for trial runs. Then, the freeze dryers failed a preliminary test administered by a Hull service technician, leading Huadu to send a list of concerns to Berg, which then forwarded the list to Hull. The Hull technician supervising the testing left China without running any performance tests. These tests would have held the freeze dryers to even more stringent standards than did the failed start-up test, and satisfaction of the performance tests was required by the Huadu Contract. Frustrated by Hull's apparent lack of cooperation, Huadu threatened to cancel the contract; Berg, in turn, threatened to sue Hull.

In an effort to salvage the project and persuade Huadu not to terminate the contract, representatives of Berg and Hull traveled to China in October 1997 to negotiate a compromise. The result was an agreement among Huadu, Berg, and Hull, modifying certain terms in the original contract (the "Modified Agreement"). The Modified Agreement provided, among other things, that Berg and Hull would arrange, at their own cost, modifications to the freeze dryers so they would meet the through-put requirements of the original Huadu contract. It also obligated Hull to perform technical work, assembly work, testing work, and production work on the freeze dryers according to engineering plans prepared by a Hull engineer. March 1998 was set as the date by which modifications would be completed and Huadu would grant final acceptance.

Meanwhile, in August 1997, Hull began negotiating a business deal with SPI, a Delaware corporation with its principal place of business in New Jersey. The transaction, structured as an asset purchase agreement, proposed to sell to SPI all assets, properties, rights, and businesses related to Hull's Food, Drug and Chemical ("FDC") Division. Hull's FDC Division included its freeze dryer production capacity, and consequently its rights and obligations under the Modified Agreement and the Purchase Agreement. At the time of contract negotiations, Hull had at least two other Divisions: the Emission Monitoring Systems Division and the Vacuum Components Division.

Hull and SPI entered into an asset purchase agreement dated August 25, 1997 ("Asset Purchase Agreement" or "APA"), which closed approximately one week after Huadu, Berg, and Hull signed the Modified Agreement. SPI's President and

CEO, Jack Partridge, indicated that SPI specifically intended to acquire Hull's FDC Division as an ongoing business.See *Berg Chilling Sys., Inc.v. Hull Corp., 2003 U.S. Dist. LEXIS 9936, No. 00-5075, 2003 WL 21362805, at *4 (E.D. Pa. June 10, 2003)* (hereinafter Berg I). SPI planned to combine the newly-acquired FDC Division with its own VirTis Division, which manufactured freeze dryers for research; indeed, a public release by SPI referenced a "merger agreement between the FDC division of Hull and the VirTis division of SP Industries." (A1042).

Several particular provisions of the APA are relevant to our discussion. The first is a list of purchase assets, detailed in Article 1.2, which included "all contracts and agreements, including, without limitation, sales orders and sales contracts." (A962-965). The second provision at issue is Section 7.8, entitled Product Warranties, which states that:

> Purchaser will, as appropriate, agree to repair (at the Real Estate or as necessary, at the location of the customer) or accept returns of products of the Business shipped by [Hull] on and prior to the Closing Date . . . which are defective or which fail to conform to the customer's order in accordance with the following provisions (but [SPI] does not hereby assume any liability to any third party claimant. . . .)(A986). Third, the APA's choice of law provision, set forth in Section 10.6, stated that the "agreement shall be governed and controlled as to validity, enforcement, interpretation, construction, effect and in all other respects by the internal laws of the State of New Jersey applicable to contracts made in that State." (A994). Finally, the purchase price of the contract indicated in Section 3.1 was fixed as the sum of six million dollars cash and the aggregate book amount of assumed liabilities. (A966).

As the APA's closing date approached, the remaining work on the freeze dryers for Berg was a cause of concern for all parties. After the asset transfer, it would have been impossible for Hull to complete its obligations under the Modified Agreement because Hull retained neither the personnel nor the capacity for the required work. Hull and SPI resolved the issue by simultaneously entering into a "side letter agreement" in which they agreed that SPI would complete the remaining design modifications and repairs to the freeze dryers, and that Hull would reimburse SPI for a portion of its expenses. *Berg Chilling, 369 F.3d at 750.* The letter provided that "except as amended hereby, the terms and provisions of the Asset Purchase Agreement shall remain in full force and effect." (A1098). Both Hull and SPI considered SPI's efforts to fix the freeze dryers to be warranty work, as defined and covered by Section 7.8 of the APA, and the side letter agreement made no changes to that section. Meanwhile, Berg attempted to assuage its own concerns about the project by sending a letter to Hull, inquiring about "the transfer of liabilities, and specifically who will be carrying the full financial responsibility for this project." (A1045). Hull responded by indicating that "if Hull's freeze drying division should be transferred to another entity, Hull's responsibility will of course be assumed by the successor." (A1043). At the time Hull made this representation, the APA was still under negotiation, and there was no guarantee that any asset transfer would ultimately take place. There is no indication that Hull ever informed SPI about its assurances to Berg, and Berg did not discuss the matter directly with SPI after the asset transfer was complete.

After the APA closed, SPI renamed Hull's former FDC Division "Hull Company Division," and marketing materials called the Hull Company Division the "continuation" of Hull. (A725-27, 737-39). Key former employees of Hull, including the major players in the Huadu Contract, remained involved in the project. SPI named Lewis Hull, Hull's chairman, as honorary chairman of the Hull Company Division, and employed John Hull as a consultant to the Huadu project. Both men lacked any power to legally bind SPI. Others, including Hull's chief engineer, continued to perform design and engineering work on the Huadu Project pursuant to the Modified Agreement. The Division's first order of business was to complete the remaining work on the Huadu freeze dryers to bring them into compliance with the contract.[1]

SPI's efforts to bring the freeze dryers up to performance standards were ultimately unsuccessful. Consequently, Huadu filed an international arbitration action against Berg for breach of contract in March, 1999, pursuant to its rights under the Huadu Contract, as modified by the Modified Agreement. Berg requested that Hull participate in a joint defense in the proceedings, but Hull refused to do so. Although the arbitrators found that the only deficiency in the freeze-drying system was the freeze dryers themselves, they found that Berg bore full responsibility to Huadu, and deemed Hull's liability to be outside the scope of arbitration. *Berg Chilling Sys. v. Hull Corp., 369 F.3d 745, 752 (3d Cir. 2004).* Approximately one year later, Berg informed SPI of the arbitration for the first time. Ultimately, Huadu won an arbital award of approximately $ 2.5 million against Berg, which the parties settled for a total of $ 1,000,000 in cash, and $ 650,000 in equipment value (Huadu kept the freeze dryers).

While the arbitration continued, Berg filed suit against Hull and SPI in the United States District Court for the Eastern District of Pennsylvania, asserting claims for breach of contract, breach of express warranty, breach of implied warranty, and indemnity and contribution. Hull and SPI, in turn, each filed cross- claims against each other for indemnity or contribution After a bench trial in January 2003, the District Court determined that Berg, Hull, and SPI were equally at fault for breaching the agreements with Huadu. Accordingly, the court apportioned the $ 1,000,000 arbitration settlement equally but separately among Berg, Hull, and SPI. The District Court did not allow Berg to recover any portion of the $ 650,000 equipment credit because Berg did not show that it accurately reflected the actual value of the equipment, nor did it take into account the costs Berg would have in-

1 Berg intimates that the ultimate failure of the freeze dryers to perform to Huadu's specifications was due to SPI's faulty design, not to Hull's. We, however, believe that it is more accurate to characterize SPI's work as attempting to fix flaws—including design flaws—in Hull's original work.

curred in retrieving the equipment. The District Court also found against both Hull and SPI on their respective cross-claims for indemnification.

Berg and SPI appealed, and this Court reversed, finding that Section 7.8 of the APA precluded a finding that SPI was liable to Berg on the basis of the APA. Thus, based on that indemnification clause, Hull was determined to be solely liable to Berg for the $ 1,000,000 cash settlement, the $ 650,000 equipment credit for the freeze dryers, and attorneys' fees and costs incurred in the arbitration proceedings. *Berg Chilling, 369 F.3d at 766*. This Court also found Hull liable to SPI for indemnification, including attorneys' fees and costs. The District Court was directed on remand to determine whether to void Section 7.8 as against public policy, and whether SPI is liable to Berg under the doctrine of successor liability.

On remand, Berg contended that SPI is liable for Hull's breach of contract as a successor corporation, either because the substance of their transaction—despite the label of the APA—was truly a *de facto* merger between SPI and Hull, or because the APA rendered SPI a "mere continuation" of Hull. Initially, the District Court decided that there is no material difference between New Jersey and Pennsylvania successor liability law, and therefore did not decide which state's law governed the successor liability issue. Ultimately, the District Court found that SPI did not succeed to Hull's liability under the Modified Agreement. *Berg II, 2004 U.S. Dist. LEXIS 15275, 2004 WL 1749174 at *4*. Hull Corporation did not participate in the remand proceedings, nor does it participate in this appeal, as it is no longer in business and has no assets. *Berg II, 2004 U.S. Dist. LEXIS 15275, 2004 WL 1749174 at *2*.

Next, Berg argued that Section 7.8 was void as contrary to public policy, both according to two New Jersey statutes and to New Jersey common law. *Berg Chilling Sys. v. Hull Corp., 2004 U.S. Dist. LEXIS 15275, No. 00-5075, 2004 WL 1749174, at *1 (E.D. Pa. Aug. 3, 2004)* (hereinafter Berg II). First, the District Court summarily rejected Berg's argument that N.J. Stat. § 2A:40A-1 and N.J. Stat. § 2A:40A-2 prohibited enforcement of Section 7.8. The Court reasoned that the statutes in question applied only to negligence disclaimers and were thus irrelevant to a breach of contract action. Moreover, the Court found the statutes inapplicable because they only apply in situations where damages are caused by the contracting party's sole negligence—which is not the case here, as this Court previously held that Hull was also liable. The District Court similarly rejected Berg's argument that Section 7.8 contravened New Jersey common law deeming exculpation of professionals to be against public policy. The District Court found cases on which Berg relied to be inapplicable to the situation in this case. *Berg II, 2004 U.S. Dist. LEXIS 15275, 2004 WL 1749174 at *3*.

II.

We exercise plenary review over the District Court's legal determinations, *Shire U.S. Inc. v. Barr Labs. Inc., 329 F.3d 348, 352 (3d Cir. 2003)*, and review the

District Court's findings of fact for clear error, *United States v. Bell, 414 F.3d 474, 478 (3d Cir. 2005)*. In order to constitute error, a factual finding must be "completely devoid of minimum evidentiary support displaying some hue of credibility." *Berg Chilling Sys. Inc. v. Hull Corp., 369 F.3d 745, 754 (3d Cir. 2004)* (internal citations and quotations omitted).

We must first determine which state's substantive law governs, a question over which we exercise plenary review. See *Garcia v. Plaza Oldsmobile Ltd., 421 F.3d 216, 219 (3d Cir. 2005)*. To resolve the issue of what law to apply to Berg's successor liability claims, we look to the choice of law rules of the state of Pennsylvania, because in an action based on diversity of citizenship jurisdiction, we must apply the substantive law of the state in which the District Court sat, including its choice of law rules. See *Klaxon Co. v. Stentor Elec. Mfg. Co., 313 U.S. 487, 496, 61 S. Ct. 1020, 85 L. Ed. 1477 (1941)*; *Yohannon v. Keene, 924 F.2d 1255, 1264 (3d Cir. 1991)*. Because choice of law analysis is issue-specific, different states' laws may apply to different issues in a single case, a principle known as "depecage." See, e.g., *Compagnie des Bauxites v. Argonaut-Midwest Ins. Co., 880 F.2d 685, 691 (3d Cir. 1989)*.

A.

Initially, we must determine whether a true conflict exists between the application of New Jersey law and Pennsylvania law. According to conflicts of laws principles, where the laws of the two jurisdictions would produce the same result on the particular issue presented, there is a "false conflict," and the Court should avoid the choice-of-law question. See *Williams v. Stone, 109 F.3d 890, 893 (3d Cir. 1997)*; *Lucker Mfg. v. Home Ins. Co., 23 F.3d 808, 813 (3d Cir.1994)* (applying Pennsylvania choice-of-law rules). The District Court determined that there was no material difference between New Jersey and Pennsylvania successor liability law, and therefore did not decide which state's law governs the successor liability issue. *Berg II, 2004 U.S. Dist. LEXIS 15275, 2004 WL 1749174 at *4*. Berg now argues that New Jersey law controls, because courts in that state find successor liability under less compelling circumstances, but asserts that applying Pennsylvania law is not fatal to its claim; SPI contends that choice of law analysis is unnecessary, but argues in favor of Pennsylvania law if the Court is obligated to choose.

Choice of law analysis is necessary because Berg's claim is more likely to fail under Pennsylvania law. District Courts applying Pennsylvania law hold that a "*de facto* merger or consolidation cannot exist unless the shareholders of the predecessor become shareholders of the successor through the successor's use of stock in payment for the predecessor's assets." *Glynwed, Inc. v. Plastimatic, Inc., 869 F. Supp. 265, 277 (D.N.J. 1994)* (noting the Pennsylvania law before proclaiming the opposing view under New Jersey law); see also *Forrest v. Beloit Corp., 278 F. Supp. 2d 471, 477 (E.D. Pa. 2003)*, rev'd on other grounds, *424 F.3d 344, 2005 WL 2245640 (3d Cir., Sept. 15, 2005)* (finding that *de facto* merger claim failed as a matter of law because there was no stock transfer between the so-called predecessor and successor corporations); *Tracey v. Winchester Repeating Arms Co., 745 F. Supp. 1099, 1109-10 (E.D. Pa. 1990)* (finding continuity of stock ownership to be the "essential element" to application of de facto merger exception). Thus, as the District Court noted, "the lack of a stock transfer is probably fatal to Berg's *de facto* merger argument" under Pennsylvania law. Berg II, 2004 U.S. Dist. LEXIS 15275, 2004 WL 1749174 at *4 n.5.

Berg has a much better chance under New Jersey law because its courts have adopted a broader standard of successor liability that de-emphasizes continuity of shareholder interest. See, e.g., *Woodrick v. Jack J. Burke Real Estate, 306 N.J. Super. 61, 74-77, 703 A.2d 306 (App. Div. 1997)*. This line of cases elevates the intent of the contracting parties to primary importance, id., and may disregard entirely whether the selling corporation continues in business, see *Koch Materials Co. v. Shore Slurry Seal, Inc., 205 F. Supp. 2d 324, 337 (D.N.J. 2002)*. In Koch, the District Court allowed for the possibility that a corporation purchasing an entire division may meet the requirements of a "mere continuation," despite the fact that all other divisions of the selling corporation remain extant and viable. Id. According to that court, it "makes little sense" to consider whether the selling corporation continues in business "in the context of modern business, where a corporation might easily sell an entire division and carry on dutifully in another area." Id. Because SPI, like the corporation in Koch, also purchased an entire division of another corporation, Koch would be an influential, perhaps dispositive, case if we were to apply New Jersey law. Thus, because Pennsylvania and New Jersey courts focus on such disparate elements in determining successor liability, we must engage in choice of law analysis.

B.

Once it is determined that an actual conflict exists, Pennsylvania follows a "flexible rule," that "permits analysis of the policies and interests underlying the particular issue before the court." *Griffith v. United Air Lines, 416 Pa. 1, 203 A.2d 796 (1964)*; see also *Myers v. Commercial Union Assurance Cos., 506 Pa. 492, 485 A.2d 1113 (1984)* (reiterating importance of "policies and interests" analysis); *Cipolla v. Shaposka, 439 Pa. 563, 267 A.2d 854 (1970)* (advising that relevant factors be viewed qualitatively, not quantitatively). The federal courts of the Third Circuit have interpreted Griffith to mean that a court applying Pennsylvania law should use the Second Restatement of Conflict of Laws as a starting point, and then flesh out the issue using an interest analysis. See *Compagnie des Bauxites, 880 F.2d at 688*; *Melville v. American Home Assurance Co., 584 F.2d 1306, 1308-09 (3d Cir. 1978)*; *American Contract Bridge League v. Nationwide Mut. Fire Ins. Co., 752 F.2d 71, 74 (3d Cir. 1975)*; see also *United Brass Works, Inc. v. American Guarantee & Liability Ins. Co., 819 F. Supp. 465 (W.D. Penn. 1992)* (providing historical analysis of federal courts' determination of Pennsylvania choice of law approach).

The Second Restatement dictates different approaches depending on the substantive law at issue. Thus, to properly apply the Second Restatement and remain true to the spirit of Pennsylvania's "flexible approach," we must first characterize the particular issue before the court as one of tort, contract, or corporate law—or some hybrid—in order to settle on a given section of the Restatement for guidance. See *Ruiz v. Blentech Corp., 89 F.3d 320, 324 (7th Cir. 1996)* ("To properly apply the Second Restatement method, a court must begin its choice-of-law analysis with a characterization of the issue at hand in terms of substantive law."). Here, the practical effect of characterizing successor liability may be significant. This case arose from the effects of SPI's purchase of an entire division of the Hull Corporation, and the Asset Purchase Agreement between those parties—the centerpiece of the transaction—contains a provision that chooses New Jersey law to govern the contract. According to the Restatement, if we characterize the issue as purely contractual, and strictly apply the rules governing choice of law in contracts interpretation cases, the APA's choice of law provision would likely stand unless:

> (a) the chosen state has no substantial relationship to the parties or the transaction and there is no other reasonable basis for the parties' choice, or (b) application of the law of the chosen state would be contrary to a fundamental policy of a state which has a materially greater interest than the chosen state in the determination of the particular issue and which, under the rule of § 188, would be the state of the applicable law in the absence of an effective choice of law by the parties.

Restatement (Second) of Conflicts of Law § 187(2).

The ordinary rule of successor liability is rooted in corporate law, and it states that a firm that buys assets from another firm does not assume the liabilities of the seller merely by buying its assets. See, e.g., *Luxliner P.L. Export Co. v. RDI/Luxliner, Inc., 13 F.3d 69 (3d Cir. 1993)*; *Polius v. Clark Equip. Co., 802 F.2d 75 (3d Cir. 1986)* (noting that the general rule of corporate successor liability was "designed for the corporate contractual world where it functions well"); 15 William Meade Fletcher et al., Fletcher Cyclopedia of the Law of Private Corporations § 7122. The problem of characterization lies in the mottled nature of the exceptions to the ordinary rule in successor liability law because they are not uniformly characterized as wholly based in tort, contract, or corporate law. See, e.g., *United States v. General Battery Corp., 423 F.3d 294, 301 (3d Cir. 2005)* (noting that the choice of law framework governing successor liability remains "unsettled"); *Savage Arms, Inc. v. Western Auto Supply Co., 18 P.3d 49, 53 (Alaska 2001)* (analyzing other states' approaches to successor liability law and concluding that successor cases dealing with products liability are appropriately charaterized as torts questions); *Ruiz, 89 F.3d at 326* (noting that many courts have "struggled to decide whether [successor liability] is part of corporate law or tort law"); *Webb v. Rodgers Machinery Mfg. Co., 750 F.2d 368, 374 (5th Cir. 1985)*; *In re Asbestos Litigation (Bell), 517 A.2d 697, 699 (Del. Super. 1986)* (holding that contract/corporate law applied to successor liability case based on legal effect of contract between corporations).

While the basic tenet of successor liability law is based in corporate law, the exceptions span a loose substantive continuum from contract to corporate to tort law. There are four traditional exceptions, all founded in corporate and contract law. See *Ruiz, 89 F.3d at 326*. The first exception covers situations where the buyer either expressly or implicitly agrees to assume some or all of the seller's liabilities. It is usually straightforward in application. Because this exception is based on interpreting the terms of the parties' agreement, it is characterized most strictly as contract law. See, e.g., *T.H.S. Northstar Associates v. W.R. Grace & Co.-Conn., 840 F. Supp. 676, 677-78 (D. Minn. 1993)* (indicating that the Court would enforce the contractual choice of law clause under an "express assumption of liability" theory of successor liability). The second exception applies where a transaction is entered into fraudulently in order to evade liability.[2] The third and fourth exceptions, *de facto* merger and mere continuation, are generally treated identically, see, e.g., *Luxliner, 13 F.3d at 73* (stating that "much the same evidence is relevant to each determination," and listing the same factors as necessary to determine "whether either of these exceptions applies"), as both arise where there is continuity of identity between the buyer and seller, see *Ruiz, 89 F.3d at 325* ("In effect, the de facto merger and continuation exceptions are identical; each exception depends upon an identity of ownership between the seller and purchaser"). "Mere continuation" analysis focuses on whether the new corporation is merely a restructured form of the old, while *de facto* merger analysis inquires whether a transaction—though structured as an asset purchase—factually amounts to a consolidation or merger.

Additionally, many states have adopted rules expanding successor liability in products liability cases. See *Dawejko v. Jorgensen Steel Co., 290 Pa. Super. 15, 434 A.2d 106, 111 (Pa. Super. 1981)*; *Ramirez v. Amsted Industries, Inc., 86 N.J. 332, 431 A.2d 811, 824-825 (N.J. 1981)*; see also *Ray v. Alad Corp., 19 Cal. 3d 22, 560 P.2d 3, 136 Cal. Rptr. 574 (Cal. 1977)* (departing, for the first time, from traditional corporate law grounding of successor liability). Under the so-called "product line" theory, the successor corporation remains strictly liable in tort for the defective products of its predecessor. We need not, and do not here, characterize the substantive law of the product line exception, but merely note the confusing effect of introducing an explicitly tort-based exception to a traditionally corporate- and contract-based doctrine. Thus, at one extreme lies the explicit and implicit assumption of liability exception, interpreted solely based on contract. At the other lies the product line exception, which is generally analyzed using torts choice of law principles. The *de facto* merger/continuation exception to successor liability rests somewhere in the middle.

---

2 Some states recognize transfer for inadequate consideration as an additional exception, see, e.g., *Lopata v. Bemis Co., Inc., 383 F. Supp. 342 (E.D. Pa. 1974)*; however, this seems more properly viewed as a form of constructive fraud, see, e.g., Marie T. Reilly, Making Sense of Successor Liability, 31 Hofstra L. R. 745, 757 (2003).

The *de facto* merger exception is not strictly contractual because it is an equitable principle, ultimately designed to look beyond the contract. As an initial matter, the Restatement itself suggests that we consider whether the parties could have contracted about the subject matter at issue. A contractual choice of law provision applies, with certain limitations, to issues that the parties "could have resolved by an explicit provision" of the contract. Restatement (Second) of Conflicts of Law § 187 (1) ; see also *Chestnut v. Pediatric Homecare of America, Inc., 420 Pa. Super. 598, 604, 617 A.2d 347 (1992)* (applying Pennsylvania law to an issue according to Restatement (Second) of Conflicts of Law § 187(2)(b), while recognizing that parties did not have the power to contract as to the issue); *Schifano v. Schifano, 324 Pa. Super. 281, 471 A.2d 839, 843 n.5 (Pa. Super. Ct. 1984)*. A *de facto* merger inquiry investigates whether a transaction labeled "Asset Purchase Agreement" in fact constituted a merger—a determination that does not arise purely from the agreement itself. Thus, SPI and Hull could not have controlled, through express contractual language, whether their agreement in fact constituted a merger. Though strict adherence solely to the Restatement might lead to a different result, under Pennsylvania's flexible combination of Restatement and interest-based analysis, the contractual choice of law provision should not apply to the issue. Cf. *T.H.S. Northstar Associates, 840 F. Supp. at 678.*

Our cases have acted upon this principle, although none has explicitly addressed it. See *SmithKline Beecham Corp. v. Rohm & Haas Co., 89 F.3d 154, 162 (3d Cir. 1996)* (using law chosen by contract to interpret contract terms, but engaging in Pennsylvania choice of law analysis to determine successor liability); *Rego v. ARC Water Treatment Co., 181 F.3d 396, 401 (3d Cir. 1999)* (observing that successor liability is "derived from equitable principles"). Other federal courts have explored the issue in more detail. See, e.g., *Source One Enterprises. v. CDC Acquisition Corp., 2004 U.S. Dist. LEXIS 11674, No. 02-4925, 2004 WL 1453529 at *1 (D. Minn. June 24, 2004)* (indicating that contractual choice of law clause did not apply to successor liability); *East Prairie R-2 School District v. U.S. Gypsum Co., 813 F. Supp. 1396 (E.D. Miss. 1993)* (using the Restatement-based choice of law rules of Missouri to determine that, while contractual choice of law clause applied to contract terms, Mississippi law controlled successor liability issue).

In general, while it makes sense to allow the parties to a contract to control which law applies to their agreement, it does not follow that the contract provisions should control an inquiry that, by its nature, looks beyond the contract. In a strict Restatement analysis, we would be guided towards giving effect to the contractual choice of law by considerations such as protecting the parties' justified expectations and assuring certainty, predictability and uniformity of results. Restatement 2d of Conflicts of Laws § 6(2)(d) & (f). These factors, however, do not apply to the equitable application of successor liability. Here, there is no protection of justified expectations because SPI and Berg did not bargain with each other; Berg brought a third-party action.[3] Cf. *International Paper Co. v. Midvale-Heppenstall Co., 63 Pa. D. & C.2d 627, 1973 WL 15333 (Pa. Com. Pl.)* (applying freely bargained-for contractual choice of law provision but failing to characterize individual issues as required by depecage). Even when we consider that SPI and Hull bargained over the provisions of the Asset Purchase Agreement, the fact remains that they bargained for New Jersey law to apply to interpretation of the provisions of the contract, not to their real-world effect. In short, the nature of an inquiry into the *de facto* merger exception to successor liability speaks against following the APA's choice of law provision. As we acknowledged in Polius, the court steps in "when the form of the transfer does not accurately portray substance." *802 F.2d at 78.* Ultimately, in conducting choice of law analysis for this situation, we should look to the substance of the transaction, rather than to the form of the agreement; therefore, the APA's choice of law provision does not control.

C.

Yet, there is more than one contract to consider. The few courts applying choice of law analysis to this highly specific situation—a third-party breach of contract suit based on successor liability—have generated somewhat confusing opinions. This is because there is no clear line of reasoning specifying *which* contract is the anchor point for a choice of law analysis. Though we have already examined the APA, some courts ignore similar documents entirely. Some courts use the breached contract as the exclusive basis for their analysis of which state's successor liability law to apply. See, e.g., *Johnson v. Ventra Group, Inc., 191 F.3d 732, 739-40 (6th Cir. 1999)* (using employee's breached contract with former employer to supply proper state law to apply to potential liability of employer's "successor," primarily because employee bargained for choice of law clause). Other courts avoid looking at any contracts. See, e.g., *Schwartz v. Pillsbury Inc., 969 F.2d 840, 845 (9th Cir. 1992)* (applying California law, despite New York choice of law clause in breached franchise agreement, "because the issue does not involve the interpretation or enforcement of the franchise agreement;" and failing to mention corporate "successor" transaction altogether).

The overarching problem is that, however many transactions interlock to form a factual nucleus, there is no one contract to which all the involved entities are parties. That is assuredly true in this case, where, unpacking the contractual relations among the parties, there are somewhere between two and four relevant contracts. The first relevant contract is the APA, which we have already discussed. The second is the Modified Agreement, the contract that Berg sued Hull and SPI for breaching. SPI did not even sign the Modified Agreement; it became effective one week before Hull and SPI finalized the sale of Hull's FDC Division. The Modified Agreement, however, does not stand on its own. It is a relatively short document,

3 In fact, as we determined in Berg Chilling Systems, Inc. v. SP Industries, SPI bargained with Hull to construct the Asset Purchase Agreement specifically to avoid liability to third parties such as Berg. *369 F.3d 745, 757-58 (3d Cir. 2004).*

and it specifically refers back to the original Huadu Contract, giving each signatory to the Modified Agreement all the rights each held under the Huadu Contract. As to Huadu and Berg, it is clear that all terms of the Huadu Contract that were not superceded by the Modified Agreement remained in full effect. This is confirmed by the fact that Huadu and Berg adhered to the agreement by submitting to arbitration in Sweden, as provided by the Huadu Contract, for Berg's breach of the Modified Agreement. Hull, however, had a previous legal relationship only with Berg, via the Purchase Agreement. Because Hull did not bargain for rights under the Huadu Contract, and was not a signatory to it, Hull remained liable only under the Modified Agreement.

In order to properly follow the flexible approach articulated in Griffith and since followed by this Court in Compagnie des Bauxites and its progeny, it makes sense to consider both the APA and the Modified Agreement (and, to the extent relevant, the Huadu Contract and Purchase Agreement) in conducting our choice of law analysis. Because it was impossible for any of these contracts to have made an effective choice of law on successor liability, we will look to the grouping of contacts with the various concerned jurisdictions. See *Restatement 2d of Conflicts of Laws § 188*; *Compagnie des Bauxites, 880 F.2d at 689* (interpreting Griffith to mean that proper choice of law analysis involves "grouping of contacts with the various concerned jurisdictions and the interests and policies that may be validly asserted by each jurisdiction."). Relevant contacts in a contract case[4] include: "(a) the place of contracting, (b) the place of negotiation of the contract, (c) the place of performance, (d) the location of the subject matter of the contract, (e) the domicil, residence, nationality, place of incorporation and place of business of the parties. These contacts are to be evaluated according to their relative importance with respect to the particular issue." *Compagnie des Bauxites, 880 F.2d at 689*. Here, we will analyze only factors (c), (d), and (e), as the place of contracting and of negotiation are of minor importance to the issue.

The initial factor in our analysis is place of performance. Regarding the APA, the performance was the sale of Hull's FDC Division to SPI, making this factor essentially a combination of the location of the Division's assets and the places of business of the seller and buyer. The Modified Agreement envisioned essentially two places of performance: Pennsylvania, the situs of Hull's freeze dryer manufacturing facilities, and China, the location where the freeze dryers were erected and subjected to performance testing.

The second factor is the location of the subject matter of the contract. The subject matter of the APA is the assets, properties, rights, and businesses related to the conduct of the "Business," defined in the contract as: "manufacturing, remanufacturing, installing, servicing, marketing, selling, and distributing standard and customized vacuum drying, freeze drying, and vacuum shelf drying equipment

---

4 Although Griffith was a tort action, its analysis has been regularly applied to contract actions. See, e.g., *Compagnie de Bauxites, 880 F.2d at 689*.

and related products, equipment and systems for customers involved in the pharmaceutical, animal health, diagnostic, biotech and food industries." (A962). Many of these activities, conducted exclusively through Hull's FDC Division, don't have an easily identifiable "location." To the extent that Hull Corporation's FDC division—the subject matter of the Asset Purchase Agreement—has a "location," it is primarily in Pennsylvania: tangible purchased assets included equipment, inventory, and real estate located in Pennsylvania. The freeze dryers were the subject matter of the Modified Agreement. Manufactured by Hull in Pennsylvania under the original Purchase Agreement, by the time of the Modified Agreement the freeze dryers were already installed, albeit imperfectly, at Huadu's facilities in China. Berg had delivered the freeze dryers from Hull's Pennsylvania site to Huadu's site in China, where they remain, pursuant to the arbitration settlement between Berg and Huadu.

The third factor is the domicil, residence, nationality, place of incorporation and place of business of the parties. There are two sets of parties: Hull and SPI, parties to the APA; and Hull, Berg, and Huadu, parties to the Modified Agreement. Hull is incorporated in Pennsylvania. SPI is a Delaware corporation. While SPI's primary place of business is in New Jersey, it operated the freeze dryer business that it bought from Hull from the same premises in Pennsylvania that it leased from Hull Corporation. Berg is a Canadian Company whose legal address and place of business is in Ontario, Canada. Huadu is a Chinese company whose legal address and place of business is in Beijing, China.

We view the relevant contacts qualitatively and in their totality. See *Cipolla, 439 Pa. 563, 267 A.2d 854*. Although much of the relevant activity took place in China, the only company actually located there is Huadu, which is not a party to the present action. The next most relevant location is Pennsylvania: Hull's place of incorporation and the location of the site where the freeze dryers were manufactured. Accordingly, we will apply the successor liability law of the state of Pennsylvania.

III.

Where one company sells or otherwise transfers all of its assets to another company, the latter is not normally liable for the debts and liabilities of the transferor. However, if circumstances indicate that there was a *de facto* consolidation or merger of the corporations or that the purchasing company was a "mere continuation" of the selling company, liability may attach. The *de facto* merger exception is similar to the continuation exception, save that the latter focuses on situations in which the purchaser is merely a restructured or reorganized form of the seller. Although the parties separate their analyses, we follow the trend of the courts here and treat the exceptions identically.

We now turn to the *de facto* merger analysis. In determining whether a transaction is a *de facto* merger or continuation, we look to the following factors:

> (1) There is a continuation of the enterprise of the seller corporation, so that there is continuity of management, personnel, physical location, assets, and general business operations.
>
> (2) There is a continuity of shareholders which results from the purchasing corporation paying for the acquired assets with shares of its own stock, this stock ultimately coming to be held by the shareholders of the seller corporation so that they become a constituent part of the purchasing corporation.
>
> (3) The seller corporation ceases its ordinary business operations, liquidates, and dissolves as soon as legally and practically possible.
>
> (4) The purchasing corporation assumes those obligations of the seller ordinarily necessary for the uninterrupted continuation of normal business operations of the seller corporation.

Philadelphia Electric Co. v. Hercules, Inc., 762 F.2d 303, 310 (3d Cir. 1985) (applying Pennsylvania law).

As noted earlier, the District Courts in this Circuit consider the second factor—continuity of ownership—to be critical to a successful successor liability claim under Pennsylvania law. See *Forrest v. Beloit Corp., 278 F. Supp. 2d 471, 477 (E.D. Pa. 2003)* (finding that *de facto* merger claim failed as a matter of law because there was no stock transfer between the so-called predecessor and successor corporations), rev'd on other grounds, *424 F.3d 344, 2005 WL 2245640 (3d Cir. Sept. 15, 2005)*; *Glynwed, Inc. v. Plastimatic, Inc., 869 F. Supp. 265, 277 (D.N.J. 1994)*; *Tracey v. Winchester Repeating Arms Co., 745 F. Supp. 1099, 1109-10 (E.D. Pa. 1990)* (finding continuity of stock ownership to be the "essential element" to application of de facto merger exception). In fact, only one District Court applying Pennsylvania law has been willing to find liability despite a partial-cash sale. *Fiber-Lite Corp. v. Molded Acoustical Products of Easton, Inc., 186 B.R. 603 (E.D. Pa. 1994)*, aff'd mem. *66 F.3d 310 (3d Cir. 1995)*. However, the most recent Pennsylvania court decision on the matter did not specifically adopt the Pennsylvania District Courts' formulation of stock ownership as the "essential element." Yet, it also did not take the opportunity to disagree with the District Courts, and lists "continuity of ownership" as the first factor in the four-factor test. *Cont'l Ins. Co. v. Schneider, Inc., 2002 PA Super 323, 810 A.2d 127, 134-36 (Pa. Super. Ct. 2002),* aff'd, 582 Pa. 591, 873 A.2d 1286 (Pa. 2005). If we were to strictly apply the reasoning of the District Courts, this inquiry would be over, as there is no continuity of stock ownership between Hull and SPI. Given the Pennsylvania state courts' failure to specifically adopt such a bright-line standard, however, we will instead conduct a full analysis that emphasizes the ownership factor but does not rely on it alone.

First, we determine whether there was continuity of ownership between Hull and SPI. The objective of this requirement is usually to identify situations in which shareholders of a seller corporation unfairly attempt to impose their costs or misdeeds on third parties by retaining assets that have been artificially cleansed of liability. See *General Battery, 423 F.3d at 306-07* (evaluating corporate successor liability under CERCLA); see also *SmithKline Beecham, 89 F.3d at 164*. Here, there was no continuity of stock ownership between Hull and SPI, as the APA fixed consideration at $ 6 million in cash. Berg II, 2004 U.S. Dist. LEXIS 15275, 2004 WL 1749174 at *4. Based on this key factor, we continue the remainder of the analysis with a strong presumption against imposing successor liability.

Next, we investigate whether SPI "continued the enterprise of the seller corporation" Hull, an inquiry that depends on how we define the term "enterprise." There is ample evidence to support the conclusion that SPI, through its VirTis/Hull Company Division, continued the business operations of Hull's FDC Division. SPI purchased all of the FDC Division's equipment and inventory, assumed tenancy of the Division's manufacturing facilities (though eventually did not purchase the associated real estate), manufactured the same products, took over many contractual obligations, and used the same personnel, telephone number, and fax number. SPI also renamed its VirTis Division "Hull Company" specifically to take advantage of the Hull name's acceptance in the community, and purchased the Hull logo for the same purpose. On the corporate level, however, there is no indication that SPI continued Hull's enterprise; indeed, until recently, Hull was extant and master of its own corporate destiny. There was no continuity of corporate management: no member of Hull's Board of Directors held a position on SPI's Board of Directors. Although Hull's Chairman, Lewis Hull, became "Chairman of the Hull Company Division," the title was solely honorary and he had no capacity to bind SPI or its Hull Company Division. John Hull, a corporate officer at Hull Corporation, became a temporary consultant to the Hull Company Division, also with no authority to bind either SPI or the Hull Company Division. Thus, while it is clear that two divisions combined operations as a result of the APA, there is no support for the proposition that SPI continued Hull's corporate enterprise.

Third, we look to whether the seller corporation ceases operation and liquidates. The *de facto* merger doctrine recognizes that an essential characteristic of a merger is that one corporation survives while the other ceases to exist. See *General Battery, 423 F.3d at 308* (citing *Knapp v. N. Am. Rockwell Corp., 506 F.2d 361, 367 (3d Cir. 1974)* (applying Pennsylvania law)). Here, the FDC Division of Hull Corporation ceased its freeze drying operations and agreed not to compete with SPI's Hull Company Division. Yet, Hull continued to exist as a corporate entity, and continued to operate its other divisions, for years after the APA closed. Berg II, 2004 U.S. Dist. LEXIS 15275, 2004 WL 1749174 at *4. Thus, this factor does not support a *de facto* merger.

Finally, we determine whether the seller corporation has assumed the obligations ordinarily necessary for uninterrupted continuation of normal business operations. Here, the APA unambiguously provided that SPI acquire all accounts receivable and all contracts relating to the operation of the FDC Division of Hull. It is equally unambiguous that SPI did not assume any of Hull's obligations relating to any other division: the APA itself defined the subject matter of the contract as only the FDC Division, and specifically excluded all other corporate assets and liabilities. Moreover, the APA provided that SPI assume only limited liabilities from Hull; for example, SPI did not assume Hull's pre-closing contractual liabilities to third parties. *Berg Chilling, 369 F.3d at 758.*

In sum, the APA resulted in a combination of like corporate *divisions*, but not of corporate *entities*. Thus, the *de facto* merger exception to the rule of successor non-liability will not render SPI liable for Hull's breach of the Modified Agreement.

IV.

This court found that the APA operated to exculpate SPI from any liability arising from Hull's work, or from its own attempts to cure defects in Hull's work, on the freeze dryers for the Huadu Contract. *Berg Chilling, 369 F.3d at 745.* Berg now presents the same arguments it put forward to the District Court in Berg II; namely, that the so-called "exculpatory" clause in Section 7.8 is void as against public policy. Applying New Jersey law, per Section 10.6 of the APA, the District Court held that public policy did not void the clause. For the following reasons, we agree.

Berg first argues that two sections of the New Jersey Code act to void Section 7.8. The first section invalidates any agreement "purporting to indemnify or hold harmless the promisee against liability for damages arising out of bodily injury to persons or damage to property caused by or resulting from the sole negligence of the promisee . . . .." N.J. Stat. Ann. § 2A:40A-1 (2005). The second voids any agreement indemnifying an architect, engineer, or surveyor for "damages, claims, losses, or expenses" caused either by preparing reports or specifications; or by giving or failing to give instructions. N.J. Stat. Ann. § 2A:40A-2 (2005) (emphasis added).

Neither statute is applicable to the clause at issue in Section 7.8. First, the clause does not fall under the purview of Section 2A:40A-1 because it does not relate to negligence. By its plain language, Section 2A:40A-1 is limited to prohibit clauses through which a party seeks to be indemnified for damages resulting from "sole negligence." Further, while Berg seeks to recover damages related to the breached contract with Huadu,[5] Section 2A:40A-1 only applies to traditional negligence recovery; that is, "damages arising out of bodily injury to persons or damage to property." Moreover, the clause at issue does not absolve SPI of responsibility for

---

5 Berg notes in its brief that it did assert tort claims for contribution and common law indemnification against SPI. However, neither of these claims relate to the clause in Section 7.8, nor do they relate to negligence.

its own negligence; rather, it is a disclaimer of liability to third parties for faulty products shipped by Hull prior to the date SPI took over the business. The term, therefore, only assures that SPI will not be liable to third parties based on Hull's actions. Therefore, because the clause does not relate to SPI's negligence—much less to its sole negligence—and because both statutes are limited to actions in tort, neither New Jersey statute voids Section 7.8.

Second, both statutes were intended to apply to construction contracts. Berg II, 2004 U.S. Dist. LEXIS 15275, 2004 WL 1749174 at *3. Legislative history confirms the District Court's interpretation by introducing both statutes as "amend[ing] a recently-enacted law, P.L.1981, c. 317, which prohibits hold harmless clauses in *construction contracts* which indemnify the promisee for any damages regardless of the extent of his negligence." Assembly, No. 590-L.1983, c.107 (emphasis added); accord *Ryan v. Biederman Indust. 223 N.J. Super. 492, 500, 538 A.2d 1324; 223 N.J. Super. 492, 538 A.2d 1324, 1329 (1988)* (indicating that stated purpose of the amendment was "to clarify the purpose behind the original enactment."). We find unconvincing Berg's argument that New Jersey courts would find the Huadu freeze dryers to be within the scope of "appliances or appurtenances" in Section 2A:40A-1. Berg assumes that the New Jersey courts would term the freeze dryers appliances or appurtenances based on a Georgia District Court decision interpreting a similar statute. See *Federal Paper Bd. Co., Inc. v. Harbert-Yeargin, Inc., 53 F. Supp. 2d 1361 (N.D. Ga. 1999)* (finding paper mills to be "appliances or appurtenances" under similar Georgia statute). This is unlikely, as the Georgia District Court specifically noted the "expansive" way that Georgia state courts interpreted the statute to include leases and maintenance agreements, a view that the New Jersey state courts do not demonstrably share. Id.

Berg additionally claims that Section 7.8 violates New Jersey public policy because it violates common law dictating that "professionals" be held to the standards of their profession. See, e.g., *Erlich v. First Nat'l Bank, 208 N.J. Super. 264, 505 A.2d 220 (N.J. Super. Ct. Law Div. 1984)*. This argument is unpersuasive. The New Jersey common law is based on the principle that "courts will not enforce an exculpatory clause if the party benefiting from exculpation is subject to a positive duty imposed by law or is imbued with a public trust, or if exoneration of the party would adversely affect the public interest." Erlich, 208 A.3d at 232. Thus, as part of New Jersey's basic doctrine disallowing liability limitation in areas of the public interest, exculpation clauses are disfavored in contracts for professional services in order to protect the individual relying on the professional's expertise. See *Lucier v. Williams, 366 N.J. Super 485, 496, 841 A.2d 907 (2004)* (determining that exculpation clause in contract for home inspection was invalid as violating public policy). This doctrine is not applicable in a situation in which two sophisticated corporations deliberately rely on one another's expertise, yet are able to allocate liability through contract. Further, Section 7.8 is not voided by the common law because it does not absolve SPI of liability for its *own* actions; it merely indicates that SPI does not assume any of *Hull's* liability to third parties. Berg is seeking to characterize the disputed clause in Section 7.8 as "exculpatory," yet it is not, because it does not relate to SPI's own negligence. See *Valhal Corp. v. Sullivan Assocs., 44 F.3d 195 (3d Cir. 1995)* (defining "exculpatory" as absolving a party from his own negligence). Thus, because the public trust is not at issue, and because the Section 7.8 does not seek to exonerate SPI for its own actions, the common law does not apply.

V.

Finally, Berg argues that because SPI did not specifically appeal the District Court's original order finding that Berg had a right to contribution from SPI, the District Court erred by vacating that order on remand. However, that order was predicated on the finding that "Berg, SPI, and Hull Corporation were equally at fault" in breaching the Huadu Contract. *Berg I, 2004 U.S. Dist. LEXIS 15275, 2004 WL 1749174 at *11*. As the District Court explained, contribution is "an attempt by equity to distribute equally among those who have a common obligation, the burden of performing that obligation." Id. at *11 n.15 (citation omitted). Thus, Berg can no longer assert a right to contribution because this Court reversed that order and determined that SPI was not at fault. See *Berg Chilling, 369 F.3d at 745*. SPI, therefore, cannot be liable to Berg for contribution.

VI.

We recognize that this judgment places Berg in an untenable situation. Based on the last several years of litigation, it appears that Hull Corporation bears the greatest responsibility for breaching the Modified Agreement; but Hull is now out of business and lacks assets. For these reasons, we affirm.

DISSENT

AMBRO, Circuit Judge, Dissenting

Although the majority ably argues for the application of Pennsylvania law to preclude Berg's successor liability claim, I respectfully dissent because (1) I am not convinced that Pennsylvania law should apply to this dispute and, (2) even if it does, I do not believe that Pennsylvania law precludes a finding of successor liability.

There is no question that, for contractual matters arising under the Asset Purchase Agreement ("APA") between SPI and Hull, New Jersey law would apply pursuant to the agreement's explicit choice of law. In this case, of course, we are not faced with a dispute between the parties to the APA, but rather with a third-party successor liability claim. Notwithstanding this distinction, I am of the view that the successor liability claim involved here relates to the "interpretation, construction, [and] effect" of the asset purchase transaction, and is, therefore, within the scope of the broad choice of law provision contained in the APA. I am thus unpersuaded that, as the majority states, "SPI and Hull . . . bargained for New Jersey law to apply to interpretation of the provisions of the contract, not to their real-world effect."

To the contrary, in deciding whether the APA accomplished a de facto merger of SPI and Hull, the "effect[s]" of the APA fall squarely within SPI's choice of New Jersey law. Since we have already held that Berg, a non-party to the APA, is nonetheless bound by the APA's exculpatory provisions, see *Berg Chilling Systems, Inc. v. Hull Corp., 369 F.3d 745, 757-58 (3d Cir. 2004)*, I find it incongruous for SPI to argue on this appeal, and for the majority to agree, that Berg's successor liability claim against SPI for Hull's obligations is not "contractual" because Berg was not a party to the APA and therefore the choice of law provision is irrelevant. In sum, because SPI agreed in the APA to apply New Jersey law to all effects of the asset purchase transaction, and Berg's successor liability claim clearly implicates the effects of the APA, I would hold that SPI is bound by the choice of law it made, especially since it has already benefitted from that choice in successfully using the APA's exculpatory provision as a shield against direct liability to Berg.

Applying the choice of law clause as written, this dispute should be governed by New Jersey law[6]—which, as the majority correctly notes, would almost certainly result in a victory for Berg. Not only does New Jersey's successor liability standard place great importance on the parties' intent and de-emphasize continuity of ownership, see, e.g., *Woodrick v. Jack J. Burke Real Estate, 306 N.J. Super. 61,*

---

6 Pennsylvania law states that "choice of law provisions in contracts will generally be given effect," *Smith v. Commonwealth Nat'l Bank, 384 Pa. Super. 65, 557 A.2d 775, 777 (Pa. Super. Ct. 1989)*, and "Pennsylvania courts will only ignore a contractual choice of law provision if that provision conflicts with strong public policy interests," *Kruzits v. Okuma Mach. Tool, Inc., 40 F.3d 52, 56 (3d Cir. 1994)*.

703 A.2d 306, 313 (N.J. App. Div. 1997), but it provides that the mere fact a purchaser acquires a division of another company, and the seller maintains its operations in other respects, does not defeat a finding of successor liability with respect to the acquired division. See, e.g., *Koch Materials Co. v. Shore Slurry Seal, Inc., 205 F. Supp. 2d 324, 337 (D.N.J. 2002)*. This answers the majority's reliance on the fact that "the APA resulted in a combination of like corporate divisions, but not of corporate entities" as support for its conclusion that the de facto merger doctrine is inapplicable.

Even assuming, however, that the majority is correct and Pennsylvania law applies, I am unconvinced that Pennsylvania would not find successor liability in this case. Contrary to the majority's interpretation, the case upon which it principally relies as evidence of Pennsylvania law, *Continental Insurance Co. v. Schneider, Inc., 2002 PA Super 323, 810 A.2d 127 (Pa. Super. Ct. 2002)*, does not "emphasize[]" the continuity of ownership factor nor does it stand for the proposition that the absence of such continuity yields a "strong presumption against imposing successor liability." Rather, Continental Insurance states:

> When determining if a de facto merger has occurred, courts generally consider four factors: (1) continuity of ownership; (2) cessation of the ordinary business by, and dissolution of, the predecessor as soon as practicable; (3) assumption by the successor of liabilities ordinarily necessary for uninterrupted continuation of the business; and (4) continuity of the management, personnel, physical location, and the general business operation. Although each of these factors is considered, all need not exist before a de facto merger will be deemed to have occurred. Id. at 135 (internal citations omitted; emphasis added).

As the majority states, there is "ample evidence" that SPI sought to, and did, continue the business operations of Hull's FDC Division. SPI used the same facilities, equipment, personnel, logo, and telephone and fax numbers as Hull's FDC Division. SPI continued to manufacture the same products as Hull and maintained Hull's contractual obligations. SPI retained Hull's Chairman, Lewis Hull, and held him out in its promotional materials as "Chairman" of the new Hull Division, and retained Hull's Executive Vice President, Bernard Kashmer, for two years as Executive Vice President of the Hull Division. Hull ceased doing the type of business its FDC Division had been doing and agreed not to compete with SPI. SPI's President and CEO, John Partridge, testified that he was interested in Hull's FDC Division as an ongoing business, intended to operate it as an ongoing business, and wanted to "continue to use the name of Hull because of its acceptance in the marketplace." SPI represented in its promotional materials that its Hull Division was founded in 1952 and was approaching its 50th anniversary, and Partridge testified that SPI "was saying by way of this [that it was] counting all the years that the Hull Corporation had been in existence," and was "tak[ing] it back to when that company was founded and tak[ing] credit for that length of service." When asked if he was taking credit for Hull's 50 years of business "because you were really continuing what had been the FDC freeze-drying business," Partridge replied, "Yes."

Perhaps most tellingly, SPI and Hull represented to their customers and employees that the transaction was a merger; indeed, Hull informed Berg before the APA was concluded that Hull's responsibilities under the agreement with Berg would "of course be assumed by the successor," and Lewis Hull referred to the transaction in a Hull newsletter after the APA was concluded as a "textbook strategic merger."

Based on this evidence, I am unpersuaded that Pennsylvania law would not find successor liability in this case. Continental Insurance, which the majority describes as "the most recent Pennsylvania court decision on the matter," does not privilege the continuity of ownership factor above all others; rather, in keeping with the modern view of successor liability, it counts continuity of ownership as one of several factors to consider, and notes that all factors need not exist. Here, there can be little question that SPI's continuation of Hull's business satisfies the third and fourth factors listed in Continental Insurance: SPI sought to, and did, continue Hull's business, and in doing so assumed the necessary contractual liabilities and retained key management, personnel, facilities, trademarks, telephone numbers, etc. As for the second factor, Hull immediately ceased the business of its FDC Division—the only Hull property that has anything to do with this appeal—upon conclusion of the APA and agreed not to resume such business, and the FDC Division was dissolved. Although Hull continued to operate unrelated divisions for a short time after it sold its FDC Division to SPI, Hull, too, eventually ceased to exist. Indeed, the only factor that clearly does not weigh in favor of a finding of successor liability here is the continuity of ownership. Contrary to the majority, I would find that these circumstances should result in a finding of successor liability under Pennsylvania law.

At base, I am troubled by the consequences of concluding that successor liability does not exist in this case. SPI purchased an entire division of Hull and operated that division as an ongoing business, holding the division out to the world as a continuation of Hull, and presumably reaping substantial rewards by doing so. That division was almost entirely responsible for serious deficiencies in freeze dryers sold to Berg, but SPI disclaimed any resulting liabilities in an asset purchase agreement that was negotiated without Berg's participation, all while Berg was being assured by Hull that "of course" SPI would assume full liability. Shortly after the sale of Hull's FDC Division to SPI, Hull went out of business. The result, therefore, is that SPI gets the benefit of the continuation of Hull's business without any attendant liabilities, Hull effectively avoids liability by selling off its assets, and, because of our holding today, Berg is left to bear all the liabilities for a problem it did not create. As my majority colleagues note, this "places Berg in an untenable situation." As I do not perceive a compelling reason why we must do so, I respectfully dissent.

ADRIAN RODRIGUEZ
v.
UNITED STATES

No. 05-370C (Fed. Cl. 2006)
Decided January 30, 2006

Sale on behalf of the Customs Service of a seized vehicle containing hidden drugs; alleged breach of contract; motion to dismiss; subject matter jurisdiction; standing; privity of contract; third party beneficiary; implied warranty; covenant of good faith and fair dealing

Teresa Trucchi, Suppa, Trucchi & Henein, LLP, San Diego, CA, for plaintiffs.

Andrew P. Averbach, Trial Attorney, Commercial Litigation Branch, Civil Division, United States Department of Justice, Washington, D.C., for defendant. With him on the briefs were Peter D. Keisler, Assistant Attorney General, Civil Division, David M. Cohen, Director, Commercial Litigation Branch, and Kathyrn A. Bleecker, Assistant Director, United States Department of Justice, Washington, D.C. Of counsel was Erik J. Gantzel, Attorney, Office of Assistant Chief Counsel, United States Customs and Border Protection, San Diego, CA.

OPINION AND ORDER

LETTOW, Judge.

This case arises from the auction sale to plaintiff Ali Jazmin Rodriguez of a vehicle that had been seized by government customs agents. Subsequent to the sale, her husband, Adrian Rodriguez, legally drove the vehicle into Mexico where he and the vehicle were seized by Mexican officials upon the discovery that the vehicle contained a hidden cache of illegal drugs. The plaintiffs filed their complaint against the United States in this court on April 15, 2005, alleging breach of implied warranty, breach of contract, and breach of the implied covenant of good faith and fair dealing. The government filed a motion to dismiss, or in the alternative for summary judgment, asserting that this court does not have subject matter jurisdiction over claims grounded in tort, that plaintiff Adrian Rodriguez lacks standing under either a theory of privity of contract or as an intended third party beneficiary, that both plaintiffs have failed to state a valid claim, and otherwise that summary judgment in the government's favor is appropriate on the ground that no implied warranty of any kind existed in connection with the sale of the vehicle.

The court conducted a hearing on the government's motion on December 22, 2005. For the reasons stated below, the government's motion to dismiss is granted with respect to plaintiff Adrian Rodriguez, but that motion and the alternative motion for summary judgment are denied with respect to plaintiff Ali Jazmin Rodriguez.

BACKGROUND[1]

On or about June 6, 2001, a 1991 Volkswagen Passat with Vehicle Identification Number WVWFB4316ME017877 (the "vehicle") was sold to an individual who registered it in Tijuana, Mexico. Compl. ¶¶ 6-7. The individual drove the vehicle into the United States at the San Ysidro, California port of entry on November 18, 2002. Compl. ¶ 8. At the port, the vehicle was seized by the United States Customs Service ("Customs Service")[2] after an officer searched the vehicle and discovered 32 packages of marijuana hidden in the rear bumper and dashboard, in total weighing approximately 33 pounds. Compl. ¶ 9; Defendant's Motion to Dismiss or, in the Alternative, for Summary Judgment ("Def.'s Mot.") at 3. On February 20, 2003, the Customs Service declared the vehicle forfeited pursuant to 19 U.S.C. § 1595a and in accordance with 19 U.S.C. §§ 1608, 1610. Compl. ¶¶ 10, 12; *see* Def.'s Mot. at 3.

On March 5, 2003, a U.S. Customs Select Consignors and Bankruptcy Public Vehicle Auction ("auction") was conducted on behalf of the United States by McCormack Auction Company ("McCormack"), in conjunction with EG&G Technical Services ("EG&G") which organized the forfeiture sale and to whom the vehicles were consigned. Def.'s Mot. at 3. EG&G published a brochure that advertised this and ten other auctions that were conducted between November 6, 2002 and September 3, 2003; the brochure included the terms and conditions of the sales. *Id.*; Appendix in Support of Defendant's Motion to Dismiss or, in the alternative, for Summary Judgment ("Def.'s App.") at 47-48 (Public Auctions Brochure (2002)). At the auction, Ali Jazmin Rodriguez, as a condition of participation, completed and signed an EG&G bidder registration form. Def.'s Mot. at 4; *see* Def.'s App. at 50 (Bidder Registration Form (March 5, 2003)). A sales catalog also was available at the auction that included the terms and conditions of the sale along with a listing of the vehicles that would be sold. Def.'s App. at 51-60 (Sales Catalog); *see* Def.'s

---

1 The recitations that follow do not constitute findings of fact by the court. Rather, the recited factual elements are taken from the parties' filings and are either undisputed or alleged and assumed to be true for purposes of the pending motions.

2 The Customs Service is now part of the Border and Transportation Security component of the Department of Homeland Security and is known as the Bureau of Customs and Border Protection. *See* 19 U.S.C. § 2703 note (quoting Pub. L. No. 108-429, Title V, § 5001, 118 Stat. 2604 (Dec. 3, 2004)).

Mot. at 4. Ali Jazmin Rodriguez successfully bid on and ultimately purchased the vehicle in question for $600, as well as a 1982 Volvo GL for $200. *See* Def.'s Mot. at 4; Def.'s App. at 61 (Invoice (Mar. 6, 2003)). An invoice, printed by McCormack, included a listing of the vehicles on which Mrs. Rodriguez bid, the total bids, any remaining balance due, and certain terms and conditions. *Id.* Title to the vehicle was officially transferred to Mrs. Rodriguez from the Customs Service on March 5, 2003. Def.'s App. at 62 (Certificate to Obtain Title to a Vehicle (Mar. 5, 2003)).[3]

Thereafter, Adrian Rodriguez, Ali Jazmin Rodriguez's husband, drove the vehicle to a mechanic in Tijuana on or about July 15, 2003 for repairs "because it [the vehicle] was making an unusual sound." Compl. ¶ 15; *accord* Def.'s Mot. at 4 & n.4. In the process of the mechanic's inspection of the vehicle, he discovered 33 pounds of marijuana in a box affixed to the underside of the vehicle's body. Compl. ¶ 16; Def.'s Mot. at 4-5. The manager of the repair shop contacted the municipal police of Tijuana who subsequently arrested Adrian Rodriguez and seized the vehicle. Compl. ¶ 16; Def.'s Mot. at 5. The municipal police transferred both Mr. Rodriguez and the vehicle into the custody of the Mexican Federal Agency of Investigations in Tijuana. Compl. ¶ 16.

On July 17, 2003, Adrian Rodriguez was formally indicted for violating various provisions of the Mexican criminal code. Compl. ¶ 17. A Mexican district court on July 23, 2003, ordered him imprisoned, suspended his political rights, and issued an Official Notice to the Federal Immigration Services of Mexico. Compl. ¶ 18.[4] On August 14, 2003, Mr. Rodriguez's counsel demonstrated to the Mexican district court that Mrs. Rodriguez had purchased the vehicle from a public auction of seized vehicles conducted on behalf of the U.S. Customs Service and that Mrs. Rodriguez was unaware of the fact that illegal narcotics were hidden in the vehicle.

Compl. ¶¶ 19-20. As a result, the Mexican district court found Adrian Rodriguez innocent of all charges and ordered him released from prison. Compl. ¶ 20.

---

3 Only Ali Jazmin Rodriguez's name is printed on the title of the vehicle. Def.'s App. at 62 (Certificate to Obtain Title to a Vehicle). In their pleadings, the plaintiffs inconsistently allege that either Ali Jazmin Rodriguez purchased the vehicle or that both Ali Jazmin and Adrian Rodriguez purchased the vehicle. *Compare* Plaintiff's Response to Defendant Proposed Findings of Uncontroverted Facts ¶ 1 (filed Oct. 31, 2005) (not disputing defendant's assertion that Ali Jazmin Rodriguez purchased the vehicle), *with id.* ¶ 11 (alleging that both plaintiffs purchased the vehicle). *See* Plaintiff Adrian Rodriguez and Ali Jazmin Rodriguez's Opposition to Defendant USA's Motion to Dismiss, or in the alternative, for Summary Judgment ("Pls.' Amended Response") at 2; Plaintiffs' Appendix in Opposition to Motion to Dismiss and for Summary Judgment ("Pls.' App.") Ex. 8 (Declaration of Adrian Rodriguez (Nov. 18, 2005)) ¶ 2.

4 Article 33 of the Constitution of the United Mexican States allows for the immediate expulsion from Mexico of any individual who is not a Mexican national and "whose remaining [the Federal Executive] may deem inexpedient." Constitución Política de los Estados Unidos Mexicanos, art. 33 (Mex.).

On October 22, 2003, the plaintiffs submitted a claim to the U.S. government for compensation, but that claim was "denied by operation of law on or about April 22, 2004." Compl. ¶ 22. On April 30, 2004, the plaintiffs sought relief in the United States District Court for the Southern District of California ("District Court") from the United States, McCormack, and EG&G. Def.'s App. at 17-29 (Complaint, *Adrian Rodriguez and Ali Jazmin Rodriguez v. United States of America, et al.*, No. 04-CV-0905 JAH (BLM) (S.D. Cal. filed Apr. 30, 2004)). The plaintiffs asserted six causes of action for negligence, fraud and intentional misrepresentation, negligent misrepresentation, negligent infliction of emotional distress, intentional infliction of emotional distress, and violations of California's Consumer Legal Remedies Act. *Id.* The District Court, on December 7, 2004, dismissed all of plaintiffs' claims, but did grant the plaintiffs' request for leave to amend their complaint to assert contractual claims pursuant to the Tucker Act. Def.'s App. at 30-40 (Order of Dec. 7, 2004, *Adrian Rodriguez and Ali Jazmin Rodriguez v. United States of America, et al.*, No. 04-CV-0905 JAH (BLM)). The parties subsequently stipulated that plaintiffs would file a second amended complaint asserting three contract claims and that the case would be transferred to the United States Court of Federal Claims. Def.'s App. 41-43 (Stipulation to Transfer and Dismiss Appeal (Feb. 3, 2005), *Adrian Rodriguez and Ali Jazmin Rodriguez v. United States of America, et al.*, No. 04-CV-0905 JAH (BLM) (S.D. Cal.)).

Plaintiffs filed their complaint in this court on April 15, 2005.[5]

STANDARDS FOR DECISION

Jurisdiction must established before this court may proceed to the merits of the case. *Steel Co. v. Citizens for a Better Env't*, 523 U.S. 83, 88-89 (1998). Plaintiffs have the burden of establishing the court's subject matter jurisdiction over their respective claims. *See McNutt v. General Motors Acceptance Corp. of Ind.*, 298 U.S. 178, 189 (1936); *Reynolds v. Army and Air Force Exch. Serv.*, 846 F.2d 746, 748 (Fed. Cir. 1988). The court must "draw all reasonable inferences in favor of the plaintiff[s]" and accept as true the facts as they are asserted in the complaint when determining whether it has jurisdiction over a particular case. *Goel v. United*

---

5 At least two other cases have been filed in which similar facts have been alleged. In *Agredano and Leon v. United States*, No. 05-608C (Fed. Cl. filed June 17, 2005), a purchaser of a previously seized vehicle that still contained drugs was arrested along with a passenger by Mexican officials who discovered drugs in the vehicle, and the purchaser and passenger were incarcerated in a Mexican jail. In a second case, *Cervantes v. United States*, 330 F.3d 1186 (9th Cir. 2003), the plaintiff tried to cross the U.S.-Mexican border in a previously seized vehicle that he had purchased, but which still contained contraband. *Id.* at 1187-88. The Ninth Circuit held that the plaintiff's alleged causes of action against the United States for false arrest and false imprisonment were precluded because customs agents had probable cause to arrest the plaintiff upon the discovery of hidden narcotics, but his claim under the Federal Tort Claims Act ("FTCA") was remanded because the 'detention of goods' exception to the government's waiver of sovereign immunity under the FTCA did not apply. *Cervantes*, 330 F.3d at 1188-90.

States, 62 Fed. Cl. 804, 806 (2004) (citing *Henke v. United States*, 60 F.3d 795, 797 (Fed. Cir. 1995)); *see also Hamlet v. United States*, 873 F.2d 1414, 1415-16 (Fed. Cir. 1989). The court must deny defendant's motion to dismiss if the undisputed facts in the complaint reveal any possible basis on which plaintiffs might prevail. *See Scheuer v. Rhodes*, 416 U.S. 232, 236 (1974) (citing *Conley v. Gibson*, 355 U.S. 41, 45-46 (1957)); *Ex parte McCardle*, 74 U.S. (7 Wall.) 506, 514 (1868) (concluding that if a court lacks jurisdiction to decide the merits of a case, then, as a matter of law, the court must dismiss the claim).

A court may grant summary judgment "if . . . [the record] show[s] that there is no genuine issue as to any material fact and that the moving party is entitled to a judgment as a matter of law." Rules of the Court of Federal Claims ("RCFC") 56(c); *see Anderson v. Liberty Lobby, Inc.*, 477 U.S. 242, 247-48 (1986). The moving party bears the burden of establishing that no genuine issue of material fact exists. *See Celotex Corp. v. Catrett*, 477 U.S. 317, 322-25 (1986). A dispute is "genuine" if it "may reasonably be resolved in favor of either party." *Anderson*, 477 U.S. at 250. A fact is deemed "material" if it "might affect the outcome of the suit under the governing law." *Id.* at 248. A court must resolve all inferences "'in the light most favorable to the party opposing the motion'" when deciding these issues. *Matsushita Elec. Indus. Co. v. Zenith Radio Corp.*, 475 U.S. 574, 587-88 (1986) (quoting *United States v. Diebold, Inc.*, 369 U.S. 654, 655 (1962)). If a rational finder could reach only one reasonable conclusion, then a genuine issue of material fact does not exist. *See, e.g.*, *Matsushita*, 475 U.S. at 587.

ANALYSIS

A. Adrian Rodriguez's Claims

The government avers that Mr. Rodriguez lacks standing to raise claims based on breach of contract. First, the government alleges that this court lacks jurisdiction over any of plaintiff Adrian Rodriguez's claims because he was not in privity of contract with the United States.

Def.'s Mot. at 9-10. The government specifically cites the Certificate to Obtain Title to a Vehicle whereby the United States certified that title to the vehicle was transferred to Ali Jazmin, not Adrian, Rodriguez. *Id.*; Def.'s App. at 62. Mr. Rodriguez counters that he is "arguably a party to the contract" with the United States "due to his status as a spouse in a community property state [California]." Plaintiffs' Response to Motion to Dismiss, or in the alternative, for Summary Judgment ("Pls.' Original Response") at 10. Secondarily, Mr. Rodriguez asserts that he is an intended third-party beneficiary of either an agreement between the United States and EG&G or the contract between the government and Mrs. Rodriguez, *see id.* at 10-11; Pls.' Amended Response at 1, 16-17, while the government contends that Mr. Rodriguez has not satisfied the requirements for establishing a third-party beneficiary status. *See* Defendant's Consolidated Reply to Plaintiffs' Opposition to Defendant's Motion [to] Dismiss, or in the Alternative, for Summary Judgment,

Response to Plaintiffs' Motions for Joinder, and Reply to Response to Motions to Strike ("Def.'s Reply") at 4-5.

1. Privity of contract.

Generally, "the 'government consents to be sued only by those with whom it has privity of contract.'" *First Hartford Corp. Pension Plan & Trust v. United States*, 194 F.3d 1279, 1289 (Fed. Cir. 1999) (quoting *Erickson Air Crane Co. of Wash. v. United States*, 731 F.2d 810, 813 (Fed. Cir. 1984)). In the present case, despite the contradictory allegations in the plaintiffs' filings, *see supra*, at 3 n.3, only Ali Jazmin Rodriguez is in privity of contract with the United States pursuant to the transfer of title. *See* Def.'s App. at 62 (Certificate to Obtain Title to a Vehicle).[6] Adrian Rodriguez asserts that because he and his wife reside in a community property state, California, which also served as the location of the contract's execution, he possesses rights under the contract. *See* Pls.' Original Response at 10. Mr. Rodriguez's argument is unavailing. Under California state law, Mr. Rodriguez had no property rights either with respect to the executory contract for the vehicle or to the vehicle itself.[7] He was not a signatory to the contract with the United States

6 "[W]hen a question of the [court's] jurisdiction is raised . . . the court may inquire by affidavits or otherwise, into the facts as they exist." *Land v. Dollar*, 330 U.S. 731, 735 n.4 (1947) (citing *Wetmore v. Bymer*, 169 U.S. 115, 120 (1898)); *see Reynolds*, 846 F.2d at 747; *Ware v. United States*, 57 Fed. Cl. 782, 783 n.1 (2003). The procedure to reach a determination on an issue of jurisdiction "is left to the trial court." *Land*, 330 U.S. at 735 n.4 (quoting *Gibbs v. Buck*, 307 U.S. 66, 71-72 (1939)). Where, as in the present case, "a motion to dismiss for lack of subject matter jurisdiction . . . challenges the truth of the jurisdictional facts alleged in the complaint, the . . . court may consider relevant evidence in order to resolve the factual dispute." *Reynolds*, 846 F.2d at 747 (citing *Land*, 330 U.S. at 735; *Zunamon v. Brown*, 418 F.2d 883, 886 (8th Cir. 1969)). The court has considered the evidence presented by the parties and has concluded that only Mrs. Rodriguez held title to the vehicle.

7 In California, "[e]xcept as otherwise provided by statute, all property, real or personal, wherever situated, acquired by a married person during marriage while domiciled in this state is community property." Cal. Fam. Code § 760. However, "the affirmative act of specifying a form of ownership in the conveyance of title . . . removes such property from the more general [community property] presumption." *In re Marriage of Lucas*, 614 P.2d 285, 288 (Cal. 1980), *superseded in part by statute*, Cal. Fam. Code § 2640, *as recognized in In re Marriage of Walrath*, 952 P.2d 1124, 1130 (Cal. 1998); *see also In re Allustiarte*, 786 F.2d 910, 915-16 (9th Cir. 1986) (noting that the rebuttable record-title presumption is "stronger" than the general rebuttable presumption with respect to community property); William P. Hogoboom & Donald B. King, *California Practice Guide: Family Law* §§ 8:31-8:43 (a married couple acquires a motorboat using community property but takes title in the wife's name as her "sole and separate property" with the consequence that the boat is "rebuttably presumed [to be the w]ife's separate property"). An exception to superiority of the record-title presumption to the general community-property presumption arises in cases involving "a spousal property dispute." *In re Marriage of Haines*, 33 Cal. Rptr. 2d 673 (Cal. Ct. App. 1995); *see also* 5 Harry D. Miller & Marvin B. Starr, *Miller and Starr California Real Estate 3D* § 12:41 (stating that the record-title presumption "applies only in proceedings with third parties, and does not apply in actions between spouses."). The presumption that "[t]he owner of the legal title . . . is . . . the owner of the full beneficial title" can itself by rebutted by "clear and convincing proof." Cal. Evid. Code § 662.

and thus cannot exercise any rights under that contract. *See* Def.'s App. at 62; *Pacetti v. United States*, 50 Fed. Cl. 239, 252 (2001) (concluding that the plaintiff did not have standing to raise claims arising from the government's breach of an agreement with his spouse that pertained to her ability to reinvest sale proceeds in which he claimed a one-half interest under California marital property law); *see also Restatement (Second) of Contracts* § 2 (defining the parties to a contract). Therefore, Mr. Rodriguez may not invoke the Tucker Act, 28 U.S.C. § 1491(a)(1), to raise a claim for breach of contract because he was not in privity of contract with the United States.

2. Third-party beneficiary claims.

Adrian Rodriguez could maintain a claim against the United States if he was an intended third-party beneficiary pursuant to an existing contract between the government and another party. *See Flexfab, L.L.C. v. United States*, 424 F.3d 1254, 1259 (Fed. Cir. 2005) (addressing as a matter of standing, and thus as a jurisdictional issue, the question of whether a plaintiff was an intended third-party beneficiary of a contract). To be considered an intended third-party beneficiary, a "contract must 'reflect [] the express or implied intention of the parties to benefit the third-party.'" *Montana v. United States*, 124 F.3d 1269, 1273 (Fed. Cir. 1997) (quoting *Schuerman v. United States*, 30 Fed. Cl. 420, 433 (1994)). "The intended beneficiary need not be specifically or individually identified in the contract, but must fall within a class clearly intended to be benefited thereby." *Montana*, 124 F.3d at 1273. The Federal Circuit reiterated this test in *Glass v. United States*, 258 F.3d 1349 (Fed. Cir. 2001), and extended the reasoning of *Montana* by stating that the contract must also reflect the intention to benefit the third party "directly." *Id.* at 1354 ("Third party beneficiary status is an 'exceptional privilege' and . . . a party must 'at least show that [the contract] was intended for his *direct* benefit.'") (quoting *German Alliance Ins. Co. v. Home Water Supply Co.*, 226 U.S. 220, 230 (1912) (emphasis added)); *see also Restatement (Second) of Contracts* § 302.

To determine whether Adrian Rodriguez is a third-party beneficiary, the court must consider whether he "'would [have] be[en] reasonable in relying on the promise as manifesting an intention to confer a right on him.'" *Flexfab*, 424 F.3d at 1260 (quoting *Montana*, 124 F.3d at 1273). Mr. Rodriguez asserts that he is an intended third-party beneficiary of a contract between the government and EG&G, and that this alleged contract was breached due to the inadequate search for illegal narcotics in the vehicle. *See* Pls.' Amended Response at 1. For purposes of acting on the pending motion, the court accepts that the United States and EG&G had a form of contract in place. *See* Hr'g Tr. 18:20 to 20:5 (Dec. 22, 2005) (statement by the government's counsel commenting that "any contract that might have existed between the United States and EG&G [as] basically [] an agency arrangement . . . [is] a fair characterization"). Mr. Rodriguez also provides statements from Customs Service officials that imply the possibility that the search of the vehicle was not conducted as thoroughly as regulations and policy required. Pls.' Amended Response at 3-7.

Nonetheless, even if the government had undertaken a duty with respect to EG&G to properly search the vehicle prior to sale, Mr. Rodriguez was not an intended third-party beneficiary. When a member of the public alleges standing to sue as an intended third-party beneficiary of a government contract, the purpose of which is to render a public service, the public citizen is "considered to be [an] incidental third-party beneficiar[y] unless [he] can show a direct right to compensation." *Montana*, 124 F.3d at 1273 n.6 (citing *Schuerman*, 30 Fed. Cl. at 430); *see also Restatement (Second) of Contracts* § 315 ("An incidental beneficiary acquires by virtue of the promise *no right* against the promisor or the promisee." (emphasis added)). In the present case, the government had removed contraband from the vehicle to satisfy the federal government's societal purpose to protect the public and ensure that illegal drugs are outside the general stream of commerce. *See Gonzales v. Raich*, __ U.S. __, 125 S. Ct. 2195, 2202-04 (2005) (summarizing aspects of the federal government's anti-drug policy); *see also* Pls.' App. Ex. 1 (Deposition of Jason Ahern (June 4, 2004), in *Rivera Agredano, et al. v. United States, et al.*, No. 02-CV-2243 B (NLS) (S.D. Cal.)) at 7:4-18 (stating that the "principal responsibility" of "narcotics enforcement" within the Customs Service was "[t]o interdict the narcotics coming into the country").[8] In short, Mr. Rodriguez has failed to establish any direct right to compensation arising from a breach of an agreement between the Customs Service and EG&G. *See Montana*, 124 F.3d at 1273 n.6. Consequently, he did not "stand to directly benefit under" a contract between the United States and EG&G, and thus he can only be considered, at most, an incidental, not intended, third-party beneficiary. *See Glass*, 258 F.3d at 1355.

Mr. Rodriguez also claims the status of an intended third-party beneficiary with respect to the contract between the United States and Ali Jazmin Rodriguez. Compl. ¶ 36; Pls.' Amended Response at 1. The documents associated with the sale from the United States to Mrs. Rodriguez, including the Certificate to Obtain Title to a Vehicle, signed bidder registration form, invoice, and sales catalog, do not show

---

8 The exhibits the plaintiffs include in the appendix to their opposition to the defendant's motion were generated as part of a separate legal proceeding, *Rivera Agredano, et al. v. United States, et al.*, No. 02-CV-2243 B (NLS) (S.D. Cal. filed Nov. 14, 2002), that has since been dismissed and was unrelated to the present case. For purposes of addressing the pending motion, the court has accepted these exhibits pursuant to Fed. R. Evid. 801(d)(2)(d) which defines as not hearsay a statement that "is offered against a party and is . . . a statement made by the party's agent or servant concerning a matter within the scope of the agency or employment, made during the existence of the relationship." Under that rule, the proffering party need not prove that the witness is unavailable nor does the party need also to invoke RCFC 32(a)(2) regarding admissibility of deposition testimony. *See Globe Sav. Bank, F.S.B. v. United States*, 61 Fed. Cl. 91, 94-97 (2004). In the present matter, all five deponents are current employees of the United States and they limited the subject matter of their statements to the scope of their employment. Pls.' App. Exs. 1-5. Their deposition testimony accordingly falls within Fed. R. Evid. 801(d)(2)(D). *See Globe*, 61 Fed. Cl. at 97 (citing *Aliotta v. National R.R. Passenger Corp.*, 315 F.3d 756, 761 (7th Cir. 2003)); *see also PR Contractors, Inc. v. United States*, __ Fed. Cl. __, 2006 WL 163226, at *5 (Jan. 20, 2006).

any intent on the part of the government directly to benefit Adrian Rodriguez. *See* Def.'s App. at 49-62.

To shore up his argument, Mr. Rodriguez points to the court's decision in *Sullivan v. United States*, 54 Fed. Cl. 214 (2002). *See* Pls.' Original Response at 10. In that case, the contract mandated that a government contractor who transported mail for the United States Postal Service had to possess vehicle insurance. *Sullivan*, 54 Fed. Cl. at 215. The court held that there was a triable issue as to whether the purpose of this contractual provision was to confer any rights as a third-party beneficiary upon a person who was injured by the contractor while he operated the vehicle. *Id.* at 216-17. Unlike *Sullivan*, however, in the present case the context of the vehicle sales contract provides no indication that the government intended directly to benefit any third party. *See also Restatement (Second) of Contracts* § 315 ("Effect of a Promise of Incidental Benefit"). Consequently, Adrian Rodriguez is not an intended third-party beneficiary of the contract between the United States and Mrs. Rodriguez.

In sum, this court does not have subject matter jurisdiction to entertain any of Mr. Rodriguez's claims. He has no privity of contract with the government, and he is not an intended third-party beneficiary of an agreement between the government and EG&G or the contract between the Customs Service and Ali Jazmin Rodriguez. The government's motion to dismiss the claims of Adrian Rodriguez is accordingly granted because Mr. Rodriguez has no standing to pursue claims grounded in contract.

B. Ali Jazmin Rodriguez's Claims

1. Breach of an implied contractual term and of an implied warranty.

Mrs. Rodriguez seeks relief from the government on the ground that the Customs Service violated an implied warranty in the contract "that the [vehicle] was reasonably clear of contraband before releasing the same for sale to plaintiffs." Compl. ¶ 25.[9] From the breach, Mrs. Rodriguez alleges she suffered "damages including, but not limited to, loss of liberty, pain and suffering, physical injuries, lost wages, loss of future earning capability, emotional distress, mental anguish, property damages, and other general and special damages." Compl. ¶ 41. The government counters that this court lacks subject matter jurisdiction over Mrs. Rodriguez's claim because the damages she seeks sound in tort and thus should be dismissed.

---

9 Mrs. Rodriguez asserts two separate causes of action: a breach of an implied term in the contract, Compl. ¶¶ 33-41, and a breach of an implied warranty of the contract. Compl. ¶¶ 23-32. The plaintiff avers that both the implied term and implied warranty in the contract were promises made by the government that it would conduct a "complete and thorough" search of the vehicle to ensure that it was "reasonably clear" of contraband prior to its sale. Compl. ¶¶ 25, 34. The existence of an implied warranty in the contract would, itself, be an implied term. Therefore, because the court concludes that there is no practical difference in the scope of the alleged implied term and the alleged implied warranty, it treats the first two causes of action in the plaintiff's complaint as a single claim.

Def.'s Mot. at 7-9. Alternatively, should this court find that it does possess jurisdiction over her claim, the government seeks summary judgment on the ground that the terms and conditions of the contract disclaimed any implied warranties. *Id.* at 15-17.

The Tucker Act explicitly states that this court "shall have jurisdiction to render judgment upon any claim against the United States . . . for liquidated or unliquidated damages in cases not sounding in tort." 28 U.S.C. § 1491(a)(1). Correlatively, this court has very limited juridical power to award damages that are shaped by tort law in an action based on breach of contract. "The court lacks jurisdiction to award . . . damages for emotional distress and pain and suffering. Except in limited circumstances . . . not applicable here, the court cannot award damages for the emotional consequences of a breach of contract because such consequences are speculative as a matter of law." *Pratt v. United States*, 50 Fed. Cl. 469, 482 (2001) (citing *Bohac v. Dep't of Agriculture*, 239 F.3d 1334, 1340 (Fed. Cir. 2001); *Kania v. United States*, 650 F.2d 264, 269 (Ct. Cl. 1981); *H.H.O., Inc. v. United States*, 7 Cl. Ct. 703, 708 (1985)); *see also Restatement (Second) of Contracts* § 353. *But see Chain Belt Co. v. United States*, 115 F. Supp. 701, 712 (Ct. Cl. 1953) ("A tortious breach of contract is not a tort independent of the contract so as to preclude an action under the Tucker Act.").

Mrs. Rodriguez argues that the contract was breached when the government sold the vehicle to her without discovering 33 pounds of marijuana in a box hidden on the underside of the vehicle because the circumstances of the sale had created an implied warranty that a "thorough and adequate search" had been conducted. Compl. ¶¶ 35, 37-38. The damages she alleges, however, center on the injuries Adrian, not Ali Jazmin, Rodriguez, suffered when he "was arrested and imprisoned by the Mexican authorities." Compl. ¶¶ 31, 39, 54; *see* Def.'s Mot. at 10. As a plaintiff, Mrs. Rodriguez's claims for damages must be analyzed only with respect to the harm that she herself may have incurred. *See Restatement (Second) of Contracts* § 346 ("The *injured party* has a right to damages.") (emphasis added). The government is correct that Mrs. Rodriguez fails to specify damages that she actually suffered, except for generalized property damages. Def.'s Mot. at 10. Thus, most of the damages that Mrs. Rodriguez seeks are outside the subject matter jurisdiction of this court as they arise from conduct independent of the alleged breach of contract. Def.'s Mot. at 9; *see L'Enfant Plaza Properties, Inc. v. United States*, 645 F.2d 886, 892 (Ct. Cl. 1981) (citing *Burtt v. United States*, 176 Ct. Cl. 310, 313-14 (1966)); 28 U.S.C. § 1491(a)(1). Mrs. Rodriguez has implicitly recognized this deficiency because she has sought leave to amend her complaint to elaborate her request for general property damages. Hr'g Tr. 74:19 to 75:2. In this instance, because no answer has been filed, an amended complaint may be submitted as a matter of course by Mrs. Rodriguez. RCFC 7, 15(a). Even if the government had filed an answer, RCFC 15(a) would obligate the court to grant leave to file an amended complaint "freely . . . when justice so requires." The Supreme Court has listed a variety of factors that a court should consider when determining whether to grant leave to amend, such as undue delay, bad faith, repeated failure to cure prior deficiencies, undue prejudice, and futility. *Foman v. Davis*, 371 U.S. 178, 182 (1962) (interpreting Federal Rule of Civil Procedure 15(a), which is identical to RCFC 15(a)). In effect, "[i]f the underlying facts or circumstances relied upon by a plaintiff may be a proper subject of relief, [s]he ought to be afforded an opportunity to test h[er] claim on the merits." *Foman*, 371 U.S. at 182.

The government has argued that it would be futile for Mrs. Rodriguez to file an amended complaint because even if she did amend her complaint she would still not be entitled to any relief. Hr'g Tr. 76:22 to 77:7. Def.'s Reply at 11-12. However, contrary to the government's assertions, Mrs. Rodriguez could be entitled to relief if she were to amend her complaint and seek damages based purely upon contractual remedies, whether premised upon expectancy, reliance, or restitutionary theories. *See Restatement (Second) of Contracts* §§ 347, 371; *Restatement (Third) of Restitution and Unjust Enrichment (Tentative Draft No. 3 (March 22, 2004))* § 37(1)(b) ("a decree of rescission may require the defendant . . . to repay amounts received on account of the contract price"); *see also* Hr'g Tr. 75:21-24.

Even Mrs. Rodriguez's general allegations of property damages suffice to supply the court with subject matter jurisdiction over her claims for breach of contract premised upon the Tucker Act, 28 U.S.C. § 1491(a)(1). Nonetheless, such subject matter jurisdiction does not preclude the government from seeking either dismissal for failure to state a claim or a summary judgment, on the ground that the sale's terms and conditions disclaimed any warranty. Def.'s Mot. at 15-17. Therefore, the issue remaining before the court is whether Mrs. Rodriguez has stated a claim upon which relief can be granted for breach of an implied warranty.

The terms and conditions of the sale of the vehicle in question are set out in several documents. Prior to the auction, EG&G produced a pamphlet advertising eleven different government sales, listing their dates and locations. Def.'s App. at 47-48 (Public Auctions Brochure). That brochure also contained a section entitled "Terms and Conditions" that included the payment terms, how one registered to bid, and how vehicles that were successfully purchased should be removed. *Id.* at 48. In addition, under the "Terms and Conditions," the brochure stated that "[a]ll merchandise is sold 'As is, Where is' without warrant, or guarantee of any kind, stated, implied or otherwise. Please bid from your personal observations!" *Id.* Mrs. Rodriguez asserts that she never received or read the brochure printed by EG&G. Pls.' App. Ex. 7 (Declaration of Ali Jazmin Rodriguez (Nov. 18, 2005)) ¶ 4.

To participate in the auction conducted on March 5, 2003, an individual had to register to bid by completing and executing a Bidder Registration Form. Def.'s App. at 45 (Declaration of Charles F. Fulghum, West Region Director, EG&G (July 28, 2005)) ¶ 6; *see* Def.'s App. at 49 (Blank Bidder Registration Form). Mrs. Rodriguez did complete and sign such a form, and was assigned bidder number 167. Def.'s App. at 50 (Completed Bidder Registration Form). The form stated that the individual "agree[d] to comply with the terms of sale contained in the sale catalog for this sale." *Id.* The sale catalog listed a description of all the vehicles that would be available at the auction and the terms and conditions of the sale. Def.'s App. at 51-60 (Sales Catalog). The "Warranty-Guarantee" section of the terms and conditions in the catalog stated that "[a]ll merchandise is sold on an 'AS IS/WHERE IS' basis, without warranty or guarantee as to condition, fitness to use, or merchantability stated, implied or otherwise. Please bid from your personal observations." *Id.* at 51. In the catalog, the Volkswagen Passat that the plaintiff bought from the Customs Service was listed as lot number 96. *Id.* at 55.

Following the "auction, successful bidders [we]re presented with an invoice" that listed the vehicles purchased, total bids, remaining outstanding balance, and advised that "all merchandise [was] sold on an 'as is/where is' basis with no warrantees or guarantees as to condition, fitness to use, or merchantability stated or implied." Def.'s App. at 61 (Invoice). "In order to take possession of the [vehicle], the bidder must . . . present the invoice to McCormack personnel." Def.'s App. at 46 (Declaration of Fulghum) ¶ 10.

Mrs. Rodriguez alleges that "[t]o the best of [her] recollection, at no time did [she] see the sales catalog for the auction," Pls.' App. Ex. 7 (Declaration of Ali Jazmin Rodriguez) ¶ 5, even though a catalog was "generally and customarily made available by McCormack to bidders at the auction." Def.'s App. at 46 (Declaration of Fulghum) ¶ 9. Furthermore, Mrs. Rodriguez asserts that despite being the successful bidder on the two vehicles listed on the invoice, Def.'s App. at 61 (Invoice), and having received both vehicles and the Certificate to Obtain Title to a Vehicle, she does "not recall receiving an invoice with a disclaimer on it." Pls.' App. Ex. 7 (Declaration of Ali Jazmin Rodriguez) ¶ 6. Ultimately, however, "[f]ailure to read the terms of a contract, particularly when so directed," such as by the signed Bidder Registration Form, "cannot be used as a defense." *Richardson Camera Co. v. United States*, 467 F.2d 491, 496 (Ct. Cl. 1972) (citing *Schoeffel v. United States*, 193 Ct. Cl. 923, 935 (1971)); *see also Fraas Surgical Mfg. Co. v. United States*, 571 F.2d 34, 40 (Ct. Cl. 1978).

The government argues that in light of the repeated "as is/where is" disclaimer language, Mrs. Rodriguez cannot state a claim for breach of contract. Def.'s Reply at 8-10, 12. The disclaimer language, the government avers, "simply means that the purchaser took the vehicle as it was and where it was at the time of sale, after the completion of whatever search was performed." *Id.* at 10. Mrs. Rodriguez counters that the fact that the vehicle was sold in a forfeiture sale conducted on behalf of the United States itself creates an implied warranty that the vehicle had been properly searched for contraband prior to its public availability. Pls.' Amended Response at 19. Moreover, she contends that the scope of the warranty disclaimer is not wide enough to incorporate the alleged failure of the government to properly search the vehicle. *Id.* at 20.

An "as is/where is" disclaimer has been held to be an enforceable contractual provision "sufficient to transfer the risk of loss to a purchaser of government property." *Pratt*, 50 Fed. Cl. at 477 (citing *Varkell v. United States*, 334 F.2d 653, 654 (Ct. Cl. 1964)). In a variety of circumstances, the United States has inserted "as is/where is" disclaimers in contracts for the sale of government property. *See, e.g., Edward Levy Metals, Inc. v. United States*, 485 F.2d 603, 604- 605 (Ct. Cl. 1973) (sale of two traveling crane gantries); *Varkell*, 334 F.2d at 654 (sale of surplus property); *United States v. Hathaway*, 242 F.2d 897, 899-900 (9th Cir. 1957) (sale of four sets of steel lock gates located below water); *Barstow Truck Parts & Equip. Co. v. United States*, 5 Cl. Ct. 224, 225 (1984) (sale of surplus property). The specific language used in the aforementioned cases, however, ostensibly disclaims more than the clause in the contract in the present case. *Compare Barstow Truck Parts*, 5 Cl. Ct. at 225 ("[A]ll property . . . is offered for sale 'as is' and 'where is.' The description of the property is based on the best information available . . . [and] the Government makes no warranty, . . . expressed or implied as to quantity, kind, character, quality, weight, size or description of any of the property, or its fitness for any use of purpose."), *with* Def.'s App. at 51 ("All merchandise is sold on an 'AS IS, WHERE IS' basis without warranty or guarantee as to condition, fitness to use, or merchantability stated, implied or otherwise."). Moreover, the government's counsel conceded that in seizure sales and auctions conducted on behalf of the Customs Service after the auction in the present case, the government used language that contained "stronger disclaimers . . . or, at least, more clear disclaimers." Hr'g Tr. 35:12-16.[10]

Based upon the contractual documents presented to the court in this case, the court concludes that plaintiff has stated a rudimentary claim for damages arising from an alleged breach of contract and that an amendment of her claim to elucidate further the damages alleged to be due would not be futile. The catalog that was made available to all registered bidders by McCormack indicated that the auction would offer for sale vehicles that had been seized by the Customs Service, Def.'s App. at 51 (Sales Catalog), a federal agency whose "principal responsibility" is to "interdict the narcotics coming into the" United States. Pls.' App. Ex. 1 (Deposition of Ahern) at 7:4-18. Moreover, the advertising brochure that EG&G produced stated that the public auction would sell vehicles seized by the government. Def.'s App. at 47 (Public Auctions Brochure). The prospective buyers, including Mrs. Rodriguez, were aware that the vehicles were available after being seized as a result of drug or other violations. Hr'g Tr. 20:18 to 21:19; *see* Pls.' App. Ex. 7 (Declaration of Ali Jazmin Rodriguez) ¶ 7. Therefore, an implied warranty respecting a reasonable search for drugs may have arisen in the contract between the government and plaintiff based upon the acknowledged context of how the vehicle had been obtained by the government.

---

10 The court has failed to discover, nor have the parties identified, any prior opinion from any court in which the exact disclaimer language at issue in the present case was interpreted or contested. Hr'g Tr. at 40:1-10, 59:15 to 60:6.

The government contends that the "as is/where is" language disclaimed any implied warranty of the type asserted, Def.'s Reply at 10, but the court cannot agree based upon the plain meaning of the disclaimer. *See Record Steel and Constr., Inc. v. United States*, 62 Fed. Cl. 508, 513 (2004) ("If the language [of a contract] is explicit and unambiguous, the court must give effect to its plain meaning") (citing *L.W. Matteson, Inc. v. United States*, 61 Fed. Cl. 296, 307- 308 (2004)). The contract specifically disclaimed express and implied warranties, but only respecting the vehicle's "condition, fitness to use, or merchantability." Def.'s App. at 51 (Sales Catalog). The plain meaning of the terms "condition, fitness to use and merchantability" refers to the construction and maintenance of the vehicle and its utility for transportation, including how it operates mechanically.[11] These terms would not necessarily apply to whether the vehicle had been modified in a way that had no effect on its ability to function for transportation and introduced an attribute not ordinarily associated with such a vehicle, including affixing a box containing illegal drugs to the vehicle's underside. Thus, an implied warranty that the vehicle would be properly searched prior to its sale would fall outside the scope of the excluded terms.

This straightforward interpretation is strengthened by the fact that the disclaimer warned bidders that they should "bid from [their] personal observations." Def.'s App. at 51 (Sales Catalog). According to the record as it presently stands before the court, a bidder had a limited opportunity to inspect the vehicle prior to purchase. Hr'g Tr. 60:7 to 62:5 (indicating that all bidders were "allowed to get within a certain radius of the cars" but were not "allowed to touch them at all"). In at least one case that interpreted an "as is/where is" disclaimer, although the exact language covered a much wider scope than in the present matter, the plaintiff's failure to properly inspect the property that it purchased was held fatal to its claim of breach of contract. *See Varkell*, 334 F.2d at 655. The present record does not support any defense that the box containing the contraband would have been visible to a reasonable person performing a visual inspection at a distance from the vehicle.

Accordingly, an issue remains before the court that cannot be resolved at this procedural juncture. There may well have been an implied warranty that the vehicle had been reasonably searched for drugs, based upon the context in which the vehicles sold at auction were obtained.[12] Such an implied warranty would fall outside the scope of the contract's "as is/where is" disclaimer. Consequently, the government's motion to dismiss, or in the alternative, for summary judgment on Mrs.

---

11 The terms "fitness to use" and "merchantability" substantially overlap; an implied warranty of merchantability is a warranty that the property is fit for the ordinary purposes for which it is used. *See* Black's Law Dictionary 1582 (7th ed. 1999).

12 Submissions to the court indicate that the Customs Service had a policy in place respecting how a search of a seized vehicle should be conducted prior to its public sale. Pls.' Amended Response at 3-7; *see, e.g.,* Pls.' App. Ex. 4 (Deposition of Joseph Marilao (June 9, 2004), *Rivera Agredano, et al. v. United States, et al.*, No. 02-CV-2243 B (NLS) (S.D. Cal.)) at 25:2-8 (stating that the search policy was a seven-point inspection).

Rodriguez's claim is denied. She may amend her complaint to restate the damages she has allegedly suffered.

2. Breach of the implied covenant of good faith and fair dealing.

Mrs. Rodriguez also alleges that the government violated the contract's implied covenant of good faith and fair dealing when it failed to "thoroughly inspect" the vehicle for contraband before it became available to the public at auction. Compl. ¶ 43. She in effect contends that the Customs Service did not follow its policy on properly searching the vehicle for illegal drugs because the Service "decided to limit searches for the purpose of increasing [the] resale value of the vehicle" without disclosing this decision to potential purchasers. Pls.' Amended Response at 21. The United States counters that the plaintiff has failed to state a claim because she has not offered sufficient proof that the government intended to injure her. Def.'s Mot. at 13. In addition, the government avers that the "as is/where is" warranty language in the contract disclaims any obligation on the part of the Customs Service. *Id.* at 15-17.

"[I]n every contract there exists an implied covenant of good faith." *Southern Cal. Edison v. United States*, 58 Fed. Cl. 313, 325 (2003) (quoting 13 *Williston on Contracts* § 38:15 at 437); *accord Asco-Falcon II Shipping Co. v. United States*, 18 Cl. Ct. 484, 491 (1989); *Restatement (Second) of Contracts* § 205. The covenant obligates both parties "not to interfere with the other party's performance and not to act so as to destroy the reasonable expectations of the other party regarding the fruits of the contracts." *Centex Corp. v. United States*, 395 F.3d 1283, 1304 (Fed. Cir. 2005); *see also First Nationwide Bank v. United States*, 431 F.3d 1342, 1349-51 (Fed. Cir. 2005). For a plaintiff to successfully assert a claim for breach of the implied covenant of good faith and fair dealing respecting a contract with the government, she "must allege and prove facts constituting a specific intent to injure [the] plaintiff on the part of a government official." *Pratt*, 50 Fed. Cl. at 479 (citing *Texas Instruments, Inc. v. United States*, 991 F.2d 760, 768 (Fed. Cir. 1993)); *see Southern Cal. Edison*, 58 Fed. Cl. at 325 ("'plaintiff[] must allege facts which if proved would constitute malice or an intent to injure'" (internal citations and quotation marks omitted)). The intended injury may be as simple and straightforward as elimination of tax benefits previously granted. *See First Nationwide Bank*, 431 F.3d at 1350-51.

For some time, litigation about the covenant of good faith and fair dealing has been infused with disagreement about the effect of the presumption that government officials act in good faith. *See Am-Pro Protective Agency v. United States*, 281 F.3d 1234, 1239 (Fed. Cir. 2002) (citing *Knotts v. United States*, 121 F. Supp. 630 (Ct. Cl. 1954)). In *Am-Pro*, the Federal Circuit recognized that courts in the circuit were using two different descriptions of the appropriate standard of proof necessary to overcome the presumption that a government official had acted in good faith. *Am-Pro*, 281 F.3d at 1239-40; *compare Schaefer v. United States*, 633 F.2d 945, 948-49 (Ct. Cl. 1980) (requiring "well-nigh irrefragable proof") *with*

George v. United States, 166 Ct. Cl. 527, 531 (1964) (necessitating "clear evidence"). Ultimately, the court of appeals equated "well-nigh irrefragable proof" with the traditional clear and convincing standard of proof,[13] and held that the latter legal standard "most appropriately describes the burden of proof applicable to the presumption of the government[']s good faith." *Am-Pro*, 281 F.3d at 1239; *see also Galen Medical Assoc., Inc. v. United States*, 369 F.3d 1324, 1330 (Fed. Cir. 2004).[14] Questions about the meaning and strength of the presumption of the government's good faith are presented by Mrs. Rodriguez's allegations.

Mrs. Rodriguez proffers the testimony of a number of government officials regarding the policy guidance that was distributed to customs officers at ports of entry in Southern California, including San Ysidro where plaintiff's vehicle was initially obtained, setting out the manner in which seized vehicles were to be searched. Pls.' App. Ex. 1 (Deposition of Ahern) at 49:8 to 52:17 (confirming that a policy memo was issued by the Field Director of customs operations in Southern California), Ex. 2 (Deposition of Robert Root (June 24, 2004), *Rivera Agredano, et al. v. United States, et al.*, No. 02-CV-2243 B (NLS) (S.D. Cal.)), at 29:6 to 32:17 (describing how canines would inspect vehicles for illegal narcotics on multiple occasions). Inspectors for the Customs Service are taught in training and by their supervisors to inspect seized vehicles and clear any illegal narcotics and other contraband that they discover. *See* Pls.' App. Ex. 4 (Deposition of Marilao) at 25:2-17 (detailing a seven-point inspection that was taught to customs inspectors), Ex. 5 (Deposition of Robert Bickers (June 9, 2004), *Rivera Agredano, et al. v. United States, et al.*, No. 02-CV-2243 B (NLS) (S.D. Cal.)), at 26:21 to 27:7 (describing how as a contraband enforcement team supervisor the deponent would correct inspectors who "were under the impression they were not supposed to tear the vehicle up"). De-

---

13 The Federal Circuit has described the clear and convincing standard as a heavier burden than preponderance evidence but a lighter burden than proof beyond a reasonable doubt, and as a level of proof that "produces in the mind of the trier of fact an abiding conviction that the truth of a factual contention is highly probable." *Am-Pro*, 281 F.3d at 1240 (quoting *Price v. Symsek*, 988 F.2d 1187, 1191 (Fed. Cir. 1993)).

14 In *Tecom, Inc. v. United States*, 66 Fed. Cl. 736 (2005), Judge Wolski of this court reviewed the history in this circuit of the presumption of good faith on the part of government officials and concluded that it "poses no special obstacle to parties alleging" a breach of the implied covenant of good faith and fair dealing. *Id.* at 771. Instead, [w]hen a government official acts under a duty to employ discretion, . . . and a lack of good faith is alleged that does not sink to the level of fraud or quasi-criminal wrongdoing, clear and convincing evidence is not needed to rebut the presumption [of good faith]. Instead, this may be inferred from a lack of substantial evidence, gross error, or the like. And when the government actions that are alleged are not formal, discretionary decisions, but instead the actions that might be taken by any party to a contract, the presumption of good faith has no application. *Tecom*, 66 Fed. Cl. at 769 (citing *Moore v. United States*, 46 Ct. Cl. 139, 172-74 (1910)). Accordingly, he respectfully disagreed with opinions that have adopted and applied the clear and convincing evidence standard broadly when analyzing a potential breach of the implied covenant. Instead, Judge Wolski would limit applicability of the strong presumption elucidated in *Am-Pro* to situations where matters of fraud or quasi-criminal wrongdoing are alleged. *Tecom*, 66 Fed. Cl. at 771 n.41.

spite this policy in the Customs Service, at least one former senior inspector stated that he is aware that other inspectors had been told to minimize the damage when inspecting a seized vehicle "for resale purposes." Pls.' App. Ex. 4 (Deposition of Marilao) at 26:2 to 27:2. Furthermore, another employee who worked at the San Ysidro border crossing had heard other inspectors discuss minimizing the amount of damage to seized vehicles during inspections. Pls.' App. Ex. 5 (Deposition of Bickers) at 26:23 to 27:23.

Resolving all inferences "in the light most favorable" to plaintiff in deciding whether to grant defendant's motion for summary judgment, *Matsushita*, 475 U.S. at 587-88 (1986) (internal citations and quotation marks omitted), the court concludes that Mrs. Rodriguez has stated a valid claim for breach of the implied warranty of good faith and fair dealing over which this court has jurisdiction. 28 U.S.C. § 1491(a)(1). Therefore, the government's motion to dismiss, or in the alternative, for summary judgment on Mrs. Rodriguez's claim that the Customs Service breached the implied covenant of good faith and fair dealing is denied. As with Mrs. Rodriguez's first cause of action, she should amend her claim to clarify the damages sought.

CONCLUSION

For the reasons set forth, the government's motion to dismiss, or in the alternative, for summary judgment, is GRANTED IN PART and DENIED IN PART. The government's motion to dismiss is GRANTED with respect to plaintiff Adrian Rodriguez's claims. The government's motion to dismiss, or in the alternative, for summary judgment with respect to plaintiff Ali Jazmin Rodriguez's claims is DENIED. Mrs. Rodriguez should amend her claims to clarify the damages sought, as explained above.[15]

Mrs. Rodriguez shall file an amended complaint by February 15, 2006. The government shall file an answer to Mrs. Rodriguez's Complaint on or before March 1, 2006. Thereafter, a status conference shall be held in this case on March 16, 2006, commencing at 2:00 p.m. EST by telephonic means.

IT IS SO ORDERED.

---

15 Plaintiffs' Motion to File Revised Brief and Supplemental Documents is GRANTED. Defendant's Motion to Strike is DENIED. Plaintiff Ali Jazmin Rodriguez's two Motions for Joinder in (1) Plaintiff Adrian Rodriguez's Response to Defendant's Motion to Dismiss, or in the alternative, for Summary Judgment, and Statement of Uncontroverted Facts, and in (2) Plaintiff Adrian Rodriguez's Response to Motion to Strike and Request to File Revised Brief and Supplemental Pleadings, are hereby DENIED as moot because both Mr. and Mrs. Rodriguez have been co-plaintiffs in this action.

SOMPO JAPAN INSURANCE COMPANY OF AMERICA
v.
UNION PACIFIC RAILROAD COMPANY

456 F.3d 54 (2d Cir. 2006)
Decided July 10, 2006

Before: WESLEY and HALL, Circuit Judges, and TRAGER,[1] District Judge.

OPINION

WESLEY, Circuit Judge:

A shipment of thirty-two tractors, en route from Tokyo, Japan to Swanee, Georgia, was severely damaged when the train carrying the cargo derailed in Texas. The cargo owner, Kubota Tractor Corporation ("Kubota"), collected the full value of the tractors—$ 479,500—from its insurer, Sompo Japan Insurance Co. of America ("Sompo"). Subrogating Kubota's claim, Sompo then brought this suit against defendant-appellee Union Pacific Railroad Co. ("Union Pacific" or "the Railroad") in the Southern District of New York. The district court (Duffy, J.) granted partial summary judgment in favor of Union Pacific, giving effect to the contract for carriage, which incorporates by reference the Carriage of Goods by Sea Act ("COGSA"), Pub. L. No. 74-521, 49 Stat. 1207 (1936) (codified at *46 U.S.C. app. §§ 1301-1315*), and effectively limits Union Pacific's liability to $ 500 per tractor, or $ 16,000. *See Sompo Japan Ins. of Am. v. Union Pac. R.R., 2003 U.S. Dist. LEXIS 19757, No. 03-1604, 2003 WL 22510361, at *4 (S.D.N.Y. Nov. 5, 2003).*[2]

On appeal, Sompo argues that the district court erred in finding that another statute, the Carmack Amendment to the Interstate Commerce Act of 1887 ("Carmack"), Act of June 29, 1906, ch. 3591, 34 Stat. 584 (1906) (current version at *49 U.S.C.*

1 The Honorable David G. Trager, Judge of the United States District Court for the Eastern District of New York, sitting by designation.

2 After the district court denied Sompo's motion for reconsideration, the parties stipulated to a final judgment subject to Sompo's right to appeal. See Sompo Japan Ins. of Am. v. Union Pac. R.R. Co., No. 03-1604 (S.D.N.Y. Nov. 18, 2003); Sompo Japan Ins. Co. of Am. v. Union Pac. R.R. Co., No. 03-1604 (S.D.N.Y. March 31, 2004)

§ 11706), does not govern the Railroad's liability in this case. We agree and accordingly vacate the district court's order for partial summary judgment and remand this case for further proceedings.

BACKGROUND

In July 2002, Kubota hired Mitsui OSK Line Ltd. ("MOL"), an ocean shipping company, to ship thirty-two tractors from Tokyo, Japan to Swanee, Georgia. As evidence of this agreement, MOL issued three identical bills of lading, contracts that "record[] that a carrier has received goods from the party that wishes to ship them, state[] the terms of carriage, and serve[] as evidence of the contract for carriage." *Norfolk S. Ry. Co. v. Kirby, 543 U.S. 14, 18, 125 S. Ct. 385, 160 L. Ed. 2d 283 (2004)*. The bills of lading were "through" bills: they covered the entire journey from start to finish, including both the ocean and land legs. *See* id. at 25-26. Further, they were "intermodal" through bills, meaning that they contemplated multiple modes of transportation, including ocean and rail carriage. Pursuant to the bills of lading, MOL shipped the tractors by ocean transit from Tokyo to Los Angeles, California where the cargo was then transferred from MOL's ship to MOL's subcontractor, Union Pacific,[3] for rail carriage to Georgia. Union Pacific issued electronic waybills[4] covering the rail carriage to Georgia. While Union Pacific was transporting the cargo, the tractors were damaged in a train derailment in Texas.

In the district court, Union Pacific argued that, pursuant to the MOL bills of lading, its liability should be limited to $ 500 per package. In particular, Union Pacific relied upon two provisions in the bills, Clause 29 and Clause 4. Clause 29 is a "clause paramount," which identifies the law that will govern the rights and liabilities of all parties to the bill of lading. Stephen G. Wood, *Multimodal Transportation: An American Perspective on Carrier Liability and Bill of Lading Issues*, 46 Am. J. Comp. L. 403, 408 n. 37 (1998). The clause paramount in the MOL bills recognizes COGSA as the governing law for the ocean leg of the journey and further includes a "period of responsibility clause," *see* id. at 408 n. 36, a contractual provision extending COGSA's reach beyond "the period from the time when the goods are loaded on to the time when they are discharged from the ship." *46 U.S.C. app. § 1301(e)*. The period of responsibility clause in the MOL bills of lading provides that "[MOL] shall be entitled to the benefits of the defences [sic] and limitations in the U.S. COGSA, whether the loss or damage to the Goods occurs at sea or not." *Sompo, 2003 U.S. Dist. LEXIS 19757, 2003 WL 22510361, at *2* (quoting MOL bills of lading) (second alteration in *Sompo*; emphasis removed).

---

3 There is some confusion as to how exactly the rail shipment was subcontracted to Union Pacific. See Sompo, 2003 U.S. Dist. LEXIS 19757, 2003 WL 22510361, at *1 n. 2. How the subcontract was entered is of no moment to the resolution of this appeal.

4 Like bills of lading, waybills are contracts for the carriage of goods. 1 T. SCHOENBAUM, ADMIRALTY LAW § 10-11 (4th ed. 2006). But in contrast to bills of lading, waybills are non-negotiable. Id.

Clause 4 of the MOL bills of lading constitutes what is referred to as a "himalaya clause,"[5] a contractual provision "extend[ing] to third parties the defenses, immunities, limitations or other protections a law or a bill of lading confers on a carrier." Wood, supra, at 408 n. 35. The himalaya clause in the MOL bills expressly authorizes MOL to subcontract the carriage of Kubota's tractors and grants all subcontractors "the benefit of all provisions herein benefiting the Carrier [MOL] as if such provisions were expressly for their benefit." Sompo, 2003 U.S. Dist. LEXIS 19757, 2003 WL 22510361, at *2 (quoting MOL bills of lading) (emphasis removed). Combining the Clause 29 period of responsibility clause with the Clause 4 himalaya clause, Union Pacific argued that its liability as a subcontractor was limited to $ 500 per tractor.

The district court agreed with Union Pacific. It rejected Sompo's contention that two other federal statutes—Carmack and the Staggers Rail Act of 1980 ("Staggers"), Pub. L. No. 96-448, 94 Stat. 1895 (codified at *49 U.S.C. § 11706*)—governed the liability of Union Pacific in this case. Sompo argues on appeal, as it argued below, that Carmack and Staggers together take precedence over the COGSA liability limitation that the MOL bills of lading extend to Union Pacific. Although the district court recognized that Carmack and Staggers apply in certain circumstances to impose full liability upon a rail carrier for any losses caused by the railroad, it nevertheless ruled that, because MOL employed through bills of lading containing period of responsibility and himalaya clauses, the Carmack/Staggers statutory regime was inapplicable to this case. Sompo, 2003 U.S. Dist. LEXIS 19757, 2003 WL 22510361, at *4. We disagree. Carmack applies to the domestic rail portion of a continuous intermodal shipment originating in a foreign country, like the one at issue here. While the through bills attempt to extend COGSA's sweep inland, that contractual extension lacks the force of statute. And in our view, the intermodal through bills, written in the context of COGSA, falls short of the Staggers prerequisite for limiting a rail carrier's Carmack liability. Carmack controls; a remand is required.

DISCUSSION

I. The Statutory Landscape

The issues presented in this case arise out of the confluence of two fairly complex federal statutory schemes that govern different aspects of international commerce.

A. COGSA

COGSA "was lifted almost bodily from the Hague Rules of 1921, as amended by the Brussels Convention of 1924." *Robert C. Herd & Co. v. Krawill Mach.*

5 The clause derives its name "from the steamship 'Himalaya' which was involved in Adler v. Dixon, [1955] 1 Q.B. 158 (C.A. 1954)." Toshiba Int'l Corp. v. M/V "SEA-Land Express", 841 F. Supp. 123, 125 n. 4 (S.D.N.Y. 1994) (alteration in original).

Corp., 359 U.S. 297, 301, 79 S. Ct. 766, 3 L. Ed. 2d 820 (1959). The purpose of the Hague Rules was to establish "international uniformity in the law governing the carriage of goods by sea." Michael F. Sturley, *Uniformity in the Law Governing the Carriage of Goods By Sea*, 26 J. Mar. L. & Com. 553, 556 (1995) (hereinafter "Uniformity in the Law"). "COGSA is the culmination of a multilateral effort 'to establish uniform ocean bills of lading to govern the rights and liabilities of carriers and shippers *inter se* in international trade . . . ." *Vimar Seguros y Reaseguros, S.A. v. M/V Sky Reefer, 515 U.S. 528, 537, 115 S. Ct. 2322, 132 L. Ed. 2d 462 (1995)* (quoting Robert C. Herd & Co., 359 U.S. at 301).

COGSA establishes a negligence-based liability regime.[6] The statute also explicitly permits a carrier to limit its liability for loss or damage to the cargo it is carrying to $ 500 per "package." *46 U.S.C. app. § 1304(5)*.[7] A carrier cannot avail itself of the COGSA $ 500-per-package liability limitation unless the shipper is given a "fair opportunity" to declare a higher liability value for its cargo. *Gen. Elec. Co. v. MV Nedlloyd, 817 F.2d 1022, 1028 (2d Cir. 1987)*. Thus, as long as the shipper is given a fair opportunity to declare a value higher than $ 500 per package—the higher value need not be the full value of the goods—the carrier's maximum liability is limited to whatever value the shipper declares. If the shipper declares no value, the carrier's liability is defaulted to $ 500 per package. But if the carrier fails to give the shipper a fair opportunity to declare a value, then the carrier is liable for the full value of the cargo.

By its terms, COGSA only applies to "the period from the time when the goods are loaded on to the time when they are discharged from the ship," *46 U.S.C. app. § 1301(e)*, the so-called "tackle-to-tackle" period. But the statute also contemplates that parties will enter into agreements extending COGSA's terms beyond the tackle-to-tackle period:

> Nothing contained in [COGSA] shall prevent a carrier or a shipper from entering into any agreement, stipulation, condition, reservation, or exemption as to the responsibility and liability of the carrier or the ship for the loss or damage to or in connection with the custody and care and handling of goods prior to the loading on and subsequent to the discharge from the ship on which the goods are carried by sea.46 U.S.C. app. § 1307. Thus, COGSA does not prevent a carrier in its bill of lading from choosing "to extend the [COGSA] default rule to the entire period in which the [cargo] would be under its responsibility, including the period of the inland transport." Kirby, 543 U.S. at 29.

---

6 Under COGSA, a carrier may avoid liability on a number of grounds, including "due diligence" with respect to damage caused by unseaworthiness. See 46 U.S.C. app. §1304(1). With respect to damage caused by something other than unseaworthines, the carrier can avoid liability by proving among other things that he was without actual fault and privity and that his agents or servants were without fault or neglect. See id. § 1304(2)(q).

7 The statute itself does not define the term "package," which is a term that is largely fact-dependent. See 2A-XVI BENEDICT ON ADMIRALTY § 167 (7th ed. 1998). In any case, the definition of "package" is not at issue in this case.

B. The Carmack Amendment and the Staggers Rail Act of 1980

In 1887, Congress passed the Interstate Commerce Act ("ICA") and created the Interstate Commerce Commission ("ICC"). The ICA empowered the ICC to regulate railroad rates, a responsibility that in 1995 Congress transferred to the Surface Transportation Board ("Board"). *See* Interstate Commerce Commission Termination Act of 1995, Pub. L. No. 104-88, 109 Stat. 803 (codified generally at Title 49). Congress added Carmack to the ICA in 1906, *see* Act of June 29, 1906, ch. 3591, 34 Stat. 584 (1906), in an effort "to create a national scheme of carrier liability for goods damaged or lost during interstate shipment under a valid bill of lading." *Ting-Hwa Shao v. Link Cargo (Taiwan) Ltd., 986 F.2d 700, 704 (4th Cir. 1993).* Carmack applies to carriage by railroad or "by railroad and water" if the carriage is "under common control, management, or arrangement for a continuous carriage or shipment," including "transportation in the United States between a place in . . . the United States and a place in a foreign country." *49 U.S.C. § 10501(a).* In enacting Carmack, Congress also intended "to relieve shippers of the burden of searching out a particular negligent carrier from among the often numerous carriers handling an interstate shipment of goods." *Reider v. Thompson, 339 U.S. 113, 119, 70 S. Ct. 499, 94 L. Ed. 698 (1950).* Thus, Carmack allows a shipper to recover for damage or loss from either the delivering carrier or the carrier issuing the bill of lading or receipt.

Whereas COGSA establishes a negligence-like liability regime, Carmack "imposes something close to strict liability upon originating and delivering carriers." *Rankin v. Allstate Ins. Co., 336 F.3d 8, 9 (1st Cir. 2003).* Indeed, Carmack effectively codified the strict liability rule that governed the liability of common carriers at common law. *See Missouri P. R. Co. v. Elmore & Stahl, 377 U.S. 134, 137, 84 S. Ct. 1142, 12 L. Ed. 2d 194 (1964).* Once the shipper establishes a prima facie case of Carmack liability by showing "delivery in good condition, arrival in damaged condition, and the amount of damages," id. at 138; *see also 49 U.S.C. § 14706(a)(1)*, the carrier is liable "for the actual loss or injury to the property" it transports, *49 U.S.C. § 14706(a)(1)*, unless there is an available defense.[8]

By 1976, the extensive regulatory scheme created by the ICA had prevented rail carriers from effectively competing with other modes of transportation. *See Tokio Marine & Fire Ins., Co. v. Amato Motors, Inc., 996 F.2d 874, 877 (7th Cir. 1993)*; *Western Coal Traffic League v. United States, 694 F.2d 378, 384 (5th Cir. 1982).* As part of an expansive deregulation effort, Congress enacted the Staggers Rail Act of 1980, Pub. L. No. 96-448, 94 Stat. 1895 (codified at *49 U.S.C. § 11706*),

---

8 The Supreme Court has indicated that Carmack preserved the defenses available to common carriers at common law. See Missouri Pac. R.R., 377 U.S. at 137-38. Thus, even under Carmack, a carrier is relieved of liability if it can prove (1) that it was free from negligence, and (2) that the damage to the cargo was caused by one of five excusable factors: (a) an act of God, (b) the public enemy, (c) an act of the shipper himself, (d) public authority, or (e) the inherent vice or nature of the goods. Id.

which, among other things, authorized the ICC "to exempt transportation that is provided by a rail carrier as part of a continuous intermodal movement." *49 U.S.C. § 10502(f)*. Pursuant to this authority, the ICC exempted from regulation rail carriers, like Union Pacific, that operate one leg of a continuous intermodal movement. *See* 49 C.F.R. § 1090.2.

While this exempt order relieved certain rail carriers of rate regulation, it did not free them from all legal obligations to shippers. In particular, exempt rail carriers must satisfy the requirements of *49 U.S.C. § 10502(e)*, which states:

> No exemption order issued pursuant to this section shall operate to relieve any rail carrier from an obligation to provide contractual terms for liability and claims which are consistent with the provisions of section 11706 of this title. Nothing in this subsection or section 11706 of this title shall prevent rail carriers from offering alternative terms nor give the Board the authority to require any specific level of rates or services based upon the provisions of section 11706 of this title.

Section 11706 is the Carmack provision governing the liability of rail carriers. It provides, among other things, that the "rail carrier and any other carrier that delivers the property and is providing transportation or service subject to the jurisdiction of the Board under this part are liable to the person entitled to recover under the receipt or bill of lading. The liability imposed under this subsection is for the actual loss or injury to the property." *49 U.S.C. § 11706(a)*. Thus, exempt rail carriers, including those operating under an intermodal bill may limit their liability under Carmack by negotiating "alternative terms." However, the combined effect of § 10502(e) and § 11706(a) is that rail carriers that wish to limit their liability must offer the shipper the option of full Carmack coverage, which includes both the Carmack version of strict liability and full coverage for loss. *See Tokio Marine, 996 F.2d at 879* ("rail carriers still must offer full rates"); *Am. Trucking Ass'ns v. ICC, 656 F.2d 1115, 1124 (5th Cir. 1981)* ("the exemption does not and could not relieve rail carriers from the provisions of [§ 11706[9]]"); *Co-Operative Shippers, Inc. v. Atchison, Topeka & Santa Fe Ry. Co., 613 F. Supp. 788, 791 (N.D. Ill. 1985)* ("[a]lthough freed from most regulation, [exempt rail carriers] are still subject to the liability provisions of [§ 11706]"), *overruled on other grounds, 840 F.2d 447 (7th Cir. 1988)*; *cf. Yamazen (U.S.A.), Inc. v. Chicago & Nw. Transp. Co., 790 F.2d 621, 622 (7th Cir. 1986)* (finding that *§10502(e)*, coupled with 11706(e), which states that a rail carrier or freight provider "may not provide by rule, contract, or otherwise . . . a period of less than 2 years for bringing a civil action against it under this section," requires the carrier to offer the shipper a two-year filing period before offering alternative terms); Ferrostaal, Inc. v. Union Pac. R.R. Co., 109 F. Supp. 2d 146, 149-50 (S.D.N.Y. 2000) (same). If an exempt rail carrier fails to offer the shipper the option of coverage for the actual loss or injury to the property, then the shipper may sue the carrier under Carmack. *See, e.g., Tokio Marine, 996 F.2d at 880.*

---

9 At the time these cases were decided, 49 U.S.C. § 11706 was codified at 49 U.S.C. § 11707.

As noted above, MOL's through bills of lading gave Kubota a "fair opportunity" to declare a value for the tractors in excess of $ 500 per package, and Kubota declined. Thus, MOL did all that was required under COGSA to trigger the statute's $ 500-per-package liability limitation. But Sompo argues forcefully on appeal that Carmack and Staggers apply to the domestic rail portion of a shipment that, like Kubota's, originates in a foreign country and travels under a through bill of lading. We therefore must decide whether Carmack applies to the inland portion of Kubota's shipment, a carriage of goods by rail shipped under a through bill of lading from a foreign country to a destination in the United States. If it does not, then the joint force of the period of responsibility and himalaya clauses will limit Union Pacific's liability to $ 500 per package. If, however, Carmack does apply, we must resolve a potential conflict between Carmack's possible imposition of full liability upon Union Pacific and COGSA's liability limitation incorporated by reference in MOL's bill of lading and extended to Union Pacific by virtue of the himalaya clause. If Carmack takes precedence over a contractual extension of COGSA, then we must address whether Union Pacific has complied with the requirements of Staggers so as to be permitted to limit its liability under Carmack. *See 49 U.S.C. § 11706(c)(1), (c)(3)(A)*.

II. Carmack's Applicability

Carmack applies to common carriers "providing transportation or service subject to the jurisdiction of the [Surface Transportation] Board." *49 U.S.C. § 11706(a)*. The Board's jurisdiction over rail carriers applies to "transportation in the United States between a place in . . . the United States and a place in a foreign country." *49 U.S.C. § 10501(a)(2)(F)*.

Sompo argues that "if the domestic rail transport is part of a larger transportation originating in a foreign country, then it fits the statutory requirement that it is a shipment between a place in the United States and a foreign country, and Carmack is applicable to it." Not surprisingly, Union Pacific sees things differently: "[t]he Carmack Amendment is generally inapplicable where a through bill of lading contemplated inland transportation of goods." The parties' arguments reflect a difference of opinion in the courts regarding Carmack's applicability to a through bill of lading covering a shipment of goods originating in a foreign country. *Compare, e.g., Neptune Orient Lines, Ltd. v. Burlington N. & Santa Fe Ry. Co., 213 F.3d 1118, 1119 (9th Cir. 2000)*; *Swift Textiles, Inc. v. Watkins Motor Lines, Inc., 799 F.2d 697, 698-700 (11th Cir. 1986)*; *Berlanga v. Terrier Transp., Inc., 269 F. Supp. 2d 821, 829-30 (N.D. Tex. 2003)*; *Canon USA, Inc. v. Nippon Liner Sys., Ltd., 1992 U.S. Dist. LEXIS 5699, No. 90-C-7350, 1992 WL 82509, at *6-8 (N.D. Ill. 1992), with Shao, 986 F.2d at 701-04*; *Capitol Converting Equipment, Inc. v. LEP Transp., Inc., 965 F.2d 391, 394-95 (7th Cir. 1992)*; *Toshiba Int'l Corp. v. M/V "SEA-Land Express", 841 F. Supp. 123, 128 (S.D.N.Y. 1994)*. Surprisingly, this is an issue of first impression in this Circuit.

Most courts that have answered this question tend to reiterate the Eleventh Circuit's articulation of its holding in *Swift Textiles v. Watkins Lines, Inc.* that "when a shipment of foreign goods is sent to the United States with the intention that it come to final rest at a specific destination beyond its port of discharge," *Swift, 799 F.2d at 701*, as is the case with a through bill of lading, then Carmack applies *only* if there is a separate bill of lading covering the inland portion of the shipment. *See, e.g., Shao, 986 F.2d at 703*; *Capitol Converting, 965 F.2d at 394*; *Toshiba, 841 F. Supp. at 128*. We agree with *Swift*'s mode of analysis but think that the court's articulated holding is fatally flawed.

Swift involved a shipment of textile machinery from Switzerland to LaGrange, Georgia. There was no through bill of lading. Rather, the machinery was shipped from Switzerland to Savannah, Georgia under one bill of lading and then trucked by a motor carrier from Savannah to LaGrange under a separate bill of lading. *Swift, 799 F.2d at 698*. During the Savannah-to-LaGrange leg of the journey, one of the containers housing the machinery slid off the truck, and the contents of the container was damaged. *See id.* In 1986, when the case came before the Eleventh Circuit, the ICC's jurisdiction over the shipment in question was governed by a provision that was nearly identical to that applying to rail carriers. *Compare 49 U.S.C. § 10521(a)(1)(E)* (repealed in 1995), *with 49 U.S.C. § 10501(a)(2)(F)*. The provision stated that the ICC exercised jurisdiction over transportation of motor carriers "between a place in . . . the United States and a place in a foreign country to the extent the transportation is in the United States." *49 U.S.C. § 10521(a)(1)(E)* (repealed in 1995). The ICC had no jurisdiction, however, over a purely intrastate journey.[10]

For the court in *Swift*, there was no question that Carmack applied to the domestic leg of a shipment that began in a foreign country. Indeed, the court referred in the opinion to § 10521(a)(1)(E) as "the continuation of foreign commerce provision." *Swift, 799 F.2d at 699*. Thus, the court understood that if the shipment of goods from Switzerland to LaGrange, Georgia, was one continuous foreign shipment, then Carmack applied. However, if there were two separate shipments—one from Switzerland to Savannah and another from Savannah to LaGrange—then Carmack did not apply to the inland portion of the trip. The motor carrier urged the court to view the separate domestic bill of lading covering the inland carriage as evidence of two separate, distinct shipments. The court rejected this argument and articulated an "intent test" for determining the nature of an intermodal shipment: "[t]he nature of a shipment is not determined by a mechanical inspection of the bill of lading nor by when and to whom title passes but rather by 'the essential character of the commerce,' *United States v. Erie R.R. Co., 280 U.S. 98, 102, 50 S. Ct. 51,*

10 The statute gave the ICC jurisdiction over transportation by motor carrier between "a State and a place in another State" and between "a State and another place in the same State through another State." Act to Revise the Interstate Commerce Act, Pub. L. 95-473, 92 Stat. 1337, § 10521(a)(1)(B), 1361-62 (1978). But because the entire domestic leg of the journey took place solely within one state, these provisions did not apply.

74 L. Ed. 187 (1929), reflected by the 'intention formed prior to shipment, pursuant to which property is carried to a selected destination by a continuous or unified movement,' *Great N. Ry. Co. v. Thompson, 222 F. Supp. 573, 582 (D.N.D. 1963)* (three-judge district court)." *Swift, 799 F.2d at 699.*

Applying this intent test, the court determined that the shipment represented a "continuation of foreign commerce" and therefore Carmack applied. "There was no reason for the container to come to rest in Savannah other than for the consignee's customs broker to make arrangements for the Savannah to LaGrange leg of the journey." Id. at 700. It was obvious the parties "intended [the shipment] to begin in Switzerland and end in LaGrange, Georgia." *Id.* Having adopted a view of the shipment as a single continuous transport, the court considered it irrelevant that the motor carrier had issued a separate bill of lading for the final intrastate leg of the journey. Quoting the Supreme Court in *Erie Railroad*, the *Swift* court explained that the character of the shipment is "not affected by the fact that the transaction is . . . completed under a local bill of lading which is wholly intrastate. . . ." Id. at 700 (quoting Erie R.R., 280 U.S. at 102).

Despite the clarity of *Swift*'s analysis, the court muddied the waters when it articulated its holding:

> [W]hen a shipment of foreign goods is sent to the United States with the intention that it come to final rest at a specific destination beyond its port of discharge, then the domestic leg of the journey (from the port of discharge to the intended destination) will be subject to the Carmack Amendment *as long as the domestic leg is covered by separate bill or bills of lading.*

Id. at 701 (emphasis added). The court's statement that a domestic bill of lading is *necessary* for Carmack to apply is perplexing to say the least. Indeed, it was the separate domestic bill of lading (covering a purely intrastate journey) in *Swift* that the motor carrier employed, unsuccessfully, to argue that Carmack *did not* apply. Once the *Swift* court had determined that the parties intended a continuous shipment from the foreign place of origin to the final destination, it deemed the separate domestic bill of lading to be irrelevant. Further, the version of Carmack in force at the time of *Swift* explicitly provided that a motor (or rail) carrier's failure to issue a bill of lading did not remove the carrier from Carmack's reach, *see* 92 Stat. at 1359, 1361, 1453, and that provision still exists as to rail carriers, *see 49 U.S.C. § 11706(a)*.

The disconnect between *Swift*'s reasoning and the articulation of its holding has not gone unnoticed. *See, e.g., Berlanga, 269 F. Supp. 2d at 829.* In fact, recognizing the inconsistency, one court has hypothesized that *Swift*'s use of the phrase "as long as" instead of "even if" was due to a typographical error. *See* Canon USA,

1992 U.S. Dist. LEXIS 5699, 1992 WL 82509, at *7. We are therefore reluctant to rely on any line of precedent derived from *Swift*'s articulated holding.[11]

Nevertheless, although we reject *Swift*'s articulated holding, we have no hesitation about adopting Swift's mode of analysis for determining Carmack's applicability, and in fact we have done so before. *See Project Hope v. M/V IBN SINA, 250 F.3d 67, 74-75 (2d Cir. 2001)*. Under that analysis, we must first determine the nature of the shipment in question—whether it is a single continuous intermodal shipment or multiple shipments consisting of separate ocean and domestic legs. Then we must determine whether Carmack applies to the shipment at issue.

The answer to the first question is straightforward. Under the Swift intent test, which we applied in *Project Hope*, the domestic leg of the Kubota shipment is a continuation of foreign commerce rather than a separate and distinct interstate transport of goods. Kubota's intention that the tractors travel from Japan to Swanee, Georgia was fixed at the time the shipment began in Japan, as evidenced by the through bill of lading designating Swanee, Georgia as the final destination. The fact that Union Pacific issued separate domestic waybills does not change the nature of the shipment. *Cf. Project Hope, 250 F.3d at 75* (collecting cases supporting the proposition that the foreign commerce nature of a shipment is not affected by the issuance of a domestic bill of lading covering intrastate transport).

While it is relatively clear that Kubota's shipment of tractors is a single continuous shipment of goods originating in a foreign country and destined for the United States, whether Carmack applies to the domestic rail portion of such a shipment is a more complicated question. To be clear, the source of the complexity is not the requirement of *Swift*'s articulated holding that Carmack applies to such a shipment only if there is also a separate domestic bill of lading. As we have already explained, that requirement is nonsensical in light of *Swift*'s own analysis, as well as

11 For an illustration of the confusion caused by Swift's articulated holding, one need look no further than the Seventh Circuit's opinion in Capitol Converting, 965 F.2d at 391. In an attempt to rationalize Swift's articulated holding, the court in Capitol Converting explained that Carmack only applies to a shipment of goods originating in a foreign country if there is a "separate domestic segment," as evidenced by a separate domestic bill of lading. Id. at 394. But this surely cannot be the rationale underlying Swift's articulated holding because the Swift court clearly viewed the domestic transport at issue in that case as part of a single continuous shipment rather than as a separate domestic shipment. See Swift, 799 F.2d at 700 ("[I]t cannot be disputed that the shipment was intended to begin in Switzerland and end in LaGrange, Georgia."). Further, the Swift court explicitly stated that Carmack applies to such a "continuation of foreign commerce." Id. Moreover, had the Swift court viewed the domestic shipment in that case as separate and distinct from the rest of the transport, as Capitol Converting suggests, it would clearly have held that Carmack did not apply because, unlike the domestic interstate shipment in Capitol Converting, the domestic shipment in Swift was an intrastate shipment to which Carmack clearly does not apply. Id. at 699. Thus, Capitol Converting's rationalization of Swift is wholly unpersuasive. Regrettably, it has proven to be influential. See, e.g., Tokio Marine & Fire Ins. Co. v. Kaisha, 25 F. Supp. 2d 1071, 1081 (C.D. Cal. 1997); N.Y. Marine & Gen. Ins. Co. v. S/S "Ming Prosperity", 920 F. Supp. 416, 425 (S.D.N.Y. 1996); Toshiba, 841 F. Supp. at 128.

the statute, and was likely the result of an inadvertent error. Rather, the complexity derives from the language and history of the statute itself.

"The starting point for [the] interpretation of a statute is always its language," *Community for Creative Non-Violence v. Reid, 490 U.S. 730, 739, 109 S. Ct. 2166, 104 L. Ed. 2d 811 (1989)*, and "courts must presume that a legislature says in a statute what it means and means in a statute what it says there," *Connecticut Nat. Bank v. Germain, 503 U.S. 249, 253-54, 112 S. Ct. 1146, 117 L. Ed. 2d 391 (1992)*. As pertinent to this case, Carmack applies to "transportation in the United States between a place in . . . the United States and a place in a foreign country." *49 U.S.C. § 10501(a)(2)(F)*. At first blush, the word "between" does not seem to imply a direction of travel; rather, it appears to describe simply the relationship that an object or activity bears with respect to two fixed points. Thus, the phrase "air service between the two cities" means that the air service is from one city to the other and vice versa. WEBSTER'S THIRD NEW INT'L DICTIONARY 209 (2002). Then again, the phrase "two cities" does not give priority to either of the two endpoints. Both rest on equal footing. By contrast, by providing that the Board has jurisdiction over "transportation . . . between . . . the United States and . . . a foreign country," *49 U.S.C. § 10501(a)(2)(F)*, without also granting jurisdiction over transportation between a foreign country and the United States, the ICA might be read as distinguishing between exports and imports.

In a thoughtful analysis of Carmack's applicability, a Texas district court relied in part upon a comparison of prior versions of the statute to find that Carmack applies to the domestic portion of international shipments *regardless* of the direction of travel. *Berlanga, 269 F. Supp. 2d at 826-27*. Prior to 1978, the statute did not include the word "between" and instead covered the transportation of property "*from* any point in the United States *to* a point in an adjacent country." *F. J. McCarty Co. v. S. Pac. Co., 428 F.2d 690, 692 n. 1 (9th Cir. 1970)* (quoting *49 U.S.C. § 20(11)*) (emphasis added). In 1978, Congress amended the Interstate Commerce Act, replacing the "from . . . to" construction with the word "between." Amendments to the Interstate Commerce Act, Pub. L. No. 95-473, § 10501(a)(2)(G), 92 Stat. 1337, 1359 (1978). Employing the canon of statutory construction "requiring a change in language to be read, if possible, to have some effect," *Am. Nat'l Red Cross v. S.G., 505 U.S. 247, 263, 112 S. Ct. 2465, 120 L. Ed. 2d 201 (1992)*, the court in *Berlanga* concluded that Congress, by changing this language in 1978, must have intended for Carmack's applicability to the carriage of goods traveling in foreign commerce to no longer depend upon the shipment's point of origin. *269 F. Supp. 2d at 826-27*.

However, the court in Berlanga, as well as subsequent courts, failed to notice that the 1978 amendments were adopted in a codification bill enacting the ICA into positive law, and it is well-established that courts should not "infer[] that Congress, in revising and consolidating the laws, intended to change their effect, unless such intention is clearly expressed." *Fourco Glass Co. v. Transmirra Prods. Corp., 353*

U.S. 222, 227, 77 S. Ct. 787, 1 L. Ed. 2d 786 (1957). Congress expressed no such intention in the 1978 amendments. To the contrary, Congress made clear that the bill was intended to leave the law substantively unchanged. *See* H.R. Rep. No. 1395, 95th Cong., 2d Sess. 9 (1978), *reprinted in* U.S. Code Cong. & Ad. News 3009, 3018 (cited in *In re Roll Form Prods., Inc., 662 F.2d 150, 153 & n. 5 (2d Cir. 1981))*.[12]

Nevertheless, judicial interpretations of this earlier version of the ICA, combined with well-settled principles of statutory construction, lead us to conclude that even the pre-1978 statute, which contained the "from . . . to" language, provided that Carmack applied to the transportation of goods both exiting and entering the United States. When Carmack was first enacted, it did not apply to shipments of goods destined for foreign countries but was instead limited to purely interstate commerce. *See* Act of June 29, 1906, c. 3591, 34 Stat. 593 (originally codified at *49 U.S.C. § 20(11)*); *see also J.H. Hamlen & Sons Co. v. Ill. Cent. R. Co., 212 F. 324, 327 (E.D. Ark. 1914)*. By contrast, the ICC's regulatory jurisdiction originally included transportation "from any place in the United States to an adjacent foreign country." Act to Regulate Commerce, Feb. 4, 1887, c. 104, 24 Stat. 379 (originally codified at *49 U.S.C. § 1*). Thus, as of 1906, the ICA provision establishing the ICC's jurisdiction covered a wider swathe of common carrier transportation than under Carmack, the ICA provision establishing a common carrier's liability.

Congress eliminated that distinction in 1915 when it enacted the First Cummins Amendment, which extended Carmack's application to transportation "from any point in the United States to a point in an adjacent foreign country." Act of March 4, 1915, c. 176, 38 Stat. 1196, 1197. While the First Cummins Amendment brought certain foreign shipments within Carmack's reach, there remained a question as to the precise boundaries of the "from . . . to" language.

In *Galveston, Harrisburg & San Antonio Ry. Co. v. Woodbury, 254 U.S. 357, 359-60, 41 S. Ct. 114, 65 L. Ed. 301 (1920)*, the Supreme Court interpreted the "from . . . to" language contained in the ICA's jurisdictional provision as encompassing both exports and imports. At issue in *Woodbury* was whether a railroad could avail itself of a tariff published with the ICC to limit its liability for a passenger's trunk that was lost in transit from Canada to Texas. The Court explained that even under Carmack, carriers could limit their liability by publishing a tariff with

---

12 In particular, Congress stated the following:

> Like other codifications undertaken to enact into positive law all titles of the United States Code, this bill makes no substantive change in the law. It is sometimes feared that mere changes in terminology and style will result in changes in substance or impair the precedent value of earlier judicial decisions and other interpretations. This fear might have some weight if this were the usual kind of amendatory legislation where it can be inferred that a change of language is intended to change substance. In a codification statute, however, the courts uphold the contrary presumption: the statute is intended to remain substantively unchanged.H.R. Rep. No. 1395, 95th Cong., 2d Sess. 9 (1978), *reprinted in* U.S. Code Cong. & Ad. News 3009, 3018.

the ICC and that this rule survived the First Cummins Amendment. Id. at 359. The rail passenger argued that, in order to take advantage of the tariff published with the ICC, the transportation in question had to be one over which the ICC could assert its jurisdiction. *Id.* Because the transportation in question originated in Canada rather than in the United States, the rail passenger argued, the transportation was not "from any place in the United States to an adjacent foreign country," and therefore the ICC lacked jurisdiction. *Id.* The Supreme Court rejected this argument and, in what was later described euphemistically as a "prodigious feat of interpretation," Note, *Foreign Commerce and the Interstate Commerce Act*, 40 Harv. L. Rev. 1130, 1134 (1927), read the "from . . . to" language as conferring upon the ICC jurisdiction over transportation in foreign commerce *regardless* of whether the transportation originated in the United States or in an adjacent foreign country, Woodbury, 254 U.S. at 359. Writing for the Court, Justice Brandeis reasoned that "[a] carrier engaged in transportation by rail *to* an adjacent foreign country is, at least ordinarily, engaged in transportation also *from* that country to the United States." *Id.* Justice Brandeis found support for this bi-directional reading of the language in both ICC interpretations and Supreme Court cases interpreting similar language in analogous trade contexts. *See* id. at 360.

The use of similar language, let alone identical language, in two different provisions of the same statute is, as the Supreme Court has emphasized, "a strong indication that [the two provisions] should be interpreted *pari passu*," i.e., in the same manner. *Northcross v. Bd. of Ed. of Memphis City Sch., 412 U.S. 427, 428, 93 S. Ct. 2201, 37 L. Ed. 2d 48 (1973)* (per curiam). This principle of statutory construction holds true unless "there is strong evidence that Congress did not intend the language to be used uniformly." *Smith v. City of Jackson, 544 U.S. 228, 261, 125 S. Ct. 1536, 161 L. Ed. 2d 410 (2005)* (O'Connor, J., concurring in the judgment); *see also Merrill Lynch, Pierce, Fenner & Smith, Inc. v. Dabit, 547 U.S. 71, 126 S. Ct. 1503, 164 L. Ed. 2d 179 (2006)*. Thus, while the *Woodbury* Court interpreted the "from . . . to" language only in that section of the ICA defining the ICC's jurisdiction, one would think that the same interpretation would have applied to the identical language in Carmack. In general, however, lower courts have resisted that inclination, *see, e.g., Sklaroff v. Pennsylvania R.R. Co., 184 F.2d 575, 575 (3rd Cir. 1950)*; *Strachman v. Palmer, 177 F.2d 427, 429 (1st Cir. 1949)*; *Condakes v. Smith, 281 F. Supp. 1014, 1015 (D. Mass. 1968)*, and have tended instead to adopt the reasoning of an influential Pennsylvania Superior Court decision, *Alwine v. Pennsylvania R. Co., 141 Pa. Super. 558, 15 A.2d 507 (Pa. Super. Ct. 1940)*.

The *Alwine* court provided two rationales for its decision not to extend the *Woodbury* interpretation of the "from . . . to" language of the Carmack liability provision and instead to limit that interpretation to the language in the ICC jurisdiction provision. First, the *Alwine* court noted that the ICC itself had interpreted the First Cummins Amendment as "extend[ing] the territorial application of the provisions of the Carmack amendment to . . . goods *exported* to adjacent foreign countries." Id. at 510 (quoting 52 I.C.C. 671, 683 (Apr. 14, 1919)). However, it is not clear that this quote represented the ICC's official interpretation of the ICA. And even if it was an official interpretation, the ICC did not state, and to our knowledge has never stated, that Carmack applied *exclusively* to exports.

Second, the court in *Alwine* also relied upon an inference drawn from congressional action following the *Woodbury* decision. *Id.* It explained that in *Woodbury*, after the state court's decision, which viewed the ICC jurisdiction provision as covering only exports, Congress set into motion an amendment to the ICA to make clear that the ICC had jurisdiction over the carriage of goods exported to, or imported from, an adjacent foreign country. *Id.* That amendment was finally enacted two months after the Supreme Court issued its decision in *Woodbury*. *See* Act of February 28, 1920, c. 91, 41 Stat. 456, 474. The court in *Alwine* reasoned that Congress's failure, in the course of altering the language in the jurisdiction provision, to change the parallel language in Carmack, while at the same time making other minor revisions in Carmack, *see id.* 41 Stat. at 494, supported an inference that Congress no longer intended the two provisions to be co-extensive. Alwine, 15 A.2d at 510.

We are less sanguine than the *Alwine* court about the force of that inference. The Supreme Court has on numerous occasions expressed a "reluctan[ce] to draw inferences from Congress' failure to act." *Brecht v. Abrahamson, 507 U.S. 619, 632-33, 113 S. Ct. 1710, 123 L. Ed. 2d 353 (1993)* (quoting *Schneidewind v. ANR Pipeline Co., 485 U.S. 293, 306, 108 S. Ct. 1145, 99 L. Ed. 2d 316 (1988)* (citing *Am. Trucking Ass'ns v. Atchison, T. & S. F. R. Co., 387 U.S. 397, 416-18, 87 S. Ct. 1608, 18 L. Ed. 2d 847 (1967)))*. That reluctance seems to be particularly apt in a case like *Alwine*, where the inference drawn would deny the effect of a Supreme Court precedent. Indeed, if anything, Congress's re-enactment of Carmack in the Act of February 28, 1920 without changing the "from . . . to" language would seem to reflect a congressional intent to ratify the Supreme Court's interpretation of that language in *Woodbury*. *Cf. Merrill Lynch, Pierce, Fenner & Smith, Inc. v. Curran, 456 U.S. 353, 382 n. 66, 102 S. Ct. 1825, 72 L. Ed. 2d 182 (1982)* ("Congress is presumed to be aware of an administrative or judicial interpretation of a statute and to adopt that interpretation when it re-enacts a statute without change . . . ." (quoting *Lorillard v. Pons, 434 U.S. 575, 580-81, 98 S. Ct. 866, 55 L. Ed. 2d 40 (1978)))*. We do not think that Congress, by simply making the language of the ICC jurisdiction provision more explicit in light of the *Woodbury* Court's interpretation of that language, indicated any intent to restrict Carmack's coverage solely to exports.

Nor do we think that the Supreme Court's later decision in *Reider v. Thompson, 339 U.S. 113, 70 S. Ct. 499, 94 L. Ed. 698 (1950)*, resolved the issue at hand, as the Seventh Circuit has suggested. *See Capitol Converting, 965 F.2d at 394* (characterizing *Reider* as holding that Carmack does not cover goods shipped under a through bill of lading issued in a foreign country). The issue in *Reider* was whether Carmack applied to the inland rail carriage of a shipment of goods that originated in Buenos Aires, Argentina with the final destination of Boston, by way of New Orleans, Louisiana. Importantly, the original carrier in *Reider* did not issue a through bill of lading from Buenos Aires to Boston. 339 U.S. at 117. Accordingly, the Supreme Court viewed the shipment as consisting of two distinct legs: Buenos Aires to New Orleans and New Orleans to Boston, and the Court rightly pointed out that Carmack clearly applies to the interstate leg from New Orleans to Boston. *Id.* The Court then proceeded to clarify that, because the shipment involved no through bill of lading, it would not decide whether *Alwine* was correctly decided. *See* id. at 118 ("We need not now determine whether [*Alwine*] was correctly decided. For purposes of this case it is sufficient to note that there the Pennsylvania court emphasized that the shipment came into this country on a through bill of lading from Canada. The contract of carriage did not terminate at the border, as in the instant case."). Thus, notwithstanding the Seventh Circuit's suggestion to the contrary in *Capitol Converting*, the *Reider* Court specifically reserved from its judgment the question at issue here: whether Carmack applies to the domestic rail portion of a single, continuous shipment of goods originating in a foreign country.

Where does that leave us? We know that *Woodbury* interpreted the phrase "from a place in the United States to a place in an adjacent foreign country" in the ICC jurisdiction provision as encompassing both imports and exports. As we have noted, that interpretation should also govern the "from . . . to" language in Carmack in the absence of "strong evidence" that Congress wished for the language in the ICC jurisdiction provision to be interpreted differently from that of Carmack. *See* Smith, 544 U.S. at 261 (O'Connor, J., concurring). Because we have found no evidence, let alone "strong evidence," of such congressional intent, we conclude that the Supreme Court's decision in *Woodbury* would have governed the interpretation of the "from . . . to" language in Carmack prior to 1978, the year that Congress enacted the ICA into positive law. Accordingly, we find that at that time, Carmack applied to the domestic portion of a transportation of goods originating outside of the United States.[13] Although we might question the basis for the

13 One could fairly raise the objection that, regardless of the proper interpretation of the "from . . . to" language in the pre-codification version of Carmack, the pre-codification version of the statute contained language making clear that Carmack only applied to international shipments of goods involving "an adjacent foreign country," Berlanga, 269 F. Supp. 2d at 827 (quoting 49 U.S.C. § 20(11) (1976) (emphasis added)), and that the codification bill's omission of the word "adjacent" should not be interpreted as a change in the law. Under this objection, it would follow that Carmack does not apply in this case because the Kubota shipment involved transportation from a non-adjacent country, Japan, to Georgia. This objection, however, is foreclosed by our decision in Project Hope. Focusing solely on the post-codification language, we held in Project Hope that Carmack applied to the domestic motor carriage portion of an international shipment originating in Virginia and destined for a non-adjacent country, Egypt. See Project Hope, 250 F.3d at 75. Although Project Hope involved motor, rather than rail, carriage, the post-codification language governing the Board's jurisdiction, and therefore Carmack's applicability, is identical regardless of the mode of transport. Compare 49 U.S.C. § 13501(1)(E) with 49 U.S.C. § 10501(a)(2)(F). Thus, we find ourselves bound by Project Hope's holding, which effectively extended Carmack's applicability to international shipments involving non-adjacent foreign countries.

Woodbury Court's interpretation, we cannot simply jettison a Supreme Court case because we disagree with it. "Even if a Supreme Court precedent was 'unsound when decided' . . . it remains the Supreme Court's 'prerogative alone to overrule one of its precedents.'" *Bach v. Pataki, 408 F.3d 75, 86 (2d Cir. 2005)* 42] (quoting *State Oil Co. v. Khan, 522 U.S. 3, 9, 20, 118 S. Ct. 275, 139 L. Ed. 2d 199 (1997)* (quoting *Khan v. State Oil Co., 93 F.3d 1358, 1363 (7th Cir. 1996)* (Posner, J.))). *Woodbury* has never been overruled and therefore is still good law that we are obligated to follow.

Our interpretation of Carmack—that it applies to the domestic inland portion of a foreign shipment regardless of the shipment's point of origin—also comports with Congress's view of the law when Congress codified the ICA in 1978. In the codification bill, Congress struck the "from . . . to" language from Carmack altogether and made Carmack's applicability turn on whether a "common carrier [is] providing transportation subject to the Interstate Commerce Commission." *49 U.S.C. § 11706*, 92 Stat. at 1453. Thus, Congress indicated that, in order to determine Carmack's applicability, one must consult the ICC jurisdiction provision. Because the codification bill was intended to leave the substantive law unchanged, this structural re-arrangement of Carmack reflects Congress's understanding that the boundaries of Carmack's applicability have always been co-extensive with those of the ICC's jurisdiction. *Woodbury* and the Act of February 28, 1920 (ratifying the *Woodbury* interpretation) clearly establish that the ICC's jurisdiction includes transportation from a foreign country to the United States. Because the scope of the ICC jurisdiction provision is co-extensive with the scope of Carmack's applicability and because the *Woodbury* Court interpreted the "from . . . to" language as applying to goods traveling in foreign commerce regardless of direction, it follows that the "from . . . to" language in Carmack also applies to goods in foreign commerce regardless of the direction of travel. We therefore conclude that Carmack applies to the domestic interstate leg of the Kubota shipment.[14]

III. The Carmack Amendment and COGSA

Because the period of responsibility and himalaya clauses in MOL's through bills of lading together extend COGSA's terms to subcontractors, like Union Pacific, the fact that Carmack also applies to the Union Pacific leg of the Kubota shipment creates a potential conflict between two different liability regimes. In our view, however, the conflict is not between two federal laws but rather between one federal law (Carmack) and a contract that, although incorporating the terms of another

14 We note that, even if we were to view Union Pacific's domestic, interstate carriage as a shipment entirely distinct from the rest of the transport, Carmack would still apply by virtue of 49 U.S.C. § 10501(a)(2)(A), because the Union Pacific waybill covers the interstate carriage of goods.

statute (COGSA), nevertheless lacks statute-like status. Section 1307 of COGSA states:

> Nothing contained in [COGSA] shall prevent a carrier or a shipper from entering into any agreement, stipulation, condition, reservation, or exemption as to the responsibility and liability of the carrier or the ship for the loss or damage to or in connection with the custody and care and handling of goods prior to the loading on and subsequent to the discharge from the ship on which the goods are carried by sea.*46 U.S.C. app. § 1307*. Because COGSA only applies to "the period from the time when the goods are loaded on to the time when they are discharged from the ship," *id.* § 1301(e), courts have consistently held that when COGSA is extended by contract beyond the tackles, as contemplated by *§ 1307*, the statute does not apply of its own force, or *ex proprio vigore*, but rather as a contractual term. *See Hartford Fire Ins. Co. v. Orient Overseas Containers Lines (UK) Ltd., 230 F.3d 549, 557 (2d Cir. 2000)*; *Colgate Palmolive Co. v. S/S Dart Canada, 724 F.2d 313, 315 (2d Cir. 1983)*; *Pannell v. U.S. Lines Co., 263 F.2d 497, 498 (2d Cir. 1959)*; *Inst. of London Underwriters v. Sea-Land Serv., Inc., 881 F.2d 761, 764-66 (9th Cir. 1989)*; *Croft & Scully Co. v. M/V SKULPTOR VUCHETICH, 664 F.2d 1277, 1280 (5th Cir. 1982)*; *Commonwealth Petrochems., Inc. v. S/S Puerto Rico, 607 F.2d 322, 325 (4th Cir. 1979).*

This view of COGSA finds further support in the fact that Congress explicitly provided that contracts extending the statute's reach in ways other than over land—in particular, contractual extensions covering trade between United States ports (or "coastwise trade")—do have statutory force. COGSA by its terms only applies to shipping "to or from ports of the United States" and is further limited to foreign trade. *46 U.S.C. app. § 1300.* Shipping between the ports of a single nation falls under the jurisdiction of that nation alone and therefore does not raise the uniformity concerns the Hague Rules were intended to address. *See Commonwealth Petrochems., 607 F.2d at 327*; *see also* Michael F. Sturley, *Proposed Amendments to the Carriage of Goods by Sea Act*, 18 Hous. J. Int'l L. 609, 622-27 (1996). In the United States, coastwise trade remains governed by the Harter Act.[15] Although

15 Enacted in 1898, the Harter Act imposes a duty of "proper loading, stowage, custody, care, [and] proper delivery." 46 U.S.C. app. § 190. It prohibits any exculpation clause in a bill of lading or shipping document relieving the carrier from liability arising out of negligence or fault in loading, stowage, custody, care, delivery of cargo, and the provision of a properly equipped and seaworthy vessel. See 46 U.S.C. app. §§ 190, 191. Like COGSA, the Harter Act also provides for exoneration of the carrier in certain circumstances, including "errors of navigation," "dangers of the sea," and "acts of God." 46 U.S.C. app. § 192. Although COGSA superseded the Harter Act with respect to the tackle-to-tackle period of international shipments, the Harter Act nevertheless continues to govern the carrier's duties in international shipments prior to the time when the goods are loaded on the ship and after the time they are discharged from the ship, until "proper delivery." See Wemhoener Pressen v. Ceres Marine Terminals, Inc., 5 F.3d 734, 741-42 (4th Cir. 1993) ("['Proper delivery' includes] actual or constructive delivery. Actual delivery consists [of] completely transferring the possession and control of the goods from the vessel to the consignee or his agent. Constructive delivery occurs where the goods are discharged from the ship upon a fit wharf and the consignee receives due and reasonable notice that the goods have been discharged and has a reasonable opportunity to remove the goods or put them under proper care and custody." (quoting B. Elliott (Canada) Ltd. v. John T.

COGSA left the Harter Act's application to domestic shipping largely unaffected, Congress created in COGSA what has become known as the "coastwise option," which authorizes carriers and shippers in domestic trade to, in effect, contractually opt out of the Harter Act and into the COGSA regime, as long as they do so with an "express statement." *46 U.S.C. app. § 1312*; *see also* 2A-V BENEDICT ON ADMIRALTY § 42 (7th ed. 1998). Thus, there is little dispute that Congress intended for certain contracts extending COGSA's reach to supersede prevailing federal statutes.

However, Congress made an important textual distinction between contracts extending the statute's terms to coastwise trade under § 1312 and contracts extending COGSA's terms beyond the tackles, pursuant to § 1307. With respect to contracts under the coastwise option, Congress made clear that such contracts "shall be subjected [to COGSA] as fully as if subject . . . by the express provisions of [the statute]." *46 U.S.C. app. § 1312*. Thus, when extended by contract to cover coastwise trade, COGSA does indeed act *ex proprio vigore*.[16] However, with respect to period of responsibility provisions, like the one in the MOL bills of lading, Congress simply stated that "[n]othing [in COGSA] shall prevent a carrier or a shipper from entering into any [such] agreement." *Id.* § 1307. "[W]here Congress includes particular language in one section of a statute but omits it in another section of the same Act, it is generally presumed that Congress acts intentionally and purposely in the disparate inclusion or exclusion." *Russello v. United States, 464 U.S. 16, 23,*

Clark & Son, 704 F.2d 1305, 1308 (4th Cir. 1983) (in turn quoting Orient Overseas Line, Inc. v. Globemaster Baltimore, Inc., 33 Md. App. 372, 365 A.2d 325, 335-36 (Md. 1976)))). "It is clear from the legislative history that Congress intended the Harter Act to continue to apply to all cases not governed by COGSA." 2A-II BENEDICT ON ADMIRALTY § 14 (7th ed. 1998). Because COGSA only applies to the tackle-to-tackle period in international shipments, see 46 U.S.C. app. § 1300 ("Every bill of lading or similar document of title which is evidence of a contract for the carriage of goods by sea to or from ports of the United States, in foreign trade, shall have effect subject to the provisions of this Act." (emphasis added)), the Harter Act continues to apply to trade between United States ports. Id. Similarly, because COGSA specifically exempts from its coverage goods stored on the deck of a ship, see 46 U.S.C. app. § 1304, courts have also held that the Harter Act applies to damage to goods in international trade during the tackle-to-tackle period, as long as the goods were carried on deck, see, e.g., Blanchard Lumber Co. v. S.S. Anthony II, 259 F. Supp. 857, 865 (S.D.N.Y. 1966).

16 Accordingly, the First and Ninth Circuits, along with the Southern District of New York, have held that COGSA applies with the force of statute when a bill of lading in domestic trade incorporates COGSA's terms with an "express statement." Hanover Ins. Co. v. Shulman Transp. Enters., Inc., 581 F.2d 268, 270 & n. 2 (1st Cir. 1978); Pan Am. World Airways v. Cal. Stevedore & Ballast Co., 559 F.2d 1173, 1175 n. 3 (9th Cir. 1977) (per curiam); Orion Ins. Co. v. M/V "Humacao", 851 F. Supp. 575, 578 (S.D.N.Y. 1994); Watermill Export, Inc. v. MV Ponce, 506 F. Supp. 612, 614-15 (S.D.N.Y. 1981). The Fourth and Fifth Circuits, on the other hand, have held that, notwithstanding § 1312's language to the contrary, COGSA applies simply as a contractual term even when extended to domestic bills of lading. Commonwealth Petrochems., 607 F.2d at 326-27; Ralston Purina Co. v. Barge Juneau & Gulf Carribean Marine Lines, Inc., 619 F.2d 374, 375-76 (5th Cir. 1980) (per curiam). But see Burdines, Inc. v. Pan-Atlantic S.S. Corp., 199 F.2d 571, 573 (5th Cir. 1952).

104 S. Ct. 296, 78 L. Ed. 2d 17 (1983) ((quoting *United States v. Wong Kim Bo, 472 F.2d 720, 722 (5th Cir. 1972)* (alteration in original)). Therefore, that Congress, in enacting § 1307, omitted language similar to the language in § 1312 is persuasive evidence that Congress did not wish for period of responsibility clauses to have the force of statute with the capability to supersede federal law.

In light of the contractual nature of period of responsibility provisions, courts have routinely held that contracts extending COGSA beyond the tackles must give way to conflicting law. *See Colgate Palmolive, 724 F.2d at 315-16* (refusing to apply COGSA $ 500-per-package limitation in view of governing state law because "provisions of COGSA incorporated by contract can be valid only insofar as they do not conflict with applicable state law"); *Wemhoener Pressen v. Ceres Marine Terminals, Inc., 5 F.3d 734, 739 (4th Cir. 1993)* ("To portions of the carriage that take place prior to loading or after discharge and therefore are not covered by the terms of COGSA, the Harter Act controls."); *Uncle Ben's Int'l Div. of Uncle Ben's, Inc. v. Hapag-Lloyd Aktiengesellschaft, 855 F.2d 215, 217 (5th Cir. 1988)* (holding that "[i]f the parties extend the provisions of COGSA to the preloading phase, any inconsistency with the Harter Act must yield to the Harter Act" but finding that the contractual incorporation of COGSA's one-year statute of limitation was not inconsistent with the Harter Act); *Toshiba Int'l Corp., 841 F. Supp. at 128* (suggesting that if Carmack applied to the inland portion of the journey, it would disallow the COGSA liability limitations incorporated by contract).[17] *But see Schramm, Inc. v. Shipco Transp., Inc., 364 F.3d 560, 565 (4th Cir. 2004)* (assuming without discussion that a contract incorporating COGSA's terms wins out over any conflict with the Harter Act).

In fact, in cases involving foreign trade where there is a conflict between a period of responsibility clause and the Harter Act—which, in international shipments, applies from the time when the goods are unloaded until "proper delivery"—the principal issue is not whether a contract incorporating COGSA's terms must give way to conflicting provisions in the Harter Act, but rather whether there is in fact a conflict. "Because COGSA and the Harter Act are so similar, it often makes no difference which statute applies." 2A-II BENEDICT ON ADMIRALTY § 14 (7th ed. 1998). Nevertheless, when courts have identified inconsistencies between the two statutes, they have held that the Harter Act supersedes the period of responsibility clause. For example, in *R. L. Pritchard & Co. v. S.S. Hellenic Laurel, 342 F. Supp. 388, 391 (S.D.N.Y. 1972)*, one of our district court's noted that "[i]nsofar as the provisions of COGSA are inconsistent with the Harter Act, they cannot be incorporated into a bill of lading to cover the responsibilities of the carrier after

17 In Norfolk Southern Ry. Co. v. Kirby, the Supreme Court held that a through bill of lading consisting of a "substantial" sea component is governed by federal law, even if the bill covers inland carriage. 543 U.S. at 27. Thus, Kirby would appear to effectively overrule those cases, like Colgate Palmolive, that hold that contracts extending COGSA's terms beyond the tackles must yield to conflicting state law, but only to the extent that the bills of lading in those cases consist of a sea component that is "substantial."

discharge and before delivery of the cargo." Id. at 391. The court held that the "fire exemption" provision of COGSA, *46 U.S.C. § 1304(2)(b)*—under which the carrier is liable for losses due to fire only if caused by certain types of negligence is inconsistent with the Harter Act and therefore "null and void." *R. L. Pritchard & Co., 342 F. Supp. at 391*. Similarly, in *United States v. Ultramar Shipping Co., 685 F. Supp. 887 (S.D.N.Y. 1987)*, the court found that the carrier's burden of proof for demonstrating due diligence in assuring seaworthiness is more relaxed under COGSA than under the Harter Act. *See* id. at 894-95. Accordingly, the court held that the period of responsibility clause must yield to the Harter Act. Finally, in *Birdsall, Inc. v. Tramore Trading Co., 771 F. Supp. 1193, 1199 (S.D. Fla. 1991)*, the United States District Court for the Southern District of Florida held that COGSA's statute of limitations cannot supersede the absence of such a limitation in the Harter Act for the pre- and post-loading phases. *See* id. at 896.

These cases are consistent with the policy motivating COGSA. The driving force behind COGSA was a need for uniformity in the law governing the contracts central to maritime commerce. *See* Vimar Seguros y Reaseguros, S.A., 515 U.S. at 537. Uniformity was considered necessary to minimize the costs arising in maritime transactions that touch the shores of, and involve parties haling from, the numerous maritime nations. For the carriers, shippers, insurers, cargo underwriters, and financial intermediaries involved in these transactions, this harmonization of the law governing the agreements that drive international shipping eliminated much of the uncertainty and unpredictability that prevailed before the adoption of the Hague Rules and COGSA, when a party would not know before the fact which law would control in the event of a lawsuit under the bill of lading. However, the Hague Rules (and by extension COGSA) only sought to achieve uniformity in the law governing the international carriage of goods *by sea*. Other types of carriage, including land-based carriage, were to be governed by the law of the individual nations that participated in the international convention at the Hague. *See* Sturley, Uniformity in the Law, supra, at 573-74. The United States' decision to preserve the application of the Harter Act did not "sacrifice international uniformity for the simple reason that the international community made no effort to establish a uniform rule" governing the carriage of goods outside of the tackle-to-tackle period. *Id.*

Consistent with the treaty's intent, Congress specifically provided in COGSA that the statute would have no effect upon laws applying to the inland carriage of goods:

> Nothing in [COGSA] shall be construed as superseding any part of [the Harter Act], or of any other law which would be applicable in the absence of [COGSA], insofar as they relate to the duties, responsibilities, and liabilities of the ship or carrier prior to the time when the goods are loaded on or after the time they are discharged from the ship. *46 U.S.C. app. § 1311*.

As Senator White explained in the Commerce Committee's report of the bill to Congress, "[COGSA] supersedes the so-called 'Harter Act' from the time the goods are loaded on the ship to the time they are discharged from the ship. Otherwise our law remains precisely as it is, unaffected and unimpaired by the proposed legislation." 1 Legislative History of the Carriage of Goods by Sea Act and the Travaux Preparatoires of the Hague Rules, at 589 (Michael F. Sturley ed., 1990). Although § 1311 makes specific reference to the Harter Act, it also preserves from COGSA's reach "*any other law* which would be applicable in the absence of [COGSA], insofar as they relate to the duties, responsibilities, and liabilities of the ship or carrier prior to the time when the goods are loaded on or after the time they are discharged from the ship." *46 U.S.C. app. § 1311* (emphasis added). Carmack is such a law. Accordingly, we hold that the contractual provision extending COGSA's terms inland must yield to Carmack. Therefore, we hold that Carmack governs Union Pacific's liability in this case.

Union Pacific would have us rely upon the Supreme Court's recent decision in *Norfolk Southern Railway Co. v. Kirby, 543 U.S. 14, 125 S. Ct. 385, 160 L. Ed. 2d 283 (2004)*, but *Kirby* does not alter our analysis. In *Kirby*, the Supreme Court held that federal law should govern the interpretation of a through bill of lading consisting of sea and land portions, as long as the sea portions are "substantial." Id. at 27. The shipper, Kirby, had hired a freight forwarder to arrange for the shipment of machinery from Switzerland to Huntsville, Alabama. The freight forwarder hired a German ocean shipping company to transport the cargo, and the ocean shipping company then contracted with a railroad, Norfolk Southern, to carry the goods by rail from the port of discharge—Savannah, Georgia—to the final destination, Huntsville, Alabama. *See* id. at 19. The bill of lading between the ocean shipping company and Norfolk Southern contained a period of responsibility clause and a himalaya clause conferring the benefit of COGSA's $ 500-per-package liability limitation on independent contractors, like Norfolk Southern. *See* id. at 19-20. When the goods were damaged after the train derailed en route to Huntsville, Norfolk Southern claimed that its liability was limited to $ 500 per package, as provided for in the bill of lading.[18] The cargo owner, Kirby, argued that the period of responsibility clause should be interpreted in light of state agency law principles, in which case the railroad was not entitled to benefit from the himalaya clause because the freight forwarder was not acting as Kirby's agent when it received the ocean shipping company's bill of lading. Id. at 22.

---

18 Norfolk Southern also sought to insulate itself by relying on the himalaya clause in the bill of lading between the freight forwarder and the ocean shipping company. However, the interpretation of that himalaya clause raised the question of the meaning of Supreme Court precedent rather than which law, federal or state, to apply. See Kirby, 543 U.S. at 30 (explaining that the interpretation "turns only on whether the Eleventh Circuit correctly applied this Court's decision in Robert C. Herd & Co. v. Krawill Machinery Corp., 359 U.S. 297, 79 S. Ct. 766, 3 L. Ed. 2d 820 (1959)"). Thus, it is less relevant to our discussion here, which is concerned with the correct law to apply when federal laws conflict with a contract extending COGSA's reach.

The Supreme Court found that the bill of lading, although covering carriage by both sea and land, was nevertheless a maritime contract to which federal law applied. *See* id. at 23-27. Adopting a conceptual approach, the Court stated that "so long as a bill of lading requires substantial carriage of goods by sea, its purpose is to effectuate maritime commerce—and thus it is a maritime contract . . . [even if] it also provides for some land carriage. . . . If a bill's *sea* components are insubstantial, [however,] then the bill is not a maritime contract." Id. at 27. The Court further explained that in applying federal law, it was avoiding the "[c]onfusion and inefficiency [that] will inevitably result if more than one body of law governs a given contract's meaning," id. at 29, and thereby was promoting "the uniformity of general maritime law," id. at 28. The Court noted that in applying a single body of law to the contract, it was also "reinforc[ing] the liability regime Congress established in COGSA." Id at 29.

Union Pacific contends that the same concern for uniformity and consistency in interpreting international maritime contracts "demands that provisions of 'through bills of lading' which extend limitations of liability to inland carriers should be analyzed under COGSA and not the Carmack Amendment." We cannot read *Kirby* so broadly. In *Kirby*, the Court was primarily concerned with the lack of uniformity and consistency that would result if *state* law were applied to contracts extending COGSA's terms inland. That is a significant concern, especially for the myriad parties potentially responsible for an inland carrier's damage to goods who cannot know before the fact which state law might define the contours of their liability. The Supreme Court's decision that national law will govern the interpretation of an international bill of lading with a substantial sea component adroitly avoids that problem.

However, in *Kirby*, the cargo owner failed to raise the issue of Carmack's applicability. *See* Brief for the United States as *Amicus Curiae* at 12, *Norfolk So. Ry. Co. v. Kirby, 543 U.S. 14, 125 S. Ct. 385, 160 L. Ed. 2d 283, 2003 WL 22762727 (2004)*. Therefore the only issue before the Court was the interaction between *state* law and contractual provisions extending COGSA's terms to a rail carrier. Consequently, *Kirby* only established the principle that maritime contracts should be interpreted in light of federal maritime law. Notwithstanding Union Pacific's argument to the contrary, it does not follow from that principle that the only federal law to apply is COGSA. Nor can we accept the argument that Carmack—what Union Pacific refers to as a "non-maritime federal law"—cannot play a role in governing the terms of the domestic carriage portion of a maritime contract. Federal maritime law consists of both federal common law and federal statutes. Although federal common law plays a more prominent role in the maritime context than in others, where it remains largely interstitial, it nevertheless only applies in the absence of a relevant statute. *See, e.g., E. River S.S. Corp. v. Transamerica Delaval, Inc., 476 U.S. 858, 864, 106 S. Ct. 2295, 90 L. Ed. 2d 865 (1986)* ("Absent a relevant statute, the general maritime law, as developed by the judiciary, applies."). What constitutes a relevant federal statute is determined solely by whether a given statute applies by its own terms to a particular set of facts. There is no additional requirement that only those federal statutes that a court deems "inherently maritime" can govern the interpretation of a maritime contract.

To apply COGSA here to the exclusion of Carmack would be to contradict well-established circuit precedent holding that period of responsibility provisions do not have statute-like status and would undermine the text of the statute itself, which explicitly states that COGSA does not affect laws governing the carriage of goods prior to loading and after discharge. *46 U.S.C. app. § 1311*.[19] We cannot interpret the Kirby Court's language concerning the policy underlying COGSA—language that at most merely supported, but was far from central, to the Court's holding that federal law should apply instead of *state* law—as implying that a contract extending COGSA inland should supersede an otherwise applicable *federal* law. Without further guidance from the Supreme Court or from Congress, we must rely on precedent and the plain language of the statutory scheme.

IV. Compliance with the Carmack Amendment and the Staggers Rail Act

Now that we have determined that Carmack applies to the domestic rail portion of an international shipment originating in a foreign country and traveling under a through bill of lading, even where the parties have extended COGSA's liability provisions to domestic rail carriers, one question remains: when Union Pacific negotiated the applicable terms of carriage of Kubota's tractors, did it provide the shipper an opportunity, consistent with Staggers, *see 49 U.S.C. §§ 10502(e)*; *11706(a)*, *(c)(3)*, to receive full Carmack liability coverage as well as "alternative terms"? If so, then under Carmack and Staggers, *see 49 U.S.C. § 11706(c)(3)*, such alternative terms would circumscribe Union Pacific's liability. If not, and in the absence of any other defense, then Union Pacific, having failed to comply with the Carmack and Staggers requirements, would be liable for the full value of the tractors. Because the district court determined that COGSA, rather than Carmack, applied to the Kubota shipment, it did not have the opportunity to address whether Union Pacific satisfied Staggers. Moreover, the question of whether Union Pacific satisfied Staggers raises potential issues of fact and law that the district court, in the first instance, is in a better position to evaluate than are we. Accordingly, we find it prudent to remand the case to the district court to address whether Union Pacific satisfied the requirements of *49 U.S.C. § 10502(e)*.

---

19 Section 1311 was irrelevant to the Court's analysis in Kirby. Once again, § 1311 states:

> Nothing in [COGSA] shall be construed as superseding any part of [the Harter Act], or of *any other law which would be applicable in the absence of [COGSA]*, insofar as they relate to the duties, responsibilities, and liabilities of the ship or carrier prior to the time when the goods are loaded on or after the time they are discharged from the ship. *46 U.S.C. app. § 1311*. Once the *Kirby* Court had determined that federal, not state, law governed the bill of lading, state law would not have been "applicable in the absence of [COGSA]," and therefore § 1311 did not require that the period of responsibility provision yield to state law.

We see no reason, however, to refrain from addressing Union Pacific's argument, advanced on appeal, that the MOL bills of lading satisfy Staggers. Union Pacific urges us to view the $ 500-per-package liability limitation in the MOL bills of lading as "alternative terms" and contends that Clause 29(2) of the MOL bills "gave Kubota the opportunity to declare the full value of the cargo and receive full value coverage as required by *49 U.S.C. § 11706*." Clause 29(2) provides:

> If the US COGSA applies as Clause 29(1) above, neither the Carrier nor the Vessel shall, in any event, be or become liable for any loss or damage to or in connection with the Goods in an amount exceeding $ 500.00 per package, lawful money of the United States or in the case of Goods not shipped in packages, per customary freight unit, unless the value of the Goods has been declared and inserted in the declared value box on the face hereof, in which case Clause 6(2) shall apply. Union Pacific's argument is without merit because, although Clause 29(2) provides the option of full coverage under COGSA, it does not provide the option of full coverage under Carmack. Of course, substituting the liability scheme available under COGSA for that available under Carmack might be a harmless error if the liability rules under COGSA and Carmack were identical. But as discussed above, COGSA liability is grounded in negligence while Carmack liability is rooted in strict liability. Thus, Union Pacific's argument that it is liable under either COGSA's or Carmack's standard of care misses the point. Because COGSA and Carmack create two different liability standards, we cannot assume that the shipper contracting with Union Pacific had the opportunity to choose among several types of liability coverage and opted not to pay a higher freight rate for full coverage under a strict liability rule.

While we hold that the MOL bills of lading do not satisfy Staggers, we express no opinion as to any other potential contention that Union Pacific complied with the requirements of Carmack and Staggers.

CONCLUSION

For the foregoing reasons, we conclude that Carmack governs Union Pacific's liability in this case. We further conclude that the MOL bills of lading do not satisfy the Staggers requirement that the shipper be given an opportunity to receive full Carmack liability coverage before accepting alternative terms. We remand this case to the district court to consider any other potential arguments that Union Pacific might raise that it complied with the requirements of Carmack and Staggers. Accordingly, we vacate the judgment of the district court and remand the case to the court for further proceedings consistent with this opinion.

TREIBACHER INDUSTRIE, A.G.
v.
ALLEGHENY TECHNOLOGIES, INC.

464 F.3d 1235 (11th Cir. 2006)
Decided September 12, 2006

Before TJOFLAT and PRYOR, Circuit Judges, and GEORGE,* District Judge.

* Honorable Lloyd D. George, United States District Judge for the District of Nevada, sitting by designation.

OPINION

Tjoflat, Circuit Judge:

I.

A.

This lawsuit arises out of two contracts, executed in November and December of 2000, respectively, whereby Treibacher Industrie, AG ("Treibacher"), an Austrian vendor of hard metal powders, agreed to sell specified quantities of tantalum carbide ("TaC"), a hard metal powder, to TDY Industries, Inc. ("TDY")[1] for delivery to "consignment." TDY planned to use the TaC in manufacturing tungsten-graded carbide powders[2] at its plant in Gurney, Alabama. After it had received some of the amount of TaC specified in the November 2000 contract, TDY refused to take delivery of the balance of the TaC specified in both contracts, and, in a letter to Treibacher dated August 23, 2001, denied that it had a binding obligation to take delivery of or pay for any TaC that it did not wish to use. Unbeknownst to Treibacher, TDY had purchased the TaC it needed from another vendor at lower prices than those specified in its contracts with Treibacher. Treibacher eventually sold the quantities of TaC of which TDY refused to take delivery, but at lower

1 TDY, a California corporation, is a subsidiary of Allegheny Technologies, Inc., a Pennsylvania corporation, which produces various metals and metal-based products.

2 TaC is a component of tungsten-graded carbide powder, which is used to harden other metals.

prices than those specified in its contracts with TDY. Treibacher then filed suit against TDY, seeking to recover the balance of the amount Treibacher would have received had TDY paid for all of the TaC specified in the November and December 2000 contracts.[3]

The case proceeded to a bench trial, where TDY and Treibacher disputed the meaning of the term "consignment"—the delivery term contained in both contracts. TDY introduced experts in the metal industry who testified that the term "consignment," according to its common usage in the trade, meant that no sale occurred unless and until TDY actually used the TaC. Treibacher introduced evidence of the parties' prior dealings to show that the parties, in their course of dealings (extending over a seven-year period), understood the term "consignment" to mean that TDY had a binding obligation to pay for all of the TaC specified in each contract but that Treibacher would delay billing TDY for the materials until TDY had actually used them. The district court ruled that, under the United Nations Convention on Contracts for the International Sale of Goods ("CISG"), *opened for signature* April 11, 1980, S. Treaty Doc. No. 9, 98th Cong., 1st Sess. 22 (1983), 19 I.L.M. 671, reprinted at 15 U.S.C. app. (1997), evidence of the parties' interpretation of the term in their course of dealings trumped evidence of the term's customary usage in the industry, and found that Treibacher and TDY, in their course of dealings, understood the term to mean "that a sale had occurred, but that invoices would be delayed until the materials were withdrawn."[4] The court therefore entered judgment against TDY, awarding Treibacher $ 5,327,042.85 in compensatory damages (including interest).

B.

TDY now appeals. TDY contends that, under the CISG, a contract term should be construed according to its customary usage in the industry unless the parties have expressly agreed to another usage. TDY argues, in the alternative, that the district

---

3 Treibacher's complaint contains six counts. Count I is a claim for "Breach of Contract under the United Nations Convention on Contracts for the International Sale of Goods." Count II is a claim for "Anticipatory Breach of Contract" under the same United Nations convention. Count III is a claim for "Breach of Contract" under Alabama law. Count IV is a claim for "Moneys Owed and Unjust Enrichment" under Alabama law. Count V is a claim for "Conversion" under Alabama law. Count VI is a claim for "Misrepresentation," alleging that TDY misrepresented that it would accept and pay for the goods Treibacher shipped to it. Counts II through VI incorporate by reference the allegations of all previous counts.[br]On TDY's motion for summary judgment, the district court isolated Treibacher's claims from the complaint and granted the motion on all counts but Counts I and VI. The court, following a bench trial, gave Treibacher judgment on Counts I and VI, awarding Treibacher $ 5,327,042.85. Since we affirm the court's judgment on Count I, we need not review the court's disposition of Count VI.

4 Although the parties presented conflicting evidence regarding the customary usage in the industry of the term "consignment," the district court did not make a finding regarding the customary usage of the term because it found that the parties had established a meaning for the term in their course of dealings, thus rendering customary usage irrelevant.

court erred in finding that, in their course of dealings, Treibacher and TDY understood the term "consignment" to require TDY to use and pay for all of the TaC specified in each contract. Finally, TDY contends that, if we uphold the district court's ruling that TDY breached its contracts with Treibacher, we should remand the case for a new trial on damages on the ground that the district court erroneously found that Treibacher reasonably mitigated its damages.

Reviewing the district court's legal conclusions *de novo* and factual findings for clear error, *Newell v. Prudential Ins. Co., 904 F.2d 644, 649 (11th Cir. 1990)*, we hold that the district court properly construed the contract under the CISG—according to the parties' course of dealings—and did not commit clear error in finding that the parties understood the contracts to require TDY to use all of the TaC specified in the contracts. As to the mitigation of damages issue, which we review for clear error, *Bunge Corp. v. Freeport Marine Repair, Inc., 240 F.3d 919, 923 (11th Cir. 2001)*, we find that the evidence before the district court supported its finding that Treibacher's mitigation efforts were reasonable under the circumstances. We therefore affirm the judgment of the district court.

II.

A.

We begin our analysis by discussing the CISG, which governs the formation of and rights and obligations under contracts for the international sale of goods. CISG, arts. 1, 4.[5] Article 9 of the CISG provides the rules for interpreting the terms of contracts. Article 9(1) states that, "parties are bound by any usage to which they have agreed and by any practices which they have established between themselves." Article 9(2) then states that, "parties are considered, unless otherwise agreed, to have impliedly made applicable to their contract . . . a usage of which the parties knew or ought to have known and which in international trade is widely known to . . . parties to contracts of the type involved in the particular trade concerned." Article 8 of the CISG governs the interpretation of the parties' statements and conduct. A party's statements and conduct are interpreted according to that party's actual intent "where the other party knew . . . what that intent was," CISG, art. 8(1), but, if the other party was unaware of that party's actual intent, then "according to the understanding that a reasonable person . . . would have had in the same circumstances," CISG, art. 8(2). To determine a party's actual intent, or a reasonable interpretation thereof, "due consideration is to be given to all relevant circumstances of the case including the negotiations, any practices which the par-

5 The parties do not dispute that the CISG governs their dispute. Article 1 of the CISG provides, in relevant part, that it "applies to contracts of sale of goods between parties whose places of business are in different States . . . when the States are Contracting States." The United States and Austria are contracting states. Article 4 of the CISG provides, in relevant part, that it "governs . . . the formation of the contract and the rights and obligations of the seller and buyer arising from such a contract." The parties dispute their respective "rights and obligations" under the contracts at issue in this case.

ties have established between themselves, usages and any subsequent conduct of the parties." CISG, art. 8(3).

In arguing that a term's customary usage takes precedence over the parties' understanding of that term in their course of dealings, TDY seizes upon the language of article 9(2), which states that, "parties are considered, unless otherwise agreed, to have made applicable to their contract" customary trade usages. TDY contends that article 9(2) should be read to mean that, unless parties to a contract expressly agree to the meaning of a term, the customary trade usage applies. In support of its argument, TDY points to the language of article (9)(1), which binds parties to "any usage to which they have agreed and by any practices which they have established between themselves." According to TDY, the drafters of the CISG, by separating the phrase "usages to which they have agreed" from the phrase "practices which they have established between themselves," intended the word "agreed," in article 9, to mean express agreement, as opposed to tacit agreement by course of conduct. Applying this definition to the language of article 9(2), TDY contends that contract terms should, in the absence of express agreement to their usage, be interpreted according to customary usage, instead of the usage established between the parties through their course of conduct.

TDY's construction of article 9 would, however, render article 8(3) superfluous and the latter portion of article 9(1) a nullity. The inclusion in article 8(3) of "any practices which the parties have established between themselves," as a factor in interpreting the parties' statements and conduct, would be meaningless if a term's customary usage controlled that term's meaning in the face of a conflicting usage in the parties' course of dealings. The latter portion of article 9(1) would be void because the parties would no longer be "bound by any practices which they have established between themselves." Instead, in the absence of an express agreement as to a term's meaning, the parties would be bound by that term's customary usage, even if they had established a contrary usage in their course of dealings. We therefore reject TDY's interpretation of article 9(2), and, like the district court, adopt a reading that gives force to articles 8(3) and 9(1), namely, that the parties' usage of a term in their course of dealings controls that term's meaning in the face of a conflicting customary usage of the term. *Cf. Gonzalez v. McNary, 980 F.2d 1418, 1420 (11th Cir. 1993)* ("A statute should be construed so that effect is given to all its provisions, so that no part of it will be inoperative or superfluous, void or insignificant.").

B.

The district court did not commit clear error in finding that, in their course of dealings, TDY and Treibacher defined the term "consignment" to require TDY to accept and pay for all of the TaC specified in each contract. The parties do not dispute that they executed, between 1993 and 2000, a series of contracts in which Treibacher agreed to sell certain hard metal powders, such as TaC, to TDY. In each instance, TDY discussed its needs with Treibacher, after which Treibacher and TDY executed a contract whereby Treibacher agreed to sell a fixed quantity of materials at a fixed price for delivery to "consignment." Treibacher then delivered to TDY the specified quantity of materials—sometimes in installments, depending upon TDY's needs.[6] TDY kept the materials it received from Treibacher in a "consignment store," where the materials were labeled as being from Treibacher and segregated from other vendors' materials. As it withdrew the materials from the consignment store for use, TDY published "usage reports," which documented the amounts of materials withdrawn. TDY sent the usage reports to Treibacher, and Treibacher, in turn, sent TDY invoices for the amounts of materials withdrawn at the price specified in the relevant contract. TDY then paid the invoices when they came due. In each instance, TDY ultimately withdrew and paid for the full quantity of materials specified in each contract.

A particularly telling interaction, the existence of which the parties do not dispute, occurred in February 2000, when a TDY employee, Conrad Atchley, sent an e-mail to his counterpart at Treibacher, Peter Hinterhofer, expressing TDY's desire to return unused portions of a hard metal powder, titanium carbonitride ("TiCN"), which Treibacher had delivered. Hinterhofer telephoned Atchley in response and explained that TDY could not return the TiCN because TDY was contractually obligated to purchase the materials; Treibacher had delivered the TiCN as part of a quantity of TiCN that it was obligated to provide TDY under a contract executed in December 1999. Atchley told Hinterhofer that TDY would keep the TiCN. TDY subsequently used the TiCN and sent a usage report to Treibacher, for which Treibacher sent TDY an invoice, which TDY paid. This interaction—evidencing TDY's acquiescence in Treibacher's interpretation of the contract—along with TDY's practice, between 1993 and 2000, of using and paying for all of the TaC specified in each contract amply support the district court's finding that the parties, in their course of dealings, construed their contracts to require TDY to use and pay for all of the TaC specified in each contract.

C.

With respect to damages, the district court did not commit clear error in finding that Treibacher reasonably mitigated its damages. Article 77 of the CISG requires a party claiming breach of contract to "take such measures as are reasonable in the circumstances to mitigate the loss." Article 77, however, places the burden on the breaching party to "claim a reduction in the damages in the amount by which the loss should have been mitigated." Treibacher's Commercial Director, Ulf Strumberger, and Hinterhofer testified that Treibacher sought to mitigate damages as soon as possible and ultimately obtained the highest prices possible for the quantity of TaC that TDY refused; their first sale in mitigation occurred on September 9, 2001, seventeen days after the date of TDY's letter denying its obli-

6 TDY would notify Treibacher as to when it wanted to take delivery of portions of the quantity of materials provided for in each contract.

gation to purchase all of the TaC. TDY, the party carrying the burden of proving Treibacher's failure to mitigate, presented no evidence showing that Treibacher did not act reasonably. The district court therefore had no basis upon which to find that Treibacher did not take reasonable steps to mitigate its losses.

III.

In sum, the district court properly determined that, under the CISG, the meaning the parties ascribe to a contractual term in their course of dealings establishes the meaning of that term in the face of a conflicting customary usage of the term. The district court was not clearly erroneous in finding that Treibacher and TDY understood their contracts to require TDY to purchase all of the TaC specified in each contract and that Treibacher took reasonable measures to mitigate its losses after TDY breached. Accordingly, the judgment of the district court is

AFFIRMED.

IX. INTERNATIONAL TRADE

3. Transportation carriers

A. Shipping

i. In General*

* Cases are indexed under this subject. The full text of these cases is published in the **volume**-page indicated.

IX. INTERNATIONAL TRADE

3. Transportation carriers

A. Shipping

iii. Carriage of Goods by Sea Act*

* Cases are indexed under this subject. The full text of these cases is published in the **volume**-page indicated.

CONTSHIP CONTAINERLINES, LTD.
v.
PPG INDUSTRIES, INC.

442 F.3d 74 (2d Cir. 2006)
Decided March 21, 2006

JOHN M. WOODS (Joseph G. Grasso, on the brief), Thacher Proffitt & Wood LLP, New York, NY, for Plaintiff-Appellant Contship Containerlines.

STANLEY McDERMOTT III (Camilo Cardozo, on the brief), DLA Piper Rudnick Gray Cary US LLP, New York, NY, for Defendant-Appellee PPG Industries, Inc.

Before: JACOBS, CABRANES, and SACK, Circuit Judges.

OPINION

DENNIS JACOBS, Circuit Judge:

This dispute arises from a fire aboard the Contship France, a carrier operated by plaintiff-appellant Contship Containerlines, Ltd. ("Contship"). The fire was caused by the overheating of a cargo of calcium hypochloride ("Cal Hypo") shipped by defendant-appellee PPG Industries, Inc. ("PPG"). Contship concedes awareness (based on published specifications) that Cal Hypo could ignite at temperatures *over* 55 [degrees] C; and PPG concedes awareness that the cargo could ignite at lower temperatures. After a bench trial, the district court found that the proximate cause of the fire was Contship's failure to consider the impact of heat on the cargo when its towed the cargo in a spot that sustained temperatures of at least 47 [degrees] C. On appeal, Contship argues that the district court erred in dismissing its claims of strict liability and duty to warn. We affirm.

BACKGROUND

This appeal considers whether a carrier may recover against a shipper in strict liability for loss caused by cargo that is known to be dangerous, and whether a shipper satisfies its duty to warn by disclosing the dangerous characteristics of cargo in less than specific terms.

Contship is an operator of ocean-going container vessels. PPG shipped 512 drums of Cal Hypo aboard the Contship France, which sailed from Charleston, South Carolina, in late September 1997. Upon the ship's arrival in Tahiti, a fire broke out. The source of the fire was one batch of Cal Hypo, consisting of 80 drums each weighing 425 pounds.

The particular type of Cal Hypo at issue, designated "UN 2880" by Department of Transportation regulations, is known to be flammable. When exposed to heat at or above its "critical temperature," Cal Hypo will generate heat from decomposition faster than the heat can dissipate, resulting in a "thermal runaway" that can ignite surrounding materials. The critical temperature of a given drum of Cal Hypo depends in part on the volume of the drum. The district court found, upon expert testimony, that the critical temperature for the 425-pound drums of Cal Hypo was 47 [degrees] C.

According to the district court, the shipped Cal Hypo was heated to ignition due to two errors committed by the crew. First, the container that caught fire was stowed directly above the bottom center fuel tank, exposing the cargo to the heat generated by the normal flow of oil on a vessel. Second, the ship's fuel was heated to abnormally high temperatures, further raising the ambient temperature. As a result, the district court found, "temperatures at the floor of the hold above the tank top and below the container caused the temperatures in some of the drums to reach . . . at least 47 [degrees] C, the self-accelerating decomposition temperature of the calcium hypochlorite hydrate." The fire was caused by 18 days of constant exposure to these conditions.

Contship undertakes to demonstrate that relevant industry guidelines provide a default maximum storage temperature of 55 [degrees] C for Cal Hypo, and thereby afford assurance that Cal Hypo is safe at temperatures below that mark. Constship argues that it acted reasonably so long as it stowed Cal Hypo at temperatures below 55 [degrees] C, and that PPG should be liable for not warning Contship that special care was needed for its shipment of (allegedly) unusually unstable Cal Hypo.

Relevant Department of Transportation regulations in force at the time of the fire incorporated the International Maritime Dangerous Goods ("IMDG") Code—adopted by the United Nations as an international regime for the classification and regulation of hazardous sea cargoes. See 49 C.F.R. § 171.12 (1998); 49 C.F.R. § 172.101 (1996). The IMDG Code required stowage of Cal Hypo "away from sources of heat where temperatures in excess of 55 [degrees] C for a period of 24 hours or more will be encountered." Contship interprets this standard as assuring safety below 55 [degrees] C, rendering stowage reasonable at temperatures below 55 [degrees] C in the absence of contrary advice from the shipper.

PPG acknowledges that it was aware before shipping that the critical temperature of its 425 pound Cal Hypo drums was lower than 55 [degrees] C. Contship, therefore, alleges that PPG owed it a duty to warn, which PPG violated by failing to disclose the atypical and unsuspected danger of the shipped Cal Hypo. Alternatively, Contship alleges that PPG is strictly liable for shipping latently dangerous cargo.

PPG argues that the quoted regulation does not guarantee that temperatures below 55 [degrees] C are safe for Cal Hypo, because Cal Hypo's critical temperature varies according to container size and therefore could not be stated categorically. PPG adds (and the district court agreed) that the IMDG Code, taken as a whole, bars storage of Cal Hypo near sources of extreme heat, such as fuel tanks. The district court found that "stowing [Cal Hypo] as Contship did, in violation of the Code and atop a constant source of heat, was not a normal condition of transport. The stowage was equally improper for a product with an actual [critical temperature] of 55 [degrees] C."

The District Court placed full blame on Contship:

> The fire . . . was not caused by Contship stowing the cargo at an appropriate location for [a critical temperature] of 55 but inappropriate for 47 [degrees] C, it was caused by Contship's stowage entirely disregarding the factor of heat. Nothing done or undone by PPG contributed in any way or degree to the fire on the Contship France. PPG adequately complied with all its obligations . . . .Trial transcript at 1366 (emphasis added). Contship appeals both the district court's fault assessment, and the dismissal of the strict liability claim.

DISCUSSION

This Court reviews the district court's findings of fact for clear error. Conclusions of law are reviewed de novo. *Senator Linie GMBH & Co. KG v. Sunway Line, Inc., 291 F.3d 145, 151 (2d Cir. 2002)*. Attributions of fault among the various parties are considered factual determinations and therefore are reviewed under the clearly erroneous standard. See *Ching Sheng Fishery Co. v. United States, 124 F.3d 152, 157 (2d Cir. 1997)* ("A district court's finding on issues of causation and on its allocation of fault among negligent parties continues to be subject only to clearly erroneous review.").

I.

Contship's strict liability claim is premised on its interpretation of the Carriage of Goods by Sea Act ("COGSA"), which distributes liability between shipper and carrier as follows:

> [for g]oods of an inflammable, explosive or dangerous nature to the shipment whereof the carrier . . . has not consented with knowledge of their nature and character . . . the shipper of such goods shall be liable for all damages and expenses directly or indirectly arising out of or resulting from such shipment.46 U.S.C. App. § 1304(6) (2004) (emphasis added).

Is strict liability a claim available to a carrier that knew the cargo was flammable but had reason to think that it was safe enough under the conditions of stowage?

Under COGSA, dangerousness is an aspect of a cargo's "nature and character." The shipper's knowledge seems to be no consideration: Shippers are strictly liable for loss caused by inherently dangerous shipments where neither the shipper nor the carrier appreciates that the cargo is inherently dangerous. *Senator Linie, 291 F.3d at 148.*

We conclude that a carrier cannot invoke strict liability if it knows that a cargo poses a danger and requires gingerly handling or stowage, and nevertheless exposes the cargo to the general condition that triggers the known danger, regardless of whether the carrier is aware of the precise characteristics of the cargo. This principle is implicit in Senator Linie (relied on by Contship), which considered generally whether the carrier (or shipper) was "on notice that an exothermic reaction . . . was possible." Id. at 152 (internal quotation marks omitted). In such a binary analysis, a party either will know that such a reaction is possible or it will not; the calibrated likelihood of an exothermic reaction under a variety of heat circumstances is not considered. Senator Linie reinforces that dichotomy in another passage, which considers whether the cargo was "considered a stable compound" on the one hand, or deemed "inherently dangerous" on the other. Id. at 149, 152-53, 156. A carrier that exposes a cargo to heat with knowledge of its flammability may or may not ultimately prevail—depending on the particulars of what it and the shipper knew and their respective duties—but it cannot prevail on strict liability. See *Ionmar Compania Naviera, S.A. v. Olin Corp., 666 F.2d 897, 904-05 (5th Cir. 1982)* (concluding that the liability of a shipper for a fire caused by CalHypo depended on whether shipper negligently violated its duty to warn of dangers the carrier could not reasonably have been expected to know).

In this case, such a "nature and character" inquiry defeats Contship's strict liability claim. The "nature and character" of Cal Hypo is that it is flammable at elevated temperatures. Knowing Cal Hypo's tendency to lose thermal stability when heated, Contship stowed it in a superheated spot. Contship may not invoke strict liability where it brought about the very danger it knew to lie latent in its cargo.

II.

In the alternative, Contship argues that PPG's superior knowledge as to Cal Hypo's specific dangerousness at temperatures under 55 [degrees] C created a duty to warn under COGSA's negligence provision: "The shipper shall not be responsible for loss or damage sustained by the carrier or the ship arising or resulting from any cause without the act, fault, or neglect of the shipper . . . ." *46 U.S.C. App. § 1304(3)(2004)* (emphasis added).

A shipper's failure to adequately inform a carrier of the foreseeable dangers posed by cargo can constitute a negligent failure to warn under § 1304(3). As the Fourth Circuit has explained, "under general maritime law a shipper has a duty to warn the stevedore and the ship owner of the foreseeable hazards inherent in the cargo of which the stevedore and the ship's master could not reasonably have been expected to be aware." *Ente Nazionale Per L'Energia Electtrica v. Baliwag Navigation, Inc., 774 F.2d 648, 655 (4th Cir. 1985)*; see also *O'Connell Mach. Co. v. M.V. "Americana", 797 F.2d 1130, 1134 (2d Cir. 1986)* (shippers have "an obligation to inform the carrier of special requirements regarding stowage location"). However, liability for a supposedly negligent omission is inappropriate where "the particular event would have occurred even without the allegedly negligent . . . omission." *Ente Nazionale, 774 F.2d at 655*. Thus, liability for failure to warn is only appropriate if there is evidence that a "warning would have altered the [carrier's] actions." Id. at 657.

Contship's negligent-failure-to-warn claim requires two showings: (1) that PPG failed to warn Contship about dangers "inherent in the cargo of which the stevedore and ship's master could not reasonably have been expected to be aware"; and (2) that an absent warning, if given, would have impacted stowage.

1. Could Contship reasonably be expected to know the inherent dangers of PPG's Cal Hypo cargo? Professional carriers might be reasonably expected to exercise caution, and not stow flammable compounds in the hottest hold on a ship, at temperatures exceeding 47 [degrees] C—that is, 115 [degrees] F; but Contship emphasizes the supposedly reliable stability of Cal Hypo at or below 55 [degrees] C, absent circumstances that PPG knew and Contship did not. This argument is dubious.

Contship concedes that it could be expected to be aware of dangers detailed in the IMDG Code. Several provisions of the Code give notice to carriers that Cal Hypo is dangerous at temperatures approaching 55 [degrees] C. Thus, the IMDG Code advises carriers to stow potentially unstable materials with critical temperatures over 35 [degrees] C in conditions at least ten degrees cooler than the critical temperature. See *In re M/V DG Harmony, 394 F. Supp. 2d 649, 659 (S.D.N.Y. 2005)*("The IMDG Code provides that cargo having an SADT [Self Accelerating Decomposition Temperature] of 'over 35 [degrees] C' (95 [degrees] F) must be transported at a 'control temperature' of 10 [degrees] C less than the SADT."). Contship's contention that it could reasonably expect danger only at or above the critical temperature of 55 [degrees] C is undermined by the cited warning in the IMDG Code against stowage at temperatures greater than 45 [degrees] C.

That said, we need not decide this appeal by interpreting which dangers are conveyed by a reasonable reading of the IMDG Code, because the district court's findings on the issue of causation are fatal to Contship and are not clearly erroneous. See *Fed. R. Civ. P. 52(a)* ("Findings of fact, whether based on oral or documentary evidence, shall not be set aside unless clearly erroneous. . . .").

2. The district court found that Contship was unconcerned with the effect of heat on Cal Hypo, and that additional warnings therefore would not have averted the loss. Specifically, the district court found that "Contship's stowage entirely disregarded the factor of heat" due to the Contship stowage planner's "unfortunate

belief that his function was only to designate whether stowage should be above or below deck." Contship's dangerous goods coordinator believed that Cal Hypo could be carried "under deck without any real consideration as to its position in the stow." Seemingly acting on this belief, Contship stowed the flammable, heat-sensitive Cal Hypo near the heated fuel tank, an area of the ship maximally subjected to fluctuations of heat. As noone involved in stowing Cal Hypo was much concerned with the IMDG Code's 55 [degrees] C warning, the court did not err in finding that no one at Contship would have reacted to warnings of a somewhat lower critical temperature.

The likely effect of a warning is a fact question best left to the finder of fact. Since the district court's finding on this point is not clearly erroneous, the court properly dismissed Contship's claim for negligent failure to warn under § 4(3) of COGSA.

CONCLUSION

We have considered the parties' remaining arguments and find each of them to be without merit. For the foregoing reasons, the judgment of the district court is affirmed.

IX. INTERNATIONAL TRADE

3. Transportation carriers

B. Warsaw Convention*

* Cases are indexed under this subject. The full text of these cases is published in the **volume**-page indicated.

EDWARD A. BLOTTEAUX
v.
QANTAS AIRWAYS LIMITED

171 F.App'x 566 (9th Cir. 2006)
Decided March 1, 2006

Before: B. FLETCHER, CALLAHAN, Circuit Judges, and ENGLAND,* District Judge.

* The Honorable Morrison C. England, Jr., United States District Judge for the Eastern District of California, sitting by designation.

OPINION

MEMORANDUM[1]

Edward A. Blotteaux ("Blotteaux") appeals the district court's grant of summary judgment in favor of Qantas Airways Limited ("Qantas") on grounds that Blotteaux's development of Deep Vein Thrombosis ("DVT") fails to qualify as an accident compensable under the terms of Article 17 of the Warsaw Convention.[2] We have jurisdiction pursuant to 28 U.S.C. § 1291, and we affirm the district court's judgment.

A grant of summary judgment is reviewed de novo. *Ocean Advocates v. United States Army Corps of Eng'rs, 402 F.3d 846, 858 (9th Cir. 2005)*. Interpretation of the Warsaw Convention, a multilateral treaty governing the liability of air carriers engaged in international transportation, is a question of law also subject to de novo review. *Hosaka v. United Airlines, Inc., 305 F.3d 989, 993 (9th Cir. 2002), cert. denied, 537 U.S. 1227, 123 S. Ct. 1284, 154 L. Ed. 2d 1089 (2003).*

On or about September 26, 2001, Blotteaux developed DVT, a condition in which blood clotting forms in the deep veins of the legs, while seated in business class

1 This disposition is not appropriate for publication and may not be cited to or by the courts of this circuit except as provided by Ninth Circuit Rule 36-3.

2 Convention for the Unification of Certain Rules Relating to International Transportation by Air, Oct. 12, 1929, 49 Stat. 3000.

aboard an international flight operated by Qantas between Australia and the United States. It is undisputed that the flight in question was uneventful, with no equipment malfunction or other anomaly occurring. It is further undisputed that Blotteaux did not request any assistance or other accommodation from Qantas personnel during the course of the flight, and while he does claim to have noticed some leg discomfort as the trip progressed, Blotteaux did not seek any medical treatment for some thirteen days after concluding his air travel.

The susceptibility of airline passengers to development of DVT, particularly on long flights, is well recognized. It is undisputed that Qantas developed an informational video on the risks of DVT, and precautionary measures to be taken in the face of that risk, for use on long-haul flights. Qantas' standard custom and practice, since March 2001, has been to show its informational video on all international flights, including the flight at issue. In addition, it is undisputed that the Qantas in-flight magazine, which was available on Blotteaux's flight, contained an article cautioning passengers on the risk of developing DVT on long flights. Finally, Qantas' in-flight audio entertainment system included a segment about the importance of maintaining blood circulation during such flights.

Blotteaux makes two primary arguments in appealing the judgment below. First, he argues that the term "accident," which triggers liability for bodily injury under Article 17 of the Warsaw Convention, should be interpreted flexibly in order to allow recovery for his DVT-related damages. Secondly, Blotteaux contends that he was not provided with any meaningful warning as to the risk of DVT, and argues that Qantas' failure to adequately warn in that regard subjects the airline to liability under the Warsaw Convention. As set forth below, neither contention has merit.

Article 17 of the Warsaw Convention makes international air carriers liable for bodily injury sustained by a passenger "if the accident so sustained took place on board the aircraft or in the course of any of the operations of embarking or disembarking." 49 Stat. 3018. Liability under Article 17 therefore hinges in the present matter on whether or not Blotteaux's development of DVT constitutes an "accident", as that term has been defined.

In *Air France v. Saks, 470 U.S. 392, 105 S. Ct. 1338, 84 L. Ed. 2d 289 (1985)*, the Supreme Court addressed the definition of "accident" for purposes of assessing Article 17 liability. In *Saks,* an airline passenger became permanently deaf in one ear after experiencing severe pain and pressure in that ear during the plane's descent into Los Angeles enroute from Paris. *Id.* at 394. The Court held that the hearing loss was not an "accident" for purposes of Article 17 liability because it resulted from "the passenger's own internal reaction to the usual, normal, and expected operation of the aircraft." *Id.* at 406. In order to trigger liability, the Court required that a passenger's injury be "caused by an unexpected or unusual event or happening that is external to the passenger." *Id.* at 405.

The rationale of *Saks* applies squarely to this case. No evidence has been presented that anything unusual occurred aboard the Qantas flight in question, or that Blotteaux's development of DVT was triggered by anything other than his own internal reaction to the prolonged sitting/inactivity attendant to any lengthy flight. Blotteaux nonetheless argues that the reasoning of a subsequent Supreme Court decision, *Olympic Airways v. Husain, 540 U.S. 644, 124 S. Ct. 1221, 157 L. Ed. 2d 1146 (2004)*, should extend to the present matter.

In *Husain,* the airline was held liable for a passenger's fatal asthma attack after the flight attendant repeatedly refused to move the passenger out of the proximity of the plane's smoking section, despite numerous requests from the passenger's wife that an allergy to cigarette smoke made that move imperative. *See Id.* at 647. The Court found that the attendant's refusal to assist the passenger was an unusual and unexpected event that satisfied the "accident" requirement of Article 17. *Id.* at 646.

The present case is factually distinguishable from *Husain* because it is undisputed that flight personnel were not asked to assist Blotteaux in any way and were not even notified of any discomfort on his part. Moreover, in *Rodriguez v. Ansett Australia Ltd., 383 F.3d 914 (9th Cir. 2004)*, this court unequivocally found that the occurrence of DVT on an otherwise unremarkable flight does not constitute an accident because, pursuant to *Saks,* the condition was precipitated not by any unexpected or unusual event or happening but instead by the passenger's own internal reaction to normal aircraft operation. *Id.* at 917. *Rodriguez* distinguished *Husain* on grounds that it involved a response by flight crew to the passenger's medical condition, a distinction equally applicable here. *Id.* at 918. Consequently, with respect to an airline passenger's development of DVT under normal flight conditions, we have already decided that no "accident" under the Warsaw Convention could have occurred.

Blotteaux's second argument is equally unavailing. He contends that Qantas failed to meaningfully inform its passengers about the risk of developing DVT on long-haul flights, and argues that such a failure can be analogized to the "accident" identified by the Supreme Court in *Husain.* As *Rodriguez* makes clear, however, *Husain* involved a response by the flight crew to the passenger's medical condition, a circumstance not present in this case. *Id.* The only question left open by *Rodriguez,* given our statement there that we need not decide the issue, is whether an airline's failure to warn of DVT can constitute an accident for purposes of Article 17. *See Id.* at 919.

There is no factual basis here for Blotteaux's claim that Qantas failed to adequately warn him about the danger of DVT. Since both video, audio, and written materials concerning DVT were provided, the fact that Blotteaux failed to heed those materials does not support any failure to warn on Qantas' part. In the face of those warnings, Blotteaux's claim that Qantas somehow "hid" the risk of developing DVT is simply untenable. Moreover, Blotteaux has failed to demonstrate any clear industry standard against which Qantas' warnings could be measured in any event. In the absence of a viable failure-to-warn claim, this case is squarely controlled by *Saks* and *Rodriguez.*

AFFIRMED.

GUY CAMAN
v.
CONTINENTAL AIRLINES, INC.

455 F.3d 1087 (9th Cir. 2006)
Decided August 2, 2006

Before: Betty B. Fletcher and Consuelo M. Callahan, Circuit Judges, and Morrison C. England, Jr., District Judge.* Opinion by Judge England

* The Honorable Morrison C. England, Jr., United States District Judge for the Eastern District of California, sitting by designation.

OPINION

ENGLAND, District Judge:

This action is brought pursuant to Article 17 of the Convention for the Unification of Certain Rules Relating to International Transportation by Air, Oct. 12, 1929, art. 17, 49 Stat. 3000, T.S. No. 876 (1934), reprinted in note following 49 U.S.C. § 40105 ("Warsaw Convention" or "Convention"). The parties agree, and we concur, that this action is governed exclusively by the Warsaw Convention. The scope of our review is limited to whether appellant Guy Caman ("Caman") can establish liability against appellee Continental Airlines ("Continental") under the Convention.[1] We hold that the district court properly granted summary judgment in favor of Continental on the ground that Continental's failure to warn Caman of the possibility of developing Deep Vein Thrombosis ("DVT") during the course of an international flight does not constitute an "accident" under the Warsaw Convention. Accordingly, we affirm.

1 A passenger whose injury is not compensable under the Warsaw Convention because it entails no "bodily injury" or was not the result of an "accident" will have no recourse to an alternate remedy. *El Al Isr. Airlines v. Tseng, 525 U.S. 155, 160-61, 119 S. Ct. 662, 142 L. Ed. 2d 576 (1999).*

BACKGROUND

Caman alleges that he developed DVT while on board an international flight operated by Continental. Caman's axial argument is that Continental's failure to advise him of the risk of DVT, which can result from immobility, dehydration and being cramped in a small pitch seat over the course of an international flight, constitutes an "accident" for purposes of establishing liability under the Warsaw Convention.

The following facts are uncontested. On May 28, 2002, Caman departed from Los Angeles, California, on a flight bound for Paris, France. The flight was uneventful with no equipment malfunction or other anomaly occurring. Caman did not receive any warning regarding the potential hazard of developing DVT on his international flight. During the course of his air travel, up to and including his disembarkation from the aircraft, Caman did not request any assistance or other accommodation from Continental personnel. Upon his arrival in France, Caman found it difficult to walk on his right leg and immediately sought medical attention. He was diagnosed with DVT and was admitted to a hospital where he remained for three days. He received therapy amounting to injections several times a week for the next month.

STANDARD OF REVIEW

Caman appeals the district court's grant of summary judgment in favor of Continental. We review the district court's grant of summary judgment de novo. *Carey v. United Airlines, 255 F.3d 1044, 1047 (9th Cir. 2001).* Interpretations of treaties, such as the Warsaw Convention, are questions of law that are also reviewed de novo. *Hosaka v. United Airlines, Inc., 305 F.3d 989, 993 (9th Cir. 2002).*

ANALYSIS

Caman seeks review of the lower court's ruling that an air carrier's failure to warn passengers of the risk of developing DVT during international air travel is not an "accident" for purposes of Article 17 liability. Article 17 of the Warsaw Convention imposes liability on an air carrier for a passenger's death or bodily injury caused by an "accident" that occurred in connection with an international flight. *Olympic Airways v. Husain, 540 U.S. 644, 124 S. Ct. 1221, 157 L. Ed. 2d 1146 (2004).* The term "accident" in the Warsaw Convention has been defined as an "unexpected or unusual event or happening that is external to the passenger," and not "the passenger's own internal reaction to the usual, normal, and expected operation of the aircraft." *Air France v. Saks, 470 U.S. 392, 405-06, 105 S. Ct. 1338, 84 L. Ed. 2d 289 (1985).*

It is well settled that the development of DVT as the result of international air travel, without more, does not constitute an "accident" for purposes of Article 17 liability. *See, e.g., Rodriguez v. Ansett Austl. Ltd., 383 F.3d 914, 919 (9th Cir. 2004)*; *Scherer v. Pan Am. World Airways, Inc., 54 A.D.2d 636, 387 N.Y.S.2d 580, 581 (App. Div. 1976).* Generally, courts reach this conclusion because the development of DVT is nothing more than a passenger's own internal reaction to the usual, normal, and expected operation of the aircraft. *Rodriguez, 383 F.3d at 917*. Since the development of DVT itself does not constitute an Article 17 "accident," Caman would have us conclude that Continental's failure to warn him of the risk of DVT constitutes an Article 17 "accident." While this issue has been expressly decided by a sister circuit as well as by sister signatories to the Warsaw Convention, it is an issue of first impression in this circuit. Given the narrow ambit of the issue coupled with the unsettled state of the law, a brief recitation of both controlling precedent as well as related domestic cases follows.

I.

The seminal case on the issue of what constitutes an accident under Article 17 of the Warsaw Convention is *Air France v. Saks, 470 U.S. 392, 105 S. Ct. 1338, 84 L. Ed. 2d 289*. In *Saks*, an airline passenger became permanently deaf in one ear after experiencing severe pain and pressure in that ear during the plane's descent into Los Angeles en route from Paris. The plaintiff sued the air carrier under the Warsaw Convention, contending that her injury was the result of an "accident" occurring during her international flight. Justice O'Connor delivered the opinion of the Court and held that Article 17 liability arises only if a passenger's injury is caused by an "unexpected or unusual event or happening that is external to the passenger." *Id.* at 405. The conditions precedent to Article 17 liability are as follows: 1) an unexpected or unusual event; 2) external to the passenger; 3) that causes the plaintiff's injury. *See id.; see also Rodriguez, 383 F.3d at 917*.

Nearly two decades after *Saks* was decided, the Supreme Court revisited the question of what constitutes an Article 17 "accident." *Husain, 540 U.S. 644, 124 S. Ct. 1221, 157 L. Ed. 2d 1146*. In *Husain*, a passenger severely allergic to tobacco smoke suffered a fatal asthma attack after the flight attendant repeatedly refused to assist him in finding a seat further away from the plane's smoking section. *Id.* at 653. With respect to whether the flight crew's refusal to reseat the decedent was "unusual or unexpected," the Court expressly declined to decide the question.[2] *Id.* at 653. Instead, the Court adopted the district court's finding that the air crew's departure from relevant industry standard was unusual or unexpected conduct satisfying part of the first condition precedent. *Id.* at 652-53. Next, the Court considered whether inaction can constitute an "event" for purposes of Article 17 liability. The Court rejected Olympic Airways' argument that only affirmative conduct can constitute an "event" under Article 17. In dismissing that argument, the majority of

---

2 The Supreme Court's discussion of this issue in *Husain* is as follows: "As an initial matter, we note that petitioner did not challenge in the Court of Appeals the District Court's finding that the flight attendant's conduct in three times refusing to move [the passenger] was unusual or unexpected in light of the relevant industry standard or petitioner's own company policy. . . . Consequently, we need not dispositively determine whether the flight attendant's conduct qualified as 'unusual or unexpected' under *Saks*, but may assume that it was for purposes of this opinion." *Husain, 540 U.S. at 652-53*.

the Court concluded that the air crew's failure to assist, or inaction, can constitute an Article 17 "event." *Id.* at 654-57. With respect to the element of causation, the Court concluded that the failure of the air crew to reseat the decedent together with exposing him to smoke were each links in the causal chain leading to his expiration and entitling his wife, the plaintiff, to relief. *Id.* at 654.

In *Blansett v. Continental Airlines, Inc., 379 F.3d 177 (5th Cir. 2004)*, the plaintiff sought relief on the identical theory presented here. Namely, Blansett argued that the airline's failure to warn him of the potential for developing DVT is an Article 17 "accident" because the decision not to warn passengers of a known risk is a departure from industry standard and is, therefore, unexpected.[3] *Id.* at 181. Based in part on *Husain*'s reasoning that inaction can constitute an event, the plaintiff urged that the air carrier's failure to warn also comprised an Article 17 "event." *Id.*

The *Blansett* court carefully abstained from creating a *per se* rule that any departure from an industry standard constitutes an Article 17 "accident." *Id.* at 182. Instead, the court pointed to the absence of any Federal Aviation Administration requirement that warnings of DVT be issued on international flights as evidence that a failure to warn of DVT is not "unexpected" and, therefore, outside the scope of Article 17. As the court explained in summation, "[i]t was not an unexpected or unusual decision for Continental merely to cleave to the exclusive list of warnings required of it by the agency that has regulatory jurisdiction over its flights." *Id.*

In *Rodriguez* this court addressed circumstances very similar to those presented here. Specifically, we considered first whether developing DVT can constitute an Article 17 "accident," and second, whether a failure to warn of the risk of DVT can constitute an Article 17 "accident." 383 F.3d 914. On the merits of the first claim, we concluded that "there was no event external to the passenger, let alone an unusual or unexpected event." *Id.* at 918. As to the failure to warn claim, we declined to decide whether failure to warn of DVT can constitute an "accident." *Id.* at 919. Rather, we decided that Rodriguez had failed to create a genuine issue of material fact by failing to submit evidence establishing the industry custom or the airline's own policy, and failing to establish whether the airline complied with either the industry standard or its own company policy. *Id.*

The foregoing decisions have left unresolved certain issues salient to this court's inquiry. Specifically, whether an air carrier's departure from either industry standard or its own company policy are the appropriate benchmark for determining whether an event is "unexpected or unusual" conduct under Article 17[4] and, more

---

3 This argument is directly drawn from the *Husain* decision. As noted *supra*, the *Husain* Court expressly declined to decide whether the refusal to assist a passenger was "unexpected." *See* n.2, *supra*. Rather, the Court adopted the district court's reasoning that the departure from industry standard made the air crew's conduct "unexpected." *Husain, 540 U.S. at 653.*

4 We recognize that there are questions as to whether an air carrier's departure from an industry standard or its own company policy is "unexpected" for the purpose of defining an Article

importantly, whether the inaction alleged here is sufficient to constitute an Article 17 "event."

II.

The starting point of our analysis is, of course, the text of the Convention and the context in which the written words are used. *Saks, 470 U.S. at 396-97*. The text of Article 17 is as follows:

> The carrier shall be liable for damage sustained in the event of the death or wounding of a passenger or any other bodily injury suffered by a passenger, if the accident which caused the damage so sustained took place on board the aircraft or in the course of any of the operations of embarking or disembarking.

Art. 17, 49 Stat. 3018. The foregoing language clearly establishes the liability of international air carriers for accidents resulting in harm to passengers sustained during any operations of the aircraft. Conversely, Article 20(1) provides a defense for air carriers. The language of Article 20(1) is as follows:

> The carrier shall not be liable if he proves that he and his agents have taken all necessary measures to avoid the damage or that it was impossible for him or them to take such measures.

Art. 20, 49 Stat. 3019.

With respect to considering these two Articles, the Supreme Court explained that "[t]he 'accident' requirement of Article 17 is distinct from the defenses in Article 20(1), both because it is located in a separate article and because it involves an inquiry into the nature of the event which *caused* the injury rather than the care taken by the airline to avert the injury." *Saks, 470 U.S. at 407*. The Court went on to clarify that, while these two inquiries may on occasion be similar, courts should decline to employ that similarity to repeal Article 20(1). *Id.* Attributing liability to an air carrier for failing to do all it can to prevent an injury that is inherent in air travel, as Caman is here requesting, improperly shifts the focus of the inquiry from the nature of the event which caused the injury to the alleged failure of the air carrier to avert the same. In addition, interpreting the term "accident" to include a failure to warn of a possible risk of flight would incorporate into Article 17 an inquiry that is properly left to analysis under Article 20(1) once it has been established that an accident has occurred. *Husain, 540 U.S. at 649 n.5* ("*After* a plaintiff has established a prima facie case of liability under Article 17 by showing that the injury was caused by an 'accident,' the air carrier has the opportunity to prove under Article 20 that it took 'all necessary measures to avoid the damage or that it was impossible for [the airline] to take such measures.'" (quoting 49 Stat. 3019) (alteration in original) (emphasis added)).

---

17 "accident." We decline to address this question as our holding today does not turn on the resolution of that issue.

Applying the treaty's text and Supreme Court precedent to the facts of this case, we hold that Caman cannot establish his DVT was the result of an "accident" because he cannot show that it resulted from an "unexpected or unusual event." *Saks, 470 U.S. at 404, 406*. Specifically, we hold that Continental's failure to warn Caman of DVT is not an "event" as that term is discussed in *Saks* and *Husain*. Rather, Continental's failure to warn was an act of *omission* (inaction that idly allows an unfolding series of events to reach their natural conclusion) as opposed to an act of *commission* (inaction that produces an effect, result or consequence) as in *Husain*'s rejection of a direct plea for help.

For the foregoing reasons, we conclude that Continental's failure to warn Caman of the risk of developing DVT is not an Article 17 "accident." Accordingly, he cannot obtain relief under the Warsaw Convention.

AFFIRMED.

TRACEY FAYE CORTEZ
v.
AIR NEW ZEALAND LIMITED (USA)

203 F.App'x 31 (9th Cir. 2006)
Decided October 2, 2006

Before: D.W. NELSON, HAWKINS, and PAEZ, Circuit Judges.

OPINION

MEMORANDUM[1]

Plaintiff Tracey Faye Cortez appeals the district court's grant of summary judgment to defendant Air New Zealand Limited (USA). We affirm.

Cortez first argues that this court wrongly decided *Rodriguez v. Air New Zealand, 383 F.3d 914, 916-19 (9th Cir. 2004)*, which held that the development of deep vein thrombosis ("DVT") was not an "accident" as that term is used in Article 17 of the Warsaw Convention. Cortez contends Rodriguez is inconsistent with the Supreme Court's decision in *Olympic Airways v. Husain, 540 U.S. 644, 124 S. Ct. 1221, 157 L. Ed. 2d 1146 (2004)*. In Rodriguez, however, we fully considered and distinguished Husain, *383 F.3d at 918*, and, moreover, as a three-judge panel, we lack the authority to disregard Rodriguez.

Cortez next argues that the airline should be liable under the Warsaw Convention because its failure to warn of the risk of DVT is an "accident," that is, an "unexpected or unusual event." See *Air France v. Saks, 470 U.S. 392, 405-06, 105 S. Ct. 1338, 84 L. Ed. 2d 289 (1985)*. We recently rejected this argument in *Caman v. Continental Airlines, 455 F.3d 1087 (9th Cir. 2006)*. In Caman, we explained the difference between the "accident" requirement of Article 17 and the defenses

1 This disposition is not appropriate for publication and may not be cited to or by the courts of this circuit except as provided by Ninth Circuit Rule 36-3.

available to a carrier under Article 20(1) when a carrier has "taken all necessary measures to avoid the damage":

> Attributing liability to an air carrier for failing to do all it can to prevent an injury that is inherent in air travel . . . improperly shifts the focus of the inquiry from the nature of the event which caused the injury to the alleged failure of the air carrier to avert the same. In addition, interpreting the term "accident" to include a failure to warn of a possible risk of flight would incorporate into Article 17 an inquiry that is properly left to analysis under Article 20(1) once it has been established that an accident has occurred.455 F.3d at 1092. We went on to conclude that the failure to warn of the DVT risk is not an Article 17 "event." Id.

Although Cortez argues the factual record in his case differs from the facts in Caman, nothing about the holding in Caman is tied to its specific evidence. Rather, the decision turns on the interpretation of two different provisions of the Warsaw Convention, and the nature of the alleged act of omission. See id. Cortez's reliance on footnote four of *Caman, 455 F.3d at 1091 n.4*, is thus misplaced. Although in Caman we declined to address the *general* question of whether an air carrier's departure from an industry standard or its own company policy is "unexpected" for the purpose of defining an Article 17 "accident," we specifically concluded that a failure to warn of the risk of DVT is not an "event" for Article 17 purposes. *Id. at 1092*. If no "event" has occurred, it matters not whether that non-event is "unusual or unexpected." Even though Caman may leave open a question for another day in another context, it definitively resolves the DVT failure to warn issue, and in a way that is fatal to Cortez's claim.

AFFIRMED.

EDO GEORGE MBABA
v.
SOCIETE AIR FRANCE

457 F.3d 496 (5th Cir. 2006)
Decided July 25, 2006

Before JONES, Chief Judge, and BARKSDALE and BENAVIDES, Circuit Judges.

OPINION

BENAVIDES, Circuit Judge:

This case concerns the preemptive effect of the Warsaw Convention as amended by Montreal Protocol No. 4. The Appellant, Edo George Mbaba, argues that his claims stemming from excess baggage fees are not preempted because such injuries are not contemplated by the Convention. The Appellee, Societe Air France ("Air France"), argues that Mbaba's claims are preempted due to the Convention's broad exclusivity. As explained below, the Convention's text and Supreme Court precedent inform our conclusion that the claims are preempted.

I. FACTUAL AND PROCEDURAL BACKGROUND

Mbaba purchased a ticket to travel on Air France from Houston, Texas to Lagos, Nigeria. The trip was scheduled for June 15, 2002, and included a layover in Paris, France. Mbaba bought the ticket from Federal Express, his employer. The parties dispute whether Federal Express sold Mbaba a "non-revenue" (complimentary) ticket. When Mbaba checked in for the flight in Houston, he paid a \$ 520.00 excess baggage fee, \$ 130.00 for each of his four extra bags. His baggage ticket indicated that the bags were to be transported from Houston to Lagos.

In Paris, Air France unloaded Mbaba's baggage. Air France says that it had to do this because Mbaba was a non-revenue passenger. Meanwhile, Mbaba missed the scheduled flight to Lagos. Mbaba reclaimed the baggage and spent a night in the airport terminal waiting for the next flight. The next day, when Mbaba checked in for the new Lagos flight, an agent said Mbaba would have to pay \$ 4048.66 for the extra bags. In Paris, Air France charges excess baggage fees based upon the weight of the bags. Mbaba alleges that the agent refused to let him send the bags back to Houston and said that if Mbaba did not pay the charge, the bags would be "taken out and burned." Mbaba payed the fee with a credit card.

Mbaba filed this suit against Air France in Texas state court, alleging breach of contract, violation of the Texas Deceptive Trade Practices Act, and common law fraud. Air France removed the case to federal court. After a period of discovery, the district court granted summary judgment to Air France, holding that the Warsaw Convention preempted Mbaba's state law claims. Mbaba appealed.

II. STANDARD OF REVIEW

This Court reviews a district court's grant of a summary judgment *de novo*, applying the same standards as the district court. *Hirras v. Nat'l R.R. Passenger Corp., 95 F.3d 396, 399 (5th Cir. 1996)*. The evidence should be viewed in the light most favorable to the nonmoving party, and the record should not indicate a genuine issue as to any material fact. *Am. Home Assurance Co. v. United Space Alliance, 378 F.3d 482, 486 (5th Cir. 2004)*.

III. DISCUSSION

A. The Warsaw Convention

This case presents the first opportunity for this Court to interpret the language of the Warsaw Convention as amended by Montreal Protocol No. 4. *See* Convention for the Unification of Certain Rules Relating to International Transportation By Air, Oct. 12, 1929, 49 Stat. 3000, T.S. No. 876 (1934) (as amended by Montreal Protocol No. 4,*as reprinted in* S. Rep. No. 105-20, at 21-32 (1998)) ("Warsaw Convention"). The "cardinal purpose" of the Warsaw Convention is "to achieve uniformity of rules governing claims arising from international air transportation." *El Al Israel Airlines, Ltd. v. Tsui Yuan Tseng, 525 U.S. 155, 169, 119 S. Ct. 662, 142 L. Ed. 2d 576 (1999)*. It applies to "all international transportation of persons, baggage, or goods performed by aircraft for hire." Warsaw Convention, *as reprinted in* S. Rep. No. 105-20, at 21 (Article 1).

The language at issue is in Paragraph 1 of Article 24. It states:

> 1. In the carriage of passengers and baggage, any action for damages, however founded, can only be brought subject to the conditions and limits set out in this Convention, without prejudice to the question as to who are the persons who have the right to bring suit and what are their respective rights.

Id. at 29. The language in Paragraph 2 of Article 24 offers some guidance in interpreting Paragraph 1. It states:

> 2. In the carriage of cargo, any action for damages, however founded, whether under this Convention or in contract or in tort or otherwise, can only be brought subject to the conditions and limits of liability set out in this Convention without prejudice to

> the question as to who are the persons who have the right to bring suit and what are their respective rights. Such limits of liability constitute maximum limits and may not be exceeded whatever the circumstances which gave rise to the liability.

Id. at 29. This version became binding in the United States March 4, 1999, after adoption of Montreal Protocol No. 4. *Tseng, 525 U.S. at 175 n.14.* The previous version of Article 24 stated:

> 1. In the cases covered by articles 18 and 19 any actions for damages, however founded, can only be brought subject to the conditions and limits set out in this Convention.
>
> 2. In the cases covered by article 17 the provisions of the preceding paragraph shall also apply, without prejudice to the questions as to who are the persons who have the right to bring suit and what are their respective rights.Warsaw Convention, *as reprinted in* note following *49 U.S.C. § 40105*, at 11 (2000).

It is undisputed that the alleged damages suffered by Mbaba do not fall within the language of Articles 17, 18, or 19. Article 17 describes carrier liability for death or bodily injury. Warsaw Convention, *as reprinted in* S. Rep. No. 105-20, at 26. Article 18 describes carrier liability for damage to passenger baggage. *Id.* Article 19 describes carrier liability for damage caused by delay in transportation of "passengers, baggage, or goods." *Id.*

Montreal Protocol No. 4 deals primarily with rules relating to cargo transportation. *Id.* at 1. For example, it reduces paperwork that must accompany cargo and redefines cargo liability. *Id.* at 3-4. The protocol languished for more than twenty years in the Senate, because Senators objected to liability limits for personal injuries and death that would be triggered by its adoption. *Id.* at 2. In 1997, the Department of Transportation approved an inter-airline agreement that waived the Convention's limits, which led to the Senate's reconsideration of the protocol. *Id.*

B. *El Al Israel Airlines, Ltd. v. Tsui Yuan Tseng*

Neither the United States Supreme Court nor the Fifth Circuit has interpreted Article 24 of the Warsaw Convention since it was altered by Montreal Protocol No. 4. The Supreme Court, however, reviewed the prior version in *El Al Israel Airlines, Ltd. v. Tsui Yuan Tseng, 525 U.S. 155, 119 S. Ct. 662, 142 L. Ed. 2d 576 (1999).*

Tseng sought damages for psychic and psychosomatic injuries resulting from "an intrusive security search" before she boarded an El Al Israel Airlines flight. *Id. at 160.* The case presented a question of the Convention's exclusivity, given that the Convention did not address psychological injuries. *Id.* The Court found that the Convention barred Tseng's recovery, holding that recovery for a personal injury "not allowed under the Convention, is not available at all." *Id. at 161.*

The Court reasoned that recourse to local law would undermine the Convention's purpose—uniformity of air carrier liability. *Id. at 161.* It relied on language in Article 1 that made the Convention apply to "all international transportation" and

Article 24, as written before adoption of Montreal Protocol No. 4. *Id. at 162.* The Court found that Article 24 was part of "a compromise between the interests of air carriers and their customers" that restricted the claims those customers could pursue. *Id. at 170-71.* It also explained that an interpretation allowing Tseng's claims would lead to "several anomalies," including cases where passengers injured physically would be subject to liability limits while passengers merely traumatized would not. *Id. at 171.* Finally, the Court concluded that other treaty signatories had interpreted the Convention as an exclusive remedy. *Id. at 176.*

The Court also addressed Montreal Protocol No. 4, which at the time of the decision had been ratified but had not taken effect. *Id. at 174.* It stated that under the amended Article 24, both parties agreed that "[t]he treaty precludes passengers from bringing actions under local law when they cannot establish air carrier liability under the treaty." *Id. at 175.* Indeed, Tseng "concede[d]" that under the protocol she would have "no recourse to an alternate remedy." *Id. at 160-61.* The Court said that the protocol "clarifies, but does not change, the Convention's exclusivity domain." *Id. at 161.* Justice Stevens, the only dissenting member of the Court, also assumed that the protocol clarified the exclusivity of the Convention. *Id. at 177* (Stevens, J., dissenting) (describing his disagreement as having limited significance because "the issue has been conclusively determined for future cases by the recent amendment [Montreal Protocol No.4] to the Warsaw Convention").

C. Analysis

Mbaba argues that his claims cannot be preempted because his injuries are not contemplated by the Convention. He focuses on the fact that his injury is not even within the broad categories of the Convention: personal injury, lost or damaged baggage, or delay. He suggests that the district court's holding in effect means that "unless an injury is specified in the Warsaw Convention, there can be no remedy for it." *Id.* He makes this point with an analogy: "An airline could, if it chose, even line up passengers on an international flight and *rob them at gunpoint* without fear of any civil liability to the victims whatsoever." Robbery is not prohibited by the Convention.

Mbaba supports his argument with the text of Article 24, specifically the language stating that claims "can only be brought subject to the conditions and limits set out in this Convention." He also relies on a portion of *Tseng* relating to a hypothetical involving an escalator. *Tseng, 525 U.S. at 171-72.* The hypothetical came from Tseng's Court of Appeals decision. The Second Circuit reasoned that if the Convention excluded Tseng's claims "then a passenger injured by a malfunctioning escalator in the airline's terminal would have no recourse against the airline, even if the airline recklessly disregarded its duty to keep the escalator in proper repair." *Id. at 171.* In response, the Supreme Court stated, "[T]he Convention's preemptive effect on local law extends no further than the Convention's own substantive scope. A carrier, therefore, is indisputably subject to liability under local law for injuries arising out of that scope: *e.g.*, for passenger injuries occurring before any of the operations of embarking or disembarking."[1] *Id. at 172* (internal quotation marks omitted). Finally, Mbaba relies on statements made by Senator Biden that describe Montreal Protocol No. 4. as "simplify[ing] cargo rules" without making "controversial" changes. *See* 144 CONG. REC. S11059-02 (1998).

Mbaba's argument fails to overcome the text of the Convention and *Tseng*. First, the text of Article 24 specifically preempts claims resulting from the carriage of baggage "however founded."[2] Second, the language in *Tseng* surrounding the escalator hypothetical does not overcome other passages of *Tseng* specifically related to Montreal Protocol No. 4. *Tseng, 525 U.S. at 175* (describing the amended Convention as "preclud[ing] passengers from bringing actions under local law when they cannot establish air carrier liability under the treaty"). Third, Senator Biden's comments are unpersuasive as they speak only to the general characteristics of the protocol. Finally, Mbaba's recitation of analogies is unhelpful. Our task is to review the Convention in relation to a tariff on the carriage of baggage. We will not consider other scenarios.

Our decision conforms with the view taken by the Second Circuit in *King v. American Airlines, Inc., 284 F.3d 352 (2d Cir. 2002)*. In *King*, the court held that the Warsaw Convention preempted a discrimination claim based on an allegation that the plaintiffs were bumped from a flight because of their race. *Id. at 358*. The *King* Court noted that the Supreme Court in *Tseng* "held that the Convention's preemptive effect on local law extends to all causes of action . . . regardless of whether a claim actually could be maintained under the provisions of the Convention." *Id. at 357*.

For these reasons, the Warsaw Convention preempts Mbaba's claims. To hold otherwise would undermine the Convention's goal of uniformity. *See Tseng, 525 U.S. at 169* ("Given the Convention's comprehensive scheme of liability rules and its textual emphasis on uniformity, we would be hard put to conclude that the delegates at Warsaw meant to subject air carriers to the distinct, nonuniform liability rules of the individual signatory nations."). Because we affirm on this ground, we do not reach Air France's alternative arguments.

---

1 Mbaba asks this Court to interpret "scope," as used in *Tseng*, as pertaining to the types of claims contemplated by the Convention. Such an interpretation, however, would directly contradict the ultimate holding in *Tseng*, which precluded claims for psychological injuries because the Convention did not include them. The Supreme Court appears to use the term "scope" to describe the specified parameters of the Convention. Indeed, Article 17 states that a carrier is liable for death or injuries that take place "onboard" or while "embarking or disembarking." Warsaw Convention, *as reprinted in* S. Rep. No. 105-20, at 26; *see also Acevedo-Reinoso v. Iberia Lineas Aereas de Espana S.A., 449 F.3d 7, 14 (1st Cir. 2006)* (remanding for a determination of whether the alleged injury "occurred on board the airplane or in the process of embarking or disembarking").

2 The amended version of Paragraph 1 uses the more broad language of "In the carriage of passengers and baggage" rather than the previously used "In the cases covered by articles 18 and 19." *Supra* Part III.A.

IV. CONCLUSION

Based on the text of the Warsaw Convention and the language in *Tseng*, we hold that Mbaba's claims are preempted. Accordingly, his injuries are not actionable in the courts of the United States. We affirm the district court's grant of summary judgment.

X. CUSTOMS

1. In General*

---

* Cases are indexed under this subject. The full text of these cases is published in the **volume**-page indicated.

CALIFORNIA INDUSTRIAL PRODUCTS
v.
UNITED STATES

436 F.3d 1341 (Fed. Cir. 2006)
Decided February 1, 2006

Mark L. Austrian, Collier Shannon Scott, PLLC, of Washington, DC, argued for plaintiff-appellee. With him on the brief was Robin H. Gilbert. Of counsel was Michael R. Kershow.

Mikki Graves Walser, Attorney, International Trade Field Office, Commercial Litigation Branch, Civil Division, United States Department of Justice, of New York, New York, argued for defendant-appellant. With her on the brief were Peter D. Keisler, Assistant Attorney General; David M. Cohen, Director, of Washington, DC; and Barbara S. Williams, Attorney in Charge, of New York, New York. Of counsel on the brief was Chi S. Choy, Attorney, Office of Assistant Chief Counsel, International Trade Litigation, United States Customs and Border Protection, of New York, New York.

Before MICHEL, Chief Judge, SCHALL, and GAJARSA, Circuit Judges.

OPINION

SCHALL, Circuit Judge.

DECISION

The United States appeals from the final decision of the United States Court of International Trade in *California Industrial Products, Inc. v. United States, 350 F. Supp. 2d 1135 (Ct. Int'l Trade 2004)*. In its decision, the court granted the motion of California Industrial Products, Inc. ("CIP") for summary judgment and denied the government's cross-motion for summary judgment. In granting CIP's motion, the court overturned the ruling of the United States Customs Service ("Customs")[1] that CIP was not entitled to manufacturing substitution drawbacks under 19 U.S.C. § 1313(b) (1994)[2] based upon its exportation of steel scrap. The court held that Customs erred in denying CIP's drawback claims because, before doing so, it failed to conduct notice and comment proceedings. Such proceedings were required under 19 U.S.C. § 1625(c), the court determined, because Customs' denial of CIP's claims represented, in the words of that statute, a modification of the favorable "treatment previously accorded by [Customs] to substantially identical transactions." The court held that Customs was bound by this previous favorable treatment. We affirm.

BACKGROUND

I.

Under 19 U.S.C. § 1313, a manufacturer is entitled to recover a portion of previously paid Customs duties on imported merchandise that is subsequently exported or destroyed. In essence, the statute operates to give a party a refund on Customs duties. The refund is called a drawback.[3] Subsection (b) of section 1313 allows for manufacturing substitution drawbacks, through which a manufacturer may receive a drawback when the manufacturer substitutes the same "kind and quality" of goods for those that were actually originally imported. Section 1313(b) provides:

> If imported duty-paid merchandise and any other merchandise (whether imported or domestic) of the same kind and quality are used in the manufacture or production of articles within a period not to exceed three years from the receipt of such imported merchandise by the manufacturer or producer of such articles, there shall be allowed upon the exportation, or destruction under customs supervision, of any such articles, notwithstanding the fact that none of the imported merchandise may actually have been used in the manufacture or production of the exported or destroyed articles, an amount of drawback equal to that which would have been allowable had the merchandise used therein been imported . . . .

---

1 Effective March 1, 2003, the United States Customs Service was renamed the United States Bureau of Customs and Border Protection. Homeland Security Act of 2002, Pub. L. No. 107-296, § 1502, 116 Stat. 2135, 2308-09 (2002).

2 Generally, the provisions of the United States Code (1994) relating to drawback that were in effect in 1995, the relevant period of time, are cited. Section 1313(b), which governs manufacturing substitution drawback, has not been amended since 1995.

3 A "drawback" is currently defined in 19 C.F.R. § 191.2(i) as "the refund or remission, in whole or in part, of a customs duty, fee or internal revenue tax which was imposed on imported merchandise under Federal law because of its importation . . . ." 19 C.F.R. § 191.2(i) (2005). In 1995, a "drawback" was defined similarly as "a refund or remission, in whole or in part, of a customs duty, internal revenue tax, or fee lawfully assessed or collected because of a particular use made of the merchandise on which the duty, tax or fee was assessed." 19 C.F.R. § 191.2(a) (1995). The purpose of allowing drawbacks is two-fold: to increase foreign commerce and to promote domestic manufacturing. *United States v. Int'l Paint Co., 35 C.C.P.A. 87, 90 (1948).*

19 U.S.C. § 1313(b). In order to receive a manufacturing substitution drawback pursuant to section 1313(b), a manufacturer files a drawback claim requesting payment. 19 C.F.R. § 191.2(i) (1995).[4]

For the purpose of simplifying the drawback claiming process for certain common manufacturing operations, Customs issues offers in the form of general manufacturing drawback contracts. Id. §§ 191.2(f), 191.41.[5] A manufacturer who meets the requirements of a general manufacturing drawback contract may accept Customs' offer by submitting a letter notifying Customs of its intent to comply with the general contract. Id. §§ 191.2(f), 191.42(b). Customs then notifies the manufacturer of its receipt of the letter of intent. Id. § 191.43. The contract is effective for fifteen years from the date of Customs' acknowledgement of receipt.[6] Id. The manufacturer may then file individual drawback claims that comply with the general drawback contract. Id. § 191.45. If an individual drawback claim is denied, the manufacturer may file a protest with Customs pursuant to 19 U.S.C. § 1514. An individual's right to a manufacturing substitution drawback under section 1313(b) is limited by 19 U.S.C. § 1313(*l*), which makes "the privileges provided for in this section . . . subject to compliance with such rules and regulations as the Secretary of the Treasury shall prescribe . . . ." 19 U.S.C. § 1313(*l*). The regulations are made binding on officers of Customs by 19 U.S.C. § 1502(b).

In addition to 19 U.S.C. § 1313(b) and the associated regulations, when dealing with drawback claims, the Secretary of the Treasury (the "Secretary") also must comply with the procedural requirements of 19 U.S.C. § 1625(c). Under section 1625(c), the Secretary must follow notice and comment procedures before issuing an interpretive ruling or decision that would change a preexisting "treatment." Section 1625(c) provides in relevant part:

> A proposed interpretive ruling or decision which would—
>
> > (1) modify (other than to correct a clerical error) or revoke a prior interpretive ruling or decision which has been in effect for at least 60 days; or
> >
> > (2) have the effect of modifying the treatment previously accorded by the Customs Service to substantially identical transactions;
>
> shall be published in the Customs Bulletin. The Secretary shall give interested parties an opportunity to submit, during not less than the 30-day period after the date of such

---

4 The regulations governing drawback were amended in 1998. See *63 Fed. Reg. 10970 (Mar. 5, 1998)*. In this opinion, we cite to the regulations as in effect in 1995. Except as otherwise noted, the current regulations, see *19 C.F.R. § 191.1 et seq. (2005)*, do not differ materially from the regulations as in effect in 1995.

5 When it amended the drawback regulations in 1998, Customs changed the name of general drawback contracts to "general drawback rulings," 63 Fed. Reg. at 10973. 19 C.F.R. §§ 191.1(p), 191.7.

6 Under the regulations currently in effect, a general manufacturing drawback contract lasts indefinitely unless no claims are filed for five years or the manufacturer or producer files a request to terminate the contract. 19 C.F.R. §§ 191.7(d), 191.8(h) (2005).

> publication, comments on the correctness of the proposed ruling or decision. After consideration of any comments received, the Secretary shall publish a final ruling or decision in the Customs Bulletin within 30 days after the closing of the comment period. The final ruling or decision shall become effective 60 days after the date of its publication.

19 U.S.C. § 1625(c) (1994).[7]

In 2002, the Secretary promulgated regulations expressly defining "treatment previously accorded by the Customs Service to substantially identical transactions" as set forth in 19 U.S.C. § 1625(c). See 19 C.F.R. § 177.12(c) (2005). Subsection (c)(1)(i) sets forth what must be shown to establish "substantially identical transactions" that give rise to a "treatment." Subsection (c)(1)(ii) establishes guidelines for case-by-case inquiries as to whether particular transactions involve sufficient Customs review to form the basis of a "treatment." The evidentiary burden for establishing a "treatment" is set forth in subsection (c)(1)(iv). This case concerns subsection (c)(1)(iii), which limits the "substantially identical transactions" that may form the basis of a section 1625(c) "treatment" to only the transactions of the person alleging entitlement to section 1625(c)'s notice and comment process. 19 C.F.R. § 177.12(c)(1)(iii) provides in relevant part:

> The issuance of an interpretive ruling that has the effect of modifying or revoking the treatment previously accorded by Customs to substantially identical transactions must be in accordance with the procedures set forth in paragraph (c)(2) of this section. The following rules will apply for purposes of determining under this section whether a treatment was previously accorded by Customs to substantially identical transactions of a person:
>
> ***
>
> (iii) Customs will not find that a treatment was accorded to a person's transactions if:
>
> (A) The person's own transactions were not accorded the treatment in question over the 2-year period immediately preceding the claim of treatment . . . .

19 C.F.R. § 177.12(c)(1)(iii) (emphases added). Thus, under the regulations enacted in 2002, a "treatment" arises only as the result of "substantially identical transactions" involving the person claiming the benefit of section 1625(c). See id. § 177.12(c)(1)(iii)(A). Also in 2002, Customs repealed 19 C.F.R. § 177.9(e). That provision contained language suggesting that transactions could be "substantially identical" so as to form a "treatment" even if they did not involve the person claiming the benefit of section 1625(c).

---

7 The statutory provisions cited are those that were in effect at the time CIP's drawback claims were formally denied in January of 1998. No substantive amendments have been made to 19 U.S.C. § 1625 have been made since that time.

II.

CIP operates steel conversion mills that manufacture flat-rolled steel sheet products. CIP purchases the steel it uses for its products from domestic trading companies, which previously paid Customs duties when importing the steel. These domestic trading companies factor the Customs duties into the price CIP pays them for the steel. In CIP's mills, cold-rolled sheets of steel are trimmed to the desired size, rolled in coils, and sold to customers. Trim or steel scrap is the material trimmed off the sheets and may be re-smelted to make new steel products. CIP ex ports the steel trim or scrap it produces in its manufacturing process and seeks to obtain drawback on this product.

On February 16, 1994, CIP sent a letter of intent to comply with Treasury Decision ("T. D.") 81-74, 15 Cust. B. & Dec. 176 (Mar. 31, 1981).[8] CIP revised its letter of intent on October 25, 1995, to add several additional factories that would be operating under T.D. 81-74. T.D. 81-74 comprises a general drawback contract for manufactured steel articles composed of duty-paid steel or steel of the same kind or quality under *19 U.S.C. § 1313(b)*. Id. at 176-77. T.D. 81-74 creates a specific exception for "waste":

> The drawback claimant understands that no drawback is payable on any waste which results from the manufacturing operation. Unless the claim for drawback is based on the quantity of steel appearing in the exported articles, the drawback claimant agrees to keep records to establish the value (or the lack of value), the quantity, and the disposition of any waste that results from manufacturing the exported articles. If no waste results, the drawback claimant agrees to keep records to establish that fact. T.D. 81-74, 15 Cust. B. & Dec. at 178. Neither CIP's original February 16, 1994 letter nor its revised October 25, 1995 letter of in tent to comply with T.D. 81-74 mentioned that CIP intended to claim a manufacturing substitution drawback for steel trim or scrap. *Cal. Indus. Prods., 350 F. Supp. 2d at 1137-38.*

Pursuant to its letter of intent to comply with T.D. 81-74, CIP filed twenty-six drawback claims between December 2, 1995 and March 7, 2002. Id. at 1138. Two of these claims are at issue in this case.[9] The bill of lading for each of these two claims stated that part of the claim involved "Iron and Steel Scrap." Id. at 1138. On January 2, 1998, Customs denied both claims on the ground that scrap was not eligible for a drawback. Id. In so doing, Customs stated, "CANNOT CLAIM ON SCRAP," and, "DRAWBACK IS NOT ALLOWED ON SCRAP."

---

8 When Customs amended the drawback regulations in 1998, it required that general drawback contracts be published in Appendix A of 19 C.F.R. Part 191, Subpart A. 19 C.F.R. § 191.7(b). T.D. 81-74 is now listed as "General Manufacturing Drawback Ruling Under 19 U.S.C. 1313(b) For Steel (T.D. 81-74)." 19 C.F.R. § 191, Subpart A, App. A, XII (2005).

9 Although only two claims are involved in the present appeal, there are eleven other claims that have been suspended pending the outcome of this litigation. *Cal. Indus. Prods., 350 F. Supp. 2d at 1138 n. 9.* CIP received accelerated payments for all thirteen of these claims. Id. Customs then demanded return of the accelerated payments on steel scrap on the ground that it was not eligible for drawback. Id. at 1138.

Prior to the denial of CIP's claims, between June of 1992 and November of 1997, Customs liquidated 145 entries for drawback on steel scrap. The entries were filed by five companies other than CIP, including Calstrip Steel Corporation ("Calstrip") and Precision Specialty Metals, Inc. ("Precision"). CIP approached the consulting firm that assisted these five companies in filing drawback claims in October of 1995 with a request for aid in obtaining drawback for steel scrap. The firm agreed to assist CIP in this endeavor. However, in 1996, after CIP filed its first claims for drawback, but before it had received any decision, Customs began denying drawback claims for steel scrap made by other companies such as Calstrip and Precision. In response to Calstrip's claims for drawback on steel scrap, Customs issued Headquarters Ruling Letter ("HQ") 227375 on October 10, 1997, denying the claims. HQ 227375, slip op. (Oct. 10, 1997), available at 1997 WL 897192. In HQ 227375, Customs ruled that steel scrap was "waste" and therefore not eligible for drawback. HQ 227375, slip op. at 1. Based on HQ 227375, Precision's claims for drawback on steel scrap also were denied. Precision successfully challenged the denial of its drawback claims for steel scrap in the Court of International Trade. *Precision Specialty Metals, Inc. v. United States, 24 C.I.T. 1016, 116 F. Supp. 2d 1350 (Ct. Int'l Trade 2000)* ("Precision I"); *Precision Specialty Metals, Inc. v. United States, 25 C.I.T. 1375, 182 F. Supp. 2d 1314 (Ct. Int'l Trade 2001)* ("Precision II").[10]

CIP responded to Customs' denial of its claims for drawback on steel scrap by timely filing a request for further review in the form of a protest. In the protest, CIP argued that Customs had impermissibly retroactively changed its practice regarding drawback claims, that certain types of valuable waste are entitled to drawback, and that Customs had erred when it found that steel scrap was waste. On March 3, 1998, Customs issued a protest review decision affirming the January 2, 1998

---

10 Like CIP, Precision filed claims with Customs for drawback on steel scrap. Although Customs initially granted 69 drawback claims to Precision, it began denying Precision's claims in 1996. *Precision I, 116 F. Supp. 2d at 1354-55.* Precision challenged Customs' decision in the Court of International Trade, alleging, among other things, that the denial of its claims without first following notice and comment procedures violated section 1625(c). Responding to cross-motions for summary judgment, the court conducted a lengthy analysis of section 1625(c) and determined that Customs' liquidation of 69 of Precision's claims for drawback on steel scrap constituted a "treatment" under section 1625(c) because they involved more than a single transaction. Id. at 1377. However, the court found that Precision had failed to come forward with evidence demonstrating the existence of other factors necessary to trigger the procedural requirements of section 1625(c), making summary judgment inappropriate. Id. at 1378-79.

As the parties were preparing for trial, the Court of International Trade decided that the issues before it were, in fact, entirely legal. It therefore directed the parties to move again for summary judgment. *Precision II, 182 F. Supp. 2d at 1316.* In Precision II, the Court of International Trade reiterated its interpretation of "treatment" under section 1625(c) from Precision I and found, again, that Customs' actions in granting Precision's claims prior to 1996 comprised a "treatment." Id. at 1328-29. It then granted summary judgment in favor of Precision on the ground that Customs had failed to comply with section 1625(c) when it denied Precision's drawback claims—thereby reversing that treatment—without first engaging in a notice and comment process. Id. at 1329-30.

denial of CIP's drawback claims. Customs based its denial of CIP's protest on HQ 227375.

III.

CIP timely filed suit in the Court of International Trade challenging Customs' denial of its protest. See 28 U.S.C. § 2636(c) (2000). The Court of International Trade exercised jurisdiction over CIP's suit pursuant to 19 U.S.C. § 1581(a).

In due course, CIP and the United States filed cross-motions for summary judgment. In its motion, CIP urged the Court of International Trade to adhere to the interpretation of the term "treatment" in 19 U.S.C. § 1625(c) that it had adopted in *Precision I, 116 F. Supp. 2d at 1374,* and *Precision II, 182 F. Supp. 2d at 1323-28.* CIP also argued that the "substantially identical transactions" that form the basis of a "treatment" in section 1625(c) may be transactions of parties other than the person claiming that section 1625(c)'s notice and comment process applies. As a result, CIP urged, under section 1625(c), Customs was required to engage in a notice and comment process before changing the favorable treatment previously accorded to claims for drawback on steel scrap. Because Customs did not do so, CIP argued, it was bound by that favorable treatment in CIP's case. Plaintiff's Motion for Summary Judgment at 9-10. Thus, CIP contended that the fact that CIP itself had not previously been afforded drawbacks on steel scrap did not preclude the Court of International Trade from finding that a "treatment" was established through Customs' actions toward the "substantially identical" claims of other steel scrap exporters. Id.

In its cross-motion for summary judgment, the government did not dispute the Court of International Trade's finding in Precision I and Precision II that Customs' grants of drawback with respect to Precision formed the basis of a "treatment" with respect to Precision. Defendant's Motion for Summary Judgment at 14. However, the government argued that because 19 U.S.C. § 1625(c) is silent as to whether the "treatment" afforded a company like Precis ion can be applied to a second company like CIP, the regulation set forth at 19 C.F.R. § 177.12(c)(1)(iii)(A) should be afforded deference under *Chevron U.S.A. Inc. v. NRDC, 467 U.S. 837, 104 S. Ct. 2778, 81 L. Ed. 2d 694 (1984)*. Defendant's Motion for Summary Judgment at 8-9. The government argued that, under 19 C.F.R. § 177.12(c)(1)(iii)(A), drawback claims file d by other companies, such as Calstrip and Precision, did not constitute "substantially identical transactions" that CIP, another company, could point to as giving rise to a "treatment" under section 1625(c). Defendant's Motion for Summary Judgment at 10.

The Court of International Trade granted CIP's motion for summary judgment and denied the government's cross-motion. The court rejected the government's suggestion that it give Chevron deference to the Customs regulation at 19 C.F.R. § 177.12(c)(1)(iii)(A). Doing so, the court concluded, would amount to impermissible retroactive application of the regulation. *Cal. Indus. Prods., 350 F. Supp. 2d at 1141-42*. Likewise, the court declined to give deference under *Skidmore v. Swift & Co., 323 U.S. 134, 65 S. Ct. 161, 89 L. Ed. 124 (1944)*, to Customs' HQ 227375 because it concluded it did not represent a consistent agency position. *Cal. Indus. Prods., 350 F. Supp. 2d at 1140-41*. Instead, the court accepted CIP's invitation to adopt the Precision I and Precision II courts' interpretation of "treatment" in section 1625(c)(2). Id. at 1142-45. The court was persuaded that a "treatment "can be established through Customs' transactions with other companies, id. at 1145, and reasoned that CIP had demonstrated that Customs had established a "treatment" under section 1625(c) with respect to drawbacks for steel scrap based on Customs' grants of drawback to other companies. Consequently, the court ruled, Customs violated the procedural requirements of section 1625(c) when, before denying CIP's drawback claims, it changed that "treatment" without following notice and comment procedures. Id. at 1147. The court therefore held that Customs was "bound by and subject to its earlier treatment of steel scrap as eligible for drawback."[11] Id. at 1148.

The government has timely appealed the Court of International Trade's decision. We have jurisdiction over the appeal pursuant to 28 U.S.C. § 1295(a)(5).

DISCUSSION

I.

The Court of International Trade properly grants summary judgment "when there is no genuine issue as to any material fact and . . . the moving party is entitled to a judgment as a matter of law." *Sea-Land Serv. Inc. v. United States, 239 F.3d 1366, 1371 (Fed. Cir. 2001)* (quoting Ct. Int'l Trade R. 56(d)). We review a grant of summary judgment by the Court of International Trade "for correctness as a matter of law, deciding de novo the proper interpretation of the governing statute and regulations as well as whether genuine issues of material fact exist." *Guess?, Inc. v. United States, 944 F.2d 855, 857 (Fed. Cir. 1991)*.

II.

On appeal, the government argues first that the alleged violation of section 1625(c) was not raised before the agency and therefore was not properly heard for the first time by the Court of International Trade. According to the government, the court "should have remanded the matter as it relates to section 1625(c)(2)) (to allow Customs to apply its regulations and carry out its administrative functions as charged by Congress." Consequently, the government argues, under the doctrine of "primary jurisdiction" we may not consider the issue.

On the merits of the section 1625(c) issue, the government raises several arguments in support of reversing the Court of International Trade's ruling that Cus-

11 The court stated that its ruling was limited to the facts of "this case" and should not be deemed precedential for claims of drawback on steel scrap filed subsequent to the publication of its opinion. Id.

toms violated 19 U.S.C. § 1625(c) when it denied CIP's claims. As seen above, section 1625(c) requires that Customs follow notice and comment procedures before issuing an "interpretive ruling or decision which would . . . have the effect of modifying the treatment previously accorded by the Customs Service to substantially identical transactions." The government contends that two provisions of section 1625(c) are not implicated by its actions regarding CIP and that, therefore, section 1625(c) is inapplicable. First, the government argues that none of Customs' actions with respect to CIP comprised an "interpretive ruling or decision" under section 1625(c). Second, the government argues that section 1625(c) does not apply in this case because the previously liquidated claims upon which CIP asserts that it relied were not "substantially identical transactions." Relying solely on the terms of Precision's contract, the government claims that there are substantial differences between the drawback contracts of the parties that previously were allowed drawback and CIP's drawback contract. The government also claims that the Court of International Trade erred when it did not afford Chevron deference to its regulation at 19 C.F.R. § 177.12(c)(1)(iii)(A). As noted, that regulation limits the reach of the notice and comment requirement of section 1625(c) to the situation in which Customs issues an interpretive ruling with respect to a person and that ruling has the effect of modifying or revoking the treatment previously accorded to "substantially identical transactions" of that person. Thus, the government argues that the Court of International Trade erred in ruling that the 145 previously liquidated claims for drawback on steel scrap, which were not claims of CIP, were "substantially identical transactions" to CIP's drawback claims.

Additionally, the government contends that the Court of International Trade erred in its interpretation of 19 U.S.C. § 1625(c) because its construction conflicts with the overall statutory scheme for drawback, particularly 19 U.S.C. § 1313(l) and 19 U.S.C. § 1502(b). Finally, the government urges that steel scrap is waste for which CIP was not entitled to a drawback and that its ruling letter to that effect, HQ 227375, should be afforded deference under Skidmore.

Responding to the government's arguments, CIP argues first that the government's violation of section 1625(c) was properly raised before the Court of International Trade. According to CIP, an alleged violation of section 1625(c) is not the type of claim that first must be raised before Customs.

Turning to the merits of the section 1625(c) issue, CIP states that, in the Court of International Trade, it was challenging a protest review decision, which CIP asserts was a "decision" within the meaning of section 1625(c). Alternatively, CIP states that Customs' decision to deny its drawback claims was based on HQ 227375, which CIP asserts also is a "ruling" within the meaning of section 1625(c) .With regard to the government's argument that Customs' prior liquidations of other companies 'claims for drawback on steel scrap did not constitute "substantially identical transactions" under section 1625(c) because there are substantial differences between the drawback contracts of those parties and CIP's drawback contract, CIP argues that there are only insubstantial differences in the other companies' letters of intent to comply with T.D. 81-74 and CIP's letter of intent. Next, CIP addresses the government's argument that Customs' previous drawback allowances were not "substantially identical transactions" so as to form the basis of a "treatment" with respect to CIP. CIP urges that we should not accord Chevron deference to the definition of what constitutes "substantially identical transactions" giving rise to a "treatment" that is contained in the regulation at 19 C.F.R. § 177.12(c)(1)(iii)(A). CIP asks us to hold that the numerous grants of drawbacks for scrap issued to other companies, like Precision, were "substantially identical transactions" vis-a-vis CIP's drawback claims so that they formed a "treatment" for purposes of 19 U.S.C. § 1625(c). CIP argues that because section 1625(c) applies to Customs' actions towards it, the Court of International Trade correctly granted summary judgment that Custom s violated section 1625(c) by denying CIP's claims for drawback without first following notice and comment procedures.

With regard to the government's assertion that the Court of International Trade's interpretation of section 1625(c) conflicts with 19 U.S.C. § 1313(l) and 19 U.S.C. § 1502(b), CIP argues that the court's ruling does not impermissibly restrict the Secretary's ability to act under either statute. Finally, CIP contends that the Court of International Trade properly gave no deference to HQ 227375, in which Customs ruled that steel scrap is not eligible for drawback because it is waste.

III.

We see no error in the Court of International Trade's holding that, pursuant to 19 U.S.C. § 1625(c), Customs was required to engage in a notice and comment process before issuing HQ 227375. We therefore affirm the court's decision granting CIP's motion for summary judgment and denying the government's cross-motion.

A.

As a preliminary matter, we reject the government's argument that the doctrine of "primary jurisdiction" is a bar to our review of whether the government violated 19 U.S.C. § 1625(c). The doctrine of "primary jurisdiction" requires that "in cases raising issues of fact not within the conventional experience of judges or cases requiring the exercise of administrative discretion, agencies created by Congress for regulating the subject matter should not be passed over." *Nippon Steel Corp. v. United States, 219 F.3d 1348, 1353 (Fed. Cir. 2000)* (quoting *Far E. Conference v. United States, 342 U.S. 570, 574, 72 S. Ct. 492, 96 L. Ed. 576 (1952))*. The government correctly notes that Customs' violation of 19 U.S.C. § 1625(c) was not explicitly raised in CIP's protest or in its summons in the Court of International Trade. It then argues that, under the doctrine of "primary jurisdiction," we should remand to Customs for it to decide in the first instance the section 1625(c) issue. We do not agree. We are not asked in this case to make any factual determinations that should be reserved for Customs under the doctrine of "primary jurisdiction." Compare *Union Pac. R.R. Co. v. United States, 125 Ct. Cl. 390, 111 F. Supp. 266,*

268 (Ct. Cl. 1953) (finding that a legal question as to which of two rates apply was not reserved exclusively for the agency), with *Nippon Steel, 219 F.3d at 1354-55* (noting that the inquiry as to whether an antidumping order was circumvented must first be heard by the agency because of "expertise and experience" required to make complex factual determinations). Instead, the alleged violation of section 1625(c) presents purely legal questions regarding the construction of "interpretive ruling or decision" and "substantially identical transactions." Therefore, the doctrine of "primary jurisdiction" does not require us to remand to Customs the issue of whether Customs violated section 1625(c) when it denied CIP's drawback claims.

B.

Turning to the merits, section 1625(c)(2) mandates that Customs follow notice and comment procedures before issuing an "interpretive ruling or decision which would . . .have the effect of modifying the treatment previously accorded by the Customs Service to substantially identical transactions." 19 U.S.C. § 1625(c)(2). As noted, two aspects of section 1625(c)'s mandate are disputed by the parties: (1) whether Customs issued an "interpretive ruling or decision" with respect to CIP, and (2) whether prior transactions of companies other than CIP were "substantially identical" to CIP's transactions with Customs so that they constituted a "treatment."

1.

Section 1625(c) only applies when Customs issues an "interpretive ruling or decision." See *Sea-Land, 239 F.3d at 1372*. We think Customs did issue an "interpretive ruling or decision" to CIP in this case. Section 1625(c) is a subsection of 19 U.S.C. § 1625, which is titled "Interpretive rulings and decisions; public information." Subsection (a) of section 1625, titled "Publication," provides as follows:

> Within 90 days after the date of issuance of any interpretive ruling (including any ruling letter, or internal advice memorandum) or protest review decision under this Act with respect to any customs transaction, the Secretary shall have such ruling or decision published in the Customs Bulletin or shall otherwise make such ruling or decision available for public inspection.19 U.S.C. § 1625(a) (emphases added). Thus, "interpretive ruling" is expressly defined as "including any ruling letter, or internal advice memorandum." Id. At the same time, two lines later, the text refers back to the previously noted "interpretive ruling . . . or protest review decision" as "such ruling or decision." "Interpretative ruling . . . or protest review decision" and the later shorthand reference to that phrase ("such ruling or decision") should be construed consistently in section 1625. See *Timex V.I., Inc .v. United States, 157 F.3d 879, 884 (Fed. Cir. 1998)* ("It is well-settled that words appearing in a statute should be read consistently: a particular word appearing multiple times in a statutory provision should be given the same reading, unless there is a clear Congressional intent to the contrary."). In short, "decision" in the phrase "ruling or decision" in 19 U.S.C. § 1625(c), includes a "protest review decision." CIP is appealing from

Customs' March 3, 1998 protest review decision. Furthermore, the March 3 protest review decision was based on a Customs' ruling letter, HQ 227375, which is a ruling letter and, therefore, also an "interpretive ruling" under section 1625(a). We hold that CIP is appealing from both a "decision" and a "ruling" within the meaning of 19 U.S.C. § 1625(c).

2.

Addressing the second issue relating to section 1625(c), we do not agree with the government that the statute does not apply because the prior liquidations of other companies' drawback claims were not "substantially identical" to CIP's claims. The government argues first that Precision's previously granted claims for drawback on steel scrap were not "substantially identical" because Precision's letter of intent to comply with T.D. 81-74 listed "trim," which is a synonym for scrap. See *Precision II, 182 F. Supp. 2d at 1329* (mentioning the contents of Precision's letter). In contrast, CIP's letter of intent did not list "trim" or "scrap" as a permissible item for which a drawback would be issued. However, the requirement that transactions be "substantially identical" does not require complete identity. While differences in the letters of intent to comply with a general drawback contract underlying two different transactions could conceivably render two transactions substantially different in another case, the claims of Precision and CIP were, in fact, "substantially identical" within the meaning of 19 U.S.C. § 1625(c). Both Precision's and CIP's drawback claim s were based on T.D. 81-74, and Precision's and CIP's letters of intent both purported to comply with the terms of T.D. 81-74. See *Precision II, 182 F. Supp. 2d at 1329*. Furthermore, both companies were denied drawbacks because their bills of lading mentioned scrap, which Customs interpreted to be "waste" and therefore not eligible for drawback. See id. at 1318. There is no evidence that the mention of "trim" in Precision's original letter of intent played any role in Customs' ruling in that case or that the lack of a mention of "trim" had any effect on its ruling on CIP's claim. We thus conclude that there was only an insubstantial difference between the two companies' claims.[12]

3.

The main issue in this case with respect to section 1625(c) is whether "substantially identical transactions" should be defined narrowly in accord with Customs' recently promulgated regulation at 19 C.F.R. § 177.12(c)(1)(iii)(A). As already seen, under section 177.12 (c)(1)(iii)(A), as far as any person is concerned, "sub-

---

12 Additionally, Precision's claims account for just 69 of the 145 successful pre-1996 claims for drawback on steel scrap on which CIP relies. In HQ 227375, Customs describes Calstrip's letter of intent as stating "its intention to adhere to and comply with the conditions of [T.D.] 81-74 [dated March 31, 1981,] drawback contract under 19 USC 1313(b), articles manufactured using steel." Unlike Precision's letter, no mention appears to have been made of scrap or trim in Calstrip's letter of intent. Thus, at least some of the letters of intent appear to have had the same content as CIP's letter of intent and were therefore "substantially identical" even under the government's interpretation.

stantially identical transactions" giving rise to a "treatment" are only those transactions between Customs and that person. See 19 C.F.R. § 177.12(c)(1)(iii)(A) ("Customs will not fin d that a treatment was accorded to a person's transactions if the per son's own transactions were not accorded the treatment in question."). Accordingly, the government contends that Customs' granting of drawbacks to other companies such as Precision could not form the basis of a "treatment" under 19 U.S.C. § 1625(c) with regard to CIP.[13]

Under Chevron, we must follow a two step inquiry to determine if deference should be given to the government's narrow definition of "substantially identical transactions" that give rise to a "treatment" in 19 C.F.R. § 177.12(c)(1)(iii)(A). First, "we must . . . carefully investigate the matter to determine whether Congress's purpose and intent on the question at issue is judicially ascertainable." *Timex V.I., 157 F.3d at 881* (citing Chevron, 467 U.S. at 842-43 & n.9). Second, if Congress has not spoken to the meaning of "substantially identical transactions," then we must give effect to Customs' regulation so long as it represents a reasonable interpretation of the statute. See Chevron, 467 U.S. at 844, 846.

When determining whether Congress has expressly spoken as to the meaning of a statutory term such as "substantially identical transactions," we must utilize the "traditional tools of statutory construction." *Timex V.I., 157 F.3d at 882*. We begin our inquiry with the plain meaning of the text of the statute itself. *Defenders of Wildlife v. Hogarth, 330 F.3d 1358, 1366 (Fed. Cir. 2003)* ("Deciphering the intent of Congress begins with the text of the statute."); *Timex V.I., 157 F.3d at 882* ("The first and foremost 'tool' to be used is the statute's text, giving it its plain meaning." (citing *VE Holding Corp. v. Johnson Gas Appliance Co., 917 F.2d 1574, 1579 (Fed. Cir. 1990))*). Section 1625(c) requires that Customs follow notice and comment procedures before issuing "[a] proposed interpretive ruling or decision" that would "have the effect of modifying the treatment previously accorded by the Customs Service to substantially identical transactions." 19 U.S.C. § 1625(c) (emphasis added). The statute provides no definition of the term "sub-

---

13 In its cross-motion for summary judgment in this case, the government agreed with the holdings in Precision I and Precision II that the 69 drawback claims of Precision, which Customs paid, comprised a "treatment" with regard to Precision. In its motion, the government wrote:

> We do not dispute the Precision court's conclusion that, in spite of Customs publications, the erroneous liquidations granting drawback to Precision's claims for exported steel scrap constituted a "treatment" under 19 U.S.C. § 1625 for Precision itself .Customs also erroneously granted drawback to other claimants (i.e., Calstrip, Combined Metals of Chicago, Thypin, and Ulbrich) for their individual claims of exported steel scrap. These claimants did not get the benefit of Precision's treatment, but were erroneously accorded their own—independent—treatment by Customs.
>
> However, these erroneous liquidations cannot be expanded to include importers who were not similarly affected and for whom such expectations could not have been created. Congress could not have intended that, having made an error, Customs must then uniformly apply that error to all importers.

Defendant's Motion for Summary Judgment at 14.

stantially identical transactions." However, the intent of Congress may be clear even in the absence of an express definition of the statutory term. See, e.g., *Chevron, 467 U.S. at 842.*

When a particular term is not expressly defined in a statute, the meaning of that term may be discerned by "looking to the provisions of the whole law, and to its object and policy." *Warner-Lambert Co. v. Apotex Corp., 316 F.3d 1348, 1355 (Fed. Cir. 2003)* (quoting *U.S. Nat'l Bank of Or. v. In dep. United States Nat'l Bank v. Independent Ins. Agents of Am., 508 U.S. 439, 455, 113 S. Ct. 2173, 124 L. Ed. 2d 402 (1993)).* Although sect ion 1625 does not define "substantially identical transactions," the language of the statute indicates that Congress clearly intended transactions between Customs and multiple parties to be "substantially identical transactions." Section 1625(c) states that when it changes a prior "treatment," Customs "shall give interested parties an opportunity to submit, during not less than the 30-day period after the date of such publication, comments on the correctness of the proposed ruling or decision." 19 U.S.C. § 1625(c) (emphasis added). We think that if the words "substantially identical transactions" in section 1625(c) were only meant to refer, in each case, to prior treatment accorded the person claiming entitlement to the notice and comment process of the statute, as provided in 19 C.F.R. § 177.12(c)(1)(iii)(A), it is unlikely that Congress would have required that "interested parties" be given notice of the change of a prior "treatment." In our view, use of the words "interested parties" indicates that Congress intended, contrary to 19 C.F.R. § 177.12(c)(1)(iii)(A), that "substantially identical transactions" forming the basis of a "treatment" include transactions other than transactions of just the person before Customs claiming the right to a notice and comment process.

Customs regulations in effect at the time of the enactment of section 1625(c) also support the view that Congress intended "substantially identical transactions" forming a single "treatment" to include the transactions of multiple parties. These regulations are appropriately considered in the construction of 19 U.S.C. § 1625(c) because Congress is presumed to be aware of pertinent existing law. *Bristol-Myers Squibb Co. v. Royce Lab., 69 F.3d 1130, 1136-37 (Fed. Cir. 1995)* ("We presume 'that Congress is knowledgeable about existing law pertinent to legislation it'" enacts. (quoting *VE Holding, 917 F.2d at 1581*)); *Goodyear Atomic Corp. v. Miller, 486 U.S. 174, 184-85, 108 S. Ct. 1704, 100 L. Ed. 2d 158 (1988)* ("We generally presume that Congress is knowledgeable about existing law pertinent to the legislation it enacts. "); *Minneapolis & St. Louis Ry. Co. v. United States, 361 U.S. 173, 187, 80 S. Ct. 229, 4 L. Ed. 2d 223 (1959)* (presuming that Congress was aware of applicable railroad regulations when enacting pertinent legislation).

In Precision I and Precision II, the Court of International Trade determined that Congress modeled 19 U.S.C. § 1625(c) after former 19 C.F.R. § 177.10. *Precision I, 116 F. Supp. 2d at 1375*; *Precision II, 182 F. Supp. 2d at 1323-28*. The court noted, in particular, the similarities between former 19 C.F.R. § 177.10(c) and 19 U.S.C. *§ 1625(c). Precision I, 116 F. Supp. 2d at 1375*. Former *section 177.10(c)(2)* provided:

> Before the publication of a ruling which has the effect of changing a position of the Customs Service and which results in a restriction or prohibition, notice that the position (or prior ruling on which the position is based) is under review will be published in the FEDERAL REGISTER and interested parties given an opportunity to make written submissions with respect to the correctness of the contemplated change. This procedure will also be followed when the change of position will result in a holding that an activity is not restricted or prohibited and the Headquarters Office determines that the matter is of sufficient importance to involve the interests of the general public.19 C.F.R. § 177.10(c)(2)((1993) (amended 2002). Similar to 19 U.S.C. § 1625(c), which requires notice and comment proceedings before Customs can change a "treatment," former 19 C.F.R. § 177.10(c)(2) required Customs to follow notice and comment procedures before changing its "position." *Precision I, 116 F. Supp. 2d at 1375.*

Former 19 C.F.R. § 177.9(e)(1), in turn, clarifies the scope of "substantially identical transactions" that form the basis of a "treatment" for purposes of section 1625(c).[14] Former section 177.9(e)(1) provided:

> The Customs Service will from time to time issue a ruling letter covering a transaction or issue not previously the subject of a ruling letter and which has the effect of modifying the treatment previously accorded by the Customs Service to substantially identical transactions of either the recipient of the ruling letter or other parties. . . .19 C.F.R. § 177.9(e)(1) (1993) (repealed 2002). Subsection (e)(1) refers to the "treatment previously accorded by the Customs Service to substantially identical transactions of either the recipient of the ruling letter or other parties." Thus, when enacting § 1625(c), Congress relied on a definition of "treatment" that encompassed actions towards "other parties." Further, we think that if Congress had intended the restrictive approach to "substantially identical transactions" embodied in 19 C.F.R. § 177.12(c)(1)(iii)(A), it would have made that intention clear with express language in the statute.

The government argues that in 19 C.F.R. § 177.9(e)(1), "the words 'other parties' clearly relate only to parties who had transactions that received the treatment in question and not to parties who did not have transactions that received treatment." We do not see such "clear" indication in the former regulation. The government also attempts to discount the language of section 177.9(e) by arguing that "had Congress intended to include the language 'or other parties' from the text of section 177.9(e) in the text of section 1625(c)(2), in order to broaden the scope of the statute to include parties who had not received a "treatment, then it could have done so; it did not." However, the regulations in effect in 1993 refer to "substantially identical transactions" of "other parties." Thus, when Congress wrote section 1625(c), it knew that under Customs regulations, "treatment" included "substantially identical transactions" of "other parties," making it unnecessary for it to

---

14 The parties are in accord that 19 C.F.R. § 177.9(e) was the basis for 19 U.S.C. § 1625(c).

specify that it was referring to "substantially identical transactions" of a single party or multiple parties.

This construction of "substantially identical transactions" is further supported by the legislative history of 19 U.S.C. § 1625(c), which demonstrates Congress' intent to increase the transparency of Customs' actions.[15] If "substantially identical transactions" were limited to only the transactions of one particular person, as the government argues, a "treatment" with respect to that person would have no effect on other parties. In other words, under Customs' interpretation, a particular company would have no interest in other parties' transactions, rendering the increase in transparency of Customs' interactions with other companies served by section 1625(c) meaningless.

Our construction of "substantially identical transactions" giving rise to a section 1625 "treatment" does not conflict with either 19 U.S.C. § 1313(l) or 19 U.S.C. § 1502(b). Both 19 U.S.C. § 1313(l) and 19 U.S.C. § 1502(b) give the Secretary of the Treasury the authority to promulgate regulations relating to drawback. Section 1313(l) makes "the privileges provided for in this section . . . subject to compliance with such rules and regulations as the Secretary of the Treasury shall prescribe . . . ." The Secretary's regulations are made binding on Customs officers through 19 U.S.C. § 1502(b), which mandates:

> It shall be the duty of all officers of the customs to execute and carry into effect all instructions of the Secretary of the Treasury relative to the execution of the revenue laws; and in case any difficulty arises as to the true construction or meaning of any part of the revenue laws, the decision of the Secretary shall be binding upon all offi-

---

15 The only legislative history pertinent to 19 U.S.C. § 1625 reveals Congress' intent to increase the transparency of Customs' actions. It provides:

> Section 623 of H.R. 3450 amends 19 U.S.C. 1625 by requiring that interpretative rulings, ruling letters or internal advice memorandum [sic] be published within 90 days in the Customs Bulletin or otherwise be made available for public inspection. Section 623 further provides that adverse interpretative rulings may be appealed within Customs, and require that a ruling modifying or revoking an existing ruling be first published in the Customs Bulletin for notice and comment. The Secretary of the Treasury will give interested parties an opportunity to submit comments and will strictly enforce the 30-day comment period in order to avoid unduly delaying the process, absent extraordinary circumstances. Also, section 623 states that Customs make available all information necessary for importers to comply with applicable laws and regulations.
>
> Section 623 requires that a decision that limits the application of a court decision shall also be published for notice and comment in the Customs Bulletin.
>
> Reasons for change
>
> Section 623 will provide assurances of transparency concerning Customs rulings and policy directives through publication in the Customs Bulletin or other easily accessible source.
>
> It is the Committee's intent that the Customs Service shall be deemed to have satisfied any publication requirements mandated by this section if it disseminates such information by the U.S. Customs Service electronic bulletin board and such information remains publicly available in an accessible, retrievable format. H.R. Rep. No. 36 103-1(I), at 24 123-(1993), reprinted in 1993 U.S.C.C.A.N. 2552.

cers of the customs. 19 U.S.C. § 1502(b). The government argues that the interpretation of "substantially identical transactions" in section 1625(c) adopted by the Court of International Trade conflicts with the Secretary's power to promulgate binding regulations. Under such an interpretation, the government states, the Secretary will be forced to follow "treatments" established by what it terms "aberrant decisions" of Customs officers. We do not agree. Section 1625(c), like 19 U.S.C. § 1313(l) and 19 U.S.C. § 1502(b), is a binding Congressional mandate that limits the Secretary's authority to make decisions when Customs officers have decided "substantially identical transactions" in a consistent manner so that a "treatment" arises. Contrary to the government's argument, the interpretation of "substantially identical transactions" that we think is correct does not limit the Secretary's authority to change a prior "treatment." It simply requires that the Secretary utilize notice and comment procedures under 19 U.S.C. § 1625(c) before doing so.

Based on the foregoing, we conclude that Congress clearly intended that "substantially identical transactions" in 19 U.S.C. § 1625 (c) include transactions of parties other than the person claiming entitlement to the statute's notice and comment process. Under Chevron, this finding ends the matter because we must give effect to this clear intent of Congress. *Chevron, 467 U.S. at 843*; *Whitman v. Am. Trucking Ass'ns, 531 U.S. 457, 471, 121 S. Ct. 903, 149 L. Ed. 2d 1 (2001)*. Because the regulation set forth at 19 C.F.R. § 177.12(c)(1)(iii)(A) is due no Chevron deference due to Congress' unambiguously expressed intent, it is unnecessary for us to reach the issue of whether the regulation is impermissibly retroactive as found by the Court of International Trade.[16] See *Cal. Indus. Prods., 350 F. Supp. 2d at 1141, 42*-(finding that no Chevron deference was due because 19 C.F.R. § 177.12(c)(1)(iii)(A) was impermissibly retroactive). In sum, we agree with the Court of International Trade that because Customs failed to comply with section 1625(c) before it denied CIP's drawback claims, it is, in CIP's case, bound by and subject to its earlier treatment of steel scrap as eligible for drawback.

IV.

We turn now to the government's final argument. As noted, the government contends that steel scrap is waste and that HQ 227375, in which Customs held that steel scrap is waste, should be given Skidmore deference. Under Skidmore, administrative rulings or decisions that are not entitled to Chevron deference may still be "eligible to claim respect according to [their] persuasiveness." *United States v. Mead Corp., 533 U.S. 218, 221, 121 S. Ct. 2164, 150 L. Ed. 2d 292 (2001)*. We need not address the government's Skidmore argument, however. The reason is that any argument in support of Customs' rejection of CIP's drawback claims is foreclosed by our holding in Part III. Because, contrary to 19 U.S.C. § 1625(c), Customs failed to engage in a notice and comment process before rejecting CIP's drawback claims, it is bound by and subject to, at least in this case, its earlier treat-

16 This court has reached a different conclusion with regard to a different portion of the regulation as applied to a different issue under 19 U.S.C. § 1625(c). See Motorola, Inc. v. United States, Nos. 05-1025, 1041, decided today.

ment of steel scrap as eligible for drawback. No argument seeking to undo that state of affairs—and that includes the government's Skidmore argument—can be heard.

CONCLUSION

For the foregoing reasons, the decision of the Court of International Trade granting summary judgment in favor of CIP is

AFFIRMED.

UNITED STATES OF AMERICA
v.
4,432 MASTERCASES OF CIGARETTES

448 F.3d 1168 (9th Cir. 2006)
Decided June 2, 2006

Before: Procter Hug, Jr. and Kim McLane Wardlaw, Circuit Judges, and James K. Singleton,* District Judge. Opinion by Judge Wardlaw.

* The Honorable James K. Singleton, Senior United States District Judge for the District of Alaska, sitting by designation.

OPINION

WARDLAW, Circuit Judge:

This appeal and cross-appeal arise from the search and seizure by the United States Customs Service of over 44 million cigarettes, contained in 4,432 mastercases, for nonpayment of California cigarette taxes. The appeals require us to determine the extent of immunity from state and federal regulatory and taxing power that businesses can expect when they operate in foreign trade zones. We hold that an importer of goods destined for domestic consumption is not exempt from state excise taxes and administrative searches by federal Customs officials simply because it stores its merchandise in a foreign trade zone.

I. FACTS AND PROCEDURAL HISTORY

Between 1998 and 2000, Intrigue Trading, Inc. ("Intrigue"), a California corporation, was licensed by the Bureau of Alcohol, Tobacco, and Firearms to import gray market cigarettes into the United States for domestic sale. The term "gray market cigarettes" refers to both American-made exported cigarettes that are re-imported into the United States, as well as American brands of cigarettes manufactured abroad for sale in foreign markets but then imported into the United States.[1] Until

1 Collier, Shannon, Rill & Scott, PLLC, Memorandum to NACS, *Questions and Answers Relating to Gray Market Cigarettes* (Sept. 10, 1999), *available at* http://www.nacsonline.com/NACS/Resource/Government/gray_market_cigs_091099.htm.

the year 2000, importing gray market cigarettes was legal, as was their sale in California. *See* Tariff Suspension and Trade Act of 2000, Pub. L. No. 106-476, tit. IV, § 4002 (effective as amended Nov. 9, 2000, at 26 U.S.C. § 5754) (banning importation of previously exported tobacco products); Act of May 5, 2000, S.B. 1038, § 1, Cal. Legis. Serv. 18 (codified as amended at Cal. Rev. & Tax. Code § 30163) (making illegal in California the importation of cigarettes in violation of 26 U.S.C. § 5754, and the importation by third parties of American-branded cigarettes manufactured abroad). Throughout most of the period of Intrigue's operations, however, California law required cigarette distributors either to obtain a state distributor's license or to pay use taxes on cigarettes placed into storage.

Intrigue is ninety percent owned by Andy Lee, who is also the majority shareholder of two other corporations that dealt in gray market cigarettes, National Trade Industry, Inc. ("NTI") and Ampac, Inc. ("Ampac"). The companies were similarly structured and shared storage facilities, but each company served a particular purpose. For instance, only NTI was licensed to sell cigarettes in California. The companies are separately incorporated.

Between 1998 and April 2001, Intrigue regularly stored gray market cigarettes, including the 4,432 mastercases at issue here, in a storage space rented under Ampac's name at the Port Services Foreign Trade Zone in Carson, California. Foreign trade zones ("FTZs") are discrete areas located adjacent to ports of entry and authorized by Congress to receive preferential treatment under United States customs laws. *BMW Mfg. Corp. v. United States, 241 F.3d 1357, 1359 n.1 (Fed. Cir. 2001).* Merchandise from foreign countries stored within an FTZ is not subject to United States customs duties so long as it remains in the FTZ. 19 U.S.C. § 81c. Congress thus allows international shippers to use American ports as a duty-free way station in international commerce. Companies operating within FTZs are also permitted to manipulate or alter these foreign goods (by repackaging, breaking up, assembling, sorting, mixing with other foreign or domestic parts, etc.) before reshipment abroad, without incurring Customs duties unless they are entered into the United States for sale. *Id.* In addition, domestic merchants may use FTZs as a holding area for eventual exports, or to store "domestic status" merchandise, imported goods on which Customs duties have already been paid. *See* 19 C.F.R. §§ 146.43; 146.44. Intrigue's mastercases of cigarettes were "domestic status" goods.[2]

Intrigue purchased the 4,432 mastercases of Marlboro brand cigarettes between August 2000 and January 2001 from three different companies that had imported them through Miami, Florida. Importation documents indicated that the cigarettes were manufactured in Switzerland. They had passed through Customs and all du-

---

2 More information on the establishment and regulation of FTZs can be found at United States Customs & Border Protection, Foreign Trade Zones Manual, http://www.cbp.gov/xp/cgov/toolbox/publications/manuals_handbooks/, and United States Customs & Border Protection, About Foreign-Trade Zones & Contact Info, http://www.cbp.gov/xp/cgov/import/cargo_control/ftz/about_ftz.xml.

ties were paid. From Miami, Intrigue shipped the cigarettes to the Carson Port Services FTZ in California, where they were placed in storage for a planned eventual sale to LPC, Inc., a Missouri-based company doing business under the name DirtCheapCigarettes.com. This transaction never occurred because the United States Customs Service seized the cigarettes.

Customs Service agents began searching FTZs in the Los Angeles and Long Beach area in early April 2001 as part of an investigation into counterfeit and contraband cigarettes they suspected were being stored there. Customs Inspector Rudolfo Villacana visited the Carson FTZ on April 3 or 4, 2001, but was informed by Zone Operator John Yeskel that there were no cigarettes on-site. A day or two later, additional Customs Service agents visited the Carson FTZ and a different zone employee, in response to the agents' questioning, led them to Intrigue's space. There, they found a fenced-in, locked storage area covered with black tarp that obscured the contents of the pallets. Zone employees did not have a key to the storage space, nor could they locate documents detailing Intrigue's admissions and removals of cigarettes from the FTZ. When the Customs inspectors threatened to cut the lock, an Intrigue employee, Nick Choi, was summoned. He had a key to the space and opened it for the inspectors to enter. During this initial search, the inspectors found mastercases of cigarettes wrapped in opaque black plastic. This combination of circumstances made one senior Customs inspector "very suspicious" of the nature of the cigarettes.

Customs Service officials returned to the FTZ again on April 5 and seized twelve sample cartons of cigarettes for testing. The next day, Apri 16, four officials at a Customs warehouse performed a series of field tests on the cigarettes. Those tests indicated that the cigarettes were "likely counterfeit," "possibly counterfeit," or at least "appeared to be counterfeit." Based on the field test results and the suspicious circumstances of the cigarettes' storage, the Customs Service decided to seize all the cigarettes in Intrigue's storage area and move them to a secure Customs warehouse.

The following Monday, April 9, 2001, Customs Specialist Trevor Rudalevige performed another test on packs of cigarettes from the sample cartons. The results of this second test (the "Rudalevige test") were inconclusive. Officer Rudalevige recommended forwarding some of the samples to Phillip Morris for further analysis. That same day, Customs officials began a detailed, week-long inventory of the cigarettes. On April 10, in the course of the inventory, agents found two boxes of cigarettes that bore Customs notations indicating that they had previously been denied importation into the United States. Sometime between April 10 and April 17, Customs officials also discovered evidence of country-of-origin violations: some of the inventoried cigarettes were not from Switzerland, as Intrigue had claimed, but rather from the Czech Republic, Germany, Holland, and Malaysia.

Phillip Morris responded to the Customs Service's inquiry on April 19. Its tests established that the cigarettes in fact were not counterfeit, but it confirmed that three of the four cartons it reviewed were incorrectly labeled as manufactured in Switzerland. The Customs Service retained control of the cigarettes, asserting that it now had probable cause to believe that a large number of the cigarettes were imported in violation of country-of-origin rules or imported despite having been previously denied entry. All but 408 mastercases ultimately were sold at a court-ordered interlocutory sale in October 2002 for $ 450,000. The estimated domestic market value of the 4,432 mastercases of cigarettes was between $ 1.7 million and $ 5.5 million.

In December 2001, the United States filed this civil forfeiture complaint against the cigarettes as goods entered into the country in violation of law. *See* 19 U.S.C. § 1595a. The United States initially alleged only country-of-origin and unlawful importation violations but amended its complaint in December 2002 to add charges under the Contraband Cigarette Trafficking Act ("CCTA"), 18 U.S.C. § 2341 et seq. The CCTA claim alleged that the cigarettes could be seized because they were "found" in California without bearing "evidence of the payment of applicable State cigarette taxes." 18 U.S.C. §§ 2341, 2344.

Intrigue moved to suppress the cigarettes as fruits of an illegal search and seizure in violation of the Fourth Amendment. The district court denied the suppression motion, holding that "there is no legitimate expectation of privacy in imported merchandise located in [an FTZ]," and that "imports released from Customs' custody may still be subject to Customs sampling or additional examination after they are released."

After the government withdrew five of its eight original claims, the parties filed cross-motions for summary judgment. The district court denied summary judgment to Intrigue on the country-of-origin and unlawful importation claims but granted summary judgment in its favor on the CCTA claim. The district court held that California cigarette taxes were not due on Intrigue's mastercases because such taxes are preempted by a provision of the Foreign Trade Zones Act ("FTZ Act") that prohibits the imposition of state and local ad valorem taxes against goods stored in FTZs. *See* 19 U.S.C. § 81o(e). It concluded that California's imposition of a tax on cigarettes destined for sale in another state "transform[s] a tax on the sale or distribution of cigarettes in California into an ad valorem property tax."

The parties entered into a consent judgment in December 2003. In return for the government's agreement to drop its remaining country-of-origin claims, Intrigue agreed that the government preserved its right to appeal the CCTA judgment. In turn, Intrigue preserved its right to appeal the denial of its motion to suppress. Thereafter, the district court awarded Intrigue $ 491,000 in attorney fees. The government appeals that award, arguing only that if we reverse the grant of summary judgment on the CCTA claim, Intrigue will not be a "prevailing party" and the fee award should be vacated. We consolidated these timely appeals.

II. MOTION TO SUPPRESS

We review the denial of a motion to suppress de novo, *see United States v. Willis, 431 F.3d 709, 713 n.3 (9th Cir. 2005)*, although we accept the district court's underlying findings of fact in the absence of clear error, *see id*. We hold that the district court properly denied Intrigue's motion to suppress the 4,432 mastercases of cigarettes as fruits of an illegal search and seizure.

Intrigue argues that the warrantless search of its locked cage and sealed cigarette cases on April 4 or 5, 2001, and the related seizure of twelve sample cartons of cigarettes for testing, violated the Fourth Amendment. It further contends that the United States lacked probable cause when it seized all 4,432 mastercases of cigarettes on April 6. Lastly, Intrigue contends that the government's continuing retention of the mastercases after the inconclusive Rudalevige test on April 9 was unconstitutional, because any probable cause that may have arisen at earlier points in the Customs Service investigation dissipated at the conclusion of the second, inconclusive test.

A. Initial Search

It is undisputed that Customs agents searched Intrigue's storage area within the Port Services FTZ and seized twelve sample cartons of cigarettes without a warrant. We conclude, however, that this initial search and sampling was a constitutional administrative search.[3]

[1] As a general rule, searches and seizures violate the Fourth Amendment unless they are based on probable cause and executed pursuant to a valid search warrant. *See Katz v. United States, 389 U.S. 347, 357, 88 S. Ct. 507, 19 L. Ed. 2d 576 (1967)*. The protection against unreasonable searches and seizures extends to commercial premises, *see Tucson Woman's Clinic v. Eden, 379 F.3d 531, 550 (9th Cir. 2004)*, and it also applies in the context of civil forfeiture proceedings, *see One 1958 Plymouth Sedan v. Pennsylvania, 380 U.S. 693, 696, 85 S. Ct. 1246, 14 L. Ed. 2d 170 (1965)*.

[2] The United States Supreme Court, however, has carved out a limited number of contexts within which a warrant is not required. Administrative searches of "closely regulated" industries are one such exception and may be conducted without a warrant, so long as they meet certain standards of reasonableness. *See, e.g., New York v. Burger, 482 U.S. 691, 702-03, 107 S. Ct. 2636, 96 L. Ed. 2d 601 (1987)*. We do not require a warrant in such situations because "the federal regulatory presence is sufficiently comprehensive and defined that the owner of the commercial property cannot help but be aware that his property will be subject to periodic inspections undertaken for specific purposes." *Donovan v. Dewey, 452 U.S. 594, 600, 101 S. Ct. 2534, 69 L. Ed. 2d 262 (1981)*. Industries deemed "close-

---

3 Intrigue does not independently contest the constitutional validity of the sampling. Therefore, we consider the initial search and sampling together.

ly regulated" under this doctrine include liquor distribution, *Colonnade Catering Corp. v. United States, 397 U.S. 72, 90 S. Ct. 774, 25 L. Ed. 2d 60 (1970)*; sale of sporting weapons, *United States v. Biswell, 406 U.S. 311, 316, 92 S. Ct. 1593, 32 L. Ed. 2d 87 (1972)*; stone quarrying and mining, *Donovan, 452 U.S. at 606*; and automobile junkyards, *Burger, 482 U.S. at 703-04*; *United States v. Argent Chem. Labs., Inc., 93 F.3d 572, 575 (9th Cir. 1996)* (veterinary drugs); *United States v. V-1 Oil Co., 63 F.3d 909, 911 (9th Cir. 1995)* (transportation of hazardous materials). The Supreme Court, in *Burger*, upheld a warrantless search and inspection regime for automobile junkyards that allowed police officers to inspect not only a company's business records but also the cars and auto parts stored on its property. In reaching its determination that automobile junkyards are closely regulated, the Court focused on "the pervasiveness and regularity of the federal regulation and the effect of such regulation upon an owner's expectation of privacy." *Burger, 482 U.S. at 701* (internal quotation marks omitted); *see also Tucson Woman's Clinic, 379 F.3d at 550.*

The United States contends that FTZs are a "closely regulated" industry and that Customs Service regulations sufficiently authorize warrantless searches. As a result, those who store property within FTZs have a diminished expectation of privacy and adequate notice of the likelihood of warrantless inspections. We agree that, given the closely regulated nature of FTZs, a warrant is not required, so long as the search is otherwise reasonable.

Although storing cigarettes in an FTZ is more akin to a "business activity" than an "industry," we have previously approved administrative searches premised on the "closely regulated" nature of a particular commercial activity, even where the entire industry might not be tightly regulated. In *V-1 Oil*, we evaluated the constitutionality of a warrantless search provision in the federal Hazardous Materials Transportation Act. Although V-1 acknowledged that it was regulated by 331 different state and federal agencies, the company argued that it could not be subject to administrative searches because it was not part of the railroad industry or any other industry that could be deemed "closely regulated." *V-1 Oil, 63 F.3d at 911.* We disagreed, focusing not on the industry to which V-1 belonged but rather on the closely regulated nature of its business activity: "V-1 has a reduced expectation of privacy because it transports, sells, and stores propane gas." *Id.*; *see also United States v. Gonsalves, 435 F.3d 64, 67 (1st Cir. 2006)* (holding that "[w]hatever the status of the [medical] profession in the abstract," the manufacture, storage, and dispensation of pharmaceuticals is closely regulated). Therefore, we need only decide whether the activity of storing merchandise in an FTZ is closely regulated.

We first note that the regulation of FTZs is pervasive. An FTZ may be established only with the consent and authorization of a federal agency, the Foreign Trade Zones Board. 19 U.S.C. § 81b. Entities seeking to admit merchandise to an FTZ must submit an application and numerous supporting documents, 19 C.F.R. § 146.32; they must do so again if they wish to manipulate, manufacture, exhibit, or destroy their merchandise, *id.* § 146.52; and they must gain permission yet again from the Port Director to remove their merchandise from a zone, *id.* § 146.71. Each of these steps is tightly controlled, requires documentation, and is subject to Customs supervision. Detailed regulations also address safety conditions, security, and recordkeeping responsibilities within FTZs. *See id.* §§ 146.4, 146.21-26; 15 C.F.R. § 400.46. Most importantly, the statute and accompanying regulations clearly authorize the Customs Service to monitor, search and inspect items stored therein. Customs Service officers have primary responsibility for policing the admission of foreign goods into customs territory. *See* 19 U.S.C. § 81d; 19 C.F.R. § 146.3. FTZ operators must "permit any Customs officer access to a zone," 19 C.F.R. § 146.4(b), and once on-site, those officers may examine any merchandise stored in an FTZ so long as "the examination is considered necessary to facilitate the proper administration of any law, regulation, or instruction which Customs is authorized to enforce." *Id.* § 146.10. The Foreign Trade Zones Manual, which serves as a comprehensive guidebook for zone users and operators, further emphasizes the breadth of the Customs Service's authority:

> To properly enforce the laws and regulations, Customs officers are given considerable authority to conduct searches, arrest suspected violators, and seize merchandise and articles. . . . Merchandise may be seized by any Customs officer who has reasonable cause to believe that any law or regulation enforced by Customs has been violated, by reason of which the merchandise has become subject to seizure or forfeiture.

United States Customs & Border Protection, Foreign Trade Zones Manual 197-98 (2003) (citing 19 C.F.R. § 162.21).[4] These numerous and specific regulations should have provided sufficient notice to Intrigue "that its property and records will from time to time be inspected by government officials," *V-1 Oil, 63 F.3d at 912* (internal quotation marks omitted), and that its goods might be subject to occasional sampling.

[4] The duration and regularity of this scheme also supports our conclusion that the commercial activity of storing merchandise in FTZs is "closely regulated." Customs supervision has been part of the scheme for FTZs since they were conceived in 1934. Section 146.10, which enables warrantless searches of merchandise in FTZs by Customs Service agents has been in place since 1969,[5] and was not modified during the period of Intrigue's operations. Moreover, the Carson FTZ zone operator testified that Customs officials inspected Intrigue's inventory and manipulation activity "two to three times a year" during the thirty months Intrigue rented space there.

---

4 http://www.cbp.gov/[tilde]xp/cgov/toolbox/publications/manuals_handbooks/.

5 From 1970 to 1984, a regulatory provision with almost identical language was located at 19 C.F.R. § 146.6. *See* 49 Fed. Reg. 28,855, 28,878 (July 17, 1984); 35 Fed. Reg. 9262, 9263 (June 13, 1970). Between 1969 and 1970, the provision authorizing Customs Service examinations of merchandise in FTZs could be found at 19 C.F.R. § 30.6. *See* 34 Fed. Reg. 4957 (Mar. 7, 1969).

Intrigue correctly points out that "domestic status" goods, like Intrigue's cigarettes, which have come through Customs and on which duties have been paid, are subject to less scrutiny and regulation than goods in international transshipment or domestic goods bound for export. That fact, however, does not relieve Intrigue from most of the FTZ regulations, including especially the search provisions of sections 146.4 and 146.10. In *Burger*, the Supreme Court held that a regulatory scheme far less comprehensive and enacted more recently nonetheless rendered automobile junkyards "closely regulated." The New York statute, less than five years old when the warrantless inspection occurred, *Burger, 482 U.S. at 705*, was comparatively limited in scope. It required junkyard owners to obtain a license and keep records of vehicles coming into and leaving their possession, and allowed police officers to examine the records or the vehicles during normal business hours. Id. at 694 nn.1 & 3. The regulatory regime for "domestic status" goods in FTZs is at least as pervasive and well-established.

Next, we disagree with Intrigue that the FTZ regulations fail to clearly authorize warrantless searches. In support of its contention, Intrigue cites a statutory provision detailing obligations for Customs Service officers:

> If any officer or person authorized to make searches and seizures has probable cause to believe that—(A) any merchandise . . . which has been otherwise brought into the United States unlawfully . . . is in any dwelling house, store, or other building or place, he may make application, under oath, to any [authorized judge], and shall thereupon be entitled to a warrant to enter . . . and to search for and seize such merchandise or other article described in the warrant.19 U.S.C. § 1595(a)(1). In *United States v. Mendoza-Ortiz, 262 F.3d 882, 885 (9th Cir. 2001)* (per curiam) we held that 19 U.S.C. § 1595(a) required Customs officers to obtain a warrant to search a private warehouse, even though they had probable cause to believe drugs were located on the site. 262 F.3d at 885. An FTZ, however, is not private property. It is a heavily regulated, government created and controlled location at which only particular commercial activity, defined by the government, is allowed. Business activities that otherwise would be private fall under extensive federal control and Customs supervision when they are conducted in FTZs. Our decision in *Mendoza-Ortiz* turned on the fact that the search involved private activity at a private facility, one that typically would be shielded from government intervention. Indeed, in *Mendoza-Ortiz*, we were careful to note that the officers could have intercepted the drugs at the border or at any place en route to the private warehouse without a warrant; it was only "[a]t the moment the planks were unloaded into Space G" that a warrant became necessary. *Id.* Furthermore, the specific statute and regulations giving Customs search and inspection power over merchandise in FTZs, 19 U.S.C. § 81d; 19 C.F.R. §§ 146.3, 146.4, 146.10, trump the more general statute requiring a warrant in the majority of situations, 19 U.S.C. § 1595. *See Bonneville Power Admin. v. FERC, 422 F.3d 908, 916 (9th Cir. 2005)* (describing the "basic principle of statutory construction . . . that the specific prevails over the general").

We also reject Intrigue's similar argument that the statute and regulations do not authorize a "warrantless search and seizure" because they do not use those particular terms. Neither of the statutes held to authorize administrative searches in *Burger* and *V-1 Oil*used the words "warrantless search and seizure." In *Burger*, the statute allowed "any police officer . . . to examine" vehicle records, vehicles, and vehicle parts. *482 U.S. at 694 n.1* (citing *N.Y. Veh. & Traf. Law § 415-a5* (McKinney 1986)). In *V-1 Oil*, the statute empowered "any officer, employee, or agent to enter upon, inspect, and examine, at reasonable times and in a reasonable manner, the records and properties of persons[relating to transportation or shipment of hazardous materials]." 63 F.3d at 912 (citing 49 U.S.C. § 1808(c) (1988)). We decline to hold that the words "warrantless search and seizure" are talismanic.

[5] Even though we conclude that the FTZ regulations clearly authorize inspections without warrants and that the storage of goods in FTZs is "closely regulated" commercial activity, to satisfy the Fourth Amendment, the administrative search must also be reasonable. In *Burger*, the Supreme Court held that a warrantless search is nevertheless reasonable if three conditions are satisfied: 1) the underlying regulatory scheme advances a substantial government interest; 2) warrantless inspections are "necessary" to further the regulatory scheme; and 3) the inspection program provides a "constitutionally adequate substitute for a warrant." *Burger, 482 U.S. at 702-03* (internal quotation marks omitted); *V-1 Oil, 63 F.3d at 911*. Each of these conditions is met here.

[6] First, the underlying regulatory scheme for FTZs advances the government's substantial interest in ensuring that duties are paid, that consumers are protected from counterfeit or adulterated cigarettes, and that country-of-origin labels are reviewed. Second, it is plain that a warrantless inspection program is necessary to further the regulatory scheme, because here, as in *V-1 Oil*, advance notice of inspections could permit those violating American customs laws "to temporarily correct violations and frustrate enforcement efforts." 63 F.3d at 912. This is particularly the case for so-called "domestic status" goods, like Intrigue's cigarettes, because they can be moved in and out of FTZs without permits. *See* 19 C.F.R. § 146.71.

[7] Third, the FTZ regulations provide a "constitutionally adequate substitute for a warrant." As the Supreme Court explained in *Burger*,

> the regulatory statute must perform the two basic functions of a warrant: it must advise the owner of the commercial premises that the search is being made pursuant to the law and has a properly defined scope, and it must limit the discretion of the inspecting officers.482 U.S. at 703; *see also Argent Chem. Labs., 93 F.3d at 576*. The FTZ regulations provide adequate notice that inspections will occur in accordance with the law. 19 C.F.R. sections 146.4 and 146.10 identify who will be performing the searches ("any Customs officer"), the object of the search ("merchandise"), the timing of searches ("at the time of admission to a zone, or at any time thereafter"), and the circumstances under which searches are allowed (only as "necessary to facilitate the proper administration of any law, regulation, or instruction which Customs is authorized to enforce"). Furthermore, the record indicates that Customs officials inspected Intrigue's storage area two to three times per year. The "certainty and

> regularity" of these searches indicate that Intrigue was aware that its property would be subject to lawful periodic inspections. *See Burger, 482 U.S. at 703*; *Donovan, 452 U.S. at 600*.

Although the FTZ regulations place few limits on the discretion of searching officers, we are confident that they are sufficient. The Supreme Court's opinion in *Burger* instructs that we should review the scheme's limitation on officer discretion in context. The *Burger* Court upheld the New York vehicle-dismantling statute, even though it did not indicate how often searches would occur, provided virtually no limitation on the scope of the search within automobile junkyards, and failed to "provide[] limits or guidance on the selection" of businesses for inspection. 482 U.S. at 722-23 (Brennan, J., dissenting). The Court instead relied on the restriction of the searches to certain types of businesses and certain types of items that could be inspected. Id. at 711 (majority opinion). The same basic limitations are present in the FTZ statute and regulations.

Moreover, because companies operating in FTZs do not have the expectation of privacy one would have in a private home or business, we require fewer safeguards to satisfy us that the search is reasonable. In *Rush v. Obledo*, we struck down as unconstitutional a regulation that enabled warrantless searches of family-home day care facilities because it failed to place any limits on the time of searches, the area that could be searched, or the regularity of searches. *756 F.2d 713, 721 (9th Cir. 1985)*. The overbroad search provision would have authorized searching anywhere within day care providers' private residences, even in areas unconnected to the provision of day care, at any time of day. As we explained, constitutionally adequate searches "must be directly connected with the environment the Legislature seeks to regulate—i.e., the areas of the home used by children when the children are present." *Id.* Similarly, in *Argent Chemical Laboratories*, we concluded that a statute authorizing warrantless FDA searches of veterinary drug manufacturers was reasonable, because notice was furnished at the time, the statute limited the scope of what could be inspected and what could be seized, and most seizures required approval from a district office before items could be seized. 93 F.3d at 576-77. In that case, allowing searches of pharmaceutical plants without those limitations would have far exceeded the FDA's interest in regulating the "safety and effectiveness" of veterinary drugs. Id. at 576. Here, unlike the situation in *Rush*, the area in which searches are authorized (FTZs) is the same area subject to regulation. There is minimal risk that Customs Service officers will go beyond the scope prescribed by the FTZ regulations, because virtually all the activities that take place within an FTZ fall within the scope of Customs inspection and monitoring. *See A.T. Cross Co. v. Sunil Trading Corp., 467 F. Supp. 47, 51 (S.D.N.Y. 1979)*.

Finally, we note the settled expectations that surround the use and control of FTZs. It is long-established and well understood that, in exchange for the benefits afforded to users of FTZs, those who store merchandise in FTZs must keep Customs apprised of their activities and afford Customs officials the right to inspect their operations. Intrigue was well aware of this trade-off when it decided to run its operations out of an FTZ.

[8] We therefore hold that the Customs Service searches authorized by the FTZ regulations are "directly connected with the environment the Legislature seeks to regulate," *Rush, 756 F.2d at 721*, and the FTZ regulatory scheme provides a constitutionally adequate substitute for a warrant. The warrantless search of Intrigue's storage area and the initial sampling constituted a valid and reasonable administrative search.

B. Probable Cause for Seizure of all 4,432 Mastercases

[9] We next conclude that, under the "totality of the circumstances" confronting the Customs Service, probable cause supported the government's seizure of all 4,432 mastercases of cigarettes on April 6, 2001. As we held in *United States v. One 1978 Piper Cherokee Aircraft*:

> The standard for probable cause in forfeiture proceedings resembles that required to support a search warrant. The determination of probable cause is based upon a "totality of the circumstances" test, and the government's evidence must be more than that which gives rise to a mere suspicion, although it need not rise to the level of prima facie proof.*91 F.3d 1204, 1208 (9th Cir. 1996)* (citations omitted).[6] Thus, probable cause to seize property does not require absolute certainty, but only a "fair probability" that the property is contraband. *See United States v. Sokolow, 490 U.S. 1, 7, 109 S. Ct. 1581, 104 L. Ed. 2d 1 (1989)*; *United States v. Alaimalo, 313 F.3d 1188, 1193 (9th Cir. 2002)*. Because judicial constructs like "probable cause" and "reasonable suspicion" are "fluid concepts that take their substantive content from the particular contexts in which the standards are being assessed," *Ornelas v. United States, 517 U.S. 690, 696, 116 S. Ct. 1657, 134 L. Ed. 2d 911 (1996)*, we give reasonable deference to the inferences and judgments of experienced agents in the field, *see id. at 700*; *United States v. $ 129,727.00 U.S. Currency, 129 F.3d 486, 489 (9th Cir. 1997)*.

The Customs Service agents encountered the following combination of circumstances when they inspected the Carson FTZ. The FTZ operator initially indicated that there were no cigarettes on-site, but an FTZ employee queried the next day led Customs officers to Intrigue's cigarette storage space. The FTZ operator could not immediately produce records for Intrigue's cigarettes, records the zone operator generally maintains and must have "readily available for Customs review." 19 C.F.R. § 146.4(d). The FTZ employees did not have a key to the storage area, and an Intrigue employee showed up with a key only when Customs was preparing to break the lock. Intrigue's storage cage was covered with a black tarp and the pallets inside were wrapped in opaque black plastic, both elements that Senior Customs Inspector Rudolfo Villacana testified he had not encountered before. When an

---

6 Although the United States points to regulatory provisions indicating that the appropriate standard might be the lesser "reasonable cause" instead of "probable cause," because we find that probable cause existed, we do not reach this issue.

Intrigue employee showed up, he was not initially able to produce any documentation that duties had been paid on the cigarettes. The next day, Customs inspectors (accompanied by a government chemist) performed field tests on sample packs of Intrigue's cigarettes, which indicated that the cigarettes were "likely counterfeit," "possibly counterfeit," or at least "appeared to be counterfeit." Inspector Villacana declared that this combination of factors caused him to be "very suspicious that the mastercases were entered illegally." Although Intrigue now offers explanations for each of these circumstances, at the time, an objectively reasonable Customs officer could properly conclude that probable cause existed for seizure. *See Ornelas, 517 U.S. at 696.*

[10] Intrigue's contention that the field test results were not sufficiently certain to support a finding of probable cause lacks merit. The Supreme Court has upheld probable cause determinations that are based on ambiguous or inconclusive field tests, even in the absence of other evidence supporting a finding of probable cause. For example, in *Illinois v. Caballes*, the Supreme Court upheld the search of a car based on a dog-sniff detection of narcotics, *543 U.S. 405, 410, 125 S. Ct. 834, 160 L. Ed. 2d 842 (2005)*, even though evidence in the record indicated that Illinois drug dogs return false positives anywhere from 12.5% to 60% of the time, id. at 412 (Souter, J., dissenting). Here, moreover, the "likely counterfeit"/"possibly counterfeit" field test results did not stand alone. They were one of a combination of circumstances giving rise to probable cause for the seizure.

[11] Once Customs officers had probable cause to believe the merchandise was counterfeit, it was within their discretion to seize all of the cigarettes. "Property may be seized, if available, by any Customs officer who has reasonable cause to believe that any law or regulation enforced by the Customs Service has been violated, by reason of which the property has become subject to seizure or forfeiture." 19 C.F.R. § 162.21(a). Similarly, 19 C.F.R. § 162.11 allows Customs officers "lawfully on any premises and [] able to identify merchandise which has been imported contrary to law [to] seize such merchandise without a warrant." We therefore hold that the seizure was based on probable cause and statutorily authorized.[7]

C. Retention of the Mastercases

Intrigue contends that even if probable cause existed for the seizure of the 4,432 mastercases, the Customs Service lacked probable cause to retain them once the Rudalevige test returned inconclusive results on April 9, 2001. Intrigue is correct as a matter of law that when there ceases to be probable cause for continuing a search or seizure, it must end immediately. *See Jacobs v. City of Chicago, 215 F.3d 758, 772 (7th Cir. 2000)*. However, because Intrigue mischaracterizes the import of the Rudalevige test, we cannot agree that probable cause evaporated with

---

7 We do not reach the United States' alternative argument that it was justified in seizing all the mastercases without a warrant because of exigent circumstances.

its failure to reach conclusive results. Probable cause existed at each step in the Customs Service's investigation of the cigarettes.

By April 19, 2001, when Phillip Morris definitively established that the cigarettes were not counterfeit, the Customs Service had developed new bases for probable cause, as its inventory of the cigarettes had turned up country-of-origin and re-importation violations. Intrigue does not dispute this fact but instead contends that there was a one-daybreak in probable cause, between the completion of the inconclusive Rudalevige test on Apri 19 and the discovery of previously-denied cigarettes on April 10. It contends that once the Rudalevige test failed to establish with certainty that the cigarettes were counterfeit, the inventory should have stopped and the cigarettes should have been returned to Intrigue.

We disagree. Intrigue asserts that the Rudalevige test "proved wrong" the initial field tests indicating that the cigarettes might be counterfeit. That is not correct. The Rudalevige test report identifies a number of characteristics of the tested cigarettes that were similar to genuine gray market cigarettes, including "the filter holes, the glue, the printing, the cigarette packing, the control number, the folding pattern of the foil, the lack of fluorescence, the placement of the material codes, and the statement 'Blend of USA.'" However, the report also notes that the lack of codes on the filter paper, the misspelling of Switzerland on two of the sample packs, and a number of "signs of poor quality control," such as uneven folds, poorly aligned bands on the filters, and loose tobacco in the packages, raised red flags about their genuineness. Due to these potentially troubling factors, the Rudalevige test report stated, "We cannot draw any conclusion based on these observations." The report recommended sending the cigarettes to Phillip Morris for further testing. The Rudalevige test results did not dispute, or even address, the findings of the initial field tests. They merely indicated that additional testing would be required to determine with any certainty whether the cigarettes were counterfeit or not.

[12] The inconclusive Rudalevige test did not extinguish probable cause. Indeed, the test report noted several additional factors that would have supported a probable cause determination. Rudalevige found these elements troubling enough that he sought further testing from the supposed manufacturer. Furthermore, virtually all of the factors that had generated support for the initial seizure, including the suspicious circumstances of Intrigue's storage and the field tests indicating that the cigarettes were "possibly" or "likely" counterfeit, remained in play and supported probable cause.

Intrigue points to one out-of-circuit district court case to support its argument that an inconclusive test result nullifies probable cause to continue seizure. *See United States v. One DLO Model A/C, 30.06 Mach. Gun, 904 F. Supp. 622 (N.D. Ohio 1995)*. *One DLO Model* dealt with the arcane issue of whether a 28 U.S.C. § 2465 "certificate of reasonable cause," which exempts federal officials from liability after a judicial determination that the government wrongly seized property for forfeiture, should be predicated on the appropriateness of the initial evidentiary seizure or alternatively on the appropriateness of the "warrant for the arrest of property" that enables forfeiture. Id. at 636, 638. The claimant had been charged with federal weapons violations and the case turned only on whether or not he had forged documents transferring ownership of the weapons to himself. Id. at 641-42. However, during the investigation that followed the initial seizure, neither the government's nor the claimant's forensic experts found anything that would indicate that the claimant had forged the documents. Id. at 642 (noting that "[t]here was no longer any evidence linking [claimant] to the forgery . . . rising above mere suspicion"). Therefore, the court held, while the government might have had probable cause to seize the weapons pursuant to the search warrant, that probable cause had evaporated by the time the government filed the complaint to forfeit them. *Id.*

[13] Even if *One DLO Model*were controlling authority, it would not compel the result Intrigue seeks. In *One DLO Model*, the forensic tests exonerated the claimant. The Rudalevige test, on the other hand, produced findings both inculpatory and exculpatory. In addition, the Customs Service still possessed evidence from the initial field test that the cigarettes might indeed be counterfeit. Intrigue was not exonerated on the counterfeiting charge until April 19, days after the new violations were discovered. *Cf. One DLO Model, 904 F. Supp. at 642* (noting that the exonerating evidence was possessed by government officials "well before the filing of the complaint and the subsequent seizure"). The probable cause that existed on April 6 did not lapse before the additional bases for probable cause (for violating other importation laws) arose on April 10.

III. CONTRABAND CIGARETTES TRAFFICKING ACT

Next we consider the United States' cross-appeal, challenging the district court's decision that the Contraband Cigarettes Trafficking Act ("CCTA") was inapplicable to Intrigue's cigarettes because the California cigarette tax is an ad valorem tax, expressly precluded by the FTZ Act from application to goods stored in FTZs. We agree with the United States that the district court misapprehended the nature of the California cigarette tax.

This dispute arises at the intersection of two federal laws: the CCTA, which authorizes the federal forfeiture of cigarettes found in a state without the appropriate state tax stamps, and the FTZ Act, which specifically limits the application of state and local taxes. The CCTA makes it unlawful "for any person knowingly to ship, transport, receive, possess, sell, distribute, or purchase contraband cigarettes," 18 U.S.C. § 2342(a), and allows the federal government to seize and forfeit such cigarettes, *id.* § 2344(c). The CCTA, at the time of the seizure, defined "contraband cigarettes" as

> a quantity in excess of 60,000 cigarettes, which bear no evidence of the payment of applicable State cigarette taxes in the State where such cigarettes are found, . . . in the possession of any person other than [a permitted manufacturer, common carrier, entity licensed to pay cigarette taxes by other means, or federal or state agency or

employee].*Id.* § 2341(2) (2005).[8] Federal liability under the CCTA is thus predicated on the non-payment of state taxes or any other violation of an applicable state cigarette tax law. *See United States v. Gord, 77 F.3d 1192, 1193 (9th Cir. 1996).* The FTZ Act, however, prohibits state and local governments from imposing ad valorem taxes on tangible personal property held in FTZs. 19 U.S.C. § 81o(e). Therefore, whether Intrigue's cigarettes were contraband and seizable for failure to pay the California tax turns on whether California's cigarette tax is properly characterized as an ad valorem tax or an excise tax.

A. Nature of Cigarette Tax

[14] We hold, contrary to the district court, that the California cigarette tax is an excise tax, not expressly precluded by the FTZ Act. 19 U.S.C. § 81o(e). An ad valorem tax is defined by its method for calculating the size of the tax. *Ad valorem* is the Latin phrase for "according to value," and it describes a tax the size of which directly correlates to the value of the item taxed. *See Quinault Indian Nation v. Grays Harbor County, 310 F.3d 645, 647 n.1 (9th Cir. 2002).* The most common example of an ad valorem tax is the local property tax. An excise tax, by contrast, is one "imposed on the performance of an act . . . or the enjoyment of a privilege." Id. at 651 (citing Black's Law Dictionary 563 (6th ed. 1990)) (alteration in original). The quintessential excise tax in our country is the sales tax. An excise tax, because it is based on a particular transaction or activity, can be imposed only once per act, whereas an ad valorem property tax can be imposed annually, as is typical of property taxes.

[15] The California cigarette tax makes no reference to value, instead calculating the tax solely according to the number of cigarettes distributed within the state. The statute provides: "Every distributor shall pay a tax upon his or her distributions of cigarettes at the rate of . . . [$ 0.006 per cigarette distributed] on and after 12:01 a.m. on January 1, 1994." Cal. Rev. & Tax. Code § 30101. The statute also imposes separate taxes of $ 0.0125 per cigarette to fund community health education and disease research, *id.* §§ 30121-30129, and $ 0.025 per cigarette to fund early child development programs, *id.* § 30131. Distributors, therefore, owe the state 4.35 cents per cigarette, whether the cigarettes are very expensive Dunhills, mid-priced Salems, or lower-priced Dorals.

[16] On its face, the California tax is not imposed ad valorem, but rather is an excise tax. *See Cal. State Bd. of Equalization v. Chemehuevi Indian Tribe, 474 U.S. 9, 10-11, 106 S. Ct. 289, 88 L. Ed. 2d 9 (1986)* (repeatedly describing California's cigarette distribution tax as an excise tax). The tax does not in any way correlate to value, and it is imposed only once, when the cigarettes are "distributed." See Cal.

---

8 A 2006 amendment to the CCTA lowered the threshold for contraband cigarettes from 60,000 to 10,000 cigarettes. *See* USA Patriot Improvement & Reauthorization Act of 2005, Pub. L. 109-177, § 121(a)(1), 120 Stat. 192, 221 (2006). Congress also amended the CCTA to include non-payment of local taxes as a source of liability. *Id.* § 121(b)(6), 120 Stat. at 222. Neither of these changes affects our analysis.

Rev. & Tax. Code § 30008 (defining "distribution"). Intrigue argues, however, that imposing the per-cigarette tax on the act of storing the cigarettes in California for future sale "transform[s]" the tax into an ad valorem tax. We reject the notion that a tax calculated in a manner other than *ad valorem* can be an ad valorem tax.

That conclusion is consistent with our case law and the language of the California statute. We have previously determined that a tax on the storage of goods for out-of-state sale may nonetheless be an excise tax. *Mount Tivy Winery v. Lewis, 134 F.2d 120 (9th Cir. 1943)*. In *Mount Tivy*, a California-based winery challenged a federal tax on wine stored for future sale as an unconstitutional direct tax. Id. at 122. The outcome of the case similarly turned on whether the tax at issue was an excise tax or an ad valorem property tax. After reviewing the Supreme Court's definition of an excise tax, "a tax imposed upon a particular use of property or the exercise of a single power over property incidental to ownership," we held that the liquor tax was indeed an excise tax. Id. at 124-25 (quoting *Bromley v. McCaughn, 27366 C.B. 392, 280 U.S. 124, 136, 50 S. Ct. 46, 74 L. Ed. 226, 1929-2 C.B. 392 (1929))*.

[17] The language of California's cigarette tax, which is imposed on "the exercise of any right or power" over cigarettes, Cal. Rev. & Tax. Code § 30009, parrots the terminology of *Mount Tivy* and of the "use taxes" common throughout the United States. *See, e.g.*, Cal. Rev. & Tax. Code § 6201; Mo. Rev. Stat. § 144.610; Tex. Tax Code Ann. § 151.011; Vt. Stat. Ann. tit. 32, § 9701(15). As B.E. Witkin explains in his foundational treatise on California law, the use tax is an "excise tax imposed . . . on the *storage, use or other consumption* in [a] state of tangible personal property." Witkin, Summary of California Law, Vol. 9, § 305 (9th ed. 1989). We therefore conclude that a tax on cigarettes placed in storage does not transform an excise tax into an ad valorem tax.

B. CCTA Application to Cigarettes Stored for Out-of-State Sale

Intrigue also argues that even if the California cigarette tax is an excise tax, by its terms, it does not reach the storage of cigarettes to be sold in another state. Because the district court found that the California tax was an ad valorem tax, it did not reach this question. We reject Intrigue's argument and hold that California law requires unlicensed distributors like Intrigue to pay cigarette taxes on cigarettes stored in California for out-of-state sale.

The plain language of the statute compels this reasoning. *See United States v. Daas, 198 F.3d 1167, 1174 (9th Cir. 1999)* ("The first step in ascertaining congressional intent is to look to the plain language of the statute."). We follow the plain meaning of a statute unless it is ambiguous or its application would lead to unreasonable results.*Id.*

[18] California taxes "distributions" of cigarettes, requiring "distributors" to either affix a pre-paid stamp on the pack of cigarettes or make direct payment to the state. Cal. Rev. & Tax. Code §§ 30101, 30161. "Distribution" is defined as either

the "sale of [previously] untaxed cigarettes or tobacco products in this state," or "[t]he use or consumption of untaxed cigarettes or tobacco products in this state." *Id.* § 30008. In turn, "use or consumption" is defined as

> the exercise of any right or power over cigarettes or tobacco products incident to the ownership thereof, other than the sale of the cigarettes or tobacco products or the keeping or retention thereof by a licensed distributor for the purpose of sale.

Id. § 30009.

We agree with the United States that California's use of the term "the exercise of any right or power over cigarettes . . . incident to [] ownership" is intended to include the act of storage. A number of courts and statutes have recognized or approved this interpretation. For example, in *D.H. Holmes Co. v. McNamara*, the United States Supreme Court upheld against a Commerce Clause challenge a Louisiana use tax that defined "use" as "the exercise of any right or power over tangible personal property incident to ownership, and includes consumption, distribution, and storage." 486 U.S. 24, 27, 108 S. Ct. 1619, 100 L. Ed. 2d 21 (1988). Similarly, in *Mount Tivy Winery*, we held that the "activity of holding wine intended for sale" could be taxed under a statute that imposed taxes on the "exercise of a single power over property incidental to ownership." 134 F.2d at 124 (internal quotation marks omitted). *See also Dept. of Revenue of State of N.M. v. United States, 408 F.2d 574, 576-77 (10th Cir. 1969)* (describing New Mexico excise tax which defined "use" as "exercise of any right or power over tangible personal property incident to . . . ownership" and laid the tax on "personal property stored, used or consumed in state"); *Texas Co. v. Siefried, 60 Wyo. 142, 147 P.2d 837, 844 (Wyo. 1944)* (holding that a tax on "use" reached the storage and withdrawal from storage of gasoline).

[19] Given the definition of "distribution" in § 30008, we cannot accept Intrigue's argument that the California statute is intended to tax only sales of cigarettes. Because California explicitly defined the term in the statute, we need not resort to dictionary definitions of "distribution." *See Konop v. Hawaiian Airlines, Inc., 302 F.3d 868, 880 (9th Cir. 2002)*. California's definition of "distribution" includes not only the "sale of untaxed cigarettes in this state" but also the use and consumption of cigarettes. All other exercises of right or power over cigarettes, including storage, fall within this second definition of "distribution." Cal. Rev. & Tax. Code § 30009. Intrigue's proposed interpretation would write out of the statute the second basis for § 30008 tax liability, something we must seek to avoid. *See Miller v. United States, 363 F.3d 999, 1008 (9th Cir. 2004)* ("Courts must aspire to give meaning to every word of a legislative enactment.").

Our interpretation of the California statute is reinforced by the exception built into § 30009. California explicitly exempts from its definition of "use or consumption" the "keeping or retention [of cigarettes] by a *licensed* distributor for the purpose of sale." Cal. Rev. & Tax. Code § 30009 (emphasis added). Thus, "use or consumption" would have to include the keeping or retention for sale of cigarettes by an *unlicensed* distributor. Intrigue concedes it was not a licensed distributor within the state of California at the time of seizure; therefore, it would not qualify for the exception.

The legislative history of the "use or consumption" definition in § 30009 further confirms our conclusion that the California cigarette tax reaches Intrigue's cigarettes. The California legislature, in 1998, amended the exception to § 30009 for "the keeping or retention thereof for the purpose of sale" to add the words "by a licensed distributor." Act of Aug. 28, 1998, ch. 420, § 4, 1998 Cal. Legis Serv. 420 (S.B. 2230) (West). The legislative history of Senate Bill 2230, which enacted this amendment, indicates that California intended to make unlicensed distributors liable for taxes on any unstamped cigarettes found in their possession. It reads: "This bill . . . revises the definition of 'use and consumption' to allow for the imposition of the tax on inventory seized while in the possession of an unlicensed distributor . . . ." California Bill Analysis, Assembly Committee, 1997-1998 Regular Session, Senate Bill 2230 (Aug. 5, 1998). Elsewhere, the legislative history offers a more thorough explanation, envisioning the precise scenario presented in this case:

> Unlicensed distributors have been known to obtain cigarettes and sell them directly to consumers without the cigarette tax having been paid. However, under current law, unlicensed distributors cannot be held liable for the cigarette tax on unstamped cigarettes that are seized because they can claim that a large portion of their inventory is being held for purposes of resale, rather than for direct sale to consumers.

This bill would draw a distinction between licensed and unlicensed distributors. Unlicensed distributors would be liable for tax on all unstamped cigarette or tobacco products found in their possession. The presumption would be that the unlicensed distributor is really in the business of selling cigarettes to consumers. Licensed distributors would not be liable for unstamped products in their possession. California Bill Analysis, Senate Floor, 1997-1998 Regular Session, Senate Bill 2230 (May 6, 1998).

Unlicensed distributors, like Intrigue, were precisely the target of the 1998 amendment. Indeed, Intrigue's owner Andy Lee testified that Intrigue kept the cigarettes in an FTZ because he believed that, by doing so, Intrigue could avoid paying California taxes. The clear implication of the statute, as amended in 1998, is that an unlicensed distributor like Intrigue owes taxes when it stores cigarettes within the state of California.

The distinction between licensed and unlicensed cigarette distributors also has practical merit. As the United States, and amicus California Board of Equalization ("BOE"), contend, the statutory scheme intentionally creates an "either/or" system that balances fairness to distributors with the government interest in combating cigarette smuggling. A distributor may choose to obtain a license, in which case it must report the cigarettes it brings into or ships out of state; or it may remain unlicensed but face liability for taxes on any cigarettes found in its possession, even if it intends to ship the cigarettes elsewhere. Contrary to Intrigue's representations at oral argument, licensed distributors are required to file regular reports with the California BOE detailing their inventories (both tax-stamped and unstamped), any distributions or sales, and the tax they believe is due. *See* Cal. Rev. & Tax. Code §§ 30182(a), 30183(a); Cal. Code Regs. tit. 18, §§ 4022, 4031. Licensed distributors must also keep a record of all cigarettes stored on a particular site, a record which must be made available to the BOE upon request. *See* Cal. Rev. & Tax. Code § 30454; Cal. Code Regs. tit. 18, § 4026. Taxing the cigarettes of unlicensed distributors is a precautionary measure to limit the state's financial risk that a distributor will claim cigarettes are destined for export, only to sell them at the lower, pre-tax price within California.

Intrigue argues that our reading of the statute would enable a system of double taxation, because it would be taxed for storing cigarettes in California and then taxed again when it sells the cigarettes in another state. We find this argument unavailing. First, any risk of double taxation would apply only to the small number of distributors who neglect to obtain a California license. Second, section 30008 makes clear that the "use or consumption" tax is due not for the sale, but rather for the privilege of storing the cigarettes within the state, a right that imposes on the state the reciprocal burdens of protecting and monitoring the cigarettes stored there. Third, California provides a legal procedure for companies like Intrigue, when they actually sell the cigarettes in another state, to petition the California BOE for a credit or refund of taxes on those cigarettes sold out of state. *See*Cal. Rev. & Tax. Code §§ 30176.1, 30178.1-2. In that way, the specter of double taxation can be avoided altogether.

Intrigue also asserts that, because the legislative history of the CCTA indicates that its purpose was to combat organized crime and bootlegging, Intrigue, as a legitimate business, should not be subject to the law. Even assuming, as we do, that Intrigue is a legitimate business, this argument lacks merit. The explicit language of the statute does not limit the CCTA to organized crime or bootlegging operations; any knowing possession, sale, or receipt of contraband cigarettes exposes one to liability under the statute. *See* 18 U.S.C. § 2342(a). Furthermore, it defies logic that, under a penal statute, a defendant who violated clear statutory provisions could escape punishment merely because his particular class of criminal offenders was unmentioned in the authorizing statute's legislative history.

For similar reasons, we reject Intrigue's argument that the CCTA is inapplicable to Intrigue because its operations were closely monitored by state and federal officials and because the United States offered no proof that it "evaded" tax laws. The CCTA does not require an intentional evasion of the law to prompt forfeiture of cigarettes. *Compare* 18 U.S.C. § 2344(a), (b) (requiring "knowing" violations to trigger criminal punishments), *with id.* § 2344(c) ("Any contraband cigarettes involved in any violation of the provisions of this chapter shall be subject to seizure and forfeiture."). We have previously held that the federal government may seize and forfeit cigarettes whenever they are found in a state in violation of that state's tax laws, regardless of the possessor's intent to evade state tax laws or its intent to distribute the cigarettes in another state. *Grey Poplars, Inc. v. 1,371,100 Assorted Brands of Cigarettes, 282 F.3d 1175, 1178 (9th Cir. 2002)*. This case is no exception.

Finally, we reject as factually unfounded Intrigue's argument that it owed no taxes because the cigarettes were in "joint possession" with NTI, Intrigue's sister corporation that was licensed to distribute cigarettes in California. Even Intrigue's CEO Andy Lee conceded during his deposition that, "Well, legally . . . Intrigue Trading, Inc. owned the product," agreeing that Intrigue "always had possession" of the cigarettes once they entered the FTZ. Intrigue offered no evidence indicating that it conveyed joint ownership rights over the cigarettes to NTI in a written document, as California law requires to establish joint ownership. *See Donovan v. Donovan, 223 Cal. App. 2d 691, 697, 36 Cal. Rptr. 225 (1964)* (citing *California Trust Co. v. Bennett, 33 Cal. 2d 694, 697, 204 P.2d 324 (1949))*. Nor did NTI demonstrate "possession" by exerting any control over or taking any action with regard to the 4,432 mastercases, other than paying the rent on the storage space where they were located. *See* Black's Law Dictionary 1201 (8th ed. 2004) (defining possession as "the exercise of dominion over property" or "[t]he right under which one may exercise control over something to the exclusion of all others"). Furthermore, there is no indication in the record that NTI reported the acquisition of the cigarettes to the California BOE, as it would have been required to do as a licensed distributor that believed itself to be a rightful owner. *See* Cal. Code Regs. tit. 18, §§ 4022, 4031. NTI does not cite to, and we cannot find, any authority suggesting that shared storage space creates this form of joint ownership or allows a company like Intrigue to piggyback on the license of a separate and independent corporation. Because there was no "joint possession" of the cigarettes, we need not decide whether "joint possession" by a licensed distributor could exempt a co-possessing unlicensed distributor from the California tax.

C. Preemption

Having concluded that California's cigarette tax applies to the storage of cigarettes in California destined for future out-of-state sale, we must reach the broader question whether the FTZ Act preempts all state and local efforts to impose taxes on merchandise stored within FTZs. We hold that it does not.

[20] Federal law may preempt state law under the Supremacy Clause of the Constitution. U.S. Const., art. VI, cl. 2. "Preemption can occur in one of three ways: express preemption by statute, occupation of the field, or conflict between state and federal regulation." *Air Conditioning & Refrigeration Inst. v. Energy Res. Conservation & Dev. Comm'n, 410 F.3d 492, 495 (9th Cir.), petition for cert. filed*, 74 U.S.L.W. (Sept. 12, 2005) (No. 05-331). In any consideration of preemption, we view the purpose and intent of Congress as the "ultimate touchstone," *Cipollone v. Liggett Group, Inc., 505 U.S. 504, 516, 112 S. Ct. 2608, 120 L. Ed. 2d 407 (1992)*,

and presume that Congress did not intend to supplant state law, *Air Conditioning & Refrigeration Inst., 410 F.3d at 496* (citing *Medtronic, Inc. v. Lohr, 518 U.S. 470, 485, 116 S. Ct. 2240, 135 L. Ed. 2d 700 (1996)).*

[21] The FTZ Act does not expressly preempt all state regulation and taxation. "Express preemption occurs when Congress enacts a statute that expressly commands that state law on the particular subject is displaced." *Gadda v. Ashcroft, 377 F.3d 934, 944 (9th Cir. 2004)*. The only express preemption in the FTZ Act is the prohibition on state and local ad valorem taxes. 19 U.S.C. § 81o(e). We view this limited statement of preemption through the canon of statutory construction *inclusio unius est exclusio alterius*, indicating Congress's lack of interest in more broadly limiting state power. *See Metrophones Telecomm., Inc. v. Global Crossing Telecomm., Inc., 423 F.3d 1056, 1072 (9th Cir. 2005)*; *United States v. Terrence, 132 F.3d 1291, 1294 (9th Cir. 1997)*; *see also 3M Health Care Ltd. v. Grant, 908 F.2d 918, 920-21 (11th Cir. 1990)* (concluding that the FTZ Act does not expressly preempt all state power over FTZs).

[22] Nor do we find that Congress has expressed an intent to occupy the entire field of activity around FTZs, such that state law should be preempted, or that state regulation creates an irreconcilable conflict with the FTZ Act and federal regulation. As the Supreme Court has explained:

> [Field preemption] may be inferred from a scheme of federal regulation . . . so pervasive as to make reasonable the inference that Congress left no room for the States to supplement it, or where an Act of Congress touch[es] a field in which the federal interest is so dominant that the federal system will be assumed to preclude enforcement of state laws on the same subject.

English v. Gen. Elec. Co., 496 U.S. 72, 79, 110 S. Ct. 2270, 110 L. Ed. 2d 65 (1990) (internal quotation marks omitted). State law may also be preempted where it would be impossible for a party to comply with both state and federal requirements or where the state law would "stand[] as an obstacle to the accomplishment and execution of the full purposes and objectives of Congress." *Id.*(internal quotation marks omitted).

As discussed above, *supra*at pp. *6029-30*, there is significant federal control over the "field" of FTZs. However, several factors militate against applying field preemption in this arena. First, the federal regulations implementing the CCTA, which Congress enacted forty-five years after the passage of the FTZ Act, envision that certain activities within an FTZ would remain subject to state cigarette taxes. Those regulations exempt from the CCTA both cigarettes in the stream of international commerce and domestic cigarettes destined for export, but not those like Intrigue's that have been entered into the United States for domestic consumption. In defining parties exempted from the CCTA, 27 C.F.R. § 646.143 includes "[a]ny person who is . . . (g) Operating within a foreign-trade zone established under 19 U.S.C., section 81b, when the cigarettes involved have been entered into the zone [pending foreign export]or, in respect to foreign cigarettes, have been admitted into the zone but have not been entered in the United States." The 4,432 mastercases at issue here do not fall within either of these exceptions. They had already passed through Customs in Miami, so they were no longer "foreign cigarettes," nor were they destined for foreign export. By implication then, the federal government has acknowledged that states retain taxing authority over some products within FTZs. Otherwise, the regulation would have exempted *every*person operating within an FTZ.

Second, the Supreme Court itself has indicated that the federal interest in domestic-bound goods stored in FTZs is not so dominant as to completely preclude state activity in this field. In a pair of cases from the 1980s, *Xerox Corp. v. Harris County, Texas, 459 U.S. 145, 103 S. Ct. 523, 74 L. Ed. 2d 323 (1982)* and *R.J. Reynolds Tobacco Co. v. Durham County, North Carolina, 479 U.S. 130, 107 S. Ct. 499, 93 L. Ed. 2d 449 (1986)*, the Supreme Court addressed this same preemption question in the context of customs-bonded warehouses. Customs-bonded warehouses ("CBWs") and FTZs are functionally quite similar and often treated as one and the same. An importer may store goods in a CBW, just as he would in an FTZ, without paying duties until the products leave the CBW for domestic consumption. Also like in an FTZ, goods in the stream of foreign commerce may be temporarily stored in a CBW, and may be manipulated, combined, or re-packaged before being sent abroad again, all without paying American duties. CBWs, however, need not be located adjacent to ports; the importer must pay a bond for the right to store merchandise in a CBW, which he gets back when the products are re-exported or domestic duties are paid; and the duties owed on goods that have been manipulated are set at the time of withdrawal from the warehouse (whereas an importer using an FTZ can choose whether to pay duties on the imported raw goods or the manipulated final product).[9] From a customs perspective though, FTZs and CBWs are far more alike than they are different.

In *Xerox*, the Supreme Court struck down an ad valorem property tax the Texas county sought to impose on copiers that had been built in Mexico and were being stored in a CBW until they could be sent to distributors in Latin America. The Court's reasoning combined elements of field preemption and conflict preemption. The Court first pointed to "the continuous control and supervision" of Customs officials over CBWs and the "[d]etailed regulations control[ling] every aspect of the manner in which the warehouses are to be operated," 459 U.S. at 150, which demonstrated a "pervasive" system of regulation, id. at 153. Then, after reviewing the legislative history of the Warehousing Act of 1846 and Congress's purpose in establishing CBWs, the Court also held that the state tax would "offset substantially the very benefits Congress intended to confer" in creating CBWs. *Id.*

[23] Four years later, in *R.J. Reynolds*, the Supreme Court clarified its preemption reasoning. The *R.J. Reynolds* Court held that a county was not preempted from

9 United States Customs & Border Protection, *U.S. Customs Bonded Warehouse* (2001), www.cbp.gov/linkhandler/cgov/toolbox/publications/trade/bonded_ 20wh2.ctt/bonded_20wh2.doc.

imposing an ad valorem tax on foreign tobacco that R.J. Reynolds was storing and aging in CBWs, because Reynolds ultimately intended to enter the tobacco into the United States for domestic manufacturing and consumption. At the beginning of its analysis, the Court explicitly pulled back from any "field preemptive" language in *Xerox*. *R.J. Reynolds, 479 U.S. at 142* ("[The *Xerox* Court] limited its preemption analysis to whether taxation would impede the congressional objectives."); *see also* id. at 149 ("[T]he [customs] regulations, while detailed, appear to contemplate some concurrent state regulation and, arguably, even state taxation."). Then, after reviewing the same legislative history of the Warehousing Act of 1846 that it had examined in *Xerox*, the Court found that local taxes on imports destined for domestic consumption would not obstruct congressional objectives. Id. at 142-43 & n.10, 148. Seven years later, the Court reiterated that Congress had not occupied the entire field of taxation with regard to CBWs:

> [W]e have not held that state taxation of goods in bonded warehouses is preempted by Congress' intent to occupy the field of bonded warehouse regulation. In fact, in *R.J. Reynolds* we specifically held that the bonded warehouse statutes and regulations did not evidence such a purpose. *Itel Containers Int'l Corp. v. Huddleston, 507 U.S. 60, 71, 113 S. Ct. 1095, 122 L. Ed. 2d 421 (1993)*. For the same reasons, we hold that state regulation and taxation of goods in FTZs are not prohibited under the doctrine of "field preemption."

[24] With respect to conflict preemption, we read *Xerox* and *R.J. Reynolds* as drawing a clear distinction between goods within the stream of international commerce and goods destined for domestic consumption. In the former case, where federal duties are not even due, local taxation would inhibit the use of American ports; in the latter, federal duties will already be required and an exemption from local taxation would provide a windfall for foreign manufacturers that domestic manufacturers do not receive, hardly the aim of the statute. *R.J. Reynolds, 479 U.S. at 144-46*. As the Court explained: "There is no indication in the legislative history of the Warehousing Act that one of the goals of the [CBW] system was to benefit imported goods in their competition with domestic goods." Id. at 145 n.14. Therefore, "[p]ermitting imposition of a tax . . . leads to equal treatment for imported and domestic tobacco." Id. at 147. This bifurcated approach to CBWs, treating goods differently depending on whether they are in foreign transshipment or destined for domestic consumption, is also consistent with the approach taken by California's courts. *See Am. Smelting & Refining Co. v. County of Contra Costa, 271 Cal. App. 2d 437, 474, 77 Cal. Rptr. 570 (1969)* (concluding that "the laws and regulations relating specifically to [CBWs] do not . . . confer an immunity from a non-discriminatory tax on property of foreign origin being processed for domestic consumption").

The reasoning of the *R.J. Reynolds* opinion applies with equal force to FTZs. Intrigue cites dicta in a footnote to the *R.J. Reynolds* opinion to argue that the holding of that case should not extend from CBWs to FTZs. In its opinion at footnote 22, the *R.J. Reynolds* Court sought to explain why the then-recently passed 19 U.S.C.

§ 81o(e), which explicitly prohibited ad valorem taxes in FTZs, did not preclude it from approving an ad valorem tax in a CBW. After noting the limited scope of the 1984 amendment that inserted § 81o(e), the Court explained:

> Foreign trade zones are valued because they actually promote domestic industry and create jobs [citing 129 Cong. Rec. 14501 (1983) (remarks of Sen. Bentsen)]. Given that the taxation of goods in foreign trade zones could arguably harm domestic industry, while exemption from taxation of the imported goods in the present case would serve to discriminate against domestic producers, there appears to be a sufficient justification for the difference in state taxation with respect to these customs entities. *R.J. Reynolds, 479 U.S. at 151 n.22.* We are unpersuaded that the dicta in footnote 22 compels the result Intrigue seeks.

We conclude that, outside the context of ad valorem taxes (which Congress expressly prohibited for property in FTZs), there is no reason to treat the two facilities differently. FTZs and CBWs serve almost identical roles in our system of interstate commerce. The legislative history of the Warehousing Act of 1846, which enabled the creation of customs-bonded warehouses, indicates that the aim of CBWs was twofold: granting flexibility to importers as to when they pay their duties (duties need only be paid when the goods are removed from the CBW and entered into the United States); and encouraging shippers to utilize American ports as a way station in international commerce (because duties are never required if the goods are re-exported directly from the CBW). *See R.J. Reynolds, 479 U.S. at 145-47* & nn.14-16 (providing detailed analysis of legislative history of Warehousing Act).

Foreign trade zones were created by Congress for the same basic purposes. Although there is no formal legislative history for the 1934 FTZ Act, its stated purpose was "to expedite and encourage foreign commerce, and for other purposes." Act of June 18, 1934, 48 Stat. 998, 998. Congress's twin aims in passing the FTZ Act, further encouraging use of United States ports in the flow of interstate commerce and enabling manipulation of foreign goods before they are imported, are apparent from the face of the statute. *See* 19 U.S.C. § 81c(a); *see also 3M Health Care, 908 F.2d at 921* ("[T]he goal of the [FTZ Act] is straightforward-to facilitate the use of U.S. ports for the transshipment of goods in foreign commerce."); *Fountain v. New Orleans Pub. Serv., Inc., 387 F.2d 343, 344 (5th Cir. 1967)* ("The purpose of [FTZs] is to expedite and encourage foreign commerce . . . without subjecting same to the customs laws of the United States."); *A.T. Cross, 467 F. Supp. at 50* (suggesting that the purpose of the FTZ Act is to allow American workers and companies to "profit from the breaking down, repacking and relabeling of the goods" temporarily stored there).

Moreover, the reasons given in *R.J. Reynolds* for distinguishing FTZs from CBWs are inapplicable here. When goods like cigarettes are bound for domestic use already, as Intrigue's were, exempting them from state cigarette taxes because they are stored in an FTZ will not adversely affect domestic industry or job creation. Indeed, like the local tobacco growers in *R.J. Reynolds*, domestic cigarette distributors would be disadvantaged by allowing Intrigue a tax exemption not afforded to unlicensed distributors storing cigarettes elsewhere in California. Allowing California to impose its tax on domestic-bound cigarettes would lead to "equal treatment for imported and domestic" cigarettes. *R.J. Reynolds, 479 U.S. at 147.*

The Eleventh Circuit similarly has found the *Xerox/R.J. Reynolds* dichotomy relevant in the context of FTZs. *See 3M Health Care, 908 F.2d 918.* The court in *3M Health Care* blocked Florida's effort to apply its Drug and Cosmetic Act to foreign pharmaceuticals being stored in an FTZ for eventual transshipment to Latin American countries. Id. at 919. Performing a similar preemption analysis, the Eleventh Circuit held that allowing Florida to regulate products that would never actually enter the domestic market would "encumber the ease of transshipment through the zones . . . [and] frustrate[] the goal of the Foreign Trade Zones Act." Id. at 921. In doing so, the Eleventh Circuit relied on the Supreme Court's *Xerox/R.J. Reynolds* distinction between goods that are in transshipment and those destined for domestic sale. Id. at 922 n.6.

[25] We find distinguishable the state and federal cases cited by Intrigue that have limited state taxing authority within FTZs. *See Hostetter v. Idlewild Bon Voyage Liquor Corp., 377 U.S. 324, 333-34, 84 S. Ct. 1293, 12 L. Ed. 2d 350 (1964)* (holding that New York lacked power to regulate duty-free liquor shops, which are technically FTZs, in airports); *McGoldrick v. Gulf Oil Corp., 309 U.S. 414, 428-29, 60 S. Ct. 664, 84 L. Ed. 840, Treas. Dec. 50200 (1940)* (holding that New York did not have the power to tax oil imported into a customs-bonded warehouse that was then reprocessed and sold to vessels in foreign commerce); *During v. Valente, 267 A.D. 383, 46 N.Y.S.2d 385, 387 (App. Div. 1944)* (holding that sale of alcohol in an FTZ "was not subject to local regulation or tax"). All of these cases addressed state regulation or taxation of goods that were in the stream of foreign commerce, as opposed to goods like Intrigue's cigarettes that were destined for domestic consumption. Moreover, all of these cases pre-date the Supreme Court's opinion in *R.J. Reynolds*. We believe that, post-*R.J. Reynolds*, the operative framework is the transshipment/domestic consumption dichotomy, and we will straightforwardly follow it. Because Intrigue's cigarettes were bound for domestic consumption and there is not "any suggestion that taxation here would conflict with the central purpose" of our country's system of foreign trade zones, *R.J. Reynolds, 479 U.S. at 148*, we fail to see any conflict between imposition of the California cigarette tax and the goals of the FTZ Act. That the CCTA regulations exempt from forfeiture all cigarettes in an FTZ except for those in the situation presented here ("domestic status" cigarettes) only confirms the correctness of this result. 27 C.F.R. § 646.143(g).

[26] We therefore hold that state excise taxes on merchandise stored in FTZs for eventual domestic consumption are not expressly preempted by federal law. Nor has the federal scheme for FTZs so occupied the field as to prohibit state taxation. Finally, imposition of California's cigarette tax does not create an irreconcilable

conflict with the FTZ laws, at least when the goods taxed are already duty-paid and bound for domestic consumption.[10]

IV. ATTORNEYS' FEES

[27] The district court awarded attorneys' fees based on its grant of summary judgment to Intrigue. Because we reverse that judgment, we vacate the fee award. *Baffert v. Cal. Horse Racing Bd., 332 F.3d 613, 617 (9th Cir. 2003)*; *Lovell v. Poway Unified Sch. Dist., 90 F.3d 367, 373-74 (9th Cir. 1996).*

V. CONCLUSION

California has made the decision to impose its cigarette tax on unlicensed distributors who store cigarettes within the state for future sale in another state, including those cigarettes stored in FTZs. That decision is not preempted by the express language of the Foreign Trade Zones Act, nor does it conflict with the general purpose or intent of Congress in establishing foreign trade zones. Though Intrigue's motives may have been pure, and it may simply be the victim of bad legal advice or a poor gamble on the outcome of unsettled law, Intrigue's cigarettes were ultimately found in California without California tax stamps. That was sufficient, under the CCTA, to allow the federal government to seize and forfeit them.

The storage of goods in foreign trade zones is "closely regulated," and Customs officials are empowered by statute to search and inspect merchandise in foreign trade zones without a warrant. Customs officials had probable cause to believe that Intrigue's cigarettes were counterfeit, and it lawfully seized them. Probable cause for the seizure never dissipated, because the Rudalevige test was not conclusive and because, by the time the cigarettes were demonstrated to be genuine, the Customs Service had developed probable cause to believe that the cigarettes otherwise violated importation laws. The search and seizure both comported with the Fourth Amendment.

We therefore **AFFIRM** the denial of the motion to suppress,

REVERSE the grant of summary judgment,

VACATE the award of attorneys' fees, and

REMAND with instructions that summary judgment be granted to the United States.

---

10 We do not reach the question of whether a state or local tax imposed on domestic-bound goods that have not yet been "entered into" the United States would conflict with the purpose of the FTZ Act.

UNITED STATES OF AMERICA
v.
STEFAN IRVING

452 F.3d 110 (2d Cir. 2006)
Decided June 23, 2006

Before: CARDAMONE, JACOBS, and CABRANES, Circuit Judges.

OPINION

REVISED OPINION

CARDAMONE, *Circuit Judge*:

The United States petitions for rehearing following our decision in *United States v. Irving, 432 F.3d 401 (2d Cir. 2005)*, that vacated two counts upon which defendant Stefan Irving was convicted. Upon consideration of the petition for rehearing, it is granted. We withdraw the majority opinion along with the concurring and dissenting opinion filed December 23, 2005, and Irving's convictions on counts two and three previously vacated are now affirmed in the revised opinion that follows.

Defendant Stefan Irving (defendant or appellant) appeals from a judgment entered on February 23, 2004 in the United States District Court for the Southern District of New York (Kaplan, J.) convicting him, following a jury trial, of two counts of traveling outside the United States for the purpose of engaging in sexual acts with children under the age of 18, in violation of 18 U.S.C. § 2423(b); one count of traveling outside the United States for the purpose of engaging in sexual acts with children under the age of 12, in violation of 18 U.S.C. § 2241(c); one count of receiving images of child pornography, in violation of 18 U.S.C. § 2252A(a)(2)(B); and one count of possessing child pornography in violation of 18 U.S.C. § 2252A(a)(5)(B). Following his conviction on all counts, Irving received a sentence of 262 months of imprisonment followed by 60 months of supervised release, a $ 200,000 fine, and a $ 500 special assessment. He appeals from his judgment of conviction and his sentence.

For the reasons stated below, we affirm defendant's convictions on all counts—count one, traveling to Mexico in violation of 18 U.S.C. § 2423(b), count two, traveling to Honduras in violation of 18 U.S.C. § 2423(b), count three, traveling to Honduras in violation of 18 U.S.C. § 2241(c), and counts four and five, receiving and possessing images of child pornography in violation of 18 U.S.C. § 2252A(a)(2)(B) and 18 § 2252A(a)(5)(B). But, because the district court treated the Sentencing Guidelines as mandatory, we remand for consideration of whether resentencing is warranted under *United States v. Crosby, 397 F.3d 103 (2d Cir. 2005).*

BACKGROUND

Defendant is a former chief pediatrician for the Middletown, New York school district. On April 29, 1983 while employed as school physician, he was convicted of attempted sexual abuse in the first degree of a seven-year-old boy that resulted in the revocation of his license to practice medicine in New York, and a sentence of 16 to 48 months imprisonment. Thirteen years later in 1996, the federal government initiated a nationwide investigation of individuals suspected of traveling to Mexico for the purpose of engaging in sexual acts with children. Defendant became a target of that investigation which ultimately led to the criminal proceedings before us on this appeal.

A. 1998 Mexico Trip

In May 1998 Irving traveled to Acapulco, Mexico to visit Castillo Vista del Mar, a guest house that served as a place where men from the United States could have sexual relations with Mexican boys. When defendant visited, seven or eight boys ranging in age from eight to 20 years old were residing there. Irving learned of Castillo Vista del Mar from Robert Decker—its then manager, and a friend from the 1970s.

Decker testified that prior to visiting, Irving asked if specific boys—whom he knew from previous visits—would be there. Decker said Irving specifically asked about an eight-year-old boy. Decker testified further that he saw Irving fondle some of the boys who lived at the guest house while swimming with them. He also stated he saw defendant go upstairs to his bedroom at various times with different boys. Decker said that during Irving's visit the two of them discussed a previous trip to Honduras that Irving had taken, trips to the beaches he took while there, and the boys he met. One of the boys at the guest house when Irving visited, Jesus Santiago Percastegui, corroborated relevant portions of Decker's testimony. Although unable to identify Irving in court, this witness stated that he saw "Esteban" (the name by which he knew Irving) at the beach caressing two other boys that lived at the guest house and twice go upstairs to his room with them.

Decker admitted while he was in Mexico he experienced financial difficulties, and that Irving gave him ATM cards, connected to an account he funded, up until

Decker's September 2000 arrest. Irving gave Decker over $ 5,000 in support over the years. The two men also communicated regularly. Irving provided Decker with Internet web addresses of sites containing child pornography and on one occasion gave him images of boys engaged in sex acts with each other, with men, or by themselves. Irving told Decker he preferred prepubescent boys, under the age of 11, and that he preferred oral sex or fondling.

Upon returning to the United States from Mexico on May 27, 1998 through the Dallas-Fort Worth Airport, defendant was stopped by United States Customs inspectors. This search was prompted by Special Agent Robert Casey who was in California investigating Irving. Special Agent Casey directed Special Agent Edwin B. Rehkopf, stationed at the Dallas-Fort Worth Airport, to search and interview Irving upon his arrival there.

The initial search of Irving's luggage revealed children's books and drawings that appeared to be drawn by children, but nothing necessarily incriminating. Nonetheless, the Customs agents questioned defendant further. Defendant admitted he was a convicted pedophile, but denied having visited Decker. Instead, he told the agents he had visited another friend. A second search of Irving's luggage revealed a disposable camera and two 3.5 inch computer diskettes, which the agents said they would need to examine. Irving denied having any child pornography on either the diskettes or the camera and refused to sign a Customs form consenting to their seizure. The film Irving was carrying turned out to have pictures taken at Castillo Vista del Mar of the defendant with Decker and with boys. Images of child erotica were found on the diskettes.

B. Arrest and Search of Defendant's Home

Jerome A. Coleman, a special agent of the United States Bureau of Immigration and Customs Enforcement (BICE), and other BICE agents arrested Irving five years later at his apartment in Brooklyn on May 6, 2003. While executing the arrest warrant at the apartment, Agent Coleman observed a personal computer and monitor. Based upon his 15 years of experience and formal training concerning the importation and distribution of child pornography, Agent Coleman knew that pedophiles often use computers to communicate and to exploit children, by making travel arrangements on the Internet to facilitate travel with the intention of engaging in sex acts with children or sharing data with other pedophiles that involves the exploitation of children.

Existence of the computer and other information led him to apply for a search warrant for defendant's apartment. In a supporting affidavit, Agent Coleman listed a number of reasons for his suspicion that Irving's apartment and specifically his computer might contain evidence of child exploitation. First, he relied on Decker's statements, which indicated that: (1) Irving used his home and office computers to communicate with fellow boy lovers and to send and receive pornographic pictures depicting children engaged in sexual acts; (2) Irving's purpose in visiting

Mexico, and specifically Castillo Vista del Mar, was to engage in sex with boys; and (3) Irving photographed boys he found attractive in Mexico, but was careful to destroy incriminating pictures before returning to the United States. Second, Coleman explained that pedophiles often use their computers to facilitate the exploitation of children. Third, he noted that Irving's work computer did not contain any incriminating material, thus suggesting, on the basis of Decker's statements, that such materials would be found on Irving's home computer. Fourth, he enumerated the items found in Irving's luggage at the Dallas-Fort Worth Airport in 1998, and noted defendant's prior conviction for attempted sexual abuse in 1983. Fifth, Agent Coleman stated that three children who had spent time at Castillo Vista del Mar identified Irving (from a photograph) as one of the men at the guest house who had sexually abused boys while there. Sixth, he described the contents of various letters Irving wrote discussing exploitation of children that had allegedly already occurred, or that Irving hoped would occur, one of which was dated as recent as 2001. Based on this affidavit a magistrate judge in the Eastern District of New York issued a search warrant two days later on May 8, 2003 for Irving's apartment.

Armed with the warrant, BICE agents searched and seized there, among other things, Irving's home computer, which contained 76 video files, or MPEG files. The trial judge allowed, over defendant's objection, two of these video files to be played for the jury for a minute or less each. Agent Coleman explained they revealed "prepubescent boys engaging in various sexual acts with each other and in other cases of sexual acts by themselves." The agent further testified that all 76 files contained essentially the same content as that revealed in the two files played for the jury.

C. 1999 Honduras Trip

During the search of Irving's apartment agents discovered Irving's passport, which showed a visit to Honduras on January 1, 1999. Defendant's bank records reflected a cash withdrawal from his account on January 4, 1999 in La Ceiba, Honduras, and his employment records indicated he was on vacation from January 1 to January 10, 1999. Although at trial Irving never explicitly admitted to being in Honduras during this period, his personal journal covering those dates discusses a trip from the United States to Honduras and details his activities while there, particularly his luring of a 12-year-old boy back to his hotel with him and the sexual activities in which they engaged.

The journal also mentions meetings with other children, the weather, getting in and out of the country, food, and other innocuous topics. The January 4, 1999 journal entry describes his attempts to make a bank withdrawal on that date in La Ceiba. The journal, employment records, bank statement, and passport constitute the government's evidence that defendant traveled to Honduras, and that he did so for the purpose of engaging in sexual acts with children.

D. Trial Proceedings

Two months prior to the start of Irving's trial on September 23, 2003 defendant moved to suppress all evidence that was obtained (1) pursuant to the May 8, 2003 search warrant, (2) through photo identifications of defendant by children in Mexico, (3) from Irving at the Dallas-Fort Worth Airport, including information from his statements to Customs agents, and (4) from defendant's correspondence or photographs regarding minors produced at any time other than those times referred to in the superseding indictment. The district court denied the suppression motion. At the close of the trial the jury convicted defendant on all counts. Irving then unsuccessfully filed a motion for a new trial on October 22, 2003. The district court sentenced him to 262 months imprisonment on each count, to run concurrently, five years of supervised release, a $ 200,000 fine, and a $ 500 special assessment. This appeal ensued.

DISCUSSION

Irving raises a number of issues on appeal, most of which we find unavailing. We turn to an analysis of the issues.

I Sufficiency of Proof

Irving contends the district court erred in denying his Fed. R. Crim. P. 29(c) motion for a judgment of acquittal because the government proffered insufficient evidence to support counts one through three, which charged him with: traveling to Mexico with intent to engage in sexual acts with minors (count one); traveling to Honduras with intent to engage in sexual acts with minors (count two); and traveling to Honduras with intent to engage in a sexual act with a person not yet 12 years of age (count three).

A. Rule 29

Rule 29(c)(2) states that "[i]f the jury has returned a guilty verdict, the court may set aside the verdict and enter an acquittal." Fed. R. Crim. P. 29(c)(2). A Rule 29 motion should be granted only if the district court concludes there is "no evidence upon which a reasonable mind might fairly conclude guilt beyond a reasonable doubt." *United States v. Taylor, 464 F.2d 240, 243 (2d Cir. 1972).*

To succeed on his challenges regarding sufficiency Irving carries a heavy burden, and must show that when viewing the evidence in its totality, in a light most favorable to the government, and drawing all inferences in favor of the prosecution, no rational trier of fact could have found him guilty. *See Jackson v. Virginia, 443 U.S. 307, 319, 99 S. Ct. 2781, 61 L. Ed. 2d 560 (1979)*; *United States v. Gaines, 295 F.3d 293, 299-300 (2d Cir. 2002)*. A jury may convict on circumstantial evidence alone. *United States v. Martinez, 54 F.3d 1040, 1043 (2d Cir. 1995)*. On appeal, we review the disposition of the *Rule 29(c)* motion *de novo*, applying the same standards as the district court. *United States v. Reyes, 302 F.3d 48, 52-53 (2d Cir. 2002).*

According to Irving the evidence was insufficient on count one, the Mexico travel count, and on counts two and three, the Honduras travel counts, because his convictions on these counts improperly relied on uncorroborated writings in his personal journal. With respect to defendant's Mexican trip there was ample evidence, including Decker's testimony and Jesus Percastegui's testimony, as well as pictures of Irving with children in Mexico, on which the jury could rely to convict him. With regard to counts two and three, we must turn to an examination of the corroboration rule.

B. Corpus Delicti/Corroboration Rule Issue

Traditionally, the corroboration rule, historically termed the *corpus delicti* rule, applied only to a defendant's confession, but over time has been expanded to apply to admissions and exculpatory statements. *See* 1 John W. Strong, *McCormick on Evidence* § 145, at 521 (5th ed. 1999); *see also Opper v. United States, 348 U.S. 84, 90-91, 75 S. Ct. 158, 99 L. Ed. 101 (1954)* (holding that "accused's admissions of essential facts or elements of the crime, subsequent to the crime, are of the same character as confessions and that corroboration should be required"). Historically, and still in many jurisdictions, courts adhering to the corroboration rule demanded that prosecutors present evidence other than the defendant's confession, admission, or exculpatory statement to prove the *corpus delicti* or "body of the crime." Strong, *supra*, § 145, at 525. Generally, the *corpus delicti* is understood to include the actual injury or harm, i.e., the dead body in a murder case, and proof that the harm or injury was caused by defendant's criminal activity. *Id.*

In *Opper*, the Supreme Court rejected this traditional understanding of the *corpus delicti* rule, and held instead that the corroborating evidence need not prove the essential elements of the crime. *See 348 U.S. at 93*. Rather, the corroboration must prove that the confession was reliable, and must prove any elements of the crime to which the defendant did not confess. But the confession, if proven reliable, may serve as the only evidence reaching the *corpus delicti*. *See* id. at 93-94; *see also Smith v. United States, 348 U.S. 147, 156, 75 S. Ct. 194, 99 L. Ed. 192, 1954-2 C.B. 225 (1954)* ("All elements of the offense must be established by independent evidence or corroborated admissions, but one available mode of corroboration is for the independent evidence to bolster the confession itself and thereby prove the offense 'through' the statements of the accused."). Although the corroborative evidence need not independently prove the injury or harm resulting from the crime, it must "support[] the *essential* facts admitted sufficiently to justify a jury inference of their truth." *Opper, 348 U.S. at 93* (emphasis added).

In applying *Opper*, we have held: "[T]he modern corroboration rule requires only that there be 'substantial independent evidence which would tend to establish the trustworthiness of the statement.'" *United States v. Bryce, 208 F.3d 346, 354 (2000)*. The corroboration rule thus serves a "gatekeeping function" in that it prevents juries from convicting on unreliable evidence. *Id.*

For purposes of the corroboration rule, there are two types of confessions or admissions:

> those that bear insufficient indicia of reliability as proof of the defendant's commission of the offense to support a finding of guilt beyond a reasonable doubt, and those that, considering the nature and the context of the defendant's words, demonstrate his commission of the offense so reliably that, without need of other supporting evidence, they can support a finding of guilt beyond a reasonable doubt.

Id. at 355. Some examples of self-corroborating statements—statements so reliable in and of themselves that they require no corroborative evidence—are statements made prior to the commission of the crime, *see Warszower v. United States, 312 U.S. 342, 347, 61 S. Ct. 603, 85 L. Ed. 876 (1941)*, and statements made between co-conspirators to accomplish the ends of their criminal enterprise, *see United States v. Simmons, 923 F.2d 934, 954 (2d Cir. 1991)*.

We need not reach the question of whether the journal is self-corroborating because we conclude that the evidence in the record provides adequate corroboration.

To determine that an admission has been adequately corroborated, we must find in the record "substantial independent evidence which would tend to establish the trustworthiness of the statement." *Opper, 348 U.S. at 93*. With respect to Irving's journal, the government points to the following corroborating evidence: (1) Decker's testimony that Irving had sexual interests in young boys, traveled to foreign nations to act on those interests, and discussed a prior trip to Honduras and the boys he met there with Decker; (2) Irving's behavior on the Mexico trip; (3) Irving's employment records and his passport, which showed he traveled to Honduras on the relevant dates; and (4) the bank records showing a withdrawal in La Ceiba, Honduras on January 4, 1999, corresponding to the journal entry on that date discussing a trip to the bank in La Ceiba.

We are persuaded that such evidence corroborates defendant's journal. First, the passport, employment and ATM records are circumstantial evidence corroborating Irving's travel to Honduras during the time of the events described in the journal. Second, evidence of Irving's acts in Mexico establishes the veracity of Irving's criminal intent as exhibited in the journal. Related to this point, we are comfortable that Irving's Mexico acts may be used to corroborate his Honduras journal without running afoul of the rule of evidence that prohibits propensity evidence. *See* Fed. R. Evid. 404(a) (generally prohibiting evidence of a defendant's character through prior or other acts "for the purpose of proving action in conformity therewith on a particular occasion"). Federal Rule of Evidence 404(b) guides us here. It provides that although evidence of other crimes or acts is usually inadmissible to prove propensity to commit the same or similar acts, such evidence "may, however, be admissible for other purposes, such as proof of motive . . . [or] *intent* . . . ." Fed. R. Evid. 404(b) (emphasis added). Because the jury may consider Irving's Mexico acts as proof of the intent element of Irving's Honduras crimes, it follows that the Mexico acts are likewise admissible to corroborate his confession in his journal to those crimes in Honduras. Accordingly, we hold the prosecution presented substantial independent evidence necessary to establish the trustworthiness of Irving's journal.

Irving's burden with respect to sufficiency of the evidence is weighty, and it has not been met in this case. Viewing the evidence in its totality and drawing all inferences in favor of the government, the evidence is sufficient to allow any reasonable juror to find defendant guilty on counts two and three beyond a reasonable doubt. The district court did not err in failing to grant Irving's Rule 29 motion with respect to those counts, and we therefore affirm appellant's conviction on them.

II Receiving and Distributing Pornographic Materials (Counts Four and Five)

Irving additionally maintains there was insufficient proof for the jury to convict him on count four, which charged him with receiving and distributing material that contains child pornography in violation of 18 U.S.C. § 2252A(a)(2)(B), and count five, which charged him with possession of an image containing child pornography in violation of 18 U.S.C. § 2252A(a)(5)(B). Irving's argument is that (1) the government failed to proffer evidence beyond the videos themselves to prove that the children in the videos were in fact real children, and (2) there was no proof that he willfully downloaded the images onto his computer. Although the trial court carefully instructed the jury using a constitutionally permissible definition of child pornography, Irving contends the jury may have convicted him for possession and receipt of child pornography that did not contain real children and thus might have violated his First Amendment right to freedom of speech. We use the same sufficiency of the evidence standard set forth earlier to determine whether Irving's challenge with respect to counts four and five should succeed.

A. Extrinsic Evidence of Use of Real Children

To convict Irving under counts four and five the prosecution had to show that appellant knowingly received or possessed materials containing child pornography. *See* 18 U.S.C. § 2252A(a)(2)(B) and (a)(5)(B). Accordingly, Irving insists the prosecution was required to prove, by expert testimony, that the 76 video files depicted real, as opposed to virtual, children. It is well established that a statute which prohibits a substantial amount of protected speech, is unconstitutional on its face. *See Ashcroft v. Free Speech Coal., 535 U.S. 234, 244, 122 S. Ct. 1389, 152 L. Ed. 2d 403 (2002)*. Yet freedom of speech is not completely without bounds. Certain categories of speech such as defamation, incitement, obscenity, and pornography produced using real children, may be barred without trespassing on individual First Amendment rights. *See* id. at 245-46.

In *Free Speech Coalition* the Supreme Court ruled that two of the definitions of child pornography adopted by the Child Pornography Prevention Act of 1996 (Act), 18 U.S.C. § 2251, et seq., were overbroad and hence violated the First Amendment on their face. *See* 535 U.S. at 258. The first, § 2256(8)(B), defined child pornography as a "visual depiction [that] is, or appears to be, of a minor engaging in sexually explicit conduct." 18 U.S.C. § 2256(8)(B) (1996) (invalidated 2002, amended 2003). The second, § 2256(8)(D), defined child pornography as a "visual depiction [that] is advertised, promoted, presented, described, or distributed in such a manner that conveys the impression that the material is or contains a visual depiction of a minor engaging in sexually explicit conduct." 18 U.S.C. § 2256(8)(D) (1996) (invalidated 2002, amended 2003). The "appears to be" and "in such a manner that" language, the Supreme Court held, reached constitutionally protected speech because these phrases did not restrict the definition of child pornography to obscene material or to material that was itself the product of sexual abuse. *See Free Speech Coal., 535 U.S. at 240, 251* (citing *Miller v. California, 413 U.S. 15, 24, 93 S. Ct. 2607, 37 L. Ed. 2d 419 (1973)*, which defines obscenity, and *New York v. Ferber, 458 U.S. 747, 761, 102 S. Ct. 3348, 73 L. Ed. 2d 1113 (1982)*, which holds that states may constitutionally prohibit the creation or promotion of child pornography not meeting the *Miller* standard).

Obscene material is that which taken as a whole, appeals to the prurient interest, is patently offensive in light of community standards, and lacks serious literary, artistic, political, or scientific value. *See Miller, 413 U.S. at 24.* In *Free Speech Coalition*, the Court explained that states may prohibit child pornography that fails to meet the *Miller* obscenity standard if it is the product of sexual abuse of actual children. *535 U.S. at 249.* In his brief to this Court, Irving urges that the holding of *Free Speech Coalition* necessarily created a bright-line rule requiring the government to present evidence, other than the unlawful images themselves, to prove beyond a reasonable doubt that the pictures were created using real children. A careful reading of the Supreme Court's opinion does not support Irving's view of it. Although the Supreme Court noted the possible evidentiary difficulty of distinguishing virtual and actual child pornography, it did not establish a bright-line rule requiring that the government proffer a specific type of proof to show the use of an actual child. *Id. at 254-56.*

Nor does Irving's interpretation of *Free Speech Coalition* find support in our sister circuits. Since the First Circuit vacated its decision in *United States v. Hilton, 363 F.3d 58 (1st Cir.), vacated, 386 F.3d 13 (1st Cir. 2004)*, which had adopted a rule similar to the one Irving urges us to adopt, it now appears that none of the circuits that have addressed the effect of *Free Speech Coalition* on the government's burden of proof in child pornography prosecutions has adopted the bright-line rule pressed by Irving in this case; that is, that *Free Speech Coalition* increased the government's burden of proof regarding the actuality requirement.

The Eighth Circuit, for example, has declined to alter its previous rule—that it would uphold "a jury's conclusion that real children were depicted even where the images themselves were the only evidence the government presented on the subject"—following *Free Speech Coalition. United States v. Deaton, 328 F.3d 454,*

455 (8th Cir. 2003) (per curiam). The Fifth, Sixth, and Tenth Circuits agree that *Free Speech Coalition* does not lay down "the absolute requirement that, absent direct evidence of identity, expert testimony is required to prove that the prohibited images are of real, not virtual, children." *United States v. Kimler, 335 F.3d 1132, 1142 (10th Cir. 2003)*; *see United States v. Farrelly, 389 F.3d 649, 653-54 (6th Cir. 2004)*; *United States v. Slanina, 359 F.3d 356, 357 (5th Cir. 2004)* (per curiam).

We have not had occasion to address the effect of *Free Speech Coalition* on the government's evidentiary burden with respect to the actuality requirement. On the basis of the facts of this case and our own interpretation of Free Speech Coalition, we reject Irving's claim that the government must present extrinsic evidence. Although Irving's objections to the presentence investigation report included a claim that the government failed to carry its burden of proving beyond a reasonable doubt that certain images did contain real children, appellant points to no evidence suggesting that the images were not created using actual children. Further, the superseding indictment specifically made reference to the constitutionally valid definition of child pornography

> any visual depiction, including any photograph, film, video, picture, or computer or computer-generated image or picture, whether made or produced by electronic, mechanical, or other means, of sexually explicit conduct, where—
>
>> (A) the production of such visual depiction involves *the use of a minor* engaging in sexually explicit conduct; 18 U.S.C. § 2256(8)(A) (emphasis added).

And, as the same definition was used by the trial court in its charge, the jury understood that it should not vote to convict unless it found the images were made using real children.

Moreover, it does not appear that video technology is so far advanced that a jury is incapable of determining whether a real child was used to make a video. *See Kimler, 335 F.3d at 1142*; Susan S. Kreston, *Defeating the Virtual Defense in Child Pornography Prosecutions, 4 J. High Tech. L. 49, 60-61 (2004)*; *see also United States v. Pabon-Cruz, 255 F. Supp. 2d 200, 207 (S.D.N.Y. 2003), vacated in part on other grounds, 391 F.3d 86 (2d Cir. 2004)* (stating that "jurors [can] draw on their own common sense and experience to recall that the most expensive digital special effects Hollywood can command only rarely generate images that can be confused with live human actors"). Even the most technologically advanced films created without the use of real people are distinguishable from those created with real people. Kreston, *supra*, at 60.

Hence, we decline to hold the government is required, after Free Speech Coalition, to present expert testimony proving the children in the unlawful images are in fact real children. Yet, we restrict today's holding to cases that present facts similar to those before us, that is, cases involving video images or MPEGs. Moreover, we are not shifting the burden of proof regarding the images onto defendant. The government must still prove the images were created using real rather than virtual children. But where, as here, the video images are such that confusing them with images of virtual children is highly unlikely—and, in any event, the defendant never actually argued that the images contained only virtual children—a reasonable jury could conclude that the images depicted real children solely on the basis of the images themselves. Consequently, Irving has not carried his heavy burden of proving the evidence was not sufficient to convict.

B. Willfully Downloaded Issue

Irving next contends the government failed to prove he willfully downloaded and stored images containing child pornography on his home computer. Although he concedes the images were on his computer, he maintains the government was not able to exclude the very real possibility that someone else put the images on the hard drive. In support of this assertion, defendant notes Agent Coleman recognized it was not Irving's usual practice to save, rather than to destroy, incriminating evidence.

This assertion has no merit. First, the government was only required to prove that Irving knowingly—not willfully—received or possessed the images. *See* 18 U.S.C. § 2252A(a)(2)(B) and (a)(5)(B). Second, ample evidence was presented to the jury from which it could find Irving knowingly received and possessed the images: There were 76 files containing such images on his computer; they were stored in the My Documents folder; someone was at Irving's home and on the Internet on the days that the images were downloaded; and Irving was not working on those days. Perhaps even more importantly, Irving made no showing that someone else lived at his apartment, or had access to his computer on the relevant dates. Drawing all inferences in favor of the prosecution, we conclude that a rational juror could find that the government proved all elements of the crime beyond a reasonable doubt.

III Searches

A. Dallas-Fort Worth Airport Interview and Search

Appellant filed a motion at trial to suppress evidence collected from his luggage and his statements made to the Customs agents at the Dallas-Fort Worth Airport. The trial court denied the motion on the grounds that the Customs agents were entitled to search Irving's belongings without reasonable suspicion and, in any event, they had such suspicion. The trial court also stated that because Irving was not in custody when questioned, the Customs agents were not required to give him *Miranda* warnings. With respect to the searches of Irving's luggage and belongings, we find no error.

With respect to denial of the motion to suppress, we review the district court's factual findings for clear error, and review its conclusions of law *de novo*. *United States v. Rodriguez, 356 F.3d 254, 257 (2d Cir. 2004)*. We apply the same standards of review regarding the district court's determination that the defendant was not in custody for *Miranda* purposes. *Id. at 257-58.*

B. Search of Irving's Belongings

The Fourth Amendment protects "[t]he right of the people to be secure in their persons, houses, papers, and effects, against unreasonable searches and seizures." U.S. Const. amend. IV. With few exceptions, warrantless searches are *per se* unreasonable. *See Cady v. Dombrowski, 413 U.S. 433, 439, 93 S. Ct. 2523, 37 L. Ed. 2d 706 (1973).* One of those exceptions is a search at our nation's borders: "Border searches . . . from before the adoption of the Fourth Amendment, have been considered 'reasonable' by the single fact that the person or item in question had entered our country from outside." *United States v. Ramsey, 431 U.S. 606, 619, 97 S. Ct. 1972, 52 L. Ed. 2d 617 (1977).* An airport is considered the functional equivalent of a border and thus a search there may fit within the border search exception. *See United States v. Gaviria, 805 F.2d 1108, 1112 (2d Cir. 1986)* (airport serving as final destination for nonstop international flight deemed functional equivalent of border).

Although routine border searches of a person's belongings are made reasonable by that person's decision to enter this country, more invasive searches, like strip searches, require reasonable suspicion. *United States v. Asbury, 586 F.2d 973, 975-76 (2d Cir. 1978).* Routine searches include those searches of outer clothing, luggage, a purse, wallet, pockets, or shoes which, unlike strip searches, do not substantially infringe on a traveler's privacy rights. *See United States v. Grotke, 702 F.2d 49, 51-52 (2d Cir. 1983)*; *Asbury, 586 F.2d at 975.* To determine whether a non-routine search is reasonable, the offensiveness of the intrusion must be weighed against the level of warranted suspicion. *Asbury, 586 F.2d at 976.*

Of the warrant exception contexts in which the Supreme Court has addressed the issue of pretextual searches, border searches seem most analogous to searches of vessels by Customs officials. And, in that context, the Court noted, "[w]e would see little logic in sanctioning such examinations of ordinary, unsuspect vessels but forbidding them in the case of suspected smugglers." *United States v. Villamonte-Marquez, 462 U.S. 579, 584 n.3, 103 S. Ct. 2573, 77 L. Ed. 2d 22 (1983).* Similarly, in the case of searches at airports, it would make little sense to allow random searches of any incoming passenger, without reasonable suspicion, *see United States v. Montoya de Hernandez, 473 U.S. 531, 538, 105 S. Ct. 3304, 87 L. Ed. 2d 381 (1985)*, but require reasonable suspicion for searches of passengers that are suspected of criminal activity. From this we reason that the validity of a border search does not depend on whether it is prompted by a criminal investigative motive.

As pretext should not determine the validity of a border search, it also should not determine whether a border search is routine (meaning it does not require reasonable suspicion). Rather, as we have earlier held, the level of intrusion into a person's privacy is what determines whether a border search is routine. And, we have long ruled that searches of a person's luggage or personal belongings are routine searches. *See Asbury, 586 F.2d at 975*. Accordingly, the search of Irving's luggage was valid regardless of whether Customs officials conducting the search had or did not have reasonable suspicion. Hence, we decline to decide whether reasonable suspicion for the search was present in this case. Our holding and reasoning that Customs officials' search of Irving's luggage upon his entry into the United States was constitutional extends to the initial search of his luggage in the sterile area of the Dallas-Fort Worth Airport, and to the secondary search of his luggage in a Customs office 40 yards from the initial inspection. The border space of an airport includes "a reasonable extended geographic area in the immediate vicinity of any entry point." *See United States v. Nieves, 609 F.2d 642, 647 (2d Cir. 1979)*. Secondary searches following initial Customs inspection are, like the initial inspection, valid border searches which, if routine, do not require reasonable suspicion. *See* id. at 646-47.

The last question we must consider in determining whether the district court erred in denying Irving's suppression motion is whether the search of the diskettes and film in his luggage was a valid search. A border search is valid under the Fourth Amendment, even if non-routine, if it is supported by reasonable suspicion. *See Asbury, 586 F.2d at 975-76*. As noted above, the question of reasonableness must be determined by balancing the level of intrusion with the level of suspicion. *See United States v. Price, 599 F.2d 494, 499 (2d Cir. 1979)* ("[T]he reasonableness of a particular stop must be gauged by comparing the degree of the intrusion with the grounds for the suspicion that intrusion is called for."). A reasonable suspicion inquiry simply considers, after taking into account all the facts of a particular case, "whether the border official ha[d] a reasonable basis on which to conduct the search." *Asbury, 586 F.2d at 976*. We have pointed to a number of factors that courts may consider in making the reasonable suspicion determination, including unusual conduct of the defendant, discovery of incriminating matter during routine searches, computerized information showing propensity to commit relevant crimes, or a suspicious itinerary. Id. at 976-77.

Here the Customs agents found both the 3.5 inch computer diskettes and the undeveloped film *after* they collected the following information: Irving was a convicted pedophile; he was the subject of criminal investigation; he had been to Mexico; he claimed that he visited an orphanage while in Mexico; and his luggage contained children's books and drawings that appeared to be drawn by children. These all constitute specific and articulable facts, and thus may serve as the basis of reasonable suspicion. *See Price, 599 F.2d at 500*. Taking all this information into account and considering the relevant *Asbury* factors noted above, we find the Customs agents had a reasonable basis for examining the diskettes and the undeveloped film. *See Asbury, 586 F.2d at 976*. This information is certainly sufficient to justify the search of items found in Irving's luggage. Because these searches were supported by reasonable suspicion, we need not determine whether they were routine or non-routine. The district court properly denied Irving's motion to suppress with respect to the Customs officials' examination of the diskettes and film found in his luggage.

C. Search of Irving's Brooklyn Apartment

Next, Irving asserts the district court erroneously denied his motion to suppress evidence seized from a search of his home, and specifically his home computer. He contended the warrant permitting the search was based on stale information and not executed in good faith. We review *de novo* the determination that there was probable cause to issue the warrant and that, regardless, the officers executing the warrant were entitled to the good faith defense. *United States v. Smith, 9 F.3d 1007, 1011 (2d Cir. 1993).*

To be valid under the Fourth Amendment a search warrant must be supported by probable cause. When making the probable cause determination, a magistrate judge must make a common sense account of all the circumstances, *Illinois v. Gates, 462 U.S. 213, 238, 103 S. Ct. 2317, 76 L. Ed. 2d 527 (1983)*, and in doing so determine whether the information in the application is current or has become stale. *See Rivera v. United States, 928 F.2d 592, 602 (2d Cir. 1991)*. The age of the supporting facts and the nature of the unlawful conduct is helpful in determining whether the information is stale, as is whether the supporting affidavit depicts continuing conduct or isolated and random instances of illegal conduct. *See id.*; *United States v. Martino, 664 F.2d 860, 867 (2d Cir. 1981)*. When a defendant is suspected of possessing child pornography, the staleness determination is unique because it is well known that "images of child pornography are likely to be hoarded by persons interested in those materials in the privacy of their homes." *United States v. Lamb, 945 F. Supp. 441, 460 (N.D.N.Y. 1996)* (citing cases).

As explained earlier, the affidavit in support of the search warrant for Irving's residence included information primarily collected from Decker and Irving's own writings, at least one of which was dated July 2001. *See supra* BACKGROUND, Part B. The affidavit also included Decker's statement that Irving took care to destroy pictures that were sexually suggestive or otherwise inappropriate. The defendant makes much of this final piece of information, but it only shows that Officer Coleman was forthcoming in his warrant application. The magistrate judge was entitled to weigh the evidence presented and determine, notwithstanding this statement, that there was a fair probability that child pornography would be found at Irving's apartment, and specifically on his home computer.

The nature of Irving's criminal activity and the age of the facts in the affidavit furnished evidence of continuing conduct and provided probable cause to issue the search warrant of Irving's home and computer. The affidavit furnished sufficient evidence for the magistrate judge to determine, at least preliminarily, that as a pedophile Irving would be likely to hoard pornographic images of children in his home for extended periods of time. Moreover, in a doubtful case, we accord preference to the warrant. *See Rivera, 928 F.2d at 602*. And, even absent probable cause, the executing officers were entitled in good faith to rely on the warrant. *See United States v. Leon, 468 U.S. 897, 922, 104 S. Ct. 3405, 82 L. Ed. 2d 677 (1984)*. The resulting evidence was therefore admissible at trial and the motion to suppress was properly 6 denied.

IV United States Sentencing Guidelines Application

Beyond challenging his convictions, Irving also argues on appeal that his sentence should be vacated and his case remanded for resentencing because the district court based his sentence on facts not found by a jury beyond a reasonable doubt and because the district court erroneously treated the Sentencing Guidelines as mandatory. Irving also contends that the district court committed various errors in determining his Guidelines sentence. Because Irving's case was pending when the Supreme Court decided *United States v. Booker, 543 U.S. 220, 125 S. Ct. 738, 160 L. Ed. 2d 621 (2005)*, and because the district court treated the Guidelines as mandatory, we must order a *Crosby* remand so that the district court may determine whether resentencing is warranted. *See Crosby, 397 F.3d at 119-20*. We refrain at this juncture from addressing the other sentencing errors alleged by Irving. *Id. at 120*.

V ERISA's Anti-alienation Provision

Finally, Irving asserts that we should vacate the $ 200,000 fine levied against him because it violated ERISA's anti-alienation provision, *see* 29 U.S.C. § 1056(d)(1). In making this argument, Irving relies primarily on *Guidry v. Sheet Metal Workers National Pension Fund*, in which the Supreme Court refused to create an exception to ERISA's anti-alienation provision, even for "employee malfeasance or for criminal misconduct," and held that only Congress could create such an exception. 493 U.S. 365, 376, 110 S. Ct. 680, 107 L. Ed. 2d 782 (1990). As noted by the government, it appears that Congress accepted the Supreme Court's invitation in *Guidry* by enacting the Mandatory Victim Restitution Act of 1996 (MVRA). *See* 18 U.S.C. § 3613(a). The relevant provision of the MVRA states

> The United States may enforce a judgment imposing a fine in accordance with the practices and procedures for the enforcement of a civil judgment under Federal law or State law. *Notwithstanding any other Federal law* (including section 207 of the Social Security Act), a judgment imposing a fine may be enforced against all property or rights to property of the person fined . . . . *Id.* (emphasis added).

District courts across the country have found 18 U.S.C. § 3613(a) permits courts to consider ERISA protected assets in determining appropriate fines and restitution. *See United States v. James, 312 F. Supp. 2d 802, 806 (E.D. Va. 2004)* (citing cases). We adopt this understanding of *§ 3613(a)* because the only property exempt from that subsection is that which the government could not reach for the payment of federal income taxes. *See* id. at 805; 18 U.S.C. § 3613(a). ERISA pension plans are not exempted from payment of taxes under 26 U.S.C. § 6334, and thus they should not be exempted from payment of criminal fines. Nothing in the text of the ERISA anti-alienation provision suggests that it needs to be specifically cited to in § 3613(a) to justify our interpretation. *Compare* 42 U.S.C. § 407 (Social Security benefits anti-alienation provision), *with* 29 U.S.C. § 1056(d)(1) (ERISA anti-alienation provision). Moreover, § 3613(c) demands that criminal fines in favor of the United States should be enforced in the same manner as a tax liability would be enforced. *James, 312 F. Supp. 2d at 805-06.* And, the government may look to an ERISA plan to collect unpaid taxes. *See id.*; 26 C.F.R. § 1.401(a)-13(b)(2) (2005). For the above reasons, we reject Irving's claim that the $ 200,000 fine levied against him violated ERISA's anti-alienation provision.

CONCLUSION

We have considered defendant's other arguments on appeal and find them to be without merit. For the reasons stated, we affirm Irving's convictions on all counts but remand for the district court to consider whether resentencing is warranted pursuant to *Crosby*.

X. CUSTOMS

2. Currency Smuggling

UNITED STATES OF AMERICA
v.
MICHAEL ELY

468 F.3d 399 (6th Cir. 2006)
Decided November 16, 2006

ON BRIEF: Randolph W. Alden, OFFICE OF THE FEDERAL PUBLIC DEFENDER FOR THE WESTERN DISTRICT OF TENNESSEE, Memphis, Tennessee, for Appellant.

Frederick H. Godwin, ASSISTANT UNITED STATES ATTORNEY, Memphis, Tennessee, for Appellee.

Before: MARTIN and COOK, Circuit Judges; BUNNING, District Judge.*

* The Honorable David Bunning, United States District Judge for the Eastern District of Kentucky, sitting by designation.

OPINION

BOYCE F. MARTIN, JR., Circuit Judge. Michael Ely was convicted by a jury of bulk cash smuggling and making a false and fictitious material statement and representation to a Customs and Border Protection officer in violation of 31 U.S.C. §§ 5316 and 5332, and 18 U.S.C. § 1001. The jury also found that Ely's interest in the property was subject to forfeiture to the United States pursuant to section 5332. The district court subsequently sentenced Ely to five months imprisonment and five months of home detention to be served as a condition of supervised release, as well as ordering the forfeiture pursuant to the jury verdict. Ely now appeals the forfeiture and his sentence.

I.

Ely's conviction arose from his attempt to bring roughly $ 24,000 in assorted currency[1] into the United States without reporting it. Ely had been working as a con-

1 This amount included $ 22,490 in United States currency, in addition to the equivalent of $ 954.30 in European Union Euros, and the equivalent of $ 642.88 in Kuwaiti Dinars.

tractor in the Middle East, and was returning to the United States on a flight from Amsterdam to Memphis on April 2, 2005. At the Memphis airport, Ely presented his Customs Declaration to Customs and Border Protection Officer Brandon Marlier. On the Declaration, Ely had answered "no" to the question of whether or not he was carrying currency valued at over $ 10,000. The Declaration explains that it is legal to carry currency into the United States, but that if the traveler is carrying more than $ 10,000 it must be reported to Customs. It also provides a clear definition of the term "currency."

Marlier asked Ely how much currency he was bringing into the United States, and Ely responded that he had between six and seven thousand dollars. Marlier then began a "routine bag examination," and discovered currency inside of Ely's luggage, mostly consisting of one-hundred dollar bills. Marlier informed Ely that it was legal to carry currency, but that it merely needed to be reported if it was over $ 10,000. Ely again informed Marlier that it was not over ten thousand dollars. Marlier then counted the money from his initial discovery, and found that it amounted to over $ 13,000. He then contacted his supervisor and two other customs agents. After a more thorough search they discovered an additional $ 7000 to $ 8000, and eventually discovered a total of $ 24,000 after taking Ely into custody. The following day, Ely was questioned by an Internal Revenue Service agent, and admitted that he knew he was carrying more than $ 10,000 and violated the requirement to report it. He claimed that he had wanted to wire the money to his wife from Kuwait, but had encountered difficulty doing so, and was thus carrying the cash with him without reporting it to keep the IRS from knowing about it.

Ely was indicted for three counts: knowingly concealing more than $ 10,000 on his person and attempting to transport it from overseas to the United States in violation of 31 U.S.C. § 5316; knowingly and willfully making a false statement to a Customs and Border Patrol officer in violation of 18 U.S.C. § 1001; and, a charge under 31 U.S.C. § 5332 (b) and (c)(3), authorizing forfeiture of the entire sum of money he was carrying upon conviction for violation of section 5316. The case was subsequently tried to a jury, which convicted Ely on all three counts, including a special verdict on count 3 authorizing the forfeiture of all the currency he was carrying.

II.

Pursuant to the special verdict on count 3, the district court ordered the forfeiture of the entire $ 24,000, which Ely argues was an excessive fine, imposed in violation of the Eight Amendment provision that "excessive fines [shall not be] imposed." Because he failed to raise an Eighth Amendment objection in the district court, we review the excessiveness of the fine for plain error. *United States v. Blackwell, 459 F.3d 739, 771 (6th Cir. 2006).* "'To establish plain error, a defendant must show (1) that an error occurred in the district court; (2) that the error was plain, i.e., obvious or clear; (3) that the error affected defendant's substantial rights; and (4) that this adverse impact seriously affected the fairness, integrity or public reputation of the judicial proceedings.'" *Id.* (citing *United States. v. Abboud, 438 F.3d 554, 583 (6th Cir. 2006)).*

Ely relies largely on the Supreme Court's decision of *United States v. Bajakajian, 524 U.S. 321, 118 S. Ct. 2028, 141 L. Ed. 2d 314 (1998)*, in which the Court upheld a district court's decision to limit a forfeiture for a violation of section 5316 to an amount significantly less than the amount of currency that the defendant was transporting. The facts of *Bajakajian* are similar to this case, save the fact that the defendant failed to report a significantly higher sum of money. The defendant was traveling through an airport with $ 357,144 in currency, knowingly avoided reporting it, and lied to a customs agent about the amount he was carrying. Id . at 325. After a search, the government seized the cash, and sought forfeiture of the entire amount. *Id.* The defendant pled guilty to the charge of failing to report, the government agreed to dismiss the false statement charge, and the court held a bench trial on the forfeiture issue. *Id.* The district court determined that the entire $ 357,144 was subject to forfeiture under 18 U.S.C. § 982(a)(1),[2] but that it would be grossly disproportionate to the offense for the entire amount to be forfeited, and instead ordered a forfeiture of $ 15,000, plus the maximum authorized fine of $ 5000 under the Federal Sentencing Guidelines. Id. at 326. The district court specifically noted that the funds were not connected to any other crime and that the defendant was carrying the money for the lawful purpose of paying a legitimate debt. *Id.* The government appealed, but the order was upheld by the Ninth Circuit, and the Supreme Court subsequently granted certiorari.

The question before the Supreme Court in *Bajakajian* was limited to whether the full forfeiture under section 982(a)(1) of the amount of money the defendant was carrying was constitutional under the *Excessive Fines Clause of the Eight Amendment. Id. at 337 n. 11.* The Court found that the forfeiture was punishment, subject to the Excessive Fines Clause, because it was "imposed at the culmination of a criminal proceeding and require[d] conviction of an underlying felony," and that it was not based on the judiciary's in rem jurisdiction over the currency itself, but rather as a result of the defendant's criminal conviction. Id. at 328-332. To qualify as an excessive fine under the Clause, the amount of the forfeiture had to be grossly disproportionate to the gravity of the criminal offense. Id. at 337. The Court stated that the defendant was merely guilty of a reporting offense, as it was permissible to transfer the money so long as it was reported and there was no connection

---

2 This statute included a forfeiture provision that was a precursor of the present version of 31 U.S.C. § 5332. The statutory language was modified as part of the USA PATRIOT Act in 2001, by moving the forfeiture provision from 18 U.S.C. § 982 (the statute authorizing the forfeiture in *Bajakajian* to 31 U.S.C. § 5332 (the statute authorizing Ely's forfeiture). The government advances this modification as a basis for us to find *Bajakajian* inapplicable. However, the forfeiture language of the two provisions is virtually identical, and even if Congress could circumvent the Eighth Amendment's limitations on excessive fines by modifying a statute, which would make little sense, cutting and pasting a provision of the United States Code from one chapter to another cannot be viewed as a meaningful change.

to other illegal activities. It also looked to the Federal Sentencing Guidelines for guidance in determining the culpability associated with a violation of the reporting statute, and found it relevant that the maximum authorized fine was $ 5000, with a maximum sentence of six months. *Id.* These considerations "confirm[ed] a minimal level of culpability." Id. at 337-38. Similarly, the defendant did not cause significant harm, as there was no fraud committed on the United States, and no loss caused to the public fisc. Id. at 339. For these reasons, the Court agreed with the lower courts that full forfeiture would have been grossly disproportionate to the gravity of the offense. Id. at 339-340.

We cannot say on appeal that the district court committed plain error by ordering forfeiture of the entire $ 24,000, even though *Bajakajian* would have supported an excessive fines argument if Ely were to have argued the issue below. Had Ely raised an excessive fines objection in the district court, he would have been entitled to an assessment of whether the forfeiture was grossly disproportionate to the gravity of his offense, in light of factors including the nature of the offense, the connection to other illegal activities, the source and likely use of the funds, whether his conduct fit into the class the statute was designed to cover (money launderers, tax evaders, terrorism financiers, or drug traffickers), and the potential fine under the advisory guideline range. *United States v. Carpenter, 317 F.3d 618, 627-628 (6th Cir. 2003), vacated on other grounds, reinstated 360 F.3d 591 (6th Cir. 2004).*

Even if the district court erred in not analyzing whether the forfeiture was an excessive fine, it is neither obvious nor clear on appeal that the amount here was grossly disproportionate to Ely's culpability in light of the factors that are relevant to examining the excessiveness of a fine. Specifically, the amount of cash subject to forfeiture is less than one-tenth of the amount at stake in Bajakajian. Further, Ely's potential fine under the now-advisory Sentencing Guidelines was $ 30,000, as compared to $ 5000 in *Bajakajian*. Thus, Ely's forfeiture is within his potential fine range under the Guidelines, whereas the defendant in *Bajakajian* stood to forfeit more than seventy times the amount of his maximum fine under the Guidelines. The forfeiture amount here is also well within the statutory maximum fine of $ 250,000 — another of the several relevant factors that can be considered in assessing gravity of the offense. *Carpenter, 317 F.3d at 627*. ("While the [*Bajakajian*] Court noted that authorized penalties are relevant, they are but one of several factors to consider in assessing the overall gravity of the offense."). Although Ely may have benefitted from a more fact-specific inquiry had he raised this issue in the district court, we cannot say at this juncture that a plain error was made in this case based on our rough comparison between the facts here and those in *Bajakajian*.

III.

Ely also appeals his sentence, claiming that the district court did not properly balance relevant factors in determining the sentence, resulting in an unreasonable sentence under *18 U.S.C. § 3553(a)*. Under the Supreme Court's decision in *United*

States v. Booker, 543 U.S. 220, 125 S. Ct. 738, 160 L. Ed. 2d 621 (2005), a district court is required to consult the sentencing range under the Federal Sentencing Guidelines for advisory purposes only. *United States v. McBride, 434 F.3d 470, 476 (6th Cir. 2006)*. The range is then treated as "just one of the numerous factors that a district court must consider when sentencing a defendant," and the district court must also address the other factors provided for in section 3553(a). *Id.* Section 3553(a) also requires the district court to impose a sentence that is "sufficient, but not greater than necessary," to advance the factors reflected in the statute. In this case, the district court addressed Ely's guideline range, which was determined without objection from Ely to be ten to sixteen months, selected the very bottom sentence from that range, and allowed for half of the sentence to be served in home detention under U.S.S.G. § 5C1.1(c), providing five months imprisonment and five months of home detention.

We review Ely's sentence for reasonableness. Booker, 543 U.S. at 260-61. While a sentence that is within the advisory guideline range, like Ely's, is entitled to a presumption of reasonableness, the record must still reflect that the district court considered the relevant sentencing factors provided in section 3553(a). *United States v. Foreman, 436 F.3d 638, 644 (6th Cir. 2006)* ("A sentence within the Guidelines carries with it no implication that the district court considered the 3553(a) factors if it is not clear from the record."). Specifically, "[w]here a defendant raises a particular argument in seeking a lower sentence, the record must reflect both that the district judge considered the defendant's argument and that the judge explained the basis for rejecting it." *United States v. Richardson, 437 F.3d 550, 554 (6th Cir. 2006)*. This requirement "assures not only that the defendant can understand the basis for the particular sentence but also that the reviewing court can intelligently determine whether the specific sentence is indeed reasonable." *Id.*

Ely concedes that the district court considered the relevant factors from section 3553(a), and our review of the record confirms as much. Specifically, the district court discussed extensively the nature and circumstances of the offense, and the need to promote respect for the law, noting that Ely's violation was deliberate and that the failure to report the funds was a "serious offense." The court also addressed the need for deterrence, stating that Ely refused to concede any wrongdoing, and could thus be considered a likely repeat offender. The district court also addressed the need to protect the public, explaining that although Ely did not represent a security threat himself, he created a distraction in an airport, and willfully violated a statute that is designed to detect and prevent the funding of terrorism as well as other serious crimes. The district court also addressed the need to provide educational or vocational training for the defendant and the benefit of incarceration. The district court went on to consider the advisory guidelines sentence, and subsequently addressed alternative available sentences and the need to avoid sentencing disparities, the need for restitution, Ely's familial responsibilities and military record, and Ely's financial situation.

Given the thoroughness of the district court's consideration of the sentencing factors, Ely does not identify any argument that he raised and the district court failed to address, but instead asks us to balance the factors *differently* than the district court did. This is simply beyond the scope of our appellate review, which looks to whether the sentence is reasonable, as opposed to whether in the first instance we would have imposed the same sentence. Because the district court considered all the relevant sentencing factors, and imposed a sentence of a reasonable length, we affirm the sentence here.

IV.

For the reasons discussed above, we affirm Ely's sentence and the full forfeiture of the currency he failed to report.

X. CUSTOMS

3. Illegal Drug Importation & Interdiction

A. In General*

* Cases are indexed under this subject. The full text of these cases is published in the **volume**-page indicated.

PDK LABORATORIES INC.
v.
UNITED STATES DRUG ENFORCEMENT ADMINISTRATION

No. 04-1432 (D.C. Cir. 2006)
Decided February 24, 2006

On Petition for Review of an Order of the United States Drug Enforcement Agency

Saul Pilchen argued the cause for petitioner. With him on the briefs were Joseph L. Barloon and David E. Carney.

Teresa A. Wallbaum, Appellate Counsel, U.S. Department of Justice, argued the cause for respondent. With her on the brief were Kenneth L. Wainstein, U.S. Attorney, and Stephen A. Sola, Trial Attorney.

Before: TATEL and GARLAND, Circuit Judges, and EDWARDS, Senior Circuit Judge.

Opinion for the Court filed by Circuit Judge TATEL.

TATEL, Circuit Judge: Pursuant to the Chemical Diversion and Trafficking Act of 1988, the Drug Enforcement Agency (DEA) "may order the suspension of any importation or exportation of a listed chemical . . . on the ground that the chemical may be diverted to the clandestine manufacture of a controlled substance." Petitioner, a pharmaceutical manufacturer, does not dispute that some of its products contain ephedrine and pseudoephedrine, both "listed chemicals" and both critical in the manufacture of methamphetamine, a "controlled substance." Nor does petitioner dispute that its ephedrine- and pseudoephedrine-containing products have been and will continue to be "diverted" to illicit methamphetamine labs. Instead, petitioner argues that when DEA suspends shipments of listed chemicals—in this case, the agency suspended two such shipments—it may act only on the basis of evidence that the raw listed chemical, not the finished product containing the listed chemical, "may be diverted." Alternatively, petitioner argues that even if DEA may act on the basis of evidence that the finished product may be diverted, the suspension orders in this case were unsupported by substantial evidence. We disagree on both counts and deny the petition for review. DEA, acting on the basis of its law enforcement experience and expertise, reasonably interpreted the phrase "listed chemical" to include ephedrine and pseudoephedrine contained in finished drug products. Moreover, a series of letters from DEA warning petitioner that thousands of bottles of its products had been found in some 140 methamphetamine labs in at least eighteen states provides more than enough evidence to support the suspension orders.

I.

A powerful and highly addictive synthetic stimulant, methamphetamine is a growing problem for law-enforcement and public-health officials across the country, particularly in western states. "Chronic methamphetamine abuse can lead to psychotic behavior including intense paranoia, visual and auditory hallucinations, and out-of-control rages that can result in violent episodes." Office of Nat'l Drug Control Policy, Methamphetamine Fact Sheet 1 (2003). Rooting out the illegal manufacture and distribution of the drug has proven especially difficult because it "can be made in a portable cooler with ingredients bought at the corner drugstore." Timothy Egan, Meth Building Its Hell's Kitchen in Rural America, N.Y. Times, Feb. 6, 2002, at A14.

Congress's first major effort to arm the federal government with adequate authority to stamp out homemade methamphetamine production came in the Chemical Diversion and Trafficking Act of 1988 (CDTA), Pub. L. No. 100-690, tit. VI, subtit. A, 102 Stat. 4312. To discourage the diversion of "listed chemicals"—including two critical methamphetamine ingredients, ephedrine and pseudoephedrine, id. § 6054(3) (codified as amended at 21 U.S.C. § 802(34)(C), (K))—the CDTA requires companies to report transactions in such chemicals to DEA, see id. § 6052(a) (codified at 21 U.S.C. § 830(b)), and imposes criminal liability on individuals who import a listed chemical "knowing, or having reasonable cause to believe, that [it] will be used to manufacture a controlled substance," see id. § 6053(c) (codified as amended at 21 U.S.C. § 960(d)(2)). Using language central to the issue before us, one section of the Act, now codified at 21 U.S.C. section 971(c)(1), also provides that DEA "may order the suspension of any importation or exportation of a listed chemical . . . on the ground that the chemical may be diverted to the clandestine manufacture of a controlled substance." Id. § 6053(a) (codified as amended at 21 U.S.C. § 971(c)(1)).

As the CDTA tightened the screws on access to raw listed chemicals, illicit methamphetamine manufacturers shifted to extracting ephedrine and pseudoephedrine from common over- the-counter medications, including Sudafed and some types of Primatene. Since the two listed chemicals are present in such medications in a chemically unchanged form, the extraction process is relatively simple. Congress sought to counter this trend with the Domestic Chemical Diversion Control Act of 1993, which (for the first time) required companies to report all transactions in FDA-approved drug products containing listed chemicals. Pub. L. No.

103-200 § 2(a)(6)(C), 107 Stat. 2333, 2333-34 (codified as amended at 21 U.S.C. § 802(39)(A)(iv)). Still dissatisfied, Congress enacted the Methamphetamine Anti- Proliferation Act of 2000, Pub. L. No. 106-310, tit. XXXVI, 114 Stat. 1227, which allocated significant funding to combating methamphetamine production, id. §§ 3623(c), 3624(b)(1), 3625(c), and imposed stiffer penalties on the operators of methamphetamine laboratories, id. § 3612.

Petitioner PDK Laboratories, Inc., a large manufacturer of generic drugs containing ephedrine and pseudoephedrine, has long known that its products have been diverted to clandestine methamphetamine labs. In March 1998, DEA sent PDK a "warning letter" documenting the appearance of the company's products at fifty-one methamphetamine labs in various states over an eight-month period. Two years later, another DEA warning letter informed PDK that its products had been found at forty-nine additional methamphetamine labs. And over the subsequent eleven months, DEA sent twenty-one additional warning letters informing the company that its ephedrine- and pseudoephedrine-containing products were still showing up at illicit drug labs across the country. In total, DEA alerted PDK to the diversion of "thousands of bottles of its previously imported [listed] chemicals to approximately 140 illicit methamphetamine laboratory-related sites located in at least 18 states." See Indace, Inc., Suspension of Shipments, 69 Fed. Reg. 67,951, 67,959 (Nov. 22, 2004).

By January 2001, DEA had had enough. Relying on the string of warning letters, as well as on PDK's failure to report several "regulated transactions," DEA flexed its section 971(c)(1) authority and issued suspension orders to two foreign manufacturers preparing to ship 6,000 kilograms of raw ephedrine to PDK. PDK challenged the suspension orders, and an administrative law judge (ALJ), siding with the company, concluded that the orders lacked adequate legal and factual support. In her analysis, the ALJ construed DEA's authority to suspend importations of "listed chemicals" to extend only to cases in which the agency has evidence that bulk listed chemicals like raw ephedrine—and not finished over-the-counter drug products that contain listed chemicals—may be diverted to clandestine drug manufacturers.

On appeal, DEA's Deputy Administrator disagreed with the ALJ. Indace, Inc., Suspension of Shipments, 67 Fed. Reg. 77,805 (Dec. 19, 2002). Reading section 971(c)(1) to permit suspension if DEA finds that finished drug products containing listed chemicals "may be diverted," the Deputy Administrator held that DEA could properly rely on the diversion of PDK products to justify suspending the ephedrine shipments. Id. at 77,806. Considering the "totality of the circumstances," including both the warning letters and the reporting violations, the Deputy Administrator concluded that substantial evidence supported the suspension orders. Id. at 77,807.

PDK filed a petition for review in this court. In considering this first appeal, we saw ambiguity as to "whether, as the suspension orders assume, [the phrase] 'the chemical may be diverted' [from section 971(c)(1)] includes the prospect that PDK's ephedrine-containing pills in retail stores will be sold to, or shoplifted by, people who then use the pills to produce methamphetamine." PDK Labs., Inc. v. DEA, 362 F.3d 786, 794 (D.C. Cir. 2004) ("PDK I"). Reasoning that the Deputy Administrator had therefore improperly concluded that section 971(c)(1) compelled a result that it did not in fact compel, we vacated and remanded to DEA to "fill in the gap" by "bring[ing] its experience and expertise to bear in light of competing interests at stake." Id. at 797-98. Although then-Judge Roberts disagreed on this point, he joined in the majority's alternative reason for vacating the Deputy Administrator's order, id. at 799 (Roberts, J., concurring in part and concurring in the judgment), namely, that it failed to address DEA's own relevant precedent in finding that PDK violated the CDTA's reporting requirements. See id. at 798-99 (providing the majority's reasoning).

On remand, a new Deputy Administrator explained that, in her view, "the totality of [Congress's] progressive enactments" reflected its "intent to provide DEA the regulatory means to monitor the domestic production, manufacture and distribution of [listed] chemicals and prevent their illicit use in manufacturing methamphetamine." 69 Fed. Reg. at 67,955. Therefore, while acknowledging that these chemicals are often found in products that have "legitimate therapeutic uses," id. at 67,954, the Deputy Administrator held that section 971(c)(1) permits suspension of imports of listed chemicals based on evidence that finished drug products containing such chemicals "may be diverted," id. at 67,957. Because "[s]ection 971(c)(1) is considered by DEA to be a significant component of the regulatory arsenal given it by Congress to combat this immense and growing problem," and because "using precursor chemicals[] obtained by theft or purchase of listed chemical products" poses an acute law-enforcement challenge, id. at 67,956, the Deputy Administrator concluded that a narrow interpretation of the statute would unnecessarily hamper the agency's efforts to prevent the diversion of listed chemicals. Id. at 67,595-96.

Defending her interpretation of section 971(c)(1), the Deputy Administrator asserted that her approach comported with the statute's text, reasoning that "[i]f Congress wanted to make an express distinction between a bulk listed chemical and a finished product . . . it could have done so." Id. at 67,955. She further explained that "listed chemical . . . should be construed broadly in light of that term's use in other parts of the same statute . . . enacted by Congress in 1988," id. at 67,954, and pointed out that the Ninth Circuit had already interpreted "listed chemical" as used in one of the CDTA's criminal provisions to cover the ephedrine and pseudoephedrine in finished drug products, id. (citing United States v. Daas, 198 F.3d 1167, 1175 (9th Cir. 1999)). The Deputy Administrator also believed that a narrow interpretation would "create an arbitrary dual standard," for if DEA could suspend shipments only if raw ephedrine were at risk of diversion, then even when DEA "had facts to show that an importer had reasonable cause to believe that a listed chemical was to be imported, tableted, and distributed to a clandestine laboratory," it could do nothing to suspend the shipment. Id. at 67,955. Such a result, she concluded, "is certainly inconsistent with the criminal penalty provisions of the law involving imports," which would allow for the imposition of lengthy prison terms on the importer. Id.

Turning to the second issue—whether substantial evidence supported the suspension orders—the Deputy Administrator again looked to the totality of the circumstances. Examining three categories of evidence—the warning letters and two types of reporting violations—she concluded that the orders were adequately supported, emphasizing that "the evidence of diversion reflected in the series of Warning Letters provides a sufficient independent basis" for sustaining the suspension orders. Id. at 67,961 n.9. In reaching this conclusion, the Deputy Administrator rejected PDK's argument that DEA's failure to compare the rate of diversion of other companies' products to PDK's diversion rate rendered the suspension orders invalid. She explained:

> DEA recognizes that it and other law enforcement agencies are aware of and able to take action against only a small number of the total clandestine methamphetamine laboratories and dump sites in this country. Accordingly, the specific universe of PDK product diverted, vis-a-vis, all other manufacturers' products, is a number which cannot be established with any specificity. . . .
>
> Given the quantities and diverse locations of PDK listed chemical products discovered at illicit sites reflected in the Warning Letters, DEA is able to draw a reasonable inference regarding the likelihood that the instant shipments may be diverted and to exercise its discretion as to the need to prohibit their import.

Id. at 67,959. The Deputy Administrator also pointed out that she had considered warning letters to be adequate grounds for taking adverse action against other drug manufacturers, and that in one case she had sustained a suspension order based on fewer warning letters than DEA had sent to PDK. Id.

Before addressing the two types of reporting violations (neither of which is relevant to our disposition of this case), the Deputy Administrator noted "[a]s a collateral matter" that Michael Lulkin, PDK's former in-house counsel "responsible for implementing PDK's operating procedures for responding to DEA Warning Letters," had been convicted of four counts of felony fraud, one of which involved PDK. Id. Yet after his conviction, Lulkin remained at PDK, "where his duties include overseeing the company's regulatory compliance." Id. The Deputy Administrator also observed that PDK's former president, Michael Krasnoff, had been convicted of similar charges, yet "continued to serve as a consultant to the company," id.—despite his statement that "it's none of my business if someone gets high off of this stuff," id. at 67,960 n.7. "Neither of these personnel decisions," she concluded, "but particularly the retention of Mr. Lulkin as a key overseer of regulatory matters . . . , generates confidence on the part of the Deputy Administrator that PDK is sufficiently committed to complying with the myriad of regulatory requirements designed to prevent diversion of listed chemicals." Id. at 67,959.

PDK again petitions for review, challenging the Deputy Administrator's interpretation of section 971(c)(1) and arguing that insufficient evidence supports the suspension orders. We address each contention in turn.

II.

When considering the legitimacy of an agency's interpretation of a statute it is charged with enforcing, we first ask "whether Congress has directly spoken to the precise question at issue." Chevron U.S.A. Inc. v. Natural Res. Def. Council, Inc., 467 U.S. 837, 842-43 (1984). In this case, PDK I has already answered this question in the negative: it concluded that section 971(c)(1) is ambiguous as to whether DEA can issue suspension orders based on the diversion of finished drug products that contain listed chemicals. See PDK I, 362 F.3d at 797 ("we do not agree that the meaning of § 971(c)(1) is as plain as DEA says it is"). This leaves us with the task of resolving at Chevron's second step whether the Deputy Administrator's resolution of that ambiguity "is based on a permissible construction of the statute," Chevron, 467 U.S. at 843, keeping in mind that "[a] court may not substitute its own construction of a statutory provision for a reasonable interpretation made by the administrator of an agency," id. at 844.

Even at Chevron's second step, we begin with the statute's language. Abbott Labs. v. Young, 920 F.2d 984, 988 (D.C. Cir. 1990) ("The 'reasonableness' of an agency's construction depends on the construction's 'fit' with the statutory language as well as its conformity to statutory purposes."). Recall that section 971(c)(1) provides that DEA "may order the suspension of any importation or exportation of a listed chemical . . . on the ground that the chemical may be diverted to the clandestine manufacture of a controlled substance." 21 U.S.C. § 971(c)(1). According to PDK, section 971(c)(1) does not "vest DEA with the authority to suspend an import based on misuse of a finished product." Pet'r's Br. 23. But nothing in the statute's spare language supports that contention. Section 971(c)(1) simply authorizes DEA to suspend an importation when it finds that a "listed chemical" may be diverted. While it's true that under the Deputy Administrator's interpretation, the listed chemical subject to diversion may be part of a finished drug, section 971(c)(1) in no way precludes her view that a listed chemical remains a listed chemical when, without any change in its chemical structure, it is incorporated into pills or tablets. As then-Judge Roberts explained in his PDK I separate opinion, the Deputy Administrator's interpretation comports with common sense. If a methamphetamine manufacturer steals, for the purpose of making methamphetamine, a bottle containing pure ephedrine, or pure ephedrine dissolved in water, or a bottle containing 50 ephedrine pills and 50 guaifenesin pills [guaifenesin is another compound present in some of PDK's products], we would not hear an argument that he did not divert a listed chemical because he also diverted a bottle, some water, or some guaifenesin. The presence of packaging materials or other extraneous items does not vitiate the existence of the listed chemical. Here, a bottle of PDK Mini Two-Way Action contains pills each consisting of 25 mg of ephedrine and 200 mg of guaifenesin and binders. For purposes of Section 971(c), the decongestant and the binders are extraneous materials, no more relevant to the analysis than the bottles and boxes in which the pills are packaged.

PDK I, 362 F.3d at 801 (Roberts, J., concurring in part and concurring in the judgment).

Absent anything in section 971(c)(1)'s language suggesting that the Deputy Administrator's interpretation is impermissible, PDK resorts to the assertion that Congress, committed to ensuring that popular cold medications remain readily available, could never have intended to give DEA authority to "shutter the industry." Although citing nothing in the CDTA's legislative history to support this contention, PDK explains that:

> Given that some misuse [of ephedrine drug products] concededly is endemic to the industry, the Deputy Administrator's interpretation . . . would allow DEA to shutter the entire [listed chemicals] industry by using Section 971 to suspend imports to any and every manufacturer whose finished goods are misused in some amount—that is, every manufacturer in the United States.

Pet'r's Br. 24-25. Invoking PDK I's statement that "no one doubts that Congress did not intend to ban, or to give DEA the authority to ban, all sales of ephedrine-containing drugs in retail stores," PDK I, 362 F.3d at 797 (emphasis added), PDK contends that the Deputy Administrator's interpretation must therefore be unreasonable. We disagree.

For starters, the Deputy Administrator has never suggested that section 971(c)(1) permits DEA to ban drug sales in retail stores. Nor has she claimed authority "to suspend imports to any and every manufacturer . . . in the United States." She has concluded only that in deciding whether to suspend a particular shipment of raw ephedrine, DEA may consider evidence that ephedrine-containing drug products are being diverted. If, as PDK asserts, DEA can readily amass evidence of diversion sufficient to warrant suspending any ephedrine shipment, that attests to the rampant nature of the diversion problem and— critically for our purposes—to section 971(c)(1)'s breadth, not to whether the Deputy Administrator's interpretation is unreasonable. As we have explained, "the Supreme Court has consistently instructed that statutes written in broad, sweeping language should be given broad, sweeping application." Consumer Elecs. Ass'n v. FCC, 347 F.3d 291, 298 (D.C. Cir. 2003).

Even under PDK's narrow interpretation, moreover, DEA would still have authority, at least in principle, to "shutter the industry." After all, there is a risk that every shipment of raw ephedrine could be diverted before delivery, just as there is a risk that finished drug products containing ephedrine could be diverted after delivery. If DEA could amass substantial evidence to support the inference that all raw ephedrine shipments "may be diverted"—a big if, of course—then no one doubts it would have the authority to suspend those shipments, thus "shuttering the industry." When even a narrow interpretation of section 971(c)(1) would authorize DEA to "shutter the industry," a more expansive interpretation could hardly be considered unreasonable on that basis. The relative ease with which DEA can document diversion of ephedrine- and pseudoephedrine-containing drugs goes to the quantum of evidence necessary to justify the inference that a shipment "may be diverted" (a question we shall turn to shortly), but it has little relevance to the interpretation of "listed chemical."

Nor do we see any merit to PDK's charge that the Deputy Administrator failed to consider the "competing interests at stake," as PDK I instructs. PDK I, 362 F.3d at 797-78. Contrary to PDK's insistence, nothing in PDK I requires the Deputy Administrator to weigh the risk that her interpretation could potentially "shutter the industry" against DEA's statutory charge to prevent ephedrine diversion. PDK I merely gives the boilerplate instruction that the Deputy Administrator, when interpreting section 971(c)(1), must "bring [her] experience and expertise to bear in light of competing interests at stake." Id.

Moreover, as PDK I directs, the Deputy Administrator did interpret section 971(c)(1) in light of her experience and expertise. See Cont'l Air Lines, Inc. v. DOT, 843 F.2d 1450, 1452 (D.C. Cir. 1988) (an agency must provide "a reasonable explanation for its conclusion that the interpretation serves the statutory objectives" (internal quotation marks and alterations omitted)). She emphasized not only that DEA considers the suspension provision a critical weapon in its anti-methamphetamine arsenal, but also that PDK's narrow reading would severely hamper the provision's usefulness. 69 Fed. Reg. at 67,956. She reasoned that PDK's interpretation would lead to an "arbitrary dual standard," i.e., an importer who delivered ephedrine knowing that it would be diverted after being processed into finished products could be held criminally liable, yet DEA would lack authority to suspend the shipment itself. Id. at 67,955. And drawing on DEA's experience with the growing problem of homemade methamphetamine, she concluded that the statute "should be construed broadly to effectuate its purpose" of protecting the public. Id. at 67,956. Far from being a case in which an agency has failed to explain its interpretive decision, see Republican Nat'l Comm. v. FEC, 76 F.3d 400, 407 (D.C. Cir. 1996) ("[W]e might determine that although not barred by statute, an agency's action is arbitrary and capricious because the agency has not considered certain relevant factors or articulated any rationale for its choice."), the Deputy Administrator's reasoning provides a more-than- adequate justification for her resolution of section 971(c)(1)'s ambiguity, see Ariz. Pub. Serv. Co. v. EPA, 211 F.3d 1280, 1287 (D.C. Cir. 2000) ("As long as the agency stays within Congress' delegation, it is free to make policy choices in interpreting the statute, and such interpretations are entitled to deference." (internal quotation marks and alterations omitted)).

In reaching this conclusion, we acknowledge that DEA could someday abuse its broad section 971(c)(1) authority to reach an outcome Congress would not have approved. Yet all congressional delegations of discretionary authority—particularly broad delegations like this one—carry such a risk. Without more, the theoretical possibility that an agency might someday abuse its authority is of limited relevance in determining whether the agency's interpretation of a congressional delegation is reasonable. Should DEA one day opt to "shutter the industry," as PDK fears, the courts remain open to consider a challenge to that action pursuant to the Administrative Procedure Act.

PDK's remaining arguments likewise lack merit. The company rightly points out that PDK I criticizes the Deputy Administrator for relying on post-CDTA legislative enactments to explicate what the CDTA plainly meant, reasoning that "the views of a subsequent Congress form a hazardous basis for inferring the intent of an earlier one." PDK I, 362 F.3d at 794 (quoting United States v. Price, 361 U.S. 304, 313 (1960)). But here, the Deputy Administrator used post-enactment legislative action for a very different purpose, namely, to help her choose among several plausible constructions of a statute Congress charged her agency with administering. We see nothing inappropriate about this. In exercising delegated authority to resolve statutory ambiguities, agencies can and should consider policy input from a wide variety of sources, including the views of private citizens, industry groups, non-governmental organizations, legal commentators, and, most certainly, Congress. Our case law supports this. For example, while we cautioned in Southern California Edison Co. v. FERC, 116 F.3d 507 (D.C. Cir. 1997), against relying on subsequent legislative history to divine an earlier Congress's intent, id. at 514, we nonetheless observed that "[w]ith respect to Congress's current policy goals, as distinguished from retrospective legislative history, we find the [subsequent] committee reports . . . quite illuminating," id. at 516; cf. McCreary v. Offner, 172 F.3d 76, 82 (D.C. Cir. 1999) ("[T]o determine whether [a statute] is reasonably susceptible to more than one meaning . . . post-enactment legislative commentary offering a plausible interpretation is certainly relevant, much like plausible interpretations from litigants, other courts, law review articles, or any other source would be."). Indeed, it would be quite peculiar to bar an agency seeking to fill a statutory gap from considering strong indications of Congress's developing preferences. Here, for example, subsequent congressional action reflects the severity of the diversion problem, as well as Congress's commitment to addressing it aggressively, both of which clearly support the Deputy Administrator's broad interpretation of her statutory authority.

PDK next points to our observation in PDK I that the 1993 Domestic Chemical Diversion Control Act (DCDCA) "drew a distinction between, on the one hand, the finished product and, on the other hand, the listed chemical." PDK I, 362 F.3d at 795. According to PDK, this "tends to indicate that Congress intended Section 971 to address diversion of raw, bulk listed chemicals from their intended destination." Pet'r's Br. 28.

Even setting aside the hypocrisy of this claim when juxtaposed with PDK's previous one—either later congressional enactments are relevant to interpreting section 971(c)(1) or they're not—the argument is without merit. True, the DCDCA does speak of "drugs" and "drug products" as distinct from "listed chemicals," see DCDCA § 2(b)(1) (codified at 21 U.S.C. § 814(a), (e)), leading us to have reasoned in PDK I that "[o]ne might say . . . that in the view of a later Congress it is PDK's 'drug' or 'drug product,' not the 'listed chemical' mentioned in § 971(c)(1), that is being diverted," PDK I, 362 F.3d at 795 (emphasis added). But the DCDCA's distinction could just as easily demonstrate that when Congress wishes to distinguish between "drugs" and "listed chemicals," it does so. Indeed, the Deputy Administrator took just this position, 69 Fed. Reg. at 67,955 ("If Congress wanted to make an express distinction between a bulk listed chemical and a finished product in section 971(c), it could have done so."), and we have no license to substitute PDK's preferred interpretation for the agency's reasonable one, see Serono Labs., Inc. v. Shalala, 158 F.3d 1313, 1321 (D.C. Cir. 1998) ("[U]nder Chevron, courts are bound to uphold an agency interpretation as long as it is reasonable—regardless whether there may be other reasonable, or even more reasonable, views.").

Finally, PDK argues that the Deputy Administrator inappropriately relied on the Ninth Circuit's decision in United States v. Daas, 198 F.3d at 1175, which held that the phrase "listed chemical" in one of the CDTA's criminal provisions encompasses listed chemicals found in drug products. Disinclined to read the same phrase in the same act to mean different things, the Deputy Administrator explained that she would resolve section 971(c)(1)'s ambiguity to comport with the Ninth Circuit's broad interpretation. See 69 Fed. Reg. at 67,954. Given this explanation, we see no basis for PDK's assertion that the "Deputy Administrator did not explain [Daas's] application . . . to Section 971," Pet'r's Br. 28-29. Nor do we see anything unreasonable about the Deputy Administrator's adoption of an approach that we previously found to have "logic" to it. PDK I, 362 F.3d at 796.

In short, as directed in PDK I, the Deputy Administrator brought her "expertise and experience" to bear in filling the gap left by Congress when it drafted section 971(c)(1). Finding her interpretation consistent with the provision's text, as well as with its manifest purpose of preventing the diversion of chemicals used in the illegal manufacture of a controlled substance, we shall defer to her reasonable, well-considered interpretation. See Chevron, 467 U.S. at 843.

III.

This leaves us with the question whether substantial evidence supports the suspension orders. Although the parties lock horns over all three categories of evidence upon which DEA rested its suspension orders—the warning letters and the two types of reporting violations—the Deputy Administrator made clear that "the evidence of diversion reflected in the series of Warning Letters provides a sufficient independent basis" for sustaining the suspension orders. 69 Fed. Reg. at 67,961 n.9. We agree and shall affirm on that basis. But before explaining why the warning letters suffice, we must address PDK's contention that the Deputy Administrator's use of a totality-of- the-circumstances test to decide whether substantial evidence exists to suspend a shipment is so formless that her conclusion is "purely results-driven." Pet'r's Br. 31.

The Totality-of-the-Circumstances Test

Although we take PDK's point that, "[i]n the absence of an explanation, the 'totality of the circumstances' can become simply a cloak for agency whim—or worse," LeMoyne-Owen Coll. v. NLRB, 357 F.3d 55, 61 (D.C. Cir. 2004), we disagree that an agency's use of the test is necessarily arbitrary and capricious. Agencies routinely employ multi-factor standards when discharging their statutory duties, and we have never hesitated to uphold their decisions when adequately explained. See, e.g., Ark Las Vegas Rest. Corp. v. NLRB, 334 F.3d 99, 105- 106 (D.C. Cir. 2003); ExxonMobil Gas Mktg. Co. v. FERC, 297 F.3d 1071, 1081, 1084-88 (D.C. Cir. 2002). Indeed, we ourselves use a totality test to make a variety of fact-intensive determinations. See, e.g., United States v. Moore, 394 F.3d 925, 930 (D.C. Cir. 2005) (whether reasonable suspicion exists for making a Terry stop); Kingman Park Civic Ass'n v. Williams, 348 F.3d 1033, 1040 (D.C. Cir. 2003) (whether state political processes "are not equally open to participation by members of a class of [protected] citizens" under the Voting Right Act). Nor is this a case, as PDK alleges, where the agency has failed to explain the basis for its decision or the relative significance of the evidence before it. See LeMoyne-Owen, 357 F.3d at 61 ("[A] thorough, careful, and consistent application of a multi-factor test is important to allow relevant distinctions between different factual configurations to emerge, and . . . appellate courts depend on it for the performance of their assigned task of review." (internal citations, quotation marks, and alterations omitted)). Quite to the contrary, the Deputy Administrator explained that the warning-letter evidence was by itself sufficient to justify suspending the shipments. What better way for the Deputy Administrator to have acknowledged the warning letters' relative importance to her decision?

To support its challenge to the Deputy Administrator's application of a totality test, PDK relies on Pearson v. Shalala, 164 F.3d 650 (D.C. Cir. 1999), and Chippewa & Flambeau Improvement Co. v. FERC, 325 F.3d 353 (D.C. Cir. 2003). According to PDK, Pearson stands for the proposition that "an unarticulated standard does not comport with . . . the APA." Pet'r's Br. 33. But that case holds only that an agency proceeding on a case-by-case basis must pour "some definitional content" into a vague statutory term by "defining the criteria it is applying." See Pearson, 164 F.3d at 660. In upholding the suspension orders on the strength of the warning-letter evidence, the Deputy Administrator did just that, giving "some definitional content" to the phrase "may be diverted": in her view, a string of warning letters documenting the diversion of thousands of pills to dozens of illicit methamphetamine labs is sufficient to warrant a finding that a drug "may be diverted." Although PDK is correct that this falls short of an exhaustive definition,

Pearson itself acknowledges that an agency is not "necessarily required to define [an open-ended] term in its initial general regulation—or indeed . . . obliged to issue a comprehensive definition all at once." Id. at 661. Rather, in fleshing out the contours of vague statutory terms, agencies are "entitled to proceed case by case," id., precisely as DEA did here, see 69 Fed. Reg. at 67,597 ("DEA need not issue an array of regulations to anticipate every situation where a [listed] chemical may be diverted. . . . The statute clearly envisions permitting the agency to proceed by adjudication.").

Worse still for PDK, Chippewa actually supports the Deputy Administrator's decision. That case touched on the Federal Energy Regulatory Commission's (FERC) statutory authorization to require a reservoir operator to procure a license whenever "necessary or appropriate in the maintenance and operation" of downstream power plants. 16 U.S.C. § 796(11). Although FERC considers the totality of the circumstances when deciding whether a license is "necessary or appropriate," over time the agency has identified "a series of relevant factors" that it "balanc[es] . . . in light of the facts of the [particular] case," the most important of which is the percentage by which the reservoir increases the power generation of downstream plants. Chippewa, 325 F.3d at 358. Rejecting a reservoir operator's claim that this standard's flexibility doomed a FERC order requiring the operator to obtain a license, we observed that the reservoir at issue increased downstream power generation more than other reservoirs FERC had also required to have licenses. Id. Because "the increase was clearly above the line of demarcation [at which FERC requires a reservoir to get a license], wherever it may lie," id. at 359, we upheld the order—even though FERC had never articulated the threshold above which licensing would be required.

Like FERC, DEA applied an all-things-considered standard to implement a statute that confers broad discretionary authority. Also like FERC, in applying that standard, DEA relied on its precedent, namely, Mediplas Innovations, 67 Fed. Reg. 41,256 (June 17, 2002), which upheld a suspension order based on less evidence of product diversion than DEA amassed against PDK. See 69 Fed. Reg. at 67,959. And also like FERC, DEA provided no clear "line of demarcation" to define an open-ended term, Chippewa, 325 F.3d at 359, instead choosing to establish the term's contours through a series of adjudications. Just as we upheld FERC's reasonable exercise of its discretion in Chippewa, so too must we uphold the Deputy Administrator's here.

The Warning Letters

This brings us to the question whether the warning-letter evidence supports DEA's inference that the ephedrine shipments "may be diverted." PDK argues that before suspending the two ephedrine shipments, the Deputy Administrator should have compared the percentage of PDK products documented in the warning letters with the percentage of other companies' products that had been diverted. Although never contesting that its products have been diverted to many illicit methamphetamine labs, PDK argues that "[t]he Deputy Administrator's failure to compare PDK to other companies in the industry . . . prevents this Court from . . . assess[ing] . . . whether DEA is treating similarly situated parties similarly." Pet'r's Br. 35. In other words, PDK seems to think that DEA may not suspend its shipments unless the agency also suspends shipments to other companies whose products are diverted in equal or greater rates.

PDK's argument lacks merit. Section 971(c)(1) offers no hint that DEA must undertake a comparative analysis before issuing a suspension order. Instead, it says that DEA may suspend "any importation . . . of a listed chemical" based on a finding that "the chemical may be diverted." 21 U.S.C. § 971(c)(1). The rate at which other companies' products are diverted has no bearing on whether PDK's products "may be diverted." As the government nicely puts it, moreover, "[a] law enforcement agency is not limited to investigating only those companies or persons who have committed comparatively more crimes than others. In the law enforcement context, absolute amounts matter." Resp't's Br. 42. And the "absolute amounts" of diverted PDK products—thousands of bottles to roughly 140 illicit labs in at least eighteen states, see 69 Fed. Reg. at 67,959—serve as a more-than-adequate foundation for the Deputy Administrator's inference that PDK's two ephedrine shipments "may be diverted" somewhere down the line. "[A]n agency's predictive judgments about areas that are within the agency's field of discretion and expertise," we have held, "are entitled to particularly deferential review, so long as they are reasonable." Milk Indus. Found. v. Glickman, 132 F.3d 1467, 1478 (D.C. Cir. 1998) (internal quotation marks omitted).

PDK challenges the Deputy Administrator's finding that "substantial amounts" of PDK products have been diverted. 69 Fed. Reg. at 67,959. According to PDK, the warning letters document only a "minuscule percentage" of its total distributed products. Pet'r's Br. 34. That may be so, but PDK is a large company, and a minuscule percentage of its products is a large amount—thousands of bottles, according to the warning letters—and absolute amounts matter.

Moreover, we think that PDK's dubious personnel decisions reinforce the Deputy Administrator's conclusion that the warning letters support DEA's finding that the two ephedrine shipments "may be diverted." 69 Fed. Reg. at 67,959. Hiring Krasnoff, a convicted felon who believes "it's none of my business if someone gets high off of this stuff," surely demonstrates "a cavalier approach toward complying with DEA regulations." Id. at 67,960 n.7. And retaining Lulkin, who had been convicted for fraud against PDK itself, as "a key overseer of regulatory matters," hardly demonstrates PDK's "commit[ment] to complying with the myriad of regulatory requirements designed to prevent diversion of listed chemicals." Id. at 67,959.

PDK objects to the Deputy Administrator's consideration of a DEA employee's statement that "PDK products were number one in terms of being seized at methamphetamine labs." Id. Although PDK did refer to the employee's statement as "hearsay" in the fact section of its opening brief, it waited until its reply to argue that the Deputy Administrator should have disregarded it. This is too late, of course, and we will not consider the claim. See City of Nephi, Utah v. FERC, 147 F.3d 929, 933 n.9 (D.C. Cir. 1998) ("By merely informing the court in the statement of facts in its opening brief [of the factual basis for a claim] . . . [petitioner] failed properly to raise this argument."); Rollins Envtl. Servs. v. EPA, 937 F.2d 649, 653 n.2 (D.C. Cir. 1991) ("Issues may not be raised for the first time in a reply brief.").

In a footnote, PDK argues that the Deputy Administrator improperly ignored factual inaccuracies that the ALJ identified in the warning letters. In support, however, PDK cites a portion of the ALJ's opinion that has nothing to do with factual errors. To be sure, elsewhere the opinion does contain a vague reference to some errors in a small number of warning letters. See In re Indace, Inc., Nos. 01-12, 01-13, slip op. at 38-39 (Apr. 5, 2002) (included at J.A. 59-60). But judging from the citations, at most six (and probably only four) letters contained any such errors. We agree with the government that "[a]ny factual inaccuracies identified by the ALJ, even if true, are de minimis." Resp't's Br. 41 n.11; see Braniff Airways, Inc. v. Civil Aeronautics Bd., 379 F.2d 453, 466 (D.C. Cir. 1967) ("A court will not reject an agency finding that is supported by substantial evidence merely because the agency also incidentally mentions incompetent or irrelevant material."). The Deputy Administrator's lapse, if any, thus provides no basis for setting aside the suspension orders. See 5 U.S.C. § 706 (instructing courts to take "due account . . . of the rule of prejudicial error"); Mass. Trs. v. United States, 377 U.S. 235, 248 (1964) (finding reversal unwarranted "when a mistake of the administrative body is one that clearly had no bearing on . . . the substance of decision reached"); Fed. Express Corp. v. Mineta, 373 F.3d 112, 118 (D.C. Cir. 2004) ("No principle of administrative law or common sense requires us to remand a case in quest of a perfect opinion unless there is reason to think that the remand might lead to a different result.").

In a similar vein, PDK argues that the Deputy Administrator "failed to address the numerous infirmities in the warning letters that led the ALJ to conclude 'it is difficult to determine what, if any, inference can be drawn from these warning-letter figures.'" Pet'r's Br. 32. Viewed in context, however, the ALJ's statement makes clear that the only infirmity she had in mind was DEA's failure to undertake a comparative analysis, and we have already explained why we think the Deputy Administrator's articulated position that DEA has no obligation to do so is perfectly reasonable.

Finally, PDK alleges that, factual inaccuracies aside, the Deputy Administrator's reliance on the warning letters was itself arbitrary because, according to the company, in deciding whether to send the letters, DEA "followed no rules, regulations, or even the most basic informal internal guidelines." Id. at 37. PDK explains that

> [t]he pertinent point here is not that it was unfair of DEA to document discoveries of PDK products in warning letters while ignoring discoveries of competitors' products. The point is that the inconsistent treatment regarding the preparation of warning letters shows that the Deputy Administrator's reliance on them . . . is arbitrary and capricious—largely because the record demonstrates that the decision to document a discovery of misused product, in a warning letter, is itself arbitrary and capricious.

Id. at 38. We disagree. Even assuming the standards for issuing warning letters are arbitrary, that does not automatically invalidate the suspension orders. To succeed on such a claim, PDK must identify exactly how defects in the standards for issuing warning letters tainted the suspension orders. See 5 U.S.C. § 706. A hypothetical shows why. Suppose it were DEA's policy, upon discovering a company's drug product at a methamphetamine lab, to send warning letters only if a coin toss came up heads. The arbitrariness of that policy would do nothing to undermine the evidence that the company's product had been diverted to clandestine methamphetamine labs. Likewise, because PDK nowhere argues that DEA's allegedly arbitrary issuance of warning letters impeaches the evidence of rampant product diversion—indeed, PDK acknowledges the diversion—any possible arbitrariness in the process for sending warning letters is of no moment.

IV.

In sum, we find the Deputy Administrator's construction of "listed chemical" reasonable and her conclusion that the two ephedrine shipments "may be diverted" supported by substantial evidence. We realize the interpretation of section 971(c)(1) we validate gives DEA significant authority over shipments of listed chemicals, but the provision's undemanding language invites such a result. Facing a persistent threat to public health and a challenging law-enforcement problem, Congress armed DEA with broad suspension authority, and only Congress, not this court, can take it away. We deny the petition for review.

So ordered.

UNITED STATES OF AMERICA
v.
TONY BARROW

448 F.3d 37 (1st Cir. 2006)
Decided May 17, 2006

Before Torruella, Circuit Judge, Hansen,* Senior Circuit Judge, and Lynch, Circuit Judge.

* Of the Eighth Circuit, sitting by designation.

OPINION

TORRUELLA, *Circuit Judge*. Defendant Tony Barrow ("Barrow") was convicted of importing 500 or more grams of cocaine into the United States, in violation of 21 U.S.C. §§ 952 and 960, and of possessing with intent to distribute 500 or more grams of cocaine, in violation of 21 U.S.C. § 841. He appeals his conviction and sentence. After careful consideration, we affirm.

I.

On November 16, 2003, Barrow flew from the island of St. Maarten (or St. Martin) to San Juan, Puerto Rico. As he was going through immigration, agents questioned him pursuant to their routine procedures. When asked about the purpose of his visit, he stated that he went to St. Maarten for business and that he was setting up a barber shop. According to the agents, Barrow avoided eye contact and appeared nervous. Barrow was carrying a box used by duty-free stores, which is not unusual for a person traveling internationally, but the box was old and broken instead of new. The agents referred Barrow to secondary inspection.

The agents ran a computer query on Barrow's plane ticket and discovered that the ticket had been purchased the day before by someone else and was paid for in cash. The agents also discovered that Barrow had a criminal history. Agents asked him further questions, to which they found Barrow's answers suspicious. Barrow stated that he had a cousin in St. Maarten, but that he did not stay with him or have his address or phone number. Agents found a phone number in Barrow's bag, and Barrow stated that it was the cell phone number of his cousin but that it did not work.

One of the agents opened the box Barrow was carrying and discovered that it contained four liquor bottles. Barrow and the government dispute whether Barrow was present during the inspection of the bottles. The agent found the bottles unusual because liquor bottles normally have some air at the top and these were filled all the way to the top, the caps of the bottles did not look new, and there were no bubbles when the bottles were shaken. The agent tested the bottles and discovered that they contained cocaine. The agents then arrested Barrow.

Further analysis revealed that the bottles contained 2.6 kilograms of cocaine. Accordingly, Barrow was charged with importing 500 grams or more of cocaine into the United States ("Count 1") and with possession with intent to distribute 500 grams or more of cocaine ("Count 2"). Barrow moved to suppress the contents of the liquor bottles, arguing that the search was unreasonable. In support of his motion to dismiss, Barrow requested an evidentiary hearing, which he argued was necessary to determine the veracity of the agents' statements and to determine whether the agents had stopped him because of his race. The district court did not allow an evidentiary hearing and denied the motion to suppress.

After a three day trial, a jury convicted Barrow of both counts. Because Barrow had prior convictions for drug trafficking crimes, the district court found that he was a career offender and sentenced him to a term of imprisonment of 262 months, which was the minimum sentence under the Guidelines.

II.

A. Motion to Suppress

Barrow argues that the search of the liquor bottles outside of his presence[1] was an unreasonable search that violated his Fourth Amendment rights. Because of the unique considerations concerning the entry of persons into the United States, routine searches at an international border are reasonable under the Fourth Amendment and do not require a warrant, probable cause, or even a reasonable suspicion. *United States v. Montoya De Hernandez, 473 U.S. 531, 538, 105 S. Ct. 3304, 87 L. Ed. 2d 381 (1985)*. Non-routine border searches include strip searches and body-cavity searches and can only be made if supported by a reasonable suspicion. *United States v. Braks, 842 F.2d 509, 512-14 (1st Cir. 1988)*. Barrow does not contend that the testing of the contents of the liquor bottles was non-routine. He merely argues that the search was unreasonable but cites no case law in support of this proposition. The testing of the contents of the liquor bottles was clearly a routine border search, and we refuse to find it unreasonable merely because Barrow may not have been present.

---

1 The parties dispute whether Barrow was present during the testing, but we need not address this issue as it does not change the outcome.

Barrow also argues that the district court erred in not granting him an evidentiary hearing to resolve factual disputes relevant to his motion to suppress. He cites three factual disputes: (1) whether he was present during the testing of the contents of the liquor bottles; (2) whether statements by government agents explaining their reasons for stopping Barrow were true; and (3) whether government agents stopped Barrow because of his race. We review the district court's decision not to hold an evidentiary hearing for abuse of discretion. *United States v. Calderon, 77 F.3d 6, 9 (1st Cir. 1996)*. The first two factual disputes do not merit attention because they are not relevant to determining whether evidence should be suppressed. As we just discussed, the search of the liquor bottles was reasonable regardless of Barrow's presence. Further, the agents did not need a reason to stop Barrow, so the truth of their statements is immaterial. Finally, the district court did not abuse its discretion in denying an evidentiary hearing to investigate bare speculation that agents may have considered Barrow's race in their decision to stop him. *See Shackelford v. DeLoitte & Touche, LLP, 190 F.3d 398, 405 (5th Cir. 1999)* (finding bare allegations of discrimination insufficient to avoid summary judgment).

B. Information Stating Prior Convictions

In order to use prior convictions as a basis for enhancing Barrow's sentence, the prosecution was required to "file[] an information with the court (and serve[] a copy of such information on the person or counsel for the person) stating in writing the previous convictions to be relied upon" before the commencement of the trial. 21 U.S.C. § 851(a)(1). The prosecution filed an information with two of Barrow's convictions the day before the trial and served it the following morning before the trial began. Barrow claims that the last-minute filing and service of the information violated the Due Process Clause. Barrow provides no legal support for this claim and has not indicated how he was prejudiced. We have previously upheld the filing and service of an information the day before trial, and we similarly find no error here. *United States v. Cartagena-Carrasquillo, 70 F.3d 706, 715 (1st Cir. 1995)*.

C. Admissibility of Evidence

Barrow contends that the district court made several errors in admitting evidence at trial. We review a district court's decision to admit evidence for abuse of discretion. *United States v. Cruz, 352 F.3d 499, 504 (1st Cir. 2003)*.

(1) Chain of Custody of the Liquor Bottles

Barrow argues that the liquor bottles should not have been allowed into evidence because the chain of custody was compromised. Under Federal Rule of Evidence 901(a), authentication is a condition precedent to admissibility. The district court must determine "if there is a reasonable probability that the evidence is what it is purported to be." *Cruz, 352 F.3d at 506* (internal quotation marks omitted). Once this is established, "[a] possible defect in the chain of custody for a certain piece of evidence factors into the weight given to the evidence rather than its admissibility." *United States v. Scharon, 187 F.3d 17, 22 (1st Cir. 1999).*

The government presented two witnesses to establish the chain of custody: Customs Agent Roderic Gurunmendi and DEA Chemist Enrique Pinero. Gurunmendi participated in the arrest of Barrow. He testified that, on the day of Barrow's arrest, he put the liquor bottles in an evidence bag, sealed the bag, and wrote his initials and badge number on the bag. His supervisor witnessed this, also signed the bag, and stored the bag in a vault. Gurunmendi also testified that the bottles in evidence at trial were the same ones that were seized from Barrow.

Pinero tested the contents of the liquor bottles. He testified that when he received the bottles they were in heat-sealed bags inside Customs boxes. After performing the tests, he put the bottles in a DEA heat-sealed bag, initialed the bag, and then placed and sealed it in a DEA box. At trial, he testified that the bottles in evidence were the same ones that he had tested.

The only coherent argument that Barrow makes is that one of the liquor bottles broke between Barrow's arrest and the trial and that this suggests that the evidence was tampered with. Pinero's testimony showed that the bottles were broken after he had tested their contents, so his analysis was not affected. Further, Barrow does not explain why a broken bottle undermines the chain of custody or indicates tampering. Accordingly, we find that the district court did not abuse its discretion in admitting the liquor bottles.

(2) Testimony by Agent Rivera and Agent Gurunmendi

Agent Jorge Rivera of U.S. Immigration and Customs Enforcement testified at trial, based on his training and experience, how drugs are usually transported or shipped across the border. Agent Gurunmendi testified that St. Maarten is a high-risk country and that agents seize a lot of drugs from people arriving from St. Maarten. Barrow objected to both agents' testimony and now argues that their testimony was improper both as lay and expert testimony and also that it should have been excluded under Federal Rule of Evidence 403.

Barrow's argument, which is difficult to understand, does not turn on whether the two agents were lay or expert witnesses, but is only that the testimony lacked foundation and as such was inadmissible and in any event was unduly prejudicial under Rule 403. While the testimony was harmful in the sense that it was relevant and probative, this does not make the testimony unduly prejudicial. *See Cruz, 352 F.3d at 506* ("[T]he district court could have concluded that the prejudice caused by such testimony was not unfair; it was, instead, merely the negative result of the testimony's probative value."); *United States v. Pitrone, 115 F.3d 1, 8 (1st Cir. 1997)* ("Virtually all evidence is prejudicial — if the truth be told, that is almost always why the proponent seeks to introduce it — but it is only *unfair* prejudice against which the law protects."). The subject of the agents' testimony was not an unusual one in criminal cases. *See, e.g., Cruz, 352 F.3d at 504-05* (officer testified that defendant was seen at a known drug point); *United States v. Garcia-Morales, 382 F.3d 12, 18-19 (1st Cir. 2004)* (officer explained "the structure and operation of a typical drug distribution conspiracy"). Further, the agents' testimony was not specific to Barrow in that it described general techniques used in international drug trafficking and the general prevalence of drug trafficking out of St. Maarten. This testimony is rather insignificant when compared with the other evidence against Barrow. Assuming arguendo that the court abused its discretion in allowing the agents' testimony, any error was harmless.

D. Sentencing Errors

Barrow claims that he is entitled to resentencing under *United States v. Booker, 543 U.S. 220, 125 S. Ct. 738, 160 L. Ed. 2d 621 (2005)*. Because he did not argue below that the Guidelines were unconstitutional or that the sentence violated *Apprendi v. New Jersey, 530 U.S. 466, 120 S. Ct. 2348, 147 L. Ed. 2d 435 (2000)*, or *Blakely v. Washington, 542 U.S. 296, 124 S. Ct. 2531, 159 L. Ed. 2d 403 (2004)*, we review for plain error. *See United States v. Antonakopoulos, 399 F.3d 68, 76 (1st Cir. 2005)*.[2] In order to meet this standard, Barrow "must point to circumstances creating a reasonable probability that the district court would impose a different sentence more favorable to the defendant under the new 'advisory Guidelines' *Booker* regime." *Id. at 75*. Barrow, however, has failed to point to anything in the record to indicate that such a reasonable probability exists.[3]

Because of his prior convictions, the sentencing judge found that Barrow was a career offender and enhanced his sentence. Barrow contends that a jury was required to find the existence of the prior convictions beyond a reasonable doubt despite Supreme Court authority to the contrary. *See Almendarez-Torres v. United States, 523 U.S. 224, 226-27, 118 S. Ct. 1219, 140 L. Ed. 2d 350 (1998)*. Barrow argues that *Almendarez-Torres* has been undermined by the Court's more recent decision in *Booker*. We have recently considered and rejected this very argument. *See United States v. Jimenez-Beltre, 440 F.3d 514, 520 (1st Cir. 2006)* (en banc).

E. Cumulative Error

Barrow's last ditch effort is to argue that the alleged errors taken cumulatively deprived him of due process. We have noted that "[i]ndividual errors, insufficient in themselves to necessitate a new trial, may in the aggregate have a more debilitating effect." *United States v. Sepulveda, 15 F.3d 1161, 1195-96 (1st Cir. 1994)*. Given that we have not found any significant prejudice from any of Barrow's alleged errors, we do not find any cumulative effect that would justify a new trial.

---

2 Barrow argues that there should be a presumption of prejudice, but this argument is foreclosed by our decision in *Antonakopoulos. 399 F.3d at 79-80* & n.11.

3 Barrow did not even mention that he received a sentence at the bottom of the applicable Guideline range. Although this is certainly a factor, it is itself not sufficient. *See United States v. Guzman, 419 F.3d 27, 33 (1st Cir. 2005)*.

F. Waived Arguments

In his brief, Barrow alleges other errors by the district court without any discussion of the relevant law or facts. We need not consider these alleged errors because "issues adverted to in a perfunctory manner, unaccompanied by some effort at developed argumentation, are deemed waived." *United States v. Zannino, 895 F.2d 1, 17 (1st Cir. 1990)*. Regardless, these alleged errors are patently meritless, and we briefly address each in turn.

Barrow states that no reasonable jury could have found that he knowingly possessed the cocaine in the liquor bottles. A jury may reasonably infer knowledge from circumstantial evidence, and we have affirmed the jury's verdict in similar situations. *See United States v. Hernandez, 218 F.3d 58, 66-67 (1st Cir. 2000)*. Barrow also contends that the district court erred in not granting a mistrial after a prosecution witness stated that he "found some criminal history in the computer" after the district court had instructed the prosecution not to introduce testimony about Barrow's prior convictions. We do not think the district court abused its discretion in not granting a mistrial based on this statement, and since Barrow testified and was impeached with a prior conviction, he cannot claim prejudice. *See United States v. Freeman, 208 F.3d 332, 339 (1st Cir. 2000)*. Further, Barrow summarily asserts that the district court violated *Federal Rules of Evidence 403* and *609* in allowing the government to impeach his credibility with a prior conviction. The district court was well within its discretion since it allowed impeachment with only one of Barrow's two prior convictions; the prior conviction was for drug trafficking, which we regard as bearing on credibility; Barrow's credibility was central to the case; and the court instructed the jury that the prior conviction could not be used as evidence of guilt but only to determine Barrow's credibility. *See United States v. Brito, 427 F.3d 53, 63-64 (1st Cir. 2005)*.

III.

For the foregoing reasons, we affirm Barrow's conviction and sentence.

Affirmed.

UNITED STATES OF AMERICA
v.
OLUYEMISI MUINAT LAWSON

461 F.3d 697 (6th Cir. 2006)
Decided August 24, 2006

Before: MOORE and SUTTON, Circuit Judges; KATZ, District Judge.*

* The Honorable David A. Katz, United States District Judge for the Northern District of Ohio, sitting by designation.

OPINION

SUTTON, Circuit Judge. Oluyemisi Lawson challenges the district court's denial of her motion to suppress evidence obtained from a search of her luggage upon her arrival from an international flight at the Cincinnati/Northern Kentucky Airport. Because customs officials did not need reasonable suspicion to x-ray her luggage during this "border" search and because they had reasonable suspicion that she possessed narcotics when they drilled a 3/8-inch hole in, and cut the liner in, her luggage, we affirm.

I.

On February 24, 2005, customs officer Heidi Tien identified Oluyemisi Lawson, a passenger on an incoming flight from Paris to the Cincinnati/Northern Kentucky Airport, as a potential drug courier. According to the flight manifest, Lawson had made her reservation the day before and had paid for her $1700 ticket in cash. Her passport had been issued overseas. And Lawson's travel history revealed that in November 2004, she had flown to Memphis and had declared her destination to be an address that agents had previously associated with "known and suspected heroin smugglers that have been intercepted in Cincinnati and other airports." JA 95. Based on this information, Tien alerted customs officers that Lawson fit the profile of a potential drug courier.

When Lawson's flight arrived later that day, Tien identified Lawson and her 16-month-old son at the baggage carousel, where she retrieved three suitcases. Along with other passengers, Lawson passed through a primary checkpoint where customs officers examined her passport and then asked her to move to a secondary inspection area. Tien and two other officers asked Lawson to verify that the luggage was hers, then asked her who had paid for the plane ticket and when. She responded that "her husband paid for her ticket in cash two weeks ago," JA 176, a response that was not consistent with the passenger manifest.

After asking these questions and receiving these answers, the officers examined the three bags. They emptied the contents of the first bag and unzipped and removed the interior liner, at which point they could see that the bag "had been tampered with." JA 110. "[A]t the bottom of the bag there was a plastic piece with hardware that was changed out"—some of the original rivets holding the piece in place had been replaced with screws—" and [the piece] was cracked down the middle." JA 178. The crack was covered with a piece of clear tape. In addition, the bag's retractable handle, which should have been long enough that "an average size person could hold it and pull [the wheeled bag] along," "only came out about 6 inches," JA 111, instead of approximately 24 inches, as the officers expected based on the size of the bag. As the officers made these discoveries, they observed Lawson grow "visibly nervous. " *Id* .

Based on this apparent tampering with the bag, the officers x-rayed it. The x-rays showed "the hollow nature of the [bag's] handle" as well as a "denser image in the [handle's] tube where it should have been just [as] hollow." JA 117. To determine the source of this anomaly, the officers removed the "cap" of the handle and peered down the tube but could not see anything. JA 182. The officers "made a small incision on the interior of the bag" to expose the handle tubes and observed that "some modification" had been made to the handle tube. JA 124. Tapping the tube elicited a "metal thump, not a hollow ping," which confirmed the officers' suspicion "that there was something in the tube." JA 183.

Unable to see into the tube, the officers drilled a 3/8-inch hole in it at the point where the x-rays showed the "denser image." JA 117, 124. "[A]n off-white powdery substance came out with the drill," JA 113, which field tests showed to be heroin. The officers also discovered heroin stored similarly in the remaining two bags. The officers arrested Lawson and charged her with conspiring to import one kilogram or more of a substance containing a detectable amount of heroin. *See* 21 U.S.C. §§ 846, 952, 960.

Lawson filed a motion to suppress the evidence. The district court rejected the motion, and Lawson entered a conditional plea to the charge reserving her right to appeal the suppression ruling. The district court imposed a (conditional) 44-month sentence.

II.

Generally speaking, border searches "are not subject to any requirement of reasonable suspicion, probable cause, or warrant." *United States v. Montoya de Her-*

nandez, 473 U.S. 531, 538, 105 S. Ct. 3304, 87 L. Ed. 2d 381 (1985). "Time and again" the Supreme Court has said "that searches made at the border, pursuant to the longstanding right of the sovereign to protect itself by stopping and examining persons and property crossing into this country, are reasonable simply by virtue of the fact that they occur at the border." *United States v. Flores-Montano, 541 U.S. 149, 152-53, 124 S. Ct. 1582, 158 L. Ed. 2d 311 (2004)* (internal quotation marks omitted); *see also United States v. Ramsey, 431 U.S. 606, 618, 97 S. Ct. 1972, 52 L. Ed. 2d 617 (1977).* This principle, however, is not without exception. Some searches—"'highly intrusive searches of the person,'" *Flores-Montano, 541 U.S. at 152*, or those carried out in a "particularly offensive manner," *id. at 154 n.2*—still require "reasonable suspicion," *see, e.g., United States v. Irving, 452 F.3d 110, 123 (2d Cir. 2006)* ("Although routine border searches of a person's belongings are made reasonable by that person's decision to enter this country, more invasive searches, like strip searches, require reasonable suspicion."); *cf. Montoya de Hernandez, 473 U.S. at 542* (requiring reasonable suspicion to detain a traveler and investigate whether she "was smuggling narcotics in her alimentary canal").

Lawson rightly concedes that this search, conducted at a customs checkpoint after the arrival of an international flight, occurred at the functional equivalent of the country's border. *See Almeida-Sanchez v. United States, 413 U.S. 266, 273, 93 S. Ct. 2535, 37 L. Ed. 2d 596 (1973).* And she rightly concedes that the officers' examination of "the contents of her luggage, including the dismantling and reassembly of the handle," was part of a "routine border search" and thus could be undertaken without any individualized suspicion. Lawson Br. at 18; *see U.S. v. Alston, 886 F.2d 1317, 1989 WL 113908, at *1 (6th Cir. 1989)* (upholding a "warrantless border search[]" of luggage "without probable cause or even articula[ble] suspicion"); *see also, e.g., Irving, 452 F.3d at 124* ("[T]he search of Irving's luggage was valid regardless of whether Customs officials conducting the search had or did not have reasonable suspicion.").

Where Lawson parts company with the government is over the customs officers' actions in (1) x-raying her bag and (2) cutting it and drilling into it. The officers did both things without reasonable suspicion, she submits, making both actions unconstitutional.

As to the x-ray of her luggage, the officers did not need reasonable suspicion before undertaking this examination, one that has become a customary feature of commercial airline travel. An x-ray examination of a *person*, it is true, may require some level of suspicion because it may present risks to health that an x-ray examination of luggage will not present and because it may permit greater intrusions into the privacy and dignity of the individual. *See, e.g., Montoya de Hernandez, 473 U.S. at 541 n.4* (expressing "no view on what level of suspicion, if any, is required for . . . strip, body cavity, or involuntary x-ray searches"); *see also United States v. Hernandez, 424 F.3d 1056, 1059 (9th Cir. 2005)* (acknowledging that x-ray searches of persons may be "potentially harmful to the health of the suspect") (internal quotation marks omitted). But "the same is not true about x-rays of objects." *United States v. Okafor,*

285 F.3d 842, 845 (9th Cir. 2002); *cf. Flores-Montano, 541 U.S. at 152* ("[T]he reasons that might support a requirement of some level of suspicion in the case of highly intrusive searches of the person—dignity and privacy interests of the person being searched—simply do not carry over to vehicles.").

As any airline traveler over the last several years well knows, luggage is routinely x-rayed at the airport, whether in connection with domestic or international flights. *See United States v. Allman, 336 F.3d 555, 557 (7th Cir. 2003)* ("[W]e have trouble seeing how, in this age of routine, soon to be universal, x-raying of containers shipped by air, the defendant could have had a reasonable expectation that his package would not be x-rayed at any point during transit."). X-ray examinations of luggage represent a "minimally intrusive" form of investigation and offer few risks of embarrassment to passengers. *See United States v. Johnson, 991 F.2d 1287, 1293 (7th Cir. 1993)* (observing that "an X-ray examination" takes "only a few minutes and [i]s minimally intrusive, causing no harm to the suitcase and no embarrassment or indignity to [the suspect]," that "thousands of airport users subject their luggage to the same procedure each day" and that the suspect "could not have reasonably expected that her suitcase would pass through customs without being subjected to an X-ray examination"); JA 131 (customs officer describing the use of the x-ray machine in this case) ("[Y]ou can't see details, like, you can't tell if that is a pair of pants and that is a shirt. . . . I can identify, based on the shape and the density, what those items might be, but it doesn't say, you know, this is a can of hair spray versus a can of shaving cream. I can just tell you that there's a can, aerosol in nature, or there's clothing or hangers."). In contrast to x-ray examinations of individuals, moreover, there are no health concerns associated with x-rays of luggage, and the risks to luggage potentially associated with x-ray examinations (*e.g.*, the destruction of film) are eminently manageable.

Perhaps most significantly, the greater intrusion to privacy and dignity that attends the routine border search that Lawson rightly concedes was appropriate in this instance (opening and reviewing the contents of luggage and occasionally removing those contents) assuredly permits the lesser intrusion that accompanies a discrete x-ray examination of one's luggage away from the "unwanted gaze" of fellow travelers. *See United States v. Vega-Barvo, 729 F.2d 1341, 1346 (11th Cir. 1984)* (noting that x-ray examinations of luggage are "less intrusive than an officer . . . personally examining the contents of the passenger's luggage"); *United States v. Henry, 615 F.2d 1223, 1227 (9th Cir. 1980)* (noting that an "x-ray scan . . . . is less intrusive than a physical search"); *cf.* Jeffrey Rosen, *The Unwanted Gaze* (2000). Indeed, several circuits have held that x-ray examinations of luggage do not require individualized suspicion even in the context of airport searches that are not at the border, a point we need not resolve today. *See United States v. Hartwell , 436 F.3d 174, 181 (3d Cir. 2006)* (Alito, J.) (upholding the x-ray examination of luggage in the context of a non-border search "even though it was initiated without individualized suspicion"); *United States v. Smith, 643 F.2d 942, 944 (2d Cir. 1981)*; *United States v. Clay, 638 F.2d 889, 890 (5th Cir. 1981)*.

Under these circumstances, we accept the commonsense (and commonly observed) conclusion that customs officers may x-ray an airline passenger's luggage at the border without reasonable suspicion—a conclusion that several other courts have embraced and that none (to our knowledge) has rejected. *See Okafor, 285 F.3d at 846* ("We hold that examination of luggage and other containers by x-ray or other technological means may be done at the border with no required showing of particularized suspicion."); *United States v. Oriakhi, 57 F.3d 1290, 1295, 1297 (4th Cir. 1995)* (holding that the "search of [the suspect] at J.F.K. Airport"—the initial step of which was "to examine [his] bags . . . with a portable x-ray machine"—was a "routine" border search and therefore could be conducted "without . . . any level of individualized suspicion"); *United States v. Udofot , 711 F.2d 831, 839-40 (8th Cir. 1983)* (upholding the "x-raying of appellant's luggage" once the court determined that the search was a border search and without analyzing what quantum of suspicion the government possessed); *United States v. Restrepo Naranja, 643 F. Supp. 154, 160 (S.D. Fla. 1986)* ("[T]he warrantless x-ray search of the Defendant's outbound baggage was reasonable and proper pursuant to the 'border search exception' . . . .").

The customs officers also did not violate Lawson's Fourth Amendment rights when they cut the liner in her luggage, then drilled a hole in it. Even assuming for the sake of argument that these acts required reasonable suspicion, a point we need not decide, *cf. United States v. Chaudhry, 424 F.3d 1051, 1053 (9th Cir. 2005)* (concluding "that a single 5/16-inch hole drilled in the bed of a pickup truck does not require reasonable suspicion"), the officers reasonably suspected that Lawson's luggage contained contraband when they performed these acts.

In prior travels, Lawson had declared her destination to be an address connected with drug smuggling. The trip in question began in Lagos, Nigeria, a city that Tien knew to be "a significant source of heroin seizures in the United States." JA 92. She claimed that her husband had purchased her ticket two weeks before the flight, while the manifest revealed that she had paid for it in cash and had done so just the day before. She appeared nervous and avoided eye contact. *See United States v. Sokolow, 490 U.S. 1, 3, 109 S. Ct. 1581, 104 L. Ed. 2d 1 (1989)* (relying on a suspect's "nervous" appearance in reasonable-suspicion calculation). Her suitcase had been tampered with in multiple ways: a plastic piece beneath the interior lining had been cracked and had been reattached using new hardware; the crack had been covered with tape; and the retractable handle extended only a fraction of its normal length. The x-ray examination revealed an unusual density within the handle tubes, which the officers confirmed by tapping on the tubes. Each incremental step by the investigating officers justified the next incremental intrusion into Lawson's property. And by the time the officers cut and drilled into the luggage, the officers' suspicion that Lawson was smuggling drugs in the handle tubes "was a common-sense conclusion about human behavior upon which [they were] entitled to rely." *Montoya de Hernandez, 473 U.S. at 542* (internal quotation marks and brackets omitted).

Lawson points out that her nervousness could have sprung from the fact that in Nigeria "women have a different social status than men." Lawson Br. at 19. What the Supreme Court said in rejecting a similar argument in *Sokolow* applies with equal force here. "Any one of these factors," the Court explained, "is not by itself proof of any illegal conduct" and may well be "consistent with innocent travel." *Sokolow, 490 U.S. at 9*. "But . . . taken together they amount to reasonable suspicion." *Id* . (rejecting Fourth Amendment argument where the suspect fit a drug courier profile, appeared nervous and had not checked any luggage).

Equally unavailing is Lawson's claim that "[t]he shortened extension of the handles was identical for all suitcases which would indicate a common manufacturer" and contraband-free luggage. Lawson Br. at 19. This of course is one inference that the customs officers could have drawn, but it is hardly the only one and hardly the most reasonable one. That *all three* pieces of luggage contained extension handles that were too short to permit the traveler to pull the luggage behind her suggests either a common (and useless) manufacturing design or that something was amiss with respect to all three pieces of luggage, which would of course increase the officers' suspicion. The officers did not act unreasonably in taking the latter view.

Lawson also points out that "[t]here is no [x-ray] image available for [her] or the Court to review to determine whether the image viewed by the agent did i[n] fact justify a further search." Lawson Br. at 19-20. Lawson offers no authority to support this argument, and the number of x-rays performed by customs officers each day, to say nothing of the uncertainty over whether this x-ray equipment could have handled such a requirement, make this proposed requirement an imposing one. *See* JA 116 ("The [x-ray] system's not capable of recording those images at this time."). For present purposes, it suffices to say that the district judge heard the officers' testimony about what the x-rays revealed, considered Lawson's cross-examination and ultimately "found each [government] witness to be highly credible"—a finding that Lawson has not contested. *See* D. Ct. Op. at 2 n.1. Under these circumstances, the district court did not err in refusing to require the government to produce the x-ray image of Lawson's luggage.

Nor did the officers act unreasonably in the way (and the extent to which) they cut and drilled into the luggage. The record shows that the bag remained as functional after the search as it was before it. The district court found that "[t]he cut was to the innermost lining of the bag, which did not render the bag unusable nor the cut even visible to the eye once the interior lining was zipped back in place. The hole drilled in the rail was small, could easily be taped or covered over if necessary, and also did not interfere with the function of the luggage." *Id. at 15*. On this record, we agree with the district court that "the manner of inspection here" was not conducted in such an "offensive or destructive manner as to be unreasonable." *Id. at 16*.

III.

For these reasons, we affirm.

UNITED STATES OF AMERICA
v.
ERNEST G.M. ROWLAND

464 F.3d 899 (9th Cir. 2006)
Decided September 13, 2006

Before: Betty B. Fletcher, Harry Pregerson, and William C. Canby, Jr., Circuit Judges.

OPINION

PREGERSON, Circuit Judge:

Defendant-Appellant Ernest G.M. Rowland appeals the denial of his motion to suppress evidence and his motion for pretrial discovery related to his conviction for possession of methamphetamine with intent to distribute in violation of 21 U.S.C. § 841(a)(1), (b)(1)(A)(viii). We have jurisdiction over this appeal under 28 U.S.C. § 1291 and we affirm. We hold that Guam Customs officers are statutorily authorized to stop any passenger arriving in Guam if the officer has reasonable suspicion to believe that the passenger is violating Guam's drug laws. We also conclude, that the totality of the circumstances in this case gave rise to reasonable suspicion of such a violation, and that the district court did not abuse its discretion when it denied Rowland's motion for pretrial discovery.

I. Factual and Procedural Background

In October 2003, Drug Enforcement Administration ("DEA") agents in Guam received a telephone tip that Rowland was planning to smuggle methamphetamine hydrochloride to Guam from Hawaii. The informant identified himself[1] to the officers, provided Rowland's name and his approximate height and weight, and remarked that Rowland was from Hawaii and was on probation. The informant told DEA Agent Jonathan Anderson that he had contacted the DEA to "bare his soul;" it is undisputed that the informant contacted the DEA voluntarily and was not motivated by a plea offer or other favorable treatment from authorities. After

1 Although the gender of the informant is unknown, we refer to the informant as a male.

receiving the tip, Agent Anderson and Agent David Taitano contacted the Hawaii Probation Department. The Probation Department confirmed that Rowland was on probation in Hawaii, provided Rowland's date of birth and his physical location, and informed the agents of Rowland's criminal history that included prior drug convictions.

About one week after receiving the tip, Agents Anderson and Taitano met with the informant for about ten minutes to discuss Rowland. In addition to that meeting, the agents spoke with the informant on the telephone about two or three other times. The informant could not tell the agents the specific date that Rowland would travel from Hawaii to Guam. The informant had no known track record of reliability on this or any other case. Agents Anderson and Taitano informed Guam Customs and Quarantine ("Guam Customs") that they were interested in Rowland; Guam Customs placed Rowland's name on a computer "watch list" at A.B. Won Pat International Airport in Guam.

On December 15, 2003, Rowland arrived at the Guam airport on a domestic flight from Honolulu, Hawaii. Although Rowland and the other passengers were not required to pass through *federal* immigration or customs checkpoints, they were required to execute a Guam Customs Agriculture Declaration Form. Rowland presented his form to a Guam Customs Officer, and stated that he would spend roughly one week in Guam and that he did not possess prohibited items or controlled substances.

Because Rowland's name was in the computer watch system, the Guam Customs officer referred Rowland to secondary inspection. At secondary inspection, Guam Customs Officer F.J. Quinata asked Rowland if he was carrying any prohibited items. Rowland responded that he was not. Officer Quinata searched Rowland's bag and found nothing. Officer Quinata observed, however, that Rowland "was nervous and sweating mildly during the inspection." Quinata then asked Rowland if he had any weapons or narcotics on his person. Rowland replied, "Yes, I have dope on me." Quinata conducted a strip-search and found 464 grams of methamphetamine hydrochloride in packets strapped around Rowland's waist.

On December 17, 2003, Rowland was indicted for possession with intent to distribute methamphetamine hydrochloride in violation of 21 U.S.C. § 841(a)(1), (b)(1)(A)(viii). Rowland filed a motion to suppress evidence on March 1, 2004, alleging, *inter alia*, that the Guam Customs officers lacked both probable cause and reasonable suspicion to believe that Rowland was engaged in criminal activity. He simultaneously filed a motion for pretrial discovery of information related to the confidential informant. In its opposition to the motions, the government argued, *inter alia*, that the search was a "border search" that did not require reasonable suspicion or probable cause. In his reply, Rowland contested the assertion that the customs search qualified as a border search. After a brief initial hearing on April 28, 2004, the district court ordered supplemental briefing on the border search issue. On October 5, 2004, the district court conducted a second hearing on the motions and heard testimony from DEA Agent Anderson about his contact with the confidential informant.

On November 3, 2004, the district court denied the motion to suppress. The district court did not reach the question whether the search was a "border search" that did not require reasonable suspicion or probable cause. Instead, the district court held that "the information supplied by the [informant] demonstrated sufficient indicia of reliability so as to provide the DEA with reasonable articulable suspicion justifying the issuance of the intelligence report and the custom[s] officer's subsequent stop of defendant." The court further concluded that Rowland's statement that he had dope on his body created probable cause that justified the search of his person.

On December 29, 2004, the U.S. magistrate judge in Guam denied Rowland's motion for discovery related to the confidential informant. The magistrate judge concluded that Rowland had not made "a sufficient showing to demonstrate that he is entitled to the information concerning the informant." The magistrate judge found relevant the fact that the government did not intend to use the informant or the information that he provided at trial.

Following the denial of his motions, Rowland entered into a conditional guilty plea with no written plea agreement. On May 6, 2005, he was sentenced to 292 months incarceration and 10 years of supervised release. Rowland filed this timely appeal of the denial of his motion to suppress and his motion for pretrial discovery.

II. Standard of Review

We review the denial of a motion to suppress *de novo*. *See United States v. Crawford, 372 F.3d 1048, 1053 (9th Cir. 2004)* (en banc). Whether an official acted within his statutory authority is a question of law that we review *de novo*. *See, e.g., United States v. Miller, 205 F.3d 1098, 1100 (9th Cir. 2000)*. We also review *de novo* whether reasonable suspicion justified a stop. *See United States v. Miguel, 368 F.3d 1150, 1153 (9th Cir. 2004)*. The trial court's factual findings are reviewed for clear error. *See United States v. Bynum, 362 F.3d 574, 578 (9th Cir. 2004)*.

The decision whether to disclose the identity of a confidential informant is reviewed for an abuse of discretion. *See United States v. Henderson, 241 F.3d 638, 646 (9th Cir. 2000)*. Nondisclosure is an abuse of discretion only if disclosure is relevant and helpful to the defense of the accused, or essential to a fair determination of the defendant's cause. *See Roviaro v. United States, 353 U.S. 53, 62, 77 S. Ct. 623, 1 L. Ed. 2d 639 (1957)*.

III. Statutory Authority to Make Stop

At the outset, we must determine whether Guam Customs officers have the statutory authority to stop an individual that they believe is violating Guam's drug laws. If the officers lack the statutory authority to make such a stop, our cases suggest that the evidence obtained as a result of the stop might be suppressed. *See, e.g., United States v. Juda, 46 F.3d 961, 968 (9th Cir. 1995)*(noting that dismissal of indictment or suppression of evidence might be appropriate remedy for statutorily unauthorized search, but declining to reach the issue); *United States v. Peterson, 812 F.2d 486, 492-93 (9th Cir. 1987)* (noting that suppression might be proper remedy for statutorily unauthorized search, but declining to reach the issue).

"Any [Guam] Customs Officer may: (1) arrest persons who violate a prohibition contained in Article 6 of Title 9 [Guam Code Annotated] Chapter 67; [and] (2) make seizures of any controlled substance imported into Guam in violation of Article 6 of Title 9 [Guam Code Annotated] Chapter 67 . . . ." 5 Guam Code Ann. § 73102(1), (2). Article 6, Chapter 67 is codified at section 67.600-.608 of title 9 of the Guam Code, and pertains to "Importation and Exportation" of controlled substances. Specifically, section 67.601 of title 9 makes it unlawful "to import into Guam any controlled substance in Schedule I or II of this Act," subject to exceptions for approved medical and scientific imports. 9 Guam Code Ann. § 67.601(a). Methamphetamine is a Schedule II substance. *See* 9 Guam Code Ann. § 67.601 (defining Schedule II drugs as those listed in Appendix B); 9 Guam Code Ann. App. B(C)(2) ("methamphetamine"). It thus appears that Guam Customs officers are statutorily authorized to arrest persons and seize methamphetamine "imported into Guam." The question then becomes whether methamphetamine arriving in Guam on a flight originating in Hawaii is "imported into Guam" within the meaning of the statutory scheme. This is a question of first impression.[2]

Rowland argues that drugs "imported into Guam" must arrive in Guam from a foreign country. Because his flight was a nonstop, *domestic* flight from Hawaii, Rowland argues that the Guam Customs officers lacked statutory authority to stop and question him about suspected violations of Guam's drug laws. In support of this interpretation, Rowland offers four arguments: (1) that the plain meaning of "imported" does not include the authority to stop "domestic" trafficking of controlled substances; (2) that our decision in *United States v. Cabaccang, 332 F.3d 622 (9th Cir. 2003)* (en banc), compels the conclusion that Rowland did not import drugs into Guam; (3) that our decision in *United States v. Mendoza-Ortiz, 262 F.3d 882 (9th Cir. 2001)*, requires that the evidence be suppressed in the instant case; and (4) that other sections of the Guam Code support his interpretation of the statute. We find these arguments unpersuasive.

It is a fundamental canon of statutory construction that, "unless otherwise defined, words will be interpreted as taking their ordinary, contemporary, common meaning." *United States v. Smith, 155 F.3d 1051, 1057 (9th Cir. 1998)* (quoting *Perrin v. United States, 444 U.S. 37, 42, 100 S. Ct. 311, 62 L. Ed. 2d 199 (1979))*.

---

2 We also observe that at least one of our decisions has *assumed* that produce sent from Hawaii to Guam is "imported" pursuant to Guam's laws concerning agricultural pests, plant disease, and quarantine. *See Guam Fresh, Inc. v. Ada, 849 F.2d 436, 436 (9th Cir. 1988)*. That decision did not address the "importation" question in any detail.

Rowland thus argues that "domestic," as set forth in section 67.601of title 9 of the Guam Code , should be defined as "of or relating to a country's internal affairs," and that importation must therefore implicate non-domestic activities. The problem with Rowland's argument is that he resorts to a common dictionary meaning before determining whether the term is "otherwise defined" in the statute. When a word is defined in a statute, "courts are not at liberty to look beyond the statutory definition." *Smith, 155 F.3d at 1057* (citation omitted).

In this case, the customs title of the Guam Code states that, "[f]or the purpose of this Article, the term *import* means, with respect to any article, any bringing in or introduction of any such article into any area on Guam." 9 Guam Code Ann. § 67.600. Thus, when the next subsection prohibits "import[ing] into Guam any controlled substance," *see* 9 Guam Code Ann. § 67.601, it prohibits bringing any controlled substances into Guam, regardless of whether the substance comes from a foreign country or from the United States. Any article brought into Guam from outside of Guam is therefore "imported" within the meaning of Guam's drug laws. Because Guam Customs officers are statutorily empowered to arrest individuals who "import" drugs into Guam, *see* 5 Guam Code Ann. § 73102(1), and because it is an act of importation to bring drugs to Guam from the United States, we hold that Guam Customs officers are statutorily authorized to stop and seize individuals they suspect of bringing drugs to Guam, even if the person arrived on a flight originating in the United States.

Even if we were not convinced by the plain language of the statute, we would reach the same conclusion based on the structure of Guam customs law. Guam is not part of the United States customs territory, and has its own customs zone. *See* 19 U.S.C. § 1401(h) (defining "United States" in the Tariff Act of 1930 as "all Territories and possessions of the United States except . . . Guam"); 19 C.F.R. § 7.2(a) (noting that Guam is "outside the customs territory of the United States"). Imports into Guam are not governed by the Tariff Act of 1930, and Guam has its own customs administration. *See* 19 C.F.R. § 7.2(b) ("The customs administration of Guam is under the Government of Guam."). Thus, although Guam is geopolitically part of the United States, an item passing from the United States into Guam leaves one customs territory, and its administration, and enters another. *See id.* It therefore makes sense that, for purposes of Guam customs law, any item arriving in Guam from outside of Guam—even if coming from the United States—is subject to customs inspection.[3]

Rowland's additional arguments in support of his interpretation cannot compete with the clarity of the statutory scheme. His reliance on our en banc decision in *United States v. Cabaccang, 332 F.3d 622*, is misplaced. In *Cabaccang*, we re-

---

3 Other sections of the customs title of the Guam Code support our conclusion. Within the customs title of the Guam Code, one section refers to "exportation to the United States" of animal products. *See* 5 Guam Code Ann. § 73106. If sending something to the United States is "exportation," then receiving something from the United States is likely "importation."

versed a conviction for importation of controlled substances in violation of 21 U.S.C. § 952(a). The Cabaccang brothers caused large amounts of methamphetamine to be shipped on nonstop commercial airline flights from California to Guam. *See Cabaccang, 332 F.3d at 623-24.* Federal law makes it unlawful "to import into the United States from any place outside thereof, any controlled substance," *see* 21 U.S.C. § 952(a), and the Cabaccangs were convicted of violating that section, *see Cabaccang, 332 F.3d at 624.* Our prior decisions had held that transporting drugs from one point in the United States to another through international airspace constituted importation. *See Guam v. Sugiyama, 846 F.2d 570, 572 (9th Cir. 1988), overruled by Cabaccang, 332 F.3d at 634-35*; *United States v. Perez, 776 F.2d 797, 801 (9th Cir. 1985), overruled by Cabaccang, 332 F.3d at 634-35.* In *Cabaccang*, we sat en banc and overruled those cases, holding that drugs that pass through international airspace on a nonstop flight from one U.S. location to another are not from "outside" the United States for purposes of 21 U.S.C. § 952(a). *See Cabaccang, 332 F.3d at 635.*

The statute in *Cabaccang* prohibited transportation of drugs into the United States, and the critical question was whether passage through international airspace rendered drugs "imported." Here, there has been no suggestion that the drugs were imported due to passage through international airspace; instead, we know that the drugs were "imported" because they were introduced "into any area on Guam" from outside of Guam. *See 9 Guam Code Ann. § 67.600.* Because Guam has its own customs zone and a different definition of "imported," importation into the United States under 21 U.S.C. § 952 and importation into Guam under Guam's customs laws are not analogous. Guam is part of the United States for purposes of federal drug law, *see* 21 U.S.C. § 802(26), (28), but not for customs purposes. *Cabaccang* is inapposite to the case at bar.

Rowland also argues that we must suppress the evidence in this case because of our prior decision in *United States v. Mendoza-Ortiz, 262 F.3d 882.* In that case, United States Customs officers inspected a truck entering the United States at Nogales, Arizona, and learned that it contained marijuana. *See Mendoza-Ortiz, 262 F.3d at 884.* Instead of seizing the drugs, the officers followed the truck to its point of delivery in Compton, California to arrest potential co-conspirators. *See id.* The officers surveilled the suspected contraband for four days, and watched as it was moved into a building. *See id.* The customs officers then entered the building without a warrant and arrested Mendoza-Ortiz. *See id.* We held that the motion to suppress should have been granted because the officers were *required by statute* to obtain a warrant. *See id. at 885.* Specifically, if a U.S. Customs officer believes that goods that violate customs laws are in a "dwelling house, store, or other building or place," he is "required to seek a warrant" to enter such building. *Id.* (citing 19 U.S.C. § 1595(a)). It was due to the statutory violation that the evidence was suppressed in that case.

The instant case is distinct from *Mendoza-Ortiz* because the Guam Customs officer did not violate a statutory command. Indeed, it appears that the officer was statutorily *authorized* to make the stop, as set forth above. We do not agree with Rowland that *Mendoza-Ortiz* compels us to order suppression in this case.

Finally, Rowland argues that section 67.601 of title 9 of the Guam Code and section 73126 of title 5 of the Guam Code support his position. First, he argues that section 67.601 indicates that an item must come from a foreign country to be imported. That argument is squarely rejected by the broad definition of "import" in the preceding subsection, a subsection that Rowland does not address. *See* 9 Guam Code Ann. § 67.600 (defining "import" as "any bringing in or introduction of any such article into any area on Guam"). Turning to his second argument, section 73126 empowers Guam Customs officers to conduct *suspicionless* searches of *baggage* arriving on flights originating outside of the United States. Rowland asserts that the corollary is that Guam Customs officers lack the statutory authority to conduct searches and seizures of passengers arriving on flights from the United States. We are not persuaded. That Guam's legislature has empowered its customs authorities to inspect *baggage* arriving on international flights is irrelevant to the question whether customs authorities may stop *persons* they reasonably suspect of violating Guam's drug laws.

In conclusion, we think it is clear that Guam Customs officers have the statutory authority to stop and question an individual suspected of smuggling drugs into Guam, so long as the person is arriving from outside of Guam. It is immaterial whether the flight originated within the United States or in some other country: the statute prohibits "any bringing in" of drugs "into any area on Guam." 9 Guam Code Ann. § 67.600. Because we conclude that the Guam Customs officer in this case was statutorily authorized to stop Rowland if he reasonably suspected that Rowland was trafficking in a controlled substance, we must next determine whether the officer had reasonable suspicion to stop Rowland.

IV. Reasonable Suspicion

An officer may stop and question an individual suspected of wrongdoing if the officer can point to "specific and articulable facts which, taken together with rational inferences from those facts, reasonably warrant that intrusion." *Terry v. Ohio, 392 U.S. 1, 21, 88 S. Ct. 1868, 20 L. Ed. 2d 889 (1968)* (footnote omitted). When a court is considering whether an informant's tip is sufficient to support a finding of probable cause or reasonable suspicion, the court must employ a "totality-of-the-circumstances approach" that takes into consideration the informant's "veracity" or "reliability" and his "basis of knowledge." *Illinois v. Gates, 462 U.S. 213, 238, 103 S. Ct. 2317, 76 L. Ed. 2d 527 (1983).*

While the probable cause requirement for a warrant requires a "fair probability that contraband or evidence of a crime will be found," reasonable suspicion is less demanding and "can arise from information that is less reliable than that required to show probable cause." *Alabama v. White, 496 U.S. 325, 330, 110 S. Ct. 2412, 110 L. Ed. 2d 301 (1990)* (citations omitted). "Reasonable suspicion, like probable cause, is dependent upon both the content of information possessed by police and its degree of reliability. Both factors—quantity and quality—are considered in the totality of the circumstances . . . ." *Id.* (internal citation omitted). "Thus, if a tip has a relatively low degree of reliability, more information will be required to establish the requisite quantum of suspicion than would be required if the tip were more reliable." *Id.*

Courts look to several factors to determine the reliability of an informant's tip. First, a known informant's tip is thought to be more reliable than an anonymous informant's tip. *See Florida v. J.L., 529 U.S. 266, 271, 120 S. Ct. 1375, 146 L. Ed. 2d 254 (2000)*; *Adams v. Williams, 407 U.S. 143, 146-47, 92 S. Ct. 1921, 32 L. Ed. 2d 612 (1972)*. That is because an anonymous informant typically cannot be questioned about the basis for knowing the information or motive for providing the tip, nor can the anonymous informant be held accountable for providing false information in violation of the law. *See J.L., 529 U.S. at 271*; *Adams, 407 U.S. at 146-47*. Second, an informant with a proven track record of reliability is considered more reliable than an unproven informant. *See Adams, 407 U.S. at 146-47*. Third, the informant's tip is considered more reliable if the informant reveals the basis of knowledge of the tip—how the informant came to know the information. *See Spinelli v. United States, 393 U.S. 410, 416, 89 S. Ct. 584, 21 L. Ed. 2d 637 (1969), abrogated on other grounds by Gates, 462 U.S. at 238*. Finally, a tip that provides detailed predictive information about future events that is corroborated by police observation may be considered reliable, even if the tip comes from an anonymous source. *See White, 496 U.S. at 329-30*; *Gates, 462 U.S. at 243-45*; *Draper v. United States, 358 U.S. 307, 313, 79 S. Ct. 329, 3 L. Ed. 2d 327 (1959)*. Predictive information that reveals a detailed knowledge of an individual's intimate affairs is more reliable than predictive information that could be observed by the general public, *see White, 496 U.S. at 332*; *J.L., 529 U.S. at 272*, and such self-verifying detail is considerably more valuable if it relates to suspicious activities than if it relates to innocent activities, *see Gates, 462 U.S. at 245 n.13*.

Here, several indicia of reliability were present that support the informant's tip. The informant in this case made himself known to the DEA agents, and the agents met with the informant personally. *See generally United States v. Romain, 393 F.3d 63, 73 (1st Cir. 2004)* (noting that face-to-face encounter with informant significantly bolsters reliability because officers may "perceive and evaluate personally an informant's mannerisms, expressions, and tone of voice" and because informant knows that he may be tracked down and held accountable for false assertions). Further, the informant did not have any apparent motive to fabricate the tip, and could presumably have been held accountable if his information proved to be false. *See United States v. Terry-Crespo, 356 F.3d 1170, 1176 (9th Cir. 2004)* (observing that exposure to legal sanction for providing false information increases reliability of tip). Regarding the basis of the informant's knowledge, the informant stated that he had personal knowledge of Rowland's activities because he had "dealt with him in the past."

The informant, although not of proven reliability, gave a general description of Rowland, predicted Rowland's future travel from Hawaii to Guam, and accurately stated that Rowland was on probation in Hawaii. The DEA agents corroborated the informant's tip when they contacted the probation office in Hawaii and confirmed that Rowland lived in Hawaii and was on probation there. Rowland's criminal background, provided by the probation office, revealed past drug convictions. The informant in this case provided sufficient detail to dispel concerns that the tip was a hoax. *See White, 496 U.S. at 333* (Stewart, J., dissenting) (expressing concern that if a generalized tip is sufficient to create reasonable suspicion, "[a]nybody with enough knowledge about a given person to make her the target of a prank, or to harbor a grudge against her, will certainly be able to formulate a tip about her").

Although the totality of the circumstances in this case might not be enough to establish probable cause, here we deal instead with the less demanding reasonable suspicion standard. *See White, 496 U.S. at 330.* We hold that the totality of the circumstances in this case provided "specific and articulable facts which, taken together with rational inferences from those facts, reasonably warrant[ed]" the stop at Guam Customs.[4] *Gates*, 462 U.S. at 238.

V. Disclosure of the Informant's Identity

Finally, Rowland asserts that the district court abused its discretion when it denied his motion for pretrial discovery of information related to the confidential informant. In *Roviaro v. United States, 353 U.S. 53, 77 S. Ct. 623, 1 L. Ed. 2d 639*, the Supreme Court held that an informant's identity must be revealed whenever it "is relevant and helpful to the defense of an accused, or is essential to a fair determination of a cause." *Id. at 60-61*. But the right is not absolute. "[N]o fixed rule with respect to disclosure is justifiable. The problem is one that calls for balancing the public interest in protecting the flow of information against the individual's right to prepare his defense." *Id. at 62*. The court must examine "the particular circumstances of each case, taking into consideration the crime charged, the possible defenses, the possible significance of the informer's testimony, and other relevant factors." *Id.* The defendant's need for information must be balanced against the value of ensuring the safety of informants. *See United States v. Napier, 436 F.3d 1133, 1136 (9th Cir. 2006)* (citing *Roviaro, 353 U.S. at 60-64*).

We have held that a defendant is *sometimes* entitled to disclosure of the informant's identity, but only after "mak[ing] specific allegations that indicate the portions of

---

4 Because we conclude that the stop was justified by reasonable suspicion, we express no opinion on whether Rowland's stop at Guam Customs was a "border search" within the meaning of *United States v. Montoyade Hernandez, 473 U.S. 531, 105 S. Ct. 3304, 87 L. Ed. 2d 381 (1985)*.

the warrant claimed to be false" and making "a contention of deliberate falsehood or reckless disregard for the truth." *See United States v. Kiser, 716 F.2d 1268, 1271 (9th Cir. 1983)*. Here, everything the informant reported turned out to be accurate. Where a defendant "has failed to articulate any substantial reason" why he should be entitled to the confidential information, disclosure is not appropriate. *Napier, 436 F.3d at 1139.*

Rowland claims that he needs the information to investigate the informant's credibility and background, but he has not articulated any specific reasons to disbelieve the informant's testimony. Our cases do not permit Rowland to go on a fishing expedition into the informant's background because "a mere suspicion that the information will prove helpful will not suffice" to demonstrate a need for disclosure. *United States v. Williams, 898 F.2d 1400, 1402 (9th Cir. 1990).*

We have little doubt that the district court did not abuse its discretion when it denied Rowland's motion. A court abuses its discretion if its decision "lies beyond the pale of reasonable justification under the circumstances." *Harman v. Apfel, 211 F.3d 1172, 1175 (9th Cir. 2000)*. Here, it appears that the district court correctly and scrupulously followed the balancing procedures set forth in *Roviaro* and by this court, and that Rowland did not carry his burden. We hold that the district court did not abuse its discretion when it denied Rowland's motion for pretrial discovery.

VI. Conclusion

We hold that under Guam law, Guam Customs officers are statutorily authorized to stop and question individuals that they reasonably suspect are violating Guam's drug importation laws, without regard for whether the flight originated in the United States or in a foreign country. In this case, the totality of the circumstances gave rise to a reasonable suspicion that Rowland was violating Guam's drug importation laws. Accordingly, the district court properly denied Rowland's motion to suppress. Finally, we hold that the district court did not abuse its discretion when it denied Rowland's motion for pretrial discovery.

The judgment of the district court is **AFFIRMED**.

Printed and bound in the UK by
CPI Antony Rowe, Eastbourne

The manufacturer's authorised representative in the EU for product safety is Oxford University Press España S.A. of El Parque Empresarial San Fernando de Henares, Avenida de Castilla, 2 - 28830 Madrid (www.oup.es/en or product.safety@oup.com). OUP España S.A. also acts as importer into Spain of products made by the manufacturer.

Printed and bound by CPI Group (UK) Ltd, Croydon, CR0 4YY

14/09/2026

02216290-0019